Ecology and Conservation of Mountain Birds

High mountain habitats are globally important for biodiversity. At least 12 per cent of bird species worldwide breed at or above the treeline, many of which are endemic species or species of conservation concern. However, due to the challenges of studying mountain birds in difficult-to-access habitats, little is known about their status and trends. This book provides the first global review of the ecology, evolution, life history and conservation of high mountain birds, including comprehensive coverage of their key habitats across global mountain regions, assessments of diversity patterns along elevation gradients and adaptations for life in the alpine zone. The main threats to mountain bird populations are also identified, including climate change, human land use and recreational activities. Written for ecologists and naturalists, this book identifies key knowledge gaps and clearly establishes the research priorities needed to increase our understanding of the ecology of mountain birds and to aid in their conservation.

DAN CHAMBERLAIN is Professor of Ecology at the University of Turin. His research is centred on the impacts of environmental change on biodiversity, including climate change, urbanization and agricultural intensification, with a particular focus on alpine birds.

ALEKSI LEHIKOINEN is the Senior Curator and Coordinator of the Finnish bird monitoring schemes at the Finnish Museum of Natural History, University of Helsinki. His research focusses on birds as indicators of environmental change, birds in changing climates, protected areas and management, and bird migration.

KATHY MARTIN is Professor of Wildlife Ecology at the University of British Columbia. She investigates how alpine birds cope with their extreme and increasingly unreliable environmental conditions. Kathy studies the adaptations, ecology, life history and conservation of alpine songbirds and grouse in the Americas.

D1555099

ECOLOGY, BIODIVERSITY AND CONSERVATION

The world's biological diversity faces unprecedented threats. The urgent challenge facing the concerned biologist is to understand ecological processes well enough to maintain their functioning in the face of the pressures resulting from human population growth. Those concerned with the conservation of biodiversity and with restoration also need to be acquainted with the political, social, historical, economic and legal frameworks within which ecological and conservation practice must be developed. The new Ecology, Biodiversity and Conservation series will present balanced, comprehensive, up-to-date and critical reviews of selected topics within the sciences of ecology and conservation biology, both botanical and zoological, and both 'pure' and 'applied'. It is aimed at advanced final-year undergraduates, graduate students, researchers and university teachers, as well as ecologists and conservationists in industry, government and the voluntary sectors. The series encompasses a wide range of approaches and scales (spatial, temporal and taxonomic), including quantitative, theoretical, population, community, ecosystem, landscape, historical, experimental, behavioural and evolutionary studies. The emphasis is on science related to the real world of plants and animals rather than on purely theoretical abstractions and mathematical models. Books in this series will, wherever possible, consider issues from a broad perspective. Some books will challenge existing paradigms and present new ecological concepts, empirical or theoretical models, and testable hypotheses. Other books will explore new approaches and present syntheses on topics of ecological importance.

Ecology and Conservation of Mountain Birds

Edited by

DAN CHAMBERLAIN
University of Turin

ALEKSI LEHIKOINEN
Finnish Museum of Natural History, University of Helsinki

KATHY MARTIN
University of British Columbia, Vancouver, and Environment and Climate Change Canada

CAMBRIDGE
UNIVERSITY PRESS

Shaftesbury Road, Cambridge CB2 8EA, United Kingdom

One Liberty Plaza, 20th Floor, New York, NY 10006, USA

477 Williamstown Road, Port Melbourne, VIC 3207, Australia

314–321, 3rd Floor, Plot 3, Splendor Forum, Jasola District Centre,
New Delhi – 110025, India

103 Penang Road, #05–06/07, Visioncrest Commercial, Singapore 238467

Cambridge University Press is part of Cambridge University Press & Assessment,
a department of the University of Cambridge.

We share the University's mission to contribute to society through the pursuit of
education, learning and research at the highest international levels of excellence.

www.cambridge.org
Information on this title: www.cambridge.org/9781108837194

DOI: 10.1017/9781108938570

First published 2023

Printed in the United Kingdom by TJ Books Limited, Padstow Cornwall

A catalogue record for this publication is available from the British Library.

Library of Congress Cataloging-in-Publication Data
Names: Chamberlain, Dan, editor. | Lehikoinen, Aleksi, 1978– editor. |
Martin, Kathy, 1949– editor.
Title: Ecology and conservation of mountain birds / edited by Dan
Chamberlain, University of Turin, Aleksi Lehikoinen, Finnish Museum of
Natural History, University of Helsinki, Kathy Martin, University of
British Columbia, Vancouver, and Environment and Climate Change Canada.
Description: Cambridge, United Kingdom ; New York, NY : Cambridge
University Press, 2023. | Series: Ecology, biodiversity and conservation |
Includes bibliographical references and index.
Identifiers: LCCN 2022062033 | ISBN 9781108837194 (hardback) |
ISBN 9781108938570 (ebook)
Subjects: LCSH: Mountain birds – Ecology. | Mountain birds – Conservation.
Classification: LCC QL677.79.M68 E26 2023 | DDC 598–dc23/eng/20230503
LC record available at https://lccn.loc.gov/2022062033

ISBN 978-1-108-83719-4 Hardback
ISBN 978-1-108-94042-9 Paperback

Contents

Colour plates can be found between pages 200 and 201.

Contributors

TOMÁS A. ALTAMIRANO
Audubon Americas, National Audubon Society, Chile and Cape Horn
International Center, Universidad de Magallanes, Punta Arenas, Chile

DOUGLAS L. ALTSHULER
Department of Zoology, University of British Columbia, Vancouver,
Canada

RAPHAËL ARLETTAZ
Conservation Biology Division, Institute of Ecology and Evolution,
University of Bern, Bern, Switzerland

ADDISU ASEFA
Department of Conservation Ecology, Faculty of Biology, Philipps-
University of Marburg, Marburg, Germany and Ethiopian Wildlife
Conservation Authority, Addis Ababa, Ethiopia

ARNAUD G. BARRAS
Conservation Biology Division, Institute of Ecology and Evolution,
University of Bern, Bern and Swiss Ornithological Institute,
Sempach, Switzerland

MATTHEW G. BETTS
Forest Biodiversity Research Network, Department of Forest
Ecosystems and Society, Oregon State University, Oregon, USA

UTE BRADTER
Norwegian Institute for Nature Research, Division for Terrestrial
Ecology, Trondheim, Norway

MATTIA BRAMBILLA
Department of Environmental Science and Policy, University
of Milan, Milan, Italy

JOHN CALLADINE
British Trust for Ornithology, Stirling, Scotland

TOMMASO CAMPEDELLI
DREAM Italia, Pratovecchio Stia (AR), Italy

ENRICO CAPRIO
Department of Life Sciences and Systems Biology, University
of Turin, Turin, Italy

DAN CHAMBERLAIN
Department of Life Sciences and Systems Biology, University
of Turin, Turin, Italy

DEVIN R. DE ZWAAN
Department of Forest and Conservation Sciences, University
of British Columbia, Vancouver, British Columbia, Canada and
Mount Allison University, Department of Biology, Sackville,
New Brunswick, Canada

WILLIAM V. DELUCA
National Audubon Society, New York, NY, USA

VIRGINIA ESCANDELL
SEO/BirdLife, Madrid, Spain

JON FJELDSÅ
Natural History Museum of Denmark, Copenhagen,
Denmark

JIŘÍ FLOUSEK[†]
Krkonose National Park, Vrchlabi, Czechia

BENJAMIN G. FREEMAN
Department of Zoology, University of British Columbia, Vancouver,
Canada

PRANAV GOKHALE
Department of Endangered Species Management, Wildlife Institute
of India, Chandrabani, Dehradun, Uttarakhand, India

DOUGLAS R. HARDY
Department of Geosciences, University of Massachusetts, Amherst,
MA, USA

SPENCER P. HARDY
Vermont Center for Ecostudies, Norwich, VT, USA

SERGI HERRANDO
Catalan Ornithological Institute, Natural History Museum of
Barcelona, Barcelona, Spain, and CREAF, Cerdanyola del Valles,
Spain, and European Bird Census Council, Nijmegen, The Netherlands

SUSANNE JÄHNIG
tier3 solutions GmbH, Leverkusen, Germany

FRÉDÉRIC JIGUET
Centre d'Ecologie et des Sciences de la Conservation (CESCO,
UMR 7204), Muséum national d'histoire naturelle (MNHN), and
Centre national de la recherche scientifique (CNRS), Sorbonne
Université, Paris, France

JOHN ATLE KÅLÅS
Norwegian Institute for Nature Research, Division for Terrestrial
Ecology, Torgarden, Trondheim, Norway

HANKYU KIM
Department of Forest and Wildlife Ecology, College of Agricultural
and Life Sciences, University of Wisconsin-Madison, Madison,
Wisconsin, USA

R. SURESH KUMAR
Department of Endangered Species Management, Wildlife Institute
of India, Chandrabani, Dehradun, Uttarakhand, India

PAOLA LAIOLO
Biodiversity Research Institute (CSIC, Oviedo University),
Mieres, Spain

ALEKSI LEHIKOINEN
The Helsinki Lab of Ornithology, LUOMUS – Finnish Museum
of Natural History, University of Helsinki, Finland

SHAOBIN LI
Department of Zoology, College of Life Sciences, Yangtze University,
Jingzhou, China

RUEY-SHING LIN
Habitats and Ecosystems Division, Endemic Species Research
Institute, Jiji, Nantou, Taiwan

ÅKE LINDSTRÖM
Department of Biology, Biodiversity Unit, Lund University, Lund,
Sweden

ROMAIN LORRILLIERE
Centre d'Ecologie et des Sciences de la Conservation (CESCO, UMR 7204), Muséum national d'histoire naturelle (MNHN), and Centre national de la recherche scientifique (CNRS), Sorbonne Université, Paris, France

KATHY MARTIN
Department of Forest and Conservation Sciences, University of British Columbia, Vancouver, and Wildlife and Landscape Science, Environment and Climate Change Canada, British Columbia, Canada

TIMOTHY D. MEEHAN
National Audubon Society, New York, NY, USA

EVGENIYA MELIKHOVA
Department of Biodiversity, All-Russian Research Institute for Environment Protection, Moscow, MKAD, Russia

INGAR JOSTEIN ØIEN
BirdLife Norway, Trondheim, Norway

JAMES W. PEARCE-HIGGINS
British Trust for Ornithology, Thetford, UK

CLARA PLADEVALL
Andorra Research + Innovation, Sant Julià de Lòria, Principality of Andorra

CARSTEN RAHBEK
Center for Macroecology, Evolution and Climate, Copenhagen, Denmark

ANTONIO ROLANDO
Department of Life Sciences and Systems Biology, University of Turin, Turin, Italy

BRETT K. SANDERCOCK
Norwegian Institute for Nature Research, Department of Terrestrial Ecology, Trondheim, Norway

THOMAS SATTLER
Swiss Ornithological Institute, Sempach, Switzerland

HANS SCHMID
Swiss Ornithological Institute, Sempach, Switzerland

DAVIDE SCRIDEL
CNR-IRSA National Research Council–Water Research Institute,
Brugherio (MB), Italy and Museo delle Scienze di Trento (MUSE),
Sezione Zoologia dei Vertebrati, Trento, Italy

BENJAMIN SEAMAN
BirdLife Österreich, Vienna, Austria

C. STEVEN SEVILLANO-RÍOS
The School for Field Studies, Center for Amazonian Studies, Loreto,
Perú and Centro de Ornitología y Biodiversidad, Corbidi, División
de Ecología Animal y Ciencias de la Conservación, Perú

LAURA SILVA
Lipu BirdLife Italia, Parma, Italy

JESPER SONNE
Center for Macroecology, Evolution and Climate, Copenhagen,
Denmark

NORBERT TEUFELBAUER
BirdLife Österreich, Vienna, Austria

SVEN TRAUTMANN
Dachverband Deutscher Avifaunisten (DDA) e.V., Geschäftsstelle,
Münster, Germany

KERRY A. WESTON
Biodiversity Group, Department of Conservation, New Zealand
Government, Christchurch, New Zealand

Preface

Humans have long held a fascination for mountains; these typically striking and beautiful landscapes are perceived as wild, challenging, and both inviting and hostile environments. For the naturalist, mountains are important as they host many iconic species that are rare or have restricted distributions. For the ecologist, mountains provide useful models to study the ecological and evolutionary mechanisms driving species diversity as environmental conditions and habitat types change dramatically across small increases in elevation, diversifying niche availability. Mountains are globally important for biodiversity as mountain regions cover one quarter of the earth's terrestrial surface, but support disproportionately high avian diversity and contain nearly one half of its biodiversity hot-spots.

Mountains host many charismatic and highly sought-after species such as giant hummingbird and glacier finch in the Andes, white-tailed ptarmigan in North America, white-winged snowfinch in the European Alps, grandala in Asia, scarlet-tufted sunbird in Africa or rosy finches in the Holarctic. Whether you are a birder or a professional ornithologist, the challenges of locating alpine birds adds to their allure given that they often have cryptic plumage and behaviour and occur in low densities in difficult to access habitats. We should stress that mountains are important for both specialist species and birds that live across elevation gradients. There is often extensive avian use all-year-round. Increasingly, mountains provide refugia for many open-country species that were formerly widespread, but are now declining in the lowlands due to increasingly intensive anthropogenic activities at low elevations. Given their sensitivity to climate change and habitat degradation, birds in high mountains can be very useful sentinels of environmental change.

Although often perceived as pristine and natural, many mountain areas have been shaped by a long history of human influence, given centuries-old management practices for hunting and agriculture, and the more recent use of mountains for recreation. Mountain biodiversity is increasingly threatened by growing pressure caused by human activities, especially climate change, that put at risk the many key ecosystem services provided by mountain habitats. Despite escalating threats, mountain biodiversity is poorly studied compared to many lowland habitats. Thus, there is a high priority to conduct further ecological and biodiversity conservation research for mountain ecosystems.

Cumulatively, we editors have spent over 75 years studying high mountain birds on four continents. We feel a strong urgency to assess the current state of mountain ornithology given the rapidly increasing pressures on high elevation ecosystems. Although there are some publications that focus on individual mountain bird species, this is the first book dedicated to research on mountain birds that addresses alpine habitats globally. In this volume, we aim to fill a large gap in the ornithology of mountain bird species and their associated ecological processes, threats and conservation.

The 10 chapters in our book focus on research at and above the treeline ecotone with an emphasis on the alpine zone, although we use examples that consider wider trends across elevation gradients from montane forest to the nival zone (the highest elevation habitats). The first chapter includes our working definition of 'mountains', global estimates of mountain habitats and an introduction to mountain bird communities and their habitats. The second chapter addresses the many adaptations that birds employ to live in high mountains. The following two chapters summarize knowledge on avian ecology in the open alpine and nival zones and the treeline ecotone. Chapter 5 assesses mountain bird population trends, mainly drawing on national-level monitoring schemes or long-term surveys in Europe and North America. Chapters 6 and 7 deal with potential threats to mountain bird populations, respectively climate change and human disturbance, assessing the evidence of likely impacts and conservation actions required to minimize those impacts and improve prospects for the future. Chapter 8 includes the current and potential future contributions of large-scale modelling approaches to mountain bird ecology and conservation. Chapter 9, as the first global treatment of alpine birds in tropical systems, reviews the impressive levels of avian species diversity and endemism, and contrasts ecological and systematic patterns with high latitude mountain avifauna.

The final chapter synthesizes the main points from each chapter and highlights the key knowledge gaps and research priorities needed to increase our knowledge of mountain birds to aid in their conservation. Our 'roadmap' to guide mountain bird research over the next decades involves improving programmes for monitoring populations, increasing our basic ecological knowledge of mountain species, identifying the key drivers of their distributions and population trends, and providing an assessment of their resilience to environmental change, in particular climate change. All of this must be accompanied by an expansion of research and funding opportunities, especially in currently under-represented mountain systems which are often hot spots of avian diversity in the Global South. Achieving the goals set by our roadmap will greatly improve the future prospects for mountain birds, and mountain biodiversity more generally, especially in the face of global environmental change.

To conclude, high mountain systems support astounding levels of avian biodiversity and provide an impressive breadth of important services. Despite the warmer future faced by mountain birds, mountain areas are becoming increasingly important climate and habitat refugia for wildlife. As the cold upper limits on distributions for birds are relaxed, formerly unsuitable habitats may potentially support species that have been lost from more productive lower elevations. Thus, despite the threats posed by climate change, mountain ecosystems may, with appropriate management, become more important centres for bird conservation in a changing climate than they are at present.

Dan Chamberlain, Aleksi Lehikoinen, Kathy Martin

Acknowledgements

We are first and foremost grateful to Rob Fuller for giving us the impetus to write this book which would not have happened without his ideas and encouragement. We wish to extend our gratitude to all authors who have contributed to this book. In particular, we acknowledge the great job done by chapter leads in assembling a diverse group of co-authors representing a broad level of expertise and experience, covering 24 countries across 6 continents. Each chapter was evaluated by at least two referees and we acknowledge the great improvements that their feedback made to the book. Cambridge University Press were ever ready to give advice and support, and we thank in particular Michael Usher, Aleksandra Serocka and Dominic Lewis.

DC wishes to thank all co-editors and authors for their input and enthusiasm. He is also grateful for the many useful discussions and insights from the field from his colleagues in Italy, especially Riccardo Alba, Camille Mermillon, Domenico Rosselli and Maria Sander. Finally, he extends his heartfelt thanks to his family, Emanuela, Giorgia and Tom, for their extreme patience during the writing of this book!

AL wishes to express his gratitude to all authors of the inspiring international network of mountain bird enthusiasts.

KM wishes to thank the many undergraduate and graduate students, postdoctoral fellows and colleagues who have inspired her with their hard work and keen insights along her journey to learn how alpine birds live successfully in their high mountain habitats. As well, many keen naturalists and hikers have contributed 'Citizen Science' observations to provide broader insights for alpine bird ecology and conservation. Kathy also thanks managers from Environment and Climate Change Canada, who have supported her alpine bird research programme over the past three decades, in particular Dr Robert Elner and Dr Elizabeth Krebs.

1 · Mountain Birds and Their Habitats

DAN CHAMBERLAIN, ALEKSI
LEHIKOINEN, DAVIDE SCRIDEL
AND KATHY MARTIN

Mountains are high relief habitats that occur across all continents. Their impressive features define landscapes and human societies. These high elevation,[1] topographically complex habitats provide key ecosystem services (Körner & Ohsawa 2006), host high levels of diversity and endemism (Antonelli et al. 2018), and are characterized by many specialized and charismatic species, in addition to many generalist species that are distributed across broad elevation gradients (Boyle & Martin 2015). Mountain regions are highly valued by people in terms of their natural beauty and wildlife, and they are common tourist destinations year-round. However, these regions are under threat from a range of factors (Alba et al. 2022), including climate change (e.g., Gottfried et al. 2012; Freeman et al. 2018), changes in livestock management (MacDonald et al. 2000; Laiolo et al. 2004), increasing pressure from tourism and recreational activities (Rixen & Rolando 2013), and exploitation of natural resources, including renewable energy (Svadlenak-Gomez et al. 2013), all of which may have implications for mountain bird populations.

In this chapter, we first define our key terms of reference, including what we consider to be 'mountains' and 'mountain birds'. We then summarize the importance of mountains to biodiversity in general and to birds in particular, focussing on key drivers of avian community assembly and variation along elevation gradients encompassing a wide range of habitats (i.e., from relatively low elevations to the highest mountain peaks). Subsequently, we provide an overview of the particular conditions faced by mountain birds at higher elevations, especially

---

[1] The term 'elevation' is used to represent the height of the ground above sea-level (e.g., a mountain summit); 'altitude' is the height above ground (e.g., a bird in flight). Both are expressed as metres above sea-level.

at and above the treeline. Finally, we identify some of the key anthropogenic pressures that have shaped high elevation habitats historically. In so doing, we set the scene for the diversity of topics covered in the following chapters.

1.1 Defining a Mountain

What is a mountain? This is a simple question for which there is no simple answer. Several researchers have attempted to define methods and delineate estimates of regional or global mountain areas, typically involving the key characteristics of elevation and steepness of terrain (e.g., Kapos *et al.* 2000; Körner *et al.* 2011; Karagulle *et al.* 2017; Körner *et al.* 2017; Sayre *et al.* 2018), although the importance put on specific characteristics varies (Körner *et al.* 2021). The definition of Kapos *et al.* (2000) and Blyth *et al.* (2002) developed for the United Nations Environmental Programme (UNEP), is based on defining different mountain classes, largely in relation to elevation, the minimum being 300 m to be included as part of a mountain system. This classification (which we term K1 following Sayre *et al.* 2018), results in 24.3 per cent of global terrestrial surface being classed as mountainous (Plate 1). This does, however, exclude areas that have many ecological characteristics of mountains. Körner *et al.* (2011) developed a different classification (termed K2) for the Global Mountain Biodiversity Assessment, mostly based on terrain ruggedness, that resulted in the inclusion of a greater area at lower elevations (particularly coastal mountains), but an overall lower area of global mountain systems (12.3 per cent of global terrestrial surface) compared to Kapos *et al.* (2000). This was due to the exclusion of high elevation plateaus, intermontane valleys and hilly forelands (Plate 2).

Using a higher resolution (250 m versus 1,000 m), Karagulle *et al.* (2017) based their classification (termed K3) for the US Geological Survey on gentle slopes (a virtual mean inclination), ruggedness and profile type (the amount of gently sloping land in upland areas), resulting in an estimate of 30.4 per cent mountain cover of global terrestrial surface (Plate 3). Testolin *et al.* (2020) used an even higher resolution (30 m) to identify a global alpine zone (areas above the treeline) based on unforested areas and modelled estimates of the limits of regional treelines, using the classification of Körner *et al.* (2011) as an initial template. Excluding Arctic and Antarctic mountains, this resulted in an estimated 2.6 per cent of the global terrestrial surface being covered by alpine zones which matches well the alpine areas defined in K2. Plate 4 shows the classification of Testolin *et al.* (2020) superimposed on a composite map of the other three main classifications (K1–K3; Kapos *et al.* 2000; Körner *et al.* 2011; Karagulle *et al.* 2017) and thus gives an estimate of the maximum extent of mountainous area combining different 'mountain' definitions.

It should be noted that only K1 includes all of Greenland or Antarctica. These areas were excluded from K2 (except for coastal mountains of Greenland) and K3 because their overall aims were not to identify ruggedness *per se* (a purely topographic view), but to apply the classifications to fields such as forestry (Kapos *et al.* 2000), biodiversity and climatic life zones on earth (Körner *et al.* 2011, 2017), and human populations living in or near mountains (Körner *et al.* 2021). We argue that Greenland and Antarctica should be included in future mountain mapping exercises as they hold relevant mountain features (high elevation sites at high latitudes), they host mountain birds (e.g., golden eagle *Aquila chysaetos* and rock ptarmigan *Lagopus muta* in Greenland, snow petrel *Pagodroma nivea* in Antarctica), and many ice-covered sites currently without birds are subject to fast ice-melting processes and are likely to become suitable in the near future.

Which of these methods is preferred depends on the objectives of a given study (Sayre *et al.* 2018), but there are situations where clear and objective definitions of mountain areas are needed (Körner *et al.* 2017). In this book, we focus on the ecology of the bird species that use these zones for at least a part of their life cycle. Our goals are most in line with the definition of Körner *et al.* (2011), that is, the K2 classification in Plate 2, in that we are primarily concerned with mountain biodiversity quantity and condition, species–habitat relationships and species–climate relationships. However, we do not formally adopt a strict and static definition of a 'mountain' which could risk the exclusion of important examples from low mountains (e.g., coastal, or where boreal mountains grade into arctic tundra) or from high elevation plateaus where species are still subject to many of the same constraints (in particular climatic) as mountain birds in steeper terrain. For example, the K2 classification does not include the whole Tibetan Plateau as it does not meet the requirements for terrain ruggedness, but ecologically we would consider this area as mountainous.

Our philosophy mirrors that of Nagy & Grabherr (2009) in that we are mainly concerned with areas that can be considered part of mountain systems from an ecological, rather than a topographic, point of view. In other words, mountain systems should have significant influences on the ecology of habitats and species due to factors associated with a combination of elevation and topography with respect to the surrounding landscape. For much of this book, we maintain a focus (albeit not exclusively) on areas above the natural elevational limit of continuous forest, where the treeline ecotone forms the lower limit of our main area of interest. Thus, the Testolin *et al.* (2020) classification probably matches that focus most closely. However, it does not include treeline ecotone areas, and in particular those that have been formed at elevations lower than the climatic limit of the treeline, which are also of interest (Chapter 4). It also underestimates the area of alpine zones that have less rock and bare ground, particularly in the tropics (Chapter 3).

1.2 Mountain Biodiversity

Mountainous areas tend to have disproportionately high biodiversity, covering around a quarter of the world's terrestrial surface (Kapos *et al.* 2000), supporting an estimated one-third of terrestrial biodiversity (Körner 2004), and harbouring almost 50 per cent of terrestrial biodiversity hot-spots globally (Myers *et al.* 2000). Mountain specialists (i.e., those dependent on and restricted to high elevation habitats for key parts of their annual cycle) often show very narrow geographic (and vertical) distributions. The range of individual species may sometimes be restricted to a single mountain or valley (Antonelli *et al.* 2018), or more typically a narrow elevational range, hence mountains are important centres of endemism (Körner *et al.* 2017) and speciation (Fjeldså *et al.* 2012; Rahbek *et al.* 2019). Mountains thus often harbour a greater proportion of threatened species than other habitats (Franzén & Molander 2012). Biodiversity is also increased by the upshifting of generalist species (those normally occurring over a wide range of elevations) that have lost their low elevation habitat due to anthropogenic impacts, such as farmland birds in France (Archaux 2007).

What drives the high biodiversity in mountains? From an evolutionary perspective, geological heterogeneity and its interaction with historical long-term fluctuations in climate has led to enhanced speciation rates and hence high diversity in mountainous regions (Rahbek *et al.* 2019). At a fairly large scale (1° latitude), tetrapod species richness is closely and positively correlated with temperature, precipitation and topographic relief (Antonelli *et al.* 2018), showing the importance of the complexity of mountain environments (evolutionary processes are considered further in Chapter 9). At finer scales, high biodiversity arises over relatively small spatial scales (e.g., one or a few kilometres) as a consequence of the steep terrain and subsequent zonation along elevation gradients (Section 1.2.1).

Species diversity, in particular species richness, varies strongly with elevation. There are competing hypotheses to explain such patterns, and typically these are linked closely to hypotheses explaining trends in relation to latitude. Moist, tropical regions have a more stable year-round climate which, over evolutionary time, may result in greater divergence and niche packing with fine-scale specialization. More fluctuating, higher latitude environments facilitate generalists with broad niches. Analogously, the more fluctuating climatic conditions at higher elevations may contribute to broader niches (Mermillon *et al.* 2022) and decreasing species richness along elevation gradients. However, the latitude gradient shows a fairly constant decrease in species richness towards the poles, whereas there is much more evidence of an intermediate peak in terms of elevation patterns, suggesting that latitudinal and elevational trends are driven, at least in part, by different factors (Rahbek 1995).

Temperature is in general the most important factor driving biodiversity trends along elevation gradients (Peters *et al.* 2016; Laiolo *et al.* 2018). Ambient temperature varies with elevation, or more strictly air pressure, in a fairly predictable way termed the adiabatic lapse rate. Typically, there is an approximately 0.6°C decrease for every 100 m increase in elevation, with local variation caused by humidity, wind exposure, cloud cover and other factors (e.g., Dillon *et al.* 2006; Colwell *et al.* 2008). Since temperature may constrain the number of organisms that a given area can support, the decrease in temperature at higher elevations may limit the richness of a given community and affect its community structure (White *et al.* 2019). Water availability (precipitation, soil water retention and evaporation) is an additional critical climatic factor (McCain 2009; Antonelli *et al.* 2018), influencing, for example, tree formation at high elevation. Primary productivity, which decreases with temperature (and hence elevation) and is also affected by precipitation, is integrated with these two abiotic drivers. High elevations have lower productivity, hence there is insufficient energy to support species rich communities (Newton 2020; Schumm *et al.* 2020). Indeed, there is evidence that bird species richness is closely correlated with measures of productivity (e.g., Acharya *et al.* 2011; Abebe *et al.* 2019). However, these relationships show considerable geographic variation – stability, *in situ* speciation and accumulation of species over a long time are considered to be more important drivers of species richness within regions with high landscape complexity (Rahbek *et al.* 2019).

A range of other hypotheses have been proposed to explain variations in species richness with elevation. Rapoport's rule states that the latitudinal range size of animals and plants is greater at higher latitudes (Stevens 1989). This has been extended to range sizes in relation to elevation, that is, species of higher elevations show a greater elevational range as they are adapted to a wider range of conditions (Stevens 1992). This results in greater species richness at lower elevations as higher elevation species are more likely to 'spill down' to lower elevations (Acharya *et al.* 2011). There are also hypotheses that are more related to spatial effects, rather than biological effects *per se*. For example, some have argued that lower species richness at higher elevations in mountains is due to the species-area relationship and the fact that a 'typical' conical-shaped mountain has a greater area at the base than close to the summit (Šekercioğlu *et al.* 2012). An alternative hypothesis is the Mid-Domain Effect (Colwell & Lees 2000), which proposes that the ranges of species are randomly distributed within a given area, thus more ranges will overlap near the middle of the area than at the edges, resulting in a mid-elevation species richness peak. There has been only limited support for Rapoport's rule (Gaston *et al.* 1998; Achayra *et al.* 2011), the species-area relationship (Elsen & Tingley 2015) and the Mid-Domain Effect (McCain 2009; Reynolds *et al.* 2021) for explaining patterns in species richness along elevation gradients. Environmental drivers (e.g., productivity and climate, in particular water and temperature) are thus likely to be more important (McCain 2009), although a range of complex factors interact to produce location-specific patterns (Reynolds *et al.* 2022).

Whilst much research on biodiversity trends along the elevation gradient has focussed on species richness, other studies have instead considered variations in functional diversity, that is, the role of organisms in communities and ecosystems (Petchey & Gaston 2006), usually expressed through the analysis of species traits (e.g., diet type, clutch size, foraging niche, migratory strategy). Trends in functional diversity along elevation gradients vary according to latitude. In the tropics, bird communities show a disproportionately high functional diversity in relation to their species richness (i.e., functional overdispersion) in stable lowland habitats, but the opposite pattern (functional clustering) in higher elevation habitats (Jarzyna *et al.* 2021). However, increasing functional overdispersion is shown in temperate and boreal bird communities at higher elevations (above *c.* 2,000 m, Martin *et al.* 2021). Temperate mountains are therefore functionally rich and distinctive ecosystems, despite their overall low species richness. These findings further suggest that higher latitude mountains are disproportionately susceptible to the loss of critical ecological functions because they harbour species assemblages with high functional distinctiveness and low species richness (Jarzyna *et al.* 2021).

1.2.1 Zonation Along the Elevation Gradient

Mountains are defined by their greater elevation with respect to the surrounding landscape, thus a key characteristic, in particular in relation to biodiversity, is the rapid change in environmental conditions along the elevation gradient – and obviously the steeper the gradient, the more rapidly conditions will change over a given spatial scale. The decrease in temperature with elevation is one of the key environmental factors that affects variation in biotic communities along elevation gradients (see earlier in section 1.2). Additionally, wind speed, air pressure, partial pressure of oxygen and UV radiation vary more-or-less predictably with elevation (Nagy & Grabherr 2009; Chapter 2).

The changing conditions over small spatial scales result in fairly distinct vegetation zones along the elevation gradient that are normally bounded by the upper limit of particular growth forms dictated by the environmental conditions. In a natural state (i.e., with little or minimal human influence), these correspond to the bioclimatic zones listed in Table 1.1. There are two features separating different zones that are of particular relevance to the scope of this book. First, the **timberline**, which is the upper limit of closed forest. Much of this book is concerned with the area above the timberline (i.e., it forms the lower limit of the bioclimatic zones considered). Second, the **treeline**, the approximate line that links the highest groups of mature trees, which is often limited by temperature (Körner & Paulsen 2004). The treeline typically represents an area of marked change in bird communities (e.g., Altamirano *et al.* 2020; Martin *et al.* 2021). Given the inconsistencies in the use of these terms to describe vegetation zones and boundaries around the treeline, we discuss them in more detail in Chapter 4.

The zones set out in Table 1.1 are, of course, generalizations – there are many situations where some of them are absent, often due to human activity (see Section 1.5), but also due to ecological or climatic conditions (e.g., the extent of treeline habitat for temperate mountains is often very limited; Nagy & Grabherr 2009). There are also regional or local climatic constraints that may influence zonation such as aspect. In dry climates, the forest may be largely absent (e.g., some central Asian ranges, Potapov 2004; the dry central Andes, Chapter 9). Furthermore, the limit of the

Table 1.1 *Habitat zonation and key divisions between zones along the elevation gradient (based largely on Nagy & Grabherr 2009), as used in this book.*

Zone	Description
Lowland	Areas not classified as mountain.
Montane forest	Closed canopy forest, mature trees – note that transitions may occur between different types of forest within this zone (e.g., subtropical and temperate broad-leaved forest; Acharya *et al.* 2011).
Timberline	The line where the closed forest ends, marking the transition between montane forest and treeline ecotone.
Treeline ecotone	The zone between the timberline and the tree species line. Also sometimes termed the upper subalpine, this is typically characterized by a mosaic of trees, shrubs and meadows.
Treeline	The approximate line that links the highest growing groups of mature trees.
Tree species line	The maximum possible elevation of tree growth (including seedlings and saplings).
Alpine	The treeless area above the tree species line that is dominated by dwarf-shrub communities (sometimes termed lower alpine) and grassland, steppe-like and meadow communities (sometimes termed upper alpine).
Snowline	The elevation at which there is permanent snow cover (often considered equal to the upper limit of the alpine zone; Körner 2012).
Nival	Patchy vegetation, often cushion or rosette plants, within a largely unvegetated landscape (some authors separate nival and subnival zones according to the snowline).
Aeolian	Beyond the elevation limit at which vascular plants grow. Wind is important in providing nutrient input and maintaining food chains.

alpine zone is influenced by slope exposure. For mountain ranges that are generally orientated from east to west (e.g., Himalayas, European Alps, Pyrenees), the alpine zone is typically lower on northern facing slopes in the northern hemisphere and on southern facing slopes in the southern hemisphere (Nagy & Grabherr 2009). There are oceanic influences on the treeline as well, mediated by precipitation patterns that influence the elevation of the different zones in major mountain chains that are orientated from north to south (e.g., the Andes, Chapter 9) and also mountains on islands. Zonation may also vary according to the geographic position of a particular location within a mountain range, whereby central areas have warmer temperatures and thus higher elevations for any given zone

Figure 1.1 Examples of the elevation zones that are the main focus of this book.
A. Suntar-Khayata Range, Eastern Siberia, showing gentle elevation gradients
resulting in a wide treeline ecotone (Photo: E. Melikhova); B. Peruvian Andes,
with patches of *Polylepis* woodland (Photo: S. Sevillano-Ríos). C. Gradient from
montane forest to the alpine zone in the Italian Alps, where grazing has a major
impact on vegetation structure and in particular on the elevation of the treeline
ecotone (Photo: D. Chamberlain). D. A high elevation lake in the Tantalus
Range, British Columbia, Canada, within a diffuse treeline ecotone transitioning
into alpine shrubs and a rocky nival zone towards the peak (Photo: D.R.
de Zwaan).

relative to external slopes (the mass elevation effect; Körner 2012). Some
examples of elevation gradients in mountains from different geographic
regions are shown in Figure 1.1. Despite these variations, the definitions
in Table 1.1 serve as a useful reference for the typical zonation found
along elevation gradients in many mountains.

At very high latitudes, Arctic mountains do not have a treeline as they
are beyond the latitudinal limit of tree growth. Indeed, latitude is the
main determinant of the elevation of these various zones (Table 1.1); the
treeline in tropical mountains can occur at very high elevations (Nagy &
Grabherr 2009), whereas in sub-arctic areas at high latitudes, the treeline
is at sea-level. Furthermore, this classification does not apply in many
areas due to human influence (see Section 1.5).

1.3 Mountain Birds

1.3.1 What Is a Mountain Bird?

Defining a mountain is difficult, so it follows that defining a mountain bird is equally challenging. Objective definitions of mountain birds have been developed based on definitions of mountain areas as outlined above and their overlap with the range maps of the geographical distribution of species. In this way, mountain birds are identified as those with a large proportion of their range in mountain areas (e.g., Scridel *et al.* 2018; Lehikoinen *et al.* 2019; Alba *et al.* 2022). However, such range maps are usually restricted to breeding season distributions and thus do not represent the use of mountains by birds throughout the year. The number of species that use mountains may be particularly high. One field study of temperate mountains in the Americas during the breeding season detected 44 to 63 per cent of the regional species pool in western Canada and southern Chile, respectively (Martin *et al.* 2021). At a continental level and including migrants, Boyle & Martin (2015) found that c. 35 per cent of the birds that breed in North America use mountains at some point in their annual life cycle.

In this book, we are interested in how mountain habitats are used by birds. We define a mountain bird in this book *as a bird species where at least some populations somewhere in their distribution spend at least one critical stage of their life cycle at or above the elevational limit of continuous forest (i.e., above the timberline).* In doing so, we recognize that our knowledge of avian use of mountains is incomplete from a seasonal point of view (as research is biased towards breeding seasons) and from a geographic point of view (as many of the world's mountain ranges are under-researched – see Section 1.3.2).

1.3.2 Extent of Knowledge of Birds using Alpine Habitats Compared to Other Systems

Given the particular logistical challenges to mountain research, it has been suggested that knowledge of mountain birds is relatively poor compared to other major habitat types (European Environment Agency 2010; Chamberlain *et al.* 2012; Scridel *et al.* 2018). For example, nearly one quarter of all alpine breeding species have no nest records or have less than five nests described, in addition to deep data deficiency for most other basic life-history traits (Chapters 2 and 3). A systematic search of published articles in the Web of Science online database between

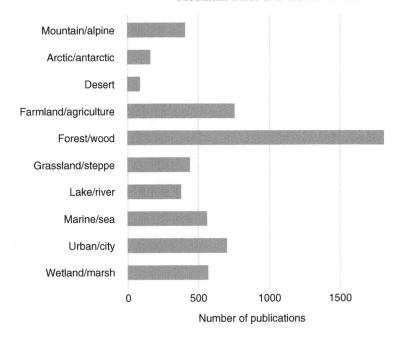

Figure 1.2 The number of research articles on Web of Science (articles referenced in the Science Citation Index, all languages) between 2011 and 2021 according to different search terms based on habitats. The general topic search (TS) term was 'TS=((bird* OR avian*) AND (HAB1* OR HAB2*) AND (ecology OR conservation))', where HAB1 and HAB2 represent the search terms on the x-axis (with the exception of desert for which there was only a single habitat term in the search). Only a maximum of two habitat-based terms were used in order to try to produce a more comparable search. A study was only included if the research therein was restricted to a given habitat (e.g., a landscape-level study including both forest and farmland would not have been included).

2011 and 2021 was undertaken to determine the level of relatively recent research on birds in mountains compared to other major habitat types. Of the ten different habitats considered, the number of publications on birds restricted to mountain/alpine habitat (n = 403) was comparable to the total from grasslands and lake/river, and was higher than Arctic/Antarctic and desert habitats (Figure 1.2). Birds associated with forests had the most publications, followed by farmland and urban habitats.

At first sight, the contention that mountain birds are under-studied compared to birds in other habitats does not seem to be supported. However, considering the number of publications in mountain/alpine habitat according to elevation zone (Table 1.1), it is clear that much

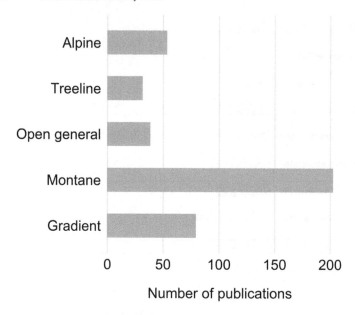

Figure 1.3 The number of research articles on mountain birds grouped according to elevation zone (Table 1.1). 'Open general' refers to largely treeless habitats that are usually anthropogenic in nature and that occur below the climatic treeline in a given location. Gradient studies encompass more than one elevation zone. N = 403.

research has been carried out exclusively in montane forests (50% of 403 studies), and on elevation gradients across zones (20%), but comparatively little has been conducted specifically in the alpine zone (13%) and even less in the treeline ecotone (8%; Figure 1.3). Hence, our knowledge of the ecology of mountain birds at high elevation does indeed seem to be lower than those in most other major habitat types based on research carried out in the last ten years. Only desert habitats (n = 83; Figure 1.2) had fewer publications than those specifically undertaken either at the treeline or in the alpine zone (n = 84).

A further examination of the 'mountain' and 'alpine' references was carried out in order to assess geographical biases in research. Most studies had been conducted in Asia and Europe, with somewhat fewer in North and South America (Figure 1.4). At the national level, there were more studies in China (n = 45) than any other country. There were very few studies (<10%) in Africa, Oceania (including Australia) or studies that

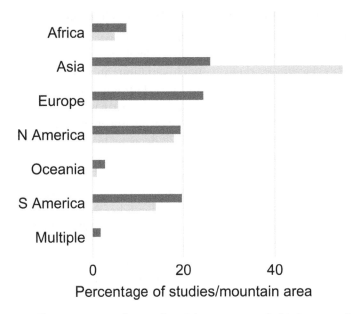

Figure 1.4 The percentage of research articles on mountain birds grouped according to the continent in which the research took place (dark grey bars) and the percent of global mountain area in each continent (light grey bars) as defined by Körner *et al.* (2017), where Australia has been combined with Oceania. 'Multiple' indicates a study that took place on more than one continent. N = 403.

were carried out in multiple continents. Similarly, a larger proportion of studies was conducted in temperate climatic zones (45%) compared to tropical (35%) or subtropical (13%) zones, and very few were undertaken in boreal or arctic mountains (<3%). These percentages were compared to the percentage of global mountain area in each continent based on the classification of Körner *et al.* (2017). There is a clear bias towards mountain bird research in Europe, which has a far higher percentage of papers relative to the percentage of global mountain area (Figure 1.4), whereas research in Asian mountains is under-represented in proportion to their global mountain coverage. Research in other continents was more-or-less representative of the contribution to global mountain coverage. We should, however, acknowledge that our search terms were in English, hence the search was biased towards publications written in English or with abstracts and titles in English, which may have underestimated representation in some regions.

1.3.3 Bird Communities Along the Elevation Gradient

The most common pattern of variation in bird species richness with elevation is that of a mid-elevation peak (Rahbek 1995; but see Quintero & Jetz 2018). However, there is much variation, and the precise pattern may be influenced by a range of factors. Humidity has a marked influence on species richness at large scales. In particular, a low-elevation plateau (i.e., species richness is constant at lower elevations and then decreases after a particular threshold) or decrease in richness with respect to elevation is shown in humid mountains, whereas a mid-elevation peak (i.e., the highest species richness at an intermediate elevation) is more likely in dry mountains (McCain 2009). At larger scales, species richness is also correlated with topographic relief, heterogeneity in soils and geological substrate properties (Antonelli *et al.* 2018; Rahbek *et al.* 2019), which are in turn related to evolutionary processes (Chapter 9). The influence of methods should also be considered, as estimates of elevational species richness are often affected by variation in sampling effort and sample size (Nogués-Bravo *et al.* 2008; Quintero & Jetz 2018). Raw species richness may give patterns that differ from those where adjustments are made to control for area considered or the geographic range of species. For example, the common intermediate peak (Rahbek 1995) is driven largely by wide ranging species. When controlling for species range size, the global elevational pattern of species richness is weakly and linearly decreasing (Quintero & Jetz 2018).

For plants, temperature and water availability typically determine the position of key vegetation zones (Körner & Paulsen 2004) and these vegetation communities are then a key determinant of animal communities. Direct effects of temperature may also limit species distributions in some animals, especially invertebrates (Hodkinson 2005), as may the other factors that vary systematically along the elevation gradient (see Section 1.2.1). There is little evidence that these factors directly affect the distribution of many birds (but see Chapter 2). Instead, it seems highly likely that they will impact birds indirectly through effects on plants (Nagy & Grabherr 2009) and invertebrates (Hodkinson 2005), influencing both nesting habitat and food supply.

There is evidence that variations in avian diversity along elevation gradients are influenced by vegetation structure (Chapters 3 and 4). For example, Acharya *et al.* (2011), working on an exceptionally long gradient (300–4,700 m) in the Eastern Himalayas, found a peak in species richness at around 2,000 m, close to the transition between subtropical and temperate broad-leaved forest. The richness patterns were best explained by vegetation characteristics (plant species richness, tree basal area, shrub density) and evapotranspiration. Ceresa *et al.* (2021) found a significant indirect effect of local temperature via vegetation on bird abundance for all 15 species considered along elevation gradients in the Italian Alps, but only generalist forest species showed evidence of direct effects of temperature. Similarly, Ferger *et al.* (2014) found evidence of both direct and indirect effects of climate on bird diversity along a gradient (870–4,550 m) on Mount Kilimanjaro extending to the alpine zone, where both vegetation structure and food resources were important indirect drivers. These studies support an indirect effect of climate (i.e., temperature and moisture) on bird diversity along the elevation gradient mediated through vegetation responses and hence food resources. Indeed, there is evidence from the Himalayas that species richness patterns are associated with declines in arthropod diversity and resource abundance along the elevation gradient (Schumm *et al.* 2020).

Interspecific competition is acknowledged as a potentially important driver of animal communities, and it likely plays a role in patterns of functional diversity along elevation gradients (Jarzyna *et al.* 2021). Although this topic has received relatively little attention, largely due to the difficulties in quantifying interactions among species (McCain & Grytnes 2010), Freeman (2020) indicates high elevation birds may be just as competitive as low elevation birds. Supriya *et al.* (2020) present intriguing evidence that the mid-elevation peak in bird diversity in the Himalayas is caused by competition with Asian weaver ants *Oecophylla smaragdina*. Songbirds and ants have a high dietary overlap, and experimental removal of ants increased arthropod prey. At mid-elevations that were beyond the elevation range of the ants, arthropod abundance was positively correlated with bird abundance. This study, carried out in montane forest, shows the potential for competition driving elevational diversity patterns.

1.4 Environmental Challenges for Mountain Birds

Mountains present various environmental challenges to birds. For breeding or year-round resident birds, these are associated with conditions that may be extreme, and are often highly variable and unpredictable. Mountain bird species, or mountain populations (i.e., compared to other populations of the same species at lower elevations), therefore often have specific adaptations to enable them to survive under the particular abiotic and biotic conditions that mountains present. This can include physiological and life-history adaptations as well as some unique behavioural strategies in high elevation specialists (Chapter 2). For example, the glacier finch *Idiopsar speculifera* nests in glaciers at elevations of up to 5,300 m in the Peruvian Andes (Hardy & Hardy 2008; Box 1.1), one of only very few species known to nest on ice (others include emperor penguin *Aptenodytes forsteri* and white-fronted ground tyrant *Muscisaxicola albifrons*; Hardy *et al.* 2018). Furthermore, mountains can influence bird migration, both as a physical barrier and as a corridor (Aschwanden *et al.* 2020), and also as a seasonal habitat that enables migratory stopovers for birds migrating both north and south (Boyle & Martin 2015; de Zwaan *et al.* 2019).

Box 1.1 *Glacier Bird of the High Andes*

Douglas R. Hardy & Spencer P. Hardy

Few birds are as well adapted to the highest alpine environments as the glacier finch *Idiopsar speculifer*, a distinctive species living in the High Andes of Peru, Bolivia, and northern Chile. Formerly known as white-winged diuca finch *Diuca speculifera*, the ecology of this species is strongly associated with glaciers (Figure B1.1). Glacier finches are among the highest nesting passerines in the Western Hemisphere, routinely constructing nests directly on glacier ice at elevations up to 5,300 m (Hardy & Hardy 2008). They also roost within glaciers (Hardy *et al.* 2018), and feed on insects on glacier surfaces (Hardy *et al.* 2020).

The glacier finch is relatively large, slate gray overall with a white throat, a white arc under red eyes, and has dark grey primaries with partially white bases that appear as a white wing patch on perched birds (Fjeldså & Krabbe 1990). Its primary foraging habitat is puna grassland, often in wetlands or bogs known as bofedales (Gibbons *et al.* 2016), where pairs or small groups move slowly over open ground looking for food. Their distinctive plumage and behaviour render the species easily identifiable, suggesting that its geographic range should be relatively accurately established. However, the 4,000 to 5,500 m elevations where glacier finches are typically found requires acclimatization by humans, hindering detailed studies of their distribution and ecology.

Each day towards dusk the birds move upslope, gathering along glacier margins in preparation for roosting within crevasses and cavities. Typically, pairs arrive at the margin and perch near or on the ice, only entering the actual roost sites when it is dark. This behaviour seems

Figure B1.1 A recently fledged glacier finch *Idiopsar speculifera* (left) being fed by an adult near the nest at Quelccaya Ice Cap, Peru (Photo: D. Hardy).

to happen year around, including during the breeding season, and was first described in 1953 (Niethammer 1953). Roosts are thought to offer protection from low night-time temperatures, snowfall and predation (Hardy *et al.* 2018).

Glacier finches may nest exclusively on glaciers. All of the c. 100 nests observed have been built on glaciers in the Cordillera Vilcanota of southern Peru (Hardy & Hardy 2008; Castañeda 2015; Hardy *et al.* 2018). Active nests have been found during April in cracks on near-vertical ice faces or deep within crevasses, with clutch sizes of two or three eggs. Nests are a massive (c. 160 g dry mass) collection of grasses and twigs. During one period of extended nest observation, feeding of chicks was evenly shared between the two parents, with both adults arriving at the nest simultaneously and regurgitating food to the chicks before departing with faecal sacs. At this nest, feeding bouts averaged just over one hour (Hardy *et al.* 2018), as most foraging flights were likely greater than 500 m. Does the species nest exclusively on glaciers? Extensive additional research is required; however, their range distribution closely coincides with that of glaciers (e.g., Dussaillant *et al.* 2019).

Glacier finch ecology appears heavily reliant upon the glacierized environment at high elevations of the Andes, for food resources and protection against both predation and the harsh climate. In the strongly seasonal precipitation regime typical of the central Andes, glacier runoff during the dry season sustains bofedales and their associated biodiversity. Even the ice morphology of glaciers appears to be important for roosting and nesting sites; extensive nest site observations at Quelccaya Ice Cap (e.g., Hardy *et al.* 2018) have revealed a strong preference for the protection of crevasses and very steep, fissured margins. Currently, however, Andean glaciers are melting and retreating upslope at an alarming rate (Rabatel *et al.* 2013; Dussaillant *et al.* 2019), and the disappearance of the Chacaltaya Glacier in Western Bolivia demonstrates the consequences for this species. Chacaltaya is where glacier finch behaviour on a glacier was first observed (Neithammer 1953), yet the glacier had disappeared by 2010 (Rabatel *et al.* 2013). There are no recent eBird reports of glacier finches from the immediate area. In light of the species' close association with glaciers, and rapid Andean environmental changes underway, the IUCN Red List Category of 'Least Concern' conservation status (BirdLife International 2021) appears inadequate. The future of the glacier finch will likely depend upon the ability of the species to adapt to a very different environment, one with a diminished number of glaciers and less meltwater runoff during the dry season to nourish bofedales.

1.4.1 Weather

Mountain birds, especially at higher latitudes, are typically subject to greater degrees of fluctuations in weather conditions, both at broad (seasonal) and fine (daily) temporal scales (Martin & Wiebe 2004). The frequency of extreme weather events increases with elevation (Martin *et al.* 2017) and can pose a significant challenge to mountain birds, in particular in terms of its impacts on nesting success. Severe storm events, often involving late season snowfalls, can cause abandonment (e.g., horned lark *Eremophila alpestris*, Martin *et al.* 2017; red-faced warbler *Cardellina rubrifrons*, Decker & Conway 2009) and direct nestling mortality (e.g., buff-bellied pipit *Anthus rubescens*, Hendricks & Norment 1991; Lapland longspur *Calcarius lapponicus*, Jehl & Hussel 1966). Similarly, prolonged rainfall can be a major cause of nest failure (e.g., in Savannah sparrow *Passerculus sandwichensis*, Martin *et al.* 2017). For high elevation specialists, hot dry weather can also have negative impacts – for example, annual survival in female white-winged snowfinch *Montifringilla nivalis* is negatively correlated with warm, dry summers (Strinella *et al.* 2020).

Unpredictable weather conditions at high elevation mean that the timing of breeding for many mountain species varies substantially from year to year, for example, up to one month's difference among years in the clutch initiation dates of ptarmigan *Lagopus* spp. in North America (Martin & Wiebe 2004). Timing of snowmelt in particular will dictate onset of nesting for alpine zone species (e.g., Martin 2001; de Zwaan *et al.* 2019; Sander *et al.* 2021, 2023), and probably also for other shrub and tree nesting species. Some migrant species, including long-distance, short-distance and altitudinal migrants, wait at lower elevations for conditions to change (e.g., ring ouzel *Turdus torquatus*, Barras *et al.* 2021). In the horned lark, birds that used staging areas relatively close to their breeding grounds for periods of 30 to 60 days on their spring migration had greater productivity, a strategy that may enable individuals to monitor environmental conditions and optimize their arrival date to their breeding site (de Zwaan *et al.* 2019). Early breeding can be risky due the possibility of nest failure caused by inclement weather. In late-onset years, reproductive success can be severely limited in comparison with birds in lower elevation habitats as the breeding window is short and there may not be the possibility to attempt re-nesting after early nest failures (Martin & Wiebe 2004). As a consequence, annual reproductive success may be highly variable. Bollmann & Reyer (2001) found that predation on water pipit *Anthus spinoletta* nests did not vary significantly from year to year. However, failure rates due to heavy rainfall and snow varied between 1 and 20 per cent annually. Such effects may have selected for slower life-histories in high elevation birds, both within and across species (physiological and behavioural adaptations to coping with conditions at high elevation are considered in detail in Chapter 2).

Clearly weather, that is, relatively short- or medium-term fluctuations in atmospheric conditions, can have major consequences for mountain bird reproductive success, survival and movement (dispersal or migration). It follows that longer term trends (over many years) in atmospheric conditions, (i.e., climate change), will also have concomitant longer term consequences for bird populations. Indeed, mountains are expected to be affected disproportionately by climate change in many regions (but predictions vary – see Pepin *et al.* 2022), and there is some evidence that this is having impacts on mountain birds (Freeman *et al.* 2018; Scridel *et al.* 2017). These impacts are likely to increase for alpine zone species in particular in the future (Chamberlain *et al.* 2013). This topic is addressed fully in Chapter 6.

1.4.2 Food Resources

For high latitude mountains, the shorter growing season is likely to be an important constraint that will limit the temporal availability of food and hence affect breeding phenology, migratory behaviour (see Section 1.4.3) and ultimately may influence life-history strategies (e.g., Bears *et al.* 2009; Sandercock *et al.* 2005). The melting snow itself may provide an important resource for a range of species (Antor 1995; Resano-Mayor *et al.* 2019; Chapter 3). The timing of snowmelt may influence the period for which food is available. For rock ptarmigan *Lagopus muta*, seasonal variation in the quality of food is important – early snowmelt leads to earlier breeding and higher breeding success. This may be influenced by the quality of plant matter in their diet, whereby earlier snowmelt leads to a longer availability of plants with high digestible protein content (García-González *et al.* 2016). For invertebrate feeders, there are numerous examples of lowland passerine species that time their breeding to coincide with peak seasonal abundance of their invertebrate prey (e.g., Both *et al.* 2006, 2009). In a mountain environment, there is little evidence of such clear seasonal peaks. Instead, food availability seems to be dictated by interactions between snowmelt and/or soil moisture (Barras *et al.* 2020) and vegetation development, and thus can vary substantially from year to year. For ground foragers of the alpine zone such as white-winged snowfinch and water pipit, it seems more likely that birds time their breeding to coincide with the peak in food availability, which may be influenced by vegetation structure (and hence access to prey), rather than prey abundance *per se* (Brodmann *et al.* 1997; Resano-Mayor *et al.* 2019; Chapter 3). In general, however, trophic links between vegetation, invertebrates and birds are poorly studied in mountains.

In tropical mountains, there are relatively more frugivores and nectivores in the bird community. Periods of bad weather that reduce their food supplies or their ability to forage successfully can pose a significant risk as these food sources are low in protein and fat and hence must be consumed frequently and in quantity (Boyle 2018), a contributory factor to altitudinal migration behaviour (see Section 1.4.3). However, tropical conditions may mean a relatively constant food supply is available year-round, hence some species have fewer constraints on timing of breeding. For example, the tropical high-elevation wetlands of the Andes generally do not freeze because of the amount of solar heating during the day (and the thermal capacity of water). This means that some waterbirds can breed all year round (Chapter 9).

1.4.3 Migration

In temperate and boreal mountains, marked seasonality is a major influence on the bird community. Most species that breed above the treeline do not remain all year round. In many temperate and boreal mountains, most species (>75 per cent) are migrants avoiding the harsh winter conditions and thus the winter communities above the forest are made up of very few species. It should be noted that aside from studies in British Columbia (Wilson & Martin 2005; Boyle & Martin 2015), there have been few published studies on temperate or boreal mountain bird communities outside the breeding season. However, there are a few studies on the winter ecology of particular mountain species (especially grouse, e.g., Artlettaz et al. 2007; Bocca et al. 2014). There is better understanding of migrants passing through mountains, and in particular passerines, thanks to long-term ringing stations in mountain passes, such as the Col de Bretolet in the Swiss Alps which has operated a ringing scheme continuously since 1958 (Hohl 2019). Data from such sites can be useful in terms of understanding species-specific seasonal migration patterns through mountains in terms of phenology and abundance (Jenni & Kéry 2003).

Migrants can be broadly defined into long-distance or short-distance migrants (although this is a simplification as there can be diverse strategies within the same species or indeed the same population; Boyle 2018). Long-distance migrants are generally classified as those species for which the whole population makes seasonal long-distance latitudinal movements, often of 1,000 km or more, to different climatic zones. Short-distance migrants generally migrate away from the breeding area, but they remain in the wider geographic region. Many short-distance migrants in mountains include species that are altitudinal migrants, that is, they make 'predictable, seasonal movements up and down-slope between breeding and wintering ranges within the same geographic region' (Boyle & Martin 2015). This is a common strategy in mountain birds (e.g., 30 per cent of North American birds and 65 per cent of Himalayan birds exhibit altitudinal migration; Boyle 2018). This behaviour is facilitated by the marked changes in conditions over small spatial scales, thus the benefits that migrants flying longer distances may accrue by changing latitudes can be achieved with relatively little cost by changing elevation (Boyle 2018). The typical altitudinal migrant is usually perceived as a species that disperses to lower elevations outside the breeding season in response to harsh weather conditions. A good example is the wallcreeper *Trichodroma muraria* which can often be found at low elevation on older buildings of European towns and cities in the winter (Box 1.2).

Whilst tropical mountains are not subject to the same level of seasonal variation in climatic conditions, migration is nonetheless a common strategy, and climate is still a main driver of migratory behaviour, in particular rainfall. Boyle (2011) found that counts of migrants in lowland forests were positively correlated with montane rainfall, suggesting movements were associated with weather conditions at high elevation. In this case, heavy rain can limit foraging opportunities and hence energy intake, leading to greater propensity for altitudinal migration in wetter years (Boyle 2011). However, in much of the tropical Andes, heavy rainfall occurs commonly at lower elevations. In the alpine zone, it can rain for long periods, but it is usually not very heavy. In many areas, most small birds actually move up high to breed in the rainy season and down-slope migration happens in the dry (winter) season. The situation is similar in African mountains where most birds stay the whole year in the upper montane forest, but some insectivores disappear during the peak of the dry season (J. Fjeldså, pers. comm.).

Box 1.2 *Wallcreeper – An Iconic Mountain Bird*

The wallcreeper *Tichodroma muraria* (Figure B1.2) is probably the most sought-after species by birdwatchers in European Mountains. In part, this is because it is undoubtedly a striking species, but it also has a reputation for being very difficult to find due to its preferred habitat of inaccessible rock faces. In some ways, this species is a typical mountain bird, although it is difficult to classify into any of the zones along the elevation gradient (Table 1.1), as it can breed across a range of elevations, exceptionally even to fairly low levels (e.g., it has been recorded down to 350 m in Switzerland and 500 m in Slovakia; Cramp & Perrins 1993; Saniga 2004). However, it is primarily a bird of high mountains and its restricted geographic distribution closely

Figure B1.2 Wallcreeper *Tichodroma muraria* (Photo: Bruno Dentesani).

follows the highest Eurasian mountain ranges (Cramp & Perrins 1993). Its most important requirement is the existence of sheer rock faces – it can inhabit gorges within mountain forests, although it is more widespread, but never common, on huge cliffs on mountainsides in the alpine zone at higher elevations, for example, 2,000–2,600 m in Switzerland (Keller *et al.* 2020), 2,450–3,000 m in Turkey (Cramp & Perrins 1993) and above the treeline from 1,700–2,900 m in Catalonia (Aymerich *et al.* 2012). Aside from rock faces, where it nests and obtains its prey (mostly spiders and small insects), its main requirement seems to be the proximity to water, a typical nest site being a cleft in a rock face above a torrent (Cramp & Perrins 1993). It also favours rock faces that have some vegetation rather than being completely bare, and seems to be more common on limestone cliffs (Saniga 2004; Aymerich *et al.* 2012).

The species exhibits altitudinal migration, usually moving to lower elevation valleys, plains and coastal cliffs in winter. It can even be found in towns and cities, in particular on old buildings such as ramparts, bridges and churches. The species is also capable of longer movements of a few hundred kilometres, probably following river valleys. In some records of longer movements, the species has turned up in places far from potential alpine breeding habitat, such as southern England (Dymond *et al.* 1989). It is not known what proportion of the population migrates, either altitudinally or over longer distances, and whether this tendency is more closely associated with certain individuals (e.g., according to age or sex) in the population (Cramp & Perrins 1993).

In common with many mountain birds, relatively little is known about this species. The general lack of knowledge of the ecology of mountain bird species or populations compared to their lowland counterparts is largely due to the logistic difficulties of working in mountain environments (Chamberlain *et al.* 2012). Even compared to other mountain species, the wallcreeper presents an extreme challenge due to its habitat. Despite this, there have been some studies on nesting in this species, in particular on nest site characteristics (Saniga 2004) and the nesting period (Cramp & Perrins 1993). However, we know very little about the factors that drive reproductive success. Indeed, Alba *et al.* (2022) could find no published study that assessed potential impacts of environmental change on this species. For such an iconic species, this is a gap in research that surely needs to be filled.

A further feature of mountains is the marked difference between day and night time temperatures. They may commonly experience frosts during the night and severe summer heat during the day (Nagy & Grabherr 2009). This presents a particular challenge for smaller species with relatively unpredictable food resources, especially in the tropics. Both hummingbirds and sunbirds are known to go into nocturnal torpor, substantially decreasing their metabolic rate as a strategy to cope with cold conditions at night (e.g., Carpenter 1974; Downs & Brown 2002). Alternatively, altitudinal migration may be undertaken on a diurnal rather than seasonal basis, for example, slender-billed starlings *Onychognathus tenuirostris* fly from the forests to the alpine zone in east African mountains to feed, but return to the forest at dusk (Young & Evans 1993). Whilst normally a forest nester, this species also shows an interesting flexibility in habitat selection, apparently nesting in cliffs in the alpine zone in years of mass flowering of *Lobelia deckenii keniensis* that produces copious nectar and seeds and hence attracts abundant insects.

1.5 Anthropogenic Impacts

Human land use has been a driver of vegetation dynamics and species distributions in mountains for millennia. Humans have been clearing mountain forests since at least the Neolithic period, initially for fuel collection and burning to maintain more open areas to facilitate hunting (Kessler & Herzog 1998). There is evidence that the practice of transhumance, the seasonal movement of livestock and people from the valleys to mountain pastures in the summer, has existed for c. 7,000 years in the European Alps, when Neolithic herdsmen probably burned the forests at the timberline to expand pastures for grazing (Schwörer *et al.* 2014). This practice has caused treelines to be much lower than their natural temperature-limited elevation in much of the European Alps, and as a consequence, there is often little or no treeline ecotone. Clearing for urbanization, deforestation and agriculture in the valleys have also impacted lower elevation mountain forests with often only a thin belt of mature forest remaining at mid elevations (Chapter 4). This is taken to further extremes in other mountain ranges where upper montane deforestation is almost complete (e.g., Cantabrian Mountains in Spain).

In both the Andes and the Himalayas, creating land for agriculture was also likely a motivation for clearing high elevation forests (Miehe *et al.* 2009; Valencia *et al.* 2018) which has had long-term impacts on the mountain landscape. In the arid mountains of southern Asia, the open dwarf shrubland that makes up the treeline ecotone is likely to be due to forest clearance and grazing, creating conditions from which the forest could not recover after the initial deforestation (Miehe *et al.* 2009). In the Andes, while *Polylepis* woodland is to some extent naturally fragmented, this fire- and disturbance-intolerant genus was much more widespread before the arrival of humans whose activity led to hyper-fragmentation, creating the landscape that is evident today. It is estimated that up to 97 per cent of the original *Polylepis* woodland has been lost in some areas of the Bolivian Andes due to human activities (Gareca *et al.* 2010).

Changes to the mountain habitat by humans can have positive effects on biodiversity, in particular by creating more diverse habitats, thus generating potential new ecological niche space (Araneda *et al.* 2018). For example, creation of open habitats in mountains has provided a refuge for farmland birds whose populations are declining in lowlands due to agricultural intensification (Archaux 2007). This may be the case when there are traditional and sustainable agricultural or pastoral systems in place, as in the European Alps where seasonal grazing creates ecotones that generally support more species than forest or alpine zone habitats (Laiolo *et al.* 2004). In the dry Andes, traditional Indigenous agriculture, including a diverse range of crops fed by irrigation systems, is associated with greater vegetative heterogeneity as well as high avian diversity and density (Araneda *et al.* 2018). Similarly, traditional irrigated Bedouin gardens in the South Sinai mountains have a higher bird species richness and density than the surrounding landscape, mainly due to a greater occurrence of migrant species rather than residents (Norfolk *et al.* 2015).

The extent of human impact on the world's mountains has varied over time. In the European Alps, the maximum rate of forest conversion to open landscapes occurred at the end of the Middle Ages (Gobet *et al.* 2003). Indeed, the current forest cover is probably the highest it has been for a number of centuries (Bebi *et al.* 2017). However, that is contrasted with other more recent changes that may have negative implications for biodiversity. The practice of transhumance is becoming economically unviable in many areas and as a consequence of reduced or absent grazing pressure, former ecotone habitats are being encroached by forest (Gerig-Fasel *et al.* 2007), with subsequent negative effects on the bird diversity of open habitats (Laiolo *et al.* 2004). Conversely, there are other areas where management is becoming more intensive, particularly in terms of management of grasslands for hay cutting, where applications of artificial fertilizers are increasing (Andrey *et al.* 2014; Assandri *et al.* 2019). Thus, in the Alps at least, management systems are becoming polarized into either more intensive management, or lack of any management, with likely negative impacts on birds and on biodiversity in general.

Agricultural activities have been the most significant historical anthropogenic factors that have influenced high mountain habitats and their associated bird communities (e.g., Gobet *et al.* 2003; Miehe *et al.* 2009; Schwörer *et al.* 2014). Hunting has also undoubtedly been an ever-present factor that continues to influence some mountain bird populations (Chapter 7). However, the last century has brought a number of new pressures caused by human activity. The leisure industry, and in particular skiing, developed in the latter decades of the nineteenth century and has become the main source of income for many temperate mountain communities (Elsasser & Messerli 2001). This has potential consequences for biodiversity in terms of habitat loss and degradation, and direct disturbance. Power generation is also an increasing pressure on mountain environments. The potential for hydropower has been recognized for several decades, and the associated changes to the fluvial environment can have impacts on biodiversity (e.g., Wu *et al.* 2019). Wind energy is a more recent development and indeed a more recent potential threat. The risk of collision with wind turbines has been well researched in lowland (especially coastal) habitats, and it seems likely that a similar threat will be posed to raptors in mountain regions (Chapter 7). Finally, evidence is building that climate change poses multiple challenges to mountain birds (Chapter 6). In total, direct effects from multiple stressors and, in some cases in interaction with other drivers, are projected to be a serious threat to high elevation specialist birds in the future (Chapter 8).

In order to protect potentially vulnerable populations of mountain birds, the ecological research community needs to develop strategies to safeguard the future of these species from potential threats through conservation and management actions. This should be underpinned by sound scientific research. Whether the existing knowledge base is sufficient for this relatively under-studied subject area (Section 1.3.2) is a question that underpins the objectives of this book. We aim to identify the key conservation issues and the highest priority conservation actions through our review of the ecology and conservation of birds at high elevations (Chapters 2–5 and 9), including the threats they face now and in the future (Chapters 6–8). Based on the evidence presented in this book, we develop a clear road map to guide research on the ecology and conservation of mountain birds over the next decades (Chapter 10).

Acknowledgements

We are grateful for the highly constructive comments of Jon Fjeldså and Devin de Zwaan that greatly improved the text. We are also indebted to Christian Körner, Roger Sayre, Davnah Payne, Corinna Ravilious and Riccardo Testolin for help in producing and interpreting Plates 1–4.

References

Abebe, A.F., Cai, T., Wale, M., *et al.* (2019) Factors determining species richness patterns of breeding birds along an elevational gradient in the Horn of Africa region. *Ecology & Evolution*, **9**, 9609–9623.

Acharya, B.K., Sanders, N.J., Vijayan, L. & Chettri, B. (2011) Elevational gradients in bird diversity in the Eastern Himalaya: an evaluation of distribution patterns and their underlying mechanisms. *PLoS ONE*, **6**, e29097.

Alba, R., Kasoar, T., Chamberlain, D., *et al.* (2022) Drivers of change in mountain bird populations in Europe. *Ibis*, **164**, 635–648.

Altamirano, T.A., de Zwaan, D.R., Ibarra, J.T. Wilson, S. & Martin, K. (2020) Treeline ecotones shape the distribution of avian species richness and functional diversity in south temperate mountains. *Scientific Reports*, **10**, 18428.

Andrey, A., Humbert, J.-Y., Pernollet, C. & Arlettaz, R. (2014) Experimental evidence for the immediate impact of fertilization and irrigation upon the plant and invertebrate communities of mountain grasslands. *Ecology and Evolution*, **4**, 2610–2623.

Antonelli, A., Kissling, W.D., Flantua, S.G.A., *et al.* (2018) Geological and climatic influences on mountain biodiversity. *Nature Geoscience*, **11**, 718–725.

Antor, R.J. (1995) The importance of arthropod fallout on snow patches for the foraging of high-alpine birds. *Journal of Avian Biology*, **26**, 81–85.

Archaux, F. (2007) Are mountains refuges for farmland bird species? A case study in the northern French Alps. *Bird Study*, **54**, 73–79.

Araneda, P., Sielfeld, W., Bonacic, C. & Ibarra, J.T. (2018) Bird diversity along elevational gradients in the Dry Tropical Andes of northern Chile: the potential role of Aymara indigenous traditional agriculture. *PLoS ONE*, **13**, e0207544.

Artlettaz, R., Patthey, P., Baltic, M. Leu, T., *et al.* (2007) Spreading free-riding snow sports represent a novel serious threat for wildlife. *Proceedings of the Royal Society Series B*, **274**, 1219–1224.

Aschwanden, J., Schmidt, M., Wichmann, G., *et al.* (2020) Barrier effects of mountain ranges for broad-front bird migration. *Journal of Ornithology*, **161**, 59–71.

Assandri, G., Bogliani, G., Pedrini, P. & Brambilla, M. (2019) Toward the next Common Agricultural Policy reform: determinants of avian communities in hay meadows reveal current policy's inadequacy for biodiversity conservation in grassland ecosystems. *Journal of Applied Ecology*, **56**, 604–617.

Aymerich, P., Capdevila, F., Canut, J., Roig, J. & Santandreu, J. (2012) Distribució i abundància de la població reproductora de Pela-roques *Tichodroma muraria* a Catalunya. *Revista Catalana d'Ornitologia*, **28**, 1–19.

Barras, A.G., Marti, S., Ettlin, S., *et al.* (2020) The importance of seasonal environmental factors in the foraging habitat selection of Alpine Ring Ouzels *Turdus torquatus alpestris*. *Ibis*, **162**, 505–519.

Barras, A.G., Liechiti, F. & Arlettaz, R. (2021) Seasonal and daily movement patterns of an alpine passerine suggest high flexibility in relation to environmental conditions. *Journal of Avian Biology*, **52**, e02860.

Bears, H., Martin, K.M. & White, G.C. (2009) Breeding in high-elevation habitat results in shift to slower life-history strategy within a single species. *Journal of Animal Ecology*, **78**, 365–375.

Bebi, P., Siedl, R., Motta, R., *et al.* (2017) Changes of forest cover and disturbance regimes in the mountain forests of the Alps. *Forest Ecology and Management*, **388**, 43–56.

BirdLife International (2021) Species factsheet: *Chionodacryon speculiferum* [*sic*]. www.birdlife.org Accessed on 21 October 2021.

Blyth, S., Groombridge, B., Lysenko, I., Miles, L. & Newton, A. (2002) *Mountain Watch*. Cambridge: UNEP World Conservation Monitoring Centre.

Bocca, M., Caprio, E., Chamberlain, D. & Rolando, A. (2014) The winter roosting and diet of the Black Grouse *Tetrao tetrix* in the north-western Italian Alps. *Journal of Ornithology*, **155**, 183–194.

Bollmann, K. & Reyer, H.-U. (2001) Reproductive success of Water Pipits in an alpine environment. *Condor*, **103**, 510–520.

Both, C., Bouwhuis, S., Lessells, C.M. & Visser, M.E. (2006) Climate change and population declines in a long-distance migratory bird. *Nature*, **441**, 81–83.

Both, C., van Asch, M., Bijlsma, R.M., van den Burg, A.B. & Visser, M.E. (2009) Climate change and unequal phenological changes across four trophic levels: constraints or adaptations? *Journal of Animal Ecology*, **78**, 73–83.

Boyle, A.W. (2011) Short-distance partial migration of Neotropical birds: a community-level test of the foraging limitation hypothesis. *Oikos*, **120**, 1803–1816.

Boyle, A.W. (2018) Altitudinal bird migration in North America. *Auk*, **134**, 443–465.

Boyle, A.W. & Martin, K. (2015) The conservation value of high elevation habitats to North American migrant birds. *Biological Conservation*, **192**, 461–476.

Brodmann, P.A., Reyer, H.-U. & Baer, B. (1997) The relative importance of habitat structure and of prey characteristics for the foraging success of Water Pipits (*Anthus spinoletta*). *Ethology*, **103**, 222–235.

Carpenter, F.L. (1974) Torpor in an Andean hummingbird: its ecological significance. *Science*, **183**, 545–547.

Castañeda, G.K. (2015) Primer registro de nido activo de Diuca Aliblanca (*Diuca speculifera*) sobre el hielo del nevado Quelccaya, Cuzco, Perú. *Boletín UNOP*, **10**, 40–41.

Ceresa, F., Kranebitter, P., Monrós, J.S., Rizzolli, F. & Brambilla, M. (2021) Disentangling direct and indirect effects of local temperature on abundance of mountain birds and implications for understanding global change impacts. *PeerJ*, **9**, e12560.

Chamberlain, D., Arlettaz, R., Caprio, E., *et al.* (2012) The altitudinal frontier in avian climate change research. *Ibis*, **154**, 205–209.

Chamberlain, D.E., Negro, M., Caprio, E. & Rolando, A. (2013) Assessing the sensitivity of alpine birds to potential future changes in habitat and climate to inform management strategies. *Biological Conservation*, **167**, 127–135.

Colwell, R.K. & Lees, D.C. (2000) The mid-domain effect: geometric constraints on the geography of species richness. *Trends in Ecology & Evolution*, **15**, 70–76.

Colwell, R.K., Brehm, J., Cardelús, C.L., Gilman, A.C. & Longino, J.T. (2008) Global warming, elevational range shifts, and lowland biotic attrition in the wet tropics. *Science*, **322**, 258–261.

Cramp, S. & Perrins, C.M. (1993) *Handbook of the Birds of Europe, the Middle East and North Africa*. Volume VII. Flycatcher to Shrikes. Oxford: Oxford University Press.

de Zwaan, D.R., Wilson, S., Gow, E.A. & Martin, K.M. (2019) Sex-specific spatiotemporal variation and carry-over effects in a migratory alpine songbird. *Frontiers in Ecology and Evolution*, **7**, article 285.

Decker, K.L. & C.J. Conway (2009) Effects of an unseasonable snowstorm on Red-faced Warbler nesting success. *Condor*, **111**, 392–395.

Dillon, M.E., Frazier, M.R. & Dudley, R. (2006) Into thin air: physiology and evolution of alpine insects. *Integrative and Comparative Biology*, **46**, 49–61.

Downs, C.T. & Brown, M. (2002) Nocturnal heterothermy and torpor in the Malachite Sunbird (*Nectarinia famosa*). *Auk*, **119**, 251–260.

Dussaillant, I., Berthier, E., Brun, F., *et al.* (2019) Two decades of glacier mass loss along the Andes. *Nature Geoscience*, **12**, 802–808.

Dymond, J.N., Fraser, P.A. & Gantlett, S.J.M. (1989) *Rare Birds in Britain and Ireland.* Berkhamstead: T & AD Poyser.

Elsasser, H. & Messerli, P. (2001) The vulnerability of the snow industry in the Swiss Alps. *Mountain Research and Development*, **21**, 335–339.

Elsen, P.R. & Tingley, M.W. (2015) Global mountain topography and the fate of montane species under climate change. *Nature Communications*, **5**, 772–776.

European Environment Agency (2010) *Europe's Ecological Backbone: Recognising the True Value of our Mountains.* EEA Report 6/2010. Copenhagen: European Environment Agency.

Ferger, S.W., Schleuning, M., Hemp, A., Howell, K.M. & Böhning-Gaese, K. (2014) Food resources and vegetation structure mediate climatic effects on species richness of birds. *Global Ecology and Biogeography*, **23**, 541–549.

Fjeldså, J. & Krabbe, N.K. (1990) *Birds of the High Andes.* Copenhagen: Zoological Museum and Apollo Books.

Fjeldså, J., Bowie, R.C.K. & Rahbek, C. (2012) The role of mountain ranges in the diversification of birds. *Annual Review of Ecology, Evolution and Systematics*, **43**, 249–265.

Franzén, N. & Molander, M. (2012) How threatened are alpine environments? A cross taxonomic study. *Biodiversity and Conservation*, **21**, 517–526.

Freeman, B.G. (2020) Lower elevation animal species do not tend to be better competitors than their higher elevation relatives. *Global Ecology and Biogeography*, **29**, 171–181.

Freeman, B.G., Scholer, M.N., Ruiz-Gutierrez, V. & Fitzpatrick, J.W. (2018) Climate change causes upslope shifts and mountaintop extirpations in a tropical bird community. *Proceedings of the National Academy of Sciences*, **115**, 11982–11987.

García-González, R., Aldezabal, A., Laskurain, N.A., Margalida, A. & Novoa, C. (2016) Influence of snowmelt timing on the diet quality of Pyrenean rock ptarmigan (*Lagopus muta pyrenaica*): implications for reproductive success. *PLoS ONE*, **11**, e0148632.

Gareca, E.E., Hermy, M., Fjeldså, J. & Honnay, O. (2010) *Polylepis* woodland remnants as biodiversity islands in the Bolivian high Andes. *Biodiversity and Conservation*, **19**, 3327–3346.

Gehrig-Fasel, J., Guisan, A. & Zimmermann, N.E. (2007) Tree line shifts in the Swiss Alps: climate change or land abandonment? *Journal of Vegetation Science*, **18**, 571–582.

Gaston, K.J., Blackburn, T.M. & Spicer, J.I. (1998) Rapoport's rule: time for an epitaph? *Trends in Ecology & Evolution*, **13**, 70–74.

Gibbons, R.E., Jia, Z. & Villalba, M.I. (2016) Habitat use and seasonality of birds in the Peruvian puna with an emphasis on peatlands (bofedales). *Boletín UNOP*, **11**, 1–21.

Gobet, E., Tinner, W., Hochuli, P.A., van Leeuwen, J.F.N. & Ammann, B. (2003) Middle to Late Holocene vegetation history of the Upper Engadine (Swiss Alps): the role of man and fire. *Vegetation History and Archaeobotany*, **12**, 143–163.

Gottfried, M., Pauli, H., Futschik, A., *et al.* (2012) Continent-wide response of mountain vegetation to climate change. *Nature Climate Change*, **2**, 111–115.

Hardy, D.R. & Hardy, S.P. (2008) White-winged Diuca Finch (*Diuca speculifera*) nesting on Quelccaya Ice Cap, Perú. *Wilson Journal of Ornithology*, **120**, 613–617.

Hardy, S.P., Hardy, D.R. & Castañeda Gil, K. (2018) Avian nesting and roosting on glaciers at high elevation, Cordillera Vilcanota, Peru. *Wilson Journal of Ornithology*, **130**, 940–957.

Hardy, D.R., Dufour, C. & Oosterbroek, P. (2020) High altitude crane flies (Tipuloidea) and their importance as food for birds. *Fly Times*, **65**, 15–20.

Hendricks, P. & Norment, C.J. (1991) Effects of a severe snowstorm on subalpine and alpine populations of nesting American Pipits. *Journal of Field Ornithology*, **63**, 331–338.

Hodkinson, I.D. (2005) Terrestrial insects along elevation gradients: species and community responses to altitude. *Biological Reviews*, **80**, 489–513.

Hohl, S. (2019) *Jahresbericht 2019 der Beringungsstation Col de Bretolet VS*. Sempach: Schweizerische Vogelwarte.

Jarzyna, M.A., Quintero, I. & Jetz, W. (2021) Global functional and phylogenetic structure of avian assemblages across elevation and latitude. *Ecology Letters*, **24**, 196–207.

Jehl Jr, J.R. & Hussell, D.J.T. (1966) Effects of weather on reproductive success of birds at Churchill, Manitoba. *Arctic*, **19**, 185–191.

Jenni, L. & Kéry, M. (2003) Timing of autumn bird migration under climate change: advances in long-distance migrants, delays in short-distance migrants. *Proceedings of the Royal Society Series B*, **270**, 1467–1471.

Kapos, V., Rhind, J., Edwards, M., Price, M.F. & Ravilious, C. (2000) Developing a map of the world's mountain forests. In *Forests in Sustainable Mountain Development: A State-of-Knowledge Report for 2000*. Price, M.F. & Butt, N. (eds.). Wallingford: CAB International, pp. 4–9.

Karagulle, D., Frye, C., Sayre, R., *et al.* (2017) Modeling global Hammond landform regions from 250-m elevation data. *Transactions in GIS*, 21, 1040–1060.

Keller, V., Herrando, S., Voříšek, P., *et al.* (2020) *European Breeding Bird Atlas 2: Distribution, Abundance and Change*. Barcelona: European Bird Census Council and Lynx Edicions.

Kessler, M. & Herzog, S.K. (1998) Conservation status in Bolivia of timberline habitats, elfin forest and their birds. *Cotinga*, **10**, 50–54.

Körner, C. (2004) Mountain biodiversity, its causes and function. *Ambio, Special Report*, **13**, 11–17.

Körner, C. (2012) *Alpine Treelines. Functional Ecology of the Global High Elevation Tree Limits*. Basel: Springer.

Körner, C. & Ohsawa, M. (2006) Mountain systems. In *Ecosystem and Human Wellbeing: Current State and Trends. Millennium Ecosystem Assessment*. Vol. 1. Hassan, R., Scholes, R. & Ash, N. (eds.). Washington, DC: Island Press, pp. 681–716.

Körner, C. & Paulsen, J. (2004) A world-wide study of high altitude treeline temperatures. *Journal of Biogeography*, **31**, 713–732.

Körner, C., Paulsen, J. & Spehn, E.M. (2011) A definition of mountains and their bioclimatic belts for global comparisons of biodiversity data. *Alpine Botany*, **121**, 73–78.

Körner, C., Jetz, W., Paulsen, J., *et al.* (2017) A global inventory of mountains for bio-geographical applications. *Alpine Botany*, **127**, 1–15.

Körner, C., Urbach, D. & Paulsen, J. (2021) Mountain definitions and their consequences. *Alpine Botany*, **131**, 213–217.

Laiolo, P., Dondero, F., Ciliento, E. & Rolando, A. (2004) Consequences of pastoral abandonment for the structure and diversity of the alpine avifauna. *Journal of Applied Ecology*, **41**, 294–304.

Laiolo, P., Pato, J. & Obeso, J.R. (2018) Ecological and evolutionary drivers of the elevational gradient of diversity. *Ecology Letters*, **21**, 1022–1032.

Lehikoinen, A., Brotons, L., Calladine, J., et al. (2019) Declining population trends of European mountain birds. *Global Change Biology*, **25**, 577–588.

MacDonald, D., Crabtree, J.R., Wiesinger, G., et al. (2000) Agricultural abandonment in mountain areas of Europe: environmental consequences and policy response. *Journal of Environmental Management*, **59**, 47–69.

Martin, K. (2001) Wildlife in alpine and sub-alpine habitats. In *Wildlife-Habitat Relationships in Oregon and Washington*. D. H. Johnson, & T. A. O'Neil. (eds.). (Manag. Dirs.). Corvallis: Oregon State University Press, pp. 285–310.

Martin, K. & Wiebe, K.L. (2004) Coping mechanisms of alpine and arctic breeding birds: extreme weather and limitations to reproductive resilience. *Integrative and Comparative Biology*, **44**, 177–185.

Martin, K., Wilson, S., MacDonald, E.C., et al. (2017) Effects of severe weather on reproduction for sympatric songbirds in an alpine environment: interactions of climate extremes influence nesting success. *Auk*, **134**, 696–709.

Martin, K., Altamirano, T.A., de Zwaan, D.R., et al. (2021) Avian ecology and community structure across elevation gradients: the importance of high latitude temperate mountains for conserving biodiversity in the Americas. *Global Ecology and Conservation*, **30**, e01799.

McCain, C.M. (2009) Global analysis of bird elevational diversity. *Global Ecology and Biogeography*, **18**, 346–360.

McCain, C.M. & Grytnes, J.-A. (2010) *Elevational gradients in species richness. In Encyclopedia of Life Sciences (ELS)*. Chichester: John Wiley & Sons.

Mermillon, C., Jähnig, S., Sander, M.M., et al. (2022) Variations in niche breadth and position of alpine birds along elevation gradients in the European Alps. *Ardeola*, **69**, 41–58.

Miehe, G., Miehe, S. & Schültz, F. (2009) Early human impact in the forest ecotone of southern High Asia (Hindu Kush, Himalaya). *Quaternary Research*, **71**, 255–265.

Myers, N., Mittermeier, R.A., Mittermeier, C.G., da Fonseca, G.A.B. & Kent, J. (2000) Biodiversity hotspots for conservation priorities. *Nature*, **403**, 853–858.

Nagy, L. & Grabherr, G. (2009) *The Biology of Alpine Habitats*. Oxford: Oxford University Press.

Newton, I. (2020) *Uplands and Birds*. London: Collins.

Niethammer G. (1953) Zur Vogelwelt Boliviens. *Bonner zoologische Beiträge*, **4**, 195–303.

Nogués-Bravo, D., Araújo, M.B., Romdal, T. & Rahbek, C. (2008) Scale effects and human impact on the elevational species richness gradients. *Nature*, **453**, 216–219.

Norfolk, O., Power, A., Eichhorn, M.P. & Gilbert, F. (2015) Migratory bird species benefit from traditional agricultural gardens in arid South Sinai. *Journal of Arid Environments*, **114**, 110–115.

Pepin, N.C., Arnone, E., Gobiet, A., et al. (2022) Climate changes and their elevational patterns in the mountains of the world. *Reviews of Geophysics*, **60**, e2020RG000730.

Petchey, O.L. & Gaston, K.J. (2006) Functional diversity: back to basics and looking forward. *Ecology Letters*, **9**, 741–758

Peters, M.K., Hemp, A., Appelhans, T., *et al.* (2016) Predictors of elevational biodiversity gradients change from single taxa to the multi-taxa community level. *Nature Communications*, **7**, 13736.

Potapov, R.L. (2004) Adaptation of birds to life in high mountains in Eurasia. *Acta Zoologica Sinica*, **5**, 970–977.

Quintero, I. & Jetz, W. (2018) Global elevational diversity and diversification of birds. *Nature*, **555**, 246–250.

Rabatel, A., Francou, B., Soruco, A., *et al.* (2013) Current state of glaciers in the tropical Andes: a multi-century perspective on glacier evolution and climate change. *Cryosphere*, **7**, 81–102.

Rahbek, C. (1995) The elevational gradient of species richness: a uniform pattern? *Ecography*, **18**, 200–205.

Rahbek, C., Borregaard, M.K., Antonelli, A., *et al.* (2019) Building mountain biodiversity: geological and evolutionary processes. *Science*, **365**, 1114–1119.

Resano-Mayor, J., Korner-Nievergelt, F., Vignali, S., *et al.* (2019) Snow cover phenology is the main driver of foraging habitat selection for a high-alpine passerine during breeding: implications for species persistence in the face of climate change. *Biodiversity and Conservation*, **28**, 2669–2685.

Reynolds, J.N.H., Swanson, H.K. & Rooney, R.C. (2022) Habitat area and environmental filters determine avian richness along an elevation gradient in mountain peatlands. *Journal of Avian Biology*, **2022**, e02797.

Rixen, C. & Rolando, A. (Eds.). (2013) *The Impacts of Skiing and Related Winter Recreational Activities on Mountain Environments*. Bussum: Bentham eBooks.

Sander, M.M., Chamberlain, D., Mermillon, C., *et al.* (2021) Early breeding conditions followed by reduced breeding success despite timely arrival in an alpine migratory songbird. *Frontiers in Ecology and Evolution*, **9**, article 676506.

Sander, M.M., Jähnig, S., Lisovski, S., *et al.* (2023) High nest failure but better nestling quality for early breeders in an alpine population of Northern Wheatear (*Oenanthe oenanthe*). *Ibis*, **165**, 125–141.

Saniga, M. (2004) Features of the Wallcreeper *Tichodroma muraria* breeding habitat in the West Carpathians. *Monticola*, **9**, 222–227.

Sandercock, B.K., Martin, K. & Hannon, S.J. (2005) Life history strategies in extreme environments: comparative demography of arctic and alpine ptarmigan. *Ecology*, **86**, 2176–2186.

Sayre, R., Frye, C., Karagulle, D., *et al.* (2018) A new high-resolution map of world mountains and an online tool for visualizing and comparing characterizations of global mountain distributions. *Mountain Research and Development*, **38**, 240–249.

Schumm, M., White, A.E., Supriya, K. & Price, T.D. (2020) Ecological limits as the driver of bird species richness patterns along the east Himalayan elevational gradient. *American Naturalist*, **195**, 802–817.

Schwörer, C., Colombaroli, D., Kaltenrieder, P., Rey, F. & Tinner, W. (2014) Early human impact (5000–3000 BC) affects mountain forest dynamics in the Alps. *Journal of Ecology*, **103**, 281–295.

Scridel, D., Bogliani, G., Pedrini, P., *et al.* (2017) Thermal niche predicts recent changes in range size for bird species. *Climate Research*, **73**, 207–216.

Scridel, D., Brambilla, M., Martin, K., *et al.* (2018) A review and meta-analysis of the effects of climate change on Holarctic mountain and upland bird populations. *Ibis*, **160**, 489–515.

Šekercioğlu, Ç., Primack, R.B. & Wormworth, J. (2012) The effects of climate change on tropical birds. *Biological Conservation*, **148**, 1–18.

Stevens, G.C. (1989) The latitudinal gradient in geographical range: how so many species coexist in the tropics. *American Naturalist*, **133**, 240–256.

Stevens, G.C. (1992) The elevational gradient in altitudinal range: an extension of Rapoport's latitudinal rule to altitude. *American Naturalist*, **140**, 893–911.

Strinella, E., Scridel, D., Brambilla, M., Schano, C. & Korner-Nievergelt, F. (2020) Potential sex-dependent effects of weather on apparent survival of a high-elevation specialist. *Scientific Reports*, **10**, 8386.

Supriya, K., Price, T.D. & Moreau, C.S. (2020) Competition with insectivorous ants as a contributor to low songbird diversity at low elevations in the eastern Himalaya. *Ecology and Evolution*, **10**, 4280–4290.

Svadlenak-Gomez, K., Badura, M., Kraxner, F., *et al.* (2013) Valuing Alpine ecosystems: the recharge.green project will help decision-makers to reconcile renewable energy production and biodiversity conservation in the Alps. *Management and Policy Issues*, **5**, 51–54.

Testolin, R., Attore, F. & Jiménez-Alvaro, B. (2020) Global distribution and bioclimatic characterization of alpine biomes. *Ecography*, **43**, 779–788.

Valencia, B.G., Bush, M.B., Coe, A.L., Orren, E. & Gosling, W.D. (2018) *Polylepis* woodland dynamics during the last 20,000 years. *Journal of Biogeography*, **45**, 1019–1030.

White, A.E., Dey, K.K., Mohan, D., Stephens, M. & Price, T.D. (2019) Regional influences on community structure across the tropical-temperate divide. *Nature Communications*, **10**, 2646.

Wilson, S. & Martin, K. (2005) Songbird use of high-elevation habitat during the fall post-breeding and migratory periods. *Ecoscience*, **12**, 561–568.

Wu, H., Chen, J., Xu, J., *et al.* (2019) Effects of dam construction on biodiversity: a review. *Journal of Cleaner Production*, **221**, 480–489.

Young, T.P. & Evans, M.R. (1993) Alpine vertebrates of Mount Kenya, with particular notes on the Rock Hyrax. *Journal of the East African Natural History Society and National Museum*, **82**, 55–79.

2 · *Avian Adaptations to High Mountain Habitats*

Solving the Challenges of Living in Alpine Ecosystems

KATHY MARTIN, DEVIN R. DE ZWAAN, DAVIDE SCRIDEL AND TOMÁS A. ALTAMIRANO

Globally, birds living at high elevations must contend with climatic extremes, energetic limitations and ecological challenges that can represent both constraints and opportunities (Figure 2.1; Martin 2001). Mountains consist of steep environmental gradients where abiotic and biotic factors transition rapidly over relatively short distances, often culminating in severe conditions at the highest elevations (Grabherr 2000). Habitats at and above the treeline are characterized by temperature extremes, powerful winds, frequent storm events, low partial pressures of oxygen and high ultraviolet (UV) radiation among other limitations (Martin & Wiebe 2004). Cold temperatures, wind and limited soil moisture combine to constrain the growing season, resulting in sparse, stunted vegetation among patches of rock, bare ground and perennial snow and ice (Nagy & Grabherr 2009). In temperate systems, snow cover or freezing early-season conditions result in short breeding seasons with limited opportunities to reproduce, while fluctuating weather can limit resource availability for extended periods (Camfield *et al.* 2010; Martin *et al.* 2017). A simplified, open landscape provides minimal refuge from the elements and potential predators relative to lower elevation habitats. While challenging conditions may be more pronounced in temperate or high-latitude mountains, tropical alpine habitats exhibit many similar constraints, including extreme temperature changes between night and day.

Around 12 per cent of the global avifauna breed in alpine habitats (de Zwaan *et al.* 2022a; Chapter 3), with some exhibiting life-history and functional traits that maximize productivity and survival under rigorous conditions. Only a limited number of bird species are specialized to

Figure 2.1 White-tailed ptarmigan *Lagopus leucura*, a year-round alpine resident, in mid-June during a year of delayed snow melt on Vancouver Island, Canada. Normally, at this time all birds are on territory and clutch initiation has begun (Photo: Kathy Martin).

breed exclusively at high elevations, while a far greater proportion are generalists that breed across a wide range of elevations (Boyle *et al.* 2016; Altamirano *et al.* 2020). A diverse bird community also uses high elevation habitats during post-breeding, migration or winter seasons, indicating a need to assess the year-round value of high mountain habitats for avian biodiversity (Boyle & Martin 2015). Several hypotheses attempt to explain why birds breed at high elevations in what initially appears to be a harsh, suboptimal habitat. Birds breeding at the upper limits of their elevational range may be poor quality individuals, unable to compete for high-quality territories at lower elevations (despotic distribution; Evans Ogden *et al.* 2012). Alternatively, many high mountain habitats contain abundant food resources and may offer refuge from stronger ecological processes at lower elevation (e.g., predation, parasitism, competition; Boyle *et al.* 2016). Both elevation generalists and specialists may persist or have moved to higher elevations in response to habitat loss at lower elevations (Ibarra *et al.* 2017; Scridel *et al.* 2018).

In this chapter, we outline the abiotic factors that set limits on avian life at high elevations. We then examine the key physiological, ecological, genetic and behavioural adaptations that enable birds to live and breed in challenging

Table 2.1 *Living and breeding in high mountains: constraints, avian adaptations and ecological consequences (adapted from Johnson & O'Neil 2001, reproduced with the permission of Oregon State University Press).*

A. Environmental constraints

1) Climate and weather
- Extreme temperatures
- Precipitation/drought
- Snow
- Storm events
- High winds

2) Atmospheric properties
- Hypoxia
- Solar radiation (UV-B)

3) Topography
- Fragmented habitat
- Exposed habitat
- Dispersal barrier

B. Biological adaptations

1) Morphological/structural
- Larger body size/longer wings
- Melanic plumage (UV absorption)
- Insulated feather microstructure
- Foraging/provisioning structures

2) Physiological
- Wide thermoneutral zone
- Counter-current heat exchange
- Regulated hypothermia (torpor)
- High haemoglobin concentration
- Flexible hematocrit levels
- Large gas exchange surface
- Flexible reproductive timing
- Cold-tolerant embryos

3) Behavioural
- Sub-nival roosting
- Altitudinal movements
- Thermoregulatory behaviours (i.e., shade-seeking, snow baths)
- Enclosed nests (domed/cavities)
- Nest orientation
- Large, insulated nests
- Greater nest attentiveness
- Cryptic plumage/nests
- Non-directional vocalizations

4) Genetic adaptations
- Phenotypic plasticity
- High mutation rate
- Metabolic flexibility/scope

C. Life-history adaptations

- Cryptic plumage
- Extensive moulting patterns
- Increased parental care
- Reduced extra-pair mating
- Strong seasonality in habitat use
- Increased longevity with elevation
- Strong age dependence & senescence
- Excellent dispersal/migration ability
- External recruitment for rescue

D. Ecological Consequences

- High energetic cost of breeding
- Need cooling/warming adaptations
- Patchy distribution & strong seasonality of resources
- Low levels of parasitism & disease
- Delayed breeding schedules
- Increased reproductive synchrony
- Increased reproductive stochasticity
- Fewer broods per season
- Longer development times
- Lower predation risk on young & adults
- Small, low-density populations
- Need to disperse across unsuitable habitat

high mountain conditions following the structure outlined in Table 2.1. While life at and above the treeline is considered to be shaped predominantly by abiotic conditions, biotic factors and their interactions with the environment have not been examined extensively. We therefore outline the ecological dynamics acting on birds at high elevations and highlight some of the primary knowledge gaps in mountain bird ecology globally. We conclude by integrating the various adaptations that facilitate and enable birds to live in high mountain habitats within a life-history framework.

2.1 Defining 'High' in High Mountain Birds

Birds have the exceptional ability to inhabit the full elevational range, from sea level to the highest land surfaces on earth (Mount Everest at 8,848 m). The highest breeding record for any bird is at 6,600 m in Asia, set by the colourful grandala *Grandala coelicolor*, a member of the Turdidae family (Figure 2.2; Potapov 2004). Globally, at least 12 species have been

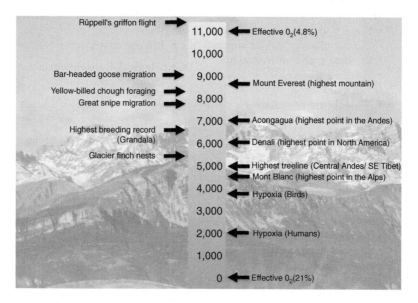

Figure 2.2 The elevation limits (m) at which birds are known to be active, relative to the world's highest mountains, oxygen concentrations and onset of hypoxia (inadequate oxygen supply to body tissues to maintain homeostatis), including maximum elevations recorded for selected species (Rüppell's vulture *Gyps rueppelli*, bar-headed goose *Anser indicus*, yellow-billed chough *Pyrrhocorax graculus*, great snipe *Gallinago media*, grandala *Grandala coelicolor* and glacier finch *Idiopsar speculifera*; Background photo: Davide Scridel).

Table 2.2 *Selection of the highest breeding bird records for all biogeographic ecozones, excluding Antarctica.*

Species	Elevation (m)†	Location
Nearctic		
White-tailed ptarmigan *Lagopus leucura*	4,268	Colorado
Horned lark *Eremophila alpestris*	4,000	Colorado
Black rosy finch *Leucosticte atrata*	3,600	Colorado
Brown-capped rosy finch *Leucosticte australis*	4,330	Colorado
Grey-crowned rosy finch *Leucosticte tephrocotis*	>5,000★	Alaska
Palearctic		
Grandala *Grandala coelicolor*	6,600	Himalayas
Yellow-billed chough *Pyrrhocorax graculus*	6,500	Himalayas
Snow pigeon *Columba leuconota*	6,000	Tibet
Tibetan lark *Melanocorypha maxima*	6,000	Tibet
Brandt's mountain finch *Leucosticte brandti*	6,000	Himalayas
Neotropical		
White-fronted ground tyrant *Muscisaxicola albifrons*	5,600	Central Andes
Glacier finch *Idiopsar speculifer*	5,330	Central Andes
Andean condor *Vultur gryphus*	>5,000	Central Andes
Rufous-bellied seedsnipe *Attagis gayi*	5,500	Central Andes
Afrotropical		
Rüppell's vulture *Gyps rueppelli*	4,500	Ethiopia
White-necked raven *Corvus albicollis*	>5,000	Tanzania
Moorland chat *Pinarochroa sordida*	>5,000	Tanzania
Australasia		
Snow Mountain robin *Petroica archboldi*	>4,000	New Guinea
Alpine pipit *Anthus gutturalis*	4,500	New Guinea
Eastern alpine mannikin *Lonchura monticola*	>3,900	New Guinea
Snow Mountain quail *Synoicus monorthonyx*	3,800	New Guinea
Western alpine mannikin *Lonchura montana*	4,150	New Guinea

★ Potential. Grey-crowned rosy finch is likely the highest nesting species in North America due to the frequency of observations on high scree, including Denali Mountain, the highest mountain on the continent. However, given difficult access, few nests have been found (MacDougall-Shackleton *et al.* 2020).

† Records accessed from Birds of the World species accounts (Billerman *et al.* 2022).

recorded breeding at elevations exceeding 5,000 m (Table 2.2), with full range limits undescribed and underestimated for many species. In the Central Andes of Peru, multiple species have been observed nesting and roosting in glacial caves up to 5,330 m (Hardy *et al.* 2018), while certain hummingbirds, including the olivaceous thornbill *Chalcostigma olivaceum*, reach similar elevations to feed on insects trapped in the ice (Sevillano-Ríos *et al.* 2020). In Nepal, the yellow-billed chough *Pyrrhocorax graculus* has been observed by mountaineers at 8,300 m (Madge *et al.* 2020). The very highest elevations used by birds represent habitats where survival and maintaining consciousness is difficult or impossible for most mammals, including humans (see Storz *et al.* 2020 for the highest dwelling mammal recorded, the yellow-rumped leaf-eared mouse *Phyllotis xanthopygus rupestris* at 6,739 m). Extreme elevation is associated with severe temperatures and hypoxic conditions (i.e., lowered partial pressure of oxygen), requiring specific anatomical, physiological and behavioural adaptations to survive and reproduce successfully (Section 2.2).

Birds also use the extensive air space above mountains. Rüppell's vulture *Gyps rueppelli* holds the record for the highest altitudinal flight of any bird at 11,277 m (Laybourne 1974). This unfortunate individual was sucked into a jet engine, a likely consequence of both bird and plane selecting the same cruising altitudes to reduce flight costs. Bar-headed geese *Anser indicus* have been recorded reaching altitudes up to 7,290 m during seasonal migration over the Himalayas (Hawkes *et al.* 2011), 6,800 m for ruddy shelduck *Tadorna ferruginea* (Parr *et al.* 2017) and 6,000 m for shorebirds like bar-tailed godwit *Limosa lapponica* (Figure 2.2; Senner *et al.* 2018). Great snipe *Gallinago media* can reach altitudes of 8,000 m during migration, with daily altitudinal variation associated with air temperatures, potentially indicating individuals are tracking cooler flight conditions or strong winds at high altitudes (Lindström *et al.* 2021; Sjöberg *et al.* 2021). Thus, a range of phylogenetically diverse species can fly or soar at extreme elevations. Senner *et al.* (2018) suggest that many species likely have the anatomical and physiological traits necessary to migrate at altitudes exceeding 6,000 m (Box 2.1).

Box 2.1   *Flight at High Altitudes*

Douglas L. Altshuler

Many birds fly at high altitudes, either during long-distance flights or by virtue of residence in high-elevation habitats. Air temperature, humidity and wind speed vary across and within altitudes, with the potential to greatly impact avian flight performance. Air pressure is the abiotic factor affecting bird flight that varies most reliably with altitude, with the consequence that both oxygen availability and air density are reduced with increasing altitude.

Reduced oxygen availability constrains metabolic input for muscle contraction necessary for locomotor activities such as flight. There are multiple mechanisms that can be used to increase oxygen delivery to tissues, and birds in general are adept in this regard. For example, the avian lung and air sac system are extraordinarily efficient for gas exchange and avian hearts tend to be large, with enhanced oxygen supply to cardiac muscle. High elevation specialist birds exhibit additional adaptations in oxygen delivery. Examples include haemoglobin with high oxygen affinity in bar-headed geese (Black & Tenney 1980) and respiratory systems that are both smaller and more compliant in high elevation ducks (York et al. 2017). Several recent reviews provide details of the oxygen delivery adaptations of birds in general and those of high elevation specialists (e.g., Scott 2011; Minias 2020; Williamson & Witt 2021).

Lower air density reduces aerodynamic forces, which can be understood through the equations for lift (L) and drag (D):

$$L = C_L \frac{1}{2} \rho v^2 S$$

$$D = C_D \frac{1}{2} \rho v^2 S$$

where ρ is air density, v is velocity, S is wing area, and C_L and C_D are the lift and drag coefficients, respectively. These equations provide insight into the availability of mechanisms to compensate aerodynamically for low air density. First, reductions in drag force during forward flight at high altitude will be offset by reductions in lift force. Lift could be enhanced through increases in wing area and especially through increases in velocity through wing flapping (due to the square term). However, there is a trade-off because wingbeat frequency is inversely proportional to wing length (Greenewalt 1962). Moreover, bird wings are constrained to be light and relatively small, likely to prevent wing damage and keep the costs of flapping low. High wingbeat frequency requires oxygen availability for muscle contractions and is thus constrained with increasing altitude. The features that vary with the lift coefficient are either the same for high and low elevation (angle of attack) or constrained within a narrow range (wing camber).

The question of whether birds flying at high altitude are more limited by oxygen availability or air density has been addressed by studying hummingbirds in physically variable gas mixtures during hovering (Chai & Dudley 1996) and manoeuvring flight (Segre *et al.* 2016). Both modes of flight are reduced at high elevation. The study on manoeuvring applied two experimental approaches. One group of hummingbirds was tested at both low and high elevation sites. Another group was tested in nitrogen/oxygen mixtures to reduce oxygen availability and in helium/oxygen mixtures to reduce air density. These experiments demonstrated that accelerations and rotational velocities are more constrained by air density than oxygen availability in hummingbirds. It thus appears that the available mechanisms for enhancing oxygen delivery to tissues are more effective than the mechanisms for increasing aerodynamic force.

Biotic factors also vary with elevation, but their influence on flight performance has received less attention. Ecosystem composition, predators, nutritional resources and vegetation structure all change dramatically across elevational gradients. These effects are of secondary importance for long-distance avian migrants, but may have substantial impacts on the flight dynamics of high-elevation residents and altitudinal migrants (Boyce *et al.* 2019).

2.2 Abiotic Challenges for Alpine Birds

The energetic cost of living in mountain habitats increases with elevation as abiotic conditions impose progressively stronger selective pressures on birds and sets limits in which biotic adaptations must develop (Table 2.1). Thus, understanding the abiotic environment provides context for the adaptive traits and life-history strategies expressed by alpine birds.

2.2.1 Climatic Conditions and Weather Events

Temperature

Arguably the most critical abiotic factor, temperature has a profound influence on high elevation birds, particularly given the magnitude of daily and seasonal variation (Williams 2020). Temperature decreases by 0.54–0.65°C per 100 m increase in elevation, although apparent temperature experienced by a bird varies with local topography, wind and humidity (Nagy & Grabherr 2009). The assimilation efficiency of energy and nutrients decreases with cold, requiring greater resource intake for a given metabolism (Schmidt-Nielsen 1997). While cold conditions are generally associated with high mountain habitats, ground-level temperatures during the breeding season can exceed 50°C and fluctuate daily by 70°C (Lauer & Klaus 1975). Both extreme and fluctuating temperatures impose thermoregulatory challenges, requiring energetically costly physiological or behavioural responses to maintain homeothermy (Chan et al. 2016; Gutierrez-Pinto et al. 2021). Seasonal temperature variation also influences primary productivity of high elevation habitats (e.g., food resources), and thus temperature has both direct and indirect effects on life-history traits of high mountain birds. As extreme temperatures (e.g., heat waves, storms) at high elevation are becoming increasingly common under climate change (Wang et al. 2018; Chapter 6), temperature will continue to be of fundamental importance in shaping avian adaptations to alpine life (Elsen et al. 2017a).

Precipitation as Snow and Rain

Unlike temperature, precipitation exhibits non-linear relationships with elevation, characterized by regional rather than global patterns. By impeding air flow, mountains generally cause clouds to rise and cluster at mid to high elevations, leading sometimes to extensive precipitation. Precipitation typically increases to a certain elevation, above which patterns vary globally depending on interactions between airflow direction, mountain range orientation and ocean proximity (Nagy & Grabherr 2009). Precipitation in the form of snow and the resulting snowpack for much of the year would be one of the strongest, if not the strongest, abiotic influences on life at high elevations. Snow is an integral feature of high mountain habitats, particularly in temperate zones. In spring, the rate and timing of snowmelt, in concert with temperature and photoperiod, dictates the duration of the growing season for alpine vegetation and breeding phenology of alpine birds (Chapter 3). Early-season snow events can return conditions to a winter-like state, covering initiated nests or limiting access to food resources, especially for insectivorous alpine passerines. However, snow dynamics can also modify resource availability positively, such as how a receding snowline exposes hibernating arthropods over an extended period across the breeding season (Resano-Mayor et al. 2019). A deep snowpack can provide thermally protective roosts for alpine winter residents such as grouse, and can increase access to forage on taller woody shrubs (Tape et al. 2010; Martin *et al.* 2020). Snow patches lasting into the breeding season are also critical sources of water and can act as microclimate temperature regulators (Rosvold 2016). Snow dynamics can therefore impose both constraints and provide benefits for birds living in high mountains. As snow plays a critical role in shaping the life-histories of alpine birds, continual declines in winter snowpack and more variability in snowmelt represent increasing fitness challenges in terms of breeding phenology, resource availability, microclimate refugia and even camouflage (Schano *et al.* 2021).

Precipitation as rain, or the lack thereof, can be an influential driver of conditions in both tropical and temperate high mountains. At the extremes, some high elevation habitats are characterized by monsoon conditions (e.g., Taiwan or New Guinea), while others are drought-limited (e.g., Central Andes; Chapter 3). Drought may be a common limiting factor for most high mountain habitats as well-drained, shallow soils and nightly frosts often lead to limited soil moisture which constrains vegetation growth, especially above the treeline (site water balance; de Andrés *et al.* 2015; Devi *et al.* 2020). Thus, high mountain habitats are increasingly water-limited given declining snowpacks and more frequent drought events (Calanca 2007).

Storms

Occurring at any point during the year, the frequency and severity of severe weather events increase with elevation (Bears *et al.* 2003; Martin *et al.* 2017). Storms are defined as periods of extreme precipitation, wind or low temperatures over one or multiple days that can constrain avian behaviour or vital rates, such as foraging, incubation, movement or off-spring development (O'Neill & Parker 1978; MacDonald *et al.* 2013; de Zwaan *et al.* 2020). While more pronounced in temperate mountains, tropical high elevation habitats also experience periods of intense precipitation (i.e., monsoons) and temperature extremes, which can shape life at high elevations. The hygric niche concept posits that species have an optimal precipitation range; above and below this range can result in suboptimal fitness and eventually mortality (Boyle *et al.* 2020).

The impacts of storms on high mountain birds vary by species and weather severity, including sub-lethal constraints on parental care and offspring growth, as well as direct nestling mortality or nest abandonment (Hendricks & Norment 1992; Decker & Conway 2009; de Zwaan *et al.* 2019a). While snow can have insulating properties, rain and freezing temperatures can impose acute thermoregulatory challenges, particularly for offspring when adults are forced to invest less in parental care. Interactions between temperature and precipitation are therefore critical, ranging from little or no impact on daily life to strong negative effects on reproduction depending on whether storms are warm or cold (Martin *et al.* 2017). While we consider precipitation to be generally influential for alpine birds, specific effects of precipitation on species distribution and life-history traits are highly variable and can be difficult to interpret (e.g., Martin *et al.* 2017; Scridel *et al.* 2021). This is particularly true for evaluating mechanisms linking storm events to effects within and outside of the breeding season (de Zwaan *et al.* 2022b), and critically, for predicting responses to future precipitation dynamics.

Wind

A prominent feature of high mountains, wind frequency and intensity generally increase with elevation and often exhibit highly stochastic seasonal as well as daily fluctuations (Nagy & Grabherr 2009). Wind speeds are correlated with differences in air temperature across elevation and are thus influenced by latitude as well as time of year (Stull 2000). In alpine habitats, wind speeds frequently exceed 100 km/h, significantly impeding bird flight and thus constraining other vital behaviours such as foraging, particularly for aerial insectivores. However, wind can also be a positive characteristic of high mountain habitats. Updrafts and wind gusts may deposit 'windfall' or large numbers of flying insects onto the snow surface, which is a vital food source for birds early in the season when resources are limited (Brambilla *et al.* 2019; Hotaling *et al.* 2019). Mountain birds also regularly take advantage of wind-assisted flights for daily movements (e.g., predator evasion) and seasonal dispersal. Overall, the influence of variable and changing wind dynamics on the movement abilities of mountain birds is poorly understood.

2.2.2 Atmospheric Properties

Atmospheric Pressure and Hypoxia

Atmospheric pressure, the moisture content of air, and the partial pressures of oxygen, decrease relatively uniformly with increasing elevation, and impact gas respiration in birds. In particular, the partial pressure of oxygen decreases by c. 11 per cent per km above sea level, translating into a c. 70–80 per cent reduction near the peak of some of the highest global ranges (Peacock 1998). Decreases in the partial pressure of oxygen with increasing altitude can increase the metabolic costs of reproduction and survival, especially affecting embryonic development and other physiological processes above 3,600 m (Carey *et al.* 1982; Section 2.3).

Solar Radiation

The intensity of solar radiation experienced by organisms increases at higher elevations (10 per cent increase per 1,000 m; McKenzie *et al.* 2001). This value varies globally with latitude, mountain slope and atmospheric properties such as air moisture content (i.e., clouds) and the ozone layer which moderates the amount of solar radiation that reaches the earth's surface (Kumar *et al.* 1997). For example, the High Andes experience the greatest solar radiation globally due to a combination of particularly clear air and an absent ozone layer (Hardy *et al.* 2018). The ultraviolet (UV) spectrum is an important component of solar radiation, particularly UV-B radiation which can cause damage to plumage structure and colour, and to internal organs, as well as being able to transmit through eggshells to damage developing embryos (Burtt 1986; Dubey & Roulin 2014; Lahti & Ardia 2016). Alpine breeding birds have developed several structural adaptations to mediate solar radiation effects (Section 2.3).

2.2.3 Topography

Mountain topography plays an important role in mediating abiotic challenges, while also creating barriers to movement and dispersal. This complex topography can facilitate and limit alpine life. Fine-scale variation in aspect and slope can provide a shield from the more intense wind and snow dynamics, providing microclimates with more benign temperature and humidity conditions for nesting birds (Chapter 3). Although soils at high elevation are generally shallow, arid and low in nutrients and organic material (Nagy & Grabherr 2009), micro-topographic features can produce variation in soil depth, type and fertility, facilitating more complex vegetation growth and greater food resource availability, thus increasing niche diversity for alpine birds to meet their life-cycle needs (Laiolo *et al.* 2015a). Extreme elevations such as those in the Andes or Himalayas can act as significant barriers to migration, forcing birds to fly to excessive heights to cross over, or to expend energy taking a longer route around. The fragmented nature and small areas of mountain peaks limit habitat availability and thus population size, while also reducing the likelihood of genetic transfer among isolated populations through dispersal (Fedy *et al.* 2008; Costanzi & Steifetten 2019).

2.3 Biological Adaptations for High Mountain Birds

Despite challenging conditions, many avian species can persist at high elevations, and in many cases maximize fitness and benefit from the unique ecological opportunities offered by these habitats. Structural or anatomical adaptations, physiological mechanisms and behavioural strategies allow birds to limit environmental stress to survive and reproduce successfully in alpine ecosystems (Table 2.1; Altshuler & Dudley 2006; Martin 2013). Adaptive functional traits represent patterns of convergent evolution across global high elevation species (Dorst & Vuilleumier 1986), but are also constrained by phylogenetic trait conservatism (Crisp & Cook 2012), leading to variation within and among high mountain habitats. In combination, these traits form coping strategies shaped by interactions between the ecology and evolutionary history of each species. For example, alpine specialists may exhibit specialized structural or morphological traits, while elevational generalists may be characterized by greater physiological or behavioural flexibility (e.g., metabolic or aerobic scope; Gutierrez-Pinto *et al.* 2021). Here, we review some of the primary biological adaptations found in high mountain birds.

2.3.1 Morphological and Structural Adaptations

Body Mass

A larger body volume to surface ratio is less susceptible to convective heat loss, allowing individuals to retain body heat while reducing the energetic cost and water loss associated with thermoregulation in cold climates (Bergmann's rule; Bergmann 1847). Thus, birds may be expected to be larger and heavier at higher elevations. In the Himalayas, alpine cardueline finches tend to be heavier at higher elevations (Landmann & Winding 1995), but Barve *et al.* (2021) found no such relationship in a phylogenetic analysis of over 250 species in the Himalayas. Likewise, a multi-continental study by Freeman (2017) found no consistent association between body mass and elevation in tropical mountains.

In contrast to inter-specific comparisons, within-species studies provide some evidence for covariation between elevation and body mass. White-tailed ptarmigan *Lagopus leucura*, an alpine specialist, were 12 per cent heavier in higher versus lower alpine habitats (Wilson & Martin 2011), while individuals from high elevation populations of horned lark *Eremophila alpestris* were also heavier than a subspecies breeding at sea level (Camfield *et al.* 2010), although these results may have been influenced by both latitudinal and subspecies differences. In the eastern Himalayas, great tits *Parus major* living at high elevation were larger, with longer wings and tarsi than populations living at low elevation in central or eastern China (Qu *et al.* 2015). In a global meta-analysis of intra-specific elevational variation for populations differing by an average of 1,000 m in elevation (including above and below treeline), there was no support for larger body mass in higher elevation populations (Boyle *et al.* 2016), similar to results from a recent analysis of 111 species across North America (Youngflesh *et al.* 2022). Although body mass does not appear to vary consistently with elevation, any covariation between body mass and elevation may ultimately be difficult to identify without controlling for alternate physiological or behavioural traits that allow birds to cope with challenging high elevation conditions (Boyle *et al.* 2016).

Wing Morphology
Wing length and shape are critical for flight at high altitudes as larger wings can provide greater lift at lower air pressures while also improving agility in a wind-dominated environment (Figure 2.3; Altshuler & Dudley 2006). In the Himalayas, alpine passerines tended to have long, pointed wings (Potapov 2004; Qu *et al.* 2015), while within-species, dark-eyed juncos *Junco hyemalis* breeding at high elevation in the Rocky Mountains, Canada had longer wings and tails compared to low elevation populations on the same mountain (Bears *et al.* 2008). Wing length was also signifi-cantly longer at higher elevations for 111 species in North America after controlling for body size (Youngflesh *et al.* 2022). This association varies with geography, as Boyce *et al.* (2019) did not find an association between wing size and elevation in the mountains of Borneo, but Graham *et al.* (2012) demonstrated that larger wing size and mass among hummingbird species tended to cluster at higher elevations in the Ecuadorean Andes. High elevation Himalayan finches and chats also have square-ended tails for flight stability and elongated hind toes (hallux) for stability on the ground while foraging in strong winds (Landmann & Winding 1995). Thus, avian morphology adaptations related to elevation (e.g., wing, tail, hallux) may be a consistent global pattern for many species to minimize energy expenditure in high wind environments.

Figure 2.3 The Andean condor *Vultur gryphus*, a high alpine specialist and the world's heaviest soaring bird, can fly without flapping for over five hours. Flapping flight represents only 1.3 per cent of all flight time, but 21 per cent of daily flight energy costs. This giant vulture with a wingspan of 2.7 to 3.2 m and a body mass of 10 to 15 kg, can achieve flights of up to 5,000 m in altitude utilizing mountain thermal forces (Williams *et al.* 2020; Photo: Tomás A. Altamirano).

Plumage Colour and Feather Structure

Plumage pigmentation can have important influences on thermoregulation and feather resistance to damage. Feather melanism has been hypothesized as a potential adaptation to cold environments, aiding thermoregulation (i.e., absorbing solar radiation), protecting organs against damaging UV-B radiation, increasing structural strength to protect feathers against abrasion (Burtt 1986), and in concert with wing muscles, improving flight efficiency by modulating temperature during flight (Rogalla *et al.* 2019, 2021). Globally, many alpine birds have darker plumage (i.e., high feather melanism), or slate-grey to blue plumage which derives from feather micro-structure and offers the highest UV absorption of any colour (e.g., grandala; Williams 2020). Dark-eyed juncos at high elevations have lighter dorsal contour feathers (less melanin) with marginally greater UV reflectance, which is consistent with greater solar radiation reflectance relative to absorption (de Zwaan *et al.* 2017). In high mountain sites, heat absorption by feathers may not be a major component of thermoregulation relative to physiological and behavioural mechanisms

(Wolf & Walsberg 1996). In fact, cold-adapted species at high elevations or latitudes may be so effective at retaining heat that overheating may be a substantial risk even in moderate temperatures, requiring mechanisms to reflect solar radiation and dissipate heat (Lustick 1984; Choy *et al.* 2021).

Feather microstructure influences the extent that plumage can trap air and reduce convection (Stettenheim 2000; Wolf & Walsberg 2000). Longer feathers with more extensive plumulaceous (downy) segments, lower barb/barbule densities and longer barbules may improve thermo-regulatory capacity by increasing space to trap and warm air against the skin (Butler *et al.* 2008; Pap *et al.* 2020). Given the need to retain heat in cold environments, one would expect feather structure to vary with elevation. The contour feathers of high elevation sparrows in China had more plumulaceous barbules than closely related low elevation species (Lei *et al.* 2002). Similarly, Barve *et al.* (2021) found more pronounced plumulaceous sections in the feathers of passerines at higher elevations in the Himalayas, as well as those with smaller body mass, indicating a potential compensation against heat loss for smaller species. This pat-tern of cold-adapted feather microstructures was also demonstrated in the only intraspecific study to date, among dark-eyed juncos breeding along a single elevational gradient (de Zwaan *et al.* 2017). Other feather traits also exist to reduce heat loss, such as to cover exposed body parts. In winter, ptarmigan legs and toes are heavily feathered, creating a 'snowshoe' effect for walking on snow while also providing insulation (Höhn 1977).

Foraging Structures to Provision Young
Some mountain passerines breeding above the Aeolian zone, but feeding in the nival or alpine zones (see Table 1.1), have developed morphologi-cal structures to transport large quantities of seeds and other foods over considerable distances to provision nestlings (Potapov 2004). In addi-tion to filling their crops, rosy finches and other mountain finches (e.g., *Leucosticte* and *Carpodacus* spp.) develop buccal sacs during the breeding season, special paired pouches beneath the tongue on the floor of the mouth, which allow parents to carry extra food with each trip to their nestlings. The increased payload makes longer flights more profitable and allows parents to search for food over a wider area (up to 4 km from the nest; Johnson 2020). Choughs *Pyrrhocorax* spp. also have an alimen-tary organ (expanded esophagus) for transporting food to their nestlings. During breeding, the upper part of the oesophagus expands into a sac that can hold considerable quantities of food (Potapov 2004).

2.3.2 Physiological Adaptations

Cold Tolerance

While feathers may play a critical role in the thermoregulation of high elevation birds, these adaptations would be ineffective without the underlying physiological mechanisms that regulate heat generation and transfer. As endotherms, bird species maintain basal metabolic rates when ambient temperatures remain within their thermoneutral zone – the temperature range where core body temperature is balanced by heat production and loss (Scholander *et al.* 1950). When ambient conditions drop below the lower critical temperature (LCT) or rise above the upper critical temperature (UCT) – thresholds which vary among species – birds increase their metabolic rate via shivering heat production or evaporative cooling, respectively (Wolf & Walsberg 1996). Given the temperature extremes in high elevation habitats, many mountain birds have developed wide thermoneutral zones with particularly low LCTs but tend to be more sensitive to heat events (i.e., cold-adapted; Swanson & Garland 2009; Khaliq *et al.* 2015; Pollock *et al.* 2019). High elevation species may also exhibit lower levels of conductance, limiting heat loss to the surrounding environment, as demonstrated in the Peruvian Andes (Londoño *et al.* 2017).

Several avian physiological traits allow high mountain birds to counter cold conditions by closely regulating core body temperature. Birds avoid frost bite while standing on snow or ice through a counter-current heat exchange circulatory system where veins and arteries in the legs run adjacent and in parallel, allowing heat to transfer from the warm blood flowing from the body to the cooled blood returning from the legs. Heat transferred in this way enables birds to maintain a core body temperature above 38°C while reducing heat loss from the extremities and maintaining sufficient nutritional blood flow to prevent tissue necrosis (Williams 2020).

High mountain birds may also regularly maintain lower body temperatures compared to species at lower elevations (Londoño *et al.* 2017). At the extreme end of this spectrum, multiple species have evolved the ability to lower core body temperature during inactive periods through 'regulated hypothermia' or torpor, with appreciable energy savings. Despite high metabolic rates, hummingbirds (Trochilidae) and sunbirds (Nectariniidae) breed and forage at high elevations in the tropics (Downs & Brown 2002; Projecto-Garcia *et al.* 2013; Arredondo-Amezcua *et al.* 2018), surviving cold temperatures by entering nocturnal torpor and decreasing metabolic rate if their energy reserves fall below a critical threshold (Carpenter & Hixon 1988; Downs & Brown 2002; Shankar *et al.* 2020). Importantly, torpor does not represent a complete abandonment of body temperature regulation, as ambient temperatures that drop too low are associated with increased metabolism and thus energy expenditure (Wolf & Hainsworth 1972).

Hypoxia

Adaptations in the cardiovascular, pulmonary and muscular systems allow birds to live at high elevations by imparting a high basic tolerance or plasticity to hypoxic conditions, even prior to any physiological adjustments after exposure to hypoxia (Box 2.2; Altshuler & Dudley 2006; Parr *et al.* 2019). These traits likely evolved due to the costly oxygen demands required to sustain long-distance flight, where metabolic rates reach 10–12 times the resting metabolic rate (Bishop *et al.* 2002). Birds have large hearts, increased haemoglobin mass, and can double their cardiac output under hypoxic conditions by increasing heart rate and stroke volume (Box 2.1; Lague *et al.* 2016; Parr *et al.* 2019). Additionally, the avian lung and air sac system is a highly efficient gas exchange organ between the avian pulmonary and circulatory systems, featuring a strong, thin blood–gas barrier that allows for oxygen extraction at twice the rate of the mammalian lung (Banzett *et al.* 1987). Combined with other anatomical features of the pulmonary and circulatory systems, avian gas exchange is enhanced by large lung-to-blood volume ratios, multiple exchanges per inspiration and high gas exchange surface area (Altshuler & Dudley 2006).

Box 2.2 *Embryonic Development at High Elevation*

Eggs contain all the resources and nutrients required for development until hatching, such that avian embryos require only external warmth and gas exchange, both limiting at high elevations. The optimal temperature for embryonic development is approximately 36–38°C with development slowing below this range, generally stalling around 24–26°C or 'physiological zero', and lethality occurring quickly above 40.5°C (Webb 1987; Cooper *et al.* 2005). The thermal gap between ambient temperatures and those required by the embryo for development, sometimes >40°C, is bridged primarily by parental incubation.

Additional adaptive traits may include larger eggs to improve heat retention (e.g., black redstarts *Phoenicurus ochruros*; Lu *et al.* 2011), or

darker eggshell pigmentation to increase heat absorption and protect embryos from damaging UV-B radiation (Lahti & Ardia 2016).
Developing embryos may have a considerable degree of cold tolerance, facilitating resilience to severe cold bouts and periods of stalled
development. Alpine horned lark, grey-crowned rosy finch *Leucosticte
tephrocotis*, Eurasian dotterel *Charadrius morinellus* and ptarmigan
embryos regularly survive extended periods of egg chilling resulting
from temporary abandonment by the incubating parent (French 1959;
MacDonald *et al.* 2013; MacDougall-Shackleton *et al.* 2020). In NW
China, female blood pheasants *Ithaginis cruentus* leave the nest for at
least six hours every morning, leading to daily embryonic hypothermia as eggs cool to c. 10°C (Jia *et al.* 2010). Egg viability is still >90
per cent, which is typical for Galliformes, although embryonic development is 8 to 10 days longer. Prolonged embryo and nestling development are typical responses to colder conditions (de Zwaan *et al.*
2020). Since predation risk increases with nest exposure time, physiological adaptations to cooler temperatures that prolong development
may carry the ecological cost of higher nest failure (Martin 1995; de
Zwaan *et al.* 2019a).

Gas exchange is critical for embryonic development as O_2 and
CO_2 must diffuse from and to the external environment through
the porous eggshell in sufficient quantities. Up to 3,600 m, eggshell
permeability to gases declines proportionally to barometric pressure,
and normal embryonic development is achieved by conserving water
vapor and CO_2 at the expense of O_2. However, birds can breed
well above 3,600 m, elevations where avian embryos require cellular oxygen tension levels that are normally lethal for tissue maintenance. White-tailed ptarmigan eggs at 3,600 to 4,100 m do not differ
in shell thickness or shell permeability to gases from arctic willow
ptarmigan *Lagopus lagopus* breeding at 720 m (Carey & Martin 1997;
Dragon *et al.* 1999). Increased shell porosity to enhance gas exchange
risks incurring elevated water loss, a potentially lethal outcome for
developing embryos. Instead, high alpine white-tailed ptarmigan
embryos exhibit elevated levels of blood hematocrit and citrate synthase enzyme in muscle tissues at a much earlier stage of development
(Figure B2.1; Martin *et al.* 2020), as well as greater oxidative capacity in heart and leg muscle tissues to improve blood oxygen affinity
and oxygen transfer to the tissues (Carey & Martin 1997; Dragon
et al. 1999; Martin *et al.* 2020). When white-tailed ptarmigan eggs are

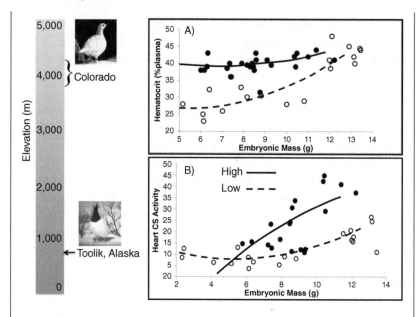

Figure B2.1 Comparison of a low (Toolik, Alaska) and high elevation (Colorado) population of willow ptarmigan *Lagopus lagopus* and white-tailed ptarmigan *L. leucura*, respectively, suggests embryonic adaptation to hypoxic conditions. (A) High elevation embryos have greater hematocrit levels during the incubation stage, and (B) the embryonic muscle tissue has a higher oxidative capacity (CS = citrate synthase, Carey & Martin unpubl.; Top Photo: Steve Ogle, Bottom Photo: Kathy Martin).

incubated artificially at lower elevations, hematocrit and red blood cell organic phosphate levels decline, indicating that for this obligate alpine species, blood biochemical levels are a physiological acclimatization to hypoxia at high elevations, rather than a genetic adaptation *per se* (i.e., phenotypic flexibility; Carey & Martin 1997; Dragon *et al.* 1999; Martin *et al.* 2020).

Since few studies have addressed the physiological traits expressed by developing embryos to cope with the cold and hypoxic conditions of high mountain environments, it is likely that other adaptations specific to alpine birds remain to be discovered. It appears facultative physiological adaptations to hypoxia and cold temperatures are possible, further facilitated by genetic adaptations to improve oxygen transfer to developing avian embryos.

Birds living in high mountain habitats make additional biochemical adjustments, such as increasing blood hematocrit concentrations or further improving blood–oxygen gas exchange efficiency (Carey 1980). These traits are flexible and can vary among species with different life histories (high elevation generalists versus specialists, residents versus migrants, or as species change elevation). In Himalayan birds, six high elevation residents and nine elevational generalist species increased haemoglobin concentrations at higher elevations to improve blood–oxygen transport capacity, but the type of erythropoietic response to hypoxia varied with the amount of time spent in hypoxic conditions: elevational migrants increased hematocrit levels at high elevation (an ancestral response of upregulating erythrocyte production), while high-elevation residents increased their mean cellular haemoglobin concentration (Barve et al. 2016). A contrasting pattern was found in Peru, where the effect of greater haemoglobin and hematocrit levels with increasing elevation was stronger for an elevational generalist, the pied-crested tit-tyrant *Anairetes reguloides* compared to a high elevation specialist species, the black-crested tit-tyrant *A. nigrocristatus* (DuBay & Witt 2014). In transplant experiments, Borras et al. (2010) found that the hematocrit levels of citril finch *Carduelis citrinella* increased by 6 per cent after ascending from 500 m to 2,000 m. Interestingly, Spence et al. (2022) found that Anna's hummingbirds *Calypte anna* exhibited lower metabolic rates, reduced hovering performance and prolonged torpor at night when transplanted to 3,800 m (the species' elevation range is 69 m to 2825 m). In general, prolonged exposure to hypoxia does not impede cerebral blood flow in birds as even at extreme elevations birds can remain conscious and high-functioning, and they are able to maintain oxygen delivery to muscles and metabolize the fatty acids necessary to sustain the energy demands of a highly mobile lifestyle (Parr et al. 2019).

2.3.3 Behavioural Adaptations

Behavioural traits are the product of genetics, physiological mechanisms and individual experience that are expressed in response to prevailing conditions. The resultant behavioural adaptations can allow mountain birds to moderate their environment to maximize survival and reproductive potential.

Thermoregulatory Behaviours

Cold extremes can occur at any point in the year in high mountain habitats, resulting in both temperature and resource constraints. During winter, galliform species in alpine habitats dig snow burrows, producing a microclimate with more benign temperatures, as well as protection from predators. Many passerines make daily altitudinal movements to lower elevation to avoid cold, inclement conditions and associated limited food availability in temperate mountain habitats, and to avoid drought or heavy rain in tropical mountains (Hsiung *et al.* 2018; Boyle *et al.* 2020; Pageau *et al.* 2020). For example, ring ouzel *Turdus torquatus* in the Alps make daily trips to lower elevations early in the season, particularly following storm events (Barras *et al.* 2021). *Tarsiger* bush-robins on the Qinghai–Tibetan Plateau vacate breeding territories or halt upslope migration in response to early-spring cold weather events; their ability to persist at high elevations under inclement conditions is tied to fast-glycolytic muscle fibers in the pectoral (flight) muscles which aid in thermoregulation but vary with body mass, sex and age (DuBay *et al.* 2020). Mountain birds near the tree-line often exhibit food-caching behaviour, including Canada jay *Perisoreus canadensis* and mountain chickadee *Poecile gambeli* in North America and black-headed jays *Garrulus lanceolatus*, tits and nuthatches in the Himalayas. Effective food caching may be a critical adaptation to high elevation residence.

While high elevation habitats appear cold-limited, ground-level temperatures can exceed 50°C during the breeding season in both temperate and tropical regions, an increasingly common phenomenon under climate change (Chapter 6) exposing mountain birds to heat stress. Several alpine birds will select cool shady sites to roost, or to take 'snow baths' during extreme heat events, while incubating ptarmigan may return to the nest with snow or water in their breast feathers to enhance evaporative cooling (Visinoni *et al.* 2015; Rosvold 2016; Martin *et al.* 2020). Additional energetically demanding behaviours to avoid the heat such as shade-seeking are also employed, but may be linked to ecological trade-offs, such as reduced foraging time, water loss or elevated exposure to predators (Huey *et al.* 2012; Pattinson *et al.* 2020). Thus, birds have adopted many effective behavioural responses to the cold and warm temperature extremes experienced in high mountains.

Nesting Strategies

As the nesting stage is stationary, nest structure and placement can be critical to mediating the more severe prevailing conditions and providing an appropriate environment for offspring development (Deeming &

Figure 2.4 Location of the earliest horned lark *Eremophila alpestris* nests on Hudson Bay Mountain, British Columbia, Canada (c. 1,800 m). Early-season nesting activity is restricted to the limited patches of exposed bare ground on windswept ridges (Photo: Devin R. de Zwaan).

Mainwaring 2015). Temperate alpine birds are largely limited to waiting for snow to melt to access potential nest sites, leading to a high proportion of open cup nests on wind exposed ridges and in rock cavities (Figure 2.4; Martin *et al.* 2021). The propensity for alpine avifauna to nest in ground nests vs cavity nests varies across continents (Figure 2.5). Enclosed nests such as cavities are likely favourable in many high elevation habitats because they provide more benign microclimates, including warmer temperatures, protection from UV-B radiation and greater humidity (Potapov 2004; Altamirano *et al.* 2022). For example, puna yellow finch *Sicalis lutea* in the Andes of Peru and Bolivia (3,800–4,500 m) and ground tit *Pseudopodoces humilis* in northern Tibet use rodent burrows or excavate nest tunnels up to 2 m long in soft ground or banks, respectively (Ke & Lu 2009; Jaramillo 2020). In tropical alpine habitats with woody vegetation, many species place nests in dense shrub cover, likely to provide protection from the external environment, or make their own protected 'cavity' by constructing globular nesting structures of plant material placed in shrubs or directly on the ground (i.e., domed nests; Chapter 3).

High mountain birds may use nest orientation and structure to moderate their nest environment (Deeming & Mainwaring 2015). In some cases, nest orientation represents a balance between sun and wind

Figure 2.5 A. Horned lark *Eremophila alpestris* nest prior to clutch initiation, highlighting extensive use of *Salix* spp. seed-down as a lining material. The surrounding matrix of lichen, short grass and stones/bare ground helps camouflage the nest from potential predators. B. A cavity entrance to the nest of a grey-flanked cinclodes *Cinclodes oustaleti* in the Andes of southern Chile. Nests are placed up to one metre inside rock cavities formed by volcanic activity (Photos: Devin R. de Zwaan).

exposure, pointing towards the rising sun and placed on the leeward side of structures such as stunted vegetation for wind protection (MacDonald *et al.* 2016; de Zwaan & Martin 2018). Robust nest structures with extensive insulation material (e.g., fur) are often recorded in high mountain habitats, weighing almost twice as much as those at low elevations (Ke & Lu 2009). Alpine breeding horned larks line their open-cup nests with *Salix* spp. seed-down (Figure 2.5; de Zwaan & Martin 2018), cavity-nesting white-winged snowfinches *Montifringilla nivalis* use ptarmigan feathers (D. Scridel, pers. comm.), while species like the ash-breasted tit-tyrant *Anairetes alpinus* in the Central High Andes use mosses, lichens and *Polylepis* foliage (Greeney 2013). At 2,700 m in the Himalayas, black-throated bushtits *Aegithalos concinnus* stuff the entrance of their nest with a ball of animal hair at night likely to increase insulation and reduce predation (S. Barve, pers. comm.). Even cavity nesters may build larger, heavier nests with increasing elevation (Kern & van Riper 1984; but see Altamirano *et al.* 2019). In the Peruvian Andes, glacier finches *Idiopsar speculifer* nesting in glacial ice caves build nests weighing up to 160 g (Hardy *et al.* 2018). Thus, birds exhibit considerable variation in nesting strategies despite the relatively simple structural features of high mountain habitats (Chapter 3).

Parental Care

Behavioural adjustments can moderate thermal conditions for developing offspring in the nest during inclement alpine weather. Most alpine birds incubate almost continuously overnight, regardless of nightly temperatures (Wiebe & Martin 1997; Camfield & Martin 2009). When exposed to cold day time temperatures, horned lark females take more frequent, shorter incubation recesses (MacDonald *et al.* 2014). Extended cold periods can force females to take recesses of 1 to 6.5 hours instead of the usual average of 8–11 mins, and in these cases of egg neglect, hatching success can decline (Camfield & Martin 2009; MacDonald *et al.* 2013). In addition, high ambient temperatures can quickly become lethal for developing offspring (Conway & Martin 2000). Female ptarmigan with no overhead nest cover take their daytime incubation recesses before or after the hottest period of the day to prevent overheating of their developing embryos (Wiebe & Martin 1997). With these effective behaviours, high mountain birds can mitigate potential negative consequences.

Crypticity

Many alpine birds have developed cryptic appearances, behaviours and vocalizations to achieve remarkable camouflage in the exposed alpine landscapes. White-tailed ptarmigan and some songbirds have territorial and social contact calls that are difficult to localize to limit detection by predators (Martin 2013). Many high mountain birds such as alpine accentor *Prunella collaris* can 'disappear' into habitat backgrounds (Figure 2.6). Ptarmigan, renowned for their cryptic plumage, moult their feathers for up to eight months of the year, turning solid white in winter and mottled brown in summer (Figure 2.1; Martin *et al.* 2020). Spring moult begins with the dorsal feathers and finishes on the breast and belly, allowing

Figure 2.6 A. An alpine accentor *Prunella collaris* with grey, brown and rusty plumage tones that allow it to blend into habitats of rock and lichen. B. Five white-winged snowfinches *Montifringilla nivalis* identified by the black circles. Their blend of grey and white plumage enables effective camouflage in their nival breeding habitats (Photos: Davide Scridel).

birds to remain cryptic from above. In fall, the pattern is reversed, with white winter feathers coming in on the legs and belly first. Ptarmigan moult phenology is sex-specific; males initiate spring moult earlier and are darker during the pre-laying period compared to the mostly white females. When together, mated pairs spend considerable time near snow field edges where both the male and female can achieve effective camouflage by matching their rock or snow-covered backgrounds, respectively.

2.3.4 Genetic Adaptations

While phenotypic traits can be considered 'adaptive' as they improve fitness in harsh or variable conditions, they do not necessarily reflect genetic processes that are heritable and can evolve. A genetic adaptation to high mountain habitats is complex to demonstrate as phenotypic responses to prevailing conditions may simply indicate physiological consequences (e.g., slow offspring development given limited resources or cold conditions). Thus, key questions remain as to whether and how high elevation species are adapted genetically to severe and stochastic conditions. At a local scale, transplant experiments can help tease apart the complex genotype-environment interactions that occur across elevational gradients. When individuals originating from a dark-eyed junco population breeding at high elevation established in a low elevation site, they fledged twice as many offspring during a breeding season that was double the length of the ancestral high elevation population (Yeh & Price 2004). In a common garden lab experiment, the larger body size and mass of high elevation dark-eyed juncos were maintained or even increased in magnitude relative to low elevation individuals (Bears *et al.* 2008). These studies support a counter-gradient effect across elevation, where birds breeding at high elevation may have evolved greater intrinsic development rates or reproductive potential to compensate for their environmental constraints, but this was not observable until those environmental constraints were released (Bears *et al.* 2009).

Some genetic adaptations derive from highly specific mutations. Six species of Andean hummingbirds living at greater than 4,000 m elevation have repeatable amino acid substitutions associated with haemoglobin forms that have greater oxygen affinity compared to the ancestral form found in closely related species below 1,000 m (Projecto-Garcia *et al.* 2013). A similar haemoglobin pattern stemming from a single point mutation was also identified in high Andean house wrens *Troglodytes aedon* relative to low elevation populations (Galen *et al.* 2015). In rufous-collared sparrows *Zonotrichia capensis* distributed along an elevational gradient on the Pacific slope of the Peruvian Andes, about 200 unique gene transcripts were differentially expressed between high-elevation (4,100 m) and low-elevation (2,000 m) populations in their native habitats, but variation in these gene expressions disappeared when placed in a low elevation common garden experiment (Cheviron *et al.* 2008). Thus, the role of variation in gene expression in adaptation and acclimation to environmental stress demonstrate substantial plasticity in the biochemical pathways that underpin cold and hypoxia compensation in *Z. capensis*, which may contribute mechanistically to enabling the broad elevational distribution of the species. Ground tit, a year-round alpine resident in the Tibetan Plateau, and great tit populations living at high elevation in the eastern Himalayas, are also known to have 'high elevation' genes that influence energy metabolism (transition from carbohydrate-based metabolism at low elevation to lipid metabolism in the alpine zone), an improved response to hypoxia and reduced immune function that improve coping abilities for living at high elevation (Qu *et al.* 2013, 2015). Studies of inter- and intraspecific populations demonstrate the role single gene mutations may play in improving performance and perhaps survival under extreme conditions.

Birds may also evolve a greater capacity to respond to fluctuating environmental stressors characterizing high mountain habitats. Individuals may be more 'robust', where phenotypic traits and reproductive success are relatively insensitive to prevailing conditions, or they may exhibit greater 'phenotypic plasticity' or 'flexibility', where different phenotypic traits are expressed (e.g., body size) or are labile (e.g., behaviour) in response to the environment (Meyers & Bull 2002; Piersma & Drent 2003). Examples are limited, but high elevation dark-eyed juncos have greater metabolic flexibility or scope than those at low elevations (Stager *et al.* 2015). While these processes are technically non-genetic, as a single genotype can produce multiple phenotypes, they are inherently more responsive to prevailing conditions than genetic processes in these highly stochastic environments where flexibility would be adaptive (i.e., mutations; Chevin & Hoffman 2017; Meyers & Bull 2002).

2.4 Seasonality, Migration and Connectivity

Many high mountain habitats represent fragmented 'sky islands', where the maintenance of connectivity across time and space is a key ecological process maintaining bird populations. Despite the tendency for small population sizes, birds adapted to isolated high mountain habitats have well-developed dispersal abilities. Although some species are year-round residents (Section 2.4.2), most high mountain birds leave their breeding habitat and move to more favourable climates during the annual cycle, either as seasonal migrants to lower latitudes or as altitudinal migrants to lower elevations (Boyle 2011; Elsen *et al.* 2017b; Altamirano *et al.* 2020). Latitudinal migration tends to be more common in temperate regions, while altitudinal migration and year-round residency is more usual in tropical mountains (Chapter 3). Because dispersal and migratory movements are a common feature of high elevation bird communities, connectivity needs to be maintained: (i) among patchy alpine habitats to aid in population persistence, (ii) along mountain corridors for north–south latitudinal migrants, and (iii) between alpine and adjacent lower elevation habitats for altitudinal migrants. Below, we address seasonal use of high mountain habitats during migration, post-breeding dispersal and winter, as well as the propensity for altitudinal movements between low and high elevations.

2.4.1 Seasonal Movements to and Through High Mountains

High mountain habitats can provide important stopover opportunities during latitudinal migration. Particularly during post-breeding migration, mountain habitats offer rich food resources when the productivity of lower elevation habitats has declined (Wilson & Martin 2005). In western Canada, post-breeding migratory songbirds gained mass faster at high elevation than at low elevation stopover sites (Evans Ogden *et al.* 2013). Baird's sandpiper *Calidris bairdii*, a shorebird which breeds in the Canadian high Arctic, uses alpine habitats as stopover sites during southward migration to their high Andean winter sites, potentially maintaining a similar climate envelope year-round (Williamson & Witt 2021). Alpine-breeding horned larks appear to 'mountain hop' during southward migration, but during spring migration when the alpine zone is snow-covered, northward stopovers occur primarily at low elevation (de Zwaan *et al.* 2019b). In fact, these pre-breeding stopovers were estimated to last from 14–66 days, suggesting individuals may be monitoring environmental conditions to better time arrival at their alpine breeding sites. Studies on how birds connect low and high elevation landscapes are required to determine whether use of low elevation habitat during migration and staging behaviour are general characteristics of alpine breeding bird life-histories.

Altitudinal migration is a common trait of high mountain birds in both temperate and tropical regions, involving predictable seasonal or daily movements up and downslope along an elevational gradient (Boyle & Martin 2015). Early in the season, when storms are frequent, many species move to lower elevations in response to suboptimal conditions and restricted food resources (e.g., ring ouzel, Barras *et al.* 2021). O'Neill & Parker (1978) recorded a dramatic downslope movement of finches, furnariids, tyrannids and Trochilidae from the puna to below the treeline and into lush temperate forest in response to a massive and severe multi-day cold front in Central and Southern Peru. These elevational movements may occur daily or over periods of several days or weeks, exploiting distinctly different conditions over small spatial scales, thus achieving the usual seasonal migration benefits with minimal energetic movement costs (Boyle 2017; Hsiung *et al.* 2018). While 30 per cent of temperate birds that overwinter in North America exhibit altitudinal migration, this proportion reaches 65 to 70 per cent in the Himalayas between temperate high mountain habitats and tropical lowland forest, indicating that altitudinal movements may be more common in tropical or subtropical birds (Dixit *et al.* 2016; Boyle 2017). Climate, especially rainfall, appears to be the main driver of migratory behaviour in tropical mountains (Boyle 2011). Heavy rain can limit foraging opportunities and hence energy intake leading to a greater propensity for altitudinal migration in wetter years (Boyle *et al.* 2020).

Avian post-breeding use of temperate high mountain habitats is mostly unmonitored. In one mountain field study in British Columbia (Canada), 95 bird species from 30 avian families were detected, including 21 altitudinal migrants from low elevation habitats (Boyle & Martin 2015). These post-breeding migrants represent over one third of the birds breeding in British Columbia that use mountains for a period of over three months, a duration that is longer than the alpine breeding season. North America wide, Boyle & Martin (2015) recorded at least 156 species of birds that move upslope to use alpine and subalpine habitats in late summer before or during migration. The rufous hummingbird *Selasphorus rufus,* one of the earliest post-breeding migrants in North America, moves to alpine meadows and defends territories of flower patches (Gass & Sutherland 1985). In fact, hummingbirds are regular late-season altitudinal migrants throughout the Americas, including Mexico and the Andes (Arredondo-Amezcua *et al.* 2018; Sevillano-Ríos *et al.* 2020). Similar avian use patterns may also occur in Europe, with 191 species recorded at high elevation in the Italian Alps across c. 40 ringing stations between 1997 and 2017 (Franzoi *et al.* 2021). Thus, temperate mountains provide important habitats for birds during post-breeding dispersal and migration, with considerable variation among- and within-species in the frequency and extent of upslope movements (Lundblad & Conway 2020; Tsai *et al.* 2021).

2.4.2 Winter Residents of High Elevation Habitats

Year-round residency is more common in tropical habitats where temperatures are relatively stable compared to temperate high mountains (Chapter 3). Rufous-collared sparrow, an elevation generalist living from sea-level to 4,600 m in South and Central America, shows variation in winter residency patterns. Individuals breeding in the high Andes in central Chile and Argentina that experience extreme cold and snow in winter are presumed to descend to lower elevations (although this is not yet studied), while mountain populations farther north in tropical alpine habitats remain year-round at their breeding sites (Rising & Jaramillo 2020). The scarlet-tufted sunbird *Nectarinia johnstoni*, a nectarivore from the Afroalpine of Mount Kenya, defends vital food resources above the treeline year-round (Evans 1996), while c. 50 furnariid species predominantly spend the winter above the treeline in the tropical Central Andes (de Zwaan *et al.* 2022a). Certain species, such as the cinnamon-bellied ground tyrant *Muscisaxicola capistratus*, even breed at low elevations and migrate to alpine habitats to spend the winter (Williamson & Witt 2021). Although mostly unstudied, seasonal altitudinal migration is considered relatively common in tropical mountains, likely driven more by seasonal precipitation patterns than temperature (Boyle *et al.* 2020). For example, *Oxypogon*, a genus of hummingbirds specialized to breed in the high páramo of the Northern Andes, descends to lower elevations during the dry season (Billerman *et al.* 2022).

In temperate mountains, little is known about the bird communities that winter in treeline and alpine habitats. Boyle & Martin (2015) classified 24 species as winter residents in North American high mountains, with only seven species occurring in alpine or subalpine habitats. Some birds, including white-tailed ptarmigan and northern raven *Corvus corax*, remain in alpine habitats year-round (Martin *et al.* 2020). Sooty grouse *Dendragapus fuliginosus* show reverse elevational seasonal migration as individuals move up from forest areas to overwinter at the treeline (Zwickel & Bendell 2020). A few Arctic species like snowy owl *Bubo scandiacus* and snow bunting *Plectrophenax nivalis* migrate to more southern alpine areas. Rosy finches form gregarious flocks foraging for seeds on windswept alpine ridges in North America (French 1959), similar to the Brandt's mountain finch *Leucosticte brandti*, one of the few hardy alpine winter residents in the Asian temperate mountains (Potapov 2004). On the Tibetan Plateau, ground tits remain in territories year-round where they excavate one burrow in spring for nesting and another in autumn for roosting over winter (Ke & Lu 2009; Li *et al.* 2015). In Europe, year-round residents are limited to species like white-winged snowfinch and yellow-billed chough which are particularly abundant around ski areas where they take advantage of artificial food sources (Laiolo *et al.* 2001). Only a few species-level studies in winter exist for high mountain temperate birds, mostly of grouse and snowfinch in Europe (e.g., Arlettaz *et al.* 2007; Bocca *et al.* 2014; Bettega *et al.* 2020), and ptarmigan, Clark's nutcracker *Nucifraga columbiana* and Canada jay in North America (Martin *et al.* 2020; Strickland & Ouellet 2020; Tomback 2020).

2.5 Ecological Consequences

As described in the preceding sections, birds exhibit a range of adaptations to cope with the challenging abiotic conditions in high mountain habitats which can impose ecological constraints on breeding phenology, predation risk, parental care and conspecific interactions (i.e., territoriality) and have profound effects on avian fitness. Here, we outline some of the ecological consequences for birds living in high mountains with implications for offspring development and reproductive success.

2.5.1 Breeding Phenology

Stochastic, early-season weather conditions lead to substantial annual variation in the timing of breeding for mountain species. It is an especially difficult challenge for long distance migrants to determine local conditions and optimal phenology on their high mountain breeding areas (Sander *et al.* 2021). Differences in annual snowmelt phenology and storms strongly influence nesting opportunities, such that clutch initiation dates for temperate alpine birds can vary by four to seven weeks annually (French 1959; Martin & Wiebe 2004). Breeding phenology also varies intra-specifically between low and high elevation populations. For dark-eyed juncos breeding in the Rocky Mountains, Canada, spring arrival time did not differ across elevations, but clutch initiation was 30 to 40 days later at higher elevations on the same mountain (Bears *et al.* 2009). Variation in breeding phenology across elevations raises questions about the cues used to initiate the physiological changes preceding clutch initiation. Day length, normally the primary cue to initiate maturation of reproductive organs in birds (Wingfield & Kenagy 1991), does not vary with elevation. Alpine breeding passerines may therefore respond more strongly to supplementary cues (e.g., temperature, snow cover, food) or respond to different day length thresholds (Hahn 1998).

Temperate mountain breeding songbirds have about 65 per cent less time to breed compared to lower elevation conspecifics because onset of breeding is delayed by several weeks and most species do not extend

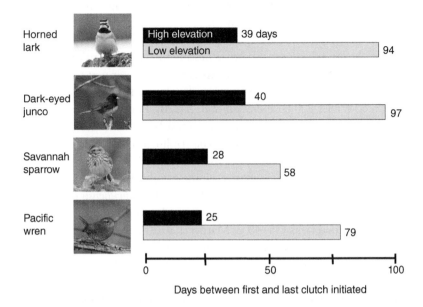

57% less time to breed in alpine habitats

Figure 2.7 Intraspecific variation in breeding times for four elevation generalist mountain songbirds in western Canada (horned lark *Eremophila alpestris*, dark-eyed junco *Junco hyemalis*, Savannah sparrow *Passerculus sandwichensis* and Pacific wren *Troglodytes pacificus*). Populations living at the high elevation sites (2,000 m) have significantly shorter times to breed each year than at the low elevation sites (1,000 m; Bears *et al.* 2009; Martin *et al.* 2009; Camfield *et al.* 2010; Evans Ogden *et al.* 2012); Photos by Meagan Grabowski (horned lark), David Bell (dark-eyed junco and Pacific wren) and Devin R. de Zwaan (Savannah sparrow).

their egg laying period beyond that of low elevation populations (Martin 2013; Altamirano *et al.* 2015). In North America, four species of alpine bird (horned lark, dark-eyed junco, Savannah sparrow and Pacific wren *Troglodytes pacificus*) initiated clutches over a period of 25 to 40 days compared to 58 to 97 days at low elevation (Figure 2.7). Therefore, both within and among species, late-onset years limit reproductive success severely in comparison with birds in lower elevation habitats as there may be insufficient time to attempt re-nesting after failures of first clutches (Martin & Wiebe 2004). However, in contrast to birds nesting at low elevations where delayed breeding results in smaller clutches, alpine breeding horned larks maintain their clutch size despite breeding delays of several weeks (Camfield *et al.* 2010), enabling birds to minimize some reproductive output costs during a late breeding season. Recently, there is evidence that alpine-nesting rock sparrows *Petronia petronia* can extend breeding activities later in the season in response to warmer temperatures under climate change (Mingozzi *et al.* 2021).

High elevation birds must balance nesting too early and risking weather-related nest failure, or too late and experiencing greater nest predation risk or running out of time for offspring to develop fully before fall migration (Martin & Wiebe 2004; de Zwaan *et al.* 2022b). For example, early-season nest failure from heavy precipitation varied between 1 and 20 per cent annually for water pipit *Anthus spinoletta* (Bollmann & Reyer 2001), while later-initiated horned lark clutches were more likely to be preyed upon (de Zwaan *et al.* 2022b). For sympatric, alpine songbirds breeding in northern British Columbia, Savannah sparrows *Passerculus sandwichensis* (c. 18 g body mass) initiated clutches over a 28-day period compared to 38.5 days for the larger horned larks (35–40 g; Martin *et al.* 2009; Camfield *et al.* 2010). A 25 per cent shorter breeding season for the smaller Savannah sparrow reflects delayed nesting, likely to avoid early-season storms (Martin *et al.* 2017; de Zwaan *et al.* 2020). Due to the longer breeding season, horned larks also have a higher probability of re-nesting following nest failure or double brooding (de Zwaan *et al.* 2020). Thus, even when breeding duration is short, some alpine songbirds alter their breeding phenology to reduce risk of clutch failure based on life-history traits such as body size and predisposition to produce single or multiple broods.

In low-latitude, tropical alpine habitats, seasonal precipitation events replace temperature in imposing temporal constraints on clutch initiation; however, at higher elevations in the nival belt, cold temperatures may still constrain initiation indirectly through seasonal resource availability (Lloyd *et al.* 2001; Hardy *et al.* 2018). In the south temperate Andes, songbird clutches were initiated over a period of a minimum of 111 days (Martin *et al.* 2021), while in the páramo of the Colombian Eastern Andes, clutch initiation extends to at least 150 days (Santiago David, unpubl. data). Breeding season phenology may vary bi-modally in the tropical alpine zone, as on the Quelccaya glacier in Peru where glacier finches nest in April, while in the same area, white-fronted ground tyrants *Muscisaxicola albifrons* nest in October, both periods occurring during the climatically comparable transitions between the dry and rainy seasons (Hardy *et al.* 2018). We note that the full range of breeding phenology has not been confirmed for most birds breeding in temperate or tropical alpine habitats outside of Europe and North America, leaving much to be discovered about the reproductive schedules of alpine birds.

2.5.2 Offspring Growth and Development

Comparative reviews on avian intra- and interspecific patterns highlight a strategy of reduced annual fecundity (i.e., smaller clutch size, fewer reproductive attempts per year), coupled with prolonged incubation and nestling stages at higher elevations (Badyaev & Ghalambor 2001; Laiolo et al. 2015b; Boyle et al. 2016). White-tailed ptarmigan at high elevations have slower laying rates, smaller clutches and longer incubation periods compared to lower elevation populations, as well as to their congener willow ptarmigan at higher latitudes (Sandercock et al. 2005; Wilson & Martin 2011). Similarly, for dark-eyed juncos in Revelstoke, British Columbia, the incubation and nestling periods on the same mountain averaged two and four days longer, respectively at high (1,900–2,200 m) compared to low elevations (450–800 m; J. Greenwood, unpubl. data). Slower development may be due to environmental constraints (e.g., cold temperatures) which can impose resource limitations or thermoregulatory challenges that prolong time within the nest (de Zwaan et al. 2019a). These responses likely vary according to the severity of weather events and among species with different life-history traits that limit exposure to prevailing conditions. For three alpine songbirds, de Zwaan et al. (2020) found that horned lark offspring were resilient to cold temperatures, but vulnerable to heavy precipitation in combination with severe cold ('cold storms' *sensu* Martin et al. 2017). Horned larks have particularly exposed nests compared to both dark-eyed juncos and Savannah sparrows, the latter of which is susceptible to moderate temperature challenges, but not to precipitation events (de Zwaan et al. 2020).

Prolonged offspring development as a consequence of prevailing weather conditions could result in greater predation rates given longer exposure times in the nest (Martin 1995; de Zwaan et al. 2019a). Yet, a meta-analysis by Boyle et al. (2016) revealed that predation rates were on average 32 per cent lower in alpine compared to low elevation habitats. Notably, slower development is hypothesized to be adaptive under uncertain, variable conditions, as rapid development disrupted by resource limitations can lead to physiological constraints on long-term fitness (Arendt 1997; Monaghan 2008). Lower predation rates at high elevation may therefore allow for longer development times and enable nestlings to reach a larger size before fledging, suggesting an ecological benefit that may improve post-fledging survival (Bears et al. 2009; Martin et al. 2018). For horned larks and Savannah sparrows, the heavier offspring raised in alpine habitats exhibited greater recruitment into the breeding population than low elevation conspecifics (Figure 2.8).

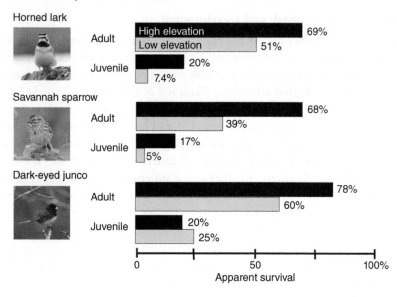

Figure 2.8 Intraspecific variation in apparent survival of elevation generalist adult, and recruitment of juvenile, songbirds (horned lark *Eremophila alpestris*, Savannah sparrow *Passerculus sandwichensis* and dark-eyed junco *Junco hyemalis*) in British Columbia, Canada. Adults and juveniles living at the high elevation sites (2,000 m), in most cases, have significantly higher local survival compared to those living at low elevation sites (1,000 m; Bears *et al.* 2009; Martin *et al.* 2009; Camfield *et al.* 2010); Photos by Meagan Grabowski (horned lark), Devin R. de Zwaan (Savannah sparrow) and David Bell (dark-eyed junco).

2.5.3 Parental Care and Mating Systems

With reduced fecundity and reproductive opportunities resulting in fewer offspring annually, mountain songbirds may increase investment in parental care to ensure higher quality offspring. In a meta-analysis of 24 phylogenetically paired passerines, high elevation species had more bi-parental care of nestlings and fledglings (Badyaev & Ghalambor 2001). During the nestling stage, the ability of parents to maintain brooding and provisioning activities is critical to buffer offspring against inclement weather. During early-season when conditions are frequently suboptimal, female horned larks in better body condition fledge larger offspring at a younger age, while females in poor condition raise smaller offspring with significantly delayed growth, suggesting females in poor condition have a reduced capacity to buffer offspring against severe conditions (de Zwaan *et al.* 2019a).

Inclement weather and variable food availability may select for elevated bi-parental care to augment the survival of a limited number of offspring, that may also have greater metabolic demands under challenging conditions. Males of several alpine specialists, such as grey-crowned rosy finch, Brandt's mountain finch and white-winged snowfinch feed their incubating mates on the nest, allowing females to spend more time warming eggs during incubation (Clement & Arkhipov 2020). Alpine breeding horned larks do not exhibit mate-feeding, but both males and females provision nestlings with equal amounts of biomass (Goullaud et al. 2018), and males invest more in post-fledging provisioning than females (de Zwaan, unpubl. data). Given challenging environmental conditions, overall low breeding densities and short, synchronous reproduction periods, alpine conditions likely shift energy allocation to parental care as opportunities for additional mates and extra-pair mating decline with increasing elevation.

The resultant changes in reproductive allocation and parental care with increasing elevation have consequences for territorial behaviour. Male Brandt's mountain finches, which breed on cliffs up to 6,000 m in Asia, defend nests and mates, but not a territory (Clement & Arkhipov 2020), similar to black rosy finches *Leucosticte atrata* in North America where males defend a floating territory around their mate, rather than a traditional territory (Johnson 2020). The expression of costly sexual characters in passerines with bi-parental care is also muted in alpine birds. To transition from mate attraction to parental care behaviours, male testosterone must be maintained at low levels or decline rapidly after hatching to facilitate increased parental investment like provisioning offspring (Badyaev & Ghalambor 2001). Badyaev (1997) and Snell-Rood & Badyaev (2008) found reduced plumage dimorphism and shorter, simpler songs in high elevation Cardueline species. Also, males showed weaker territoriality in high elevation populations of redstart *Phoenicurus* and pipit *Anthus* species (Apfelbeck & Goymann 2011; Bastianelli et al. 2015). Thus, both temperate and tropical alpine birds tend to show greater biparental care and associated reductions in territorial investment and extra-pair mating.

2.6 Life Is Slow on the High Mountains

Life-history strategies vary widely among species, shaped by key factors influencing fecundity and survival (e.g., environmental, ecological, physiological and socio-behavioural factors; Ricklefs & Wikelski 2002). The 'Pace-of-Life Syndrome' (PoLS) theory outlines a slow–fast continuum, with low reproductive rates, delayed maturity, repeated opportunities for reproduction over longer lifespans and high per capita investment in offspring at one end ('slow life-history') and the opposite traits defining 'fast life-history' (Promislow & Harvey 1990; Sæther & Bakke 2000). High mountain species may be expected to exhibit a slower life-history to cope with the stochastic weather conditions and to allow for bet-hedging in suboptimal years. This would shift investment from indi-vidual reproduction attempts to self-maintenance to minimize breeding failure costs and improve life-time reproductive success by producing fewer offspring annually and exhibiting greater longevity compared to low elevation populations (Sandercock *et al.* 2005; Londoño *et al.* 2015, 2017; Boyle *et al.* 2016).

Species comparisons generally support patterns of a slower life-history at higher elevations, particularly in temperate regions. Temperate high elevation birds consistently produce fewer offspring during short breed-ing seasons (Boyle *et al.* 2016). Reproductive rates are often lower and offspring development times longer, sometimes with accompanying increases in longevity (Bears *et al.* 2009; Martin *et al.* 2009; Boyce *et al.* 2015). Longevity is a difficult vital rate to address as it requires relatively long-term studies which are rare at high elevations. Bastianelli *et al.* (2017) assessed survival of 25 open-country species across Europe and found a positive relationship with elevation, providing support for a slower pace-of-life at higher elevations. Since data on vital rates are lacking for most tropical high mountain species (Chapter 9), it is difficult to com-pare the life-history of alpine species across latitudes. However, a study comparing 135 galliform species found an elevation–latitude interaction whereby species at high latitudes had smaller clutch sizes but larger eggs (i.e., greater per capita investment) at high elevations compared to tropi-cal species which had both larger clutches and eggs at higher elevations (150–4,250 m, Balasubramaniam & Rotenberry 2016). Therefore, only temperate galliform species appeared to follow expectations. It remains unclear whether this pattern holds for altricial songbirds or how longev-ity varies across elevation at tropical versus temperate latitudes.

Given that 85 per cent of species breeding in alpine habitats also breed at lower elevations (Chapter 3), one can assess life-history traits to evalu-ate potential trade-offs for species breeding across elevational gradients. In long-term studies in North America, birds breeding at high elevations appear well-adapted to the challenging conditions for four of five ele-vational generalist songbirds (Martin 2013). High elevation populations had 57 per cent shorter breeding seasons on average (Figure 2.7) and produced 50–60 per cent fewer offspring annually than conspecifics at

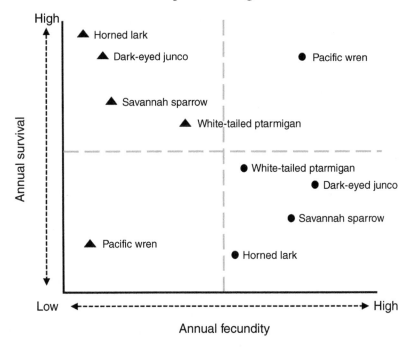

Figure 2.9 Life history variation within ten populations of five species that breed across elevation gradients in British Columbia, Canada (horned lark *Eremophila alpestris*, dark-eyed junco *Junco hyemalis*, Savannah sparrow *Passerculus sandwichensis*, Pacific wren *Troglodytes pacificus*, white-tailed ptarmigan *Lagopus leucura*). High elevation populations (c. 2,000 m) are denoted with a triangle and low elevation populations (<1,000 m) with a circle (Bears *et al.* 2009; Martin *et al.* 2009; Camfield *et al.* 2010; Wilson & Martin 2011; Evans Ogden *et al.* 2012).

lower elevations through a combination of smaller clutches, prolonged offspring development and fewer nest attempts (i.e., single-brooded). However, annual adult survival was 15–20 per cent higher for three of these species and apparent first-year survival (recruitment) was 17–20 per cent compared to ≤5 per cent at low elevations (Figure 2.8), both of which may offset lower fecundity. High elevations represent marginal habitat only for the Pacific wren, with wrens there experiencing reduced territory density, fecundity and local survival compared to birds breeding at lower elevations on the same mountain (Figure 2.9; Evans Ogden *et al.* 2012). Thus, not all species are well adapted to high mountain habitats, and some species breeding along an elevational gradient may have an optimal elevational range with populations breeding outside this range performing at suboptimal levels (Boyle *et al.* 2016).

A variety of compensatory mechanisms may improve survival in suboptimal years with important implications for longevity and lifetime fitness in long-lived organisms. However, such strategies may go undetected if the duration of a study is relatively short, especially with strong annual variation in vital rates and small sample sizes of marked birds, both conditions that are characteristic of high mountain bird studies. Juvenile survival is considered especially important for balancing life-history equations (Badyaev & Ghalambor, 2001), but survival estimates are rare given strong natal dispersal from fragmented alpine habitats. For example, Boyle *et al.* (2016) found only five studies that reported juvenile survival for conspecific populations at different elevations. In addition, while lower productivity at higher elevations seems to be a consistent pattern, only c. 40 per cent of the species studied were observed to have increased adult survival to offset reduced fecundity. Thus, unfortunately, there are almost no multi-annual studies that have rigorously examined life-history variation within species or between closely related species to determine whether life-history strategies of high mountain birds are slower and consistent with expectations from the PoLS. Identifying biotic and abiotic factors that drive variation in traits along environmental gradients is crucial to our understanding of life-history evolution for high mountain birds, especially given our imminent needs to predict species-level responses to environmental change (Martin & Wiebe 2004; Supriya *et al.* 2020; Chapter 6).

2.7 Advantages to Living and Breeding at High Elevation

Why would any bird live at high elevation given the energetic cost of breeding in an extreme environment? Despite the challenging conditions, there are probable advantages to living in high mountain environments.

2.7.1 Food Resource Availability

During the early breeding season, vast numbers of cold-numbed insects are swept up by winds from lower elevations to land on mountain snow fields while the margins of melting snow patches provide a nutritious and abundant food supply (e.g., invertebrate larvae) for many alpine birds (Norvell & Creighton 1990; Resano-Mayor *et al.* 2019; Barras *et al.* 2020). Seasonal melting of snowfields creates a gradient in plant phenology that provides an extended supply of high-quality food for birds tracking the green-up line (Evans Ogden *et al.* 2013). Leaf budding, flowering and fruiting of alpine shrubs and herbs later in the season may occur in close proximity, grading away from the snowfield edges. In winter, despite extensive snowpack, most alpine areas have wind-swept ridges with exposed herbaceous stems and seeds, and as winter progresses, increasing snow levels allow ground foraging herbivores access to the upper vegetation layers (Tape *et al.* 2010).

2.7.2 Predator Avoidance

Although it might appear that birds are more readily detected by aerial and mammalian predators in exposed alpine habitats, a meta-analysis showed nest predation risk in alpine habitats to be reduced compared to lower elevation sites (Boyle *et al.* 2016). Case studies indicate there is strong annual variation in predation risk, such that birds experience high predation in some years followed by lower-than-average rates in other years (Martin *et al.* 2000; Bowler *et al.* 2020). Alpine birds are better able to cope with high annual variability in nest mortality if they are shifted towards a slow life-history with greater longevity.

2.7.3 Minimal Parasitism and Disease

With colder temperatures, low avian densities and a compressed breeding season, the prevalence of disease and parasite infections should be relatively low in alpine habitats. Indeed, studies on several grouse species suggest that parasite occurrence is lower in species living at high elevations (Fanelli *et al.* 2020). For vector-borne diseases such as avian malaria, decreased risk along an increasing elevational gradient has been documented on several occasions and can be explained by lower vector abundance and slower parasite development at high elevations (Zamora-Vilchis *et al.* 2012). However, disease symptoms might be more detrimental in challenging environments (e.g., avian malaria in hypoxic conditions; Ishtiaq & Barve 2018) and some birds become infected when moving to lower elevations and mixing with other species during migration (Lisovski *et al.* 2018). For example, the red-necked stint *Calidris ruficollis*, which breeds in the alpine and Arctic tundra of eastern Russia, can be infected by avian flu on the wintering grounds in Australia and is thus a potential vector of the disease between non-breeding and breeding populations (Wille *et al.* 2019). In the future, disease and parasitism are likely to become increasing threats in alpine breeding bird communities under a warming climate (Chapter 6).

2.7.4 Reliable Cold

Despite their reputation for unfavourable temperatures, alpine habitats offer thermal advantages for bird species in both winter and summer. Temperate mountain winters are reliably cold, usually remaining below freezing for periods of seven to eight months. There is generally a consistent supply of snow to provide safe and well-insulated sub-nivean habitats for snow-burrowing birds (but see Chapter 6). Summers are reliably cool such that many birds may escape the late summer heat by moving upslope to forage in alpine meadows (Boyle & Martin 2015; Wilson & Martin 2005). Temperature inversions are common in mountain landscapes and provide an exception to the general rule of decreased temperature with increased elevation in temperate and tropical mountains (Potapov 2004).

2.7.5 Spatial and Temporal Habitat Considerations

In contrast to Arctic landscapes, alpine areas have alternate habitats and conditions in relatively close proximity. If conditions become too harsh, birds can avoid short-term weather events and descend to more benign conditions at lower elevations without extensive travel (Boyle 2008). Topographically complex landscapes also produce variation in microclimates that birds can exploit to modify their environmental conditions. Finally, high mountain areas, in general, represent intact habitats in natural conditions, especially compared to most other ecosystems. Although high mountains still retain considerable resilience to environmental change, these habitats are undergoing rapid change and system disruption globally (Chapters 6, 7 and 10).

2.8 Conclusions

We have much to learn about the coping mechanisms and factors enabling birds to solve the problem of living in high mountain habitats, as well as which abiotic and ecological conditions present the greatest challenges to birds. Research priorities include investigating the pathways birds have developed to live in mountain habitats, the limits to their coping mechanisms and the costs associated with these adaptations. It is critical to determine the vulnerabilities of high mountain birds to climate change and other anthropogenic stressors to manage for their persistence in high mountain habitats.

Generalizations about the relative reproductive success and survival for avian species living at high and low elevations are difficult because there are so few comparative studies of the ecology, behaviour and life-history of high mountain birds. However, the few existing studies suggest greater local adaptation and life-history diversity than realized previously. In North America, mountain habitats are used extensively by birds during the breeding and post-breeding periods, with over 40 per cent of all breeding birds using mountains for periods of 2.5 to >6 months. Furthermore, about 25 per cent of these mountain breeding species have a conservation listing of special concern or a higher level of vulnerability or endangerment (Martin *et al.* 2021). Given these roles and data gaps, we need to gather information on year-round life-history stages to evaluate accurately the status of avian biodiversity of high mountain habitats.

Acknowledgements

Special thanks to Jon Fjeldså for helpful comments on earlier editions of this chapter. Sahas Barve and Scott Wilson reviewed and greatly improved the chapter. We are also indebted to a large network of avian mountain ecologists who provided insightful observations through personal communications to integrate with the published results.

References

Altamirano, T.A., Ibarra, J.T., de la Maza, M., Navarrete, S.A. & Bonacic, C. (2015) Reproductive strategy on a secondary cavity-nester across an elevational gradient in Andean temperate ecosystems. *Auk*, **132**, 826–835.

Altamirano, T.A., Honorato M.T., Ibarra, J.T., *et al.* (2019) Elevation has contrasting effects on avian and mammalian nest traits in temperate mountains. *Austral Ecology*, **44**, 691–701.

Altamirano, T.A., de Zwaan, D.R., Ibarra, J.T., Wilson, S. & Martin, K. (2020) Treeline ecotones shape the distribution of avian species richness and functional diversity in south temperate mountains. *Scientific Reports*, **10**, e18428.

Altamirano, T.A., de Zwaan, D.R., Scridel, D., Wilson, S. & Martin, K. (2022) Rock cavity nesting as the norm: alpine breeding birds in the south temperate Andes Mountains. *Ecology*, **104**, e3931.

Altshuler, D.L. & Dudley, R. (2006) The physiology and biomechanics of avian flight at high altitude. *Integrative Comparative Biology*, **46**, 62–71.

Apfelbeck, B. & Goymann, W. (2011) Ignoring the challenge? Male black redstarts (*Phoenicurus ochruros*) do not increase testosterone levels during territorial conflicts but they do so in response to gonadotropin-releasing hormone. *Proceedings of the Royal Society Series B*, **278**, 3233–3242.

Arendt, J.D. (1997) Adaptive intrinsic growth rates: an integration across taxa. *Quarterly Review of Biology*, **72**, 149–177.

Arredondo-Amezcua, L., Martén-Rodríguez, S., Lopezaraiza-Mikel, M., *et al.* (2018) Hummingbirds in high alpine habitats of the tropical Mexican mountains: new elevational records and ecological considerations. *Avian Conservation and Ecology*, **13,** 14.

Arlettaz, R., Patthey, P., Baltic, M., *et al.* (2007) Spreading free-riding snow sports represent a novel serious threat for wildlife. *Proceedings of the Royal Society Series B*, **274**, 1219–1224.

Badyaev, A.V. (1997) Altitudinal variation in sexual dimorphism: a new pattern and alternative hypotheses. *Behavoural Ecology*, **8**, 675–690.

Badyaev, A. & Ghalambor, C.K. (2001) Avian life-history strategies in relation to elevation: evidence for a trade-off between fecundity and parental care. *Ecology*, **82,** 2948–2960.

Balasubramaniam, P. & Rotenberry, J.T. (2016) Elevation and latitude interact to drive life-history variation in precocial birds: a comparative analysis using galliformes. *Journal of Animal Ecology*, **85**, 1528–1539.

Banzett, R.B., Butler, J.P., Nations, C.S., *et al.* (1987) Inspiratory aerodynamic valving in goose lungs depends on gas density and velocity. *Respiration Physiology*, **70**, 287–300.

Barras, A.G., Marti, S., Ettlin, S., *et al.* (2020) The importance of seasonal environmental factors in the foraging habitat selection of Alpine Ring Ouzels *Turdus torquatus alpestris*. *Ibis*, **162**, 505–519.

Barras, A.G., Liechti, F. & Arlettaz, R. (2021) Seasonal and daily movement patterns of an alpine passerine suggest high flexibility in relation to environmental conditions. *Journal of Avian Biology*, **52**, jav.02860.

Barve, S., Dhondt, A.A., Mathur, V.B., Ishtiaq, F. & Cheviron, Z.A. (2016) Life-history characteristics influence physiological strategies to cope with hypoxia in Himalayan birds. *Proceedings of the Royal Society Series B*, **283**, 20162201.

Barve, S., Ramesh, V., Dotterer, T.M. & Dove, C.J. (2021) Elevation and body size drive convergent variation in thermo-insulative feather structure of Himalayan birds. *Ecography*, **44**, 680–689.

Bastianelli, G., Seoane, J., Álvarez-Blanco, P. & Laiolo, P. (2015) The intensity of male-male interactions declines in highland songbird populations. *Behavioural Ecology and Sociobiology*, **69**, 1493–1500.

Bastianelli, G., Tavecchia, G., Meléndez, L., *et al.* (2017) Surviving at high elevations: an inter-and intra-specific analysis in a mountain bird community. *Oecologia*, **184**, 293–303.

Bears, H., Smith, J. & Wingfield, J. (2003) Adrenocortical sensitivity to stress in dark-eyed juncos (*Junco hyemalis oregonus*) breeding in low and high elevation habitat. *Ecoscience*, **10**, 127–133.

Bears, H., Drever, M.C. & Martin, K. (2008) Comparative morphology of dark-eyed juncos *Junco hyemalis* breeding at two elevations: a common aviary experiment. *Journal of Avian Biology*, **39**, 152–162.

Bears, H., Martin, K. & White, G.C. (2009) Breeding in high-elevation habitat results in shift to slower life-history strategy within a single species. *Journal of Animal Ecology*, **78**, 365–375.

Bergmann, C. (1847) Ueber die Verhältnisse der Wärmeökonomie der Thiere zu ihrer Grösse. *Göttinger Studien*, **1**, 595–708.

Bettega, C., Fernández-González, Á., Ramón Obeso, J. & Delgado, M.D.M. (2020) Circannual variation in habitat use of the White-winged Snowfinch *Montifringilla nivalis nivalis*. *Ibis*, **162**, 1251–1261.

Billerman, S.M., Keeney, B.K., Rodewald, P.G. & Schulenberg, T.S. (2022) *Birds of the World*. Ithaca: Cornell Laboratory of Ornithology.

Bishop, C.M., Ward, S., Woakes, A.J. & Butler, P.J. (2002) The energetics of barnacle geese (*Branta leucopsis*) flying in captive and wild conditions. *Comparative Biochemistry and Physiology Part A*, **133**, 225–237.

Black, C.P. & Tenney, S.M. (1980) Oxygen transport during progressive hypoxia in high-altitude and sea-level waterfowl. *Respiration Physiology*, **39**, 217–239.

Bocca, M., Caprio, E., Chamberlain, D. & Rolando, A. (2014) The winter roosting and diet of Black Grouse *Tetrao tetrix* in the north-western Italian Alps. *Journal of Ornithology*, **155**, 183–194.

Bollmann, K. & Reyer, H.U. (2001) Reproductive success of Water Pipits in an alpine environment. *Condor*, **103**, 510–520.

Borras, T., Senar, J. & Cabrera, J. (2010) Hematocrit variation in response to altitude changes in wild birds: a repeated-measures design. *Condor*, **112**, 622–626.

Boyce, A.J., Freeman, B.G., Mitchell, A.E. & Martin, T.E. (2015) Clutch size declines with elevation in tropical birds. *Auk*, **132**, 424–432.

Boyce, A.J., Shakya, S., Sheldon, F.H., Moyle, R.G. & Martin, T.E. (2019) Biotic interactions are the dominant drivers of phylogenetic and functional structure in bird communities along a tropical elevational gradient. *Auk*, **136**, 1–14.

Boyle, W.A. (2008) Can variation in risk of nest predation explain altitudinal migration in tropical birds? *Oecologia*, **155**, 397–403.

Boyle, W.A. (2011) Short-distance partial migration of Neotropical birds: a community-level test of the foraging limitation hypothesis. *Oikos*, **120**, 1803–1816.

Boyle, W.A. (2017) Altitudinal bird migration in North America. *Auk: Ornithological Advances*, **134**, 443–465.

Boyle, W.A. & Martin, K. (2015) The conservation value of high elevation habitats to North American migrant birds. *Biological Conservation*, **192**, 461–476.

Boyle, W.A., Sandercock, B.K. & Martin, K. (2016) Patterns and drivers of intraspecific variation in avian life history along elevational gradients: a meta-analysis. *Biological Reviews*, **91**, 469–482.

Boyle, W.A., Shogren, E.H. & Brawn, J.D. (2020) Hygric niches for tropical endotherms. *Trends in Ecology & Evolution*, **35**, 938–952.

Bowler, D.E., Kvasnes, M.A., Pedersen, H.C., Sandercock, B.K. & Nilsen, E.B. (2020) Impacts of predator-mediated interactions along a climatic gradient on the population dynamics of an alpine bird. *Proceedings of the Royal Society Series B*, **287**, 20202653.

Brambilla, M., Scridel, D., Sangalli, B., *et al.* (2019) Ecological factors affecting foraging behaviour during nestling rearing in a high-elevation species, the White-winged Snowfinch (*Montifringilla nivalis*). *Ornis Fennica*, **96**, 142–151.

Burtt, E.H. (1986) An analysis of physical, physiological, and optical aspects of avian coloration with emphasis on wood-warblers. *Ornithological Monographs*, **38**, 1–126.

Butler, L.K., Rohwer, S. & Speidel, M.G. (2008) Quantifying structural variation in contour feathers to address functional variation and life history trade-offs. *Journal of Avian Biology*, **39**, 629–639.

Calanca, P. (2007) Climate change and drought occurrence in the Alpine region: how severe are becoming the extremes? *Global Planet Change*, **57**, 151–160.

Camfield, A.F. & Martin, K. (2009) The influence of ambient temperature on horned lark incubation behaviour in an alpine environment. *Behaviour*, **146**, 1615–1633.

Camfield A.F., Pearson, S. & Martin, K. (2010) Life history variation between high and low elevation subspecies of horned larks *Eremophila spp. Journal of Avian Biology*, **41**, 273–281.

Carey, C. (1980) Adaptation of the avian egg to high altitude. *American Zoologist*, **20**, 449–459.

Carey, C. & Martin, K. (1997) Physiological ecology of incubation of ptarmigan eggs at high and low altitudes. *Wildlife Biology*, **3**, 211–218.

Carey, C., Thompson, E.L., Vleck, C.M. & James, F.C. (1982) Avian reproduction over an altitudinal gradient: incubation period, hatchling mass, and embryonic oxygen consumption. *Auk*, **99**, 710–718.

Carpenter, F.L. & Hixon, M.A. (1988) A new function for torpor: fat conservation in a wild migrant hummingbird. *Condor*, **90**, 373–378.

Chai, P. & Dudley, R. (1996) Limits to flight energetics of hummingbirds hovering in hypodense and hypoxic gas mixtures. *Journal of Experimental Biology*, **199**, 2285–2295.

Chan, W.-P., Chen, I.-C., Colwell, R.K., *et al.* (2016) Seasonal and daily climate variation have opposite effects on species elevational range size. *Science*, **351**, 1437–1439.

Chevin, L.M. & Hoffmann, A.A. (2017) Evolution of phenotypic plasticity in extreme environments. *Philosophical Transactions of the Royal Society B*, **372**, 20160138.

Cheviron, Z.A., Whitehead, A. & Brumfield, R.T. (2008) Transcriptomic variation and plasticity in rufous-collared sparrows (*Zonotrichia capensis*) along an altitudinal gradient. *Molecular Ecology*, **17**, 4556–4569.

Choy, E.S., O'Connor, R.S., Gilchrist, H.G., *et al.* (2021) Limited heat tolerance in a cold-adapted seabird: implications of a warming Arctic. *Journal of Experimental Biology*, **224**, jeb242168.

Clement, P. & Arkhipov, V. (2020) Black-headed Mountain-Finch (*Leucosticte brandti*). In *Birds of the World. Version 1.0*. Billerman, S.M. (ed.). Ithaca: Cornell Lab of Ornithology.

Cooper, C.B., Hochachka, W.M., Butcher, G. & Dhondt, A.A. (2005) Seasonal and latitudinal trends in clutch size: thermal constraints during laying and incubation. *Ecology*, **86**, 2018–2031.

Conway, C.J. & Martin, T.E. (2000) Effects of ambient temperature on avian incubation behaviour. *Behavioural Ecology*, **11**, 178–188.

Costanzi, J.M. & Steifetten, Ø. (2019) Island biogeography theory explains the genetic diversity of a fragmented rock ptarmigan (*Lagopus muta*) population. *Ecology and Evolution*, **9**, 3837–3849.

Crisp, M.D. & Cook, L.G. (2012) Phylogenetic niche conservatism: what are the underlying evolutionary and ecological causes? *New Phytologist*, **196**, 681–694.

de Andrés, E.G., Camarero, J.J. & Büntgen, U. (2015) Complex climate constraints of upper treeline formation in the Pyrenees. *Trees*, **29**, 941–952.

de Zwaan, D.R. & Martin, K. (2018) Substrate and structure of ground nests have fitness consequences for an alpine songbird. *Ibis*, **160**, 790–804.

de Zwaan, D.R., Greenwood, J.L. & Martin, K. (2017) Feather melanin and micro-structure variation in dark-eyed junco *Junco hyemalis* across an elevational gradient in the Selkirk Mountains. *Journal of Avian Biology*, **48**, 552–562.

de Zwaan, D.R., Camfield, A.F., MacDonald, E.C. & Martin, K. (2019a) Variation in offspring development is driven more by weather and maternal condition than predation risk. *Functional Ecology*, **33**, 447–456.

de Zwaan, D.R., Wilson, S., Gow, E.A. & Martin, K. (2019b) Sex-specific spatiotemporal variation and carry-over effects in a migratory alpine songbird. *Frontiers in Ecology and Evolution*, **7**, 285.

de Zwaan, D.R., Drake, A., Greenwood, J.L. & Martin, K. (2020) Timing and intensity of weather events shape nestling development strategies in three alpine breeding songbirds. *Frontiers in Ecology and Evolution*, **8**, 359.

de Zwaan, D.R., Scridel, D., Altamirano, T.A., *et al.* (2022a) GABB: a global dataset of alpine breeding birds and their ecological traits. *Scientific Data*, **9**, 627. https://doi.org/10.1038/s41597-022-01723-6

de Zwaan, D.R., Drake, A., Camfield, A.F., MacDonald, E.C. & Martin, K. (2022b) The relative influence of cross-seasonal and local weather effects on the breeding success of a migratory songbird. *Journal of Animal Ecology*, **91**, 1458–1470.

Decker, K.L. & Conway, C.J. (2009) Effects of an unseasonable snowstorm on Red-faced Warbler nesting success. *Condor*, **111**, 392–395.

Deeming, D.C. & Mainwaring, M.C. (2015) Functional properties of nests. In *Nest, Eggs, and Incubation: New Ideas about Avian Reproduction*. Deeming, D.C. & Reynolds, S.J. (eds.). Oxford: Oxford University Press, pp. 29–49.

Devi, N.M., Kukarskih, V.V., Galimova, A.A., Mazepa, V.S. & Grigoriev, A.A. (2020) Climate change evidence in tree growth and stand productivity at the upper treeline ecotone in the Polar Ural Mountains. *Forest Ecosystems*, **7**, 1–16.

Dixit, S., Joshi, V. & Barve, S. (2016) Bird diversity of the Amrutganga Valley, Kedarnath, Uttarakhand, India with an emphasis on the elevational distribution of species. *Check List*, **12**, 1874.

Dorst, J. & Vuilleumier, F. (1986) Convergences in bird communities at high altitudes in the tropics (especially the Andes and Africa) and at temperate latitudes (Tibet). In *High Altitude Tropical Biogeography*. Vuilleumier, F. & Monasterio, M. (eds.). New York: Oxford University Press, pp. 120–149.

Downs, C.T. & Brown, M. (2002) Nocturnal heterothermy and torpor in the Malachite Sunbird (*Nectarinia famosa*). *Auk*, **119**, 251–260.

Dragon, S., Carey, C., Martin, K. & Baumann, R. (1999) Effect of high altitude and in vivo adenosine/(β)-adrenergic receptor blockade on ATP and 2, 3BPG concentrations in red blood cells of avian embryos. *Journal of Experimental Biology*, **202**, 2787–2795.

Dubay, S.G. & Witt, C.C. (2014) Differential high-altitude adaptation and restricted gene flow across a mid-elevation hybrid zone in Andean tit-tyrant flycatchers. *Molecular Ecology*, **23**, 3551–3565.

DuBay, S.G., Wu, Y., Scott, G.R., *et al.* (2020) Life history predicts flight muscle phenotype and function in birds. *Journal of Animal Ecology*, **89**, 1262–1276.

Dubey, S. & Roulin, A. (2014) Evolutionary and biomedical consequences of internal melanins. *Pigment Cell & Melanoma Research*, **27**, 327–338.

Elsen, P.R., Tingley, M.W., Kalyanaraman, R., Ramesh, K. & Wilcove, D.S. (2017a) The role of competition, ecotones, and temperature in the elevational distribution of Himalayan birds. *Ecology*, **98**, 337–348.

Elsen, P.R., Kalyanaraman, R., Ramesh, K. & Wilcove, D.S. (2017b) The importance of agricultural lands for Himalayan birds in winter. *Conservation Biology*, **31**, 416–426.

Evans, M.R. (1996) Nectar and flower production of *Lobelia telekii* inflorescences and their influence on territorial behaviour of the scarlet-tufted malachite sunbird (*Nectarinia johnstoni*). *Biological Journal of the Linnean Society*, **57**, 89–105.

Evans Ogden, L.J., Martin, M. & Martin, K. (2012) Mating and breeding success decline with elevation for the Pacific Wren (*Troglodytes pacificus*) in coastal mountain forests. *Wilson Journal of Ornithology*, **124**, 270–276.

Evans Ogden, L.J., Martin, K. & Williams, T.D. (2013) Elevational differences in estimated fattening rates suggest high-elevation sites are high quality habitats for fall migration. *Auk*, **130**, 98–106.

Fanelli, A., Menardi, G., Chiodo, M., *et al.* (2020) Gastroenteric parasite of wild Galliformes in the Italian Alps: implication for conservation management. *Parasitology*, **147**, 471–477.

Fedy, B.C., Martin, K., Ritland, C. & Young, J. (2008) Genetic and ecological data provide incongruent interpretations of population structure and dispersal in naturally subdivided populations of white-tailed ptarmigan (*Lagopus leucura*). *Molecular Ecology*, **17**, 1905–1917.

Franzoi, A., Tenan, S., Sanchez, P.L. & Pedrini, P. (2021) Temporal trends in abundance and phenology of migratory birds across the Italian Alps during a 20-year period. *Rivista Italiana di Ornitologia*, **91**, 13–28.

Freeman, B.G. (2017) Little evidence for Bergmann's rule body size clines in passerines along tropical elevational gradients. *Journal of Biogeography*, **44**, 502–510.

French, N.R. (1959) Life history of the Black Rosy Finch. *Auk*, **76**, 158–180.

Galen, S.C., Natarajan, C., Moriyama, H., *et al.* (2015) Contribution of a mutational hot spot to hemoglobin adaptation in high-altitude Andean house wrens. *Proceedings of the National Academy of Sciences*, **112**, 13958–13963.

Gass, C.L. & Sutherland, G. (1985) Specialization by territorial hummingbirds on experimentally enriched patches of flowers: energetic profitability and learning. *Canadian Journal of Zoology*, **63**, 2125–2133.

Goullaud, E.L., de Zwaan, D.R. & Martin, K. (2018) Predation risk-induced adjustments in provisioning behavior for Horned Lark (*Eremophila alpestris*) in British Columbia. *Wilson Journal of Ornithology*, **130**, 180–190.

Grabherr, G. (2000) Biodiversity of mountain forests. In *Forests in Sustainable Mountain Development: A State of Knowledge Report for 2000*. Price, M.F. & Butt, N. (eds.). Wallingford: CABI International, pp. 28–38.

Graham, C.H., Parra, J.L., Tinoco, B.A., Stiles, F.G & Mcguire, J.A. (2012) Untangling the influence of ecological and evolutionary factors on trait variation across hummingbird assemblages. *Ecology*, **93** (Suppl.), S99–S111.

Greeney, H.F. (2013) The nest of the Ash-breasted Tit-tyrant (*Anairetes alpinus*). *Ornitologia Colombiana*, **13**, 74–78.

Greenewalt, C.H. (1962) *Dimensional Relationships for Flying Animals. In Smithsonian Miscellaneous Collections*. Washington DC: Smithsonian Institution, pp. 1–46.

Gutierrez-Pinto, N., Londoño, G.A., Chappell, M.A. & Storz, J.F. (2021) A test of altitude-related variation in aerobic metabolism of Andean birds. *Journal of Experimental Biology*, **224**, 1–6.

Hahn, T.P. (1998) Reproductive seasonality in an opportunistic breeder, the red crossbill, *Loxia curvirostra*. *Ecology*, **79**, 2365–2375.

Hawkes, L., Balachandran, S., Batbayar, N., *et al.* (2011) The trans-Himalayan flights of bar-headed geese (*Anser indicus*). *Proceedings of the National Academy of Sciences*, **108**, 9516–9519.

Hardy, S.P., Hardy, D.R. & Gil, K.C. (2018) Avian nesting and roosting on glaciers at high elevation, Cordillera Vilcanota, Peru. *Wilson Journal of Ornithology*, **130**, 940–957.

Hendricks, P. & Norment, C.J. (1992) Effects of a severe snow storm on sub-alpine and alpine populations of nesting American Pipits. *Journal of Field Ornithology*, **63**, 331–338.

Höhn, E.O. (1977) The "snowshoe effect" of the feathering on ptarmigan feet. *Condor*, **79**, 380–382.

Hotaling, S., Wimberger, P.H., Kelley, J.L. & Watts, H.E. (2019) Macroinvertebrates on glaciers: a key resource for terrestrial food webs? *Ecology*, **101**, e02947.

Hsiung, A.C., Boyle, W.A., Cooper, R.J. & Chandler, R.B. (2018) Altitudinal migration: ecological drivers, knowledge gaps, and conservation implications. *Biological Reviews*, **93**, 2049–2070.

Huey, R.B., Kearney, M.R., Krockenberger, A., *et al.* (2012) Predicting organismal vulnerability to climate warming: roles of behaviour, physiology and adaptation. *Philosophical Transactions of the Royal Society B*, **367**, 1665–1679.

Ibarra, J.T., Gálvez, N., Altamirano, T.A., *et al.* (2017) Seasonal dynamics of avian guilds inside and outside core protected areas in an Andean Biosphere Reserve of southern Chile. *Bird Study*, **64**, 410–420.

Ishtiaq, F. & Barve, S. (2018) Do avian blood parasites influence hypoxia physiology in a high elevation environment? *BMC Ecology*, **18**, 1–12.

Jaramillo, A. (2020) Puna Yellow-Finch (*Sicalis lutea*). In *Birds of the World*. Version 1.0. Billerman, S.M. (ed.). Ithaca: Cornell Lab of Ornithology.

Jia, C.-X., Sun, Y.-H. & Swenson, J.E. (2010) Unusual incubation behavior and embryonic tolerance of hypothermia by the Blood Pheasant (*Ithaginis cruentus*). *Auk*, **127**, 926–931.

Johnson, R.E. (2020) Black Rosy-Finch (*Leucosticte atrata*). In *Birds of the World*. Version 1.0. Billerman, S.M. (ed.). Ithaca: Cornell Lab of Ornithology.

Johnson, D.H. & O'Neil, T.A. (2001) *Wildlife-Habitat Relationships in Oregon and Washington*. Corvallis: Oregon State University Press.

Ke, D. & Lu, X. (2009) Burrow use by Tibetan Ground Tits *Pseudopodoces humilis*: coping with life at high altitudes. *Ibis*, **151**, 321–331.

Kern, M.D. & Van Riper III, C. (1984) Altitudinal variations in nests of the Hawaiian Honeycreeper *Hemignathus virens virens*. *Condor*, **86**, 443–454.

Khaliq, I., Fritz, S.A., Prinzinger, R., *et al.* (2015) Global variation in thermal physiology of birds and mammals: evidence for phylogenetic niche conservatism only in the tropics. *Journal of Biogeography*, **42**, 2187–2196.

Kumar, L., Skidmore, A.K. & Knowles, E. (1997) Modelling topographic variation in solar radiation in a GIS environment. *International Journal of Geographical Information Science*, **11**, 475–497.

Lague, S.L., Chua, B., Farrell, A.P., Wang, Y. & Milsom, W.K. (2016) Altitude matters: differences in cardiovascular and respiratory responses to hypoxia in bar-headed geese reared at high and low altitudes. *Journal of Experimental Biology*, **219**, 1974–1984.

Lahti, D.C. & Ardia, D.R. (2016) Shedding light on bird egg color: Pigment as parasol and the dark car effect. *American Naturalist*, **187**, 547–563.

Laiolo, P., Rolando, A. & Carisio, L. (2001) Winter movements of the alpine chough: implications for management in the Alps. *Journal of Mountain Ecology*, **6**, 21–30.

Laiolo, P., Illera, J.C., Meléndez, L., Segura, A. & Obeso, J.R. (2015a) Abiotic, biotic, and evolutionary control of the distribution of C and N isotopes in food webs. *American Naturalist*, **185**, 169–182.

Laiolo, P., Seoane, J., Illera, J.C., *et al.* (2015b) The evolutionary convergence of avian lifestyles and their constrained coevolution with species' ecological niche. *Proceedings of the Royal Society Series B*, **282**, 20151808.

Landmann, A. & Winding, N. (1995) Guild organisation and morphology of high-altitude granivorous and insectivorous birds: convergent evolution in an extreme environment. *Oikos*, **73**, 237–250.

Lauer, W. & Klaus, D. (1975) Geoecological investigations on the timberline of Pico de Orizaba, Mexico. *Arctic Alpine Research*, **7**, 315–330.

Laybourne, R.C. (1974) Collision between a vulture and an aircraft at an altitude of 37,000 feet. *Wilson Bulletin*, **86**, 461–462.

Lei, F.M., Qu, Y.H., Gan, Y.L., Gebauer, A. & Kaiser, M. (2002) The feather microstructure of passerine sparrows in China. *Journal of Ornithology*, **143**, 205.

Li, Y., Li, S., Guo, C., *et al.* (2015) Nest helpers improve parental survival but not offspring production in a high-elevation passerine, the Ground Tit *Pseudopodoces humilis*. *Ibis*, **157**, 567–574.

Lindström, Å., Alerstam, T., Andersson, A., *et al.* (2021) Extreme altitude changes between night and day during marathon flights of great snipes. *Current Biology*, **31**, 3433–3439.

Lisovski, S., van Dijk, J.G., Klinkenberg, D., *et al.* (2018) The roles of migratory and resident birds in local avian influenza infection dynamics. *Journal of Applied Ecology*, **55**, 2963–2975.

Lloyd, P., Little, R.M., Crowe, T.M. & Simmons, R.E. (2001) Rainfall and food availability as factors influencing the migration and breeding activity of Namaqua Sandgrouse, *Pterocles namaqua*. *Ostrich*, **72**, 50–62.

Londoño, G.A., Chappell, M.A., Castañeda, M. del R., Jankowski, J.E. & Robinson, S.K. (2015) Basal metabolism in tropical birds: latitude, altitude, and the 'pace of life.' *Functional Ecology*, **29**, 338–346.

Londoño, G.A., Chappell, M.A., Jankowski, J.E. & Robinson, S.K. (2017) Do thermoregulatory costs limit altitude distributions of Andean forest birds? *Functional Ecology*, **31**, 204–215.

Lu, X., Ke, D., Guo, Y., *et al.* (2011) Breeding ecology of the Black Redstart *Phoenicurus ochruros* at a Tibetan site, with special reference to cooperative breeding. *Ardea*, **99**, 235–240.

Lundblad, C.G. & Conway, C.J. (2020) Testing four hypotheses to explain partial migration: balancing reproductive benefits with limits to fasting endurance. *Behavioural Ecology and Sociobiology*, **74**, 26.

Lustick, S. (1984) Thermoregulation in adult seabirds. In *Seabird Energetics*. Whittow, G.C. (ed.). Boston: Springer, pp. 183–201.

MacDonald, E.C., Camfield, A.F., Jankowski, J.E. & Martin, K. (2013) Extended incubation recesses for alpine breeding Horned Larks: a strategy for dealing with inclement weather? *Journal of Field Ornithology*, **84**, 58–68.

MacDonald, E.C., Camfield, A.F., Jankowski, J.E. & Martin, K. (2014) An alpine-breeding songbird can adjust dawn incubation rhythms to annual thermal regimes. *Auk*, **131**, 495–506.

MacDonald, E.C., Camfield, A.F., Martin, M., Wilson, S. & Martin, K. (2016) Nest-site selection and consequences for nest survival among three sympatric songbirds in an alpine environment. *Journal of Ornithology*, **157**, 393–405.

MacDougall-Shackleton, S.A., Johnson, R.E. & Hahn, T.P. (2020) Gray-crowned Rosy-Finch (*Leucosticte tephrocotis*). In *Birds of the World*. Version 1.0. Billerman, S.M. (ed.). Ithaca: Cornell Lab of Ornithology.

Madge, S. (2020) Yellow-billed Chough (*Pyrrhocorax graculus*). In *Birds of the World*. Version 1.0. Billerman, S.M. (ed.). Ithaca: Cornell Lab of Ornithology.

Martin, K. (2001) Wildlife in alpine and sub-alpine habitats. In *Wildlife-Habitat Relationships in Oregon and Washington*. Johnson, D.H., O'Neil, T.A. (Manag. Dirs.). Corvallis: Oregon State University Press, pp. 285–310.

Martin, K. (2013) The ecological values of mountain environments and wildlife. In *The Impact of Skiing on Mountain Environments*. Rixen, C. & Rolando, A. (eds.). Bussum: Bentham Science Publishers, pp. 3–29.

Martin, K. & Wiebe, K.L. (2004) Coping mechanisms of alpine and arctic breeding birds: extreme weather and limitations to reproductive resilience. *Integrative and Comparative Biology*, **44**, 177–185.

Martin, K., Stacey, P.B. & Braun, C.E. (2000) Recruitment, dispersal and demographic rescue in spatially-structured White-tailed Ptarmigan populations. *Condor*, **102**, 503–516.

Martin, K., Wilson, S., MacDonald, E.C., *et al.* (2017) Effects of severe weather on reproduction for sympatric songbirds in an alpine environment: interactions of climate extremes influence nesting success. *Auk*, **134**, 696–709.

Martin, K., Robb, L.A., Wilson, S. & Braun, C.E. (2020) White-tailed Ptarmigan (*Lagopus leucura*). In *Birds of the World*. Version 1.0. Rodewald, P.G. (ed.). Ithaca: Cornell Lab of Ornithology.

Martin, K., Altamirano, T.A., de Zwaan, D.R., *et al.* (2021) Avian ecology and community structure across elevation gradients: the importance of high latitude temperate mountains for conserving biodiversity in the Americas. *Global Ecology and Conservation*, **30**, e01799.

Martin, M., Camfield, A.F. & Martin, K. (2009) The demography of an alpine population of Savannah Sparrows (*Passerculus sandwichensis*). *Journal of Field Ornithology*, **80**, 253–264.

Martin, T.E. (1995) Avian life history evolution in relation to nest sites, nest predation, and food. *Ecological Monographs*, **65**, 101–127.

Martin, T.E., Tobalske, B., Riordan, M.M., Case, S.B. & Dial, K.P. (2018) Age and performance at fledging are a cause and consequence of juvenile mortality between life stages. *Science Advances*, **4**, eaar1998.

McKenzie, R.L., Johnston, P.V., Smale, D., Bodhaine, B.A. & Madronich, S. (2001) Altitude effects on UV spectral irradiance deduced from measurements at Lauder, New Zealand, and at Mauna Loa Observatory, Hawaii. *Journal of Geophysical Research: Atmospheres*, **106**, 22845–22860.

Meyers, L.A. & Bull, J.J. (2002) Fighting change with change: adaptive variation in an uncertain world. *Trends in Ecology & Evolution*, **17**, 551–557.

Minias, P. (2020) Ecology and evolution of blood oxygen-carrying capacity in birds. *American Naturalist*, **195**, 788–801.

Mingozzi, T., Storino, P., Venuto, G., Massolo, A. & Tavecchia, G. (2021) Climate warming induced a stretch of the breeding season and an increase of second clutches in a passerine breeding at its altitudinal limits. *Current Zoology*, **68**, 9–17.

Monaghan, P. (2008) Early growth conditions, phenotypic development and environmental change. *Philosophical Transactions of the Royal Society B*, **363**, 1635–1645.

Nagy, L. & Grabherr, G. (2009) *The Biology of Alpine Habitats*. New York: Oxford University Press.

Norvell, J.R. & Creighton, P.D. (1990) Foraging of Horned Larks and Water Pipits in alpine communities. *Journal of Field Ornithology*, **61**, 434–440.

O'Neill, J.P. & Parker, T.A. (1978) Responses of birds to a snowstorm in the Andes of southern Peru. *Wilson Bulletin*, **90**, 446–449.

Pageau, C., Vale, M.M., de Menezes, M.A., *et al.* (2020) Evolution of altitudinal migration in passerines is linked to diet. *Ecology and Evolution*, **10**, 3338–3345.

Pap, P.L., Osváth, G., Daubner, T., Nord, A. & Vincze, O. (2020) Down feather morphology reflects adaptation to habitat and thermal conditions across the avian phylogeny. *Evolution*, **74**, 2365–2376.

Parr, N., Bearhop S., Douglas D.C. *et al.* (2017) High altitude flights by ruddy shelduck *Tadorna ferruginea* during trans-Himalayan migrations. *Journal of Avian Biology*, **48**, 1–6.

Parr, N., Wilkes, M. & Hawkes, L.A. (2019) Natural climbers: insights from avian physiology at high altitudes. *High Altitude Medicine and Biology*, **20**, 427–437.

Pattinson, N.B., Thompson, M.L., Griego, M., *et al.* (2020) Heat dissipation behaviour of birds in seasonally hot arid-zones: are there global patterns? *Journal of Avian Biology*, **51**, e02350.

Peacock, A.J. (1998) Oxygen at high altitude. *British Medical Journal*, **317**, 1063–1066.

Piersma, T. & Drent, J. (2003) Phenotypic flexibility and the evolution of organismal design. *Trends in Ecology & Evolution*, **18**, 228–233.

Pollock, H.S., Brawn, J.D., Agin, T.J. & Cheviron, Z.A. (2019) Differences between temperate and tropical birds in seasonal acclimatization of thermoregulatory traits. *Journal of Avian Biology*, **50**, e02067.

Potapov, R.L. (2004) Adaptations of birds to life in high mountains in Eurasia. *Acta Zoologica Sinica*, **50**, 970–977.

Promislow, D.E.L. & Harvey, P.H. (1990) Living fast and dying young: a comparative analysis of life-history variation among mammals. *Journal of Zoology*, **220**, 417–437.

Projecto-Garcia, J., Natarajan, C., Moriyama, H., *et al.* (2013) Repeated elevational transitions in hemoglobin function during the evolution of Andean hummingbirds. *Proceedings of the National Academy of Sciences*, **110**, 20669–20674.

Qu, Y., Zhao, H., Han, N., *et al.* (2013) Ground tit genome reveals avian adaptation to living at high altitudes in the Tibetan plateau. *Nature Communications*, **4**, 2071.

Qu, Y., Tian, S., Han, N., *et al.* (2015) Genetic responses to seasonal variation in altitudinal stress: whole-genome resequencing of great tit in eastern Himalayas. *Scientific Reports*, **5**, 14256.

Resano-Mayor, J., Korner-Nievergelt, F., Vignali, S., *et al.* (2019) Snow cover phenology is the main driver of foraging habitat selection for a high-alpine passerine during breeding: implications for species persistence in the face of climate change. *Biodiversity and Conservation*, **28**, 2669–2685.

Ricklefs, R.E. & Wikelski, M. (2002) The physiology/life history nexus. *Trends in Ecology & Evolution*, **17**, 462–468.

Rising, J.D. & Jaramillo, A. (2020) Rufous-collared Sparrow (*Zonotrichia capensis*). In *Birds of the World*. Version 1.0. del Hoyo, J., Elliott, A., Sargatal, J., Christie, D.A. & de Juana, E. (eds.). Ithaca: Cornell Lab of Ornithology.

Rogalla, S., D'Alba L., Verdoodt A. & Shawkey, M.D. (2019) Hot wings: thermal impacts of wing coloration on surface temperature during bird flight. *Journal of the Royal Society Interface*, **16**, 20190032.

Rogalla, S., Patil, A., Dhinojwala, A., Shawkey, M.D. & D'Alba, L. (2021) Enhanced photothermal absorption in iridescent feathers. *Journal of the Royal Society Interface*, **18**, 20210252.

Rosvold, J. (2016) Perennial ice and snow-covered land as important ecosystems for birds and mammals. *Journal of Biogeography*, **43**, 3–12.

Sæther, B.E. & Bakke, Ø. (2000) Avian life history variation and contribution of demographic traits to the population growth rate. *Ecology*, **81**, 642–653.

Sander, M.M., Chamberlain, D., Mermillon, C., *et al.* (2021) Early breeding conditions followed by reduced breeding success despite timely arrival in an alpine migratory songbird. *Frontiers in Ecology and Evolution*, **9**, 676506.

Sandercock, B.K., Martin, K. & Hannon, S.J. (2005) Life history variation in extreme environments: comparative demography of arctic and alpine ptarmigan. *Ecology*, **86**, 2176–2186.

Schano, C., Niffenegger, C., Jonas, T. & Korner-Nievergelt, F. (2021) Hatching phenology is lagging behind an advancing snowmelt pattern in a high-alpine bird. *Scientific Reports*, **11**, 22191.

Scholander, P.F., Hock, R., Walters, V. & Irving, L. (1950) Adaptation to cold in arctic and tropical mammals and birds in relation to body temperature, insulation, and basal metabolic rate. *Biological Bulletin*, **99**, 259–271.

Schmidt-Nielsen, K. (1997) *Animal Physiology: Adaptation and Environment*. Cambridge: Cambridge University Press.

Scott, G.R. (2011) Elevated performance: the unique physiology of birds that fly at high altitudes. *Journal of Experimental Biology*, **214**, 2455–2462.

Scridel, D., Brambilla, M., Martin, K., *et al.* (2018) A review and meta-analysis of the effects of climate change on Holarctic mountain and upland bird populations. *Ibis*, **160**, 489–515.

Scridel, D., Brambilla, M., de Zwaan, D.R., *et al.* (2021) A genus at risk: predicted current and future distribution of all three *Lagopus* species reveal sensitivity to climate change and efficacy of protected areas. *Diversity and Distributions*, **27**, 1759–1744.

Segre, P.S., Dakin, R., Read, T.J.G., Straw, A.D. & Altshuler, D.L. (2016) Mechanical constraints on flight at high elevation decrease maneuvering performance of hummingbirds. *Current Biology*, **26**, 3368–3374.

Senner, N.R., Stager, M., Verhoeven, M.A., *et al.* (2018) High-altitude shorebird migration in the absence of topographical barriers: avoiding high air temperatures and searching for profitable winds. *Proceedings of the Royal Society Series B*, **285**, 20180569.

Sevillano-Ríos, C.S., Rodewald, A.D. & Morales, L.V. (2020) Alpine birds of South America. In *Encyclopedia of the World's Biomes*. Goldstein, M.I. & DellaSala, D.A. (eds.). Amsterdam: Elsevier, pp. 492–504.

Shankar, A., Schroeder, R.J., Wethington, S.M., Graham, C.H. & Powers, D.R. (2020) Hummingbird torpor in context: duration, more than temperature, is the key to nighttime energy savings. *Journal of Avian Biology*, **51**, e02305.

Sjöberg, S., Malmiga, G., Nord, A., *et al.* (2021) Extreme altitudes during diurnal flights in a nocturnal songbird migrant. *Science*, **372**, 646–648.

Snell-Rood, E.C. & Badyaev, A.V. (2008) Ecological gradient of sexual selection: elevation and song elaboration in finches. *Oecologia*, **157**, 545–551.

Spence, A.R., LeWinter, H. & Tingley, M.W. (2022) Anna's hummingbird (*Calypte anna*) physiological response to novel thermal and hypoxic conditions at high elevations. *Journal of Experimental Biology*, **225**, jeb243294.

Stager, M., Swanson, D.L. & Cheviron, Z.A. (2015) Regulatory mechanisms of metabolic flexibility in the dark-eyed junco (*Junco hyemalis*). *Journal of Experimental Biology*, **218**, 767–777.

Stettenheim, P.R. (2000) The integumentary morphology of modern birds—an overview. *American Zooogist*, **40**, 461–477.

Strickland, D. & Ouellet, H.R. (2020) Canada Jay (*Perisoreus canadensis*). In *Birds of the World*. Version 1.0. Rodewald, P.G. (ed.). Ithaca: Cornell Lab of Ornithology.

Storz, J.F., Quiroga-Carmona, M., Opazo, J.C., *et al.* (2020) Discovery of the world's highest-dwelling mammal. *Proceedings of the National Academy of Sciences*, **117**, 18169–18171.

Stull, R.B. (2000) *Meteorology for Scientists and Engineers*. Pacific Grove: Brooks/Cole.

Supriya, K., Price, T.D. & Moreau, C.S. (2020) Competition with insectivorous ants as a contributor to low songbird diversity at low elevations in the eastern Himalaya. *Ecology and Evolution*, **10**, 4280–4290.

Swanson, D.L. & Garland Jr, T. (2009) The evolution of high summit metabolism and cold tolerance in birds and its impact on present-day distributions. *Evolution*, **63**, 184–194.

Tape, K.D., Lord, R., Marshall, H.-P. & Ruess, R.W. (2010) Snow-mediated ptarmigan browsing and shrub expansion in arctic Alaska. *Ecoscience*, **17**, 186–193.

Tomback, D.F. (2020) Clark's Nutcracker (*Nucifraga columbiana*). In *Birds of the World*. Version 1.0. Billerman, S.M. (ed.). Ithaca: Cornell Lab of Ornithology.

Tsai, P.-Y., Ko, C.-J., Chia, S. Y., Lu, Y.-J. & Tuanmu, M.-N. (2021) New insights into the patterns and drivers of avian altitudinal migration from a growing crowdsourcing data source. *Ecography*, **44**, 75–86.

Visinoni, L., Pernollet, C.A., Desmet, J.F., *et al.* (2015) Microclimate and microhabitat selection by the Alpine Rock Ptarmigan (*Lagopus muta helvetica*) during summer. *Journal of Ornithology*, **156**, 407–417.

Wang, Q., Wang, M. & Fan, X. (2018) Seasonal patterns of warming amplification of high-elevation stations across the globe. *International Journal of Climatology*, **38**, 3466–3473.

Webb, D.R. (1987) Thermal tolerance of avian embryos: a review. *Condor*, **89**, 874–898.

Wiebe, K.L. & Martin, K. (1997) Effects of predation, body condition and temperature on incubation rhythms of ptarmigan. *Wildlife Biology*, **3**, 219–227.

Wille, M., Lisovski, S., Risely, A., *et al.* (2019) Serologic evidence of exposure to highly pathogenic avian influenza H5 viruses in migratory shorebirds, Australia. *Emerging Infectious Diseases*, **25**, 1903.

Williams, H.J., Shepard, E.L.C., Holton, M.D., *et al.* (2020) Physical limits of flight performance in the heaviest soaring bird. *Proceedings of the National Academy of Sciences*, **117**, 17884–17890.

Williams, T.D. (2020) *What Is a Bird?: An Exploration of Anatomy, Physiology, Behavior, and Ecology.* New Jersey: Princeton University Press.

Williamson, J.L. & Witt, C.C. (2021) Elevational niche-shift migration: why the degree of elevational change matters for the ecology, evolution, and physiology of migratory birds. *Auk*, **138**, ukaa087.

Wilson, S. & Martin, K. (2005) High elevation habitat associations of birds during fall migration. *Ecoscience*, **12**, 561–568.

Wilson, S. & Martin, K. (2011) Life-history and demographic variation in an alpine specialist at the latitudinal extremes of the range. *Population Ecology*, **53**, 459–471.

Wingfield, J.C. & Kenagy, G.J. (1991) Natural regulation of reproductive cycles. In *Vertebrate Endocrinology: Fundamentals and Biomedical Implications.* Schreibman, M. & Jones, R.E. (eds.). New York: Academic Press, pp. 181–241.

Wolf, L.L. & Hainsworth, F.R. (1972) Environmental influence on regulated body temperature in torpid hummingbirds. *Comparative Biochemistry and Physiology Part A*, **41**, 167–173.

Wolf, B.O. & Walsberg, G.E. (1996) Thermal effects of radiation and wind on a small bird and implications for microsite selection. *Ecology*, **77**, 2228–2236.

Wolf, B.O. & Walsberg, G.E. (2000) The role of the plumage in heat transfer processes of birds. *American Zoologist*, **40**, 575–584.

Yeh, P.J. & Price, T.D. (2004) Adaptive phenotypic plasticity and the successful colonization of a novel environment. *American Naturalist*, **164**, 531–542.

York, J.M., Chua, B.A., Ivy, C.M., *et al.* (2017) Respiratory mechanics of eleven avian species resident at high and low altitude. *Journal of Experimental Biology*, **220**, 1079–1089.

Youngflesh, C., Saracco, J.F., Siegel, R.B. & Tingley, M.W. (2022) Abiotic conditions shape spatial and temporal morphological variation in North American birds. *Nature Ecology and Evolution*, **6**, 1860–1870.

Zamora-Vilchis, I., Williams, S.E. & Johnson, C.N. (2012) Environmental temperature affects prevalence of blood parasites of birds on an elevation gradient: implications for disease in a warming climate. *PLoS ONE*, **7**, e39208.

Zwickel, F.C. & Bendell, J.F. (2020) Blue Grouse (*Dendragapus obscurus*). In *Birds of the World.* Version 1.0. Billerman, S.M. (ed.). Ithaca: Cornell Lab of Ornithology.

3 · *Global Bird Communities of Alpine and Nival Habitats*

DEVIN R. DE ZWAAN, ARNAUD G.
BARRAS, TOMÁS A. ALTAMIRANO,
ADDISU ASEFA, PRANAV GOKHALE,
R. SURESH KUMAR, SHAOBIN LI,
RUEY-SHING LIN, C. STEVEN
SEVILLANO-RÍOS, KERRY A.
WESTON AND DAVIDE SCRIDEL

Mountains are imposing, iconic landscape features around the globe. Yet for many, the highest mountain reaches extending well beyond the treeline are enigmatic, aptly symbolized by the frequency in which they are enshrouded by clouds. The terms 'above-treeline' or 'alpine' evoke a distinct image in our minds. This image varies regionally, but generally includes alpine meadows or tundra characterized by extensive rock, ice and snow, along with a general misconception of low diversity or ecological value. Globally, above-treeline habitats comprise c. 3.55 million km^2 or 2.6 per cent of the total landmass, excluding Antarctica (Körner *et al.* 2011; Testolin *et al.* 2020). These habitats represent varied climates and vegetation structures that provide a broad range of niches for alpine fauna, including birds. Alpine breeding bird communities consist of diverse species adapted to high elevation conditions with specialized life-history strategies and functional traits, as well as unique evolutionary histories (Boyle *et al.* 2016; Quintero & Jetz 2018). Many species that breed at low elevations venture above the treeline to forage or stopover during migration, such that across the annual cycle, alpine habitats support a greater number of species than expected based on their available area (Boyle & Martin 2015).

In this chapter, we highlight the global diversity of alpine habitats and their avifaunal communities. We first define general features of the alpine and nival zones, before providing an overview of these habitats across 12 major regions around the world. Using a global dataset of alpine breeding birds assembled from published literature and expert knowledge (de Zwaan *et al.* 2022a, b), we characterize the alpine avifauna and how communities vary regionally. We focus on a few ecological traits representing how species interact with their environment: (i) alpine breeding specialization, (ii) migration strategy, and (iii) nest type and placement. Finally, we discuss some of the main drivers that shape alpine bird communities, including climate, vegetation structure, food availability and species interactions. We conclude by discussing the critical role snow dynamics play in alpine habitats, framed within the context of an uncertain future for alpine bird communities under a rapidly changing climate.

3.1 What Defines 'Alpine' Habitat?

Habitats above the treeline can be broadly divided into alpine and nival zones. The alpine zone exists between the treeline and snowline, whereas the nival zone resides above the snowline (Körner 1999; Körner & Ohsawa 2006). Generally, the treeline and snowline are defined as the elevational limit above which upright tree growth is constrained and snow persists year-round (perennial snow), respectively (Chapter 1). Hereafter, the alpine and nival zones will be collectively referred to as 'alpine' or 'above-treeline' habitat.

Alpine habitats are characterized by climatic extremes which set the location of the treeline, thus determining available alpine habitat area (Körner 2012). Cold temperatures, high wind speeds, frequent storm events, soil erosion, precipitation and snow, which can linger late into the summer, all combine to restrict the growing season and upright tree growth in alpine habitats (Körner 2012; Chapter 1). These factors also apply at tropical latitudes where winter aridity, monsoon events and extreme temperature fluctuations between day and night are similarly limiting (Bader *et al.* 2007; Chapter 9). For example, in the north Andean páramo, where seasonality is minimal, above-treeline vegetation growth is constrained by early morning drought stemming from nocturnal frost (Meinzer *et al.* 1994). Consequently, alpine vegetation is characterized by low-profile woody shrubs, isolated tree patches (i.e., krummholz), cold-adapted perennials, graminoids (grasses, sedges), forbs and cushion plants, which form a mosaic within patches of bare ground, rock and snow. These conditions produce a simplified habitat structure and a short, temporally variable breeding season for alpine birds that is dependent on weather and snowmelt dynamics.

Despite these general features, defining alpine habitat is non-trivial given regional variation in alpine vegetation and treeline position. The treeline, which delimits the lower margin of alpine habitat, is often a relatively diffuse ecotonal gradient and sometimes it is absent altogether (Bader *et al.* 2021; Chapter 1). For example, the dry central Andes of South America lack continuous, high elevation forest, making it difficult to define where alpine habitat begins (Chapter 4). The mountainous regions of northern Canada and Eurasia represent Arctic–alpine transition zones where differences between alpine and Arctic tundra are subtle, and in some cases, ecologically indistinguishable. However, a clear and robust definition of alpine habitat is critical for effectively assessing the status of alpine ecosystems and their avifaunal communities, as well as accurately predicting habitat availability and bird community stability into the future.

Here, we define alpine habitat following Körner and Paulsen (2004) as occurring beyond the 'climatic treeline', above which tree growth is limited by climate and habitat constraints to fragmented patches <3 m in height (Chapter 1). Above 3 m, the crown of a plant is strongly associated with atmospheric conditions and remains above snow cover in habitats with extensive snowfall, whereas low-lying vegetation (<3 m) persists above the treeline by moderating its climate near the ground and is therefore strongly indicative of alpine habitats (Körner 1998; Körner 2012). By this definition, heterogeneity in microclimate, shelter and soil accumulation arising from the topography of alpine ecosystems allows for isolated patches of stunted trees or scrub to establish well above the treeline, such as *Polylepis* forest in the Andes, *Rhododendron* in the Himalayas and ericaceous (heather) trees in the Afroalpine of sub-Saharan Africa. This variation in vegetation and habitat structure above-treeline provides diverse niches for species other than ground–nesting birds (e.g., cavity or shrub nests). Our definition of alpine habitat therefore includes the upper limits of the treeline ecotone, as well as the higher elevation alpine, nival and aeolian zones (see Table 1.1). Bird communities of the treeline ecotone are specifically addressed in Chapter 4.

In certain regions where a visible treeline is lacking due to severe climate or anthropogenic effects, such as the dry Central Andes, alpine habitats can be identified using a combination of factors such as thermal belts (i.e., growing season length) and the presence of alpine plants (Körner *et al.* 2011). Alpine habitats generally occur above at least 1,500 m in elevation, although this may drop to as low as 400 m at latitudinal extremes (>55°N or 41°S) as estimated from linear associations with latitude (Testolin *et al.*

2020; Chapter 1). We refer to these regions as 'high-latitude alpine habitats' to distinguish between the ecologically distinct drier, upland tundra and the wet, coastal Arctic or Antarctic tundra at lower elevations. Importantly, the treeline has been anthropogenically modified in many parts of the world through timber harvest, livestock grazing and burning, sometimes for several centuries, leading to semi-natural subalpine grasslands well below the climatic treeline (Nagy 2006; Hope 2014). These modified ecosystems are not addressed in this chapter because they are maintained by human activity and are more representative ecologically of subalpine grasslands or steppe (but see Chapter 7).

3.2 A Global Overview of Alpine Habitats and Their Avian Communities

Mountains differ in their isolation and disturbance regimes (e.g., volcanic eruptions, glaciation), resulting in unique extinction–colonization histories that have produced variation in the alpine breeding bird communities that we observe today. Additional factors, such as elevation, latitude, topography and oceanic influence, dictate differences in treeline elevation (delimiting alpine habitat area), vegetation structure and climatic conditions that continue to shape these communities by influencing the presence and abundance of birds in alpine habitats (Chapter 1). Thus, alpine habitats represent complex ecosystems with a diversity of bird communities globally (Figure 3.1).

Below, we provide an overview of alpine habitats and the bird communities they support across global regions to highlight this diversity. Regional summaries of alpine avifauna were derived from a global dataset of alpine breeding birds that was assembled from published literature, field observations and expert knowledge (de Zwaan et al. 2022a, b). This study involved authors from six continents with expertise in mountain birds of >50 major mountain ranges representing most mountainous regions globally, excluding Antarctica and Greenland. In short, a review was conducted for all bird species with mountainous regions within their breeding range to assess evidence of above-treeline breeding using published literature, technical reports and online databases. The strength of breeding evidence was evaluated through regional expert opinions and observations from local field biologists. For each species confirmed breeding above the treeline, ecological traits (e.g., migration strategy) were sourced from databases such as Birds of the World (Billerman et al. 2020). Further details can be found in de Zwaan et al. (2022a, b).

Figure 3.1 Examples of the diversity of alpine habitats around the world.
A. Tropical Andes in Parque Nacional Lauca, Chile, showing a bofedal wetland
in the foreground and puna grassland with shrubs in the background (c. 4,500 m).
B. A gradient of stunted European larch *Larix decidua*, shrubs and alpine meadows
in the Swiss Alps (c. 2,300 m). C. Giant lobelia *Lobelia rhyncopetalum*, an endemic
giant rosette plant near a wetland in the Afroalpine of the Bale Mountains,
Ethiopia (c. 4,000 m). D. Aoraki (Mount Cook) in the Southern Alps of New
Zealand demonstrating alpine tundra, shrubs and scree from valley bottom up to
nival habitat at higher elevations (c. 3,000 m). Photos: A. Devin R. de Zwaan,
B. Niklaus Zbinden, C. Addisu Asefa and D. Kerry Weston.

3.2.1 North America – Canada, USA and Northern Mexico

High mountain systems dominate the west, extending from the Brooks
Range in Alaska and the Yukon (68°N) down into Mexico (c. 23°N).
Near the northwestern limit, the Boreal Cordillera consists of the highest mountains (>6,000 m), but a relatively low treeline (850–1,100 m),
resulting in extensive alpine tundra consisting of heather, Arctic graminoids (i.e., sedges), lichen and rock. The Western Cordillera, including
the Rocky Mountains, extends from northern British Columbia (treeline:
1,000–1,400 m) to the Sierra Nevada in California (c. 3,000 m). Moving
south, alpine vegetation becomes more diverse, with woody shrubs such
as sagebrush (*Artemisia* spp.) and juniper (*Juniperus* spp.) interspersed with
meadows of herbaceous perennials. Limited alpine habitat exists to the
east, including isolated patches in the comparatively ancient Acadian–
Appalachian range and the Labrador highlands, which represents an

Arctic–alpine transition zone with a treeline at c. 400–500 m. While the Sierra Madre Oriental and Occidental in Mexico are also prominent mountain ranges, they lack a true treeline, and high elevation habitat primarily consists of matorral scrub and open forest (Steinmann *et al.* 2021).

Within Canada and the USA, 153 species representing 37 families use alpine habitats (Boyle & Martin 2015). Of these, 113 are alpine-breeding species (Table 3.1), representing 16.1 per cent of the c. 700 species regularly breeding in North America. However, only 8 species are considered alpine breeding specialists, such as the three rosy finches (*Leucosticte* spp.), white-tailed ptarmigan *Lagopus leucura* and surfbird *Calidris virgata*. A further 14 species are restricted to tundra habitats, including higher elevation tundra within the Arctic-alpine transition zone (e.g., long-tailed jaeger *Stercorarius longicaudus*). Due to high connectivity along north–south oriented mountains, relatively few species are endemic to specific ranges, with exceptions such as black *Leucosticte atrata* and brown-capped rosy finch *L. australis* restricted to the southern Rocky Mountains. Many species that do not breed above-treeline use alpine habitats as stopover sites during migration or to forage (Boyle & Martin 2015). For example, Baird's sandpipers *Calidris bairdii* stopover in alpine habitats while migrating from their Arctic breeding grounds to the high Andes. Early in the breeding season, predominantly treeline-nesting birds, such as myrtle warbler *Setophaga coronata*, forage for windfall insects on alpine snowfields. In late summer, rufous hummingbirds *Selasphorus rufus* travel upslope to take advantage of late-season alpine blooms, while several grouse species shepherd their offspring above the treeline to forage.

3.2.2 Mesoamerica – Tropical Mexico and Central America

Confined to the upper elevations of volcanoes, isolated patches of tropical alpine habitat occur from southern Mexico to Panama. In Mexico, alpine habitats are largely restricted to the Faja Volcánica Transmexicana (Trans-Mexican Volcanic Belt), which stretches east-west around 19°N latitude (Almeida-Leñero 2007). Characterized by freezing nocturnal temperatures year-round and daily ground temperature fluctuations of up to 70°C, these alpine habitats support hardy tussock grasses, ferns and woody shrubs from 3,900 to 4,700 m (Almeida-Leñero 2007; Steinmann *et al.* 2021). The Central American Volcanic Arc, which runs from Guatemala to Panama, supports alpine habitats atop isolated peaks, particularly in Costa Rica and western Panama where the northern limit

Table 3.1 *Summary statistics for the 12 global alpine regions addressed, including select subregions with distinct alpine environments. Treeline indicates the range in treeline elevations within each region. Alpine area was estimated using a combination of published literature and shapefiles produced by Körner et al. (2011) and Testolin et al. (2020). Global represents the proportion of alpine habitat relative to the global alpine area. Counts for Families, Genera and Species were derived from de Zwaan et al. (2022a, b). See Section 3.2 for more details.*

Region Subregion	Treeline (m asl)	Area (km²)	Global (%)	Families (n)	Genera (n)	Species (n)
North America	500–3,000	318,576	8.9	30	75	113
Mesoamerica	3,300–4,000	367	0.01	15	30	34
Tropical Andes	2,500–4,900	385,862	10.8	42	173	351
Temperate Andes	600–2,000	147,684	4.1	35	79	117
Europe	400–2,700	156,967	4.4	31	78	138
Africa	1,700–4,000	34,672	1.0	50	113	217
North Africa	2,800–3,150	7,039	–	17	31	42
Afroalpine	3,300–4,000	3,500	–	33	64	91
Madagascar	2,000–2,400	500	–	20	26	28
South Africa	1,700–2,300	23,633	–	40	45	101
North Asia	400–2,700	532,308	15.0	50	128	244
Qinghai-Tibetan Plateau	3,300–4,900	1,749,822	49.1	58	160	313
Hindu Kush-Himalayan Arc	3,300–4,600	189,949	5.3	46	111	214
East Asia	2,000–3,300	54	0.002	17	20	27
Taiwan	3,300–3,600	31	–	12	13	14
Japan	2,000–2,600	23	–	12	14	19
Australasia	400–4,050	42,544	1.2	40	77	102
Australia	1,830–2,000	7,938	–	3	4	4
Tasmania	1,000–1,300	1,354	–	15	25	27
New Zealand	400–1,500	29,482	–	15	19	21
New Guinea	3,400–4,050	3,770	–	27	46	57
Islands	2,200–3,400	1,400	0.04	13	15	18
Total	400–4,900	3,560,205	100.0	120	525	1,310†

† Species, genera, and family totals do not reflect column sums because a given species may occur across multiple regions.

of páramo occurs above 3,300 m. This 'Isthmian páramo' is characterized by dense scrub, ferns and the presence of bamboo (*Chusquea* spp.), which covers over 60 per cent of the above-treeline habitat, transitioning into moss and lichen above 3,600 m (Vargas & Sánchez 2005).

Much like the montane forests below it, Central American páramo supports distinct, endemic bird communities. For example, the aptly named volcano junco *Junco vulcani* and volcano hummingbird *Selasphorus flammula* are restricted to above-treeline habitats across only a handful of volcanoes. The sooty thrush *Turdus nigrescens* breeds from the treeline to the scrub along volcanic ridges, while the rufous-collared sparrow *Zonotrichia capensis*, with an impressive range extending from the Chiapas Highlands in southern Mexico to Patagonia, also regularly breeds in these habitats. Overall, 12 species are strongly associated with Central American páramo, while an additional 34 species are frequently observed using above-treeline habitat (Kappelle & Horn 2016). These species play important ecological roles, as between 8 and 20 per cent of páramo plant species in this region are dependent on birds for pollination and seed dispersal, respectively (Barrantes 2005). While information on seasonal use of alpine habitats in Mexico is limited, 15 species breed above-treeline, including a few with North American origins, but at lower elevations (e.g., American bushtit *Psaltriparus minimus*). Of these, four hummingbird species, including the blue-throated mountain gem *Lampornis clemenciae* and broad-tailed hummingbird *Selasphorus platycercus*, forage up to 4,400 m on endemic alpine plants (Arredondo-Amezcua *et al.* 2018).

3.2.3 South America – Tropical and Sub-tropical Andes

The Andes is the longest mountain range in the world (8,900 km), 60 per cent of which is considered tropical or sub-tropical (9°N–30°S). On wetter slopes in the north and the Andean–Amazonian slopes of Peru and Bolivia, the treeline is well-defined, occurring between 2,500 and 3,000 m (Körner 2012). Here, above-treeline habitat is primarily páramo, humid ecosystems with limited seasonality, characterized by tussock grasses (*Festuca* spp., *Calamagrostis* spp.) and dense shrubs, including rosette plants (*Espeletia* spp.). The treeline is less obvious on drier, western slopes of the central Andes where continuous forest is scarce (Valencia *et al.* 2018). Here, the landscape is a savannah mosaic of several high Andean ecosystems, including puna grassland with fragmented patches of stunted *Polylepis* reaching up to 4,900 m (Kessler 2006). These highly seasonal alpine habitats are also characterized by patches of *Stipa ichu*, *Puya raimondii* ('Queen of the Andes'), and cushion plants depending on the aridity (Sevillano-Ríos *et al.* 2018). High elevation wetlands (bofedales) and saline lakes are also common landscape features.

The tropical Andes represent the most diverse alpine ecosystem in the world and is also an endemic hotspot, with 351 species from 42 families observed breeding above the treeline (Table 3.1). Species like the Mérida flowerpiercer *Diglossa gloriosa* or the critically endangered royal cinclodes *Cinclodes aricomae* are restricted to specific mountaintops, while high elevation lakes and wetlands support endemic species, such as the flightless Junin grebe *Podiceps taczanowskii* and Titicaca grebe *Rollandia microptera*, both endangered and restricted to lakes at c. 4,000 m. Many species are highly dependent on specific characteristics of high Andean ecosystems. For example, 150 Andean hummingbird species (50 per cent of all hummingbirds) have developed behavioural, physiological and anatomical adaptations to high elevations (McGuire *et al.* 2014; Chapter 9, Box 9.2). In the *Polylepis*-puna grasslands, tit-like dacnis *Xenodacnis parina* is one of 44 bird species of conservation concern that are dependent on above-treeline *Polylepis* patches (Sevillano-Ríos *et al.* 2018). Several species also regularly exceed 5,000 m to use glacial habitats. Certain hummingbirds, like the olivaceous thornbill *Chalcostigma olivaceum*, have been observed feeding on insects trapped within the ice (Sevillano-Ríos *et al.* 2020). At least five bird species have been recorded roosting in glacial caves, including the rufous-bellied seedsnipe *Attagis gayi* (Hardy *et al.* 2018). The glacier finch *Idiopsar speculifer* and white-fronted ground tyrant *Muscisaxicola albifrons* are the only known species capable of nesting in glacial walls and caves above 5,000 m, possibly as an extreme form of predator avoidance (Hardy *et al.* 2018; Chapter 1, Box 1.1).

3.2.4 South America – Mediterranean to Temperate Andes and the Sierras de Córdoba

Representing a shift in habitat and climate from the tropical Andes, the southern Andes extend c. 2,700 km to the tip of South America, consisting of both Mediterranean (30–35°S) and temperate mountain ecosystems (35–56°S; Nagy & Grabherr 2009). The treeline, primarily composed of stunted Rosaceae trees and shrubs, occurs at c. 2,000 m in the Mediterranean region, dropping to c. 1,300 m at temperate latitudes (39°S) and as low as 600 m in the extreme south, along with a shift to *Nothofagus* spp. and *Araucaria araucana* vegetation (Cavieres *et al.* 2000; Altamirano *et al.* 2020; Table 3.1). Alpine habitats in the Mediterranean Andes are characterized by sclerophyllous vegetation specialized for arid, seasonal climates, while the temperate Andes support vegetation adapted to heavy winter snow, such as tussock grasses and *Nothofagus* shrubs.

Extensive volcanic rock formations and scree are common throughout (Altamirano *et al.* 2020). Slightly east of the Andes, the isolated Sierras de Córdoba (31.5°S) support an alpine zone from c. 2,000 to 2,880 m. While proximity to the coast results in strong oceanic influences on the alpine climate of the temperate Andes, the Sierras de Córdoba are warmer and considerably drier, with tree growth limited at high elevations due to severe winter drought, nightly frost and high wind speeds. Alpine habitat consists of tussock grasses (*Poa* spp.), granite outcrops and patches of *Polylepis* scrub (*P. australis*), representing the southernmost distribution of any *Polylepis* species (Marcora *et al.* 2008).

Although alpine breeding bird communities in the Mediterranean and temperate Andes are less diverse than the tropical Andes, they are functionally and taxonomically distinct (Altamirano *et al.* 2020). The 117 species represent 35 families, of which c. 30 per cent belong to the hyper-diverse Furnariidae and Tyrannidae (Table 3.1; Section 3.3). Endemism is high, with c. 26 per cent of the 117 species restricted to either the Mediterranean or temperate mountains. The Sierras de Córdoba in particular support multiple endemic species, including two species of cinclodes restricted to the cooler, high elevation habitats, potentially representing glacial relict populations persisting since the last glaciation. Few studies of the high Andean avifauna exist in this region, limiting our understanding of seasonal alpine habitat use among species for breeding, foraging and migration. A fascinating example is the Wilson's storm petrel *Oceanites oceanicus*, which is often observed traveling between the ocean and Mediterranean Andes during the breeding season, but to date no alpine breeding colonies have been discovered (Medrano *et al.* 2018).

3.2.5 Europe – Western Europe to the Caucasus and Ural Mountains

European mountains reach elevations of >5,000 m in the Caucasus and >4,000 m in the Alps. Large patches of lower elevation alpine habitat also occur in the Pyrenees, Anatolian Highlands and Fennoscandia (Testolin *et al.* 2020), while numerous other ranges harbour distinct alpine zones (e.g., Dinaric Alps, Carpathians, Taurus Mountains). Variation in treeline elevation throughout Europe is dictated by latitude, continentality and size of the mountain massif, but also by a history of pastoralism, leading to an overall lower treeline that is now recovering in some regions due to pastoral abandonment (Nagy 2006). Above-treeline vegetation is composed of krummholz (*Pinus* spp. or *Picea* spp. in the south, *Betula* spp. in the north) and dwarf shrubs (e.g., *Juniperus* spp., *Rhododendron* spp., *Pinus mugo, Vaccinium* spp.), interspersed with graminoids or moss/lichen heaths of varying extent (Nagy 2006), again depending on the occurrence and intensity of livestock grazing.

The distributions of 138 species from 31 families currently breeding in European alpine habitats show clear glacial legacy effects (Table 3.1), shaped in part by extinction-colonization dynamics following repeated glaciation events. Populations of some species largely restricted to the north have persisted in central European mountain ranges as glacial relicts. Only a few of these 'boreo-alpine' species, such as rock ptarmigan *Lagopus muta* occur exclusively above the treeline. Many species exhibit longitudinal distributions across Eurasia, such that most alpine specialists from central and southern Europe do not occur farther north (e.g., alpine accentor *Prunella collaris*, white-winged snowfinch *Montifringilla nivalis*). As such, alpine specialization increases towards southeastern Europe, peaking in the Endemic Bird Area of the Caucasus (Keller *et al.* 2020). Endemism within mountain ranges is also low, and in fact, the Caucasian snowcock *Tetraogallus caucasicus* is the only alpine specialist in the region restricted to a mountain range. This does not include endemic subspecies, which are regularly restricted to specific ranges, such as Güldenstädt's redstart *Phoenicurus erythrogastrus erythrogastrus* in the Greater Caucasus. Since major mountain ranges tend to run west–east in Europe, alpine ecosystems also serve as foraging habitat (seasonally available invertebrates and berries) for a significant proportion of birds that must cross over mountains during migration. For example, between 1997 and 2017, 191 species were captured at ringing stations from 0 to >1,400 m in northern Italy, of which 58 species were captured crossing alpine habitats above 1,400 m (Franzoi *et al.* 2021).

3.2.6 Africa – Atlas Mountains, Afroalpine, South Africa and Madagascar

Within Africa, alpine ecosystems are represented by: (i) the High Atlas Mountains of North Africa, (ii) the Afroalpine of Ethiopia and East Africa, (iii) the Drakensberg Range in eastern South Africa, (iv) Altimontane Fynbos in western South Africa, and (v) the highest peaks of Madagascar (Table 3.1).

High Atlas alpine habitats extend from c. 2,800 m up to the highest peak (4,165 m) found on Mount Toubkal. Vegetation is limited primarily by frost dynamics and aridity, producing a matrix of steppe

(*Festuca* spp.), scattered *Juniperus* scrub and extensive rock formations (Messerli & Winiger 1992). In contrast, the Afroalpine is characterized by heathland, tussock grasses, everlasting flowers (*Helichrysum* spp.) and giant lobelia *Lobelia rhynchopetalum*, as well as lakes and wetlands which occur above an ericaceous treeline as low as 3,300 m (e.g., *Erica arborea*; Jacob *et al.* 2015). Isolated patches of ericaceous trees can also be found over 4,000 m, promoting greater avian habitat diversity (van der Hoek *et al.* 2021). The only nival habitats in Africa occur on the highest mountains of East Africa, such as the Rwenzori Mountains, Uganda, where the nival zone extends from 4,400 to >5,000 m (Rutten *et al.* 2015).

With peak elevations of 3,482 m within the mountain kingdom of Lesotho, the Drakensberg Range supports *Themeda-Festuca* grasslands (1,900–2,800 m), transitioning into Maloti Highlands or alpine heathlands above 2,800 m (Carbutt 2019). Here, the flora is characterized by tall graminoids, tussock grasses and ericoid dwarf shrubs, providing habitat for grassland-dependent birds which would not otherwise occur above the treeline. In the Western Cape of South Africa, a narrow belt of Altimontane Fynbos exists from c. 1,700–2,200 m on select ranges (i.e., the Swartberg Mountains). Characterized by restioid, ericaceous and asteraceous flowering shrubs within a sandstone rock matrix (Rebelo *et al.* 2006), the Mediterranean climate supports an alpine bird community representing the upper elevational limit of the Cape Floristic Region. Similarly isolated, above-treeline habitats in Madagascar occur on three massifs, extending from c. 2,000 to 2,876 m. Lower elevations consist of grassland savannah and ericoid shrubs transitioning into a landscape of rocks and geophytes above c. 2,400 m, with small ponds supporting aquatic breeding birds across elevations (Goodman & Rasolonandrasana 2001).

The isolated, high elevation habitats of Africa represent ecological islands with distinct avian community turnover among regions. At least 217 species, including 167 continental endemics, breed above the treeline, representing 9.4 per cent of the 2,310 breeding species and 11.9 per cent of the 1,400 species endemic to Africa (BirdLife International 2021). In Madagascar, 20 (71.4 per cent) of the above-treeline breeding species are endemic to the island, while species like the Ankober serin *Crithagra ankoberensis* and handsome spurfowl *Pternistis nobilis* are restricted to a few mountaintops in Ethiopia and the Rwenzori Mountains, respectively (Asefa *et al.* 2013; McGowan & Kirwin 2020). As in the Neotropics, nectarivores are common alpine birds, such as the scarlet-tufted sunbird *Nectarinia johnstoni* which depends on alpine lobelia flowers in East Africa (Evans 1996) and the orange-breasted sunbird

Anthobaphes violacea which relies on ericaceous fynbos in South Africa (Cheke & Mann 2020). Africa's alpine habitats are also critical stopover and wintering habitats for a significant proportion of sub-Saharan migrants from Eurasia (Billerman *et al.* 2020), adding to their importance within the global avifauna.

3.2.7 North Asia – Tian Shan, Altai and Siberian Ranges

Extensive alpine habitats occur north of the Tibetan Plateau, from the alpine steppe of the Tian Shan and Altai Mountains to the high-latitude tundra of Siberia. Alpine habitats within the Tian Shan extend from a treeline at 2,400–2,700 m to a snowline between c. 3,300–4,200 m, while the Altai range has an alpine zone residing between a treeline at 1,000–2,600 m (west-east) to the snowline at 2,600–3,800 m (Klinge *et al.* 2003). These alpine ecosystems represent transitional habitat for steppe bird communities. In the Tian Shan, vegetation consists of patches of spruce (*Picea* spp.) within extensive *Kobresia* spp. sedge meadows, while vegetation on the southern aspect is comparable to the Tibetan Plateau (Section 3.2.8). In the Altai, alpine habitats consist of *Poa* and *Festuca* grasses interspersed with *Rhododendron* patches or conifer shrubs in the drier southeast and birch (*Betula* spp.) in the wetter northwest. Siberian alpine habitat can be found from the Sayan Mountains in the south (53°N), to the Putorana Plateau in the northwest (69°N) and the Koryak Range near the Bering Strait (Romanov 2013). The treeline occurs at c. 700 m in the Putorana Plateau and is as low as 400 m in the northeast (Romanov *et al.* 2021). Above a larch treeline, this habitat is dominated by mosses and lichens, Arctic heather, wet sedge meadows and shrub patches of dwarf Siberian pine *Pinus sibirica* or alder *Alnus hirsuta*.

North Asia supports 244 alpine breeding bird species from 50 families (Table 3.1). Like North America and Europe, several high-latitude tundra specialists are included in the avifauna (n = 14), breeding from low elevation coastal plains to drier, high elevation tundra. Multiple, large alpine lakes scattered across the landscape, such as on the Putorana Plateau or Chatyr-Kohl in the Tian Shan, mean this region also supports a great diversity of waterfowl, including 18 species of Anatidae alone. The alpine avifauna include species common throughout Eurasia, but also many that are uniquely adapted to high elevation tundra or steppe habitat. Grey-tailed tattler *Tringa brevipes* nest along alpine streams in Siberia, while the Asian rosy finch *Leucosticte arctoa* is restricted to the rocky habitat of the nival zone. The endangered steppe eagle *Aquila nipalensis* reaches alpine habitat in the Altai Range, which is also home to the endemic Altai snowcock *Tetraogallus altaicus*. Notably, the endangered great knot *Calidris tenuirostris* breeds exclusively in alpine lichen meadows of northeastern Siberia (Tomkovich 1997).

3.2.8 Qinghai-Tibetan Plateau – Including the Pamir, Qinling and Hengduan Ranges

An extensive formation of high-elevation habitat, the Qinghai–Tibetan Plateau has been referred to as 'Earth's Third Pole'. Despite extreme elevations, this region hosts abundant flora and fauna in a varied landscape of snow-capped mountains, glaciers, lakes, wetlands and alpine meadows, representing 49.1 per cent of the total area above the treeline globally (Table 3.1). Multiple mountain ranges also extend beyond the Tibetan Plateau, from the Hengduan Mountains in the southeast, the Qinling Mountains in the east, and the Kunlun Mountains along the northern edge of the plateau. In the south, the highest mountains (>7,000 m) coincide with the highest treeline (c. 4,600 m), while the Kunlun and Qinling ranges support a treeline at c. 2,500–3,000 m. Across the plateau, alpine grasslands exist between 3,300 and 4,700 m, interspersed with salt lakes that provide critical habitat for waterbirds to breed or stopover during migration. To the west, the Pamir Range in Tajikistan resides at the junction between the Tibetan Plateau, the Himalayas and the Tian Shan Range, containing extensive alpine and nival zones that extend from a treeline at c. 3,300 m to over 7,000 m. Lower elevations consist of alpine meadows, heather and *Juniperus* scrub, shifting to cushion plants, lichen and extensive rock scree above 4,700 m.

The Qinghai-Tibetan Plateau and surrounding mountain ranges support 313 alpine breeding species, with 55 considered alpine breeding specialists (Table 3.1). Of note is the diversity of redstarts (*Phoenicurus*; 10 spp.) and rosefinches (*Carpodacus*; 17 spp.). The rosefinches are largely specialized on alpine scrub or boulder scree, including the rarely observed and endemic Sillem's mountain finch *C. sillemi* which occurs primarily above 5,000 m (Päckert *et al.* 2015). Abundant resources of alpine habitats during the late breeding season and fall are frequently exploited by species that are not considered alpine breeders. Whooper swan *Cygnus cygnus* breeding in the high Arctic use alpine habitats and salt lakes as important stopover sites during southward migration, along with thousands of other waterbirds (c. 40 species; Zheng 1983). Forest-dependent species, including the Darjeeling woodpecker *Dendrocopos darjellensis* and rufous-bellied woodpecker *D. hyperythrus* nest at or below the treeline, but forage in alpine habitats. Within mainland China, >300 species use alpine habitats at some point in their annual cycle, representing >30 per cent of the nearly 1,000 breeding bird species (Zheng 2011).

3.2.9 Hindu Kush-Himalayan Arc – Himalaya, Trans-Himalaya and the Hindu Kush Range

Containing many of the highest mountains globally, the Hindu Kush range and the Himalayas combine to form a monumental arc along the northern boundary of the Indian subcontinent. Extending over 3,500 km, this mountain chain blocks monsoonal rain clouds, producing a distinct gradient in alpine habitats from the lush, wet southern slopes to the drier northern slopes and cold, arid Trans-Himalaya, which more closely resembles the Tibetan Plateau. Variation in precipitation regimes has also produced a west–east treeline gradient from c. 3,300 m in the more arid Hindu Kush and western Himalayas to c. 3,800 m in the wet central and eastern range. Five distinct alpine vegetation zones are present within the Himalayas, including 'moist meadows' and 'scrub and krummholz' habitats in the core Himalaya, compared to 'desert steppe', 'dry scrub' and 'marsh meadows' in the arid Trans-Himalaya and Changthang Plateau (Rawat 2017). In the west, colder winters and greater aridity produce alpine meadows of graminoids and cushion plants, interspersed with birch (*Betula* spp.), cedar (*Cedrus* spp.) and *Juniperus* scrub, while warmer winters and greater monsoonal humidity in the east support more extensive shrub patches of *Rhododendron* and fir (*Abies* spp.; Schickhoff *et al.* 2015).

The Hindu Kush-Himalayan Arc supports high avian diversity, with 214 species breeding above the treeline, representing 46 families (Table 3.1). Of these, 75.2 per cent are Passeriformes, followed by 5.6 per cent Galliformes (e.g., snowcocks *Tetraogallus* spp., monal pheasants *Lophophorus* spp.). Notably, 33.2 per cent are considered alpine habitat specialists (Section 3.3). Most alpine breeding species share a distribution with the Tibetan Plateau, resulting in relatively few endemics, though certain species like the Himalayan monal *Lophophorus impejanus* are emblematic of the region, occurring along the entire mountain range. Many species within the Hindu Kush–Himalayan Arc also exhibit remarkable adaptations to the extreme environment, including nesting at higher elevations than anywhere else in the world (e.g., grandala *Grandala coelicolor*; 6,600 m; see Table 2.2). Mountain-finches (*Leucosticte* spp.) and snowfinches (*Montifringilla, Pyrgilauda,* and *Onychostruthus* spp.) nest within burrows dug by pika (*Ochotona* spp.) and voles (Section 3.4.4), while the black-necked crane *Grus nigricollis,* weighing 5–7 kg, is one of the largest alpine breeding birds in the world, inhabiting the marsh meadows of the Trans-Himalaya (Billerman *et al.* 2020). Due to the sharp contrast between the cold, temperate-like alpine and the subtropical habitats at lower elevations, most alpine breeders are resident, altitudinal or short-distance migrants (81.3 per cent; Section 3.3), with the remainder traveling to peninsular India or beyond.

3.2.10 East Asia – Taiwan and Japan

Taiwan and Japan are mountainous islands with elevations reaching 3,952 m (Mount Yushan) and 3,776 m (Mount Fuji), respectively. In subtropical Taiwan, alpine tundra represents a narrow zone above c. 3,300 m, less than 1 per cent of the total area of Taiwan. Annual above-treeline precipitation varies, but concentrates during the monsoon season, reaching c. 3,500 mm/year. Vegetation in lower alpine habitats is dominated by shrubs, particularly dwarf bamboo *Yushania niitakayamensis, Rhododendron* and *Juniperus* spp., while upper alpine habitats consist of sparse herbaceous plants and bare ground. In temperate Japan, the treeline varies from about 2,000 m on the western slope to 2,600 m in the east (Pacific Ocean side) in central Honshu (Gansert 2004). Like Taiwan, strong oceanic influences produce high annual precipitation, varying from 2,500 to 3,500 mm. However, in contrast to Taiwan, snow cover is more extensive, in some cases over 3.8 m deep and lasting c. 3–4 months in central Honshu (Gansert 2004). Alpine vegetation includes alpine meadows, dwarf shrubs (e.g., *Pinus pumila*), broadleaf bamboos *Sasa* spp., *Vaccinium* spp. and bog-like snowbed grasses (Yoshino 1978).

Likely due to limited alpine habitat, only a few bird species breed exclusively in alpine habitats; two species in Japan, rock ptarmigan and alpine accentor (Iijima & Morimoto 2021), and alpine accentor in Taiwan (Severinghaus *et al.* 2012). In Taiwan, 14 species breed above the treeline (Severinghaus *et al.* 2012), of which 11 are resident or exhibit altitudinal migration during winter and only three, including the Pacific swift *Apus pacificus,* are considered long-distance latitudinal migrants (Tsai *et al.* 2021). In Japan, 19 species are known to breed above the treeline, although only nine do so regularly (Iijima & Morimoto 2021). Latitudinal migration is also more common in Japan, with nine species considered long-distance, tropical migrants (Billerman *et al.* 2020). Endemism is rather high in Taiwan, with six species or 42.9 per cent of the alpine breeding birds restricted to the subtropical island, compared to only two (10.5 per cent) in Japan.

3.2.11 Australasia – Australia, Tasmania, New Zealand and New Guinea

Only 3 per cent of mainland Australia is considered as being above-treeline, restricted to the Australian Alps in the southeast (c. 36°S; Table 3.1). The Snowy Mountains support the largest contiguous alpine habitat, extending from c. 1,830–2,228 m, where snow cover lasts for 4–6 months per year and vegetation is primarily grasslands and herb-fields, with limited to no shrub cover (Green 2010). In contrast, the Central Highlands of Tasmania (c. 41.9°S) support alpine habitat extending from c. 1,000 to 1,600 m. Snow cover lasts c. 3 months due to oceanic influences, facilitating woody shrubs and stunted tree patches (e.g., pencil pine *Athrotaxis cupressoides*, *Eucalyptus* spp.), mixed with button-grass moorland, mosses and wet sedgeland (Jackson 1999).

Alpine habitats of New Zealand encompass c. 11 per cent of the total land area (O'Donnell *et al.* 2017), and are characterized by low woody shrubs, snow tussocks (*Chionochloa* spp.) and 'megaherbs' (e.g., *Bulbinella rossii*). The treeline is c. 1,500 m in the North Island around the central Volcanic Plateau (c. 39.3°S), but decreases steadily to c. 800 m in the South Island's Southern Alps (c. 44°S), and c. 400 m on Stewart Island (Rakiura; 47°S), producing an alpine zone spanning up to 1,000 m in elevation (Mark *et al.* 2000).

Extending from more contiguous areas in the western Maoke Range to smaller, isolated patches in the east, tropical alpine habitats of New Guinea occur from c. 3,600 m to the nival zone starting at 4,650 m, although subalpine forest fires during drought years have extended alpine grassland and shrub down to c. 3,200 m (Hope 2014). Annual precipitation at the summit varies from 2,500–4,000 mm, producing one of the most humid alpine habitats in the world, but with significantly different vegetation communities than other humid tropical alpine habitats, such as the páramo (Hope 2014). Alpine vegetation is predominately tussock grassland with isolated alpine mires, scattered tree ferns and stunted patches of cedar *Papuacedrus papuana*.

Variation in alpine habitats among the four sub-regions has resulted in diverse alpine bird communities with impressive endemism. In New

Zealand, 21 species breed above the treeline (Table 3.1), of which 16 (76.2 per cent) are endemic to the island. Of these, two are alpine specialists: Hutton's shearwater *Puffinus huttoni*, which form large breeding colonies in alpine habitats, spending the rest of the year at sea (Cuthbert & Davis 2002); and the New Zealand rockwren *Xenicus gilviventris*, the only year-round alpine resident. In Australia and Tasmania, no species are considered alpine specialists, although 28 breed above-treeline and many more use alpine habitats to forage year-round, such as the gang-gang cockatoo *Callocephalon fimbriatum*. In Tasmania, an alpine mosaic of heathland and shrub fosters an alpine breeding community distinct from mainland Australia, with 24 of the 28 species (85.7 per cent) breeding in Tasmanian alpine habitat only. Finally, alpine specialization and endemism in New Guinea is extremely high, especially in the Maoke Range. Of 57 alpine breeding species, 80.7 per cent are endemic to the island and five (8.8 per cent) are alpine breeding specialists (Section 3.3).

3.2.12 Island Mountains – Hawaii, Borneo, Indonesia and the Canary Islands

Globally, several islands have volcanic peaks at elevations high enough to support alpine ecosystems, yet do not easily fit within any of the major regions described above: Hawaii, Borneo, Indonesia and the Canary Islands. Alpine habitats on these islands are small in area, but they are ecologically distinct from the tropical or sub-tropical ecosystems at lower elevations.

Hawaii contains the most extensive alpine habitat (1,349 km^2), primarily on Mauna Loa and Mauna Kea, where the treeline is c. 3,000 m (Körner 1998). Above-treeline habitat is characterized by shrubland (*Dubautia*, *Chenopodium* and *Santalum* spp.) transitioning into tussock grasslands and finally arid, desert-like environments at the highest peaks, where cold-tolerant species like the Hawai'i silversword *Argyroxiphium sandwicense* grow among rocks (Sohmer & Gustafson 1987). In Indonesia, several islands support alpine habitat, including Java and Sumatra. On Mount Kerinci, Sumatra, alpine habitat extends from a treeline at c. 3,200 m to the peak at 3,800 m, while in nearby Borneo, Mount Kinabalu peaks at 4,095 m and has a treeline at c. 3,400 m (Ohsawa *et al.* 1985). These habitats support stunted *Rhododendron-Vaccinium* scrub interspersed with ferns, tussock grasses and herbs, as well as endemic pitcher plants and orchids, with rock dominating the highest elevations (Smith 1980; Ohsawa *et al.* 1985). Finally, the lowest alpine habitat of these islands occurs on the Canary Islands, existing between c. 2,200–2,426 m on La Palma and a significantly larger area from c. 2,400–3,715 m on Tenerife (Irl 2014; Bello-Rodríguez *et al.* 2019). The cold, arid above-treeline habitat is characterized by low-lying shrubs and bushy legumes (e.g., *Adenocarpus viscosus*), as well as flowering plants such as viper's bugloss *Echium wildpretii*, patchily distributed within bare ground and rock.

Combined, these island alpine habitats support 18 species from 13 families (Table 3.1). Several of these species are endemic to their respective islands and in some cases, restricted to high elevations on specific mountains. For example, the only remaining alpine breeding population of omao *Myadestes obscurus*, a Hawaiian thrush, is found on Mauna Loa, while the mountain blackeye *Zosterops emiliae* occurs primarily in Borneo, reaching its highest elevations on Mount Kinabalu. Most species are high elevation residents or altitudinal migrants (Section 3.3). Only the endangered Hawaiian petrel *Pterodroma sandwichensis*, which nests in above-treeline burrows, travels well beyond their island breeding sites during the non-breeding season. Like many alpine systems, limited data and conservation challenges are common. The volcano swiftlet *Aerodramus vulcanorum* likely breeds on volcanic ridges in Java, but no nests have been found. The only remaining natural populations of the nene *Branta sandvicensis* occur in high elevation Hawaiian grasslands, although low elevation populations are being reintroduced.

3.3 A Global Comparison of Alpine Breeding Bird Communities

Alpine habitats support distinct breeding bird assemblages that reflect a compositional shift from communities breeding below the treeline (Altamirano *et al.* 2020). Among regions, alpine breeding bird communities may be broadly comparable due to convergent evolution operating under similar environmental constraints (i.e., resource limitations, seasonal environments; Dorst & Vuilleumier 1986). However, differences in climate, vegetation structure and resource availability likely produce variation in species richness, community structure and ecological traits that a given alpine habitat can support (Quintero & Jetz 2018; Martin *et al.* 2021). Attempts have been made to compare alpine breeding bird communities across select regions, such as among Andean páramo and Afroalpine habitats (Dorst & Vuilleumier 1986) and across Holarctic ecosystems (Scridel *et al.* 2018). However, these studies are limited in scale and alpine breeding bird communities have yet to be compared at a global level.

Here, we highlight general differences in the structure and key ecological traits of alpine breeding bird communities among each major mountain region described in Section 3.2 using the global alpine breeding bird dataset (de Zwaan *et al.* 2022a, b), as well as underlining the substantial scope for research on alpine birds. Specifically, we summarize: (i) alpine habitat specialization and breeding status, (ii) migration strategy, and (iii) nest type and site. These traits were chosen to reflect alpine habitat use at different temporal and spatial scales; specifically breeding propensity (specialization and status), non-breeding use (migration strategy) and fine-scale habitat use within alpine breeding sites (nest traits).

3.3.1 Global Alpine Breeding Bird Community Overview

de Zwaan *et al.* (2022a, b) identified 1,310 species that breed above the treeline, representing 12 per cent of the 10,933 species currently recognized by the International Ornithological Congress (Gill *et al.* 2022). These species range from highly specialized or range-restricted birds, such as the giant conebill *Conirostrum binghami*, which is dependent on high elevation *Polylepis* scrub in the central Andes (Cahill *et al.* 2021), to species like the horned lark *Eremophila alpestris*, which breeds in alpine habitat on five continents, from high-latitude alpine tundra in North America and Europe, to over 4,000 m in Tibet, and isolated populations in Colombia and Morocco (Figure 3.2).

Alpine breeding species consist primarily of habitat generalists, occurring across broad elevational ranges, yet 13.3 per cent of species breed exclusively in alpine habitats and 2.1 per cent in high-latitude alpine tundra (Figure 3.3). More than 75 per cent of all alpine species breed above the treeline regularly or semi-regularly, while the remaining 24.4 per cent are considered rare alpine breeders, with either limited available data or specific habitat requirements that are currently scarce above the treeline. Over 81.4 per cent are residents or short-distance altitudinal migrants, indicating a prevalence for cold-adapted or high elevation-dependent species. Generally, nesting strategies are highly variable within the global alpine breeding bird community, with 62.6 per cent of alpine birds building open cup nests and 36.6 per cent building fully enclosed nests (cavity, domed). While open cup nests predominate, entirely exposed nests appear to be relatively rare above the treeline, with many placed within vegetation cover as evidenced by the large proportion of shrub or tree nests (39.1 per cent), likely to moderate the nest environment.

Figure 3.2 Examples of alpine bird species. A. Giant conebill *Conirostrum binghami*, dependent on *Polylepis* patches in the tropical Andes; B. white-winged snowfinch *Montifringilla nivalis*, an alpine specialist of southern Europe and Asia; C. Himalayan monal *Lophophorus impejanus* an emblematic alpine specialist of the Himalayas; D. ground tit *Pseudopodoces humilis*, endemic to the Tibetan Plateau; E. the endangered New Zealand rockwren *Xenicus gilviventris*, the only true alpine specialist in New Zealand; F. horned lark *Eremophila alpestris*, a widespread species found in alpine habitats on five continents. Photos: A. Steven Sevillano-Ríos, B. Arnaud G. Barras, C. Yuvraj Patil, D. Shaobin Li, E. Kerry Weston and F. David Bell.

3.3.2 Family and Species Diversity

Globally, 525 of 2,384 extant genera (22.0 per cent), 120 of 253 families (47.4 per cent), and 29 of 44 orders (65.9 per cent) are represented in alpine habitats. Almost half (43.3 per cent) of alpine breeding species originate

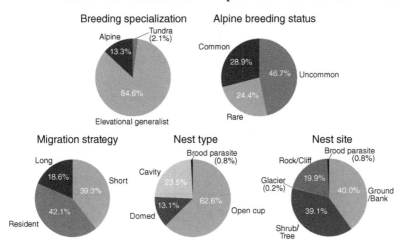

Figure 3.3 Global overview of breeding specialization and general ecological traits for alpine breeding bird species. The percentages are calculated from the total 1,310 alpine breeding bird species. Breeding specialization and alpine breeding status indicate the propensity for breeding in alpine habitats. Alpine specialists are primarily above-treeline breeders, elevational generalists both above- and below-treeline, and tundra specialists only in high-latitude alpine and polar tundra. For alpine breeding status, species classified as 'Common' nest in alpine habitats across their geographic range, 'Uncommon' species breed in alpine habitats regularly, but are more likely to breed below the treeline, while 'Rare' species are only known to breed above the treeline incidentally. Under migration strategy, 'Resident' species remain in alpine habitats year-round, 'Short-distance' migrants exhibit seasonal altitudinal movements, short latitudinal migrations, or nomadic movements, while 'Long-distance' migrants travel extensive distances (>1,000 km). *Nest type* describes the predominant nest structure, including 'open cup', 'cavity', and 'domed' nests (i.e., globular, spherical, and semi-domed). *Nest site* includes seven general locations: 'ground', 'bank', 'shrub', 'tree', 'rock', 'cliff', and 'glacier'. 'Brood parasite' is also included for parasitic species where nest type and placement depend on the host species.

from 10 families, including the hyper-diverse Fringillidae, Furnariidae, Tyrannidae and Muscicapidae, but also non-passerine families such as Anatidae and Phasianidae (Figure 3.4). In fact, 8 of the top 20 families using alpine habitats are non-passerines, representing 23.2 per cent of the overall species total (Figure 3.4). Therefore, alpine habitats support both ancient lineages (e.g., Rallidae, c. 59–75 Mya; García-R *et al.* 2014), as well as those that have undergone more recent and rapid adaptive radiations, such as Furnariidae (c. 6 Mya; Seeholzer *et al.* 2017). Notably, of the top three families, Fringillidae occur across all continents outside of Australasia and Antarctica, while Muscicapidae are confined to the

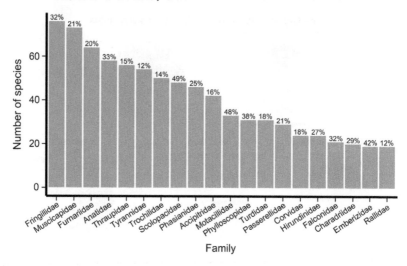

Figure 3.4 The twenty most frequent alpine breeding families. Bar height corresponds to the absolute number of alpine breeding species (y-axis), while the percentages above each bar indicate the proportion of total species within each family that breed in alpine habitats.

eastern hemisphere and Furnariidae to just Central and South America, highlighting greater diversity in alpine habitats relative to their global distribution (Figure 3.4). While most of the top families have c. 30 per cent or less of their total species represented in alpine habitats, Scolopacidae (sandpipers), Motacillidae (wagtails and pipits) and Emberizidae (buntings) have 49 per cent, 48 per cent and 42 per cent, respectively, indicating a particular specialization for these habitats (Figure 3.4).

Interestingly, the alpine avifauna of tropical mountains is comparable to north temperate mountains in terms of overall species, and although south temperate ranges support significantly fewer species (Table 3.2), the number of families represented in tropical and temperate regions are remarkably consistent (Figure 3.5A). Comparing between hemispheres, alpine habitats in the east not only support a greater number of species, but also nearly twice as many families as the west (Figure 3.5B). However, the greatest differences in species arise when comparing among biogeographic realms, where most alpine species originate from the Palearctic and Neotropics, although the number of families is again relatively consistent (Figure 3.5C). This not only represents differences in the available alpine area and thus diversity of habitat niches, but also differences in diversity within families. For example, within the

Table 3.2 *Summary of selected traits for major global regions. The total number of alpine breeding species is included in the 'n' column and then all other values are the percentage (%) of regional alpine breeding species per category. Habitat refers to breeding habitat specialization, including alpine specialists (A), elevational generalists (G) and tundra specialists (T). Status refers to alpine breeding status: common (C), uncommon (U) and rare (R). Migration strategy is split into resident (R), short- (S), and long-distance (L). Nest type includes O = open cup, C = cavity and D = domed nests, and nest site refers to G = ground/bank, V = vegetation (shrub, tree, sedge) and R = rock or cliff.*

Region	n	Habitat A/G/T	Status C/U/R	Migration R/S/L	Nest type[1] O/C/D	Nest site[1] G/V/R
Latitudinal band						
N. temperate	600	16/80/4	29/46/25	14/51/35	66/22/11	46/33/20
Tropical	575	15/85/0	34/44/22	73/26/1	61/24/14	33/46/20
S. temperate	265	11/89/0	29/44/26	43/50/7	57/29/14	42/27/30
Hemisphere						
Western	535	17/81/3	32/44/24	51/33/16	66/25/9	37/43/19
Eastern	808	13/85/3	29/44/26	36/44/20	62/22/15	43/36/20
Biogeographic realm						
Afrotropical	187	6/94/0	28/45/27	68/29/3	56/21/22	42/29/28
Australasian	102	8/92/0	27/37/35	71/28/1	67/19/13	34/50/14
Indo-Malayan	23	4/96/0	13/70/17	57/30/13	52/22/22	17/52/26
Nearctic	126	6/83/11	23/52/25	6/36/59	83/14/2	49/30/21
Neotropical	417	20/80/0	34/42/24	65/33/3	60/28/12	33/47/20
Palearctic	519	17/79/4	31/44/25	16/54/30	63/23/13	45/33/20

[1]Nest type and site percentages may not add up to 100% because of brood parasite or glacial nesting species which were not included in the depicted categories. See text for full details. All other categories may differ from 100% by a percentage point due to rounding errors.

Palearctic and Neotropics, the average species per family is 7.9 and 9.3 respectively, compared to less than 4.0 in the remaining realms.

The species–area relationship of most major regions follows an asymptotic curve, nearing a plateau of almost 2 million km^2 of alpine habitat area in Tibet (Figure 3.6). A few notable exceptions to this association are the greater than expected diversity in the tropical Andes, Africa and the Hindu Kush–Himalayan Arc (Figure 3.6). These alpine

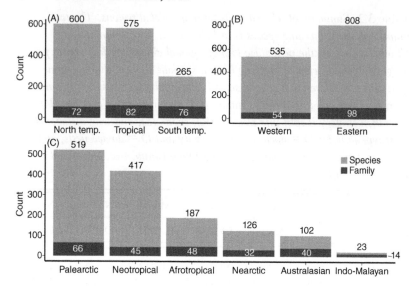

Figure 3.5 The number of species and families per major global region (Count), including: (A) latitudinal divisions, (B) longitudinal hemispheres, and (C) the six biogeographic realms or ecozones where alpine breeding species reside.

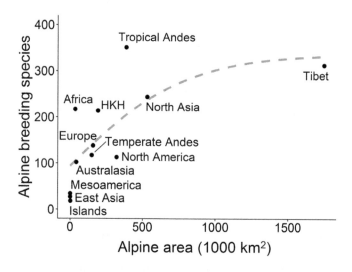

Figure 3.6 Species-area relationship for alpine breeding birds from each of the 12 major mountain regions. The dashed line is the non-linear trend fit to the 12 data points. HKH refers to the Hindu Kush-Himalayan Arc. Values for species counts and area of alpine habitat for each major mountain region are given in Table 3.1.

ecosystems may support a disproportionate number of alpine breeding species due to greater than average niche diversity. For example, *Polylepis*, *Rhododendron* and ericoid scrub in each of the Andes, Himalayas and Africa provide vegetation heterogeneity (e.g., shrubs, trees), while these regions are also characterized by rock crevices and burrowing mammals that provide nest sites for cavity nesting species (Section 3.4.2). In contrast, North America has lower than expected diversity for its available alpine habitat area (Figure 3.6). North America has one of the highest proportions of open cup, ground nesting species in its alpine breeding avifauna (Table 3.3), potentially indicating less vegetation and topographic complexity in alpine habitats to support species dependent on shrubs or rock crevices to nest.

3.3.3 Alpine Breeding Specialization

The overall proportion of alpine habitat specialists (13.3 per cent) is maintained across most biogeographic realms except for the Afrotropical, Australasian and Nearctic realms where specialization reaches lows of 5.9 per cent, 7.8 per cent and 6.3 per cent, respectively (Table 3.2). For Australasia, this low value is primarily driven by Australia and Tasmania, where no species are considered alpine specialists, while Madagascar and South Africa drive the value down for Africa (Table 3.3). Similarly, low specialization occurs in Taiwan, Japan and Mesoamerica (Table 3.3), likely a result of limited available alpine habitat and thus the likelihood of alpine specialization evolving and species persisting. In North America, Europe and North Asia, alpine habitat specialization is relatively low, but tundra specialists are prevalent, highlighting the contribution of Arctic–alpine transition zones to the overall alpine avifauna in these regions (Table 3.3). The Himalayas and Andes are centres of alpine habitat specialization, with 33.2 per cent and 20.5 per cent of species respectively residing predominantly above the treeline (Table 3.3). This high specialization may reflect the sharp contrast between tropical habitat at lower elevations and cold, temperate high elevation habitats, leading to distinct clade separation (White *et al.* 2019). In addition, certain genera from families like Furnariidae (e.g., *Upucerthia* spp.) and Tyrannidae (*Muscisaxicola* spp.) in the Andes, or Fringillidae (*Carpodacus* spp.) in the Himalayas, appear particularly well-adapted to high elevations and may have undergone rapid diversification in alpine habitats (Päckert *et al.* 2015; Harvey *et al.* 2020). Habitat complexity, as mentioned with respect to the species-area relationship above, may also play a role.

Table 3.3 Summary statistics for the 12 mountainous regions, divided into sub-regions for select areas. All variable definitions are the same as in Table 3.2.

Region	n	Habitat A/G/T	Status C/U/R	Migration R/S/L	Nest type[1] O/C/D	Nest site[1] G/V/R
North America	113	7/81/12	25/52/23	4/31/65	84/15/1	52/27/20
Mesoamerica	34	6/94/0	18/59/24	50/50/0	74/12/15	24/56/21
Tropical Andes	351	21/79/0	39/409/21	73/26/0	60/28/12	32/48/19
Temperate Andes	117	19/81/0	36/43/21	32/57/10	56/38/5	40/23/36
Europe	138	9/80/11	28/57/15	17/39/44	75/18/7	59/17/23
Africa	217	8/92/0	31/43/25	65/31/4	54/25/21	39/27/34
North Africa	42	21/79/0	52/31/17	43/45/12	48/43/10	19/10/71
Afroalpine	91	8/92/0	36/43/21	71/27/1	59/21/19	40/26/33
Madagascar	28	0/100/0	11/57/32	68/32/0	54/29/18	39/29/32
South Africa	101	5/95/0	23/50/28	54/41/5	55/20/24	44/27/29
North Asia	244	10/84/6	28/53/19	8/34/59	69/22/8	52/21/27
Tibet	313	17/83/0	35/44/21	19/62/19	56/30/13	41/33/25
Hindu Kush–Himalayan Arc	214	33/67/0	46/39/15	12/70/19	50/32/16	33/38/27
East Asia	27	7/93/0	26/63/11	22/44/33	41/22/26	30/30/30
Taiwan	14	7/93/0	7/86/7	29/50/21	43/29/21	14/43/36
Japan	19	11/89/0	37/47/16	11/42/47	26/26/32	37/11/37
Australasia	102	8/92/0	27/37/35	71/28/1	67/19/13	34/50/14
Australia/Tasmania	28	0/100/0	11/46/43	43/57/0	61/14/21	24/54/18
New Zealand	21	14/86/0	48/29/24	43/52/5	67/33/0	67/19/14
New Guinea	57	9/91/0	26/40/33	89/11/0	70/14/12	28/58/11
Islands	18	0/100/0	11/61/28	89/11/0	61/28/11	28/39/33

[1]Nest type and site percentages may not add up to 100% because of brood parasite or glacial nesting species which were not included in the depicted categories. See text for full details. All other categories may differ from 100% by a percentage point due to rounding errors.

3.3.4 Alpine Migration Strategies

Globally, alpine species are predominantly resident or short-distance migrants (Figure 3.3), meaning most species either remain in their breeding habitat year-round or move altitudinally to avoid suboptimal conditions (Chapter 2). In the tropics, 73.2 per cent of species are resident, as expected with more mild alpine environments and greater climatic stability where species can maintain a consistent climate envelope year-round (Table 3.2; Chapter 9). The higher proportion of long-distance migrants in north temperate mountains is driven by Arctic-alpine nesting species like shorebirds that migrate to the southern hemisphere (Table 3.2). This pattern is most pronounced in North America and North Asia, where 65.5 per cent and 58.6 per cent of alpine breeding species, respectively, migrate to either Central and South America or Southeast Asia, compared to Europe where alpine birds are less likely to be sub-Saharan migrants (Table 3.3). This may be associated with a greater proportion of alpine breeding shorebirds in North Asia and North America relative to Europe. Alternatively, latitudinal climate gradients differ between the Americas and across Eurasia due to oceanic influences, such that high-latitude species in the Americas and Asia would have to migrate farther south than European species to maintain a similar climate envelope (Williamson & Witt 2021). Ultimately, differences in the migratory behaviour of alpine birds among major regions are likely dictated by both current climate and evolutionary history (Chapter 2).

3.3.5 Alpine Nest Traits

While open cup, ground nests predominate overall in alpine habitats, variation in the relative proportions of nest traits among regions suggest potential drivers acting on species-level traits. The proportion of alpine cavity nesters reaches a regional high of 37.6 per cent in the Southern Andes, followed by the Himalayas, Tibet and the Tropical Andes (Table 3.3). Commonalities among these regions include relatively young mountain ranges and large areas of rock/cliffs. Extreme environmental conditions at the highest elevations in the Himalayas and Andes may drive species to seek cavities to moderate the nest environment (e.g., greater humidity and temperature; Chapter 2). Alpine habitats in each region also support patches of trees well above the treeline, including *Betula*, *Polylepis* and *Araucaria* spp. in the Himalayas, tropical Andes and southern Andes, respectively, providing niches for tree cavity nesting species. Finally, several cavity nesting birds appear dependent on rodent burrows, particularly in Tibet, the Andes and South Africa, a species interaction which may be linked to soil type or which may represent a form of co-evolution (Section 3.4.4).

Phylogenetic trait conservatism may also play a role in nesting strategies, such as greater proportions of domed nests in Africa (Table 3.3). For example, Cisticolidae place domed nests low in shrubs or on the ground in the absence of vegetation (Billerman *et al.* 2020). However, rock cavities do not appear to be limited as proportions of cavity nests and rock/cliff substrate are relatively high (Table 3.3), suggesting domed nests are a possible conserved trait originating from lower elevations.

Nest placement is also indicative of the type of alpine habitat and niche availability. Extensive volcanic activity in the Andes likely facilitates rock cavity formation and the high propensity for rock cavity nests in this region (Altamirano *et al.* 2022). Regions like North America or Europe with extensive alpine tundra habitats have limited shrub cover compared to more tropical mountain ranges or those with strong oceanic influences where alpine shrubs and trees are more prevalent (e.g., Tasmania; Table 3.3). These conditions allow many treeline-dependent species to expand into shrub patches above the treeline and are primarily driven by climate, such as average annual temperatures and precipitation, which determine the length of the growing season (Körner 2012).

3.4 Ecology of Alpine Habitats

Global variation in alpine habitat niches, species traits and life-history strategies have evolved and been maintained by multiple, interacting factors, such as climate, predation risk and interspecific competition. In this section, we highlight some of the main ecological and environmental conditions currently operating on alpine breeding bird communities. The adaptations allowing birds to breed in alpine habitats are addressed in Chapter 2.

3.4.1 Weather

As outlined previously (Section 3.1; Chapter 1), long-term climatic conditions are *the* most important factor delimiting alpine habitat, structuring alpine breeding bird communities and generally influencing most of the other factors discussed below. However, short-term weather conditions can also drive variation in avian community composition. Variation in temperature or precipitation, such as severe storms, drought and annual variation in the snowpack, lead to temporal fluctuations in alpine bird communities within and among years (Strinella *et al.* 2020). In the tropics, glacial melt dynamics and annual precipitation influence the water level and presence of lakes and wetlands in the Bolivian high Andes, with reduced wetland areas linked to sharp declines in breeding species richness (Cardenas *et al.* 2022). Over time, precipitation and temperature interact to shape alpine bird communities, defining early season conditions and breeding season length in the short-term (i.e., annual variation in snowmelt) or long-term (i.e., water storage as ice and snow; Section 3.5).

Severe winter weather and associated resource scarcity limit the species capable of being year-round residents of alpine habitats. This specialized set of species may use energy-saving strategies to remain above the treeline. Ground tits *Pseudopodoces humilis*, which are resident on the Tibetan Plateau, dig communal roosting burrows post-breeding that have smaller entrances than their nesting burrows, presumably to improve heat retention (Ke & Lu 2009). More commonly, however, resident species will make short, altitudinal movements to avoid extreme winter conditions, sometimes taking refuge within the treeline (Hsiung *et al.* 2018). The extent and occurrence of altitudinal migrations are highly variable among years and depend on winter severity, thus influencing the non-breeding alpine community from year-to-year, as well as the influx of birds to lower elevations. The alpine specialist white-winged snowfinch is a partial migrant, with the prevalence and extent of altitudinal migration increasing in years with severe winter conditions (Resano-Mayor *et al.* 2020). In subtropical Taiwan, species richness and density decline with colder temperatures as birds move to lower elevations, although certain hardy species may remain above the treeline year-round (Walther *et al.* 2017).

3.4.2 Vegetation Structure and Topography

The structural complexity of alpine habitats stems from multi-scale variation in vegetation composition and topography (e.g., aspect, slope). At a broad scale, the rugged, discontinuous nature of mountain ranges set dispersal limitations and produce steep climate gradients, which can facilitate pronounced community turnover even among adjacent mountains (Cadena *et al.* 2012). The arid, western slopes of the Central Andes, for example, support a distinct alpine breeding bird community compared to the more humid Andean-Amazon slopes (Sevillano-Ríos *et al.* 2018). The relatively simple vegetation structure and open habitat above the treeline limit birds to nest predominantly at or near ground level. Above-ground nesting opportunities vary substantially among mountains depending on the prevalence of alpine scrub and isolated krummholz or tree patches, which is facilitated by topography and suitable microclimates (Giaccone *et al.* 2019). For cavity nesting species, the presence, rock type and erosion of cliffs or scree dictate nest site availability, while soil depth and the presence of burrowing mammals provide the opportunity to nest in tunnels (Section 3.4.4). These factors determine habitat niche availability, contributing to variation in the diversity of alpine breeding birds and their nest traits globally.

Ecological factors such as temperature, predation risk and resource availability can vary dramatically within alpine habitats due to vegetation and topographic complexity, such that microhabitat selection is a key process influencing fine-scale species distributions (Visinoni *et al.* 2015; Jähnig *et al.* 2020). On the Tibetan Plateau, songbird species richness and the abundance of species like rufous-necked snowfinch *Pyrgilauda ruficollis* were associated positively with patches of sward (short grass) following the removal of cattle grazing pressure, highlighting the combined influences of fine-scale habitat characteristics and anthropogenic stressors (Arthur *et al.* 2008). The more open nature of alpine habitats is associated with greater exposure to severe weather conditions and predators which can strongly influence breeding success (Martin *et al.* 2017; de Zwaan *et al.* 2019; Chapter 2). Horned lark nests placed in patches of bare-ground or short grass benefit from warmer microclimates that are conducive to offspring development, but also suffer greater predation than nests placed in less exposed heather patches (de Zwaan & Martin 2018). Thus, microclimate variation stemming from vegetation structure or topography can allow birds to minimize certain environmental stressors (Rauter *et al.* 2002).

3.4.3 Resource Availability

Many alpine ecosystems are characterized by marked temporal and spatial fluctuations in resources. These conditions are most pronounced in temperate or high-latitude regions, but also characterize tropical alpine habitats. For example, in the Ecuadorian páramo, nectar production from *Puya* plants varies daily and among flowers, such that hummingbirds inhabiting páramo exhibit more flexible foraging behaviour than at lower elevations (Woods & Ramsay 2001). Snow is a crucial driver of alpine food availability, particularly in temperate regions. Warm, early season updrafts from lower elevations deposit insects on snowfields as 'windfall', a critical food source for adults and early offspring of some species (Antor 1994; Hotaling *et al.* 2020). For insectivores and herbivores, snowmelt provides an extended 'wave' of food rather than a peak, as vegetation and hibernating arthropods are exposed progressively (García-González *et al.* 2016). Later in the season, alpine habitats harbour a diversity of abundant insects, wildflowers and berries which benefit the offspring of alpine breeding birds, as well as species moving upslope to exploit this delayed resource surge (Boyle & Martin 2015). Dusky grouse *Dendragapus obscurus* in western North America bring their broods up to forage in alpine habitats (Zwickel & Bendell 2020), as do yellow-browed warblers *Phylloscopus inornatus* in Siberia (Clement 2020). Migrating birds may also benefit from late season resources, as some species exhibit greater fattening rates at high versus low elevation stopover sites within the same mountains (Evans Ogden *et al.* 2013). In the Andean Altiplano, lakes >4,000 m support shorebird species that have migrated from northern breeding grounds, including lesser yellowlegs *Tringa flavipes* and Baird's sandpiper. Late season alpine bird communities are therefore characterized by pronounced peaks in species diversity through an influx of non-breeding species from lower elevations or higher latitudes in search of resources (Boyle & Martin 2015).

3.4.4 Species Interactions

The strength of species interactions may be reduced in alpine compared to low elevation habitats within the same region (Boyle *et al.* 2016). However, these biotic factors can still play an important role in shaping alpine breeding bird communities.

Competition

Interspecific competition over limited resources can drive fine-scale variation in alpine community structure. In the temperate alpine zone of northwestern Canada, all three ptarmigan species are stratified across elevation when inhabiting the same mountain, with white-tailed ptarmigan restricted to the highest elevations, willow ptarmigan *Lagopus lagopus* near the treeline, and rock ptarmigan in the middle (Wilson & Martin 2008). In the absence of rock ptarmigan, white-tailed ptarmigan occupy a broader elevational niche, suggesting competitive release (Scridel *et al.* 2021). Limited co-occurrence of water pipits *Anthus spinoletta* and tree pipits *A. trivialis* in alpine habitats of the Cantabrian Mountains, Spain, have been attributed to potential interspecific competition (Bastianelli *et al.* 2017). In the south temperate Andes, blue-and-white swallow *Pygochelidon cyanoleuca* and white-browed ground tyrant *Muscisaxicola albilora* nest in rock cavities with similar dimensions, and territorial disputes are observed frequently (Altamirano *et al.* 2022).

Competitive interactions may occur at greater rates in tropical mountains, especially if multiple species occupy similar niches. Higher phylogenetic clustering in tropical alpine habitats relative to over-dispersion at high latitudes indicates greater co-existence and possibly competition among tropical species (Jarzyna *et al.* 2021). However, the more stable climate and diverse resources of tropical mountains are also likely to support avian communities with highly specialized niches that have evolved over a longer time-period, reducing niche overlap and thus competition (Price *et al.* 2014; Schumm *et al.* 2020). Territoriality decreases in intensity at higher elevations for water pipits in Spain (Bastianelli *et al.* 2015). However, in *Polylepis* fragments of the tropical Andes, giant conebills switch their foraging niche from branches to preferred trunk substrates when in a mixed flock, potentially as a form of fine-scale resource defence (Cahill *et al.* 2021). Scarlet-tufted sunbirds in the Afroalpine of Mount Kenya are highly dependent on *Lobelia tekkii* inflorescences, which can contain up to 2,000 individual flowers each. Year-round, individuals defend c. 4 times more flowers than they can feed on in a day, with breeding males defending twice as many flowers as non-breeding males (Evans 1996). While these examples suggest stronger territoriality in tropical alpine habitats, our understanding of inter- and intra-specific competition is limited, and it is likely that there are many unreported competitive interactions.

Facilitation

In some cases, alpine birds may depend on interspecific relationships to breed above the treeline. In the Andes, two genera of Furnariidae dig tunnels c. 0.5–3 m long into earthen banks with a nest chamber at the end: *Geositta* spp. (miners) and *Upucerthia* spp. (earthcreepers). However, the slender-billed miner *Geositta tenuirostris* is likely to use existing tunnels built by earthcreepers (Remsen 2020). The few documented nests of white-fronted ground tyrants, occurring above 5,000 m in glacial cavities, appear to be re-used glacier finch nests (Hardy *et al.* 2018). The colonial Andean flicker *Colaptes rupicola* of the Central Andes and the near-threatened ground woodpecker *Geocolaptes olivaceus* of South Africa are the only terrestrial alpine woodpeckers, digging burrows that provide nesting opportunities for a diverse alpine community of secondary cavity nesters (Dorst & Vuilleumier 1986). In the Andes and Tibet, several bird species also nest in burrows dug by rodents. These associations can be remarkably specific. In Tibet, the rufous-necked snowfinch primarily nests in Brandt's vole *Microtus brandti* burrows, while the white-rumped snowfinch *Onychostruthus taczanowskii* predominantly uses burrows of the black-lipped pika *Ochotona curzoniae* (Summers-Smith *et al.* 2020). In Africa, the blue swallow *Hirundo atrocaerulea* can nest up to 5 m along aardvark *Orycteropus afer* tunnels (Turner 2020). These forms of facilitation networks are conceptually comparable to nestwebs where excavating woodpeckers provide nest sites for a wide range of secondary cavity nesters in forest ecosystems (Martin & Eadie 1999), highlighting the intriguing potential for inter-dependent nest webs in alpine ecosystems.

Predation Risk

It has been hypothesized that bird species may brave the harsh conditions of high mountain habitats to benefit from a less diverse and abundant predator community (Skutch 1985; Boyle 2008). Alternatively, the more exposed, simple structure of alpine habitats may elevate predation risk as predators can locate prey more easily (Badyaev 1997). Meta-analyses and reviews have found an overall trend of lower predation rates for higher elevation populations in both temperate and tropical regions (Jankowski *et al.* 2013; Boyle *et al.* 2016). However, few of these studies include alpine habitats, and thus, patterns of reduced predation risk may not hold across the full elevational range given limited data. For example, Ims *et al.* (2019) found higher predation risk in the high-latitude alpine tundra of Scandinavia compared to lower elevations. In many cases, predators can have locally strong impacts on the reproduction and survival of alpine bird populations (Bowler *et al.* 2020). Proximity to the lower limit of the alpine zone (i.e., near the treeline) may increase predation risk through an edge effect resulting from the larger reservoir of potential nest predators in forested habitat (Masoero *et al.* 2016). For water pipits in the Swiss Alps, cavity nests in open areas were less likely to be lost to snake predation than nests surrounded by shrubs (Rauter *et al.* 2002). Alpine birds may therefore stratify within alpine communities from the treeline to the nival zone depending on their vulnerability to treeline predators, highlighting the potential for predation risk to drive fine-scale variation in community structure as well.

3.5 Snow Dynamics and the Changing Alpine Environment

Snow and snowmelt phenology play a vital role in maintaining alpine habitats and their avifauna. Snow dynamics can determine the vegetation structure of alpine habitats, set constraints on breeding season length and productivity, and function as an integral component of resource availability, thermal regimes and predation risk (Scridel *et al.* 2018). While more obvious in temperate regions, snow and ice have important implications for many tropical alpine habitats, particularly as sources of water to maintain hyper-diverse alpine wetlands, such as in the Altiplano or Afroalpine (Chignell *et al.* 2019; Cardenas *et al.* 2022; Chapter 9). Here, we discuss how current snow dynamics shape alpine breeding bird communities and highlight the concerning implications of increasingly unreliable snow phenology under a rapidly changing climate.

3.5.1 The Importance of Snow and Ice

Perennial snow covers c. 10 per cent of the globe's surface and is fundamental in regulating global climate patterns, from a strong albedo effect that reflects heat back into the atmosphere to melt water that regulates river flow and temperature (Rosvold 2016). The location of snow and phenology of snowmelt annually are critical to maintaining alpine and nival habitats as well as biological productivity. Yet, the processes by which snow dynamics may influence alpine bird communities vary by season, regional climate and species traits.

Snow dynamics determine and maintain the amount of available habitat for alpine breeding birds. Winter snowfall (snow depth), combined with the timing and rate of snowmelt, sets limits on vegetation growth, and helps dictate treeline location over the long-term. Snow-related disturbances, such as avalanches, may modify the treeline at local scales and influence vegetation structure over the short-term. This is particularly important for open-country, ground-nesting species which avoid taller vegetation. Small scale variation in topography, such as slope, aspect and depressions produce variation in snowmelt, allowing patches of snow to last until late in the breeding season (snowbeds). These micro-dynamics are critical to promoting variation in above-treeline habitat structure, such as low-profile, woody shrubs within snowbeds and drier ridges (fell-fields) that become exposed earlier in the season, characterized by frost- and drought-resistant graminoids (Körner 1999). Alpine birds segregate among these micro-habitats, resulting in more diverse alpine breeding bird communities. For example, in northern British Columbia, horned larks nest early in the season along fellfield ridges, while Savannah sparrows *Passerculus sandwichensis* nest later in the season in snowbed depressions once they become snow-free (de Zwaan *et al.* 2020).

Snow dynamics also structure alpine bird communities temporally. Early season conditions are characterized by frequent snowstorms which can set alpine habitats back into a winter-like state (Martin *et al.* 2017). Species differing in their resilience to early-season conditions partition their breeding phenology, resulting in temporal turnover of the breeding community (de Zwaan *et al.* 2020). Snow cover moderates resource availability over the season, providing an early source of food for invertivores (i.e., insect windfall, invertebrates dependent on wet soils) and regulating a resource surge that increases with vegetation growth late into the breeding season (Section 3.4.3). Long-lasting snow patches or glaciers offer snow baths at high temperatures, melt water to counter drought, and high-quality larvae for foraging along the snowline (Rosvold 2016; Scridel *et al.* 2018). Finally, snow cover can be extensive in alpine habitats during winter, limiting resources for all but the hardiest species that resort to digging for vegetation or burrowing for warmth (e.g., *Lagopus* spp.). The amount of winter snow also dictates snowpack depth in the following spring, with implications for breeding phenology, food resources and water budget (de Zwaan *et al.* 2022c).

In tropical alpine habitats, snow and glaciers also influence vegetation structure and food availability, in some cases playing a highly specialized role in the ecology of certain species. In the Ethiopian Afroalpine, the ephemeral wetlands above 3,800 m are important breeding sites for many alpine species, nearly doubling in size between the wet and dry season in response to snowmelt and associated precipitation (Chignell *et al.* 2019). In the Andes, several bird species move upslope to forage on insects trapped in glaciers, including multiple hummingbirds (Sevillano-Ríos *et al.* 2020). Of the c. 50 glacier finch nests recorded to date, all were in glacial cavities, suggesting the potential for this species to be dependent on glaciers and the permanency of ice (Hardy *et al.* 2018). Generally, a close association with snow and ice makes many alpine birds highly vulnerable to changing snow conditions (Rosvold 2016).

3.5.2 Snow Dynamics in a Changing World

Snow is intricately linked to the distribution and productivity of many alpine birds and thus rapidly changing snow regimes threaten to drastically alter alpine bird communities. Between 2000 and 2018, 78 per cent of global mountains experienced severe reductions in snow, involving a 13 per cent loss of total snow cover and up to 43 more snow-free days per year (Notarnicola 2020). In the south temperate Andes, the snow line receded by 10–30 m annually over the same period (Saavedra *et al.* 2018) and in more tropical regions, like East Africa (e.g., Mount Kilimanjaro), glacial recession has increased by c. 2.5 per cent per year over the last several decades, resulting in a >85 per cent total reduction in mass (Thompson *et al.* 2009). In fact, under current projections, glaciers with an area <10 km^2 are expected to disappear by 2050, including all remaining glaciers in Africa (UNESCO, IUCN 2022).

Essentially, this means global reductions in snow (and water) reservoirs and longer breeding or growing seasons. This may have a positive short-term influence by increasing breeding opportunities (Saracco *et al.* 2019; Chapter 6). However, receding snow conditions due to climate change are also characterized by more stochastic, unpredictable snow dynamics. Early or rapid snowmelt can lead to a mismatch between snowmelt and breeding phenology, with potentially negative consequences for reproductive success (Barras *et al.* 2021; Schano *et al.* 2021). Earlier breeding attempts following rapid snowmelt may be an ecological trap, as more severe and frequent snowstorms put early initiated nests at higher risk of failure (Martin *et al.* 2017; de Zwaan *et al.* 2020). While alpine breeding species may be flexible in their breeding phenology to match annual variability in snowmelt, it is unclear how increasingly unpredictable early-season conditions will impact long-term survival and reproduction (Schano *et al.* 2021; de Zwaan *et al.* 2022c).

In the long-term, reduced snow depth and more snow-free days prolong the growing season for alpine vegetation, promoting shrub and tree encroachment into alpine habitats (Jackson *et al.* 2016). This advancing treeline may elevate predation risk as alpine breeding birds are forced to nest in greater proximity to treeline-associated predators (Masoero *et al.* 2016), while shrinking alpine habitat will eventually lead to mountain-top extirpation for many open–country specialists (Freeman *et al.* 2018). These direct and indirect effects of alpine habitat loss are particularly concerning for isolated, range-restricted communities such as those in New Guinea (Section 3.3). Alpine breeding species have persisted through multiple glaciation events, including in the páramo habitats of South America, Africa and New Guinea where available alpine habitat has expanded and contracted drastically to its current extent (Buytaert *et al.* 2011; Hope 2014). However, many alpine breeding species are now experiencing climatic conditions beyond what they have experienced in their evolutionary history (Gulev *et al.* 2021). Understanding how species depend on snow dynamics and how this relationship is changing is pivotal to predicting the impacts of climate change on alpine bird communities (Chapter 6).

3.6 Conclusions

In this chapter, we have highlighted the diversity of alpine habitats and breeding bird communities globally, challenging the concept of an ecologically depauperate habitat. According to our classification, at least 1,310 species representing 120 families breed in alpine habitats, approximately 12.0 per cent and 47.4 per cent of extant species and families, respectively. Since only c. 2.6 per cent of the global landmass is considered as being above-treeline (Testolin *et al.* 2020), alpine habitats support a remarkable avian diversity given their available area. Ecological factors that shape and maintain current alpine breeding bird communities generally are linked directly or indirectly to climate, particularly snow dynamics, but biotic interactions such as predation risk and competition are also influential. Despite the general summaries presented in this chapter, many alpine species lack accurate data on distributions and even basic life-history traits (de Zwaan *et al.* 2022a, b). This is concerning given a rapidly changing climate and increasingly unpredictable snow dynamics, as many alpine breeding bird communities may be at significant risk. Climate change is already impacting the distribution and demographic parameters of alpine breeding birds, while alpine habitats are also at risk from anthropogenic effects, including habitat loss or degradation from tourism resorts, mining, renewable energy development and wildfires (Chapters 6 and 7). Alpine habitats may represent refugia for the substantial proportion of species that rarely or incidentally breed above the treeline. These species may benefit from increasing nesting opportunities at higher elevations, either due to climate change-driven shrub encroachment or pastoral abandonment. We therefore stress the importance of addressing knowledge gaps for the unique set of global avian biodiversity represented in alpine habitats to better assess conservation needs and track changes in alpine habitats or breeding communities over time (Chapter 10).

Acknowledgements

We are grateful to the long list of field researchers and local experts with extensive knowledge of alpine birds and their habitats who contributed information regarding alpine breeding birds. In particular, we are indebted to Thane Pratt, Bruce Beehler, Krista Oswald, Libertad Arredondo-Amezcua and Ken Green for detailed discussions on alpine ecosystems in their regions of expertise. We would also like to thank Michał Ciach, Jon Fjeldså, Ben Freeman and Trevor Price for constructive feedback that greatly improved the text and reasoning.

References

Almeida-Leñero, L., Escamilla, M., Giménez de Azcárate, J., González-Trápaga, A. & Cleef, A.M. (2007) Vegetación alpina de los volcanes Popocatépetl, Iztaccíhuatl y Nevado de Toluca. In *Biodiversidad de la Faja Volcánica Transmexicana.* Luna, I., Morrone, J.J. & Espinosa, D. (eds.). Mexico City: Universidad Nacional Autónoma de México, pp. 179–198.

Altamirano, T.A., de Zwaan, D.R., Ibarra, J.T., Wilson, S. & Martin, K. (2020) Treeline ecotones shape the distribution of avian species richness and functional diversity in south temperate mountains. *Scientific Reports,* **10,** 1–13.

Altamirano, T.A., de Zwaan, D.R., Scridel, D., Wilson, S. & Martin, K. (2022) Rock cavity nesting as the norm: alpine breeding birds in the south temperate Andes Mountains. *Ecology,* **104,** e3931.

Antor, R.J. (1994) Arthropod fallout on high alpine snow patches of the Central Pyrenees, northeastern Spain. *Arctic, Antarctic, and Alpine Research,* **26,** 72–76.

Arredondo-Amezcua, L., Martén-Rodríguez, S., Lopezaraiza-Mikel, M., *et al.* (2018) Hummingbirds in high alpine habitats of the tropical Mexican mountains: new elevational records and ecological considerations. *Avian Conservation and Ecology,* **13,** 14.

Arthur, A.D., Pech, R.P., Davey, C., Yanming, Z. & Hui, L. (2008) Livestock grazing, plateau pikas and the conservation of avian biodiversity on the Tibetan plateau. *Biological Conservation,* **141,** 1972–1981.

Asefa, A., Richman, E., Admassu, B. & Baggallay, T. (2013) *Bale Mountains National Park Birding Booklet.* Addis Ababa: Ethiopian Wildlife Conservation Authority.

Bader, M.Y., Rietkerk, M. & Bregt, A.K. (2007) Vegetation structure and temperature regimes of tropical alpine treelines. *Arctic, Antarctic, and Alpine Research,* **39,** 353–364.

Bader, M.Y., Llambí, L.D., Case, B.S., *et al.* (2021) A global framework for linking alpine-treeline ecotone patterns to underlying processes. *Ecography,* **44,** 265–292.

Badyaev, A.V. (1997) Avian life history variation along altitudinal gradients: an example with cardueline finches. *Oecologia,* **111,** 365–374.

Barrantes, G. (2005) Aves de los páramos de Costa Rica. In *Páramos de Costa Rica.* Kappelle, M. & Horn, S.P. (eds.). San José, Costa Rica: Instituto Nacional de Biodiversidad, pp. 521–532.

Barras, A.G., Niffenegger, C.A., Candolfi, I., Hunziker, Y.A. & Arlettaz, R. (2021) Nestling diet and parental food provisioning in a declining mountain passerine reveal high sensitivity to climate change. *Journal of Avian Biology,* **52,** e02649.

Bastianelli, G., Seoane, J., Álvarez-Blanco, P. & Laiolo, P. (2015) The intensity of male-male interactions declines in highland songbird populations. *Behavioral Ecology and Sociobiology,* **69,** 1493–1500.

Bastianelli, G., Wintle, B.A., Martin, E.H., Seoane, J. & Laiolo, P. (2017) Species partitioning in a temperate mountain chain: segregation by habitat vs. interspecific competition. *Ecology and Evolution*, **7**, 2685–2696.

Bello-Rodríguez, V., Cubas, J., Del Arco, M.J., Martín, J.L. & González-Mancebo, J.M. (2019) Elevational and structural shifts in the treeline of an oceanic island (Tenerife, Canary Islands) in the context of global warming. *International Journal of Applied Earth Observation & Geoinformation*, **82**, 101918.

Billerman, S.M., Keeney, B.K., Rodewald, P.G. & Schulenberg, T.S. (2020) *Birds of the World*. Ithaca: Cornell Laboratory of Ornithology.

BirdLife International (2021) www.birdlife.org/africa/partnership/about-birdlife-africa

Bowler, D.E., Kvasnes, M.A., Pedersen, H.C., Sandercock, B.K. & Nilsen, E.B. (2020) Impacts of predator-mediated interactions along a climatic gradient on the population dynamics of an alpine bird. *Proceedings of the Royal Society B*, **287**, 20202653.

Boyle, W.A. (2008) Can variation in risk of nest predation explain altitudinal migration in tropical birds? *Oecologia*, **155**, 397–403.

Boyle, W.A. & Martin, K. (2015) The conservation value of high elevation habitats to North American migrant birds. *Biological Conservation*, **192**, 461–476.

Boyle, W.A., Sandercock, B.K. & Martin, K. (2016) Patterns and drivers of intraspecific variation in avian life history along elevational gradients: a meta-analysis. *Biological Reviews*, **92**, 469–482.

Buytaert, W., Cuesta-Camacho, F. & Tobón, C. (2011) Potential impacts of climate change on the environmental services of humid tropical alpine regions. *Global Ecology and Biogeography*, **20**, 19–33.

Cadena, C.D., Kozak, K.H., Gomez, J.P., *et al.* (2012) Latitude, elevational climatic zonation and speciation in New World vertebrates. *Proceedings of the Royal Society B*, **279**, 194–201.

Cahill, J.R., Merckx, T., Van Dyck, H., Fernández, M. & Matthysen, E. (2021) Lower density of arthropod biomass in small high-Andes *Polylepis* fragments affects habitat use in insectivorous birds. *Ecosphere*, **12**, e03401.

Carbutt, C. (2019) The Drakensberg Mountain Centre: a necessary revision of southern Africa's high-elevation centre of plant endemism. *South African Journal of Botany*, **124**, 508–529.

Cardenas, T., Naoki, K., Landivar, C.M., *et al.* (2022) Glacier influence on bird assemblages in habitat islands of the high Bolivian Andes. *Diversity and Distributions*, **28**, 242–256.

Cavieres, L.A., Peñaloza, A. & Arroyo, M.K. (2000) Altitudinal vegetation belts in the high-Andes of central Chile (33°S). *Revista Chilena de Historia Natural*, **73**, 331–344.

Cheke, R. & Mann, C. (2020) Orange-breasted Sunbird (*Anthobaphes violacea*). In *Birds of the World*. Version 1.0. Billerman, S.M. (ed.). Ithaca: Cornell Lab of Ornithology.

Chignell, S.M., Laituri, M.J., Young, N.E. & Evangelista, P.H. (2019) Afroalpine wetlands of the Bale Mountains, Ethiopia: distribution, dynamics and conceptual flow model. *Annals of the American Association of Geographers*, **109**, 791–811.

Clement, P. (2020) Yellow-browed Warbler (*Phylloscopus inornatus*). In *Birds of the World*. Version 1.0. del Hoyo, J., Elliott, A., Sargatal, J., Christie, A. & de Juana, E. (eds.). Ithaca: Cornell Lab of Ornithology.

Cuthbert, R. & Davis, L.S. (2002) The breeding biology of Hutton's Shearwater. *Emu*, **102**, 323–329.

de Zwaan, D.R. & Martin, K. (2018) Substrate and structure of ground nests have fitness consequences for an alpine songbird. *Ibis*, **160**, 790–804.

de Zwaan, D.R., Camfield, A.F., MacDonald, E.C. & Martin, K. (2019) Variation in offspring development is driven more by weather and maternal condition than predation risk. *Functional Ecology*, **33**, 447–456.

de Zwaan, D.R., Drake, A., Greenwood, J.L. & Martin, K. (2020) Timing and intensity of weather events shape nestling development strategies in three alpine breeding songbirds. *Frontiers in Ecology and Evolution*, **8**, 359.

de Zwaan, D.R., Scridel, D., Altamirano, T.A., *et al.* (2022a) GABB: a global dataset of alpine breeding birds and their ecological traits. *Scientific Data*, **9**, 627. https://doi.org/10.1038/s41597-022-01723-6

de Zwaan, D.R., Scridel, D., Altamirano, T.A., *et al.* (2022b) GABB: global alpine breeding bird database. *Figshare*. https://doi.org/10.6084/m9.figshare.20556750

de Zwaan, D.R., Drake, A., Camfield, A.F., MacDonald, E.C. & Martin, K. (2022c) The relative influence of cross-seasonal and local weather effects on the breeding success of a migratory songbird. *Journal of Animal Ecology*, **91**, 1458–1470.

Dorst, J. & Vuilleumier, F. (1986) Convergences in bird communities at high altitudes in the tropics (especially the Andes and Africa) and at temperate latitudes (Tibet). In *High Altitude Tropical Biogeography*. Vuilleumier, F. & Monasterio, M. (eds.). New York: Oxford University Press, pp. 120–149.

Evans, M.R. (1996) Nectar and flower production of *Lobelia telekii* inflorescences and their influence on territorial behaviour of the scarlet-tufted malachite sunbird (*Nectarinia johnstoni*). *Biological Journal of the Linnean Society*, **57**, 89–105.

Evans Ogden, L.J., Martin, K. & Williams, T.D. (2013) Elevational differences in estimated fattening rates suggest that high-elevation sites are high-quality habitats for fall migrants. *Auk*, **130**, 98–106.

Franzoi, A., Tenan, S., Sanchez, P.L. & Pedrini, P. (2021) Temporal trends in abundance and phenology of migratory birds across the Italian Alps during a 20-year period. *Rivista Italiana di Ornitologia*, **91**, 13–28.

Freeman, B.G., Scholer, M.N., Ruiz-Gutierrez, V. & Fitzpatrick, J.W. (2018) Climate change causes upslope shifts and mountaintop extirpations in a tropical bird community. *Proceedings of the National Academy of Sciences*, **115**, 11982–11987.

Gansert, D. (2004) Treelines of the Japanese Alps–altitudinal distribution and species composition under contrasting winter climates. *Flora*, **199**, 143–156.

García-González, R., Aldezabal, A., Laskurain, N.A., Margalida, A. & Novoa, C. (2016) Influence of snowmelt timing on the diet quality of Pyrenean rock ptarmigan (*Lagopus muta pyrenaica*): implications for reproductive success. *PLoS ONE*, **11**, e0148632.

García-R, J.C., Gibb, G.C. & Trewick, S.A. (2014) Deep global evolutionary radiation in birds: diversification and trait evolution in the cosmopolitan bird family Rallidae. *Molecular Phylogenetics and Evolution*, **81**, 96–108.

Giaccone, E., Luoto, M., Vittoz, P., *et al.* (2019) Influence of microclimate and geomorphological factors on alpine vegetation in the Western Swiss Alps. *Earth Surface Processes and Landforms*, **44**, 3093–3107.

Gill, F., Donsker, D. & Rasmussen, P. (2022) *IOC World Bird List.* Version 12.1. doi: 10.14344/IOC.ML.12.1.

Goodman, S.M. & Rasolonandrasana, B.P. (2001) Elevational zonation of birds, insectivores, rodents and primates on the slopes of the Andringitra Massif, Madagascar. *Journal of Natural History*, **35**, 285–305.

Green, K. (2010) Alpine taxa exhibit differing responses to climate warming in the Snowy Mountains of Australia. *Journal of Mountain Science*, **7**, 167–175.

Gulev, S.K., Thorne, P.W., Ahn, J., *et al.* (2021) Changing state of the climate system. In *Climate Change 2021: The Physical Science Basis. Contribution of Working Group I to the Sixth Assessment Report of the Intergovernmental Panel on Climate Change.* Masson Delmotte, V., Zhai, P., Pirani, A., *et al.* (eds.). Cambridge: Cambridge University Press, pp. 287–422.

Hardy, S.P., Hardy, D.R. & Gil, K.C. (2018) Avian nesting and roosting on glaciers at high elevation, Cordillera Vilcanota, Peru. *Wilson Journal of Ornithology*, **130**, 940–957.

Harvey, M.G., Bravo, G.A., Claramunt, S., *et al.* (2020) The evolution of a tropical biodiversity hotspot. *Science*, **370**, 1343–1348.

Hope, G. (2014) The sensitivity of the high mountain ecosystems of New Guinea to climatic change and anthropogenic impact. *Arctic, Antarctic, and Alpine Research*, **46**, 777–786.

Hotaling, S., Wimberger, P.H., Kelley, J.L. & Watts, H.E. (2020) Macroinvertebrates on glaciers: a key resource for terrestrial food webs? *Ecology*, **101**, e02947.

Hsiung, A.C., Boyle, W.A., Cooper, R.J. & Chandler, R.B. (2018) Altitudinal migration: ecological drivers, knowledge gaps and conservation implications. *Biological Reviews*, **93**, 2049–2070.

Iijima, D. & Morimoto, G. (2021) Bird community heterogeneity along four gradients of different orientations on a temperate mountain. *Ornithological Science*, **20**, 65–82.

Ims, R.A., Henden, J.A., Strømeng, M.A., *et al.* (2019) Arctic greening and bird nest predation risk across tundra ecotones. *Nature Climate Change*, **9**, 607–610.

Irl, S.D.H. (2014) Patterns and Disturbance-induced Drivers of Plant Diversity and Endemism on High Elevation Islands. PhD thesis, University of Bayreuth, Bayreuth, Germany.

Jackson, W.D. (1999) The Tasmanian environment. In *Vegetation of Tasmania.* Reid, J.B., Hill, R.S., Brown, M.J. & Hovendon, M.J. (eds.). Canberra: Environment Australia, pp. 11–38.

Jackson, M.M., Topp, E., Gergel, S.E., *et al.* (2016) Expansion of subalpine woody vegetation over 40 years on Vancouver Island, British Columbia, Canada. *Canadian Journal of Forest Research*, **46**, 437–443.

Jacob, M., Annys, S., Frankl, A., *et al.* (2015) Tree line dynamics in the tropical African highlands–identifying drivers and dynamics. *Journal of Vegetation Science*, **26**, 9–20.

Jähnig, S., Sander, M.M., Caprio, E., *et al.* (2020) Microclimate affects the distribution of grassland birds, but not forest birds, in an Alpine environment. *Journal of Ornithology,* **161,** 677–689.

Jankowski, J.E., Londoño, G.A., Robinson, S.K. & Chappell, M.A. (2013) Exploring the role of physiology and biotic interactions in determining elevational ranges of tropical animals. *Ecography,* **36,** 1–12.

Jarzyna, M.A., Quintero, I. & Jetz, W. (2021) Global functional and phylogenetic structure of avian assemblages across elevation and latitude. *Ecology Letters,* **24,** 196–207.

Kappelle, M. & Horn, S.P. (2016) The Paramo ecosystem of Costa Rica's highlands. In *Costa Rican Ecosystems.* Kappelle, M. (ed.). Chicago: University of Chicago Press, pp. 492–523.

Ke, D. & Lu, X. (2009) Burrow use by Tibetan Ground Tits *Pseudopodoces humilis*: coping with life at high altitudes. *Ibis,* **151,** 321–331.

Keller, V., Herrando, S., Voríšek, P., *et al.* (2020) *European Breeding Bird Atlas: Distribution, Abundance and Change.* Vol. 2. Barcelona: Lynx Edicions.

Kessler, M. (2006) Bosques de *Polylepis.* In *Botánica Económica de los Andes Centrales.* Moraes R.M., Øllgaard, B., Kvist, L.P., Borchsenius, F. & Balslev, H. (eds.). La Paz: Universidad Mayor de San Andrés, pp. 110–120.

Klinge, M., Böhner, J. & Lehmkuhl, F. (2003) Climate pattern, snow-, and timberlines in the Altai Mountains, Central Asia. *Erdkunde,* **57,** 296–308.

Körner, C. (1998) A re-assessment of high elevation treeline positions and their explanation. *Oecologia,* **115,** 445–459.

Körner, C. (1999) *Alpine Plant Life: Functional Plant Ecology of High Mountain Ecosystems.* Berlin: Springer.

Körner, C. (2012) *Alpine Treelines: Functional Ecology of the Global High Elevation Tree Limits.* Berlin: Springer.

Körner, C. & Ohsawa, M. (2006) Mountain systems. In *Ecosystem and Human Wellbeing: Current State and Trends.* Vol. 1. Hassan, R., Scholes, R. & Ash, N. (eds.). Washington DC: Island Press, pp. 681–716.

Körner, C. & Paulsen, J. (2004) A world-wide study of high-altitude treeline temperatures. *Journal of Biogeography,* **31,** 713–732.

Körner, C., Paulsen, J. & Spehn, E.M. (2011) A definition of mountains and their bioclimatic belts for global comparisons of biodiversity data. *Alpine Botany,* **121,** 73–78.

Marcora, P., Hensen, I., Renison, D., Seltmann, P. & Wesche, K. (2008) The performance of *Polylepis australis* trees along their entire altitudinal range: implications of climate change for their conservation. *Diversity and Distributions,* **14,** 630–636.

Mark, A.F., Dickinson, K.J. & Hofstede, R.G. (2000) Alpine vegetation, plant distribution, life forms and environments in a perhumid New Zealand region: oceanic and tropical high mountain affinities. *Arctic, Antarctic, and Alpine Research,* **32,** 240–254.

Martin, K. & Eadie, J.M. (1999) Nest Webs: a community wide approach to the management and conservation of cavity nesting birds. *Forest Ecology and Management,* **115,** 243–257.

Martin, K., Wilson, S., MacDonald, E.C., *et al.* (2017) Effects of severe weather on reproduction for sympatric songbirds in an alpine environment: interactions of climate extremes influence nesting success. *Auk,* **134,** 696–709.

Martin, K., Altamirano, T.A., de Zwaan, D.R., *et al.* (2021) Avian ecology and community structure across elevation gradients: the importance of high latitude temperate mountain habitats for conserving biodiversity in the Americas. *Global Ecology and Conservation*, **30**, e01799.

Masoero, G., Maurino, L., Rolando, A. & Chamberlain, D. (2016) The effect of treeline proximity on predation pressure: an experiment with artificial nests along elevational gradients in the European Alps. *Bird Study*, **63**, 395–405.

McGowan, P.J.K. & Kirwan, G.M. (2020) Handsome Francolin (*Pternistis nobilis*). In *Birds of the World*. Version 1.0. del Hoyo, J., Elliott, A., Sargatal, J., Christie, D.A. & de Juana, E. (eds.). Ithaca: Cornell Lab of Ornithology.

McGuire, J.A., Witt, C.C., Remsen Jr, J.V., *et al.* (2014) Molecular phylogenetics and the diversification of hummingbirds. *Current Biology*, **24**, 910–916.

Medrano, F., Barros, R., Norambuena, H.V., Matus, R. & Schmitt, F. (2018) *Atlas de las Aves Nidificantes de Chile*. Santiago: Red de Observadores de Aves.

Meinzer, F.C., Goldstein, G. & Rundel, P.W. (1994) Comparative water relations of tropical alpine plants. In *Tropical Alpine Environments: Plant Form and Function*. Rundel, P.W., Smith, A.P. & Meinzer, F.C. (eds.). Cambridge: Cambridge University Press, pp. 61–76.

Messerli, B. & Winiger, M. (1992) Climate, environmental change and resources of the African mountains from the Mediterranean to the equator. *Mountain Research and Development*, **12**, 315–336.

Nagy, L. (2006) European high mountain (alpine) vegetation and its suitability for indicating climate change impacts. *Biology and Environment*, **106B**, 335–341.

Nagy, L. & Grabherr, G. (2009) *The Biology of Alpine Habitats*. New York: Oxford University Press.

Notarnicola, C. (2020) Hotspots of snow cover changes in global mountain regions over 2000–2018. *Remote Sensing of Environment*, **243**, 111781.

O'Donnell, C.F., Weston, K.A. & Monks, J.M. (2017) Impacts of introduced mammalian predators on New Zealand's alpine fauna. *New Zealand Journal of Ecology*, **41**, 1–22.

Ohsawa, M.P.H.J., Nainggolan, P.H.J., Tanaka, N. & Anwar, C. (1985) Altitudinal zonation of forest vegetation on Mount Kerinci, Sumatra: with comparisons to zonation in the temperate region of east Asia. *Journal of Tropical Ecology*, **1**, 193–216.

Päckert, M., Martens, J., Sun, Y.H. & Tietze, D.T. (2015) Evolutionary history of passerine birds (Aves: Passeriformes) from the Qinghai–Tibetan plateau: from a pre-Quaternary perspective to an integrative biodiversity assessment. *Journal of Ornithology*, **156**, 355–365.

Price, T.D., Hooper, D.M., Buchanan, C.D., *et al.* (2014) Niche filling slows the diversification of Himalayan songbirds. *Nature*, **509**, 222–225.

Quintero, I. & Jetz, W. (2018) Global elevational diversity and diversification of birds. *Nature*, **555**, 246.

Rauter, C.M., Reyer, H.U. & Bollmann, K. (2002) Selection through predation, snowfall and microclimate on nest-site preferences in the Water Pipit *Anthus spinoletta*. *Ibis*, **144**, 433–444.

Rawat, G.S. (2017) The Himalayan vegetation along horizontal and vertical gradients. In *Bird Migration Across the Himalayas: Wetland Functioning Amidst Mountains and Glaciers*. Prins, H.T. & Namgail, T. (eds.). Cambridge: Cambridge University Press, pp. 189–204.

Rebelo, A.G., Boucher, C., Helme, N., Mucina, L. & Rutherford, M.C. (2006) Fynbos Biome. In *The Vegetation of South Africa, Lesotho and Swaziland*. Mucina, L. & Rutherford, M.C. (eds.). Pretoria: South African National Biodiversity Institute, pp. 53–219.

Remsen Jr, J.V. (2020) Slender-billed Miner (*Geositta tenuirostris*). In *Birds of the World*. Version 1.0. Billerman, S.M. (ed.). Ithaca: Cornell Lab of Ornithology.

Resano-Mayor, J., Bettega, C., del Mar Delgado, M., *et al.* (2020) Partial migration of white-winged snowfinches is correlated with winter weather conditions. *Global Ecology and Conservation*, **24**, e01346.

Romanov, A.A. (2013) *Bird Fauna of the Mountains of the Asian Subarctic: Principles of Development and Dynamics*. Moscow: Russian Society for the Preservation and Study of Birds.

Romanov, A.A., Melikhova, E.V., Zarubina, M.A., Tarasov, V.V. & Yakovlev, V.O. (2021) Analysis of the avifauna structure in the alpine belt of the Northwestern Putorana Plateau, Central Siberia. *Biology Bulletin*, **48**, 1513–1527.

Rosvold, J. (2016) Perennial ice and snow-covered land as important ecosystems for birds and mammals. *Journal of Biogeography*, **43**, 3–12.

Rutten, G., Ensslin, A., Hemp, A. & Fischer, M. (2015) Vertical and horizontal vegetation structure across natural and modified habitat types at Mount Kilimanjaro. *PLoS ONE*, **10**, e0138822

Saavedra, F.A., Kampf, S.K., Fassnacht, S.R. & Sibold, J.S. (2018) Changes in Andes snow cover from MODIS data, 2000–2016. *Cryosphere*, **12**, 1027–1046.

Saracco, J.F., Siegel, R.B., Helton, L., Stock, S.L. & DeSante, D.F. (2019) Phenology and productivity in a montane bird assemblage: trends and responses to elevation and climate variation. *Global Change Biology*, **25**, 985–996.

Schano, C., Niffenegger, C., Jonas, T. & Korner-Nievergelt, F. (2021) Hatching phenology is lagging behind an advancing snowmelt pattern in a high-alpine bird. *Scientific Reports*, **11**, 1–11.

Schickhoff, U., Bobrowski, M., Böhner, J., *et al.* (2015) Do Himalayan treelines respond to recent climate change? An evaluation of sensitivity indicators. *Earth System Dynamics*, **6**, 245–265.

Schumm, M., White, A.E., Supriya, K. & Price, T.D. (2020) Ecological limits as the driver of bird species richness patterns along the east Himalayan elevational gradient. *American Naturalist*, **195**, 802–817.

Scridel, D., Brambilla, M., Martin, K., *et al.* (2018) A review and meta-analysis of the effects of climate change on Holarctic mountain and upland bird populations. *Ibis*, **160**, 489–515.

Scridel, D., Brambilla, M., de Zwaan, D.R., *et al.* (2021) A genus at risk: predicted current and future distribution of all three *Lagopus* species reveal sensitivity to climate change and efficacy of protected areas. *Diversity and Distributions*, **27**, 1759–1774.

Seeholzer, G.F., Claramunt, S. & Brumfield, R.T. (2017) Niche evolution and diversification in a Neotropical radiation of birds (Aves: Furnariidae). *Evolution*, **71**, 702–715.

Severinghaus, L.L., Ding, T.-S., Fang, W.-H., *et al.* (2012) *The Avifauna of Taiwan. Version 2*. Taipei, Taiwan: Forestry Bureau, Council of Agriculture.

Sevillano-Ríos, C.S., Rodewald, A.D. & Morales, L.V. (2018) Ecología y conservación de las aves asociadas con *Polylepis*: qué sabemos de esta comunidad cada vez más vulnerable? *Ecología Austral*, **28**, 216–228.

Sevillano-Ríos, C.S., Rodewald, A.D. & Morales, L.V. (2020) Alpine birds of South America. In *Encyclopedia of the World's Biomes*. Goldstein, M.I. & DellaSala, D.A. (eds.). Amsterdam, Netherlands: Elsevier, pp. 492–504.

Skutch, A.F. (1985) Clutch size, nesting success and predation on nests of neotropical birds, reviewed. *Ornithological Monographs*, **36**, 575–594.

Smith, J.M. (1980) The vegetation of the summit zone of Mount Kinabalu. *New Phytologist*, **84**, 547–573.

Sohmer, S.H. & Gustafson, R. (1987) *Plants and Flowers of Hawai'i*. Honolulu: University of Hawaii Press.

Steinmann, V.W., Arredondo-Amezcua, L., Hernández-Cárdenas, R.A. & Ramírez-Amezcua, Y. (2021) Diversity and origin of the Central Mexican alpine flora. *Diversity*, **13**, 31.

Strinella, E., Scridel, D., Brambilla, M., Schano, C. & Korner-Nievergelt, F. (2020) Potential sex-dependent effects of weather on apparent survival of a high-elevation specialist. *Scientific Reports*, **10**, 1–13.

Summers-Smith, D. (2020) White-rumped Snowfinch (*Montifringilla taczanowskii*) & Rufous-necked Snowfinch (*Montifringilla ruficollis*). In *Birds of the World*. Version 1.0. Billerman, S.M. (ed.). Ithaca: Cornell Lab of Ornithology.

Testolin, R., Attorre, F. & Jiménez-Alfaro, B. (2020) Global distribution and bioclimatic characterization of alpine biomes. *Ecography*, **43**, 779–788.

Thompson, L.G., Brecher, H.H., Mosley-Thompson, E., Hardy, D.R. & Mark, B.G. (2009) Glacier loss on Kilimanjaro continues unabated. *Proceedings of the National Academy of Sciences*, **106**, 19770–19775.

Tomkovich, P.S. (1997) Breeding distribution, migrations and conservation status of the Great Knot *Calidris tenuirostris* in Russia. *Emu*, **97**, 265–282.

Tsai, P.-Y., Ko, C.-J., Chia, S.Y., Lu, Y.-J. & Tuanmu, M.-N. (2021) New insights into the patterns and drivers of avian altitudinal migration from a growing crowdsourcing data source. *Ecography*, **44**, 75–86.

Turner, A. (2020) Montane Blue Swallow (*Hirundo atrocaerulea*). In *Birds of the World*. Version 1.0. Billerman, S.M. (ed.). Ithaca: Cornell Lab of Ornithology.

UNESCO, IUCN (2022) *World Heritage Glaciers: Sentinels of Climate Change*. Paris, UNESCO & Gland, IUCN.

Valencia, B.G., Bush, M.B., Coe, A.L., Orren, E. & Gosling, W.D. (2018) *Polylepis* woodland dynamics during the last 20,000 years. *Journal of Biogeography*, **45**, 1019–1030.

van der Hoek, Y., Sirami, C., Faida, E., Musemakweli, V. & Tuyisingize, D. (2021) Elevational distribution of birds in an Eastern African montane environment as governed by temperature, precipitation and habitat availability. *Biotropica*, **54**, 334–345.

Vargas, G. & Sánchez, J.J. (2005) Plantas con flores de los páramos de Costa Rica y Panamá: El páramo ístmico. In *Páramos de Costa Rica*. Kappelle, M. & Horn, S.P. (eds.). San José, Costa Rica: Instituto Nacional de Biodiversidad, pp. 397–435.

Visinoni, L., Pernollet, C.A., Desmet, J.F., Korner-Nievergelt, F. & Jenni, L. (2015) Microclimate and microhabitat selection by the Alpine Rock Ptarmigan (*Lagopus muta helvetica*) during summer. *Journal of Ornithology,* **156,** 407–417.

Walther, B.A., Chen, J.R.J., Lin, H.S. & Sun, Y.H. (2017) The effects of rainfall, temperature and wind on a community of montane birds in Shei-Pa National Park, Taiwan. *Zoological Studies,* **56,** e23.

White, A.E., Dey, K.K., Mohan, D., Stephens, M. & Price, T.D. (2019) Regional influences on community structure across the tropical-temperate divide. *Nature Communications,* 10, 1–8.

Williamson, J.L. & Witt, C.C. (2021) Elevational niche-shift migration: why the degree of elevational change matters for the ecology, evolution and physiology of migratory birds. *Auk,* **138,** ukaa087.

Wilson, S. & Martin, K. (2008) Breeding habitat selection of sympatric White-tailed, Rock and Willow Ptarmigan in the southern Yukon Territory, Canada. *Journal of Ornithology,* **149,** 629–637.

Woods, S. & Ramsay, P. M. (2001) Variability in nectar supply: implications for high-altitude hummingbirds. In *The Ecology of Volcán Chiles: High-altitude Ecosystems on the Ecuador-Colombia Border.* Ramsay, P.M. (ed.). Plymouth: Pebble & Shell, pp. 209–217.

Yoshino, M.M. (1978) Altitudinal vegetation belts of Japan with special reference to climatic conditions. *Arctic and Alpine Research,* **10,** 449–456.

Zheng, Z. (1983) *The Avifauna of Xizang: The Comprehensive Scientific Expedition to Qinghai-Xizang Plateau.* Beijing: Academia Sinica.

Zheng, G.M.A. (2011) *Checklist on the Classification and Distribution of the Birds of China.* Beijing: Science Press.

Zwickel, F.C. & Bendell, J.F. (2020) Dusky Grouse (*Dendragapus obscurus*). In *Birds of the World.* Version 1.0. Rodewald, P.G. (ed.). Ithaca: Cornell Lab of Ornithology.

4 · *Birds of Treeline Ecotones*

DAN CHAMBERLAIN, EVGENIYA
MELIKHOVA, SUSANNE JÄHNIG
AND C. STEVEN SEVILLANO-RÍOS

4.1 Introduction

The mountain treeline ecotone represents the zone between continuous montane forest and the alpine zone (as defined in Chapter 1, Table 1.1). Ecotones are defined as areas of transition between two (or more) vegetation communities or habitat types (Odum & Barrett 2005) and they often have high diversity compared to adjacent zones as they share many of the species from each of the overlapping communities (Kark *et al.* 2007). The natural elevation limit of the treeline is usually determined by climatic factors, but in many regions the treeline ecotone has been shaped by human influence over the centuries, especially through grazing and fire. The position of the treeline ecotone is likely to be highly sensitive to environmental change, especially climate change. Indeed, evidence already exists that many mountain treelines are shifting towards higher elevations due to warmer temperatures (e.g., Harsch *et al.* 2009). Despite this, treeline bird communities have received little research focus compared to adjacent montane forest and alpine zones.

In this chapter, we first define the treeline ecotone and assess the factors that affect its location along the elevation gradient. We then consider some characteristics of bird communities in the treeline ecotone, including patterns in avian species richness, measures of diversity and key traits in relation to adjacent zones. In particular, we determine the extent to which the birds of the treeline ecotone form a distinct and characteristic community, including specialist treeline species, in mountains generally. Finally, we also consider some of the anthropogenic drivers that have affected treeline ecotone bird communities and identify those that are likely to represent important threats in the future.

4.2 Defining the Treeline Ecotone

In a natural state (i.e., without human influence), the treeline ecotone is the transitional zone between closed forest and the upper elevational limit of tree growth, irrespective of a tree's physical structure or age (Figure 4.1; Nagy & Grabherr 2009; Körner 2012). There have been various definitions of exactly what constitutes the treeline ecotone. According to some classifications, it corresponds to the upper subalpine zone (Nagy & Grabherr 2009), although the definition of 'subalpine' shows variation among sources (Körner 2012). Mollet *et al.* (2018) distinguish this zone from the montane forest zone primarily on the basis of dominance of, respectively, coniferous and broadleaved trees, although they also explicitly include the treeline ecotone in the subalpine. However, several studies define the subalpine on the basis of the density or cover of trees, and the extent of shrubs and grassland habitats. Romanov *et al.* (2016), for example, used a fairly broad definition of the subalpine zone as sparse mountain forests and shrubs, as distinct from the coniferous forest zone,

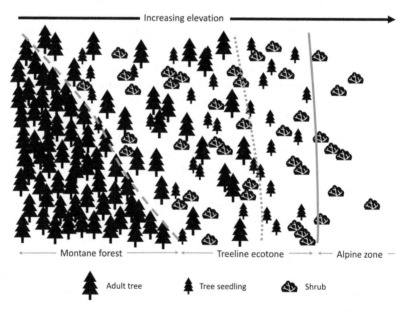

Figure 4.1 A representation of the treeline ecotone in relation to other important zones and boundaries along an elevation gradient. The grey dashed line is the timber line, the grey dotted line is the treeline and the grey continuous line is the tree growth limit. Whilst tree seedlings occur throughout the treeline ecotone, they do not survive above the tree growth limit.

which hence comes within our definition of the treeline ecotone. Other authors are more specific – Boyle & Martin (2015) define the subalpine zone as being composed of herbaceous plants and shrubs interspersed with sparse trees and krummholz trees. Krummholz trees typically have a stunted and deformed appearance because their growth is limited due to the climatic conditions (temperature, wind and snow) close to the maximum elevation for the species (Nagy & Grabherr 2009). Similarly, Altamirano *et al.* (2020) describe the subalpine zone as an ecotonal habitat characterized by a mix of herbaceous meadows, shrubs and sparse patches of trees and/or krummholz existing between the forest-line and the treeline. The breadth of the ecotone area is obviously influenced by the steepness of the terrain at a local scale (i.e., steeper slopes mean a narrower zone), and can range from a few metres to many kilometres wide in flat terrain (Körner 2012), but this will also be influenced by other factors, including aspect and exposure, and there is much geographic variation (see Table 6.4 in Nagy & Grabherr 2009). For example, climatic and topographic influences lead to a complex zonation along the Andean mountain chain (Box 4.1 and Plate 5).

Box 4.1   *Factors Influencing the Position and Structure of the Treeline Ecotone in the Andes*

Although the treeline ecotone can be clearly distinguishable as a particular ecosystem in many places in the world, this can be a challenge in some mountain systems because different factors can influence its location, structure and extent. The Andes have a topographically complex latitudinal and elevational distribution, which can help us understand how factors such as climate, topography and human activities influence treelines (Plate 5).

One main limiting factor is the average annual temperature (Figure B4.1). Globally, temperatures below 5°C strongly restrict tree growth (Körner 2003). In humid Andean slopes, which include parts of Venezuela, Colombia and Ecuador and the Amazon slopes of the Peruvian and Bolivian Andes, the treeline ecotone is climatically defined by minimum temperature. This usually occurs between 3,000 m and 3,600 m (Figure B4.1A), increasing in equatorial latitudes, below which a great diversity of trees characterize large areas of continuous montane forests (Borsdorf & Stadel 2015). However, in the Andean dry slopes (Figure B4.1B & C), the average annual precipitation is

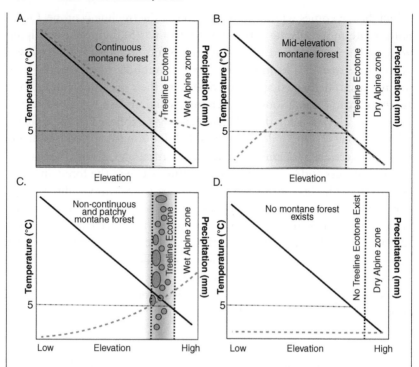

Figure B4.1 How temperature and precipitation drive the location of the treeline along the elevation gradient. In wet slopes (A), the treeline ecotone is mainly defined by minimum temperature. In dry slopes, different precipitation patterns (B,C) interact with temperature to define the treeline boundary, and even whether it occurs at all (D). Solid black lines represent average annual temperature, dashed-dotted horizontal lines are temperatures below 5°C, shading indicates forested areas and dashed grey lines indicate average annual precipitation.

also a key limiting factor that interacts with temperature to define the position and structure of the treeline ecotone.

On dry Pacific slopes and the inter-Andean valleys of Peru, Bolivia, Chile and Argentina, precipitation rarely exceeds 1,000 mm per year and, unlike in wet slopes (Plate 5), it does not necessarily decrease with elevation, but may peak at intermediate elevations (2,500–3,500 m) in the inter-Andean valleys (Figure B4.1B), or it may increase with elevation on dry Pacific slopes (Figure B4.1C). Additionally, the inter-valleys are topographically very complex, as can be seen in the cross sections of northern and southern Peru (Plate 5), causing a naturally fragmented treeline ecotone (Valencia *et al.* 2018). As a result, mid-elevation and non-continuous/patchy montane forest dominated by several native tree species (like *Polylepis*) are common in these areas (shaded patches in Figure B4.1C). In the Atacama region of Chile, annual precipitation is amongst the lowest on the planet (15 mm) and only increases to about 300 mm between 4,200 m and 5,000 m, resulting in an absence of forests along most of the gradient, except for the highest elevations where the treeline is formed by *Polylepis tarapacana* (Hoch & Körner 2005). No montane forest is expected to exist at lower levels of annual precipitation (Figure B4.1D). Hence, identifying the treeline ecotone can be challenging in dry slopes where forests are restricted by a highly heterogeneous landscape creating a mosaic of diverse ecosystems in the wet and dry puna landscapes.

Human activities that include the extensive use of fire, logging and the domestication of animals, have greatly fragmented high Andean forests and lowered the treeline in many regions (Valencia *et al.* 2018). Some pre-Columbian cultures, like the Inca, seem to have preferred savannah-type ecosystems in the high plateaus or inter-valleys that allowed the best development of agriculture and grazing (Borsdorf & Stadel 2015). This may be visible in some areas of south-east Peru and Bolivia where the limits of human-impacted areas are often found at around 2,600 m, 300–400 m below non-impacted or difficult to access areas that are usually located around 3,000 m where *Alnus* and *Podocarpus* trees are more common.

The treeline itself is typically defined as a line connecting the highest growing groups of large trees and is considered as the dividing line between alpine and non-alpine environments. It is thus distinct from the timberline, which forms the lower limit of the ecotone area, and is defined as the point where closed forest ends. Formal definitions of the treeline vary – for example what constitutes a 'large' tree varies among authors (e.g., >3 m, Körner 2007, Nagy & Grabherr 2009; >2 m, Bader *et al.* 2020), which has led to attempts for a more formal and objective definition of different types of treelines (Bader *et al.* 2020). This is important from a point of view of analysing treelines, and especially their shifts in response to environmental change, but from an ornithologist's point of view, a more general definition will suffice. We define the treeline ecotone as the area between the more or less continuous forest and the open alpine zones; it is typically characterized by a mosaic of shrubs, trees of varying age and dimension, including krummholz, but

Figure 4.2 Examples of treeline ecotone habitat. A. Natural treeline in the Kolyma Uplands, Eastern Siberia (Photo: Evgeniya Melikhova). B. Treeline subject to low-intensity grazing, Italian Alps (Photo: Dan Chamberlain). C. *Polylepis weberbaweri* in the Central Peruvian Andes (Photo: Steven Sevillano-Ríos). D. Natural, scrubby treeline in the Hazelton Mountains, British Columbia, Canada, maintained by heavy winter snowfall (Photo: Devin R. de Zwaan).

usually scattered or in isolated clumps, and more open areas of dwarf-shrub heath and grassland with unvegetated rocky areas. Examples are shown in Figure 4.2.

Vegetation zones in mountains are often defined by 'lines' (timber-line, treeline, tree growth line; Figure 4.1). These terms are used for convenience, the borders between zones being difficult to define precisely as they are usually characterized by gradual change in vegetation communities. There are circumstances where the transitions are abrupt and form a more-or-less evident line (Körner 2012). In other cases, the ecotonal areas are highly fragmented, such as patches of *Polylepis* forest in the high Andes (Sevillano-Ríos *et al.* 2020; Figure 4.2C).

In this chapter, we are primarily interested in the birds living at the upper elevational limit of the forest, and those of adjacent treeline eco-tonal habitats that include shrub-dominated areas above the treeline that grade into the alpine zone (i.e., the full range of habitat types encompassed by the treeline ecotone depicted in Figure 4.1). We include 'subalpine' habitat as part of the treeline ecotone when the definition provided in a given reference clearly indicates the habitat above the timberline. However, for the sake of consistency, we use 'treeline ecotone' when referring to the area between the timberline and the upper limit to tree growth (Figure 4.1), and also to more complex ecotones representing high elevation mosaic habitats that do not necessarily conform to the model in Figure 4.1, but which include some elements of woody vegetation (shrubs, bushes and trees), e.g., *Polylepis* forest fragments in the High Andes, where lower elevation continuous forest may be lacking. In some mountains, human activities have created forest edge habitats below the natural treeline that are similar to those occurring in natural treeline ecotones; these are also considered.

4.2.1 What Determines the Position of the Treeline?

Climate is a common determinant of the elevation of the treeline. Körner & Paulsen (2004) found that seasonal mean ground temperature of the growing season at the treeline was fairly constant at $6.7 \pm 0.8°C$ (sd) globally, with variations caused by taxonomic, and to a lesser extent regional, influences. Not surprisingly therefore, the elevation limit of the treeline varies fairly predictably according to latitude, i.e., it occurs at much higher elevations in the tropics than in temperate mountains, and is lower in boreal mountains. Indeed, the highest recorded treelines occur above 5,000 m in the tropical Andes (Hoch & Körner 2005), whereas they become progressively lower towards the poles, eventually grading into Arctic tundra at sea-level at the highest latitudes. Moisture is also important in dictating the elevation of the treeline in a given area. Cloudiness is associated with cooler temperatures; hence, in general, treelines are lower in moist areas and higher in drier areas (Körner 2012).

Many other factors influence the position of the treeline, and their importance varies spatially causing marked variation in its elevation, both within and among mountain ranges (Lu *et al.* 2021; Appendix 4.1). These include limits set by climatic factors such as lack of water, snow cover and wind (Körner 2007), but also unsuitable substrate for tree colonization (steep rocks, loose gravel), fire (e.g., Naccarella *et al.* 2020) and anthropogenic influences. The significance of these varies geographically. For example, human disturbance has been one of the main influences on the treeline in the European Alps, whereas fire has greater importance in the Rocky Mountains (Körner 2012).

At a local scale, favourable conditions caused by microtopography often allow isolated pioneer trees to grow to full stature as outliers

Figure 4.3 Examples of small-scale topography in treeline ecotone habitat. A. Natural treeline in the Peruvian Andes showing the highest extent of trees in sheltered gulleys (Photo: Steven Sevillano-Ríos). B. Avalanche track in the Italian Alps (Photo: Riccardo Alba).

beyond the treeline. Sheltered gullies and ravines promote tree growth at tropical treelines, hence the treeline reaches maximum elevation in these areas (Figure 4.3A). Conversely, in temperate climates, snow typically accumulates in gullies thereby supressing tree growth, hence treelines reach their highest elevations on ridges (Körner 2012). Avalanches can create edge habitats and open treeless areas (Figure 4.3B), especially where they regularly occur (Nagy & Grabherr 2009), and there is evidence that such areas below the treeline create bird habitats analogous to those of the treeline ecotone (Requena *et al.* 2022).

Anthropogenic impacts determine the position of the treeline in many mountain ranges of Europe and Asia. Grazing has a significant impact on treeline elevation, especially in European mountains (Section 4.6.1). In some areas, grazing is also associated with deliberate burning to maintain open habitat (Section 4.6.2). Ski-pistes usually form an abrupt barrier between open pistes and mature forest, and act as barriers for a range of fauna (Laiolo & Rolando 2005; Chapter 7). Due to these influences, more anthropogenically impacted, high elevation habitat mosaics are often represented by exceptionally fragmented areas of shrubs and open forest at elevations much below the climatic limit of the treeline (Figure 4.4). This contrasts with more natural situations with no or low grazing pressure characterized by a zonation of continuous forest, forest-shrub mosaics, krummholz and low shrubs, finally grading into the alpine zone (Figure 4.2).

Figure 4.4 Examples of fragmented ecotone habitat created by grazing of domestic animals. A. Peruvian Andes (Photo: Steven Sevillano-Ríos). B. Italian Alps (Photo: Dan Chamberlain).

The clear link between climate (especially temperature) and the elevational limit of the treeline suggests that its position could be a useful indicator of climate change impacts on terrestrial ecosystems (Lu *et al.* 2021). Indeed, there is mounting global evidence of upslope treeline shifts in many regions (Harsch *et al.* 2009; Lu *et al.* 2021). However, in some cases such shifts may be due to the removal of other limiting factors, in particular, grazing. In the European Alps for example, the contribution of abandonment of traditional livestock practices is estimated to have had a much greater impact on treeline shifts than climate change (Gehrig-Fasel *et al.* 2007).

4.3 Treeline Ecotone Bird Communities

Lloyd *et al.* (2012) state that high elevation treelines 'represent one of the most obvious yet little studied vegetation boundaries in ecology'. Whilst there has been an increase in research on treeline bird communities in the period since that statement was written, we feel that in relation to other habitats, it still rings true. Given their known sensitivity to climate change, and environmental change more broadly (Nagy & Grabherr 2009), the need for further research on treelines is greater than ever.

Dedicated studies on birds of the treeline ecotone are scarce compared with those of the adjacent zones. Alpine zone species are often quoted as being especially vulnerable to climate change (see Chapter 6), and they include several charismatic species (rock ptarmigan *Lagopus muta*, white-tailed ptarmigan *L. leucura*, white-winged snowfinch *Montifringilla nivalis*) that no doubt add to their attraction as study systems. Studies on mountain forest birds tend to focus on forest specialists, or communities associated with mature closed-canopy forest (e.g., Mollet *et al.* 2018). The treeline is perceived as a dividing line between forest and alpine birds (e.g., Alatamirano *et al.* 2020; Martin *et al.* 2021), and while often included in studies on associations between diversity indices and elevation (e.g., Acharya *et al.* 2011; Abebe *et al.* 2019; García-Navas *et al.* 2020), the treeline bird community is often not explicitly described. Treeline birds therefore tend to fall into a gap between the montane and alpine zones. This certainly seems to be the case in the European Alps, where amongst the most common species of the treeline, dunnock *Prunella modularis*, lesser whitethroat *Curruca curruca* and common linnet *Linaria cannabina*, the only published ecological studies are those of Jambor *et al.* (2011) and Jähnig *et al.* (2018, 2020), although all of these species, and especially the dunnock, have been very well-studied in non-mountain habitats (e.g., Davies 1992).

Whilst each geographic region has its own particular community of birds and plants, there are some generalizations that can be made. Temperate ecotones of the northern hemisphere typically have quite narrow treeline ecotones (e.g., Lewis & Starzomski 2015). The European Alps probably have the treeline ecotone that has been impacted by human activities more than any other mountain range, in particular by grazing (see Section 4.6.1), which as a consequence means that it is lower than would be expected based on climatic constraints, and this further influences its extent. Many areas of the Andes (Kessler & Herzog 1998) and the Himalayas (Miehe *et al.* 2009) also have a long history of anthropogenic influence.

Where the treeline ecotone occurs in rather flat terrain, in particular in boreal mountains, bird communities often have a high proportion of aquatic and semi-aquatic species. In Finland for example, waders such as wood sandpiper *Tringa glareola* and common greenshank *T. nebularia* are common in more open, wetter areas of the ecotone. On the Putorana Plateau in central Russia, there is a high proportion of Charadriiformes in the avifauna (21 per cent of all bird species recorded in this zone), including species such as common ringed plover *Charadrius hiaticula* on openings with tundra vegetation and grey-tailed tattler *Tringa brevipes* along streams and rivers (Romanov 2013). By contrast, there are few if any breeding waders in the European Alps and the temperate Andes, and only a few species are associated with aquatic habitats in British Columbia (e.g., solitary sandpiper *Tringa solitaria* and Wilson's snipe *Gallinago delicata*; Martin *et al.* 2021), likely because there is insufficient space for wetland areas in the narrow temperate treeline ecotone.

The Andes is the longest mountain chain in the world and hence covers the greatest range in latitude. That, and the marked climatic and topographic influences (Box 4.1), mean that there is not a 'typical' Andean treeline bird community. In most regions, the treeline ecotone corresponds to the pattern shown in Figure 4.1. (e.g., Lloyd et al. 2012). In some areas, however, especially in the dry Andean tropics where continuous forest is absent along many elevational gradients, vegetation patterns at high elevation are spatially more complex. In particular, *Polylepis* forest is formed of the highest growing trees in the world, and typically grows as islands within more open habitats (Figure 4.2C; Sevillano-Ríos et al. 2020). It occurs both within dry and moist puna grasslands between 3,700–5,200 m in Bolivia and Peru, and within the páramos of the northern Andes, in addition to bordering cloud forest in the eastern central Andes (Quispe-Melgar et al. 2020; Sevillano-Ríos et al. 2020). It hosts a high biodiversity (Sevillano-Ríos et al. 2018) and a number of highly specialized, endemic and threatened species including white-browed tit-spinetail *Leptasthenura xenothorax* and ash-breasted tit-tyrant *Anairetes alpinus*. *Polylepis* forest is sensitive to anthropogenic activities, especially fire, hence it is a threatened habitat (Valencia et al. 2018; Sevillano-Ríos et al. 2020).

In the Eastern Himalayas, the treeline ecotone is broad and distinct, and changes in bird and vegetation communities occur gradually. Some of the characteristic ecotone species (e.g., variegated laughingthrush *Trochalopteron variegatum*, olive-backed pipit *Anthus hodgsoni*) are not strongly linked to a natural ecotone, but are particularly associated with large clearings that occur when primary forests are disturbed as a result of human development. Also important are the shrub species barberry *Berberis* spp. and dwarf rhododendron (e.g., *Rhododendron anthopogon*, *R. setosum* and *R. lepidotum*) for which several bird species show a close association (e.g., *Phylloscopus* spp., *Prunella* spp.; Laiolo 2004; Mikhailov 2020).

4.3.1 Species Richness

The treeline ecotone is typically a relatively narrow zone compared to the adjacent montane and alpine zones and is characterized by a rapid change in vegetation structure with increasing elevation, and usually, in species composition. It is perhaps then surprising that there is not much evidence for a higher richness, nor overall bird abundance, in this zone relative to adjacent habitats (e.g., Lewis & Starzomski 2015; Romanov et al. 2016, 2019a, b; Iijima & Morimoto 2021). Considering the whole elevation gradient (e.g., including lowlands), there is much evidence of peaks in bird richness or diversity at intermediate elevations, but these are typically much lower than the treeline (García-Navas *et al.* 2020) and seem more closely correlated with temperature or productivity than habitat structure (e.g., Acharya *et al.* 2011; Abebe *et al.* 2019). However, Altamirano *et al.* (2020) did find a peak in bird diversity at the upper montane (old growth forest) and the subalpine zone, that is, the treeline ecotone and just below.

To understand the variation in species richness with elevation, a complete gradient is needed, ideally that includes natural habitats represented along each part of the gradient (Rahbek 1995). The most common pattern in such studies is a non-linear association between diversity (usually species richness) and elevation, but the peak is often around the ecotone between different forest types (Rahbek 1995; Acharya *et al.* 2011; Iijima & Morimoto 2021; see Chapters 1 and 9). Such studies are mostly based on long gradients covering several elevation zones. However, we may expect a different pattern if we focus only on our zones of interest, that is, is there evidence of a peak in diversity at the treeline if only the adjacent habitats are considered? This is a relevant question given that we expect impacts of climate change to be greater at higher elevations, and are likely to act in particular through changes to the treeline. Longer gradients may obscure more subtle patterns at finer scales.

Using the datasets summarized in Appendix 4.1, species richness was compared across a relatively short gradient. This comprised montane forest, treeline ecotone and alpine zones at two different measurement scales: point (e.g., mean richness calculated at the point count or transect scale within a given site) and site (total species richness summed across all samples for a given zone). As species richness varies geographically, it was expressed relative to richness in montane forest for each study and the means were calculated separately for site and point-scale estimates.

There was no overall evidence for a peak in avian species richness in the treeline ecotone in the breeding season (Figure 4.5). However, there was wide variation in treeline species richness patterns (Appendix 4.1), and there were a few studies undertaken over broad geographic areas showing evidence of an intermediate peak at the treeline ecotone. In most cases, the lowest richness was found in the alpine zone, although there were some exceptions. For example, species richness in this zone was higher than in the treeline ecotone on the Anabar Plateau and the Putorana Plateau, while in Finland, forest had the lowest species richness.

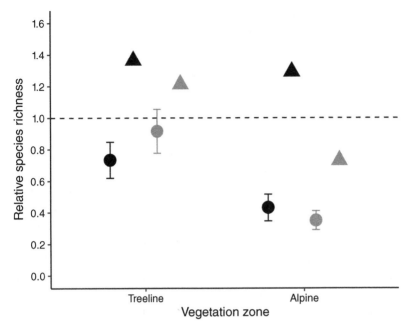

Figure 4.5 Avian species richness of treeline and alpine zones relative to forest species richness (the horizontal dashed line, i.e., set equal to 1) at site (black symbols) and point (grey symbols) scales in the late summer and autumn (British Columbia, triangles, data from Boyle & Martin 2015) and in the breeding season (circles, all other estimates in Appendix 4.1). Means and standard errors are presented from 19 (site level) and 6 (point level) estimates of species richness for breeding season data. See Appendix 4.1 for further details.

Only a single study was undertaken outside the breeding season, in late summer and autumn in the Coastal Mountains of British Columbia (Boyle & Martin 2015). This found generally higher species richness above the montane forest, only richness in the alpine zone at the point level having lower species richness (Figure 4.5). This contrasts with breeding season site-level richness estimates in the same region (Martin *et al.* 2021), suggesting that higher elevations may be more important in terms of the number of species using them during migration. This may represent an analogous situation to some lowland successional forests (with a similar open structure to the mountain treeline ecotone) that are preferentially selected by many species during stopover (Rodewald & Brittingham 2004), which in turn may be linked to higher resource abundance in such habitats (Martin & Karr 1986).

The way in which species richness, and more broadly diversity, is expressed, may affect conclusions regarding bird community characteristics along the elevation gradient. For example, Martin *et al.* (2021) found slightly different patterns between unadjusted species richness and richness estimates adjusted for sampling effort using species accumulation curves – in the south temperate Andes, adjusted richness was highest in the treeline ecotone and lowest in the montane zone. Furthermore, spatial scale of a given survey may be important (Martin *et al.* 2021). Examining the three studies for which both site and point-level estimates of species richness were available (Appendix 4.1) shows evidence of scale-dependent responses. In both the western and central European Alps, the peak in species richness was in the treeline ecotone at the site level, (i.e., pooling multiple survey points across a study area). In contrast, it was highest in the forest at the survey point level, i.e., species richness was higher for any given location in montane forest, but it was more uniform. However, the pattern was opposite in the central western Peruvian Andes where point level richness peaked in the treeline ecotone, but richness was highest in the forest at the site level (Appendix 4.1).

In conclusion, despite some evidence of clear peaks in species richness (Appendix 4.1) or other diversity measures at the treeline (Altamirano *et al.* 2020), there appears to be no universal pattern. Indeed, according to the data collated here, a decrease in species richness from montane forest to the alpine zone is the most common trend at the site level (Figure 4.5, Appendix 4.1). Only studies for which species richness estimates for all three elevation zones (i.e., montane forest, treeline and alpine) were available are included in Figure 4.5. Other studies that considered shorter gradients (from forest to the treeline) also support a decline in species richness or diversity with elevation, that is, there is no evidence of an intermediate peak at the treeline (e.g., Able & Noon 1976; Sabo 1980; Kendeigh & Fawver 1981).

There are likely to be many factors that influence variation in these patterns, such as vegetation structure, anthropogenic impacts (see below), local and regional climatic constraints including aspect (Iijima & Morimoto 2021), and differences in survey methods. The best way to fully understand patterns of avian diversity around the treeline would be to adopt consistent survey methods across widely separated geographic regions, but with the exception of Martin *et al.* (2021), such data are not currently available.

4.3.2 Other Community Measures

Traditional measures of diversity usually comprise either measures of species richness (sometimes adjusted for abundance or sampling effort) or indices of diversity. However, these measures do not take into account the distinctiveness of different communities, the shared evolutionary history of different species, or the diversity of ecological roles played by different species in a community. These can be measured by estimating, respectively, beta diversity (the turnover of species from one location to another), phylogenetic diversity (the accumulated evolutionary history of different genotypes and phenotypes that persists within lineages) and functional diversity (the range of behavioural, morphological and physiological traits in a given community) as demonstrated by Martin *et al.* (2021) for multiple mountain sites in North and South America.

Several studies have found an abrupt change in the species composition of communities at the treeline (e.g., Lloyd *et al.* 2012; Altamirano *et al.* 2020; García-Navas *et al.* 2020; Martin *et al.* 2021). In both the temperate and tropical Andes, a clear divide exists along the elevation gradient in terms of beta diversity, thus communities above and below the treeline are relatively distinct with little overlap (Lloyd *et al.* 2012; Altamirano *et al.* 2020; García-Navas *et al.* 2020). Romanov *et al.* (2019b) similarly found a higher overlap of species between the montane and treeline ecotone zones (47 per cent) than between the treeline ecotone and alpine zones (34 per cent) in the North–East Siberian Mountains. However, this pattern is not universal. Whilst Patterson *et al.* (1993) found zones of high species turnover along an extended gradient in the Peruvian Andes (340–3,450 m), these zones did not correspond to ecotone locations, including that of the treeline.

There have been fewer studies on phylogenetic or functional diversity. Martin *et al.* (2021) found that there was a clear divide in terms of phylogenetic diversity, which was higher below the treeline in both temperate northern mountains of British Columbia and the temperate southern Andes. However, evolutionary distinctiveness showed different patterns in the two regions, being higher above the treeline in the north and higher below the treeline in the south, indicating that species in the south have on average more unique evolutionary histories. Altamirano *et al.* (2020) found that alpine zone bird communities in the temperate Andes showed distinct life history traits relative to those below the treeline, as birds breeding in the alpine zone were mainly migratory, inhabited a restricted elevational range and nested in rock cavities. The subalpine zone had higher functional diversity than adjacent alpine and montane zones; in other words, the species in the treeline zone community represented a greater diversity of life history traits. Similarly, functional divergence changed markedly at the treeline in the Swiss Alps, declining steeply in the alpine zone (García-Navas *et al.* 2020).

Martin *et al.* (2021) compared nesting traits of mountain birds in two different temperate regions, British Columbia and Southern Chile. They found that the proportion of cavity nesters (including both tree and rock cavities) in the treeline ecotone was low (16 per cent) compared to those using open cup nests, and intermediate between montane (27 per cent) and alpine zones (13 per cent) in British Columbia. In Southern Chile, about 50 per cent of birds nested in cavities and reached a peak (56 per cent) in the ecotone. Based on the data in Appendix 4.1, these patterns were explored over a larger sample of studies by determining the proportion of species using a particular nesting strategy (tree, shrub or 'ground', the latter including cliff and rock cavity nesters) for each zone in each location. Overall patterns suggest that, as expected, species in the treeline ecotone are intermediate with relatively more ground nesters and fewer tree nesters than the forest zone and the reverse for birds breeding in the alpine zone (Figure 4.6). The shrub nesting strategy is comparatively less common than the other two behaviours and decreased with increasing elevation. This supports the contention that treeline communities are largely composed of either forest or alpine zone species, and there is little evidence for treeline specialists that more commonly nest in shrubs (see Section 4.3.3). Most species detected in the alpine zone used ground nests (85 per cent), as expected. The distribution of species across the three nest site types was more equal in forest; there were more tree-nesters than in the other zones, but even in this habitat there are species groups that commonly nest on the ground, such as grouse and several passerines (e.g., a number of *Phylloscopus* spp. in Europe and Asia and *Atlapetes* spp. in the Andes).

The data in Figure 4.6 are derived from surveys and are not associated with proof of breeding, hence they relate to habitat use rather than nesting habitat, and some tree nesters in the alpine zone are species with flexible nesting requirements (e.g., redwing *Turdus iliacus*, common cuckoo *Cuculus canorus* classed according to its different hosts). Also noteworthy is that some species can show different nesting requirements according to region: dunnock and lesser whitethroat always nest in shrubs (mostly rhododendron, sometimes juniper or other shrubs) in the Western Italian Alps where larch *Larix decidua* is the dominant tree. However, where

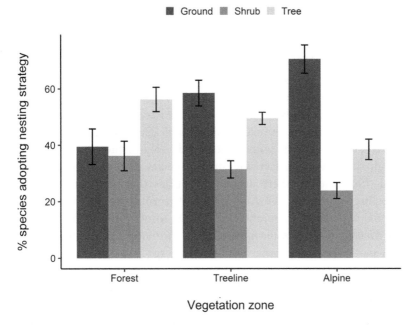

Figure 4.6 Percentage of total species recorded in each zone according to their nesting substrate, e.g., of species found in the alpine zone, 71 per cent can nest on the ground, 21 per cent can nest in shrubs and 38 per cent can nest in trees. Note that totals can sum to more than 100 for a given habitat because species can be assigned more than one nesting substrate. The data are derived from 22 studies (those listed in Appendix 4.1, and sources used in Sevillano-Ríos *et al.* 2020).

spruce *Picea* spp. is common, as in the Ural Mountains, they also nest on tree branches, presumably because spruce offers them a denser foliage and hence a more appropriate structure that is not present in larch.

4.3.3 Treeline Specialists

There are few examples of genuine treeline specialists, that is, those that are found only in the treeline ecotone. Lewis & Starzomski (2015) found that treeline species in Labrador, Canada, were generally those that were widespread across a range of elevations – they did not find evidence of any treeline specialists. Sabo (1980) found generally widespread species in krummholz in treeline ecotones of the White Mountains in New Hampshire USA, including generalist species such as the blackpoll warbler *Setophaga striata* (the most abundant species in that zone), and species of more open habitats, in particular myrtle warbler *S. coronata* and dark-eyed junco *Junco hyemalis*. Martin *et al.* (2021) also did not find any treeline ecotone specialists (which they defined as species found only breeding in that zone) in British Columbia, and found only four in the temperate Andes in Chile, although these included species such as buff-winged cinclodes *Cinclodes fuscus* that were not found elsewhere in their mountain study sites, but that are widespread in open habitats at lower elevations. Similarly, Lloyd *et al.* (2012) classified two species as treeline specialists within their study area in the tropical Andes, although these were in fact widespread species of woodland edges in general. Nonetheless, there are a few species that are found only in the treeline ecotone of the Andes, e.g., Patagonian forest earthcreeper *Upucerthia saturatior* (Altamirano *et al.* 2020), some hummingbirds of the genus *Metallura* and *Oreotrochilus* (García-Moreno *et al.* 1999), and 23 species particularly associated with *Polylepis* forest (e.g., giant conebill *Conirostrum binghami*, royal cinclodes *Cinlodes aricomae*; Sevillano-Ríos *et al.* 2018). In New Zealand and Australia, there are no treeline specialists, and there is little evidence of zonation according to elevation in bird communities, with most forest species occurring from lowlands to the treeline (Green & Pickering 2002; Kerry Weston pers. comm.).

In part, the geographic variation in the occurrence of treeline specialists may be explained by evolutionary processes. In the tropical Andes, rates of endemism are high in the treeline ecotone zone, suggesting it has played an important role in diversification of the avifauna (Fjeldså & Irestedt 2009), which may explain why there are apparently more Andean treeline specialists. In temperate mountains, the treeline ecotone may simply be too narrow to promote speciation (Lewis & Starzomski 2015). For some, such as the boreal mountains of North Asia, the avifauna may have developed as an independent geological complex very recently and has not yet had time to evolve specialist species (Kishchinsky 1980).

In temperate and boreal mountains, there are some species that might be considered treeline specialists at a regional scale, that is, they are restricted to treelines within a particular geographical area, but they may be more generalist in other parts of their range. Climate-limited species may find suitable conditions in mountains at lower latitudes that are equivalent to lower elevation conditions at higher latitudes. For example, dunnock and lesser whitethroat are treeline species in the European Alps, but are widespread species of lowland ecotone habitats (including in farmland and gardens) in northern Europe. The grey-cheeked thrush *Catharus minimus* is particularly associated with the treeline ecotone (krummholz) in northeastern North American mountains (Sabo 1980), but has a widespread distribution, occurring in a range of forested habitat. Similarly, in boreal mountains at higher latitudes, there are many species that are local treeline specialists. In the North-East Siberian Mountains, the Siberian accentor *Prunella montanella* is one of the most abundant birds of the treeline ecotone, where whinchat *Saxicola rubetra* and Siberian rubythroat *Calliope calliope* are also characteristic species (Romanov *et al.* 2019a). Pallas's reed bunting *Emberiza pallasi* is the most typical species of subalpine shrub tundra of the Polar Urals (Golovatin & Paskhalny 2005), while bluethroat *Luscinia svecica* is the only species preferring the treeline ecotone in Finnish Mountains. In central Russia, bluethroat is also an ecotone species, being especially associated with Siberian alder *Alnus hirsuta* in the Putorana Plateau (Romanov 2003). Nevertheless, this species, like most of the above, can also be found in lowland habitats in other parts of its range.

In general, treeline species are therefore either widespread generalists, or they are associated with adjacent habitats. Lloyd *et al.* (2012) reported that the treeline community in the tropical Andes of southern Peru was mainly composed of cloud forest specialists, habitat generalists and a few puna grassland species. A similar pattern was found in the temperate Andes (Altamirano *et al.* 2020), where the treeline community was made up of mostly montane species, with a few alpine species. In Asian boreal mountains, most treeline ecotone species are montane species that also inhabit the sparser forests around the treeline (e.g., red-flanked bluetail *Tarsiger cyanurus*, dusky thrush *Turdus eunomus*, Siberian jay *Perisoreus infaustus*), or shrub nesting species not associated with any particular vegetation zone (e.g., yellow-browed warbler *Phylloscopus inornatus*, dusky warbler *P. fuscatus*), and there are few species that descend from the alpine zone to the treeline ecotone (Romanov 2013; Romanov *et al.* 2019a). In the Eastern Himalayas, Romanov *et al.* (2016) found a 52 per cent similarity between coniferous forest and treeline ecotone bird communities, and a 32 per cent similarity between ecotone and alpine zones. Here, although the treeline ecotone community was still mostly influenced by forest species, there was nonetheless a reasonable proportion of alpine zone birds found around the treeline. Martin *et al.* (2021) found that the ratio of forest to alpine species in the treeline ecotone varied according to geographic location, with comparable numbers of species (25–31 per cent) using both upper montane and subalpine habitats, but with a greater proportion of alpine species in the ecotone in the southern temperate Andes (24 per cent) compared to temperate mountains in northern Canada (10 per cent). Thus, while the evidence suggests that the treeline ecotone mostly consists of forest birds at their upper elevational limit, there are regions where this zone is dominated by species at their lower elevational limit.

There are some sub-species that can be considered as treeline specialists. For example, krummholz vegetation is preferred by the 'timberline' sub-species of Brewer's sparrow *Spizella breweri taverneri* at the treeline in the Rocky Mountains of Montana (Griffin *et al.* 2003) and in northern British Columbia. Subspecies of spotted nutcracker *Nucifraga caryocatactes kamtschatkensis* and pine grosbeak *Pinicola enucleator kamtschatkensis* are particularly associated with sparse 'elfin' forest around the treeline in Russia's far east (Kishchinsky 1980, Romanov *et al.* 2019c, d). The Alpine subspecies of ring ouzel *Turdus torquatus alpestris* is restricted to mosaic habitats around the treeline in central and southern European mountains and apparently also overwinters in similar habitats in Iberia and north Africa (Box 4.2).

Box 4.2   *Ecological Requirements of Alpine Ring Ouzels in Treeline Ecosystems and Implications of a Changing Environment*

Arnaud G. Barras & Raphaël Arlettaz

The alpine ring ouzel *Turdus torquatus alpestris* (Figure B4.2) qualifies as a treeline ecotone specialist, as it has a strong association with the mosaic of coniferous patches and alpine grasslands for breeding (von dem Bussche *et al.* 2008; Ciach & Mrowiec 2013). Although migratory, it also appears to be a mountain bird throughout its annual cycle, with stopover and wintering sites located in areas above 1,000 m, the latter in Iberia and North Africa (Barras *et al.* 2021a). The long tradition of cattle grazing in European mountain ranges, by expanding and maintaining the specific habitat mosaic of the treeline ecotone, has probably benefited ring ouzels. Progressive forest closure that follows pastoral abandonment thus represents a clear threat that may have contributed to recently observed population declines in Germany (Anger *et al.* 2020; Fumy & Fartmann 2021) and Switzerland (Knaus *et al.* 2018).

The species requires foraging sites with soft and rather moist soils, where a short and sparse grass layer facilitates access to the ground

Figure B4.2 Ring ouzel *Turdus torquatus* (Photo: A. Barras).

(Barras *et al.* 2020). Earthworms form the most important component of nestling diet, both in terms of total abundance (>80 per cent) and biomass (>90 per cent; Barras *et al.* 2021b). Earthworm availability can explain the species' habitat selection patterns, as well as the reported reduction in provisioning activity and efficiency of parental birds in dry and warm weather (Barras *et al.* 2021b). Overall, results from fine-grained studies underline the brevity of the optimal time window for ring ouzel reproduction – specific microhabitat characteristics vanish as the season advances due to the rapid growth of ground vegetation and progressive soil desiccation that follows the melt of the snow-pack. The species is thus likely to be particularly sensitive to rapid climatic shifts, both due to impacts on prey availability and to changes in the structure of its preferred habitat (Barras *et al.* 2021c; Fumy & Fartmann 2021).

Managed treeline ecotones, by providing a diverse and finely structured habitat matrix maintained through extensive livestock grazing, might buffer negative seasonal effects on food availability caused by warmer, drier conditions as the season progresses. Based on a country-wide predictive model from Switzerland, it appears that average ambient spring temperature is the main determinant of habitat suitability for ring ouzels, even at the home-range scale (Barras *et al.* 2021c), occurrence probability being highest at 5–10°C. Habitat variables including forest cover, low-productivity grasslands and the number of isolated trees, all of which showed non-linear associations with ring ouzel occurrence, were still ranked among the top predictors, although they were of much lower importance compared to temperature. Notably, realistic scenarios of pastoral abandonment are projected to have only a limited impact on the future distribution and abundance of breeding ring ouzels in Switzerland (Barras *et al.* in 2021c), despite their potentially marked effects on habitat structure at treeline elevations (Gehrig-Fasel *et al.* 2007). The potential spatial mismatch between the optimal climatic niche and a suitable habitat configuration, due to the predicted lag of treelines behind climate change (Körner 2012), could actually represent a more serious threat for ring ouzels in the long run. This raises the question of what type of habitat management might constitute the most appropriate conservation strategy for the ring ouzel in the European Alps, and for treeline bird species in general.

The evidence for true treeline specialist species (i.e., species that breed exclusively in the treeline ecotone) is generally weak, although there appear to be more potential candidate species in the Andes than in either Eurasia or North America. Treeline communities are thus for the most part made up of overlapping communities of forest and alpine zone species, rather than of species particularly associated with the ecotone. Nevertheless, this mixture of species from adjacent habitat zones can form distinct treeline bird communities.

4.4 Vegetation Structure

It has been hypothesized that the diversity of plant growth form and structure is a key element in influencing the bird community of the treeline ecotone (Jähnig *et al.* 2018). Correlations between measures of vegetation complexity and bird diversity (Terborgh 1977; Altamirano *et al.* 2020) or vegetation richness (Lewis & Starzomski 2015) have been found along broad elevation gradients, and in mountain scrub and steppe habitats (although not specifically treeline; Estades 1997). Altamirano *et al.* (2020) suggested that greater structural diversity at the treeline explained the peak in species and functional diversity in their study. However, there is no evidence that vegetation heterogeneity is associated with bird diversity within treeline ecotones (Laiolo *et al.* 2004; Jähnig *et al.* 2018). Furthermore, although foliage height diversity seemed a reasonable explanation for the patterns in diversity along the c. 3,000 m gradient considered in Terborgh's (1977) study, the patterns were actually more complex when considered according to different foraging guilds of birds which showed divergent responses. Foliage height diversity may therefore explain patterns in species diversity over gradients on a fairly large scale where there is a marked variation in gross vegetation structure.

It seems difficult to generalize about the effect of vegetation structural diversity on treeline bird diversity. Nevertheless, it is clear that the diversity of plant growth form and structure is a key element in influencing the abundance of some individual species of the treeline ecotone (Jähnig *et al.* 2018). The black grouse *Lyrurus tetrix* is a species typical of mosaic habitats around the treeline ecotone in the European Alps (Patthey *et al.* 2012). The likelihood of presence of this species declines as a single vegetation type becomes more dominant (Braunisch *et al.* 2016), which usually happens with both increasing and decreasing elevation (respectively, towards the alpine zone and towards closed canopy forest). Vegetation structure may also influence the choice of mating display strategy for black grouse, where greater shrub cover probably promotes solitary display rather than lekking (Chamberlain *et al.* 2012). Jähnig *et al.* (2018) similarly found associations between shrub cover and species occurrence of dunnock and Eurasian wren *Troglodytes troglodytes*, and shrub height heterogeneity was positively associated with the presence of tree pipit *Anthus trivialis* and wren presence.

4.5 Drivers of Reproductive Success and Survival

There have been few studies investigating factors that influence reproductive success of treeline ectone species. Nest predation was identified as the main cause of nest failure for three species (lesser whitethroat, common linnet and dunnock) within the treeline ecotone in the Western Italian Alps over a three-year period (Jähnig 2019). Nest failure due to predation has also been identified as a key driver of reproductive success for other ecotone species such as Szechenyi's monal-partridge *Tetraophasis szechenyii* (Pamuling Mountains; Zhang *et al.* 2011), mountain white-crowned sparrow *Zonotrichia leucophrys oriantha* (Sierra Nevada; Morton *et al.* 1993), Wilson's warbler *Cardellina pusilla* and Lincoln's sparrow *Melospiza lincolnii* (Rocky Mountains; Ammon 1995). In the European

Alps, parasitism by common cuckoos was also a significant cause of nest failure in dunnocks. Within a three-year period, annual parasitism rate varied between 12 and 36 per cent for dunnock nests (Jähnig 2019), although parasitism was not observed for dunnocks in the Malá Fatra Mountains, Slovakia (Jambor *et al.* 2011).

Masoero *et al.* (2016) hypothesized that nest predation could be higher in the proximity of the forest edge; using an artificial nest approach, they demonstrated that overall nest survival increased further away from the treeline. A similar result was found by Jähnig (2019) who assessed if nesting success within the ecotone was linked to habitat characteristics in the nest surroundings. The probability of daily nest failure was associated positively with the number of mature trees in the proximity of the nest for lesser whitethroat and dunnock. Similarly, lower reproductive success (juveniles/pair) was observed for willow ptarmigan *Lagopus lagopus* in survey areas dominated by mountain birch *Betula pubescens* than areas without or with little birch (Kvasnes *et al.* 2017). Masoero *et al.* (2016) suggested that these patterns may arise as more forested areas act as reservoirs for predators, which has potentially important implications regarding elevational shifts in treelines. However, other studies such as that by Klausen *et al.* (2010), who used artificial nests to estimate predation rates on ground nests of willow ptarmigan, demonstrated that along an elevational gradient from birch forest to low-alpine tundra, low-alpine habitat tended to have the highest predation rates which declined with decreasing elevation. Furthermore, no difference in predation risk among different habitat types (open forest, clearing and forest edge) was identified by Cukor *et al.* (2021) who used artificial nests to investigate nest predation risk on black grouse in mountain ranges in Czechia. It should be noted, however, that caution is needed in drawing inferences from studies on artificial nests (e.g., Willebrand & Marcström 1988).

Given the geographic variation observed for treeline-associated predation risk, it seems unlikely that particular habitat characteristics within the ecotone might be generally associated with nest failure. For some species such as willow ptarmigan, predation risk in certain geographic regions might even be linked with the population dynamics of alternative prey such as rodents (Angelstam *et al.* 1984), although these relationships seem to have weakened in recent decades (Henden *et al.* 2017; Ims *et al.* 2019).

As for many mountain birds, local weather conditions and stochastic events such as storms have been identified as additional causes of nest failure or reduced reproductive success for several ecotone species. Periods of harsh weather can cause increased nestling mortality (white-crowned sparrows; Morton 1993; DeSante & Saracco 2021) and abandonment of nesting attempts (dunnock; Jambor *et al.* 2011). Temperature and precipitation during the breeding season can also affect nesting productivity. In the European Alps, local weather conditions were found to affect reproductive success indirectly by influencing parental food provisioning rate and delivered biomass in ring ouzels (Box 4.2; Barras *et al.* 2021b). In a treeline ecotone breeding bird community in the Sierra Nevada, fledging success and fledgling numbers tended to be higher in years with cooler mean spring temperatures and higher minimum summer temperature (DeSante & Saracco 2021), with particularly marked effects in white-crowned sparrow (fledging success), American dusky flycatcher *Empidonax oberholseri* and dark-eyed junco (number of fledglings). The authors speculated that warm summer temperatures could have led to increased food resources during the chick-rearing period and that cold spring temperatures could have influenced predation rates due to reduced survival of nest predators such as the Belding's ground squirrel *Spermophilus beldingi*, lodgepole chipmunk *Tamias speciosus* and Douglas squirrel *Tamiasciurus douglasii*. Nevertheless, population change of treeline ecotone species was positively related to higher spring temperatures, which was possibly driven by upslope recruitment of first-year breeders and to a lesser extent dispersing adults. Nevertheless, there have been few published studies on either adult or juvenile survival rates in treeline species, with the exception of mountain white-crowned sparrows *Zonotrichia leucophrys oriantha*, where males often withdrew parental care for late-fledging nests. This resulted in significantly higher return rates of adult males in the following season, but also led to increased brood reduction and late-season nestlings which fledged at a smaller mass (Morton *et al.* 2004).

In summary, only a small number of studies of a limited geographic range (mainly Europe and North America) have focused on the mechanisms shaping reproductive success or adult and juvenile survival of ecotone species. Further research of a wider geographic range, especially in tropical treelines, is needed to understand whether demographic mechanisms that underpin population trends are acting on local scales or if similar mechanisms operate over wider geographic areas. Whilst there is some evidence that vegetation complexity and the proximity of the treeline influence predation rates of treeline birds, there is little evidence to suggest that treeline species are subject to any particular pressures on reproductive success or survival that are not widespread in mountain environments generally. Intensive studies that monitor nest success and estimate post-fledging and adult survival are needed to better understand the demographic factors driving population size and trend in treeline bird communities.

4.6 Anthropogenic Influences on the Treeline Ecotone Bird Community

4.6.1 Grazing

Livestock grazing has been practiced for several thousands of years in many mountain regions (e.g., the Andes, Kessler & Herzog 1998; the European Alps, Lichtenberger 1994), with a significant influence on the landscape. One of the most common effects is that the treeline is maintained at a lower elevation than its climatic limit (Gehrig-Fasel *et al.* 2007), in some cases, considerably so (e.g., Bazzi *et al.* 2015). Grazing may also serve to maintain open habitats when trees and shrubs have previously been cleared by logging or burning, resulting in largely deforested mountain habitats, as in many parts of the Scottish Highlands and the Picos di Europa, Spain.

Given that grazing tends to maintain habitat openness, its effects are generally positive for grassland nesting species, and negative for forest and shrub nesting species. For example, Laiolo *et al.* (2004) found that the abundance of shrub-nesting species (including dunnock, lesser whitethroat and garden warbler *Sylvia borin*) increased with increasing shrub cover and vegetation height, and declined with increasing grazing pressure. Bazzi *et al.* (2015) found positive effects of grazing on grassland species richness, but interestingly also on tree pipit density. This species seems to prefer 'parkland' habitats with mature trees and open grassland, hence grazing probably maintains a suitable ground layer by suppressing understory shrubs. Grazing can also affect trophic relationships; for example, reindeer *Rangifer tarandus* can limit the regeneration and growth of arctic willow *Salix glauca* in the mountains of Finnish Lapland which in turn reduces food availability for willow ptarmigan (den Herder *et al.* 2008).

Within mountain forests, edges created or maintained by pastoral activities had higher species richness than those created by ski-pistes (Laiolo & Rolando 2005). In part, this is due to the high-contrast edges created by ski runs, whereas transitional shrub-dominated areas, closer in character to that of the natural treeline ecotone, are more common in forest fragmented by pastoral activity. Some typical ecotone species were less abundant or absent from ski-piste edges, for example, whinchat and rock bunting *Emberiza cia.*

4.6.2 Land Abandonment

In some regions, in particular in the European Alps, traditional grazing practices involving transhumance are declining, meaning that treelines are moving rapidly upslope (Gehrig-Fasel *et al.* 2007). The effect of this will likely increase species richness as forests encroach on more open habitats (Laiolo *et al.* 2004; see above). However, land abandonment is likely to have negative effects on non-forest species (Chamberlain *et al.* 2016), in particular by impacting ground-nesting grassland birds through habitat loss. Grazing abandonment may also have implications for more typical treeline species. For example, increases in shrub cover reduce habitat suitability for black grouse by reducing spatial vegetation complexity (Braunisch *et al.* 2016). Laiolo *et al.* (2004) also found that ecotone species were more abundant in lightly grazed areas above 1,900 m, suggesting that low intensity grazing may benefit species dependent on a habitat mosaic.

4.6.3 Fire

Fire may be a natural driver of forest fragmentation at treelines, for example in the Rocky Mountains (Körner 2012). It is, however, more commonly caused by human intervention and may be used as a management tool to maintain open habitats for livestock, as happens in the Andes (Kessler & Herzog 1998). Indeed, the vegetation of the páramo/forest ecotone in the northern Andes has been almost completely modified by burning (Robbins *et al.* 1994). Uncontrolled burning is an important factor responsible for the degradation of Andean habitats, which has a major effect on habitat structure (e.g., Novoa *et al.* 2021). In unburnt areas, the transition from forest to alpine zone grasslands is gradual, and extends over several hundred metres, whereas in burnt areas, closed forest changes abruptly to open grassland, with sometimes fire-resistant adult *Polylepis* trees remaining, while young trees are killed by fire (Kessler & Herzog 1998). This has implications for the bird community as the reduction or removal of the natural ecotone causes reduced abundance of many species, and disappearance in a few (e.g., scribble-tailed canastero *Asthenes maculicauda*, grass wren *Cistothorus platensis*; Kessler & Herzog 1998).

In Siberia, fires take on enormous proportions. Large areas of forest are burnt every year (Tsvetkov & Buryak 2014), mostly from anthropogenic sources (often accidental). For example, in 2019, fires occurred on more than 13 million hectares of the Siberian taiga (Bondur *et al.* 2020). Such fires not only affect the continuous forest belt, but also occur up to the treeline ecotone. Indeed, the onset of fires is associated with more open habitats on treeless southern slopes. Fire frequency in mountain forests is, however, generally lower than in lowland forests, but the effects are more pronounced (Farber 2012). If the treeline is formed by coniferous trees such as larch which have some resistance to fire, a significant change in the vegetation appearance occurs with relatively intense fires, while dark coniferous species (fir, cedar) are killed even in low intensity fires. In the treeline ecotones formed of elfin cedar communities, the fires can reach a high intensity due to the habitat characteristics of this vegetation community (dry stony ground with very weak soils, a high density of elfin shrubs). As a result, the recovery of the elfin trees is slower than that of trees in the forest zone (Gamova 2014). Episodic intense fires in such Siberian habitats lead to a lowering of the upper forest boundary (Evdokimenko 2009) and thus can serve to maintain the mosaic of the treeline ecotone, although effects on birds are dependent on the frequency and severity of fires. For example, the greatest abundance of olive-backed pipits has been recorded in fairly recently burned areas, where shrub thickets occur with standing dead trees, from which the pipits perform songflights (Romanov *et al.* 2019a).

4.6.4 Climate Change

One of the main impacts of climate change on mountain birds is likely to be the effects on habitats due to treelines shifting towards higher elevations (Freeman *et al.* 2018), which will impact on grassland birds in particular, as their habitats shrink towards mountain summits (Chamberlain *et al.* 2013; Lewis & Starzomski 2015). However, not all mountain species are shifting distributions in the same way – evidence from both western and eastern North America has shown several species shifting downslope (Tingley *et al.* 2012; DeLuca & King 2017). Similarly, the consequences of climate change for treeline zone birds are unclear, and evidence thus far suggests a variety of responses (e.g., Rocchia *et al.* 2018), with no consistent predictions of future distribution (Chamberlain *et al.* 2013). However, potential mechanisms that might cause impacts on suitable nesting habitat and on prey availability have been identified. For example, dunnock appear to prefer nesting in rhododendron and do not use juniper in the Western Italian Alps (Jähnig *et al.* 2018), but model projections suggest rhododendron will decrease in the future (Komac *et al.* 2016) and thus dunnock may decline unless they can shift their nesting substrate preferences to other species. Similarly, the ring ouzel's current dependence on damp, penetrable soils for foraging could potentially be compromised if climate change leads to drier conditions in early spring (Box 4.2; Barras *et al.* 2020). Changing temperature and precipitation regimes under future climate change could also influence the distribution and productivity of predator species as well as the availability of suitable nesting and foraging habitat. These issues and potential consequences are addressed comprehensively in Chapter 6.

4.7 Conclusions

Treeline bird communities do not show evidence of consistent characteristics in different geographic areas. There was no evidence of an overall higher species richness in the treeline ecotone compared to adjacent habitats; rather, the most common pattern was of a decline from the montane forest zone to the alpine zone, but there was nevertheless a wide range of altitudinal responses in species richness (Appendix 4.1). There was also no evidence that particular nesting behaviour, in terms of nest site selection, was associated with this zone. Furthermore, outside the Andes there are very few, if any, treeline ecotone specialist species. The bird communities of the treeline ecotone therefore seem to have few typical characteristics that are common to mountain treelines globally. Rather, they show a fairly marked degree of geographic variation that likely depends on many factors, including both larger scale and local climatic and topographic factors that lead to a wide variation in treeline ecotone types, as well as the evolutionary history of the species in a given location.

The mountain treeline ecosystem is important as a barometer of environmental change (Nagy & Grabherr 2009; Körner 2012), yet from an ornithological perspective, it is not especially well served by existing research. Several studies have put the treeline ecotone bird community in the broader context of the elevation gradient (e.g., see references in Appendix 4.1), although these represent a wide range of survey methods, from small-scale point counts to larger-scale species inventories, and a range of classifications (mostly descriptive, a few quantitative). Understanding what causes the broad geographic variation in patterns could be achieved by adopting consistent survey methods and analytical approaches in treeline ecotones of different geographic regions (as per Martin *et al.* 2021), which would thus ensure that comparisons are not confounded by different methodological biases or different definitions of the treeline ecotone. Furthermore, there is very little information, in terms of finer-scale studies, on the precise habitat features that dictate species occurrence and abundance, or on the key drivers of reproductive success or annual survival in the treeline ecotone. In order to better understand the capacity of the treeline ecotone to cope with future environmental changes, and its potential role to buffer these effects of change in the habitats above and below, it is essential that the research community develops a better understanding of the demographic mechanisms underpinning population changes in this diverse and interesting habitat.

Acknowledgements

We would like to thank Rob Fuller and Bill DeLuca for their highly constructive comments on an earlier version of this chapter. We are very grateful to the following for giving us advice and helping us track down data on treeline ecotone birds: Tomás Altamirano, Chiara Bettega, Mattia Brambilla, Aleksi Lehikoinen and Kerry Weston. We would also like to thank Laura Morales Moreno whose help was essential in producing Plate 5. We owe a particular debt of gratitude to Alexey Romanov for making available information from the many expeditions he has led in the eastern Asian mountains.

Appendix 4.1

Species richness of treeline ecotone bird communities and adjacent forest and alpine zones. Studies were included which estimated species richness separately for montane forest, treeline ecotone and alpine zones according to our definitions, following a systematic search on Web of Science. Region: Arc = Arctic, Bor = boreal, Tem = temperate, Tro = tropical or subtropical. Latitude is the approximate central point where multiple sites in a region were covered. Region is based largely on latitude, although in some cases, this is also dictated in part by longitude (e.g., the boreal zone is at lower latitudes in eastern than in western Canada). [P]point-level estimate; all others are site-level. ★Martin et al. (2021) and Altamirano et al. (2020) were carried out in the same geographic region, but covered different study sites; ★★the same for Boyle & Martin (2015) and Martin et al. (2021). ★★★In some cases, different maximum and minimum treeline elevations are given to represent the variation caused by local climate and topography within a given mountain range.

Location	Latitude	Region	Elevation of treeline ecotone (m)	Bird species richness (no. species)			References
				Forest	Treeline	Alpine	
Central-Western Peruvian Andes	9.0°	Tro	2,100–3,300	190	110	10	Sevillano-Ríos & Rodewald 2017, 2021
				20[P]	30[P]	5[P]	
Cuzco, Peru eastern Andes slope	13.0°	Tro	2,500–3,000	65	40	20	Jankowski et al. 2012
South-Eastern Peruvian Andes	13.2°	Tro	2,500–2,900	50.4[P]	51.1[P]	20[P]	Lloyd et al. 2012; Dehling et al. 2014
Bolivian Andes	17.8°	Tro	3,000–3,500	60	20	0	Kessler et al. 2001; Herzog et al. 2005
Eastern Himalayas	27.9°	Tro	3,400–3,860	68	51	15	Romanov et al. 2016
South temperate Andes, Chile★	38.9°	Tem	1,300–1,768	39	46	39	Martin et al. 2021
South temperate Andes, Chile★	39.0°	Tem	1,300–1,768	6.73[P]	6.80[P]	2.55[P]	Altamirano. et. al. 2020
Western Italian Alps	45.0°	Tem	2,000–2,300	27	44	17	Jähnig et al. 2018, 2020
				6.25[P]	4.58[P]	2.04[P]	
Central Italian Alps	46.0°	Tem	1,700–2,250	22	41	21	Brambilla & Pedrini 2016
				6.14[P]	3.55[P]	1.49[P]	

(cont.)

(cont.)

Location	Latitude	Region	Elevation of treeline ecotone (m)	Bird species richness (no. species)			References
				Forest	Treeline	Alpine	
Altai	47.8°	Tem	1,200/1,800–1,500/2,200★★★	194	135	103	Tsybulin 2009
British Columbia, Canada★★	51.0°	Tem	1,500	55 / 19.75[P]	75 / 23.95[P]	71 / 14.39[P]	Boyle & Martin 2015
Mealy Mountains, Canada	53.4°	Bor	510–982	5.2[P]	3.4[P]	2.6[P]	Lewis & Starzomski 2015
British Columbia, Canada★★	54.8°	Tem	1,543	59	37	31	Martin et al. 2021
Aldan Highlands	58.6°	Bor	800–1,500	165	60	28	Shemyakin et al. 2021
Polar and Subpolar Urals	62.5°	Bor	555/615–810/820★★★	120	61	52	Selivanova 2002; Golovatin & Paskhalny 2005
Koryak Upland	62.5°	Bor	200/250–360/560★★★	90	81	24	Romanov 2013; Romanov et al. 2019a, c
Suntar-Khayata Range (North)	62.6°	Bor	1,300–1,500	61	10	9	Melikhova 2018; Romanov et al. 2019c
Kolyma Upland (South)	63.0°	Bor	600–1,300	110	36	22	Melikhova 2018; Romanov et al. 2019 b, c
Chersky Range (South)	64.7°	Bor	600–1,300	73	36	16	Melikhova 2018; Romanov et al. 2019c
Verkhoyansk Range (South)	67.0°	Bor	1,000–1,300	56	38	15	Melikhova 2018; Romanov et al. 2019c
Putorana Plateau	68.7°	Bor	550–800	129	52	68	Romanov et al. 2018, 2019c
Finnish mountains	69.0°	Bor/Arc	150–550	21	34	31	Lehikoinen et al. 2014
Anabar Plateau	70.0°	Bor/Arc	200–250	69	14	18	Pospelov 2007

References

Abebe, A.F., Cai, T., Wale, M., *et al.* (2019) Factors determining species richness patterns of breeding birds along an elevational gradient in the Horn of Africa region. *Ecology and Evolution*, **9**, 9609–9623.

Able, K.P. & Noon, B.R. (1976) Avian community structure along elevational gradients in the Northeastern United States. *Oecologia*, **26**, 275–294.

Acharya, B.K., Sanders, N.J., Vijayan, L. & Chettri, B. (2011) Elevational gradients in bird diversity in the Eastern Himalaya: an evaluation of distribution patterns and their underlying mechanisms. *PLoS ONE*, **6**, e29097.

Altamirano, T.A., de Zwaan, D.R., Ibarra, J.T., Wilson, S. & Martin, K. (2020) Treeline ecotones shape the distribution of avian species richness and functional diversity in south temperate mountains. *Scientific Reports*, **10**, 18428.

Ammon, E.M. (1995) Reproductive Strategies and Factors determining Nest Success in Subalpine Ground-Nesting Passerines. PhD Thesis, University of Colorado, Boulder.

Angelstam, P., Lindström, E. & Widén, P. (1984) Role of predation in short-term population fluctuations of some birds and mammals in Fennoscandia. *Oecologia*, **62**, 199–208

Anger, F., Dorka, U., Anthes, N., Dreiser, C. & Förschler, M.I. (2020) Bestandsrückgang und Habitatnutzung bei der Alpenringdrossel *Turdus torquatus alpestris* im Nordschwarzwald (Baden-Württemberg). *Ornithologischer Beobachter*, **117**, 38–53.

Bader, M.Y., Llambì, L.D., Case, B.S., *et al.* (2020) A global framework for linking alpine-treeline ecotone patterns to underlying processes. *Ecography*, **43**, 1–24.

Barras, A.G., Marti, S., Ettlin, S., *et al.* (2020) The importance of seasonal environmental factors in the foraging habitat selection of Alpine Ring Ouzels *Turdus torquatus alpestris*. *Ibis*, **162**, 505–519.

Barras, A.G., Liechti, F. & Arlettaz, R. (2021a) Seasonal and daily movement patterns of an alpine passerine suggest high flexibility in relation to environmental conditions. *Journal of Avian Biology*, **52**, e02860.

Barras, A.G., Niffenegger, C.A., Candolfi, I., Hunziker, Y.A. & Arlettaz, R. (2021b) Nestling diet and parental food provisioning in a declining mountain passerine reveal high sensitivity to climate change. *Journal of Avian Biology*, **52**, e02649

Barras, A.G., Braunisch, V. & Arlettaz, R. (2021c) Predictive models of distribution and abundance of a threatened mountain species show that impacts of climate change overrule those of land use change. *Diversity and Distributions*, **27**, 989–1004.

Bazzi, G., Foglini, C., Brambilla, M., Saino, N. & Rubolini, D. (2015) Habitat management effects on Prealpine grassland bird communities. *Italian Journal of Zoology*, **82**, 251–261.

Bondur, V.G., Mokhov, I.I., Voronova, O.S. & Sitnov, S.A. (2020) Satellite monitoring of Siberian wildfires and their effects: features of 2019 anomalies and trends of 20-year changes. *Doklady Earth Sciences*, **492**, 370–375.

Borsdorf, A. & Stadel, C. (2015) *The Andes: A Geographical Portrait.* Cham: Springer.

Braunisch, V., Patthey, P. & Arlettaz, R. (2016) Where to combat shrub encroachment in Alpine timberline ecosystems: combining remotely sensed vegetation information with species habitat modelling. *PLoS ONE*, **11**, e0164318.

Brambilla, M. & Pedrini, P. (2016) Modelling at the edge: habitat types driving the occurrence of common forest bird species at the altitudinal margin of their range. *Ornis Fennica*, **93**, 88–99.

Boyle, A.W. & Martin, K. (2015) The conservation value of high elevation habitats to North American migrant birds. *Biological Conservation*, **192**, 461–476.

Chamberlain, D.E., Bocca, M., Migliore, L., Caprio, E. & Rolando, A. (2012) The dynamics of alternative male mating tactics in a population of Black Grouse *Tetrao tetrix* in the Italian Alps. *Journal of Ornithology*, **153**, 999–1009.

Chamberlain, D.E., Negro, M., Caprio, E. & Rolando, A. (2013) Assessing the sensitivity of alpine birds to potential future changes in habitat and climate to inform management strategies. *Biological Conservation*, **167**, 127–135.

Chamberlain, D.E., Pedrini, P., Brambilla, M., Rolando, A. & Girardello, M. (2016) Identifying key conservation threats to Alpine birds through expert knowledge. *PeerJ*, **4**, e1723.

Ciach, M. & Mrowiec, W. (2013) Habitat selection of the Ring Ouzel *Turdus torquatus* in the Western Carpathians: the role of the landscape mosaic. *Bird Study*, **60**, 22–34

Cukor, J., Linda, R., Andersen, O., *et al.* (2021) Evaluation of spatio-temporal patterns of predation risk to forest grouse nests in the central European mountain regions. *Animals*, **11**, 316.

Davies, N.B. (1992) *Dunnock Behaviour and Social Evolution*. Oxford: Oxford University Press.

Dehling, D.M., Fritz, S.A., Töpfer, T., *et al.* (2014) Functional and phylogenetic diversity and assemblage structure of frugivorous birds along an elevational gradient in the tropical Andes. *Ecography*, **37**, 1047–1055.

DeLuca, W.V. & King, D.I. (2017) Montane birds shift downslope despite recent warming in the northern Appalachian Mountains. *Journal of Ornithology*, **158**, 493–505.

den Herder, M., Virtanen, R. & Roininen, H. (2008) Reindeer herbivory reduces willow growth and grouse forage in a forest-tundra ecotone. *Basic and Applied Ecology*, **9**, 324–331.

DeSante, D.F. & Saracco, J.F. (2021) Climate variation drives dynamics and productivity of a subalpine breeding bird community. *Ornithological Applications*, **123**, 1–16.

Estades, C.F. (1997) Bird-habitat relationships in a vegetational gradient in the Andes of central Chile. *Condor*, **99**, 719–727.

Evdokimenko, M.D. (2009) Pyrogenic digression of larch forests of Transbaikalia and Northern Mongolia. *Forest Journal*, **4**, 12–18. [In Russian]

Farber, S.K. (2012) Impact of fires on forests of Eastern Siberia. *Forest Taxation and Forest Management*, **1**, 131–141. [In Russian]

Fjeldså, J. & Irestedt, M. (2009) Diversification of the South American avifauna: patterns and implications for conservation in the Andes. *Annals of the Missouri Botanical Garden*, **96**, 398–409.

Freeman, B.G., Scholer, M.N., Ruiz-Gutierrez, V. & Fitzpatrick, J.W. (2018) Climate change causes upslope shifts and mountaintop extirpations in a tropical bird community. *Proceedings of the National Academy of Sciences*, **115**, 11982–11987.

Fumy, F. & Fartmann, T. (2021) Climate and land-use change drive habitat loss in a mountain bird species. *Ibis*, **163**, 1189–1206.

Gamova, N.S. (2014) Post-fire vegetation changes of Central Khamar-Daban (Southern Baikal Region). *Problems of Botany of South Siberia and Mongolia – XII International Scientific and Practical Conference*, pp. 55–59. [In Russian]

García-Moreno, J., Arctander, P. & Fjeldså, J. (1999) A case of rapid diversification in the Neotropics: phylogenetic relationships among Cranioleuca spinetails (Aves: Furnariidae). *Molecular Phylogenetics and Evolution*, **12**, 273–281.

García-Navas, V., Sattler, T., Schmid, H. & Ozgul, A. (2020) Temporal homogenization of functional and beta diversity in bird communities of the Swiss Alps. *Diversity and Distributions*, **26**, 900–911.

Gehrig-Fasel, J., Guisan, A. & Zimmermann, N.E. (2007) Tree line shifts in the Swiss Alps: climate change or land abandonment? *Journal of Vegetation Science*, **18**, 571–582.

Golovatin, M.G. & Paskhalny, S.P. (2005) *Birds of the Polar Urals*. Ekaterinburg: Ural University Publishing House. [In Russian]

Green, K. & Pickering, C.M. (2002) A scenario for mammal and bird diversity in the Snowy Mountains of Australia in relation to climate change. In *Mountain Biodiversity. A Global Assessment*. Körner, C. & Spehn, E.M. (eds.). London: Parthenon, pp. 239–248.

Griffin, S.C., Walker, B.L. & Hart, M.M. (2003) Using GIS to guide field surveys for timberline sparrows in northwest Montana. *Northwest Science*, **77**, 54–63.

Harsch, M.A., Hulme, P.E., McGlone, M.S. & Duncan, R.P. (2009) Are treelines advancing? A global meta-analysis of treeline response to climate warming. *Ecology Letters*, **12**, 1040–1049.

Henden, J.A., Ims, R.A., Fuglei, E. & Pedersen, Å.Ø. (2017) Changed Arctic-alpine food web interactions under rapid climate warming: implication for ptarmigan research. *Wildlife Biology*, **SP1**, 1–11.

Herzog, S.K., Kessler, M. & Back, K. (2005) The elevational gradient in Andean bird species richness at the local scale: a foothill peak and a high-elevation plateau. *Ecography*, **28**, 209–222.

Hoch, G. & Körner, C. (2005) Growth, demography and carbon relations of *Polylepis* trees at the world's highest treeline. *Functional Ecology*, **19**, 941–951.

Iijima, D. & Morimoto, G. (2021) Bird community heterogeneity along four gradients of different orientations on a temperate mountain. *Ornithological Science*, **20**, 65–82.

Ims, R.A., Henden, J.-A., Strømeng, M.A., *et al.* (2019) Arctic greening and bird nest predation risk across tundra ecotones. *Nature Climate Change*, **9**, 607–610

Jähnig (2019) Effects of Vegetation Structure and Microclimate on the Bird Community of an Alpine Treeline Ecotone. PhD Thesis, University of Turin.

Jähnig, S., Alba, R., Vallino, C., *et al.* (2018) The contribution of broadscale and finescale habitat structure to the distribution and diversity of birds in an Alpine forest-shrub ecotone. *Journal of Ornithology*, **159**, 747–759.

Jähnig, S., Sander, M.M., Caprio, E., *et al.* (2020) Microclimate affects the distribution of grassland birds, but not forest birds, in an alpine environment. *Journal of Ornithology*, **161**, 677–689.

Jambor, R., Baláž, M. & Kocian, L. (2011) Contribution to the knowledge of nest success of the Hedge Sparrow (*Prunella modularis*) in a sub-alpine zone of the Malá Fatra Mts. (NW Slovakia). *Tichodroma*, **23**, 7–12.

Jankowski, J.E., Merkord, C.L., Farfan Rios, W., *et al.* (2012) The relationship of tropical bird communities to tree species composition and vegetation structure along an Andean elevational gradient. *Journal of Biogeography*, **40**, 950–962.

Kark, S. Allnutt, T.S., Levin, N., Manne, L.L. & Williams, P.H. (2007) The role of transitional areas as avian biodiversity centres. *Global Ecology and Biogeography*, **16**, 187–196.

Kendeigh, S.C. & Fawver, B.J. (1981) Breeding bird populations in the Great Smoky Mountains, Tennessee and North Carolina. *Wilson Bulletin*, **93**, 218–242.

Kessler, M. & Herzog, S.K. (1998) Conservation status in Bolivia of timberline habitats, elfin forest and their birds. *Cotinga*, **10**, 50–54.

Kessler, M., Herzog, S.K., Fjeldså, J. & Bach, K. (2001) Species richness and endemism of plant and bird communities along two gradients of elevation, humidity and land use in the Bolivian Andes. *Diversity and Distributions*, **7**, 61–77.

Klausen, K.B., Pedersen, Å.Ø., Yoccoz, N.G. & Ims, R.A. (2010) Prevalence of nest predators in a sub-Arctic ecosystem. *European Journal of Wildlife Research*, **56**, 221–232.

Kishchinsky, A.A. (1980) *Birds of the Koryak Upland*. Moscow: Nauka. [In Russian]

Knaus, P., Antoniazza, S., Wechsler, S., *et al.* (2018) Swiss Breeding Bird Atlas 2013–2016. *Distribution and Population Trends of Birds in Switzerland and Liechtenstein*. Sempach: Swiss Ornithological Institute.

Komac, B., Esteban, P., Trapero, L. & Caritg, R. (2016) Modelization of the current and future habitat suitability of *Rhododendron ferrugineum* using potential snow accumulation. *PLoS ONE*, **11**, e0147324.

Körner, C. (2003) *Alpine Plant Life*. Berlin: Springer.

Körner, C. (2007) Climatic treelines: conventions, global patterns, causes. *Erdkunde*, **61**, 316–324.

Körner, C. (2012) Alpine Treelines. *Functional Ecology of the Global High Elevation Tree Limits*. Basel: Springer.

Körner, C. & Paulsen, J. (2004) A world-wide study of high altitude treeline temperatures. *Journal of Biogeography*, **31**, 713–732.

Kvasnes, M.A.J., Pedersen, H.C., Storaas, T. & Nilsen, E.B. (2017) Vegetation type and demography of low density willow ptarmigan populations. *The Journal of Wildlife Management*, **81**, 174–181.

Laiolo, P. (2004) Diversity and structure of the bird community overwintering in the Himalayan subalpine zone: is conservation compatible with tourism? *Biological Conservation*, **115**, 251–262.

Laiolo, P. & Rolando, A. (2005) Forest bird diversity and ski-runs: a case of negative edge effect. *Animal Conservation*, **7**, 9–16.

Laiolo, P., Dondero, F., Ciliento, E. & Rolando, A. (2004) Consequences of pastoral abandonment for the structure and diversity of the alpine avifauna. *Journal of Applied Ecology*, **41**, 294–304.

Lehikoinen, A., Green, M., Husby, M., Kålås, J.A. & Lindström, Å. (2014) Common montane birds are declining in northern Europe. *Journal of Avian Biology*, **45**, 3–14.

Lewis, K.P. & Starzomski, B.M. (2015) Bird communities and vegetation associations across a treeline ecotone in the Mealy Mountains, Labrador, which is an understudied part of the boreal forest. *Canadian Journal of Zoology*, **93**, 477–486.

Lichtenberger, E. (1994) Die Alpen in Europa. Österreochiske Academie der Wissenshaften. *Veröffentlichungen der Kommision für Humanökologie*, **5**, 53–86.

Lloyd, H., Sevillano-Ríos, S., Marsden, S.J. & Valdéz-Velásquez, A. (2012) Bird community composition across an Andean tree-line ecotone. *Austral Ecology*, **37**, 470–478.

Lu, X., Liang, E., Wang, Y., Babst, F. & Camarero, J.J. (2021) Mountain treelines climb slowly despite rapid climate warming. *Global Ecology and Biogeography*, **30**, 305–315.

Martin, T.E. & Karr, J.R. (1986) Patch utilization by migrating birds: resource orientated? *Ornis Scandinavica*, **17**, 165–174.

Martin, K.M., Altamirano, T.A., de Zwaan, D.R., *et al.* (2021) Avian ecology and community structure across elevation gradients: the importance of high latitude temperate mountain habitats for conserving biodiversity in the Americas. *Global Ecology and Conservation*, **30**, e01799.

Masoero, G., Maurino, L., Rolando, A. & Chamberlain, D. (2016) The effect of treeline proximity on predation pressure: an experiment with artificial nests along elevational gradients in the European Alps. *Bird Study*, **63**, 395–405.

Miehe, G., Miehe, S. & Schültz, F. (2009) Early human impact in the forest ecotone of southern High Asia (Hindu Kush, Himalaya). *Quaternary Research*, **71**, 255–265.

Melikhova, E.V. (2018) *Geography of Bird Fauna of North-East Siberia Mountains.* PhD thesis, Lomonosov Moscow State University, Moscow. [In Russian]

Mikhailov, K.E. (2020) Small songbirds in the high belts of the Himalayas (Nepal): vertical distribution and biotope selection mechanism. In *Nepal: A View from Russia. Collection of Scientific and Popular Science Articles*, pp. 163–181. [In Russian]

Mollet, P., Bollmann, K., Braunisch, V. & Arlettaz, R. (2018) Subalpine coniferous forests of Europe. Avian communities in European high-altitude woodlands. In *Ecology and Conservation of Forest Birds*. Mikusiński, G., Roberge, J.-M. & Fuller, R.J. (eds.). Cambridge: Cambridge University Press, pp. 231–252.

Morton, M.L., Sockman, K.W. & Peterson, L.E. (1993) Nest predation in the Mountain White-Crowned Sparrow. *Condor*, **95**, 72–82.

Morton, M.L., Pereyra, M.E., Crandall, J.D., MacDougall-Shackleton, E.A. & Hahn, T.P. (2004) Reproductive effort and return rates in the Mountain White-Crowned Sparrow. *Condor*, **106**, 131–138.

Naccarella, A., Morgan, J.W., Cutler, S.C. & Venn, S.E. (2020) Alpine treeline ecotone stasis in the face of recent climate change and disturbance by fire. *PLoS ONE*, **15**, e0231339.

Nagy, L. & Grabherr, G. (2009) *The Biology of Alpine Habitats.* Oxford: Oxford University Press.

Novoa, F.J., Altamirano, T.A., Bonacic, C., Martin, K. & Ibarra, J.T. (2021) Fire regimes shape biodiversity: responses of avian guilds to burned forests in Andean temperate ecosystems of southern Chile. *Avian Conservation and Ecology*, **16**, 22.

Odum, E.P. & Barrett, G.W. (2005) *Fundamentals of Ecology* (5th Edition). Belmont: Brooks/Cole.

Patterson, B.D., Stolz, D.F., Solari, S., Fitzpatrick, J.W. & Pacheco, V. (1993) Contrasting patterns of elevational zonation for birds and mammals in the Andes of southeastern Peru. *Journal of Biogeography*, **25**, 593–607.

Patthey, P., Signorell, N., Rotelli, L. & Arlettaz R. (2012) Vegetation structural and compositional heterogeneity as a key feature in Alpine Black Grouse micro-habitat selection: conservation management implications. *European Journal of Wildlife Research*, **58**, 59–70.

Pospelov, I.N. (2007) Avifauna of the Western part of the Anabar Plateau. In Biodiversity of Ecosystems of the Putorana Plateau and Adjacent Territories. Collection of Scientific Papers, pp. 114–153. [In Russian]

Quispe-Melgar, H.R., Sevillano-Ríos, C.S., Romo, *et al.* (2020) The Central Andes of Peru: a key area for the conservation of *Polylepis* forest biodiversity. *Journal of Ornithology*, **161**, 217–228.

Rahbek, C. (1995) The elevational gradient of species richness: a uniform pattern? *Ecography*, **18**, 200–205.

Requena, E., Alba, R. & Chamberlain, D. (2022) Avalanche tracks are key habitats for the Rock Bunting *Emberiza cia* in the Alps. *Ardeola*, **69**, 203–217.

Robbins, M.B., Krabbe, N., Rosenberg, G.H. & Molina, F.S. (1994) The treeline avifauna at Cerro Mongus, Prov. Carchi, Northeastern Ecuador. *Proceedings of the Academy of Natural Sciences of Philadelphia*, **145**, 209–216.

Rocchia, E., Luppi, M., Dondino, O., Orioli, V. & Bani, L. (2018) Can the effect of species ecological traits on birds' altitudinal changes differ between geographic areas? *Acta Oecologica*, **92**, 26–34.

Rodewald, P.G. & Brittingham, M.C. (2004) Stopover habitats of landbirds during fall: use of edge-dominated and early-successional forests. *Auk*, **121**, 1040–1055.

Romanov, A.A. (2003) *Avifauna of the Lake Basins of the Western Putorana Plateau.* Moscow: Chermetinformatsiya Printing House. [In Russian]

Romanov, A.A. (2013) *Bird Fauna of the Mountains of the Asian Subarctic: Principles of Development and Dynamics.* Moscow: Birds Russia. [In Russian]

Romanov, A.A., Koblik, E.A., Melikhova, E.V., *et al.* (2016) Richness in bird species of the Eastern Himalayas in early spring. *Contemporary Problems of Ecology*, **9**, 529–534.

Romanov, A.A., Tarasov, V.V., Melikhova, E.V., Timchenko, A.S., Zarubina, M.A. & Yakovlev V.O. (2018) Avifauna of the Lake Bogatyr-Khuolu basin (the northwest of the Putorana Plateau, the Krasnoyarsk region). *Fauna of the Urals and Siberia*, **2**, 92–104. [In Russian]

Romanov, A.A., Melikhova, E.V. & Zarubina, M.A. (2019a) *Birds of North Asia Mountains: 2010–2018 Research Results.* Moscow: Birds Russia. [In Russian]

Romanov, A.A., Melikhova, E.V., Zarubina, M.A., Miklin, N.A. & Yakolev, V.O. (2019b) Avifauna of mountains in Northeastern Siberia. *Contemporary Problems of Ecology*, **12**, 339–345.

Romanov, A.A., Astakhova, M.A., Miklin, N.A. & Shemyakin E.V. (2019c) Geography of avifauna in the northern parts of the Koryak Highland. *Moscow University Bulletin. Series 5. Geography*, **1**, 53–60. [In Russian]

Romanov, A.A., Melikhova, E.V., Miklin, N.A. & Yakovlev, V.O. (2019d) An analysis of the bird fauna and population in the southern spurs of Kolyma Highland. *Zoological Journal*, **98**, 915–927. [In Russian]

Sabo, S.R. (1980) Niche and habitat relations in bird communities of the White Mountains of New Hampshire. *Ecological Monographs*, **50**, 241–259.

Selivanova, N.P. (2002) Current status and distribution of birds in the altitudinal belts of the Subpolar Urals. *Komi Institute of Biology SC UB RAS Bulletin*, **7**, 10–13. [In Russian]

Sevillano-Ríos, C.S. & Rodewald, A.D. (2017) Avian community structure and habitat use of *Polylepis* forests along an elevation gradient. *PeerJ*, **5**, e3220.

Sevillano-Ríos, C.S. & Rodewald, A.D. (2021) Responses of *Polylepis* birds to patch and landscape attributes in the High Andes. *Neotropical Biodiversity*, **7**, 5–22.

Sevillano-Ríos, C.S., Rodewald, A.D. & Morales, L.V. (2018) Ecología y conservación de las aves asociadas con *Polylepis*: ¿qué sabemos de esta comunidad cada vez más vulnerable? *Ecología Austral*, **28**, 216–228.

Sevillano-Ríos, C.S., Rodewald, A. & Morales, L.V. (2020) Alpine birds of South America. In *Encyclopedia of the World's Biomes*. Goldstein, M.I. & DellaSalla, D.A. (eds.). Amsterdam: Elsevier.

Shemyakin, E.V., Vartapetov, L.G., Isaev, A.P., Larionov, A.G. & Egorov, N.N. (2021) An analysis of the avifauna of the Aldan Highlands, northeast of the Baikal Mountainous Country. *Zoological Journal*, **100,** 770–789. [In Russian]

Terborgh, J. (1977) Bird species diversity on an Andean elevational gradient. *Ecology*, **58**, 1007–1019.

Tingley, M.W., Koo, M.S., Moritz, C., Rush, A.C. & Beissinger, S.R. (2012) The push and pull of climate change causes heterogeneous shifts in avian elevational ranges. *Global Change Biology*, **18**, 3279–3290.

Tsvetkov, P.A. & Buryak, L.V. (2014) Studies of fire nature in the forests of Siberia. *Siberian Journal of Forest Science*, **3**, 25–42. [In Russian]

Tsybulin, S.M. (2009) *The Birds of Altai: The Spatiotemporal Differentiation and the Community Structure and Organization*. Novosibirsk: Nauka. [In Russian]

Valencia, B.G., Bush, M.B., Coe, A.L., Orren, E. & Gosling, W.D. (2018) *Polylepis* woodland dynamics during the last 20,000 years. *Journal of Biogeography*, **45**, 1019–1030.

von dem Bussche, J., Spaar, R., Schmid, H. & Schröder, B. (2008) Modelling the recent and potential future spatial distribution of the Ring Ouzel (*Turdus torquatus*) and Blackbird (*T. merula*) in Switzerland. *Journal of Ornithology*, **149**, 529–544.

Willebrand, T. & Marcström, V. (1988) On the danger of using dummy nests to study predation. *Auk*, **105**, 378–379.

Zhang, K., Yang, N., Xu, Y., *et al.* (2011) Nesting behaviour of Szechenyi's Monal-Partridge in treeline habitats, Pamuling Mountains China. *Wilson Journal of Ornithology*, **123**, 93–96.

5 · *Population Trends of Mountain Birds in Europe and North America*

ALEKSI LEHIKOINEN, ÅKE LINDSTRÖM,
JOHN CALLADINE, TOMMASO
CAMPEDELLI, WILLIAM V. DELUCA,
VIRGINIA ESCANDELL, JIŘÍ FLOUSEK[†],
SERGI HERRANDO, FRÉDÉRIC JIGUET,
JOHN ATLE KÅLÅS, ROMAIN
LORRILLIERE, TIMOTHY D. MEEHAN,
INGAR JOSTEIN ØIEN, CLARA
PLADEVALL, BRETT K. SANDERCOCK,
THOMAS SATTLER, BENJAMIN SEAMAN,
LAURA SILVA, HANS SCHMID, NORBERT
TEUFELBAUER AND SVEN TRAUTMANN

5.1 Introduction

Population trends of species form a cornerstone of biodiversity conservation. Stable or increasing population trends suggest a desirable status in conservation. In contrast, declining population trends, including broad-scale declines of common species, can indicate important changes in an ecosystem's health (Gregory *et al.* 2005; Butchart *et al.* 2010). Understanding the scale of and reasons for population change is also vital when prioritising resources for conservation actions. In recent years, an increasing number of studies have investigated the characteristics of species that are more vulnerable to anthropogenic changes, especially climate and land use change (Eglington & Pearce-Higgins 2012; Howard *et al.* 2020).

Although direct human influence on high elevation mountain habitats is often weaker compared to lowland habitats, mountain birds still experience many threats (Archaux 2007; Elsen *et al.* 2020).

Climate change is thought to be pushing species distributions upslope, as their climatic niches shift (Chen *et al.* 2011; Chapter 6, but see Scridel *et al.* 2018). Upshifting can cause population declines as the amount of suitable habitat may decrease for topographic reasons (e.g., in a mountain with a conical form, the area available decreases with increasing elevation). Furthermore, climate change may also have indirect effects due to changes in species interactions, such as food availability, predation and parasitism (Pearce-Higgins & Green 2014). Human land use changes also affect the quantity and quality of alpine habitats with well-established effects on bird populations (van der Wal *et al.* 2003; Britton & Fisher 2007; Ims & Henden 2012). For instance, changes in forest cover, including at the treeline, and grazing pressure, can affect the amount of alpine habitat and lead to population changes (Herrando *et al.* 2016). More accessible mountain areas may undergo intensification (mainly agricultural, locally also urban), while remote areas are more commonly left for forest regrowth (Knaus *et al.* 2018). The latter can favour large fires in some parts of the world, especially due to a warming climate (Kelly *et al.* 2020). Most temperate mountain birds show either latitudinal or altitudinal migration because of harsh climatic conditions during winter. Threats to migratory species that breed in mountains may also occur outside mountain areas. For instance, long-distance migrants have declined more than other species in Europe, which suggests that they are experiencing problems in their wintering grounds and along the migratory flyway (Vickery *et al.* 2014).

Gathering population trend information from mountain areas is a difficult task. These areas are often situated far from populated areas, where most bird watchers live, and often suffer from infrastructure constraints (e.g., poor road networks), limiting access by professional avian surveyors or citizen scientists. Finding suitable weather for bird monitoring in a relatively short breeding season may also be difficult as weather forecasts tend to be less reliable, and weather conditions are more extreme than in lowlands. Alpine species typically have low breeding densities, which means that gathering adequate sample sizes for trend analyses for even common species requires a large number of survey routes (Lehikoinen *et al.* 2019). For all of these reasons, data to calculate population trends and corresponding multi-species indices are usually limited and time series are often short. Despite the existing challenges, there have been positive developments in the common bird monitoring of mountain species in recent years, including published population trends of common mountain birds in Europe from four different areas (the Alps, Fennoscandia, Iberia and the UK uplands) during the period 2002–2014 (Lehikoinen *et al.* 2014, 2019). However, these published time series are relatively short and can be influenced by stochastic processes. Elsewhere in the world, population trends of mountain bird species are poorly known, including North America where bird monitoring has a long tradition, but mainly for lower latitudes and low elevations (Rosenberg *et al.* 2019).

Overall, international data analyses of mountain birds were rare prior to the last decade. Lehikoinen *et al.* (2014, 2019) published European-level analyses which suggested moderate population declines in some mountain areas (Fennoscandia and Iberia). Population trend analyses of high elevation species were very rare before the twenty-first century and almost all were local studies with often short time series (Järvinen & Rajasärkkä 1992; but see Svensson & Andersson 2013; Flousek *et al.* 2015). Furthermore, the early studies were also restricted to the lower elevations of mountain areas (Haney *et al.* 2001). In more recent years, several other smaller-scale case studies have been conducted which have also suggested declining population trends in several continents. Flousek *et al.* (2015) showed that species breeding at higher elevations had more negative trends than species breeding at lower elevations in the Giant Mountains in Czechia between 1984 and 2011. Decreasing bird population trends have also been found for birds in mountainous spruce-fir forests in a large-scale study in NE and Midwestern United States, where 4 out of 14 species showed a declining trend, and none increased, in the period 1989–2013 (Ralston *et al.* 2015). King *et al.* (2008) found similar negative trends in 3 out of 10 species in spruce-fir forests of the Northern Appalachians, USA in the period from 1993 to 2003. The total number of mountain birds also declined in NW Cameroon between 2003 and 2016 (Riegert *et al.* 2021). However, not all studies have shown declines. For instance, a long-term case study of a mountain specialist, the white-tailed ptarmigan *Lagopus leucura*, showed a stable population trend in Colorado, North America in the period from 1968 to 2010 (Wann *et al.* 2014). Despite these published local studies, the overall population status of mountain bird species globally is poorly known.

The aim of this chapter is to present as much information as possible about population trends of high elevation mountain bird species, and to identify the most important knowledge gaps. First, we review the literature on case studies of mountain bird trends in scientific journals. Second, we update earlier European population trend estimates (Lehikoinen *et al.* 2019) by adding six years of data, and present information from two local long-term monitoring sites. Third, we extend the geographical scope by exploring and presenting recent abundance trends for mountain birds in North America, based on several different monitoring schemes. Fourth, we investigate whether there are major changes in the geographical distribution of European species (from the 1980s to the 2010s) using information from the recently published second European Breeding Bird Atlas (EBBA2; Keller *et al.* 2020). Last, we explore whether species traits can help to explain species-specific population abundance and range changes among European mountain species. Based on previous studies, we predict that migratory behaviour, species climatic niche and the degree of specialization for mountain habitats may explain observed population changes. Long-distance migrant birds in particular have experienced recent declines in Europe (Gregory *et al.* 2005; Vickery *et al.* 2014). Furthermore, 'cold-dwelling' species are expected to decline more compared to 'warm-dwelling' species (Devictor *et al.* 2008; Jiguet *et al.* 2010; Tayleur *et al.* 2016; Scridel *et al.* 2017), and species breeding only in mountains, so called mountain specialists, may have experienced more negative population trends than mountain generalists (Lehikoinen *et al.* 2019), that is, species that breed in mountains as well as lowland habitat.

5.2 Methods

5.2.1 Literature Review of Population Trends

We searched for scientific papers on population trends of bird species breeding in alpine or mountain ecotone habitats from the Web of Knowledge (webofknowledge.com), using the keywords 'mountain or montane + bird + population + trend' and 'mountain or montane + bird + population + dynamics' and 'mountain or montane + bird + increase or decline'. The search was conducted on 22 May 2022 and resulted in 2,983 publications. We went through all of the publications and explored whether they dealt with population trends ($\geq$5 years) of mountain birds at higher elevations.

5.2.2 Large Scale Abundance Trends in Europe

We followed the methodology of an earlier paper by Lehikoinen *et al.* (2019), which covered 12 countries and four geographically separate mountain areas in Europe: the Alps (including smaller mountain areas in the surroundings; Austria, Czechia, France, Germany, Italy, Switzerland),

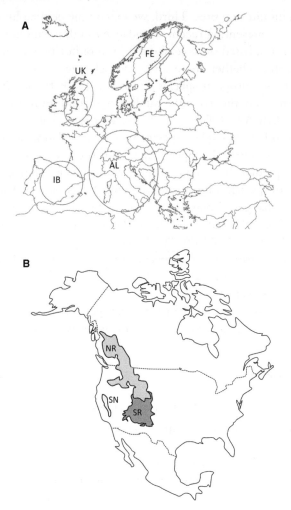

Figure 5.1 Map of the mountain regions in (A) Europe (AL = Alps, FE = Fennoscandia, IB = Iberia, UK = United Kingdom) and (B) North America (NR = Northern Rockies, SR = Southern Rockies, SN = Sierra Nevada), where monitoring data have been collected.

Fennoscandia (Finland, Norway, Sweden), Iberia (Andorra, France, Spain) and the UK uplands (Figure 5.1A). We calculated population trends from 2002 to 2020 for 44 species (16 mountain specialists, 28 generalists), which are common breeding birds in high elevation alpine and alpine-forest transitional (ecotone) habitats in the study regions. We used survey-level elevation data and information from the literature on species' habitat selection to identify the high elevation species in each mountain range. Only high elevation species preferring open or semi-open habitats were selected. The species list is the same as that in Lehikoinen *et al.* (2019), where the species selection is described in more detail.

The analysis was restricted to data from survey sites within mountain areas, that is, survey sites needed to be in higher elevation areas and include open or semi-open habitat (the elevation threshold varied between mountain ranges; for more detailed information on site selection see Lehikoinen *et al.* 2019). The annual number of survey sites varied from 412 to 840 in the Alps, from 44 to 264 in Fennoscandia, from 35 to 107 in Iberia and from 45 to 163 in the UK. The number of sampling sites increased during the study period, but there was a substantial drop in Iberia and the UK in 2020 (57 per cent and 70 per cent less than in 2019, respectively) caused by the public lockdown due to the COVID-19 pandemic (Harris *et al.* 2021; Hochachka *et al.* 2021). We did not, however, remove data from 2020 from the analyses, because all four areas are needed for the Pan-European analyses and sampling in other European areas was not affected. The results for 2020 in Iberia and the UK should, however, be treated with some caution because of the reduced sample size, but for the overall European mountain area, its effect was unlikely to have been great.

The long-term population trends and annual population abundance indices (where the initial year is set as 100), including standard errors, were calculated using log-linear Poisson regressions (Bogaart *et al.* 2018). The response variable was raw abundance which was analysed in relation to year and survey site. For Europe, we calculated population trends separately for four regions, but also species-level trends for the whole dataset. Furthermore, we combined population trend information to create multi-species indicators, which summarize annual population changes of all the studied species into a single index value. The value of a single index is that it describes the general development of all species considered and is thus easier to understand than potentially complex dynamics of a large set of individual species (Gregory *et al.* 2005; Fraixedas *et al.* 2020). This calculation was conducted using the Multi-Species Indicator-tool (MSI; Soldaat *et al.* 2017). The MSI-tool utilizes the annual abundance indices and their standard errors to calculate annual indicator values using geometric mean and bootstrapped standard errors.

In the second analysis, we aimed to investigate which factors affected the regional population trends of bird species (Table 5.1). We used

Table 5.1 Population abundance (Abu) and distribution (Range) trends (± standard error) of birds in European mountain areas. The abundance changes from 2002–2020 are annual slopes and the data are combined from four mountain regions, which are also presented separately. The range change is only presented from the whole European area from the 1980s to the 2010s. Significant abundance changes are in bold.

Species	Abu whole	Abu Alps	Abu Fennos	Abu Iberia	Abu UK	Range whole
Long-tailed duck *Clangula hyemalis*	**-0.030 ± 0.012**	—	**-0.030 ± 0.012**	—	—	0.4%
Willow grouse *Lagopus lagopus*	-0.005 ± 0.003	—	**-0.024 ± 0.005**	—	**-0.011 ± 0.004**	-8.7%
Rock ptarmigan *Lagopus muta*	**0.018 ± 0.005**	**0.023 ± 0.007**	0.013 ± 0.007	—	—	-2.9%
Black grouse *Lyrurus tetrix*	**0.025 ± 0.005**	**0.022 ± 0.005**	—	—	—	-6.9%
Rock partridge *Alectoris graeca*	**0.030 ± 0.012**	**0.030 ± 0.012**	—	—	—	-10.8%
Common buzzard *Buteo buteo*	**0.016 ± 0.007**	—	—	—	**0.016 ± 0.007**	1.1%
Rough-legged buzzard *Buteo lagopus*	0.014 ± 0.014	—	0.014 ± 0.014	—	—	-5.9%
Bearded vulture *Gypaetus barbatus*	—	—	—	—	—	10.4%
Common kestrel *Falco tinnunculus*	0.004 ± 0.004	0.004 ± 0.005	—	0.006 ± 0.012	—	0.5%
Gyrfalcon *Falco rusticolus*	—	—	—	—	—	2.1%
Common ringed plover *Charadrius hiaticula*	**0.036 ± 0.009**	—	**0.036 ± 0.009**	—	—	1.0%
Eurasian dotterel *Charadrius morinellus*	**0.029 ± 0.012**	—	**0.053 ± 0.013**	—	—	-10.1%
European golden plover *Pluvialis apricaria*	0.000 ± 0.002	—	-0.001 ± 0.003	—	-0.005 ± 0.006	-3.1%
Dunlin *Calidris alpina*	**0.040 ± 0.009**	—	**0.042 ± 0.011**	—	—	-18.6%
Common snipe *Gallinago gallinago*	0.003 ± 0.007	—	—	—	0.003 ± 0.007	-5.7%

Species					
Common redshank *Tringa totanus*	**0.029 ± 0.005**	—	**0.029 ± 0.005**	—	-1.5%
Bar-tailed godwit *Limosa lapponica*	—	—	—	—	-1.7%
Temminck's stint *Calidris temminckii*	—	—	—	—	-8.9%
Purple sandpiper *Calidris maritima*	—	—	—	—	-16.4%
Red-necked phalarope *Phalaropus lobatus*	-0.013 ± 0.016	—	-0.013 ± 0.016	—	-14.9%
Long-tailed jaeger *Stercorarius longicaudus*	**0.026 ± 0.009**	—	**0.026 ± 0.009**	—	-5.9%
Snowy owl *Bubo scandiacus*	—	—	—	—	-44.0%
Common cuckoo *Cuculus canorus*	**-0.033 ± 0.003**	—	**-0.033 ± 0.003**	—	0.1%
Eurasian skylark *Alauda arvensis*	**-0.007 ± 0.002**	**0.011 ± 0.005**	—	**-0.013 ± 0.005**	**-0.007 ± 0.003**	-2.7%
Horned lark *Eremphila alpestris*	—	—	—	—	-12.4%
Eurasian crag martin *Ptyonoprogne rupestris*	**0.028 ± 0.005**	**0.031 ± 0.006**	—	**0.025 ± 0.012**	—	6.1%
Meadow pipit *Anthus pratensis*	0.003 ± 0.002	—	**0.012 ± 0.002**	—	**-0.004 ± 0.002**	-0.8%
Water pipit *Anthus spinoletta*	**0.005 ± 0.002**	**0.006 ± 0.002**	—	**-0.020 ± 0.009**	—	-7.2%
Alpine accentor *Prunella collaris*	0.001 ± 0.004	0.000 ± 0.004	—	—	—	-11.8%
Bluethroat *Luscinia svecica*	**-0.010 ± 0.005**	—	**-0.010 ± 0.005**	—	—	11.1%
Black redstart *Phoenicurus ochruros*	**0.010 ± 0.002**	**0.011 ± 0.002**	—	0.000 ± 0.005	—	5.3%
Common redstart *Phoenicurus phoenicurus*	-0.002 ± 0.004	—	-0.002 ± 0.004	—	—	-0.4%
Whinchat *Saxicola rubetra*	**-0.016 ± 0.005**	**-0.019 ± 0.005**	—	0.017 ± 0.028	—	-4.1%
Northern wheatear *Oenanthe oenanthe*	**0.004 ± 0.002**	**0.016 ± 0.003**	0.005 ± 0.004	**-0.014 ± 0.006**	**-0.025 ± 0.005**	-3.0%

(cont.)

Table 5.1 (cont.)

Species	Abu whole	Abu Alps	Abu Fennos	Abu Iberia	Abu UK	Range whole
Common rock thrush *Monticola saxatilis*	**-0.023 ± 0.008**	**-0.024 ± 0.011**	—	**-0.031 ± 0.015**	—	-0.5%
Ring ouzel *Turdus torquatus*	**0.006 ± 0.002**	0.005 ± 0.003	**0.034 ± 0.009**	0.009 ± 0.014	-0.016 ± 0.010	-3.7%
Redwing *Turdus iliacus*	-0.005 ± 0.003	—	-0.005 ± 0.003	—	—	-7.6%
Lesser whitethroat *Sylvia curruca*	**0.020 ± 0.004**	**0.020 ± 0.004**	—	—	—	0.4%
Willow warbler *Phylloscopus trochilus*	**-0.011 ± 0.002**	—	**-0.011 ± 0.002**	—	—	-1.0%
Wallcreeper *Tichodroma muraria*	—	—	—	—	—	-11.6%
Alpine chough *Pyrrhocorax graculus*	**-0.018 ± 0.007**	-0.012 ± 0.007	—	-0.039 ± 0.022	—	-1.8%
Red-billed chough *Pyrrhocorax pyrrhocorax*	**0.045 ± 0.009**	—	—	**0.041 ± 0.011**	—	-0.9%
Carrion crow *Corvus corone*	**-0.015 ± 0.007**	—	—	—	**-0.015 ± 0.007**	0.0%
Northern raven *Corvus corax*	-0.006 ± 0.009	—	—	—	-0.006 ± 0.009	5.9%
White-winged snowfinch *Montifringilla nivalis*	0.004 ± 0.007	0.004 ± 0.007	—	—	—	-0.5%
Brambling *Fringilla montifringilla*	**-0.010 ± 0.003**	—	**-0.010 ± 0.003**	—	—	-8.8%
Citril finch *Carduelis citrinella*	-0.007 ± 0.008	-0.005 ± 0.023	—	-0.006 ± 0.010	—	-0.7%
Common linnet *Linaria cannabina*	**0.021 ± 0.004**	**0.029 ± 0.007**	—	**0.020 ± 0.006**	—	-0.1%
Twite *Linaria flavirostris*	—	—	—	—	—	-5.6%
Common / Lesser redpoll *Acanthis flammea / cabaret*	**-0.011 ± 0.004**	**-0.049 ± 0.007**	-0.002 ± 0.005	—	—	5.7%
Lapland longspur *Calcarius lapponicus*	**-0.042 ± 0.005**	—	**-0.042 ± 0.005**	—	—	-14.2%
Snow bunting *Plectrophenax nivalis*	-0.005 ± 0.008	—	-0.005 ± 0.008	—	—	-11.0%
Rock bunting *Emberiza cia*	**-0.018 ± 0.005**	0.000 ± 0.008	—	**-0.025 ± 0.006**	—	-1.2%

generalized linear mixed models (GLMMs) with a Gaussian distribution (see below). The response variables were the regional, species-specific, long-term, log-linear population trends. The explanatory variables were: 1) region (four categories – Alps, Fennoscandia, Iberia and UK; Lehikoinen et al. 2019); 2) migratory behaviour (long-distance migrant or short-distance migrant/resident according to Cramp et al. 1977–1994); 3) whether the species was a mountain specialist or not (specialization), where specialists occur only in the mountains in the study regions (according to Lehikoinen et al. 2019); and, 4) the climatic niche of species. We used the Species Temperature Index (STI) as a measure of a species' climatic niche, which is the average breeding season temperature within the breeding range of a given species covering both its latitudinal and elevational range (Devictor et al. 2008). We used the STI values published in Lehikoinen et al. (2021). As northern regions have more species with lower STI values than southern regions, we centred the STI values (to a mean of zero) within each region to remove the collinearity between these two variables. Furthermore, we included interactions between region and mountain specialization, and between region and species climatic niche. The explanatory variables did not show any clear collinearity (Pearson correlation, $|r| < 0.22$, when two level factorial variables were converted to binomial variables). Species identity was added as a random factor in the models as some species occur in multiple regions. Because closely related species may have similar responses due to common ancestry, we took this into account by adding a phylogenetic correlation structure of the species into the model. We downloaded one phylogeny tree of all the study species from www.birdtree.org (Jetz et al. 2012). Statistical details of the analyses are found in Appendix 5.1. More information about European population trends and indices can be found on the website of the PECBMS programme (http://pecbms.info).

5.2.3 Local Trend Analyses from Europe

In addition to large-scale monitoring from the 2000s onwards, some single sites had half-century-long time series on population dynamics of mountain species. Here, we were able to use data from two sites, one in the surroundings of Ammarnäs in Swedish Lapland (about 66°N, 16°E; LUVRE-project) and one in the Giant Mountains (Czechia, 50°44′N 15°44′E), to explore patterns at a more local scale.

The Swedish LUVRE-project included three separate survey types, though in each one all birds heard and seen were recorded. First, territory mapping and line transects within 9 km^2 of primeval subalpine birch forest were carried out yearly in 1963–2020, the data being combined into density estimates (pairs per km^2; Enemar *et al.* 2004). We multiplied these density estimates with the total survey area and used the estimated number of pairs as input values, rounded to the nearest integer. Second, territory mapping of two 1 km^2 squares, situated in the low alpine zone (above the tree line, at c. 800 and c. 900 m, respectively), were carried out yearly between 1964 and 2020 (Svensson 2006). We used the species sums from the two squares as input values. Third, six permanent line transects (total length of 90 km) located in the low alpine zone (above the tree line, 800–1,000 m) were counted yearly in the period 1972–2020 (Svensson & Andersson 2013). Data from a few missing surveys were extrapolated from surrounding years (Svensson & Andersson 2013). We used the species sums from the six transects as input values. Data from these three schemes were merged, and we used the data for the same 23 species in the analysis as used for Fennoscandia by Lehikoinen *et al.* (2019).

The data from the Giant Mountains, Czechia, included 29 survey points in the period 1983–2019, but excluding 1999, 2004 and 2012–14 (Reif & Flousek 2012; Lehikoinen *et al.* 2019). Altogether, seven high elevation species were analyzed using the mountain bird list of Lehikoinen *et al.* (2019). The population trends and annual indices for Sweden and Czechia were calculated using log-linear Poisson regressions (Bogaart *et al.* 2018), and multi-species indicators were calculated using the MSI-tool (Soldaat *et al.* 2017).

5.2.4 Population Trends in North America

We used two continental scale monitoring schemes from the United States and Canada, the North American Breeding Bird Survey (BBS) and the Audubon Christmas Bird Count (CBC). The BBS routes are roadside transects in the continental United States and Canada. Each transect is roughly 40 km long and includes fifty 3-minute point counts, which are spaced approximately 800 m apart. All birds heard or seen within 400 m of the point are counted by a single observer. The routes are surveyed once a year between 28 May and 7 July depending on latitude. We did not use raw BBS count data for our analyses, but used abundance indices and trends in relative abundance (and 95 per cent credible intervals) derived from the standard BBS analysis without site selection (Sauer & Link 2011). We included BBS abundance indices and trends from the years 1968–2019 in the analyses from three North American Bird Conservation Regions: 1) Northern Rockies; 2) Southern Rockies and Colorado Plateau; and, 3) Sierra Nevada (Figure 5.1B). We calculated species trends both within and across these four mountain regions of North American. BBS abundance indices and trends were accessed from Sauer *et al.* (2019).

For each region, we included species that commonly use high-elevation mountain habitats. Based on expert opinion, we divided North American mountain bird species into five categories depending on their habitat preferences during the breeding season (Appendix 5.2): A) alpine or montane species where the majority of the breeding range is at high elevation (above the tree line); B) alpine species that use alpine habitats at temperate latitudes, but coastal tundra at Arctic latitudes; C) alpine species at temperate latitudes that are common as breeding birds at high elevations in the mountains, but also have populations that breed at low elevation sites; D) ecotone species associated with shrub habitats at or above the treeline, montane meadows and forest openings; and, E) montane species associated with forests at mid or high elevations. With the BBS data, we used species with sufficient data to calculate trends in categories A through E, covering species which primarily occur in mountain tundra, ecotone and high elevation forest habitats based on expert opinion. The main point of the analyses was to evaluate the population trends of high elevation species in the three Western North American regions.

During the Christmas Bird Count (CBC), birds are counted within fixed circles of 24.1 km diameter, conducted annually on a single day between December 14 and January 5. All birds seen or heard within the boundary of the circle are recorded by observers. For our analysis, we used data from the years 1970–2019 for those species with a majority of the population breeding in high-elevation alpine habitats (category A in Appendix 5.2), although the majority of the winter counts are conducted in the lowlands. As with the BBS, we did not use raw CBC data for our analyses, but used abundance indices and population trends (and 95 per cent credible intervals) resulting from standard analyses described in Soykan *et al.* (2016). CBC abundance indices and trends were accessed from Meehan *et al.* (2020).

In addition, populations of mountain bird species were surveyed in the Northern and Southern Rockies Bird Conservation Regions of Colorado, Montana and Wyoming (the United States), as part of the Integrated Monitoring in Bird Conservation Regions (IMBCR) programme. In total, 832 point count stations were surveyed during the breeding season from 2008 onwards (Pavlacky *et al.* 2017). However, we only used the raw data from 2009 onwards, since 2008 was a pilot year of the programme. According to our classification, we calculated population trends using log-linear Poisson regressions (Soldaat *et al.* 2017) for five species classified as alpine and mountain ecotone birds in North America (Appendix 5.2).

We used the MSI-tool to calculate multi-species indicators for BBS data in three separate regions: Northern Rockies, Southern Rockies Colorado Plateau and the Sierra Nevada. The 95 per cent credible intervals were transformed into standard error estimates of the annual abundance indices of species to calculate the confidence intervals for multi-species indicators. This matched with the procedure used for indicators in different European mountain ranges (see Section 5.2.2). Similar to Europe, we also calculated the multi-species indicator with the combined data of three regions which we term the mountain bird indicator for Western North America. We used the change point option of the MSI-tool in cases of clear non-linear trends to evaluate trends before and after a certain year, that is, two linear regressions for different time periods (a broken stick regression).

5.2.5 Changes in European Distributions

Estimates of species-specific distribution changes of breeding mountain birds in Europe over approximately three decades were presented by Keller *et al.* (2020). They showed the percentage change in the total number of 50 x 50 km squares occupied by a species between the first (data collection in the 1980s) and second (2013–2017) European breeding bird atlases (Hagemeijer & Blair 1997; Keller *et al.* 2020). Volunteer observers collected data on the evidence of breeding for each species in each grid using breeding scores, which are summarized in four categories: (i) confirmed, (ii) probable, (iii) possible and (iv) unlikely breeding. The first three categories were used to classify the range size of species, and only squares that were surveyed sufficiently in both atlas periods were compared to measure the range-size change (Keller *et al.* 2020), though it must be stressed that there can be at least local differences in observation effort between atlas periods. We compiled these changes for the mountain specialist and generalist species listed by Lehikoinen *et al.* (2019), for which there are recent population trends (Table 5.1). Distribution changes between the atlas periods were also estimated for a number of mountain species with very low population densities (Keller *et al.* 2020), such as gyrfalcon *Falco rusticolus* and wallcreeper *Tichodroma muraria*, for which there are no large-scale population trends from common bird monitoring schemes (Table 5.1). Based on the assumption that changes in distribution area are roughly proportional to population changes (Koleček & Reif 2011; Jiguet *et al.* 2013), we also included the uncommon species with low densities in our range analyses in Europe. We used the overall changes in range size provided by the atlas (Keller *et al.* 2020) and thus for generalists, the range changes also included lowland habitats.

We first tested if the mean change in range size of all species differed from zero using a t-test. Then we investigated the species-specific range changes using the same explanatory variables, phylogenetic approach, linear regression (R function gls) and model-selection procedure as that used in the population trend analyses (Section 5.2.2, Appendix 5.1). However, since we had European level changes in range size, we did not include any (regional) interactions between variables. The full model therefore included (i) migratory behaviour, (ii) mountain specialization, (iii) species climatic niche (STI) and iv) the interaction between specialization and STI, as explanatory variables. More information about changes in European distribution areas of species can be found on the EBBA2 website (http://ebba2.info).

5.3 Results

5.3.1 Literature Review

The literature search produced 23 articles (all articles listed in Table 5.2), which dealt with population trends of species from high elevation areas. We additionally included papers from Africa, Asia and South America, with a focus on high-elevation forest, as few studies from these areas investigated population changes in alpine areas. The largest number of studies was from Europe (13) and North America (5). Of 23 studies, 16 were multi-species analyses and the rest dealt with single species of special conservation concern. Overall, most studies in both Europe and North America showed declining population trends in abundance or range size. Of 18 studies, 16 showed declining trends in at least one of the studied groups. Only four studies showed generally increasing or stable populations (Table 5.2). In the Mediterranean area, the studies also indicated increases in warm-dwelling generalists as well as shrubland and forest species (Regos *et al.* 2016; Scridel *et al.* 2017; Hernando *et al.* 2022).

Table 5.2 *Summary of the population trend articles of high elevation mountain birds based on the literature review. Location, time span, number of study species, and a short description of the trends for each article are shown.*

Location	Years	Species and overall trend	Citation
Europe			
Finland	1979–1986	20 spp.; increases	Järvinen & Rajasärkkä 1992
Alps, France	1979–2018	*Tetrao tetrix*; declines in 3 out of 11 sites, no increases	Canonne *et al.* 2021
Sierra Nevada, Spain	1981/1985–2008/2012	17 spp.; overall decline in juniper scrub, but not on high elevation summits	Zamora & Barea-Azcón 2015
Alps, Italy	1983/86–2012	12 spp.; negative range size change in alpine open habitat species, a positive correlation between long-term changes in range size and species' thermal niche	Scridel *et al.* 2017
Giant Mountains, Czechia	1984–2011	50 spp.; high elevation species had more negative trends than low elevation species	Flousek *et al.* 2015
Black Forest, Germany	1986/1987–2017	*Turdus torquatos*; more extinctions than colonizations	Fumy & Fartmann 2021
United Kingdom	1987–2014	*Charadrius morinellus*; decline	Ewing *et al.* 2020
United Kingdom	1987/1988–2011	*Charadrius morinellus*; decline	Hayhow *et al.* 2015
Alps, France and Switzerland	1999–2009 (FRA), 2015–2020 (CH)	*Turdus torquatus*; decline in France, increase in Switzerland	Barras *et al.* 2021a
NW Spain	2000–2010	17 spp.; increase of shrubland and forest species, decline of ecotone and open-habitat species	Regos *et al.* 2016

Location	Period	Description	Reference
Fennoscandia	2002–2012	14 spp.; declining, short-distance migrants declining more than long-distance migrants	Lehikoinen et al. 2014
Alps, Fennoscandia, Iberia, UK	2002–2014	44 spp.; declining in Fennoscandia and Iberia	Lehikoinen et al. 2019
Cantabrian mountains, NW Iberia	2008–2017	6 spp.; generalists increasing, alpine specialists declining	Hernando et al. 2022
North America			
Wyoming, USA	1952/1954–1993/1995	26 spp.; 11 out of 26 species declined in spruce–fir forests	Jones et al. 2008
Colorado, USA	1968–2010	Lagopus leucura; stable	Wann et al. 2014
NE and Mid-Western USA	1989–2013	14 spp.; 4 declining, the rest stable	Ralston et al. 2015
New Hampshire, USA	1993–2003	Catharus bicknelli; decline	Lambert et al. 2008
Northern Appalachians, USA	1993–2003	10 spp.; 3 declining, the rest stable	King et al. 2008
Africa			
South Africa	1960/1999–2000/2012	Gypaetus barbatus; decline	Krüger et al. 2014
Usambara Mountains, Tanzania	1987–2016	21 spp.; population growth rates negatively associated with increasing temperature	Neate-Clegg et al. 2021
Mount Kilimanjaro, Tanzania	1991–2011	45 spp.; increase of understorey species	Dulle et al. 2016
Bale Mountains, Ethiopia	2011–2016	18 spp.; 1 species increased, 17 stable	Kittelberger et al. 2021
Asia			
Eastern Himalayas, India	2011–2018	15 spp.; increasing and decreasing survival rates for low and high elevation species, respectively	Srinivasan & Wilcove 2021
South America			
Southern Andes of Ecuador	2006–2016	24 spp.; proportional abundance of the highest ranked species had increased	Tinoco et al. 2021

Publications on population trends of mountain species (single species or multi-species studies) from outside Europe and North America proved to be rare. Four studies were situated in Africa, one in Asia and one in South America. Interestingly, only one out of five multi-species papers was based on bird counts; four others used mist-netting of birds in the high elevation forest understorey. These studies are summarized below.

Population growth rates of 21 Afrotropical understorey species were studied in the forests of the Usambara Mountains between 1,000 m and 1,300 m in Tanzania between 1987 and 2016. Population growth rates of over half the species were negatively associated with higher temperatures. Neate-Clegg *et al.* (2021) found that growth rates were higher in species preferring lower elevations compared to those preferring higher elevations, which indicates climate driven population changes. However, the population growth rates of the species were more connected with changes in recruitment than with changes in apparent survival. Also in Tanzania, trends of 45 resident understorey bird species were investigated on Mount Kilimanjaro between 1,600 and 2,900 m (below the tree line) from 1991 to 2011. Bird abundance increased, especially at higher elevations, potentially due to climate change. The increase was mainly caused by an upsurge in the numbers of generalists, omnivores and herbivores (Dulle *et al.* 2016).

In an Afromontane ecosystem near Big Babanki in NW Cameroon, population changes of 64 species were evaluated using 29 point counts between 2003 and 2016 (Riegert *et al.* 2021). The total number of birds decreased over this period, which was driven especially by declining numbers of shrubland species, mainly nectarivores and granivores. The changes were at least partly linked to habitat change, as the authors found a decrease in bush cover and an increase in the herb layer, whereas tree cover did not change.

Trends in survival rates of 15 understorey insectivorous mountain bird species were studied in the Indian Himalayas in both primary and logged forest in 2011–2018 using mist-netting and capture-recapture analyses. The survival rates of species measured at 2,000 m were increasing for species preferring lower elevations and decreasing for species preferring higher elevations in primary forests, but this pattern was not found in logged forests (Srinivasan & Wilcove 2021).

The relative abundance of species was monitored in Cajas National Park and Mazán Reserve in the southern Andes of Ecuador using standardized mist netting from 2006 to 2016 (Tinoco *et al.* 2021). Species

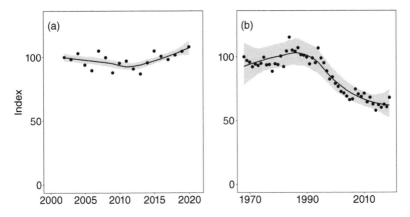

Figure 5.2 The mountain bird indicator for (a) Europe in 2002–2020 and (b) Western North America in 1968–2019. The dots are the annual values, the black line shows the smoothed trend and the grey area covers the 95 per cent confidence intervals.

richness remained stable over time across habitats, but community composition changed in the native forest. The species that were most common initially became more abundant compared to scarce species, indicating homogenization of the bird community.

5.3.2 Population Abundance Changes in Europe

The European Mountain Bird Indicator describes the average population change of European mountain birds as a group. While it initially slightly decreased from 2002 to 2012, the trend then turned positive so that the index up until 2020 showed a weak but significant increase (annual rate of change 0.0031 ± 0.0014 SE; Figure 5.2a). However, the population trends differed among the four European regions. Species-specific trends are shown in Table 5.1.

The mountain bird indicator of the Alps (including 20 species) showed a moderate annual increase of 0.0053 ± 0.0026 SE (Figure 5.3a). Populations of 11 species significantly increased and only three decreased in the Alps (Table 5.1). The indicator had a non-significant trend in Fennoscandia (23 species; annual rate of change 0.0035 ± 0.0023 SE; Figure 5.3b) and Iberia (14 species; annual rate of change -0.0022 ± 0.0049 SE; Figure 5.3c). In Fennoscandia, seven species significantly increased and seven declined, and in Iberia three species increased and five species

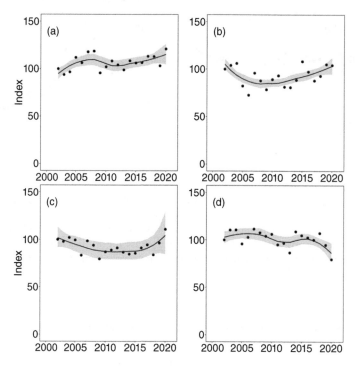

Figure 5.3 The regional European mountain bird indicators for (a) the Alps, (b) Fennoscandia, (c) Iberia and (d) the UK uplands in 2002–2020. The dots are the annual values, the black line shows the smoothed trend and the grey area covers the 95 per cent confidence intervals.

declined significantly (Table 5.1). The UK indicator showed a moderate decline (−0.0067 ± 0.0027 SE; Figure 5.3d). Four species declined in the UK, whereas only one showed a significantly increasing trend (Table 5.1).

The regional population trends were best explained by a model that included the positive effect of species' climatic niche (Table 5.3), meaning that warm-dwelling species (such as Eurasian crag martin *Ptyonoprogne rupestris* and common linnet *Linaria cannabina*) were doing better than cold-dwelling species (such as long-tailed duck *Clangula hyemalis* and willow ptarmigan *Lagopus lagopus*).

The local population analyses in Ammarnäs, Sweden showed a stable mountain bird indicator (annual slope 0.002 ± 0.002 SE) for 23 species, with some fluctuations during the period 1973–2020 (Figure 5.4a). However, the species-specific trends showed contrasting patterns as, out of 23 species, 15 increased and 3 species declined significantly in

Table 5.3 *Parameter estimates (B) and 95% confidence intervals (CI) of a model explaining the regional population trends of mountain bird species in Europe (see Table 5.1). Significant coefficients (P < 0.05) are in bold.*

Parameter	B	95% CI	P
(Intercept)	−0.008	−0.029 to 0.014	0.470
Specialists vs generalists	−0.010	−0.026 to 0.008	0.230
Region, Fennoscandia	0.007	−0.012 to 0.026	0.422
Region, Iberia	0.014	−0.007 to 0.031	0.170
Region, UK	−0.010	−0.027 to 0.009	0.244
Temperature preference, STI	**0.003**	**0.000 to 0.006**	**0.028**
Mig, Short-distance	0.014	−0.004 to 0.028	0.098
SpecialistY:Region, Fennos.	0.024	−0.003 to 0.047	0.076
SpecialistY:Region, Iberia	−0.017	−0.038 to 0.008	0.146
SpecialistY:Region, UK	0.003	−0.037 to 0.041	0.880

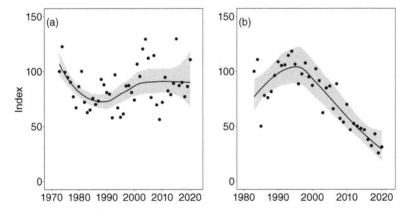

Figure 5.4 The local European mountain bird indicators for (a) Ammarnäs in Northern Sweden in 1973–2020 and (b) Giant Mountains, Czechia in 1983–2020. The dots are the annual values, the black line shows the smoothed trend and the grey area covers the 95 per cent confidence intervals.

numbers. Snow bunting *Plectrophenax nivalis* disappeared from the survey area, whereas long-tailed duck colonized.

In the Giant Mountains of Czechia, the mountain bird indicator first showed a stable trend (0.033 ± 0.019 SE) during the period 1983–1993, but then showed a decline between 1993 and 2020 (−0.049 ± 0.007 SE; Figure 5.4b). Two out of seven species increased and five species declined. Water pipit *Anthus spinoletta* almost disappeared from the survey area over the survey period.

5.3.3 Population Trends of North American Mountain Birds

The general mountain bird indicator for Western North America (seven species) showed a long-term decline of c. −30 per cent between 1968 and 2019 (annual rate of change −0.0108 ± 0.0017 SE; Figure 5.2b). The trend was, however, not linear, as the decline started from the mid-1990s (trends 0.0028 ± 0.0017 SE and −0.0166 ± 0.0048 SE for 1968–1995 and 1995–2019, respectively). Two species declined significantly (Canada jay *Perisorius canadensis* and Cassin's finch *Haemorhous cassinii*) and none increased (Table 5.4).

The regional indicator of the Northern Rockies (seven species) showed a moderate long-term decline during the study period, 1968–2019 (annual rate of change −0.0127 ± 0.0019 SE; Figure 5.5a). The abundance trends remained stable until the mid-1990s (annual rate of change 0.0016 ± 0.0051 SE in 1968–1995), whereas the recent trend was significantly negative (−0.0171 ± 0.0057 SE in 1995–2019; Figure 5.5a). The regional mountain bird indicator of the Southern Rockies (seven species) also showed a non-linear pattern, where the numbers increased significantly from the 1960s to the mid-1990s (annual rate of change 0.0133 ± 0.0061 SE in 1968–1995), followed by a decline (−0.0156 ± 0.0069 SE in 1995–2019; Figure 5.5b). The overall trend in 1968–2019 was stable (0.0008 ± 0.0024 SE; Figure 5.5b).

In the Sierra Nevada, the mountain bird indicator of six species declined significantly over the whole study period (annual rate of change −0.0127 ± 0.0044 SE in 1968–2019; Figure 5.5c). However, the indicator remained stable until the start of the 2000s (0.0052 ± 0.0083 SE in 1968–2000), and a decline, although not significant, started thereafter (−0.0246 ± 0.0182 SE in 2000–2019; Figure 5.5c). The species-specific slopes of each region are shown in Table 5.4.

Specific breeding surveys in the mountain areas of Colorado, Montana and Wyoming revealed that one species out of four, dark-eyed junco *Junco hyemalis*, had a significant positive trend in 2009–2020; the three others did not show a significant trend (Table 5.5). There was sufficient data to model trends for six high elevation bird species based on North American CBC data. One of these (wandering tattler *Tringa incana*) showed a significantly negative trend during 1970–2019 (Table 5.6), while the remainder showed no significant trends.

5.3.4 Distribution Changes in Europe

The size of the distribution areas on average decreased significantly in the set of 54 mountain species in Europe between the 1980s and

Table 5.4 *Annual population growth rates, their credibility intervals and sample sizes (number of routes) of seven mountain bird species in the Northern Rockies, Southern Rockies and Sierra Nevada in 1968–2019. In addition, general population trends in the BBS surveys of North America in 1966–2019 are given (according to Sauer et al. 2020). Species with significant population trends ($P < 0.05$) are in bold.*

Species	All 3 areas	N Rockies	S Rockies	Sierra Nevada	BBS whole N Am
Canada jay *Perisoreus canadensis*	**-0.009** **(-0.020 to 0.000)**	**-0.009 (162)** **(-0.021 to 0.000)**	-0.003 (53) (-0.024 to 0.018)	—	-0.003 (1076) (-0.014 to 0.006)
Clark's nutcracker *Nucifraga columbiana*	-0.008 (-0.016 to 0.000)	-0.008 (152) (-0.020 to 0.003)	-0.007 (129) (-0.020 to 0.005)	-0.001 (13) (-0.021 to 0.021)	-0.006 (746) (-0.016 to 0.001)
Pine grosbeak *Pinicola enucleator*	-0.008 (-0.026 to 0.007)	-0.013 (71) (-0.036 to 0.006)	-0.003 (53) (-0.024 to 0.028)	-0.015 (5) (-0.062 to 0.029)	-0.014 (273) (-0.043 to 0.001)
Cassin's finch *Haemorhous cassinii*	**-0.012** **(-0.026 to -0.001)**	-0.014 (144) (-0.029 to 0.000)	-0.001 (127) (-0.014 to 0.014)	-0.008 (32) (-0.025 to 0.009)	-0.008 (490) (-0.019 to 0.001)
Red crossbill *Loxia curvirostra*	-0.008 (-0.033 to 0.010)	-0.007 (180) (-0.033 to 0.012)	0.003 (112) (-0.028 to 0.030)	-0.010 (25) (-0.053 to 0.030)	-0.005 (875) (-0.064 to 0.012)
Pine siskin *Spinus pinus*	-0.015 (-0.045 to 0.008)	-0.013 (223) (-0.037 to 0.005)	-0.008 (150) (-0.025 to 0.008)	-0.016 (37) (-0.059 to 0.034)	-0.022 (1544) (-0.049 to 0.005)
White-crowned sparrow *Zonotrichia leucophrys*	0.001 (-0.005 to 0.008)	0.004 (150) (-0.003 to 0.012)	-0.006 (104) (-0.017 to 0.005)	**0.017 (17)** **(-0.035 to -0.001)**	-0.002 (565) (-0.007 to 0.002)

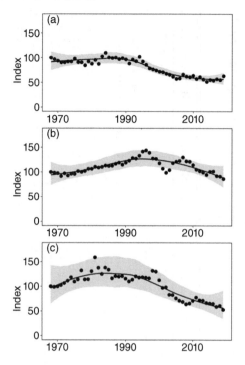

Figure 5.5 The regional North American mountain bird indicators for (a) Northern Rockies, (b) Southern Rockies and (c) Sierra Nevada in 1968–2019. The dots are the annual values, the black line shows the smoothed trend and the grey area covers the 95 per cent confidence intervals.

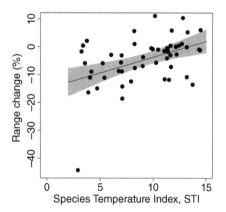

Figure 5.6 Range size change (%) in European mountain species according to European Breeding Bird Atlas data from the 1980s till 2013–2017 in relation to species thermal niche (Species Temperature Index). Note that a large number of species have a reduction in range size.

Table 5.5 *Annual population growth rates of four alpine bird species in Colorado, Montana and Wyoming, USA, in 2009–2020. Overall sample sizes (N, number of observed birds) and standard errors of the annual slopes (SE) are also given. Species with significant population trends (P < 0.05) are in bold.*

Species	N	Slope	SE
Buff-bellied pipit *Anthus rubescens*	5434	0.019	0.014
Dark-eyed junco *Junco hyemalis*	**42646**	**0.072**	**0.005**
Horned lark *Eremophila alpestris*	16896	0.001	0.006
White-tailed ptarmigan *Lagopus leucura*	328	0.133	0.069

Table 5.6 *Winter population trends (Slope) and their confidence intervals (CI) of six high elevation mountain bird species based on Christmas Bird Count data from Canada and United States during the period 1970–2019. Significant changes are in bold.*

Species	Slope (CI)
White-tailed ptarmigan *Lagopus leucura*	−0.029 (−0.069 to 0.015)
Wandering tattler *Tringa incana*	**−0.046 (−0.053 to −0.041)**
Surfbird *Calidris virgata*	−0.013 (−0.032 to 0.003)
Gray-crowned rosy finch *Leucosticte tephrocotis*	−0.063 (−0.176 to 0.014)
Black rosy finch *Leucosticte atrata*	0.001 (−0.079 to 0.113)
Brown-capped rosy finch *Leucosticte australis*	0.044 (−0.016 to 0.150)

2013–2017 according to European Breeding Bird Atlas data (one sample t-test, mean = −4.6 per cent decline, 95 per cent CIs from −2.2 to −6.9, t = −3.86, df = 52, P < 0.001; Table 5.1). The species-specific range size change was best explained by a model including mountain specialization and species' climatic niche (STI; Table 5.7). The positive connection between STI and range size change means that warm-dwelling species showed more positive range size changes than cold-dwelling species (Table 5.7; Figure 5.6). Climatic preference was not standardized regionally here as in the abundance analyses, because there was only one whole European range value (Table 5.7; Figure 5.6).

Interestingly, the population abundance changes of mountain bird species included in the European indicator were not correlated with the range size changes in Europe (Table 5.1; b = −0.0002 ± 0.0006 SE, t = −0.354, df = 42, P = 0.725). There was also no interaction between mountain specialization and range size change in explaining the

Table 5.7 *Parameter estimates (B) and 95% confidence intervals (CI) of a model explaining the range size change of mountain bird species in Europe (see Table 5.1). Significant coefficients (P < 0.05) are in bold.*

Parameter	B	95% CI	P
(Intercept)	−2.97	−10.65 to 4.85	0.291
Specialists vs generalists	−3.59	−8.00 to 0.03	0.075
Species temperature index (STI)	**0.872**	**0.18 to 1.59**	**0.020**

population abundance change (P = 0.329). This suggests that range size changes and abundance shifts were poorly connected in both mountain specialists and generalists.

5.4 Discussion

Our findings paint a complex picture of the changes in population trends for mountain bird species in Europe and Western North America, particularly in recent decades. It is good to keep in mind that the articles included in the review (Table 5.2) may include publication biases, and also that the data behind European and North American indicators differ clearly from each other and thus a direct comparison is not possible. The North American indicator is based on a smaller set of species occurring only in high elevation areas (7 species), whereas in Europe (44 species), mountain generalists were also included in the analyses. North American BBS sampling sites are likely biased towards lower elevations of mountain ranges and are only undertaken at roadsides, whereas in Europe the sampling designs are more systematic and sampling is also conducted in mountain top areas far from roads (e.g., Lehikoinen *et al.* 2019). Nevertheless, the data presented here give a useful first insight into population trends of North American mountain birds, and also act as the basis for the development of more formal indicators, and possibly the development of monitoring methods (see below). Whilst formal comparisons between Europe and North America are not realistic, the data still give some indications of similarities and differences that may act as the impetus for further research.

5.4.1 European Trends

European species have experienced long-term range contractions since the 1980s – the mountain bird indicator for Europe based on average abundance showed a slight increase from 2002 to 2020. However,

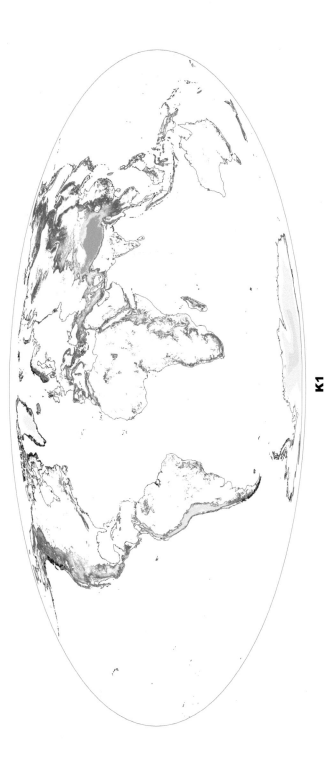

K1

Elevation >4,500; 1.2% of g.l.s ▪ Elevation 3,500–4,500; 1.8% of g.l.s □ Elevation 2,500–3,500; 4.7% of g.l.s ▪ Elevation 1,500–2,500 & slope >2°; 3.6% of g.l.s

▪ Elevation 1,000–1,500 & slope >5°; 4.2% of g.l.s ▪ Elevation 300–1,000 & LER >300m & isolated inner basins/plateau <25 sq.km; ca. 8.8% of g.l.s

Plate 1 Classification of global mountain areas based on Kapos *et al.* (2000; K1), grouped into seven elevation strata (two strata are combined in the figure). The 7th class (isolated inner basins/plateau < 25 sq. km) was introduced in the 2002 revision of the original 2000 system and is excluded from the calculation of global land surface (g.l.s). Every grid cell above 2500 m asl was considered 'mountain' and all land below 300 m asl was considered as non-mountainous. At intermediate elevations, the classification was based on combinations of elevation, slope and local elevation range (a 7 km radius around each cell). According to this typology, **24.3%** of global land surface (g.l.s) outside Antarctica is classified as 'mountain'. Note that, unlike K2 and K3 (Plates 2 & 3), K1 mapped relief both for Greenland and Antarctica. Map downloadable at: https://rmgsc.cr.usgs.gov/gme/ (USGS 2021). See Chapter 1 for citations.

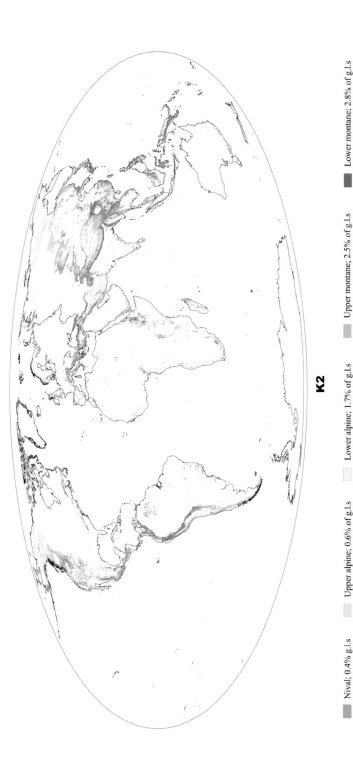

K2

■ Nival; 0.4% of g.l.s   ☐ Upper alpine; 0.6% of g.l.s   ☐ Lower alpine; 1.7% of g.l.s   ■ Upper montane; 2.5% of g.l.s   ■ Lower montane; 2.8% of g.l.s

■ Mountain area with frost; 1% of g.l.s   ■ Mountain area without frost; 3.3% of g.l.s

Plate 2 Classification of global mountain areas into seven climatic belts, based on Körner *et al.* (2011; K2). K2 was developed using ruggedness as the determining factor. According to this classification, **12.3%** of the terrestrial surface (outside Antarctica) is mountainous, less than half of the mountain area reported in K1. Körner *et al.* (2017) attributed the larger area identified as mountainous in K1 to inclusion of high plateaus, intermontane valleys and hilly forelands. Greenland was retained in the mapping for its coastal mountain ranges. GIS raster layer downloadable at: https://ilias.unibe.ch/goto_ilias3_unibe_cat_1000514.html; release 2016 version 3. See Chapter 1 for citations.

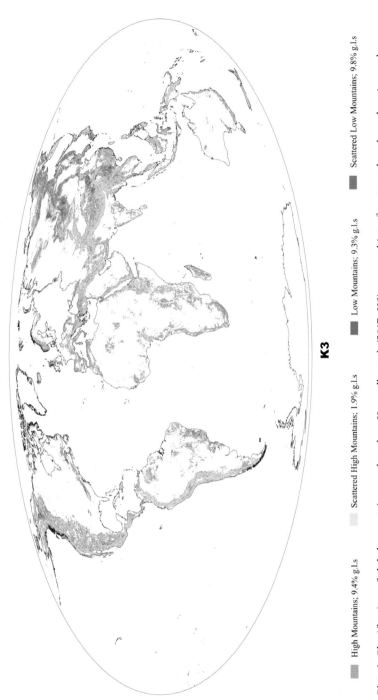

K3

■ High Mountains; 9.4% g.l.s　　□ Scattered High Mountains; 1.9% g.l.s　　■ Low Mountains; 9.3% g.l.s　　■ Scattered Low Mountains; 9.8% g.l.s

Plate 3 Classification of global mountain areas based on Karagulle *et al.* (2017; K3), grouped into four types based on elevation and isolation (high mountains; scattered high mountains; low mountains; scattered low mountains). The former two classes cover 11.3% of the Earth's land surface (excluding Antarctica), while the latter two cover 19.1%, for a total of **30.4%** (Sayre *et al.* 2018). K3 was developed at a finer spatial resolution (250 m) than K1 and K2 and was based on global landforms characterized using three classification parameters: slope, ruggedness and profile. Data downloadable at https://rmgsc.cr.usgs.gov/gme/ (USGS 2021). See Chapter 1 for citations.

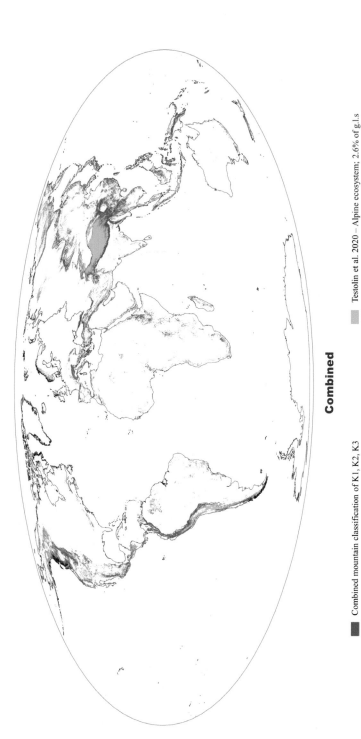

Combined

■ Combined mountain classification of K1, K2, K3　　■ Testolin et al. 2020 – Alpine ecosystem; 2.6% of g.l.s

Plate 4 Classification of global alpine areas (green) based on Testolin *et al.* (2020), overlaid onto a map representing all other mountain areas (brown) that combines the other three classifications (K1-3; Plates 1–3). Testolin *et al.* (2020) characterized alpine biomes according to climate, NDVI and satellite images (Google Earth Engine) at a 30 m spatial resolution to exclude forested areas (all pixels with forest cover > 0% were removed). This approach matches well the alpine areas defined in K2 (Plate 2). See Chapter 1 for citations.

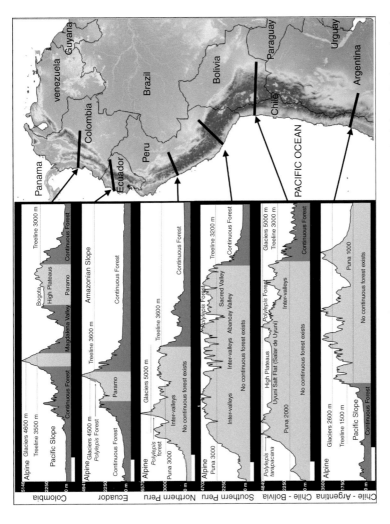

Plate 5. Transversal sections of six altitudinal gradients along the Andes mountain chain. The left panels show the elevational relief from the western (Pacific slope) to eastern slopes, the approximate elevation of the treeline and areas of continuous forest (dark shading) and where no continuous forest exists (light shading), and highlights some particular habitats, including *Polylepis* forest. Inter-valleys refer to Inter-Andean (Mountain) valleys. The white bar to the bottom left of each graph is a scale bar representing 50 km. The right panel shows the location of each section (thick black lines) along the Andes mountain chain. See Chapter 4.

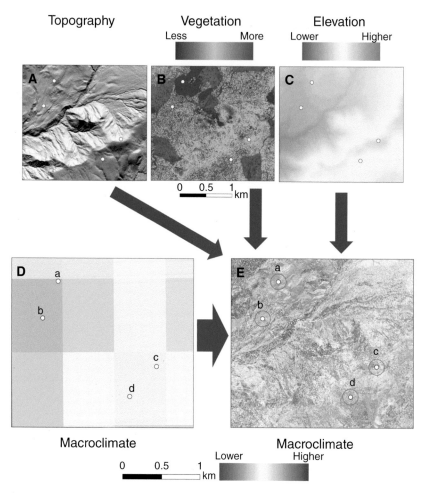

Plate 6 Mountain landscapes are composed of complex topographic features (A topography), vegetation (B forest biomass), and the elevation gradient (C). These features, combined with regional, broad-scale macroclimate, create complex microclimates across the landscape. With coarse grain (30″) climatic models (D), it is often difficult to capture the complex microclimatic conditions of mountain environments that birds experience on grid (E). Points a, b, c and d represent hypothetical avian point count survey locations, with 100m radius buffers showing the potential detection range of songbirds in a dense forest environment. These circles (E) are 3.14 hectares, which can include a few small songbird breeding territories. Points a and b, and c and d, are on warmer and cooler macroclimatic grids (D), respectively. It is more likely that birds breeding at points b and c are experiencing cooler microclimate on the ground, while birds at points a and d are located in a warmer microclimate. Reflecting ecological realism on mountain bird distributions and abundances is challenging due to these mismatches in the scale of available environmental data. Maps show MacRae Creek and Roswell Ridge in H.J. Andrews Experimental Forest, west Cascades mountains, Oregon, USA.

Plate 7 Boggy habitats (*bofedales*) in the bottom of Andean glacial valleys and around alpine lakes support a unique assemblage of birds. In the foreground, communities of compact cushion plants with diademed sand-piper plover *Phegornis mitchellii* on the left, glacier finch *Idiopsar speculifer* (actually a tanager) and grey-breasted seedsnipe *Thinocorus orbignyianus*. In the background, Andean avocet *Recurvirostra andina* and giant coots *Fulica gigantea* at their enormous nest. A silvery grebe *Podiceps occipitalis* is attaching its floating nest at the margin of the coot nest. See Chapter 9. (Jon Fjeldså)

Plate 8 Upper panel: Hummingbirds of the Andean highlands (a, purple-backed thornbill *Ramphomicron microrhynchum*; b, green-bearded helmetcrest *Oxypogon guerinii*; c, mountain avocetbill *Opisthoprora euryptera*; d, buff-winged starfrontlet *Coeligena lutetiae;* e, sword-billed hummingbird *Ensifera ensifera;* f, mountain velvetbreast *Lafresnaya lafresnayi*). Lower panel: Early-divergent lineages from the tropical lowlands (Phaethornithinae – Hermits): a, white-tipped sicklebill *Eutoxeres Aquila*; b, tooth-billed hummingbird *Androdon aequatorialis;* c, long-billed hermit *Phaethornis longirostris*; d, grey-chinned hermit *Phaethornis griseogularis*; e, rufous-breasted hermit *Glaucis hirsutus*. (b) is among the few morphologically specialized non-hermit hummingbirds from the humid lowlands. This species' toothed bill tip could be an adaptation for capturing spiders in their webs. See Box 9.2 in Chapter 9. (Jon Fjeldså)

there were also regional differences between mountain areas. We found a generally increasing average abundance index in the European Alps and general declines in the UK uplands and in the Giant Mountains in Czechia. The relatively low mountains of the UK and Czechia are likely to be at the lower edge of climate suitability for cold-loving northern species (Massimino *et al.* 2017), and are also likely to be sensitive to land use changes (Calladine *et al.* 2013).

In Europe, the recent positive indicator trends are evident in the Alps, Fennoscandia and Iberia, that is, in areas which are situated relatively far away from each other. Population trends can be driven by changes in climatic conditions or human land use (Newbold 2018). Land use practices are typically weaker in mountain areas compared to lowlands and land use changes are also likely to differ between regions leading to non-parallel trends.

The species-specific abundance trend and the range change analyses in Europe suggested that population changes were not similar for all species. In Europe, warm-dwelling species had more positive population changes than cold-dwelling species. This is in line with climate change predictions (Chapter 6) and with findings from numerous studies of European and North American birds in general (Devictor *et al.* 2008; 2012; Lindström *et al.* 2013; Lehikoinen *et al.* 2021), as well as from local European mountain bird studies from Italy (Scridel *et al.* 2017) and Czechia (Flousek *et al.* 2015). In Italy, range size changes of mountain species were positively related to species' thermal niche, which was measured using the STI. This means that cold-dwelling species experienced greater range losses compared to warm-dwelling species, and that these losses typically occurred in the low elevation peripheral sites (Ewings *et al.* 2020).

One potential reason for the simultaneous increases in regional European indicators could be similar drivers during the non-breeding season, such as winter weather conditions. Many mountain species are migratory and many overwinter in Southern Europe, where the common wintering conditions could influence a parallel increase in numbers. Warmer winters could, for instance, result in improved survival of many species and thus lead to increasing population sizes and hence positive trends in indicators (Pearce-Higgins *et al.* 2015), despite the species composition being different across mountain ranges. Weather conditions during the breeding season may also affect population dynamics. Mizel *et al.* (2021) showed that warmer temperature during the brood rearing period had a positive effect on population dynamics of mountain species in subarctic Alaska. It is possible that some mountain species experience at least short-term benefits from ongoing climate warming leading to population increases, even though the species are found in generally colder environments. This potential paradox should be investigated in more detail. The timescale of the potential negative indirect effects of warming, such as habitat change, are likely longer than the direct effects of climate change (Duclos *et al.* 2019). An alternative hypothesis could be that changes in population size are partly linked with precipitation. In southern Europe, rainfall is a more important climatic variable influencing population trends than temperature (Herrando *et al.* 2019). Higher precipitation levels in Iberia in recent years (Agencia Estatal di Meteorología 2022) could also positively influence the overwintering populations that breed in other mountain regions.

These patterns in population trends could also be driven by land use changes such as land abandonment and afforestation, especially in Mediterranean areas (Herrando *et al.* 2016; Regos *et al.* 2016; Hernando *et al.* 2022). Therefore, both climate and land use can drive populations in the same direction. However, the positive connection between species' climatic niche and population trend is not only limited to European sites, as similar results have been found in African and Himalayan mountains (Dulle *et al.* 2016; Neate-Clegg *et al.* 2021; Srinivasan & Wilcove 2021), which suggests that cold-dwelling species that prefer high elevation areas are at the highest risk worldwide (see Chapter 6).

There was no correlation between the long-term changes in species' distribution area in the whole of Europe and short-term changes in species abundance in mountain areas. The poor correlation between these two may be because of different time periods and because the areas included in the analyses were not exactly the same (the analyses of distribution data cover various mountain chains that are not included in the population data, e.g., the Balkans). It should also be noted that there can be at least local differences in observation effort and/or the tendency to record occasional breeding between the two atlases. In addition, distribution area changes were not limited to mountain areas, but included range changes in lowlands, where some mountain generalists also occur. Overall, a higher number of distribution losses compared to abundance losses may mean that mountain birds are losing ground in the peripheral areas of their distribution while their population/abundance in core areas remains more stable.

5.4.2 North American Trends

In Western North America, the overall mountain bird indicator showed a negative trend between 1968 and 2019. This decline started in the

1990s, a pattern also visible in the regional indicators. The special North American mountain bird surveys in Colorado, Montana and Wyoming showed that one out of four species had a positive trend in 2009–2020. Based on the literature review, earlier studies have shown declining population trends in high elevation spruce-fir forests of the Northeast and Mid-Western USA since the twentieth century (Jones *et al.* 2008; King *et al.* 2008; Lambert *et al.* 2008; Ralston *et al.* 2015). The recent declines of regional Western North American indicators after a period of stable or increasing trends could support the idea that populations may experience short-term benefits, but longer term negative consequences, of climate change. As North American BBS sampling sites are situated along roads, they cover mostly or only lower elevation sampling sites. Negative consequences of climate change for cold-dwelling species are expected to occur first at lower elevation sites (Ewing *et al.* 2020) leading to elevational shifts, which are discussed more extensively in Chapter 6. We are not aware of any clear land use changes in the North American mountain areas which could have led to the observed population changes.

Overall, the negative Western North American indicator and the reduced range sizes in Europe, as well as published literature, indicate somewhat long-term declines in populations of mountain birds. However, there are also contrasting results as the recent abundance trends in Europe have been weakly positive. The regional population trends showed similar tendencies both in North America (recent declines) and in Europe (recent increases). This could indicate that similar broad scale continental drivers are behind the changes. The reasons for these recent changes are not fully understood, and drivers of population trends of a single species can differ even within a single mountain range (Furrer *et al.* 2016).

We should stress that most of our European population trend estimates are based on relatively short time series (<20 years) and, accordingly, trends are sensitive to stochastic processes. Long-term trend analyses are simply rare. There are both negative (range changes in Europe and indicators in North America and UK) and positive (European mountain bird indicator) trends, but also quite a few stable situations.

5.5 Future Directions

Our results suggest that changes in population sizes of mountains species are, at least in the short-term and in our limited datasets, not as highly negative as could be expected from ongoing climate and habitat change. However, the patterns vary regionally, and several case studies have indicated population declines. Some of the variation in trends may be due to publication biases in the trend analyses, where declining trends are published more often than stable ones. Nevertheless, cold-dwelling specialist species in particular may be the most vulnerable group of mountain species. We should also keep in mind potential climate debt effects, where climate-driven changes in the population sizes occur with a time lag (Devictor *et al.* 2008).

We must emphasize that the monitoring situation of mountain species is far from ideal. There are many challenges compared to monitoring at low elevation sites, such as more difficult accessibility, a lower number of potential volunteers and in general lower bird densities. This has led to poor knowledge of population trends for alpine species even in areas such as Europe and North America where there is well organized common bird monitoring at low elevations. For example, population trends are almost completely unknown for wallcreeper in Europe and for white-tailed ptarmigan, grey-crowned rosy finch *Leucosticte tephrocotis*, black rosy finch *L. atrata* and brown-capped rosy finch *L. australis* in North America. However, the greatest need for improvement is in mountain areas outside these two continents. Successful monitoring of mountain areas will demand relatively large resources, not least in terms of strong financial support for both observers and organizers of bird monitoring programmes (Chapter 10). Both within- and across-continent comparisons would require that the selection of mountain bird species for the analyses is conducted similarly in all regions.

To overcome these challenges, we recommend the following improvements in mountain bird monitoring for the current gap areas, taking into account limited resources:

- The breeding season is usually shorter in mountain areas compared to the lowlands and thus one or two annual visits can be enough for monitoring purposes.
- If resources do not allow annual visits to an area, consideration should be given to investing effort for monitoring at fixed time intervals (e.g., repeat survey sites every three or five years; Wauchope *et al.* 2019; Drake *et al.* 2021). Of course, this should not prevent annual surveys of more accessible sites.
- Try to establish a systematic or a stratified random sampling design if this is logistically possible (e.g., Lehikoinen *et al.* 2014). That said, one should avoid establishing monitoring networks that are too ambitious

because they may be difficult to maintain over the long term. A monitoring scheme does not need to cover all areas and all the uncommon species. It is already a big improvement if the scheme is able to produce trends for just a limited number of common mountain species. The network can be expanded and intensified in later years.

- Investments for capacity building are important, especially in countries with limited monitoring effort. In addition, be creative, for example high elevation mountain areas are often protected and local managers, wardens and gamekeepers as well as tourists, could be potential surveyors (Jackson *et al.* 2015; Scridel *et al.* 2021). Diversity and densities of bird species are usually low at high elevations, which makes it potentially more appealing and plausible for new volunteers to learn the species and the survey methods rapidly.
- It would be useful to collect information about habitat type and quality from the survey sites (including remote sensing data) that could be used to understand wider environmental changes in mountain environments and reasons for population trends.
- We recommend the adoption of the same or similar methods both for bird and habitat recording in all mountain ranges, so that the population trends can be more comparable across different geographic locations.
- The demographics behind the population changes of mountain birds, such as breeding success and survival rates, are often poorly known (but see Wann *et al.* 2014; Strinella *et al.* 2020; Barras *et al.* 2021b; Mizel *et al.* 2021). Clearly, basic research on the population ecology of mountain species, including work outside the breeding season, is needed to understand the factors behind changes in populations.

Acknowledgements

We are most grateful to the many hundreds of people who censused birds in mountain areas! The national bird surveys in European mountain regions have been economically supported by the Catalan Ornithological Institute and the Government of Catalonia, the Andorra Research + Innovation, the German Federal Ministry for Environment, Nature Conservation and Nuclear Safety and the Federal Agency for Nature Conservation, the Austrian Federal Ministry of Agriculture, Forestry, Regions and Water Management, the Italian Ministry of Agriculture through the NRN 2014–2020 programme – European

Agricultural Fund for Rural Development (EAFRD), the Norwegian Climate and Environment Ministry and the Norwegian Environment Agency, the Swedish Environmental Protection Agency in collaboration with all 21 County Administrative Boards of Sweden, the Federal Office for the Environment of Switzerland and the Finnish Ministry of the Environment. We thank Colleen M. Handel for invaluable help with initiating contacts and Jennifer Timmer with the Bird Conservancy of the Rockies for providing IMBCR data for alpine species and also the IMBCR funding partners for supporting the monitoring programme. This research was also funded through the 2017–2018 Belmont Forum and BiodivERsA joint call for research proposals, under the BiodivScen ERA-Net COFUND programme, and with the funding organizations Academy of Finland (Helsinki: 326338), Swedish Research Council (Lund: 2018–02441), the Research Council of Norway (RCN, NINA: 295767) and the National Science Foundation (CLO, ICER-1927646). John R. Sauer helped with the North American breeding bird survey data and Göran Paulson, Martin Green, Thomas Andersson and Sören Svensson kindly provided updated data from the ongoing surveys in Ammarnäs, Sweden. Comments from Richard Gregory, James Pearce-Higgins, Jiří Reif and Devin de Zwaan improved the clarity of the manuscript. We wish to thank our co-author Jiří Flousek, who sadly passed away during the writing process, for his long-term contribution to research on mountain birds.

Appendix 5.1

Statistical Details in R

The long-term population trends and annual population abundance indices were calculated using the rtrim-package (Bogaart *et al.* 2018) in R (version 4.0.5., R Core Team 2021). Furthermore, population trend information to create multi-species indicators was calculated using the MSI package in R (Soldaat *et al.* 2017). In the multi-species trait analyses, we took the phylogenetic correlation structure of the species into account in the model using the MCMCglmm-package in R (Hadfield 2010). We first ran the full model and did backwards model selection, where we dropped the least significant variables until there were only significant ($P < 0.05$) variables left (Zuur *et al.* 2009). The modelling was conducted using 5,030,000 iterations, where the first 30,000 were used for 'burning in' and the thinning interval was 5,000. We used the following priors: R-structure: V=1, nu=0.00, G-structure: V=1, nu=0.02.

We investigated the trace plots of the model and found the chains to be randomly distributed.

Appendix 5.2

List of alpine and ecotone bird species in five habitat preference categories in Western North America based on expert opinion (William DeLuca, Brett Sandercock & Kathy Martin).

A) Alpine or montane species where the majority of the breeding range is at high elevation

    White-tailed ptarmigan *Lagopus leucura* (Rocky Mountains, higher elevations than willow ptarmigan *L. lagopus* and rock ptarmigan *L. muta* in northern British Columbia and Yukon)

    Wandering tattler *Tringa incana* (alpine sites and braided river channels, western Alaska)

    Surfbird *Calidris virgata* (alpine sites in Alaska)

    Gray-crowned rosy finch *Leucosticte tephrocotis* (Rocky Mountains, especially Colorado, high elevation specialists, altitudinal migrants)

    Black rosy finch *Leucosticte atrata* (Rocky Mountains, especially Colorado, high elevation specialists, altitudinal migrants)

    Brown-capped rosy finch *Leucosticte australis* (Rocky Mountains, especially Colorado, high elevation specialists, altitudinal migrants)

B) Alpine species that use alpine habitats at temperate latitudes but coastal tundra at arctic latitudes

    Rock ptarmigan *Lagopus muta* (mid elevation range between willow and white-tailed ptarmigan in northern British Columbia and Yukon)

    Red knot *Calidris canutus* (alpine ridges on Seward Peninsula near Nome, Alaska)

    Long-tailed jaeger *Stercorarius longicaudus*

    Smith's longspur *Calcarius pictus* (mountain passes in northern British Columbia)

    Snow bunting *Plectrophenax nivalis*

C) Alpine species that are common as breeding birds at high elevations in the mountains but also have populations that breed at low elevation sites at temperate latitudes

    Harlequin duck *Histrionicus histrionicus* (mountain streams in the Rocky Mountains, coastal streams in Labrador)

Golden eagle *Aquila chrysaetos*
Gyrfalcon *Falco rusticolus*
Upland sandpiper *Bartramia longicauda* (mountain sites in Alaska/ Yukon, and a prairie species elsewhere)
Short-billed gull *Larus brachyrhynchus* (uses small ponds in the mountains, but also low elevation sites).
Horned lark *Eremophila alpestris*
American dipper *Cinclus mexicanus* (altitudinal migrant)
Buff-bellied pipit *Anthus rubescens* (Rocky Mountains)
Savannah sparrow *Passerculus sandwichensis*

D) Ecotone species associated with shrub habitats at or above the treeline, montane meadows and forest openings
Willow ptarmigan *Lagopus lagopus* (also uses coastal tundra)
American tree sparrow *Spizelloides arborea*
Brewer's sparrow *Spizella breweri taverneri* (timberline sparrow subspecies)
Fox sparrow *Passerella iliaca*
Lincoln's sparrow *Melospiza lincolnii*
White-crowned sparrow *Zonotrichia leucophrys* (*oriantha* subspecies, population study by M.L. Morton)
Golden-crowned sparrow *Zonotrichia atricapilla*
Dark-eyed junco *Junco hyemalis* (wide elevational range)

E) Montane species associated with forests at mid or high elevations
Mountain quail *Oreortyx pictus*
Dusky grouse *Dendragapus obscurus*
Sooty grouse *Dendragapus fuliginosus* (also at low elevations)
Band-tailed pigeon *Patagioenas fasciata*
Boreal owl *Aegolius funereus*
Calliope hummingbird *Selasphorus calliope*
Broad-tailed hummingbird *Selasphorus platycercus*
Lewis's woodpecker *Melanerpes lewis*
Williamson's sapsucker *Sphyrapicus thyroideus*
White-headed woodpecker *Leuconotopicus albolarvatus*
American three-toed woodpecker *Picoides dorsalis*
Black-backed woodpecker *Picoides arcticus*
Olive-sided flycatcher *Contopus cooperi*
Hammond's flycatcher *Empidonax hammondii*
American dusky flycatcher *Empidonax oberholseri*
Cassin's vireo *Vireo cassinii*

Canada jay *Perisoreus canadensis*
Clark's nutcracker *Nucifraga columbiana*
Mountain chickadee *Poecile gambeli*
Boreal chickadee *Poecile hudsonicus*
Pygmy nuthatch *Sitta pygmaea*
Mountain bluebird *Sialia currucoides*
Townsend's solitaire *Myadestes townsendi*
Grace's warbler *Setophaga graciae*
Pine grosbeak *Pinicola enucleator*
Cassin's finch *Haemorhous cassinii*
Red crossbill *Loxia curvirostra*
Pine siskin *Spinus pinus*

References

Agencia Estatal di Meteorología (2022) www.aemet.es/en/serviciosclimaticos/ accessed 29/08/2022.

Archaux, F. (2007) Are mountains refuges for farmland bird species? A case study in the northern French Alps. *Bird Study*, **54**, 73–79.

Barras, A.G., Blache, S., Schaub, M. & Arlettaz, R. (2021a) Variation in demography and life-history strategies across the range of a declining mountain bird species. *Frontiers in Ecology and Evolution*, **9**, 780706.

Barras, A.G., Niffenegger, C.A., Candolfi, I., Hunziker, Y.A. & Arlettaz, R. (2021b) Nestling diet and parental food provisioning in a declining mountain passerine reveal high sensitivity to climate change. *Journal of Avian Biology* **52**, e02649.

Bogaart, P., van der Loo, M. & Pannekoek, J. (2018) rtrim: Trends and Indices for Monitoring Data. *R package version 2.0.6.* https://CRAN.R-project.org/package=rtrim

Britton, A.J. & Fisher, J.M. (2007) Interactive effects of nitrogen deposition, fire and grazing on diversity and composition of low-alpine prostrate *Calluna vulgaris* heathland. *Journal of Applied Ecology*, **44**, 125–135.

Butchart, S.H.M., Walpole, M., Collen, B., *et al.* (2010) Global biodiversity: indicators of recent declines. *Science*, **328**, 1164–1168.

Calladine, J., Bielinski, A. & Shaw, G. (2013) Effect on bird abundance and species richness of edge restructuring to include shrubs at the interface between conifer plantations and open moorland. *Bird Study*, **60**, 345–356.

Canonne, C. (2021) Drivers of black grouse trends in the French Alps: the prevailing contribution of climate. *Diversity and Distributions*, **27**, 1338–1352.

Chen, I.C., Hill, J.K., Ohlemüller, R., Roy, D.B. & Thomas, C.D. (2011) Rapid range shifts of species associated with high levels of climate warming. *Science*, **333**, 1024–1026.

Cramp, S., Simmons, K.E.L. & Perrins, C.M. (1977–1994) *Handbook of the Birds of Europe, Middle East and North America: Birds of the Western Palaearctic.* Oxford: Oxford University Press.

Devictor, V., Julliard, R., Couvet, D. & Jiguet, F. (2008) Birds are tracking climate warming, but not fast enough. *Proceedings of the Royal Society B*, **275**, 2743–2748.

Devictor, V., van Swaay, C., Brereton, T., *et al.* (2012) Differences in the climatic debts of birds and butterflies at a continental scale. *Nature Climate Change*, **2**, 638–639.

Drake, A., de Zwaan, D.R., Altamirano, T.A., *et al.* (2021) Combining point counts and autonomous recording units improves avian survey efficacy across elevational gradients on two continents. *Ecology and Evolution*, **11**, 8654–8682.

Duclos, T.R., DeLuca, W.V. & King, D.I. (2019) Direct and indirect effects of climate on bird abundance along elevation gradients in the Northern Appalachian mountains. *Diversity and Distributions*, **25**, 1670–1683.

Dulle, H.I., Ferger, S.W., Cordeiro, N.J., *et al.* (2016) Changes in abundances of forest understorey birds on Africa's highest mountain suggest subtle effects of climate change. *Diversity and Distributions*, **22**, 288–299.

Eglington, S.M. & Pearce-Higgins, J.W. (2012) Disentangling the relative importance of changes in climate and land-use intensity in driving recent bird population trends. *PLoS ONE*, **7**, e30407.

Elsen, P.R., Monahan, W.B. & Merenlender, A.M. (2020) Topography and human pressure in mountain ranges alter expected species responses to climate change. *Nature Communications*, **11**, 1974.

Enemar, A., Sjöstrand, B., Andersson, G. & von Proschwitz, T. (2004) The 37-year dynamics of a subalpine passerine bird community, with special emphasis on the influence of environmental temperature and *Epirrita autumnata* cycles. *Ornis Svecica*, **14**, 63–106.

Ewing, S.R., Baxter, A., Wilson, J.D., *et al.* (2020) Clinging on to alpine life: investigating factors driving the uphill range contraction and population decline of a mountain breeding bird. *Global Change Biology*, **26**, 3771–3787.

Flousek, J., Telenský, T., Hanzelka, J. & Reif, J. (2015) Population trends of Central European montane birds provide evidence for adverse impacts of climate change on high-altitude species. *PLoS ONE*, **10**, e0139465.

Fraixedas, S., Lindén, A., Piha, M., *et al.* (2020) A state-of-art review on birds as indicators of biodiversity: advances, gaps, challenges, and future directions. *Ecological Indicators*, **118**, 106728.

Fumy, F. & Fartmann, T. (2021) Climate and land-use change drive habitat loss in a mountain bird species. *Ibis*, **163**, 1189–1206.

Furrer, R., Schaub, M., Bossert, A., *et al.* (2016) Variable decline of Alpine Rock Ptarmigan (*Lagopus muta helvetica*) in Switzerland between regions and sites. *Journal of Ornithology*, **157**, 787–796.

Gregory, R.D., van Strien, A., Voříšek, P., *et al.* (2005) Developing indicators for European birds. *Philosophical Transaction of the Royal Society B*, **360**, 269–288.

Hadfield, J.D. (2010) MCMC methods for multi-response Generalized Linear Mixed Models: the MCMCglmm R package. *Journal of Statistical Software*, **33**, 1–22.

Hagemeijer, W.J.M. & Blair, M.J. (1997) *The EBCC atlas of European Breeding Birds: Their Distribution and Abundance.* Calton: Poyser.

Haney, J.C., Lee, D.S. & Wilbert, M. (2001) A half-century comparison of breeding birds in the southern Appalachians. *Condor*, **103**, 268–277.

Harris, S.J., Massimino, D., Balmer, D.E., *et al.* (2021) *The Breeding Bird Survey 2020. BTO Research Report 736.* Thetford: British Trust for Ornithology.

Hayhow, D.B., Ewing, S.R., Baxter, A., *et al.* (2015) Changes in the abundance and distribution of a montane specialist bird, the Dotterel *Charadrius morinellus*, in the UK over 25 years. *Bird Study*, **62**, 443–456.

Hernando, M.D., Roa, I., Fernández-Gil, J., *et al.* (2022) Trends in weather conditions favour generalists over specialist species in rear-edge alpine bird communities. *Ecosphere*, **13**, e3953.

Herrando, S., Brotons, L., Anton, M., *et al.* (2016) Assessing impacts of land abandonment on Mediterranean biodiversity using indicators based on bird and butterfly monitoring data. *Environmental Conservation*, **43**, 69–78.

Herrando, S., Titeux, N., Brotons, L., *et al.* (2019) Contrasting impacts of precipitation on Mediterranean birds and butterflies. *Scientific Reports*, **9**, 5680.

Hochachka, W.M., Alonso, H., Gutiérrez-Expósito, C., Miller, E. & Johnston, A. (2021) Regional variation in the impacts of the COVID-19 pandemic on the quantity and quality of data collected by the project eBird. *Biological Conservation*, **254**, 108974.

Howard, C., Stephens, P.A., Pearce-Higgins, J.W., *et al.* (2020) Disentangling the relative roles of climate and land cover change in driving the long-term population trends of European migratory birds. *Diversity and Distributions*, **26**, 1442–1455.

Ims, R.A. & Henden, J.-A. (2012) Collapse of an arctic bird community resulting from ungulate-induced loss of erect shrubs. *Biological Conservation*, **149**, 2–5.

Jackson, M.M., Gergel, S.E. & Martin, K. (2015) Citizen science and field survey observations provide comparable results for mapping Vancouver Island white-tailed ptarmigan (*Lagopus leucura saxatilis*) distributions. *Biological Conservation*, **181**, 162–172.

Järvinen, A. & Rajasärkkä, A. (1992) Population fluctuations in two northern land bird communities: effect of habitat, migration strategy and nest site. *Ornis Fennica*, **69**, 173–183.

Jetz, W., Thomas, G.H., Joy, J.B., Hartmann, K. & Mooers, A.O. (2012) The global diversity of birds in space and time. *Nature*, **491**, 444–448.

Jiguet, F., Devictor, V., Ottvall, R., *et al.* (2010) Bird population trends are linearly affected by climate change along species thermal ranges. *Proceedings of the Royal Society B*, **277**, 3601–3618.

Jiguet, F., Barbet-Massin, M., Devictor, V., Jonzén, N. & Lindström, Å. (2013) Current population trends mirror forecasted changes in climatic suitability for Swedish breeding birds. *Bird Study*, **60**, 60–66.

Jones, S.L. (2008) A forty-year comparison of the breeding avifauna in Grand Teton National Park, Wyoming. *American Midland Naturalist*, **159**, 172–189.

Keller, V., Herrando, S., Vorisek, P., *et al.* (2020) *European Breeding Bird Atlas 2: Distribution, Abundance and Change.* Barcelona: European Breeding Bird Council & Lynx Edicions.

Kelly, L.T., Giljohann, K.M., Duane, A., *et al.* (2020) Fire and biodiversity in the Anthropocene. *Science* **370**, eabb0355.

King, D.I., Lambert, J.D., Bounaccorsi, J.P. & Prout, L.S. (2008) Avian population trends in the vulnerable montane forests of the Northern Appalachians, USA. *Biodiversity and Conservation*, **17**, 2691–2700.

Kittelberger, K.D., Neate-Clegg, M.H.C., Buechley, E.R. & Şekercioğlu, C.H. (2021) Community characteristics of forest understory birds along an elevational gradient in the Horn of Africa: a multi-year baseline. *Ornithological Applications*, **123**, duab009.

Knaus, P., Antoniazza, S., Guélat, J., *et al.* (2018) *Swiss Breeding Bird Atlas 2013–2016. Distribution and Population Trends of Birds in Switzerland and Liechtenstein.* Sempach: Swiss Ornithological Institute.

Koleček, J. & Reif, J. (2011) Differences between the predictors of abundance, trend and distribution as three measures of avian population change. *Acta Ornithologica*, **46**, 143–153.

Krüger, S.C., Allan, D.G., Jenkins, A.R. & Amar, A. (2014) Trend in territory, distribution and density of the Bearded Vulture *Gypaetus barbatus meridionalis* in southern Africa. *Bird Conservation International*, **24**, 162–177.

Lambert, J.D., King, D.I., Buonaccorsi, J.P. & Prout, L.S. (2008) Decline of a New Hampshire Bicknell's Thrush population 1993–2003. *Northeastern Naturalist*, **15**, 607–618.

Lehikoinen, A., Green, M., Husby, M., Kålås, J.A. & Lindström, Å. (2014) Common montane birds are declining in northern Europe. *Journal of Avian Biology*, **45**, 3–14.

Lehikoinen, A., Brotons, L., Calladine, J., *et al.* (2019) Declining population trends of European mountain birds. *Global Change Biology* **25**, 577–588.

Lehikoinen, A., Lindström, Å., Santangeli, A., *et al.* (2021) Wintering bird communities are tracking climate change faster than breeding communities. *Journal of Animal Ecology*, **90**, 1085–1095.

Lindström, Å., Green, M., Paulson, G., Smith, H.G. & Devictor, V. (2013) Rapid changes in bird community composition at multiple temporal and spatial scales in response to recent climate change. *Ecography*, **36**, 313–322.

Massimino, D., Johnston, A., Gillings, S., Jiguet, F. & Pearce-Higgins, J.W. (2017) Projected reductions in climate suitability for vulnerable British birds. *Climatic Change*, **145**, 117–130.

Meehan, T.D., LeBaron, G.S., Dale, K., *et al.* (2020) *Abundance Trends of Birds Wintering in the USA and Canada, from Audubon Christmas Bird Counts, 1966–2019.* Version 3.0. New York: National Audubon Society. www.audubon.org/conservation/where-have-all-birds-gone accessed 29/08/2022.

Mizel, J.D., Schmidt, J.H. & Mcintyre, C.L. (2021) Climate and weather have differential effects in a high latitude passerine community. *Oecologia*, **195**, 355–365.

Neate-Clegg, M.H.C., Stanley, T.R., Şekercioğlu, Ç.H. & Newmark, W.D. (2021) Temperature-associated decreases in demographic rates of Afrotropical bird species over 30 years. *Global Change Biology*, **27**, 2254–2268.

Newbold, T. (2018) Future effects of climate and land-use change on terrestrial vertebrate community diversity under different scenarios. *Proceedings of the Royal Society London B*, **285**, 20180792.

Pavlacky Jr, D.C., Lukacs, P.M., Blakesley, J.A., *et al.* (2017) A statistically rigorous sampling design to integrate avian monitoring and management within Bird Conservation Regions. *PLoS ONE*, **12**, e0185924.

Pearce-Higgins, J.W. & Green, R.E. (2014) *Birds and Climate Change: Impacts and Conservation Responses*. Cambridge: Cambridge University Press.

Pearce-Higgins, J.W., Eglington, S.M., Martay, B. & Chamberlain, D.E. (2015) Drivers of climate change impacts on bird communities. *Journal of Animal Ecology*, **84**, 943–954.

R Core Team. (2021) *R: A Language and Environment for Statistical Computing*. Vienna: R Foundation for Statistical Computing. Retrieved from www.R-project.org/

Ralston, J., King, D.I., DeLuca, W.V., *et al.* (2015) Analysis of combined data sets yields trend estimates for vulnerable spruce-fir birds in northern United States. *Biological Conservation*, **187**, 270–278.

Regos, A., Dominguez, J., Gil-Tena, A., Brotons, L., Ninyerola, M. & Pons, X. (2016) Rural abandoned landscapes and bird assemblages: winners and losers in the rewilding of a marginal mountain area (NW Spain). *Regional Environmental Change* **16**, 199–211.

Reif, J. & Flousek, J. (2012) The role of species' ecological traits in climatically driven altitudinal range shifts of central European birds. *Oikos*, **121**, 1053–1060.

Riegert, J., Chmel, K., Vlček, J., *et al.* (2021) Alarming declines in bird abundance in an Afromontane global biodiversity hotspot. *Biodiversity and Conservation*, **30**, 3385–3408.

Rosenberg, K.V., Docter, A.M., Blancher, P.J., *et al.* (2019) Decline of the North American avifauna. *Science*, **366**, 120–124.

Sauer, J.R. & Link, W.A., (2011) Analysis of the North American breeding bird survey using hierarchical models. *Auk*, **128**, 87–98.

Sauer, J.R., Niven, D.K., Hines, J.E., *et al.* (2019) *The North American Breeding Bird Survey, Results and Analysis 1966–2019*. Version 2.07. Laurel, MD: USGS Patuxent Wildlife Research Center. www.mbr-pwrc.usgs.gov accessed 29/08/2022.

Sauer, J.R., Link, W.A. & Hines, J.E. (2020) *The North American Breeding Bird Survey, Analysis Results 1966–2019*. U.S. Geological Survey data release. https://doi.org/10.5066/P96A7675.

Scridel, D., Bogliani, G., Pedrini, P., *et al.* (2017) Thermal niche predicts recent changes in range size for bird species. *Climate Research*, **73**, 207–216.

Scridel, D., Brambilla, M., Martin, K., *et al.* (2018) A review and meta-analysis of the effects of climate change on Holarctic mountain and upland bird populations. *Ibis*, **160**, 489–515.

Scridel, D., Brambilla, M., de Zwaan, D.R., *et al.* (2021) A genus at risk: predicted current and future distribution of all three Lagopus species reveal sensitivity to climate change and efficacy of protected areas. *Diversity and Distributions*, **27**, 1759–1774.

Soldaat, L.L., Pannekoek, J., Verweij, R.J.T., van Turnhout, C.A.M. & van Strien, A.J. (2017) A Monte Carlo method to account for sampling error in multi-species indicators. *Ecological Indicators*, **81**, 340–347.

Soykan, C.U., Sauer, J., Schuetz, J.G., *et al.* (2016) Population trends for North American winter birds based on hierarchical models. *Ecosphere*, **7**, e01351.

Srinivasan, U. & Wilcove, D.S. (2021) Interactive impacts of climate change and land-use change on the demography of montane birds. *Ecology*, **102**, e03223.

Strinella, E., Scridel, D., Brambilla, M., Schano, C. & Korner-Nievergelt, F. (2020) Potential sex-dependent effects of weather on apparent survival of a high-elevation specialist. *Scientific Reports*, **10**, 8386.

Svensson, S. (2006) Species composition and population fluctuations of alpine bird communities during 38 years in the Scandinavian mountain range. *Ornis Svecica*, **16**, 183–210.

Svensson, S. & Andersson, T. (2013) Population trends of birds in alpine habitats at Ammarnäs in southern Swedish Lapland 1972–2011. *Ornis Svecica*, **23**, 81–107.

Tayleur, C., Devictor, V., Gaüzère, P., *et al.* (2016) Regional variation in climate change winners and losers highlights the rapid loss of cold-dwelling species. *Diversity and Distributions*, **22**, 468–480.

Tinoco, B., Latta, S.C., Astudilo, P.X., Nieto, A. & Graham, C.H. (2021) Temporal stability in species richness but reordering in species abundances within avian assemblages of a tropical Andes conservation hot spot. *Biotropica*, **53**, 1673–1684.

Vickery, J.A., Ewing, S.R., Smith, K.W., *et al.* (2014) The decline of Afro-Palaearctic migrants and an assessment of potential causes. *Ibis*, **156**, 1–22.

van der Wal, R., Pearce, I., Brooker, R., *et al.* (2003) Interplay between nitrogen deposition and grazing causes habitat degradation. *Ecology Letters*, **6**, 141–146.

Wann, G.T, Aldridge, C.L. & Braun, C.E. (2014) Estimates of annual survival, growth, and recruitment of a white-tailed ptarmigan population in Colorado over 43 years. *Population Ecology*, **56**, 555–567.

Wauchope, H.S., Amano, T., Sutherland, W.J. & Johnston, A. (2019) When can we trust population trends? A method for quantifying the effects of sampling interval and duration. *Methods in Ecology and Evolution*, **10**, 2067–2078.

Zamora, R. & Barea-Azcón, J.M. (2015) Long-term changes in mountain passerine bird communities in the Sierra Nevada (Southern Spain): a 30-year case study. *Ardeola*, **62**, 3–18.

Zuur, A., Ieno, E.N., Walker N., Saveliev, A.A. & Smith, G.M. (2009) *Mixed Effects Models and Extensions in Ecology with R*. New York: Springer-Verlag.

6 · *Climate Change Impacts on Mountain Birds*

JAMES W. PEARCE-HIGGINS AND KATHY MARTIN

Climate change involves shifts in the long-term weather patterns that tend to occur over decades. With global climate warming exceeding 1°C since pre-industrial times, the evidence that the climate has changed is *unequivocal* (IPCC 2021). Depending on the trajectory of future emissions, global temperature increases are projected to range from 1.4 to 4.4°C above pre-industrial levels by the end of the century, with global impacts on climatic means and variability (IPCC 2018, 2021). There is growing evidence that these climatic changes are impacting biological systems at all scales, from genetics to individual behaviour, altering the survival and fecundity of individuals to drive changes in local populations and ecological communities and inducing predictable and unpredictable shifts in species distributions (Scheffers *et al.* 2016; Srivastava *et al.* 2021). Depending on the combination of exposure of species to climate change, the sensitivity of species to that environmental change and the capacity of species to adapt to these changes, climate change may threaten species with severely reduced distribution or extinction, whilst others may expand their distribution in response to warming (Foden *et al.* 2019). The magnitude of any change is closely tied to the magnitude of climate change (Urban 2015).

The observed response patterns to climate change and projected future impacts across biodiversity are apparent in birds (reviewed by Pearce-Higgins & Green 2014; Dunn & Møller 2020). Birds are breeding and migrating earlier in the spring, by up to 2.2 days per decade (Cohen *et al.* 2018). Avian populations are changing (Pearce-Higgins *et al.* 2015a; Martin *et al.* 2017) and species' distributions are generally shifting poleward (Chen *et al.* 2011; Gillings *et al.* 2015), although with more varied directions of change in the tropics (VanDerWal *et al.* 2013). Avian communities are reshuffling across continents (Stephens *et al.* 2016), for example warm-associated species are tending to increase in abundance relative to cold-associated species (Devictor *et al.* 2012). The latest global projections suggest c. 7 per cent of bird species are at risk of losing climatic suitability across 50 per cent of their global range with 2°C warming, but this risk increases to 40 per cent of species with 4.5°C warming, assuming 'realistic' dispersal estimates (Warren *et al.* 2018). Overall, c. 5 per cent of bird species are threatened with extinction due to climate change (Urban *et al.* 2015), but projections vary considerably among studies depending upon the assumptions made, projected magnitude of environmental change and model uncertainty (Pearce-Higgins & Green 2014; Srivastava *et al.* 2021).

By promoting warm-associated over cold-associated species, climate change has the potential to particularly disadvantage the birds of cooler climates, such as those living in mountain environments, whilst allowing other, warm-associated species to colonize areas that were previously too cold. However, climate change is not the only driver of importance altering bird populations, particularly in human-dominated landscapes. As noted in Chapters 1 and 7, changes in agricultural management and the consequent expansion or contraction of treeline extent have long influenced mountain birds, and other stressors may exacerbate climate change impacts.

In this chapter, we review the impacts of climate change on birds living in mountain environments, first by characterizing mountain climates and recent climatic trends across global regions. We then review the types of climate change impacts on mountain birds, from individuals to populations and communities, including changes in species distributions, drawing on detailed individual studies to identify the likely main mechanisms that underpin these changes. Next, we assess the future vulnerability of mountain birds to climate change before finally considering how conservationists can respond to the present and future climate change-driven threats to mountain avifauna.

6.1 A Changing Mountain Climate

A mountain is a landmass rising above the general landscape that induces a change in climate that affects vegetation and animal life (Price 1981; Chapter 1). In line with the rest of the book, we focus on the bird species associated with open, treeless high elevation habitats, which in many mountain systems are the alpine habitats above the treeline (Nagy & Grabherr 2009), but we also draw examples from high elevation montane forests, particularly in the tropics. Outside of the tropics, mountains are highly seasonal with a growing season limited by winter cold, when the habitat is often snow covered. It is this cold which limits the treeline, particularly mediated through soil temperature (Körner & Hoch 2006; Chapter 4). In the tropics, alpine habitats are characterized by large daily variation in temperature from early morning frost, which is often limiting, to afternoon heat. In more arid mountains, treelines may be moisture-, rather than temperature-determined. Conversely, on high elevation peatlands, excessive moisture and waterlogging may limit tree growth. In exposed situations, high wind speeds can promote alpine vegetation over other types (Chapter 3). Aside from these climatic limits, various human activities artificially reduce the treeline across mountain environments, for example through excessive burning, tree felling or browsing pressure (Chapter 4).

The relationship between air temperature and elevation is described by the lapse rate, which averages -0.6°C for every 100 m increase in elevation, although this varies with humidity, wind exposure, cloud cover and other factors (Dillon et al. 2006). At ground level, aspect influences temperature with south-facing slopes being warmer than north-facing slopes in the Northern Hemisphere (Suggitt et al. 2011). The combined effect of lapse rate and aspect in topographically complex mountain environments causes temperatures to vary considerably over relatively small distances, leading to highly heterogeneous microclimates. Precipitation also varies with elevation, but this is highly dependent upon the wider climatic context (Veblen et al. 2007). In oceanic climates, prevailing marine winds will drive moist air upwards as they hit coastal mountain slopes, creating orographic rainfall that will increase with elevation until the cloud zone, but then decline above it. As a result, the landward, more continental, side of mountain ranges can be much drier (Plate 5). Other abiotic constraints on species also change with elevation, including oxygen concentration, solar radiation and air-pressure (Spence & Tingley 2020; Chapter 2).

Due to their remote nature, the availability of weather observations in mountain environments is often much lower than in more settled areas. Limited meteorological data combined with topographical complexity can mean that both observations and climatic projections may be associated with particularly high uncertainty (Baker et al. 2017). Despite this, the IPCC Special Report on the Ocean and the Cryosphere in a Changing Climate reports warming of 0.3 ± 0.2°C per decade across mountains of North America, the European Alps and High Mountain Asia (Hock et al. 2019), which is greater than the global rate of 0.2 ± 0.1°C per decade

(IPCC 2018), suggesting that warming rates are greatest at high elevations. More recent analysis (Pepin *et al.* 2022) emphasizes the complexity in these data, with variation among studies and regions. Although local comparisons of paired stations tend to show faster warming in mountains compared to lowlands, they found no overall significant difference in temperature trends between high and low elevations globally.

Precipitation patterns in mountain environments show no overall trend (medium confidence), but instead vary across decades and in response to large-scale shifts in atmospheric circulation patterns (e.g., Hartmann & Andresky 2013; Hock *et al.* 2019; Pepin *et al.* 2022). Increases in precipitation at lower elevations are reducing the effect of elevation on precipitation rates, although again with regional differences (Pepin *et al.* 2022). Storms and extreme weather events (cold temperatures and precipitation anomalies) typically increase with elevation in high mountain habitats, but are highly variable across mountain regions (Hock *et al.* 2019). Climate change may increase the frequency and intensity of such events (Beniston 2006), reducing environmental predictability for the species that live there. Increases in the intensity of heavy winter precipitation have been observed in the western Himalayas from 1979–2010 (Cannon *et al.* 2016), but no such pattern is apparent in the Swiss Alps (Brönnimann *et al.* 2018). Overall, there is high confidence that snow cover duration has declined at low elevations by an average of five days per decade, along with declines in snow depth and accumulated mass since the middle of the twentieth century (Hock *et al.* 2019). Trends at higher elevations are less clear. Changes in snow characteristics may impact the frequency and severity of avalanches, which have increased in some regions such as parts of the Himalayas due to an increased frequency of wet snow (Ballesteros-Cánovas *et al.* 2018), but declined in the Alps due to a smaller snow pack (Eckert *et al.* 2013). These climatic trends may have significant impacts upon mountain birds which need to be able to cope with increased variability (i.e., survive a multi-day snow or rainstorm during nesting, Martin *et al.* 2017), as well as long-term trends.

The shrinkage of glaciers is one of the most striking signals of climate change, reported with high confidence (Zemp *et al.* 2015), which is apparent on every continent and in most countries with mountains. Glacier mass loss impacts the subsequent rates and seasonality of runoff affecting the flow of glacier-fed streams and rivers, and therefore affecting downstream freshwater availability across large parts of East Asia and the Americas.

Future projections suggest with a very high confidence that current rates of warming are likely to continue in mountain environments to at least the middle of this century, estimated with a likely range of 0.3 ± 0.2°C per decade (Hock *et al.* 2019). Anticipated precipitation changes are less certain and more variable with projected increases in the Himalayas, East Asia, East Africa, the European Alps and the Carpathian region, and declines in the southern Andes and Mediterranean (with only medium confidence, Hock *et al.* 2019). Underlying these mean changes are potentially more significant shifts in the type of precipitation, which in the Himalayas is projected to become more monsoonal in intensity, whilst increases in precipitation in the European Alps are projected, particularly in winter. In common with current trends, further declines in snow cover are projected with high confidence at low elevations, but at high elevations where temperature is not limiting, snow cover trends may be more variable or could even increase in coastal mountains, at least in the short-term. The nature of snow and the resulting snow-pack may also change as a result of changes in temperature and precipitation patterns (Kausrud *et al.* 2008). Projected changes in the duration of snow cover and snow depth match observed trends, with 25 per cent declines (range −10 per cent to −40 per cent) anticipated by the middle of this century, after which the rate of loss is dependent upon future greenhouse gas emission pathways, ranging from 80 per cent declines (RCP8.5) to 30 per cent (RCP2.6). At higher elevations, projected declines in snow cover, depth and duration are smaller, or in some places, may even increase as a result of increased precipitation. Current declines in glacier mass and extent are also projected to continue into the future, with regional variation.

6.2 Climate Change Impacts Observed on Birds in High Mountain Habitats

In this section, we review the climate change impacts specifically for mountain birds, starting with changes in the timing of breeding, one of the most widely recognized signals of climate change. We next consider impacts on other key demographic parameters that impact individuals and populations, and we then review evidence for the scaling up of climate change impacts to affect distributions and abundance for mountain bird species and communities.

It is worth noting at this stage that the definition of high mountain birds is broad (La Sorte & Jetz 2010; Chapters 1, 2 and 3). About 85 per cent of species are widespread generalists that occupy multiple environments, including mountains (e.g., golden eagle *Aquila chrysaetos*, Eurasian skylark *Alauda arvensis*, horned lark *Eremophila alpestris*), whilst others are highly specialized and adapted to extreme mountain climates (e.g., white-tailed ptarmigan *Lagopus leucura* and white-winged snowfinch *Montifringilla nivalis*). These adaptations are summarized in Chapter 2, but as noted later, they may affect the vulnerability of these species to climate change.

6.2.1 Impacts on Breeding Phenology

One of the strongest signals of climate change has been the change in the timing of biological events. This has been particularly apparent at medium and high latitudes in the Northern Hemisphere, driven by earlier springs (Menzel *et al.* 2006). Advances in phenology generally have been associated with warmer temperatures, with the strongest response in plants, then in primary consumers such as insects, followed by secondary or higher consumers, like most birds (Thackeray *et al.* 2016).

Mountains are highly seasonal environments with short windows of opportunity for breeding (Chapter 2). Above the treeline in temperate mountains, the onset of avian breeding is generally dependent upon the timing of snow melt, as shown for high elevation species such as white-winged snowfinch and ring ouzel *Turdus torquatus* breeding in the Alps (Resano-Mayor *et al.* 2019; Barras *et al.* 2020). Alpine breeding waders, such as European golden plover *Pluvialis apricaria* in Norway, also rely upon snow melt to create areas of exposed vegetation to place their ground nests (Byrkjedal 1980). The timing of breeding in mountain grouse such as rock ptarmigan (Novoa *et al.* 2008; Imperio *et al.* 2013; García-González *et al.* 2016), willow ptarmigan *Lagopus lagopus* and white-tailed ptarmigan show similar associations with snow cover, although the strength of response varies among species (Hannon *et al.* 1988; Martin & Wiebe 2004). Delayed snow melt usually results in a shortened breeding season. In Colorado, late spring snowfall and delayed snow melt in 1995 resulted in white-tailed ptarmigan delaying their first clutch initiation by 18 days later than the study mean for normal years (n = 8 years), but the latest clutch initiation in 1995 was only four days later than any other year (Martin & Wiebe 2004).

At lower elevations, the timing of breeding is correlated with temperature (Bison *et al.* 2020), as shown for both red grouse *Lagopus lagopus scotica* (Fletcher *et al.* 2013) and European golden plover (Pearce-Higgins *et al.* 2005) in the UK, a feature apparent across UK upland birds (Moss *et al.* 2005). The temperature influence means that elevation has a strong impact on breeding phenology. In Yosemite National Park, there was a 12-day delay in timing of breeding (measured by the first capture date of juvenile birds) between elevations of 1300 m and 2400 m, although this varied among species (Saracco *et al.* 2019).

Phenology patterns are more complex in migratory bird species, where timing of arrival and breeding onset may be influenced by carry-over effects of climatic conditions on the wintering grounds, or on migration, as well as on the breeding grounds, although not in every species (Ockendon *et al.* 2013; Finch *et al.* 2014; de Zwaan *et al.* 2022). Many temperate mountain birds winter at lower elevations and can potentially respond quite rapidly to environmental change as they approach high elevation breeding grounds; the first arrivals of American robins *Turdus migratorius* returning to their breeding grounds in the Colorado Rocky Mountains advanced by 14 days from 1980 to 1999 (Inouye *et al.* 2000). In cold years or years with late snow cover, individuals either delay their return to high elevation breeding territories and remain at lower elevations (e.g., Morton 2002; de Zwaan *et al.* 2019a), or arrive at high elevation breeding territories, but delay development of breeding structures until conditions ameliorate (Bears *et al.* 2009).

Mountain avifaunas also contain a proportion of long-distance continental migrants (Boyle & Martin 2015) which may have less flexibility and can suffer high mortality if they arrive on the breeding grounds too early. Earlier arrival in response to warmer temperatures can increase exposure to late snow-fall or cold-spells that are often a feature of alpine environments (Bears *et al.* 2009), conditions that may become less predictable in the future (Beniston 2006). The mortality of two thirds of a population of common sandpipers *Actitis hypoleuca* in 1981, caused by late snow fall in the Peak District, UK, illustrates this potential (Holland & Yalden 1991, Pearce-Higgins *et al.* 2009). Martin *et al.* (2017) found for two sympatric alpine breeding passerines that body size influenced whether birds incurred the risk of early storm events, as horned larks (35 g) started breeding two weeks earlier than the smaller Savannah sparrows *Passerculus sandwichensis* (18 g). These breeding delays in the sparrows resulted in a 25 per cent shorter breeding season.

Species face two choices in order to maintain their association with a particular temperature regime in a warming climate (i.e., thermal niche tracking). In strongly temperature-driven seasonal environments, they can either advance the timing of key biological events so that they maintain a temperature match, or they can shift their distribution to higher latitudes or elevations to maintain the same association with temperature. In the Sierra Nevada and Coast Ranges of California covered by the Grinnell Resurvey Project, Socolar *et al.* (2017) observed an average 5–12 day advance in the estimated timing of breeding between 1911–1940 and 2003–2010, helping the birds to keep pace with the 1°C of warming that occurred. This simple pattern of phenological thermal niche tracking is likely to be most apparent in single-brooded species (most mountain birds; Chapter 2).

There are almost no breeding phenology studies for tropical mountain birds, where birds are more likely to respond to changes in precipitation than temperature (Pearce-Higgins *et al.* 2015a). These environments are also highly seasonal, and are particularly driven by the timing of wet and dry seasons (Boyle *et al.* 2020; Neate-Clegg *et al.* 2021a), with a number of intricate interactions that depend on phenology, from highly specialized plant-nectarivore associations important for sunbirds and hummingbirds, to birds that breed and moult in synchrony with the rainy season. A shift in phenology here could lead to a breakdown of these relationships. Birds at high elevation on Mount Cameroon breed during the dry season, while those at lower elevation breed during the wet season (Tye 1992), highlighting different drivers. The breeding season is also shorter and more constrained at higher elevations than lower elevations in the tropics (Young 1994; Peh *et al.* 2012). Ultimately, responses of species will be driven by the selection pressures that climate change imposes on individuals, such as through impacts on breeding success, the subject to which we now turn.

6.2.2 Impacts on Breeding Success

Reproductive success in mountain bird species tends to be driven either by variation in (i) weather, (ii) prey availability or (iii) predation, all of which can be affected by climate change. There is also evidence of (iv) disease and (v) competition being important in some circumstances.

Direct Impacts of Weather

It is remarkable that for many species, despite their association with cold climates, there are positive responses between breeding success and temperature (Pearce-Higgins 2011). For alpine breeding passerines, breeding success can be higher in early warm years because with more time, songbirds such as horned larks nest earlier, have a greater probability of first nest success, raise nestlings that grow faster and larger, have a higher probability of second broods and of renesting after failure of their first clutch (Camfield *et al.* 2010; de Zwaan *et al.* 2019b, 2020, 2022). The breeding success across 25 passerines in the montane zone of Yosemite National Park was shown to be correlated positively with temperature (Saracco *et al.* 2019). Annual fluctuations in the abundance of 7 of 10 high latitude passerine populations in Denali National Park, Alaska were also positively correlated with temperature during the previous breeding season (Mizel *et al.* 2021). Precocial species exhibit similar positive patterns with temperature, as shown for the breeding success of dunlin *Calidris alpina* (Beale *et al.* 2006) and rock ptarmigan (Watson *et al.* 1998), as well as the growth rates of Eurasian dotterel *Charadrius morinellus* chicks (Thomson 1994).

Rainfall can be an important driver of breeding success, particularly in gamebirds which appear more sensitive to negative effects of rainfall than other precocial species (Pearce-Higgins & Green 2014). Heavy rain when the chicks are young reduces the breeding success of black grouse *Lyrurus tetrix* (Summers *et al.* 2004; Pearce-Higgins *et al.* 2019) and rock ptarmigan (Novoa *et al.* 2008). Birds of prey such as hen harriers *Circus cyaneus* are similarly vulnerable to heavy rainfall, due to a combination of poorer foraging conditions for the adults and increased risk of chilling for the chicks (Redpath *et al.* 2002). For alpine breeding Savannah sparrows, precipitation prior to clutch initiation has a positive effect on nestling growth, while in horned larks, heavy precipitation (storm events) during the nestling period has a negative influence on offspring development (de Zwaan *et al.* 2020). In the tropics, the relatively positive impacts of precipitation on bird populations (Pearce-Higgins & Green 2014; Pearce-Higgins *et al.* 2015a) may be mitigated at higher elevations where cooler temperatures reduce rates of evaporation and evapotranspiration (Boyle *et al.* 2020). For example, white-ruffed manakins *Corapipo altera* in mid-elevational Central American forests undergo metabolic changes symptomatic of short-term fasting during rainstorms which are not apparent at lower elevations (Boyle *et al.* 2010).

Prey Availability
Whilst mountain birds can show surprisingly positive responses to temperature during the breeding season, warming may have negative impacts on species by disrupting the timing of related biological events, such as periods of peak food demand and availability, or by directly

altering the size of prey populations. Many mountain bird species rely on a highly seasonal ephemeral resource for successful reproduction, often invertebrates (e.g., tipulids, chironomids, earthworms or caterpillars) or nectar which are available for only short periods (Pearce-Higgins 2010; McKinney et al. 2012; Barras et al. 2022). The timing of prey availability will be driven by temperature (Pearce-Higgins et al. 2005; Thackeray et al. 2016), either as a result of direct impacts of invertebrate growth rates and activity, or particularly in high alpine environments, the indirect impacts on prey availability due to the timing of snow melt and subsequent evaporation of soil moisture (Barras et al. 2022). In the tropics, changes in moisture availability may be more important (Boyle et al. 2020). When warmer temperatures also speed a reduction in food availability later in the season as resource patches dry out, this could drive a negative mismatch impact on late nests or fledglings (e.g., reductions in tipulid availability for white-winged snowfinches, Resano-Mayor et al. 2019; earthworm availability for ring ouzels, Barras et al. 2020; or, ephemeral nectar resources for broad-tailed hummingbirds, *Selasphorus platycercus*, McKinney et al. 2012).

The timing of snowmelt impacts rock ptarmigan breeding success; in years of late snowmelt, clutch size is reduced in northern Canada and in the Pyrenees, hens are in poorer body condition, both situations resulting in reduced breeding success (Wilson & Martin 2010; García-González et al. 2016). In the tropics, snow or glacial melt can substantially affect the presence and size of ephemeral wetland areas which are highly productive breeding sites for a diversity of alpine birds (Chapter 3). The accelerated glacier ice mass loss on high mountain wetland areas reduces productivity in the tropical high Andes of Bolivia (Cardenas et al. 2021). Similar processes likely affect wetland areas in other tropical mountains; for example, in the Bale Mountains of Ethiopia where wetland extent more than doubles in the wet season versus the dry season (Chignell et al. 2019).

Aside from timing, warming may more directly reduce the abundance of key prey for mountain birds. Summer warming reduces the abundance of craneflies (Tipulidae) emerging the following spring, affecting European golden plover chick survival, breeding success and subsequent population changes (Pearce-Higgins & Yalden 2004; Pearce-Higgins et al. 2010; Carroll et al. 2011). Ring ouzels, which rely on earthworm-rich patches of short, damp grassland, are also affected negatively by the soil drying out during the breeding season (Burfield 2002; Beale et al. 2006; Barras et al. 2020), as this reduces earthworm availability

(Pearce-Higgins 2010; Martay & Pearce-Higgins 2018). Glaciers may also provide important sources of macroinvertebrate food for grey-crowned rosy finches *Leucosticte tephrocotis* in Mount Rainer, Washington that feed on glacier ice worms *Mesenchytraeus solifugus* (Hotaling *et al.* 2020). Despite the potential vulnerability to warming of mountain birds which rely on soil invertebrates (Pearce-Higgins 2010), European golden plover, ring ouzel or common sandpiper do not appear to be declining in mountain ranges across Europe (Beale *et al.* 2006; Pearce-Higgins *et al.* 2009, 2010; Lehikoinen *et al.* 2019; Chapter 5).

Very limited data are available for the tropics, where changes in rainfall are likely to be more important than temperature in altering insect populations (Pearce-Higgins *et al.* 2015a). There are strong elevational shifts in species richness suggesting climate change is altering tropical insect communities. Geometrid moths and stream invertebrates are highly seasonal and show the strongest responses to changes in precipitation, compared to much less variable dung beetles and Arctiid moths (Larsen *et al.* 2011). Geometrid moth populations in the humid tropics of Borneo have also shifted upward by an average of 67 m from 1967 to 2007 (Chen *et al.* 2009), with potential impacts on their avian predators.

The effect of extreme heat events on food availability or ability to forage is another potentially important factor, particularly in the tropics or subtropics. For example, mountain breeding Cape rockjumpers *Chaetops frenatus* in South Africa reduce foraging and parental provisioning efforts during heat waves to invest more time in shade-seeking, resulting in reduced nestling growth rates (Oswald *et al.* 2021). Thus, while we tend to focus on cold events, in the alpine environment 'extreme heat events' will also become more common and may negatively impact developing nestlings in a cold-adapted bird.

A full understanding of the impacts of climate change on mountain bird species depends on good ecological understanding, particularly of species diet and habitat associations. Although we describe a number of detailed case-studies, these are highly biased spatially, particularly towards lower elevations. At present, too few studies document long-term changes in prey abundance and bird populations to be able to make confident generalisations.

Predation

The breeding success of mountain birds is often limited by predation, particularly in ground-nesting species, and factors that lead to an increase in predation can cause widespread population declines (Jahren *et al.* 2016; Roos *et al.* 2018; Alba *et al.* 2022). There is the potential for climate change to affect predation rates, either directly through impacts on predator populations, or indirectly by altering the habitat.

Generalist predator populations tend to increase most where human activity artificially subsidizes predators (e.g., Pringle *et al.* 2019), or in response to meso-predator release associated with the loss of top predators (Newsome *et al.* 2017). Away from such influences, warmer conditions or shorter winters may allow predators that are common in lower elevations to expand into mountain environments. For example, climate change has helped red foxes *Vulpes vulpes* spread through Fennoscandia and the Canadian Arctic, negatively affecting Arctic fox *Vulpes lagopus* populations (Elmhagen *et al.* 2017), although a relaxation in hunting pressure and increased human subsidy of wild red fox populations may be the primary cause of increase in some areas (Gallant *et al.* 2020). These changes have the potential to disrupt the complex predator–prey dynamics of Arctic mountain systems (Henden *et al.* 2021).

In cold-dominated environments, there is increasing evidence for bottom-up regulation of predation mediated through the impact of snow cover on rodent cycles and predator populations. Deep snow provides protection from predation for rodents enabling ongoing population growth during the winter, which boosts rodent numbers during the increasing phase of the population cycle (e.g., Kausrud *et al.* 2008). Conversely, warmer winters are associated with reduced population cycling and a wide-spread dampening of rodent cycles across Europe (Cornulier *et al.* 2013), with particular implications for the breeding success of waders (Lehikoinen *et al.* 2016). Although most of the literature on such impacts on birds is from Arctic tundra, vole cycles are also dampening in the mountain regions of Europe (e.g., the Southern Uplands in the UK, Finnish and Czech Mountains; Cornulier *et al.* 2013). Thus, climate change could be significantly impacting the predation rates of ground-nesting birds, as well as the breeding success of predatory raptors and owls that rely on those rodents (Korpimäki 1994).

In addition to potential direct impacts on predator populations, climate change may also indirectly affect predation rates by changing habitat suitability. Given that the risk of predation can be linked to the vegetation characteristics around the nest (Laidlaw *et al.* 2020), climatic impacts on vegetation structure may alter nest concealment and subsequent predation rates (Wiebe & Martin 1998). Advancing treelines may also increase predation risk for ground nesting bird species which will come into contact with a higher density of treeline-associated predators (Chapter 3).

Late season storms, which are increasing in frequency and severity, can increase the risk of predation on grouse and songbirds because ground nesting birds are more readily detected after a snowstorm (Martin *et al.* 2000, 2017). Changes in snowpack may also more directly affect habitat suitability for some predators, such as the wolverine *Gulo gulo* which is associated with deeper snow (Glass *et al.* 2021), affecting their foraging distribution and potential impacts on bird populations.

Disease Processes

While the prevalence of diseases and parasites is traditionally low in alpine habitats (Chapter 2), climate change may increase disease and parasite incidence. In a mountain context, perhaps the best studied example is that of red grouse populations where high-density populations managed for sports shooting can fluctuate in response to cycles in the abundance of the nematode parasite *Trichostrongylus tenuis*. Rates of infestation are enhanced by warm, wet summer weather which increases the survival of the parasite eggs and early larval stages (Cattadori *et al.* 2005). The abundance of louping ill, carried by ticks, is another disease positively correlated with temperature and negatively with elevation (Gilbert 2010). Both diseases may increase in prevalence as a result of climate warming, although as they are largely diseases of artificially maintained high-density game populations it is unclear how much they may impact other mountain bird species. Recent evidence from Scotland suggests that the rate of tick infestation on European golden plover chicks is correlated positively with temperature and has a negative impact on chick survival (Douglas & Pearce-Higgins 2019). In South America, blood parasites are found in a high proportion of sampled bird species in the Colombian high Andes (Rodriguez *et al.* 2009), hummingbirds are reservoirs of blood parasites in the Ecuadorian mountains (Moens *et al.* 2016) and avian flu is prevalent in the Peruvian high Andes (Williams *et al.* 2012). Benning *et al.* (2002) have expressed concerns regarding the potential for avian malaria to expand upslope in Hawaii and threaten native bird species in the remaining areas of native forest at high elevations. Thus, the extent that other mountain bird species are vulnerable to disease processes and parasites may be greater than expected and likely is increasing with warming climates.

Competition

Competition is thought to be one of the main processes that limits species range margins, particularly for species in mountains where narrow elevational ranges are maintained by interspecific aggression. This has been suggested from playback experiments in *Catharus* thrushes and *Henicorhina* wrens (Jankowski *et al.* 2010). Although the evidence for competition driving responses to climate change in mountain bird populations is weak, there is circumstantial evidence that competition could still be important. Lowland species in Borneo occur at higher elevations on two small mountains which lack montane specialists compared to two larger mountains (Burner *et al.* 2020). Species richness is a better predictor of mountain bird elevation range than climate (Freeman *et al.* 2022). These studies are on montane forest species, but the same mechanisms could operate at the range boundaries of species above the treeline and merit some research.

These examples show that impacts of climate change on mountain systems can be variable and complex, and that despite many short-term positive responses to warmer temperatures, there are a variety of biotic mechanisms through which warming can have detrimental long-term impacts on mountain bird populations and communities (Hanz *et al.* 2019; Boyce *et al.* 2019). These concepts are even more complex in migratory birds which may also be affected by the same or other climate change-driven processes away from their mountain breeding grounds in a range of different ways, as we will now consider.

6.2.3 Impacts Away from Mountain Breeding Grounds

Globally, about 58 per cent of bird species breeding above the treeline vacate their mountain breeding grounds for lower elevations or warmer climates after the breeding season; about 27 per cent in the tropics and 86 per cent of species breeding in the north temperate mountains of North America, Europe and Asia (Figure 3.3, Tables 3.2 and 3.3, Chapter 3).

Beale *et al.* (2006) noted the impact that changes in rainfall conditions on the north African wintering grounds can have on ring ouzel populations breeding in the UK, potentially mediated through changes in the size of the juniper berry crop. Weather impacts on the wintering grounds affect over-winter survival rates (Pearce-Higgins & Green 2014), but can also carry-over to impact breeding parameters, although the evidence that they are sufficiently important to influence populations is relatively weak (Ockendon *et al.* 2013; Finch *et al.* 2014).

For an alpine breeding population of horned lark, cold temperatures at stopover sites can influence timing of breeding, nestling development rate and ultimately breeding success (de Zwaan *et al.* 2022). In the short-term, warming on the wintering grounds may increase the abundance of many short- and medium-distance migrants by reducing cold-related mortality, whilst the impacts on long-distance migrants may be more equivocal, depending on changes in rainfall conditions in their tropical wintering grounds (Pearce-Higgins & Green 2014; Pearce-Higgins *et al.* 2015b). However, for many migratory birds breeding in high mountains, especially the generalists, specific post-breeding locations and habitats have not been determined, hampering our ability to understand these processes further (Chapter 10).

With many migratory mountain birds only occupying their breeding sites for about two months, their populations are heavily influenced by conditions away from the breeding grounds, which if unsuitable can cause significant increases in mortality. In summary, as climate change reduces the suitability of warmer, lower elevational sites for mountain birds, we expect to find evidence of upward shifts in the distribution and abundance of species, with more relative increases predicted for warm-associated rather than cold-associated species, through the various mechanisms outlined above and changes in natal dispersal and settlement. Interactions between land-use change and climate change are also apparent at larger spatial scales, with potential impacts on the distribution and occurrence of mountain bird populations and communities, covered in detail in the next section.

6.3 Impacts at Larger Spatial Scales

Typically, data are limited to monitor the status and population trends within mountain bird communities, but fortunately coverage by Citizen Science data is increasing in a number of countries, enabling the production of robust trends for some mountain bird populations (Lehikoinen *et al.* 2019). Across Europe, mountain bird populations show a weak but significantly increasing trend from 2002–2020, but with trends varying among regions (declining trends only in the UK; Chapter 5). Regional population trends in Europe are associated positively with the climatic niche of the species, such that warm-dwelling species are doing better than cold-associated species. Over a 50-year period in Western North America, mountain bird populations showed an overall long-term decline (Chapter 5).

Here, we focus on elevational and latitudinal shifts in distribution, and relative changes in abundance across species that might be expected in response to climate change.

6.3.1 Elevational and Latitudinal Shifts in Distribution

Rates of elevational shifts in birds correlate with the shifts expected from warming globally, although the spatial magnitude of such shifts is relatively small, averaging 11 m/decade upward across all taxa compared to 16.9 km poleward shift/decade (Chen *et al.* 2011). These average values combine both upward and downward shifts, and therefore underestimate the magnitude of shift in circumstances where some species move upslope and others downslope (see below).

Table 6.1 summarizes the data from published studies of changes in the elevational distribution of species. When converted to decadal rates of change and averaged across studies, the 16 studies which present mean shifts in elevation (excluding Maggini *et al.* 2011 – see Table 6.1), give an average rate of upslope shift of 18 m/decade (Figure 6.1), although this figure masks considerable variation among studies, and even among species at the same location. For example, although 84 per cent of species shifted their elevational distribution in the Sierra Nevada mountains of California, only 51 per cent of shifts were upslope as expected from warming. Overall, 82 per cent of range shifts were in a direction predicted by changes in either temperature, pushing species upslope, or precipitation, pulling species downslope (Tingley *et al.* 2012). Estimates for 421 bird species from eight study sites across the tropics (Americas, Africa and Oceania) indicate an upslope shift of 1.63 ± 0.30 m/yr (Neate-Clegge *et al.* 2021a), similar to our global average (Figure 6.1).

Some of the variation among species appears to be linked to life-history, with small, short-lived *r*-selected species showing more rapid shifts than longer-lived species (Couet *et al.* 2022; Hallman *et al.* 2022). Larger-species in the tropics are more likely to shift downslope (Neate-Clegge *et al.* 2021a). Rates of change appear fastest for species with high dispersal ability, long-distance migrants, low foraging strata, habitat generalists and wide elevational ranges (Neate-Clegge *et al.* 2021a; Hallman *et al.* 2022).

Some of the variation may also be attributable to changes in vegetation. In the White Mountains of New Hampshire (USA), elevational shifts in the upper-range margins for 9 of 16 low-elevation forest species were consistent with expected upslope shifts in response to warming,

Table 6.1 *Published studies of elevational shifts (m ± standard errors when available) in mountain birds over the past century, for trailing (lower elevation), mean (or central optima) and leading (upper elevation) limits where presented. Studies that provide estimates for multiple locations are listed sequentially.*

Country	Start	End	No. spp.	Mean	Trailing	Leading	Reference
Europe / N America							
Czechia	1986–1998	2006–2008	50	30.5 ± 11.8			Reif & Flousek 2012
France	1973/4–1978/80	2000/1–2001/2	29	-2.4 ± 8.0			Archaux et al. 2004
Italy	1992–1994	2003–2005	11	29			Popy et al. 2010
Italy	1982	2017	29	102.2 ± 18.9	302.8 ± 75.6	194.6 ± 36.1	Bani et al. 2019
Scandinavia	1999–2002	2015–2018	76	12.3 ± 2.9			Couet et al. 2022
Switzerland	2003	2010		42			Roth et al. 2014
Switzerland	1999–2002	2004–2007	33*	40	82	94	Maggini et al. 2011
Switzerland	1996	2016	71	31.07 ± 8.8	20.7 ± 4.7	18.4 ± 9.5	Hallman et al. 2022
UK	1968–1972	1988–1991	22	-2.1 ± 20.0			Hickling et al. 2006
UK	1994	2009	<48	-9.7	14.6	0	Massimino et al. 2015
USA, Alaska	1995	2019		90.5			Mizel et al. 2021
USA, California	1900–1930	1980–2006	78		36.5 ± 25.1	97.2 ± 46.0	Tingley et al. 2012
			78		-19.3 ± 40.0	203.7 ± 57.5	
			73		-129.7 ± 46.9	143.7 ± 78.6	
USA, NY State	1980–1985	2000–2005	129		-11.6 ± 7.7	5.7 ± 9.4	Zuckerberg et al. 2009
USA, NY State	1974	2014	42	82.8	85.9	123	Kirchman & van Keuren 2017

(cont.)

Table 6.1 (cont.)

Country	Start	End	No. spp.	Mean	Trailing	Leading	Reference
Tropics							
Honduras	2007	2016	18	14.2			Neate-Clegg et al. 2018
Papua New Guinea	1969	2013	47		95 ± 190	113 ± 197	Freeman & Freeman 2014
			44		123 ± 200	153 ± 184	
Peru	1985	2017	32	40 ± 98	117 ± 170	68 ± 152	Freeman et al. 2018
Peru	1969	2010	55	49.0 ± 17.3			Forero-Medina et al. 2011
Puerto Rico	1998	2015	20		-62.2	51.8	Campos-Cerqueira et al. 2017
Rwanda	1997	2011	51	26.2 ± 19.7	61.7 ± 28.3	-42.8 ± 35.6	Neate-Clegg et al. 2020
Tanzania, Africa	1979–1981	2019	29	92.5 ± 84.9	182.8 ± 71.8	71.8 ± 117.8	Neate-Clegg et al. 2021b

* Estimates for Maggini et al. (2011) are for species with a significant shift in their elevational range only and are therefore excluded from the summary statistics presented in the text.

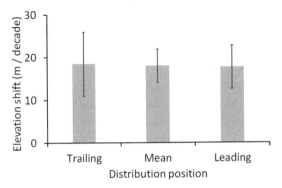

Figure 6.1 Mean (m ± se) elevational shifts in mountain birds, averaged across 15, 16 and 14 estimates respectively (presented in Table 6.1).

whilst downslope shifts were observed in the lower-elevation margin in 9 of 11 high-elevation forest species (DeLuca & King 2017). Such changes could be due to changes in forest structure, or due to declines in red spruce *Picea rubens* and paper birch *Betula papyrifera* through a mix of potential climate change, land-use change and acid deposition. At high latitudes, Mizel *et al.* (2021) recorded significant upslope shifts in 7 of 10 high altitude Arctic passerines, potentially linked to changes in erect shrub distribution (Brodie *et al.* 2019). Overall, upward elevational shifts tend to be more common at locations where warming is greatest (Chen *et al.* 2011; Scridel *et al.* 2018). However, latitude may complicate this simple global picture as elevation shifts in the tropics appear to follow warming trends, but only one-third of studies in temperate mountain areas match these expectations (Freeman & Freeman 2014; Neate-Clegge *et al.* 2021a). Tropical birds show much stronger tracking of temperature than temperate species (Freeman *et al.* 2021). This might be because many temperate mountain species are elevational generalists (Boyle *et al.* 2015) with greater niche breadth than tropical mountain species.

Further analysis by Guo *et al.* (2018), although not focussed on birds, provides a potential answer by linking elevational change to forest loss. In the tropics and at lower elevations, where many mountain species are associated with forests, the rates of elevation shift across both plant and animal taxa are enhanced by forest loss. Deforestation at low elevations accelerates the upward elevational movement of species into higher elevation areas of remaining intact habitat (Ibarra *et al.* 2017; Altamirano *et al.* 2020; Elsen *et al.* 2020). Conversely, at higher-elevations and latitudes, rates of elevation shift are reduced by forest loss which may counter the upwards push of climate change, particularly for open country species by lowering treelines. Although an alluring hypothesis, many temperate and boreal treelines are also advancing upwards, suggesting a complex interaction between anthropogenic and climatic treeline limits, which obfuscates the detection of elevation responses to climate change. The potential for land-use and climate change to interact is further illustrated by the fact that survival rates of species have increased at cold-range margins and declined at warm-range margins in Himalayan primary forest, but not in logged forests (Srinivasan & Wilcove 2021).

The rates of elevation shift across studies are at the scale of tens of metres over several decades, and thus may appear realistic for individuals to keep pace. However, for many species, relatively small shifts may mask an increasing climate debt (the relative distance between a species range and the optimal climate conditions in which it is adapted to live; Visser 2012), as habitat or topographical constraints may prevent species keeping pace with climate change. Climate variability in the form of extreme events may reverse the success of multiple upshifting movements for some species. Also, the access to climate refugia may be more limited for species with narrow elevational limits.

Many studies document asymmetrical changes in leading and trailing range margins (Table 6.1). Although our global analysis suggests there is no significant difference overall in the mean rates of change between leading and trailing edges (Figure 6.1), Neate-Clegge et al. (2021a) report that in the tropics, upper limits may have upshifted by 1.62 m ± 0.38 m/yr, but considerably more at their lower limits (2.81 ± 0.42 m/yr). Contrasts between tropical and non-tropical mountains could be another consequence of variation in rates of habitat change at upper and lower elevations across the globe.

To summarize, there is robust evidence of generally upward shifts in mountain bird distributions in response to recent warming, although these patterns are not universal; at some locations and for many species, there is little evidence of change. Also, downslope shifts have been observed, particularly in response to changes in rainfall in arid climates (Tingley et al. 2012). In the short-term, the relaxation of cold limits at leading range margins may be more rapid than change in the biotic processes that limit trailing range margins (Neate-Clegg et al. 2021b), with short-lived species having responded most rapidly (Couet et al. 2022). Climate change has therefore already changed bird community composition, altering the proportion of generalists and specialists in mountain avifaunal communities, and even increasing the elevational distribution of at least some low elevation species at some locations (Neate-Clegg *et al.* 2021b). At the species level, there will be winners and losers. Avian communities might increase in species richness if alpine specialists can co-exist with the recently upshifted lower elevation generalist species. However, if competition or predation processes increase, avian communities might also transition to higher proportions of generalist species. We next discuss what models suggest about the future impacts of climate change on mountain bird species over a much longer timescale.

6.4 Future Vulnerability

6.4.1 Climatic Limits to Distribution and Abundance

It is generally assumed that alpine birds are particularly vulnerable to climate change because they are associated with cold climates that are likely to warm. As they move upslope in response to warming, they are anticipated to have less land available to occupy (Şekercioğlu *et al.* 2008; Freeman *et al.* 2022). However, this general pattern is complicated by variation in the topography of different mountain ranges (Elsen & Tingley 2015; Chapter 3). Only about one third of mountains, such as the European Alps, follow a simple pyramidal shape in which climate warming is expected to reduce the extent of climatically suitable range as species move upslope. Thirty-nine percent of mountains have a diamond-shaped profile of land area against elevation which means that low elevation species are likely to benefit from warming with an increase in habitat area, but intermediate and high elevation species will risk habitat decline. Mountain ranges with an hourglass profile (c. 25 per cent) have low land area at intermediate elevations and 6 per cent are classed as inverse pyramids with the greatest spatial extent being high-elevation plateaus (Figure 6.2). Models assume that species found below those plateaus may expand their distribution in response to climate change due to the greater land area at high elevations, although this depends on such species not being restricted by habitat variation associated with topography.

Accounting for elevational variation in the distribution of intact natural habitats (i.e., not under intense human pressure that negatively impacts species persistence) significantly alters the proportion of mountains classified into the four topographical types; reducing the number of mountains classed as pyramidal to 17 per cent from 32 per cent, diamond-shaped mountains to 30 per cent from 39 per cent and

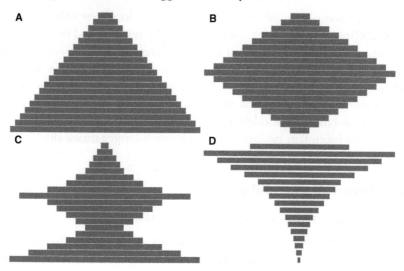

Figure 6.2 The available surface at each elevation for each class of mountain topography *sensu* Elsen & Tingley (2015). A. represents a typical mountain form where the area of land available decreases with elevation, D. represents high mountain plateaus, where high elevation area exceeds low elevation, while B. and C. represent intermediate classes.

inverse-pyramids to 2 per cent from 6 per cent (Elsen *et al.* 2020). The proportion of hourglass mountains increases slightly to 28 per cent from 23 per cent, whilst the remaining one quarter of ranges have no natural habitat left and are reclassed as 'intensified', emphasising that in these cases, most mountain species may be more threatened by land-use than by climate change, or the potential interactions between climate and land-use change. The net result is that while there is an overall reduction in alpine habitat, a greater proportion of mountain species are regarded as likely to experience an increase in the extent of climatically suitable areas of natural habitat in response to climate change than previously thought, due to the fact that the proportion of mountain habitat in a natural state is generally greater at higher elevations than in lowlands (Ibarra *et al.* 2017). Climate change processes may therefore 'rescue' low and medium-elevation generalists currently occupying heavily modified human landscapes from negative human pressure by reducing thermal limits to their distribution and facilitating colonisation of higher elevations with less human-modified habitat.

Recent reviews suggest that whilst climate is a key driver of species richness, measures of vegetation productivity linked to climate are more important than simple measures of temperature (McCain & Grytnes 2010; Pearce-Higgins & Green 2014). At medium and high latitudes where temperature tends to be limiting, warmer temperatures are associated with greater vegetation complexity, niche opportunities and avian species richness, although this simple pattern can be complicated by the location of the treeline, which adds additional heterogeneity, sometimes leading to a peak in the richness of species associated with ecotones (Martin *et al.* 2021; Chapter 4). In tropical environments, where moisture is limiting (Pearce-Higgins *et al.* 2015a), measures such as net primary productivity or actual evapotranspiration are the best predictors of species richness (Pearce-Higgins & Green 2014). This explains why in dryland systems the relationship between elevation and species richness can show a mid-range peak (Araneda *et al.* 2018), and why changes in the elevational distribution of species in such environments can be downward (Tingley *et al.* 2012). The elevational profile of species richness of the Guararrama Mountains (600–2,400 m) in Central Spain changed from a mid-range peak typical of dryland environments in 1976–80 to a monotonic decline with elevation in 2014–15, more characteristic of humid mountains (Tellería 2020). Additional studies of changes in the elevational profile of bird communities in response to climate change are required to improve our ability to project future responses to climate change.

Although habitat and climate interact to drive the elevational profiles of species and communities, the importance of those drivers varies with climate, and particularly among the humid tropics, dryland tropics and higher latitudes. In Europe, where authors have attempted to disentangle the relative importance of climate and habitat in shaping bird community assemblages, climate alone tends to be less important than habitat condition (Chamberlain *et al.* 2016; Buchanan *et al.* 2017). Similarly, habitat structure is relatively more important than climate for the south temperate Andes (Altamirano *et al.* 2020). In the Himalayas, the converse appears true (Elsen *et al.* 2017).

The importance of climate and land-use or habitat availability may also vary with elevation. Temperature is the main limitation on water pipit *Anthus spinoletta* abundance at low elevations, whilst at high elevations where the climate is suitable, habitat is the main driver (Melendez & Laiola 2014). The importance of microclimate, as measured by variation in solar insolation, may vary with overall climatic suitability. Meadow pipits *Anthus pratensis* become increasingly restricted to cooler, north-facing slopes as climatic suitability deteriorates (Massimino *et al.* 2020), whilst whinchats *Saxicola rubetra* are increasingly associated with warmer, south-facing slopes at high-elevations (Calladine & Bray 2012). Thus, across both latitudinal and elevational species ranges, climate is likely to be the ultimate determinant of occurrence and abundance, whilst within suitable climates, habitat extent and quality will influence finer-scale variation in populations.

6.4.2 Projected Impacts of Climate Change

A range of studies have attempted to project the impacts of future climate change upon the vulnerability, persistence or extinction risk of species (Chapter 8). Şekercioğlu et al. (2008) modelled the impacts of warming on the extinction risk of landbirds, mediated through changes in elevational distribution and habitat-loss. Under 2.8°C warming, 400–550 species were estimated to become extinct, with an additional 100–500 species added for every further degree of warming. Across the Western Hemisphere, projected extinction rates varied from 1.3 per cent under 1.1°C of warming to 30 per cent with an increase of 6°C temperature (Şekercioğlu et al. 2008), with tropical mountain endemics particularly vulnerable. These models are based on assumed rates of elevational change with temperature mediated through lapse rates. Although they did assume a lower lapse rate for tropical species, they may not fully account for the greater importance of precipitation than temperature in driving bird distributions and communities in the tropics (Pearce-Higgins et al. 2015a; Neate-Clegg et al. 2021a). More specific modelling for over 1,000 mountain bird species supports the conclusion that species with narrow elevational distributions, especially tropical mountain endemics, are highly threatened if they are dispersal constrained (La Sorte & Jetz 2010). At least one third of mountain bird species are projected to suffer more than 50 per cent declines in range extent, reducing their range extent to less than 20,000 km^2. Allowing species to undergo elevational shifts in distribution reduced projected losses, particularly in areas with high elevation plateaus. If long-distance dispersal to other mountain systems is also factored into the models, species vulnerability becomes more closely linked to mountain-range isolation, in which case mountain birds in Australasian, Nearctic and Afrotropical regions are most vulnerable. Other global modelling studies are not specific in modelling elevational shifts in response to climate change, but show a strong link between global temperature increase and projected reductions in range extent or increases in extinction risk or vulnerability of species to climate change (Urban 2015; Warren *et al.* 2013, 2018). In combination, these studies suggest that climate change vulnerability in mountain birds is a combination of the magnitude of climate change, mountain topography, isolation and habitat extent.

Many studies have attempted to project future climate change impacts on individual species or groups of species in particular mountain environments. Some focus just on the effects of temperature (e.g., Şekercioğlu *et al.* 2008; Pearce-Higgins *et al.* 2010), whilst most also attempt to account for variation in habitat (von dem Bussche *et al.* 2008; Braunisch *et al.* 2014) and some consider responses to multiple climate change and land-use change scenarios (Chamberlain *et al.* 2013; Barras *et al.* 2021). Many studies project significant reductions in high mountain specialists (Brambilla *et al.* 2016; Scridel *et al.* 2021), but others show more mixed results, particularly when covering a wider range of forest and open-country species (Chamberlain *et al.* 2013; Ralston & Kirchman 2013). Observed changes in community response or elevation distributions generally match those expected on the basis of warming, but the rate of change is less than would be expected from the magnitude of warming (e.g., Chen *et al.* 2011; Devictor *et al.* 2012). This suggests that a 'climate debt' may build-up through time (Devictor *et al.* 2012), although evidence of negatively impacted mountain bird population trends is not yet very strong (Chapter 5). An alternative explanation is that species may be less sensitive to climate than the models suggest, perhaps due to inadequacies in the models, or because the topographical heterogeneity of mountain environments may provide cool climate refugia where species may persist.

Across studies, projected impacts on high mountain specialists and generalists appear to be more severe than for low elevation species (Scridel *et al.* 2018). White-winged snowfinch is projected to decline by 52–97 per cent in the Italian Alps (Brambilla *et al.* 2016, 2018), and rock ptarmigan by 78 per cent in the Italian Alps by 2050 (Imperio *et al.* 2013), up to 69 per cent in the Swiss Alps (Reverman *et al.* 2012) and by 80 per cent in British Colombia, Canada (Scridel *et al.* 2021). Ring ouzel populations are projected to decline to extinction in Bavaria by 2100 (Bässler *et al.* 2010) and by 30–40 per cent under a high emissions (RCP 8.5) climate change pathway in the Swiss Alps (von dem Bussche *et al.* 2008; Barras *et al.* 2021). Significant declines in the range extent of endemic mountain top species are predicted in Brazil (Hoffman *et al.* 2020), the Andes (Velasquez-Tibeta *et al.* 2013; del Rosario Avalos & Hernandez 2015) and central America (Gasner *et al.* 2010). In contrast, elevational generalists such as Eurasian sky-lark and dunnock *Prunella modularis* in the European Alps, or Eurasian three-toed woodpecker *Picoides tridactylus* and bay-breasted warbler *Setophaga castanea*, may well increase their elevational range and distribution in response to climate change (Chamberlain *et al.* 2013; Ralston & Kirchman 2013).

A range of traits has been suggested to be associated with climate change vulnerability, most of which apply to mountain birds (Table 6.2). Many mountain birds are dietary and habitat specialists, potentially vulnerable to climate change through impacts of warming upon food availability, habitat structure, disease and predator populations. The upwards push of climate change for low elevation populations through a variety of mechanisms means that high-elevation specialists in particular will need to compete with or be replaced by generalist species associated with warmer temperatures.

Projecting the future is difficult. Not only do different models make different projections, but the precise details for which species are most vulnerable to climate change are highly uncertain (Pearce-Higgins & Green 2014; Wheatley *et al.* 2017; Foden *et al.* 2019). Despite this, there is a pretty good consensus that the increasing magnitude of warming will result in significant reductions in range extent and abundance for many species, potentially threatening some with extinction. High-elevation and cold-adapted species are thought to be particularly vulnerable to warming. Whilst patterns may be more complex in the tropics due to the increasing importance of variation in precipitation (more difficult to predict than temperature; Baker *et al.* 2017), and which may result in downward as well as upward elevational changes (Tingley *et al.* 2012), tropical mountain birds do seem to be responding rapidly to warming (Freeman *et al.* 2021) and models suggest that many tropical high elevation endemics are indeed threatened by climate change. Given uncertainties, good monitoring data from mountain environments are required to properly monitor and model present and future climate impacts for avian populations (Chapters 5 and 8). Validating the predictions from models linking climate to the distribution and abundance of birds in mountain environments requires detailed autecological studies to understand species requirements and how those are changing in response to climate change. We require a step-change in research effort to achieve our information needs for mountain birds as this is vital information to determine how to alter our management of mountain habitats to help mountain birds adapt to climate change.

Table 6.2 Indicative ecological traits associated with increased vulnerability of species to climate change (adapted from Pearce-Higgins & Green 2014) and their applicability to mountain birds.

Trait	Applicability to mountain birds	Example (if available)	Reference
Dependence on seasonal availability of ephemeral food	Mountain environments highly seasonal	White-winged snowfinch *Montifringilla nivalis* dependent upon snow patches for tipulid prey	Resano-Mayor *et al.* 2019
Long-distance migrant	Increases vulnerability to changes in phenology of mountain environments	Advancing timing of flowering may affect migratory broad-tailed hummingbirds *Selasphorus platycercus*	McKinney *et al.* 2012
Limited dispersal	Rates of dispersal influence opportunities for elevational range shift or dispersal across mountain ranges	Alpine habitat patches will become smaller and further apart for white-tailed ptarmigan *Lagopus leucura*	La Sorte & Jetz 2010; Martin *et al.* 2000, 2020; Jackson *et al.* 2015
Precocial, semi-altricial/semi-precocial species vulnerable to weather-related reductions in prey availability	Breeding season rainfall or storms can have a large impact on reproductive success	Black grouse *Lyrurus tetrix* productivity negatively correlated with June rainfall	Pearce-Higgins *et al.* 2019
Small or fragmented populations	Climate change increasingly fragments and reduces the size of high-elevation species	Rock ptarmigan *Lagopus muta*, white-tailed ptarmigan *L. leucura*	Novoa *et al.* 2014 Jackson *et al.* 2015
Vulnerable to storm events	Storms can reduce annual breeding success given short breeding season	Cold storms have strong impact on alpine songbird nesting success	Martin *et al.* 2017
Specialized diet on prey whose availability is threatened by climate change	Warming can reduce the availability of cold-adapted prey	European golden plover *Pluvialis apricaria* populations vulnerable to declines in tipulid abundance with hot, dry summers	Pearce-Higgins *et al.* 2010

(cont.)

Table 6.2 (cont.)

Trait	Applicability to mountain birds	Example (if available)	Reference
Vulnerable to predation by range-expanding predators	Increasing meso-predators linked to climate change	Ground-nesting waders vulnerable to red fox *Vulpes vulpes* predation	Roos *et al.* 2018
Vulnerable to disease which may increase in response to warming	Many pathogens showing elevational expansion with rising temperatures	High elevation Hawaiian endemics threatened by avian malaria	Benning *et al.* 2002
Vulnerable to climate-related expansion of potential competitor	Biotic interactions interact with abiotic conditions to determine species range limits in tropical mountains	Lowland birds occur at higher elevations in low mountains where they have fewer competitors	Burner *et al.* 2020
Sensitive to heat stress	May exceed thermal tolerance of cold-adapted species	Heat reduces foraging and chick provisioning in Cape rockjumpers *Chaetops frenatus*	Oswald *et al.* 2021
Habitat specialist	Many mountain birds are specialists of natural habitats or low-intensity management. High-elevation specialists particularly vulnerable to warming	White-tailed ptarmigan *Lagopus leucura* – a high-elevation specialist associated with cold temperatures	Scridel *et al.* 2021
Wetland specialist	Mountain species associated with wetland habitats on plateaus are likely to shift their distribution upwards	Dunlin *Calidris alpina* strongly associated with pools and peatland hydrology	Carroll *et al.* 2015

6.5 Conservation Strategies to Adapt to Climate Change

A key tenet of conservation action over the last century has been the concept of protected areas; designated areas of land with restrictions placed on the conversion of natural or semi-natural habitats to more intensive management, damaging human activities such as hunting or exploitation, or the promotion of positive conservation management to benefit species of conservation concern. There is growing evidence that protected areas effectively target current important areas for bird conservation (Pellissier *et al.* 2020), and result in more positive population trajectories for birds (Donald *et al.* 2007). There is also building evidence that fixed protected areas remain important in a changing climate because they provide colonization locations for range-expanding habitat specialists (Thomas & Gillingham 2015; Scridel *et al.* 2021). Protecting areas of natural and semi-natural habitat in mountain environments will be important for low- and mid-elevation species that are expanding their elevational distribution upwards and northwards.

The other benefit of protected sites is to reduce rates of extinction and loss. Northern species in Finland have persisted more in protected areas than in non-protected sites (Lehikoinen *et al.* 2019), leading to temperature-related bird community changes in protected compared to non-protected sites (Lehikoinen *et al.* 2021). In the UK, interactions between protected area extent and both elevation and latitude further suggest that protected areas have facilitated the persistence of cold-adapted northern species at low elevations and latitudes (Gillingham *et al.* 2015).

Given the scale of projected impacts of climate change on mountain bird species and the anticipated elevational and latitudinal range shifts required for them to keep pace with changing climatic conditions, conservation planning for these species should operate across landscapes (Brambilla *et al.* 2020). Although the elevational shifts observed in mountain birds have thus far been relatively modest (Table 6.1), the anticipated future shifts may significantly reduce the overlap between species distributions and protected sites, as projected for high-elevation range-restricted birds in the Andes (del Rosario Avalos & Hernandez 2015). Thus, new protected areas may need to be established, as suggested for the near-threatened satyr tragopan *Tragopan satyra* in the Himalayas (Chhetri *et al.* 2018), for endemic birds in the Highlands of eastern Brazil where areas of projected stability should be prioritized for protection as a 'no-regrets' strategy (Hoffman *et al.* 2020), and in Colombia, where high-elevation cloud forest should be protected for the high-elevation species that are most likely to persist (Gasner *et al.* 2010). In Peru, large fragments of mature *Polylepis* forest should be protected at lower elevations given their diverse avifaunas, and at higher elevations all *Polylepis* fragments should be protected to maximize the persistence of threatened species now and in the future. Conservation restoration should also seek to increase connectivity among patches, and to protect and improve the matrix of grassland and shrubland habitats (Sevillano-Ríos & Rodewald 2017; Sevillano-Ríos *et al.* 2018). In British Columbia, the existing protected areas network appears relatively well-designed to respond to future climate change impacts for white-tailed, rock and willow ptarmigan assuming these protected areas remain intact (Scridel *et al.* 2021).

There is growing evidence that active conservation management can also play an important role in reducing negative impacts of climate change (Bowgen *et al.* 2022). Eight years of extensive habitat management in the Welsh mountains, combined with legal predator control, reduced the vulnerability of young black grouse chicks to heavy June rainfall, enabling the population to respond positively to habitat management (Pearce-Higgins *et al.* 2019). In the USA, Martin & Maron (2012) showed how reduced snow cover increased winter browsing pressure by elk *Cervus canadensis*, destroying the shrub layer, leading to increases in nest predation and reduced habitat suitability for migratory birds. Using experimental exclosures, Martin & Maron (2012) demonstrated how excluding elk led to the rapid recovery of the shrub layer, and an increase in songbird breeding success. The use of exclosures may not be a long-term solution, but it emphasizes how management to reduce browsing pressure may help that system adapt to climate change.

In the context of vulnerable mountain species, what remains uncertain is the extent to which such management may provide a long-term strategy to protect vulnerable species in the face of climate change, or whether it is simply a short-term solution to 'buy time' for the most vulnerable species to shift to areas of more suitable climate. Interventions such as ensuring the maintenance of extensive pasturing in the European Alps to promote short swards for climate-vulnerable species that rely upon them like ring ouzel and white-winged snowfinch (Brambilla *et al.* 2018; Barras *et al.* 2021) are likely to deliver benefits, but more research is required to identify any potential limits to their effectiveness. Interventions that are only able to help species cope with 2°C warming, for example, may still help vulnerable populations to persist to the end of the century (Pearce-Higgins 2011) or longer, depending on the magnitude of future warming. In the longer-term and for stronger warming levels, more radical options will be required for the most vulnerable species.

Translocation is one such radical option under discussion, where individuals from a population threatened by climate change are moved to suitable locations with improved climatic suitability. Conceptually, the optimal time for such translocation would be as conditions deteriorate at the source population before species imperilment, and as the translocation site is improving in condition (McDonald-Madden *et al.* 2011). Given stochasticity in the weather and variable and uncertain responses to climate change, this is extremely challenging to achieve. Despite this, translocation trials for birds have been undertaken (e.g., Burger *et al.* 2013), including on rock ptarmigan (Kaler *et al.* 2010; Gregory *et al.* 2012; Novoa *et al.* 2014), showing that such interventions can be done. Mountain bird populations usually require dispersal and recruitment from other isolated mountain habitat patches for population persistence. In North America, translocations of white-tailed ptarmigan to unoccupied historically suitable habitat can persist for a number of years, especially if dispersal and recruitment processes are feasible (Martin *et al.* 2000, 2020). A recent review suggested that the most successful translocations of birds to protected sites occur over multiple years, involve a range of age classes and occur over shorter geographical distances (Skikne *et al.* 2020). The last point may seem to be a particular constraint for translocations in a changing climate and could argue for a gradual and phased approach to this intervention.

6.6 Conclusions

Mountain environments are characterized by cooler climates than the surrounding landscapes, but have warmed in recent decades, altering the biology of mountain birds in a range of different ways. Each of these individual population-level impacts combine to change the distribution of mountain birds, and therefore mountain bird assemblages. There is a widespread signal of elevational shifts in the distribution of species, although the rate of response may vary above and below treelines, and between tropical and temperate areas.

Modelling suggests some 1–30 per cent of mountain bird species are vulnerable to extinction depending upon the magnitude of climate change considered and the assumptions made. High-elevation specialists are regarded as the most vulnerable, whilst mid-elevation species are generally projected to increase in abundance in response to warming. Climate vulnerability is determined by a combination of the magnitude of climate change (mean conditions and anomalies), topography and land-cover and interactions with other drivers such as habitat quality and predation. High mountain birds exhibit many of the traits widely regarded as being associated with high vulnerability to climate change. Anthropogenic impact on habitat suitability is one of most influential factors changing the distribution and abundance of species, and will interact with climate to drive future changes. This provides a strong rationale for suggesting that conservation management may be used to increase the resilience of vulnerable species or populations to climate change.

Protected areas are likely to remain a key tenet of conservation in a changing climate, particularly to maintain areas of natural and semi-natural habitat for mountain habitat specialists to colonize. Regarding national and international targets to expand protected area coverage, the protection of mountain environments with their topographical heterogeneity should be prioritized, particularly where models suggest these areas are likely to act as climate refugia. Actively restoring damaged habitats is likely to increase resilience to future climate change. Although recent evidence suggests that targeted management can reduce negative climate change impacts, more work is required to identify the potential future limits to the likely effectiveness of such action. In extreme circumstances, translocation outside of the species current range may be considered to prevent extinction, with highly uncertain consequences.

Given all of this, what does a warmer future hold for mountain birds? Many cold-adapted temperate high elevation species have wide geographical ranges and should therefore persist in cold refugia, particularly if they are able to shift their distributions, which will depend upon how areas of climate suitability interact with areas of suitable habitat and other pressures (Chapter 10). They will however, probably occupy smaller ranges than before. Climate change may pose greater challenges for range-restricted mountain birds in the tropics, where the twin impacts of warming and changes in rainfall patterns may cause considerable changes in climate suitability. Maintaining an effective protected area network targeted at protecting complex mountain environments and areas of key habitat, supporting the maintenance of areas of suitable habitat across unprotected landscapes and reducing other threats through ongoing conservation action, will maximize the long-term resilience of such species. Active management can help vulnerable populations persist in an altered climate, but achieving this in remote high mountain environments will be extremely challenging or impossible. At the same time, mountain environments are likely to become increasingly important refuges for elevational generalists that currently occupy low-elevations where they may be increasingly threatened by human activity. To conclude, although mountain ecosystems may be vulnerable to climate change processes, if managed appropriately, they may become even more important centres for bird conservation in a changing climate than they are at present.

Acknowledgements

We thank Luis Brotons, Morgan Tingley, Devin de Zwaan and others for their careful and comprehensive reviews of earlier versions of the chapter.

References

Alba, R., Kasoar, T., Chamberlain, D., *et al.* (2022) Drivers of change in mountain and upland bird populations in Europe. *Ibis*, **164**, 635–648.

Altamirano, T.A., de Zwaan, D.R., Ibarra, J.T., Wilson, S. & Martin, K. (2020) Treeline ecotones shape patterns of avian species richness and functional diversity in south temperate mountains. *Scientific Reports*, **10**, 1–13.

Araneda, P., Sielfeld, W., Bonacic, C. & Ibarra, J.T. (2018) Bird diversity along elevational gradients in the Dry Tropical Andes of northern Chile: the potential role of Aymara indigenous traditional agriculture. *PLoS ONE*, **13**, e0207544.

Archaux, F. (2004) Breeding upwards when climate is becoming warmer: no bird response in the French Alps. *Ibis*, **146**, 138–144.

Baker, D.J., Hartley, A.J., Pearce-Higgins, J.W., Jones, R.G. & Willis, S.G. (2017) Neglected issues in using weather and climate information in ecology and biogeography. *Diversity and Distributions*, **23**, 329–340.

Ballesteros-Cánovas, J.A., Trappmann, D., Madrigal-Gonzalez, J., Eckert, N. & Stoffal, M. (2018) Climate warming enhances snow avalanche risk in the Western Himalayas. *Proceedings of the National Academy of Sciences*, **115**, 3410–3415.

Bani, L., Massimiliano, L., Rocchia, E., Dondina, O. & Orioli, V. (2019) Winners and losers: how the elevational range of breeding birds on Alps has varied over the past four decades due to climate and habitat changes. *Ecology and Evolution*, **9**, 1289–1305.

Barras, A.G., Marti, S., Ettlin, S., *et al.* (2020) The importance of seasonal environmental factors in the foraging habitat selection of Alpine Ring Ouzels *Turdus torquatus alpestris*. *Ibis*, **162**, 505–519.

Barras, A.G., Braunsich, V. & Arlettaz, R. (2021) Predictive models of distribution and abundance of a threatened mountain bird species show that impacts of climate change overrule those of land use change. *Diversity and Distributions*, **27**, 989–1004.

Barras, A.G., Candolfi, I. & Arlettaz, R. (2022) Spatio-temporal patterns of earth-worm abundance suggest time-limited food availability for a subalpine bird species. *Pedobiologia*, **93–94**, 150826.

Bässler, C., Müller, J., Hothorn, T., *et al.* (2010) Estimation of the extinction risk for high-montane species as a consequence of global warming and assess-ment of their suitability as cross-taxon indicators. *Ecological Indicators*, **10**, 341–352.

Beale, C.M., Burfield, I.J., Sim, I.M.W., *et al.* (2006) Climate change may account for the decline in British ring ouzels *Turdus torquatus*. *Journal of Animal Ecology*, **75**, 826–835.

Bears H., Martin, K. & White, G.C. (2009) Breeding in high-elevation habitat results in shift to slower life-history strategy within a single species. *Journal of Animal Ecology*, **78**, 365–375.

Beniston, M. (2006) Mountain weather and climate: a general overview and a focus on climatic change in the Alps. *Hydrobiologia*, **562**, 3–16.

Benning, T.L., LaPointe, D., Atkinson, C.T. & Vitousek, P.M. (2002) Interactions of climate change with biological invasions and land use in the Hawaiian Islands: modeling the fate of endemic birds using a geographic information system. *Proceedings of the National Academy of Sciences*, **99**, 14246–14249.

Bison, M., Yoccoz, N.G., Carlson, B., *et al.* (2020) Best environmental predic-tors of breeding phenology differ with elevation in a common woodland bird species. *Ecology and Evolution*, **10**, 10219–10229.

Bowgen, K.M., Kettle, E.F., Butchart, S.H.M., *et al.* (2022) Conservation interven-tions can benefit species impacted by climate change. *Biological Conservation*, **269**, 109524.

Boyce, A.J., Shakya, S., Sheldon, F.H., Moyle, R.G. & Martin, T.E. (2019) Biotic interactions are the dominant drivers of phylogenetic and functional structure in bird communities along a tropical elevational gradient. *Auk*, **136**, 1–14.

Boyle, W.A. & Martin, K. (2015) The conservation value of high elevation habitats to North American migrant birds. *Biological Conservation*, **192**, 461–476.

Boyle, W.A., Norris, D.R. & Guglielmo, C.G. (2010) Storms drive altitudinal migration in a tropical bird. *Proceedings of the Royal Society Series B*, **277**, 2511–2519.

Boyle, W.A., Shogren, E.H. & Brawn, J.D. (2020) Hygric niches for tropical endotherms. *Trends in Ecology & Evolution*, **35**, 938–952.

Brambilla, M., Pedrini, P., Rolando, A. & Chamberlain, D.E. (2016) Climate change will increase the potential conflict between skiing and high-elevation bird species in the Alps. *Journal of Biogeography*, **43**, 2299–2309.

Brambilla, M., Resano-Mayor, J., Scridel, D., *et al.* (2018) Past and future impact of climate change on foraging habitat suitability in a high-alpine bird species: management options to buffer against global warming effects. *Biological Conservation*, **221**, 209–218.

Brambilla, M., Gustin, M., Cento, M., Ilahiane, L. & Celada, C. (2020) Habitat, climate, topography and management differently affect occurrence in declin-ing avian species: implications for conservation in changing environments. *Science of the Total Environment*, **742**, 140663.

Braunisch, V., Coppes, J., Arlettaz, R., *et al.* (2014) Temperate mountain forest biodiversity under climate change: compensating negative effects by increasing structural complexity. *PLoS ONE*, **9**, e97718.

Brodie, J.F., Roland, C.A., Stehn, S.E. & Smirnova, E. (2019) Variabilty in the expansion of trees and shrubs in boreal Alaska. *Ecology*, **100**, e02660.

Brönnimann, S., Rajczak, J., Fischer, E.M., *et al.* (2018) Changing seasonality of moderate and extreme precipitation events in the Alps. *Natural Hazards and Earth System Sciences*, **18**, 2047–2056.

Buchanan, G.M., Pearce-Higgins, J.W., Douglas, D.J.T. & Grant, M.C. (2017) Quantifying the importance of multi-scale management and environmental variables on moorland bird abundance. *Ibis*, **159**, 744–756.

Burfield, I.J. (2002) *The Breeding Ecology and Conservation of the Ring Ouzel Turdus torquatus in Britain*. PhD Thesis, University of Cambridge.

Burger, C., Nord, A., Nilsson, J-Å., Gilot-Fromont, E. & Both C. (2013) Fitness consequences of northward dispersal as possible adaptation to climate change, using experimental translocation of a migratory passerine. *PLoS ONE*, **8**, e83176.

Burner, R.C., Boyce, A.J., Bernasconi, D., *et al.* (2020) Biotic interactions help explain variation in elevational range limits of birds among Bornean mountains. *Journal of Biogeography*, **47**, 760–771.

Byrkjedal, I. (1980) Nest predation in relation to snow-cover – a possible factor influencing the start of breeding in shorebirds. *Ornis Scandinavica*, **11**, 249–252.

Calladine, J. & Bray, J. (2012) The importance of altitude and aspect for breeding Whinchats *Saxicola rubetra* in the uplands: limitations of the uplands as a refuge for a declining, formerly widespread species? *Bird Study*, **59**, 43–51.

Camfield, A.F., Pearson, S. & Martin, K. (2010) Life history variation between high and low elevation subspecies of horned larks *Eremophila spp. Journal of Avian Biology*, **41**, 273–281.

Campos-Cerqueira, M., Arendt, W.J., Wunderle, J.M. & Aide, T.M. (2017) Have bird distributions shifted along an elevational gradient on a tropical mountain? *Ecology and Evolution*, **7**, 9914–9924.

Cannon, F., Carvalho, L.M.V., Jones, C. & Norris, J. (2016) Winter westerly disturbance dynamics and precipitation in the western Himalaya and Karakoram: a wave-tracking approach. *Theoretical and Applied Climatology*, **125**, 27–44.

Cardenas, T., Naoki, K., Landivar, C.M., *et al.* (2021) Glacier influence on bird assemblages in habitat islands of the high Bolivian Andes. *Diversity and Distributions*, **28**, 242–256.

Carroll, M.J., Dennis, P., Pearce-Higgins, J.W. & Thomas, C.D. (2011) Maintaining northern peatland ecosystems in a changing climate: effects of soil moisture, drainage and drain blocking on craneflies. *Global Change Biology*, **17**, 2991–3001.

Carroll, M.J., Heinemeyer, A., Pearce-Higgins, J.W., *et al.* (2015) Ecosystem processes and the survival of species under climate change. *Nature Communications*, **6**, 7851.

Cattadori, I.M., Haydon, D.T. & Hudson, P.J. (2005) Parasites and climate synchronize red grouse populations. *Nature*, **433**, 737–741.

Chamberlain, D., Negro, M., Caprio, E. & Rolando, A. (2013) Assessing the sensitivity of alpine birds to potential future changes in habitat and climate to inform management strategies. *Biological Conservation*, **167**, 127–135.

Chamberlain, D., Brambilla, M., Caprio, E., Pedrini, P. & Rolando, A. (2016) Alpine bird distributions along elevational gradients: the consistency of climate and habitat effects across geographic regions. *Oecologia*, **181**, 1139–1150.

Chen, I.C., Shiu, H.J., Benedick, S., et al. (2009) Elevation increases in moth assemblages over 42 years on a tropical mountain. *Proceedings of the National Academy of Sciences*, **106**, 1479–1483.

Chen, I.-C., Hill, J.K., Ohlemüller, R., Roy, D.B. & Thomas, C.D. (2011) Rapid range shifts of species associated with high levels of climate warming. *Science*, **333**, 1024–1026.

Chhetri, B., Badola, H.K. & Barat, S. (2018) Predicting climate-driven habitat shifting of the near threatened Satyr Tragopan (*Tragopan satyra*; Galliformes) in the Himalayas. *Avian Biology Research*, **11**, 221–230.

Chignell, S.M., Laituri, M.J., Young, N.E. & Evangelista, P.H. (2019) Afroalpine wetlands of the Bale Mountains, Ethiopia: distribution, dynamics, and conceptual flow model. *Annals of the American Association of Geographers*, **109**, 791–811.

Cohen, J.M., Lajeunesse, M.C. & Rohr, J.R. (2018) A global synthesis of animal phenological responses to climate change. *Nature Climate Change*, **8**, 224–228.

Couet, J., Marjakangas, E.-L., Santangeli, A., et al. (2022) Short-lived species move uphill faster under climate change. *Oecologia*, **198**, 877–888.

Cornulier, T., Yoccoz, N.G., Bretagnolle, V., et al. (2013) Europe-wide dampening of population cycles in keystone herbivores. *Science*, **340**, 63–66.

DeLuca, W.V. & King, D.I. (2017) Montane birds shift downslope despite recent warming in the northern Appalachian Mountains. *Journal of Ornithology*, **158**, 493–505.

de Zwaan, D.R., Wilson, S.D., Gow, E. & Martin, K. (2019a) Sex-specific spatiotemporal variation and carry-over effects in a migratory alpine songbird. *Frontiers in Ecology and Evolution*, **7**, article 285.

de Zwaan, D.R., Camfield, A.F., MacDonald, E.C. & Martin, K. (2019b) Variation in offspring development is driven more by weather and maternal condition than predation risk. *Functional Ecology*, **33**, 447–456.

de Zwaan, D.R, Drake, A., Greenwood, J.L. & Martin, K. (2020) Timing and intensity of weather events shape nestling development strategies in three alpine breeding songbirds. *Frontiers in Ecology and Evolution*, **8**, 570034.

de Zwaan, D.R, Drake, A., Camfield, A., MacDonald, E. & Martin, K. (2022) The relative influence of cross-seasonal and local weather effects on the breeding success of a migratory songbird. *Journal of Animal Ecology*, **91**, 1458–1470.

del Rosario Avalos, V. & Hernandez, J. (2015) Projected distribution shifts and protected area coverage of range-restricted Andean birds under climate change. *Global Ecology and Conservation*, **4**, 459–469.

Devictor, V., van Swaay, C., Brereton, T., et al. (2012) Differences in the climate debts of birds and butterflies at a continental scale. *Nature Climate Change*, **2**, 121–124.

Dillon, M.E., Frazier, M.R. & Dudley, R. (2006) Into thin air: physiology and evolution of alpine insects. *Integrative and Comparative Biology*, **46**, 49–61.

Donald, P.F., Sanderson, F.J., Burfield, I.J., et al. (2007) International conservation policy delivers benefits for birds in Europe. *Science*, **317**, 810–813.

Douglas, D.J.T. & Pearce-Higgins, J.W. (2019) Variation in ecoparasitic sheep tick *Ixodes ricinus* infestation on European Golden Plover chicks *Pluvialis apraciaria* and implications for growth and survival. *Bird Study*, **66**, 92–102.

Dunn, P.O. & Møller, A.P. (2020) *Effects of Climate Change on Birds*. Oxford: Oxford University Press.

Eckert, N., Keylock, C.J., Castebrunet, H., Lavigne, A. & Naaim, M. (2013) Temporal trends in avalanche activity in the French Alps and subregions: from occurrences and runout altitudes to unsteady return periods. *Journal of Glaciology*, **59**, 93–114.

Elmhagen, B., Berteaux, D., Burgess, R.M., et al. (2017) Homage to Hersteinsson and Macdonald: climate warming and resource subsidies cause red fox range expansion and Arctic fox decline. *Polar Research*, **36**, 3.

Elsen, P.R. & Tingley, M.W. (2015) Global mountain topography and the fate of montane species under climate change. *Nature Climate Change*, **5**, 772–776.

Elsen, P.R., Tingley, M.W., Kalyanaraman, R., Ramesh, K. & Wilcove, D.S. (2017) The role of competition, ecotones, and temperature in the elevational distribution of Himalayan birds. *Ecology*, **98**, 337–348.

Elsen, P.R., Monahan, W.B. & Merenlender, A.M. (2020) Topography and human pressure in mountain ranges alter expected species responses to climate change. *Nature Communications*, **11**, 1974.

Finch, T., Pearce-Higgins, J.W., Leech, D.I. & Evans, K.L. (2014) Carry-over effects from passage regions are more important than breeding climate in determining the breeding phenology and performance of three avian migrants of conservation concern. *Biodiversity and Conservation*, **23**, 2427–2444.

Fletcher, K., Howarth, D., Kirby, A., Dunn, R. & Smith, A. (2013) Effect of climate change on breeding phenology, clutch size and chick survival of an upland bird. *Ibis*, **155**, 456–463.

Foden, W.B., Young, B.E., Akçakaya, H.A., et al. (2019) Climate change vulnerability assessment of species. *WIREs Climate Change*, **10**, e551.

Forero-Medina, G., Terborgh, J., Socolar, S.J. & Pimm, S.L. (2011) Elevational ranges of birds on a tropical montane gradient lag behind warming temperatures. *PLoS ONE*, **6**, e28535.

Freeman, B.G. & Freeman, A.C. (2014) Rapid upslope shifts in New Guinean birds illustrate strong distributional responses of tropical montane species to global warming. *Proceedings of the National Academy of Sciences*, **111**, 4490–4494.

Freeman, B.G., Scholar, M.N., Ruiz-Gutierrez, V. & Fitzpatrick, J.W. (2018) Climate change causes upslope shifts and mountaintop extirpations in a tropical bird community. *Proceedings of the National Academy of Sciences*, **115**, 11982–11987.

Freeman, B.G., Song, Y., Feeley, K.J. & Zhu, K. (2021) Montane species track rising temperatures better in the tropics than in the temperate zone. *Ecology Letters*, **24**, 1697–1708.

Freeman, B.G., Strimas-Mackey, M. & Miller, E.T. (2022) Interspecific competition limits bird species' ranges in tropical mountains. *Science*, **377**, 416–420.

Gallant, D., Lecomte, N. & Berteaux, D. (2020) Disentangling the relative influences of global drivers of change in biodiversity: a study of the twentieth-century red fox expansion into the Canadian Arctic. *Journal of Applied Ecology*, **89**, 565–576.

García-González, R., Aldezabal, A., Laskurain, N.A., Margalida, A. & Novoa, C. (2016) Influence of snowmelt timing on the diet quality of Pyrenean rock ptarmigan (*Lagopus muta pyrenaica*): implications for reproductive success. *PLoS ONE*, **11**, e0148632.

Gasner, M.R., Jankowski, J.E., Ciecka, A.L., Kyle, K.O. & Rabenold, K.N. (2010) Projecting the local impacts of climate change on a central American montane avian community. *Biological Conservation*, **143**, 1250–1258.

Gilbert, L. (2010) Altitudinal patterns of tick and host abundance: a potential role for climate change in regulating tick-borne diseases? *Oecologia*, **162**, 217–225.

Gillingham, P.K., Bradbury, R.B., Roy, D.B., et al. (2015) The effectiveness of pro-tected areas in the conservation of species with changing geographical ranges. *Biological Journal of the Linnean Society*, **115**, 707–717.

Gillings, S., Balmer, D.E. & Fuller, R. J. (2015) Directionality of recent bird distribu-tion shifts and climate change in Britain. *Global Change Biology*, **21**, 2155–2168.

Glass, T.W., Breed, G.A., Liston, G.E., et al. (2021) Spatiotemporally variable snow properties drive habitat use of an Arctic mesopredator. *Oecologia*, **195**, 887–899.

Gregory, A.J., Kaler, R.S.A., Prebyl, T.J., Sandercock, B.K. & Wisely, S.M. (2012) Influence of translocation strategy and mating system on the genetic structure of a newly established population of island ptarmigan. *Conservation Genetics*, **13**, 465–474.

Guo, F., Lenoir, J. & Bonebrake, T.C. (2018) Land-use interacts with climate to determine elevational species redistribution. *Nature Communications*, **9**, 1315.

Hallman, T.A., Guélat, J., Antoniazza, S., Kéry, M. & Sattler, T. (2022) Rapid ele-vational shifts of Switzerland's avifauna and associated species traits. *Ecosphere*, **13**, e4194.

Hannon, S.J., Martin, K. & Schieck, J.O. (1988) Timing of reproduction in two populations of Willow Ptarmigan in northern Canada. *Auk*, **105**, 330–338.

Hanz, D.M., Böhning-Gaese, K., Ferger, S.W., et al. (2019) Functional and phylogenetic diversity of bird assemblages are filtered by different biotic fac-tors on tropical mountains. *Journal of Biogeography*, **46**, 291–303.

Hartmann, H. & Andresky, L. (2013) Flooding in the Indus River basin – a spatio-temporal analysis of precipitation records. *Global Planetary Change*, **107**, 25–35.

Henden, J.-A., Ehrich, D., Soininen, E.M. & Ims, R.A. (2021) Accounting for food web dynamics when assessing the impact of mesopredator control on declining prey populations. *Journal of Applied Ecology*, **58**, 104–113.

Hickling, R., Roy, D.B., Hill, J.K., Fox, R. & Thomas, C.D. (2006) The distribu-tions of a wide range of taxonomic groups are expanding polewards. *Global Change Biology*, **12**, 450–455.

Hock, R., Rasul, G., Adler, C., et al. (2019) High mountain areas. In *IPCC Special Report on the Ocean and Cryosphere in a Changing Climate*. Pörtner, H.-O., Roberts, D.C., Masson-Delmotte, V., et al. (eds.). Cambridge and New York: Cambridge University Press, pp. 131–202.

Holland, P.K. & Yalden, D.W. (1991) Population dynamics of Common Sandpipers *Actitis hypoleucos* breeding along an upland river system. *Bird Study*, **38**, 151–159.

Hoffman, D., de Vasconcelos, M.F. & Fernandes, G.W. (2020) The fate of endemic birds of eastern Brazilian mountaintops in the face of climate change. *Perspectives in Ecology & Conservation*, **18**, 257–266.

Hotaling, S., Wimberger, P.H., Kelley, J.L. & Watts, H.E. (2020) Macroinvertebrates on glaciers: a key resource for terrestrial food webs? *Ecology*, **101**, e02947.

Ibarra, J.T., Martin, M., Cockle, K.L. & Martin, K. (2017) Maintaining ecosystem resilience: functional responses of tree cavity nesters to logging in temperate forests of the Americas. *Scientific Reports*, **7**, 4467.

Imperio, S., Bionda, R., Viterbi, R. & Provenzale, A. (2013) Climate change and human disturbance can lead to local extinction of alpine rock ptarmigan: new insight from the western Italian Alps. *PLoS ONE*, **8**, e81598.

Inouye, D.W., Barr, B., Armitage, K.B. & Inouye, B.D. (2000) Climate change is affecting altitudinal migrants and hibernating species. *Proceedings of the National Academy of Sciences*, **97**, 1630–1633.

IPCC (2018) Annex I: Glossary. In *Global Warming of 1.5°C. An IPCC Special Report on the Impacts of Global Warming of 1.5°C above Pre-Industrial Levels and Related Global Greenhouse Gas Emission Pathways, in the Context of Strengthening the Global Response to the Threat of Climate Change, Sustainable Development, and Efforts to Eradicate Poverty.* Masson-Delmotte, V., Zhai, P., Pörtner, H.-O., et al. (eds.). Cambridge: Cambridge University Press, pp. 541–562.

IPCC (2021) Summary for Policymakers. In *Climate Change 2021: The Physical Science Basis: Contribution of Working Group I to the Sixth Assessment Report of the Intergovernmental Panel on Climate Change.* Masson-Delmotte, V., Zhai, P., Pirani, A., et al. (eds.). Cambridge: Cambridge University Press, pp. 3–32.

Jackson, M.M., Gergel, S.E. & Martin, K. (2015) Effects of climate change on habitat availability and configuration for an endemic coastal bird. *PLoS ONE*, **10**, e0142110.

Jahren, T., Storaas, T., Willebrand, T., Moa, P.F. & Hagen, B.-R. (2016) Declining reproductive output in capercaillie and black grouse – 16 countries and 80 years. *Animal Biology*, **66**, 363–400.

Jankowski, J.E., Robinson, S.K. & Levey, D.J. (2010) Squeezed at the top: inter-specific aggression may constrain elevational ranges in tropical birds. *Ecology*, **91**, 1877–1884.

Kaler, R.S.A., Ebbert, S.E., Braun, C.E. & Sandercock, B.K. (2010) Demography of a reintroduced population of Evermann's Rock Ptarmigan in the Aleutian Islands. *Wilson Journal of Ornithology*, **122**, 1–14.

Kausrud, K.L., Mysterud, A., Steen, H., et al. (2008) Linking climate change to lemming cycles. *Nature*, **456**, 93–97.

Kirchman, J.J. & Van Keuren, A.E. (2017) Altitudinal range shifts of birds at the southern periphery of the boreal forest: 40 years of change in the Adirondack Mountains. *Wilson Journal of Ornithology*, **129**, 742–753.

Korpimäki, E. (1994) Rapid or delayed tracking of multi-annual vole cycles by avian predators? *Journal of Animal Ecology*, **63**, 619–628.

Körner, C. & Hoch, G. (2006) A test of treeline theory on a montane permafrost island. *Arctic, Antarctic and Alpine Research*, **38**, 113–119.

La Sorte, F.A. & Jetz, W. (2010) Projected range contractions of montane biodiversity under global warming. *Proceedings of the Royal Society of London Series B*, **277**, 3401–3410.

Laidlaw, R.A., Gunnarsson, T.G., Mendez, V., *et al.* (2020) Vegetation structure influences predation rates of early nests in subarctic breeding waders. *Ibis*, **162**, 1225–1236.

Larsen, T.H., Brehm, G., Navarette, H., *et al.* (2011) Range shifts and extinctions driven by climate change in the tropical Andes: synthesis and directions. In *Climate Change and Biodiversity in the Tropical Andes*. Herzog, S.K., Martínez, R., Jørgensen, P.M. & Tiessen, H. (eds.). Paris: IAI-SCOPE, pp. 47–67.

Lehikoinen, A., Fraixedas, S., Burgas, D., *et al.* (2016) The impact of weather and the phase of the rodent cycle on breeding populations of waterbirds in Finnish Lapland. *Ornis Fennica*, **93**, 31–46.

Lehikoinen, P., Santangeli, A., Jaatinen, K., Rajasärkkä, A. & Lehikoinen, A. (2019) Protected areas act as a buffer against detrimental effects of climate change – evidence from long term abundance data. *Global Change Biology*, **25**, 304–313.

Lehikoinen, P., Tiusanen, M., Santangeli, A., *et al.* (2021) Increasing protected area coverage mitigates climate change driven community changes. *Biological Conservation*, **253**, 108892.

Maggini, R., Lehmann, A., Kéry, M., *et al.* (2011) Are Swiss birds tracking climate change? Detecting elevational shifts using response curve shapes. *Ecological Modelling*, **222**, 21–32.

Martay, B. & Pearce-Higgins, J.W. (2018) Using data from schools to model variation in soil invertebrates across the UK: the importance of weather, climate, season and habitat. *Pedobiologia*, **67**, 1–9.

Martin, T.E. & Maron, J.L. (2012) Climate impacts on bird and plant communities from altered animal-plant interactions. *Nature Climate Change*, **2**, 195–200.

Martin, K. & Wiebe, K.L. (2004) Coping mechanisms of Alpine and Arctic breeding birds: extreme weather and limitations to reproductive resilience. *Integrative and Comparative Biology*, **44**, 177–185.

Martin, K., Stacey, P.B. & Braun, C.E. (2000) Recruitment, dispersal and demographic rescue in spatially structured White-tailed Ptarmigan populations. *Condor*, **102**, 503–516.

Martin, K., Wilson, S.D., MacDonald, E.C., *et al.* (2017) Effects of severe weather on reproduction for sympatric songbirds in an alpine environment: interactions of climate extremes influence nesting success. *Auk*, **134**, 696–709.

Martin, K., Robb, L.A., Wilson, S. & Braun, C.E. (2020) White-tailed ptarmigan (*Lagopus leucura*). In *Birds of the World*. Version 1.0. Rodewald, P.G., (ed.). Ithaca: Cornell Lab of Ornithology.

Martin, K., Altamirano, T.A., de Zwaan, D.R., *et al.* (2021) Avian ecology and community structure across elevation gradients: the importance of high latitude temperate mountains for conserving biodiversity in the Americas. *Global Ecology and Conservation*, **30**, e01799.

Massimino, D., Johnston, A. & Pearce-Higgins, J.W. (2015) The geographical range of British birds expands during 15 years of warming. *Bird Study*, **62**, 523–534.

Massimino, D., Beale, C.M., Suggitt, A.J., *et al.* (2020) Can microclimate offer refuge to an upland bird species under climate change? *Landscape Ecology*, **9**, 1907–1922.

McCain, C.M. & Grytnes, J.-A. (2010) Elevational gradients in species richness. In *Encyclopedia of Life Sciences (ELS)*. Chichester: John Wiley & Sons.

McDonald-Madden, E., Runge, M.C., Possingham, H.P. & Martin, T.G. (2011) Optimal timing for managed relocation of species faced with climate change. *Nature Climate Change*, **1**, 261–265.

McKinney, A.M., CaraDonna, P.J., Inouye, D., *et al.* (2012) Asynchronous changes in phenology of migrating broad-tailed hummingbirds and their early-season nectar resources. *Ecology*, **93**, 1987–1993.

Melendez, L. & Laiolo, P. (2014) The role of climate in constraining the elevational range of the Water Pipit *Anthus spinoletta* in an alpine environment. *Ibis*, **156**, 276–287.

Menzel, A., Sparks, T.H., Estrella, N., *et al.* (2006) European phenological response to climate change matches the warming pattern. *Global Change Biology*, **12**, 1969–1976.

Mizel, J.D., Schmidt, J.H. & Mcintyre, C.L. (2021) Climate and weather have differential effects in a high latitude passerine community. *Oecologia*, **195**, 355–365.

Moens, A.J., Valkiūnas, G., Paca, A., *et al.* (2016) Parasite specialization in a unique habitat: hummingbirds as reservoirs of generalist blood parasites of Andean birds. *Journal of Animal Ecology*, **85**, 1234–1245.

Morton, M.L. (2002) The mountain white-crowned sparrow: migration and reproduction at high altitude. *Studies in Avian Biology*, no. 24, Camarillo: Cooper Ornithological Society.

Moss, D., Joyce, A.C., Clark, J.A., *et al.* (2005) Timing of breeding of moorland birds. *BTO Research Report* No. 362, Thetford: British Trust for Ornithology.

Neate-Clegg, M.H.C., Jones, S.E.I., Burdekin, O., Jocque, M. & Şekercioğlu, Ç.H. (2018) Elevational changes in the avian community of a Mesoamerican cloud forest park. *Biotropica*, **50**, 805–815.

Neate-Clegg, M.H.C., O'Brien, T.G., Mulindahabi, F. & Şekercioğlu, Ç.H. (2020) A disconnect between upslope shifts and climate change in an Afrotropical bird community. *Conservation Science and Practice*, **2**, 1–11.

Neate-Clegg, M.H.C., Jones, S.E.I., Tobias, J.A., Newmark, W.D. & Şekercioğlu, Ç.H. (2021a) Ecological correlates of elevational range shifts in tropical birds. *Frontiers in Ecology and Evolution*, **9**, 621749.

Neate-Clegg, M.H.C., Stuart, S.N., Mtui, D., Şekercioğlu, Ç.H. & Newmark, W.D. (2021b) Afrotropical montane birds experience upslope shifts and range contractions along a fragmented elevational gradient in response to global warming. *PLoS ONE*, **16**, e0248712.

Nagy, L. & Grabherr, G. (2009) *The Biology of Alpine Habitats*. Oxford: Oxford University Press.

Newsome, T., Greenville, A., Ćirović, D., *et al.* (2017) Top predators constrain mesopredator distributions. *Nature Communications*, **8**, 15469.

Novoa, C., Besnard, A., Brenot, J.F. & Ellison, L.N. (2008) Effect of weather on the reproductive rate of Rock Ptarmigan *Lagopus muta* in the eastern Pyrenees. *Ibis*, **150**, 270–278.

Novoa, C., Bech, N., Resseguier, J., *et al.* (2014) A translocation experiment for improving the genetic diversity of an isolated population of Pyrenean rock ptarmigan (*Lagopus muta pyrenaica*). *Grouse News*, **47**, 11–18.

Ockendon, N., Leech, D. & Pearce-Higgins, J.W. (2013) Climate effects on breeding grounds are more important drivers of breeding phenology in migrant birds than carry-over effects from wintering grounds. *Biology Letters*, **9**, 20130669.

Oswald, K.N., Smit, B., Lee, A.T.K., *et al.* (2021) Higher temperatures are associated with reduced nestling body condition in a range-restricted mountain bird. *Journal of Avian Biology*, **52**, e02756.

Pearce-Higgins, J.W. (2010) Using diet to assess the sensitivity of northern and upland birds to climate change. *Climate Research*, **45**, 119–130.

Pearce-Higgins, J.W. (2011) How ecological science can help manage the effects of climate change: a case study of upland birds. In *The Changing Nature of Scotland*. Marrs, S.J., Foster, S., Hendrie, C., Mackey, E.C. & Thompson, D.B.A. (eds.). Edinburgh: TSO Scotland, pp. 397–414.

Pearce-Higgins, J.W. & Green, R.E. (2014) *Birds and Climate Change: Impacts and Conservation Responses*. Cambridge: Cambridge University Press.

Pearce-Higgins, J.W. & Yalden, D.W. (2004) Habitat selection, diet, arthropod availability and growth of a moorland wader: the ecology of European Golden Plover *Pluvialis apricaria* chicks. *Ibis*, **146**, 335–346.

Pearce-Higgins, J.W., Yalden, D.W. & Whittingham, M.J. (2005) Warmer springs advance the breeding phenology of golden plovers *Pluvialis apricaria* and their prey (Tipulidae). *Oecologia*, **143**, 470–476.

Pearce-Higgins, J.W., Yalden, D.W., Dougall, T.W. & Beale, C.M. (2009) Does climate change explain the decline of a trans-Saharan Afro-Palaearctic migrant? *Oecologia*, **159**, 649–659.

Pearce-Higgins, J.W., Dennis, P., Whittingham, M.J. & Yalden, D.W. (2010) Impacts of climate on prey abundance account for fluctuations in a population of a northern wader at the southern edge of its range. *Global Change Biology*, **16**, 12–23.

Pearce-Higgins, J.W., Ockendon, N., Baker, D.J., *et al.* (2015a) Geographical variation in species' population responses to changes in temperature and precipitation. *Proceedings Royal Society Series B*, **282**, 20151561.

Pearce-Higgins, J.W., Eglington, S.M., Martay, B. & Chamberlain, D.E. (2015b) Drivers of climate change impacts on bird communities. *Journal of Animal Ecology*, **84**, 943–954.

Pearce-Higgins, J.W., Lindley, P.J., Johnstone, I.G., *et al.* (2019) Site-based adaptation reduces the negative effects of weather upon a southern range margin Welsh black grouse *Tetrao tetrix* population that is vulnerable to climate change. *Climatic Change*, **153**, 253–265

Peh, K.S.-H., Soh, M.C.K., Yap, C.A.-M. & Şekercioğlu, Ç.H. (2012) Correlates of elevational specialisation in Southeast Asian tropical birds. *Raffles Bulletin of Zoology*, **25** (Suppl.), 249–257.

Pellissier, V., Schmucki, R., Pe'er, G., et al. (2020) Effects of Natura 2000 on nontarget bird and butterfly species based on citizen science data. *Conservation Biology*, **34**, 666–676.

Pepin, N.C., Arnone, E., Gobiet, A., et al. (2022) Climate changes and their elevational patterns in the mountains of the world. *Reviews of Geophysics*, **60**, e2020RG000730.

Popy, S., Bordignon, L. & Prodon, R. (2010) A weak upward elevational shift in the distributions of breeding birds in the Italian Alps. *Journal of Biogeography*, **37**, 57–67.

Price, L.W. (1981) *Mountains and Man: A Study of Process and Environment*. Berkeley: University of California.

Pringle, H., Wilson, M., Calladine, J. & Siriwardena, G.M. (2019) Associations between gamebird releases and general predators. *Journal of Applied Ecology*, **56**, 2102–2113.

Ralston, J. & Kirchman, J.J. (2013) Predicted range shifts in North American boreal forest birds and the effects of climate change on genetic diversity in blackpoll warblers (*Setophaga striata*). *Conservation Genetics*, **14**, 543–555.

Redpath, S.M., Arroyo, B.E., Etheridge, B., et al. (2002) Temperature and hen harrier productivity: from local mechanisms to geographical patterns. *Ecography*, **25**, 533–540.

Reif, J. & Flousek, J. (2012) The role of species' ecological traits in climatically driven altitudinal range shifts of central European birds. *Oikos*, **121**, 1053–1060.

Resano-Meyer, J., Korner-Nievergelt, F., Vignali, S., et al. (2019) Snow cover phenology is the main driver of foraging habitat selection for a high-alpine passerine during breeding: implications for species persistence in the face of climate change. *Biodiversity and Conservation*, **28**, 2669–2685.

Revermann, R., Schmid, H., Zbinden, N., Spaar, R. & Schröder, B. (2012). Habitat at the mountain tops: how long can Rock Ptarmigan (*Lagopus muta helvetica*) survive rapid climate change in the Swiss Alps? A multi-scale approach. *Journal of Ornithology*, **153**, 891–905.

Rodriguez, O.A., Moya, H. & Matta, N.E. (2009) Parásitos sanguíneos de aves en el Parque Nacional Natural Chingaza: Andes de Colombia. *El Hornero*, **24**, 1–6.

Roos, S., Smart, J., Gibbons, D.W. & Wilson, J.D. (2018) A review of predation as a limiting factor for bird populations in mesopredator-rich landscapes: a case study of the UK. *Biological Reviews*, **93**, 1915–1937.

Roth, T., Plattner, M. & Amrhein, V. (2014) Plants, birds and butterflies: short-term responses of species communities to climate warming vary by taxon and with altitude. *PLoS ONE*, **9**, e82490.

Saracco, J.F., Siegel, R.B., Helton, L., Stock, S.L. & DeSante, D.F. (2019) Phenology and productivity in a montane bird assemblage: trends and responses to elevation and climate variation. *Global Change Biology*, **25**, 985–996.

Scheffers, B.R., De Meester, L., Bridge, T.C.L., et al. (2016) The broad footprint of climate change from genes to biomes to people. *Science*, **354**, aaf7671.

Scridel, D., Brambilla, M., Martin, K., et al. (2018) A review and meta-analysis of the effects of climate change on Holarctic mountain and upland bird populations. *Ibis*, **160**, 489–515.

Scridel, D., Brambilla, M., de Zwaan, D.R., *et al.* (2021) A genus at risk: predicted current and future distribution of all three *Lagopus* species reveal sensitivity to climate change and efficacy of protected areas. *Diversity and Distributions*, **27**, 1759–1744.

Şekercioğlu, Ç.H., Schneider, S.H., Fay, J.P. & Loarie, S.R. (2008) Climate change, elevational range shifts and bird extinctions. *Conservation Biology*, **22**, 140–150.

Sevillano-Ríos, C.S. & Rodewald, A.D. (2017) Avian community structure and habitat use of *Polylepis* forests along an elevation gradient. *PeerJ*, **5**, e3220.

Sevillano-Ríos, C.S., Rodewald, A.D. & Morales, L.V. (2018) Ecología y conservación de las aves asociadas con Polylepis: ¿qué sabemos de esta comunidad cada vez más vulnerable? *Ecología Austral*, **28**, 216–228.

Skikne, S.A., Borker, A.L., Terrill, R.S. & Zavaleta, E. (2020) Predictors of past avian translocation outcomes inform feasibility of future efforts under climate change. *Biological Conservation*, **247**, 108597.

Socolar, J.B., Epanchin, P.N., Beissinger, S.R. & Tingley, M.W. (2017) Phenological shifts conserve thermal niches in North American birds and reshape expectations for climate-driven range shifts. *Proceedings of the National Academy of Sciences*, **114**, 12976–12981.

Spence, A.R. & Tingley, M.W. (2020) The challenge of novel abiotic conditions for species undergoing climate-induced range shifts. *Ecography*, **43**, 1571–1590.

Srinivasan, U. & Wilcove, D.S. (2021) Interactive impacts of climate change and land-use change on the demography of montane birds. *Ecology*, **102**, e03223.

Srivastava, D.S., Coristine, L., Angert, A.L., *et al.* (2021) Wildcards in climate change biology. *Ecological Monographs*, **91**, e01471.

Stephens, P.A., Mason, L.R., Green, R.E., *et al.* (2016) Consistent responses of bird populations to climate change on two continents. *Science*, **352**, 85–87.

Suggitt, A.J., Gillingham, P.J., Hill, J.K., *et al.* (2011) Habitat microclimates drive fine-scale variation in extreme temperatures. *Oikos*, **120**, 1–8.

Summers, R.W., Green, R.E., Proctor, R., *et al.* (2004) An experimental study of the effects of predation on the breeding productivity of capercaillie and black grouse. *Journal of Applied Ecology*, **41**, 513–525.

Tellería, J.L. (2020) Altitudinal shifts in forest birds in a Mediterranean mountain range: causes and conservation prospects. *Bird Conservation International*, **30**, 495–505.

Thackeray, S.J., Henrys, P.A, Hemming, D., *et al.* (2016) Phenological sensitivity to climate across taxa and trophic levels. *Nature*, **535**, 241–245.

Thomas, C.D. & Gillingham, P.K. (2015) The performance of protected areas for biodiversity under climate change. *Biological Journal of the Linnean Society*, **115**, 718–730.

Thomson, D.L. (1994) Growth and development of Dotterel chicks *Charadrius morinellus*. *Bird Study*, **41**, 61–67.

Tingley, M.W., Koo, M.S., Moritz, C., Rush, A.C. & Beissinger, S.R. (2012) The push and pull of climate change causes heterogeneous shifts in avian elevational ranges. *Global Change Biology*, **18**, 3279–3290.

Tye, H. (1992) Reversal of breeding season by lowland birds at higher altitudes in western Cameroon. *Ibis*, **134**, 154–163.

Urban, M.C. (2015) Accelerating extinction risk from climate change. *Science*, **348**, 571–573.

VanDerWal, J., Murphy, H.T., Kutt, A.S., *et al.* (2013) Focus on poleward shifts in species' distribution underestimates the fingerprint of climate change. *Nature Climate Change*, **3**, 239–243.

Veblen, T.T., Young, K.R. & Orme, A.R. (2007) *The Physical Geography of South America*. New York: Oxford University Press.

Velasquez-Tibata, J., Salaman, P. & Graham, C.H. (2013) Effects of climate change on species distribution, community structure and conservation of birds in protected areas in Colombia. *Regional Environmental Change*, **13**, 235–248.

Visser, M. (2012) Birds and butterflies in climatic debt. *Nature Climate Change*, **2**, 77–78.

von dem Bussche, J., Spaar, R., Schmid, H. & Schrider, B. (2008) Modelling the recent and potential future spatial distribution of the Ring Ouzel (*Turdus torquatus*) and Blackbird (*T. merula*) in Switzerland. *Journal of Ornithology*, **149**, 529–544.

Warren, R., VanDerWal, J., Price, J., *et al.* (2013) Quantifying the benefit of early climate change mitigation in avoiding biodiversity loss. *Nature Climate Change*, **3**, 678–682.

Warren, R., Price, J., Graham, E., Forstenhaeusler, N. & VanDerWal, J. (2018) The projected effect on insects, vertebrates and plants of limiting global warming to 1.5°C rather than 2°C. *Science*, **360**, 791–795.

Watson, A., Moss, R. & Rae, S. (1998) Population dynamics of Scottish rock ptarmigan cycles. *Ecology*, **79**, 1174–1192.

Wheatley, C.J., Beale, C.M., Bradbury, R.B., *et al.* (2017) Climate change vulnerability for species – assessing the assessments. *Global Change Biology*, **23**, 3704–3715.

Wiebe, K.L. & Martin, K. (1998) Costs and benefits of nest cover for ptarmigan: changes within and among years. *Animal Behaviour*, **56**, 1137–1144.

Williams, R.A.J., Segovia-Hinostrova, K., Ghersi, B.M., *et al.* (2012) Avian influenza infections in nonmigrant land birds in Andean Peru. *Journal of Wildlife Diseases*, **48**, 910–917.

Wilson, S. & Martin, K. (2010) Variable reproductive effort for two ptarmigan species in response to spring weather in a northern alpine ecosystem. *Journal of Avian Biology*, **41**, 319–326.

Young, B.E. (1994) The effects of food, nest predation and weather on the timing of breeding in tropical House Wrens. *Condor*, **96**, 341–353.

Zemp, M., Frey, H., Gartner-Roer, I., *et al.* (2015) Historically unprecedented global glacier decline in the early twenty-first century. *Journal of Glaciology*, **61**, 745–762.

Zuckerberg, B., Woods, A.M. & Porter, W.F. (2009) Poleward shifts in breeding bird distributions in New York State. *Global Change Biology*, **15**, 1866–188.

7 · *Anthropogenic Activities and Mountain Birds*

ENRICO CAPRIO, ANTONIO
ROLANDO, RAPHAËL ARLETTAZ
AND DAN CHAMBERLAIN

7.1 Introduction

High elevation ecosystems are sensitive to a vast number of environmental changes (Böhm *et al.* 2001; Maggini *et al.* 2014; Flousek *et al.* 2015) and in addition, they are subject to increasingly intense human-driven alterations which impact the natural environment (Arlettaz *et al.* 2007; Braunisch *et al.* 2011; Viterbi *et al.* 2013). For centuries, mountain ecosystems and communities have played an important role in maintaining a sustainable flow of natural resources to the plains below, including timber, minerals (ore for mineral extraction and stone for building), water and agricultural products (especially dairy and meat from livestock farming) and game (meat from hunting). Over the course of the last century, there have been great social changes in mountain areas, reflecting a general shift in the human population of many parts of the world from rural areas to cities. This shift has changed the economic situation, with many traditional practices no longer economically viable. At the same time, alternative industries have developed in mountain areas.

In this chapter, we focus on some of the main current human activities in mountains, including tourism, hunting and energy generation, and assess their potential impacts on mountain and high elevation birds. Agriculture, and especially pastoral practices, have shaped mountain habitats for millennia in many mountain ranges and can thus be viewed as a major source of impacts (Chapter 1). The effects of livestock grazing on habitat structure in the alpine zone and on mountain birds are discussed elsewhere in this book (Chapters 1 and 4). We maintain a broad habitat scope across the elevation gradient from montane forest to alpine and nival zones as sources of impact are often linear features that cross multiple elevation zones (e.g., hiking trails and ski-pistes).

Before addressing impacts of different sources of disturbance, it is important to define what we mean by the term 'disturbance'. The concept of disturbance identifies a set of events that can alter any ecological level, any abiotic component or the biological cycle of organisms (Pickett *et al.* 1989). The general term disturbance includes two different kinds of impact. *Disturbance per se* refers to a temporally and spatially discrete event, that leads to: quantitative and/or qualitative changes in ecosystems, biocenoses or populations; distinct changes in the availability of resources; and/or to measurable and abrupt changes in state variables such as a storm, an avalanche, or the construction of a ski-piste or road (Grime 1979; White & Pickett 1985; Wohlgemuth *et al.* 2019). Disturbance can be direct if it directly influences a target component (like the survival of individuals, the density of a population or the species richness in a community; Battisti *et al.* 2016), or indirect, affecting specific ecological targets through other environmental components (Pickett & Thompson 1978; Hobbs & Huenneke 1992) such as the main prey type or resource availability. A consequence of disturbance can be a physiological response termed *stress* which has a cost in terms of energy that is traded-off with other vital functions (e.g., immune function, growth, reproduction) and thus may potentially have negative impacts (Arlettaz *et al.* 2015). Although stress can be more broadly defined as an event that interrupts or modifies activities such as feeding, breeding, reproduction and other behaviours (Grime 1979), here we use the term stress to refer to strictly physiological responses (as per Arlettaz *et al.* 2015).

7.1.1 Socio-Economic Changes in Mountains

By 2050, the population of Europe's urban regions is projected to increase by 24.1 million people and will provide home to almost half of the EU-28 population (Eurostat 2017). By contrast, the population of predominantly rural regions is projected to fall by 7.9 million. Similar trends are evident in the United States where depopulating rural counties lost more than 34 per cent of their original population between 1950 and 2016 (Johnson & Lichter 2019). Increased movement of people from rural to urban areas is expected to continue in many Asian and Latin American countries (Østby 2016; Dobbs *et al.* 2019; Hoffman *et al.* 2019). This general trend is likely to be even more marked in mountain areas due to their geographic isolation and the economic challenges of mountain agriculture and other sectors. Human populations of many mountain areas are shrinking as agriculture has been restructured and populations and employment have become increasingly concentrated in urban centres at lower elevations

(Maharjan *et al.* 2020; Dax *et al.* 2021). Abandonment of traditional grazing practices in particular has had significant impacts on the mountain landscape in many regions, resulting in re-forestation of areas formerly maintained as pastures and treelines shifting upwards in elevation (Brändle *et al.* 2015). Such changes have had significant impacts on the avifauna (Laiolo *et al.* 2004) and on mountain biodiversity in general (Chapter 4).

Tourism in rural areas that are not yet subject to massive development of recreation can provide a useful economic supplement to agricultural and other traditional commercial activities. In some cases, the economic disparities between traditional and new activities (i.e., tourism-related) can favour the latter. For example, in Montenegro, 6 per cent of the population is engaged in agriculture, but the sector only contributes 0.8 per cent to the gross domestic product, and 18 per cent of people in rural areas are poor, while tourism contributes about 25 per cent to the GDP – a share that is increasing with time (Montenegro Statistical Office 2012).

Tourism is now a major industry in many mountain ranges around the world. It is estimated that mountain tourism accounts for 15–20 per cent of the global tourism industry, with a value of US\$ 70–90 billion per year, and it has been reported that the European Alps alone account for an estimated 7–10 per cent of annual global tourism turnover (Mountain Agenda 1999). Long recognized as places of sanctuary and spiritual renewal, mountains will become even more attractive as places of escape in a rapidly urbanizing world. Two key changes, human depopulation in some areas and increased tourism and population in others, are therefore having profound socioeconomic effects. On the one hand, depopulation is causing a loss of open habitats of high ecological value and of rural activities, which is driven in part by the limited economic gain they create. On the other hand, mountain tourism creates new economic opportunities, and fosters the development of tourist infrastructures that increase urban cover through development of buildings, the road network and skiing facilities, and impact higher elevations that before were largely undisturbed by human pressure. In general, resident human populations have decreased, except in some major tourist resorts, while seasonal visitors have increased, periodically enlarging the local population, typically by 5–10 times (e.g., Clivaz & Savioz 2020).

Recreational activities in natural areas may have a number of impacts on birds, most of which are negative (Steven *et al.* 2011). Depending on the level of human disturbance, wildlife responses can include behavioural changes in individuals (Vallino *et al.* 2019, 2020) and physiological responses (Arlettaz *et al.* 2007, 2015; Thiel *et al.* 2008). If human

Table 7.1 *List of winter recreational activities having potential impacts on mountain birds.*

Winter activity	Brief description	References
Skiing (on- and off-piste), snowboarding	Alpine skiing (sliding downhill) needs infrastructures such as ski lifts and maintained ski-pistes; Nordic skiing consists of cross country skiing and may be practiced on groomed trails or in undeveloped backcountry areas	Laiolo *et al.* 2005; Arlettaz *et al.* 2007, 2015; Rolando *et al.* 2007; Patthey *et al.* 2008; Thiel *et al.* 2008; Caprio *et al.* 2011, 2016
Snow shoeing	Hiking on trails on the snow	Summers *et al.* 2007; Braunisch *et al.* 2011
Dog sledding	Travelling on trails on a sled pulled by dogs	
Ice climbing	Ascending inclined ice formations, usually in roped areas which enables climbing on icefalls, frozen waterfalls and cliffs and rock slabs covered with ice	Brambilla *et al.* 2004
Snowcat tours	Guided tours aboard a snowcat	
Helicopter flights	Helicopters are used both for sightseeing and to reach the top of the slopes for freeriders (heliski)	Grubb *et al.* 2010; Arroyo *et al.* 2021
Alpinism	Includes a number of activities such as climbing, trekking, scrambling and even crossing glaciers	Summers *et al.* 2007
Paragliding	Paragliding is the activity of gliding through the air on a parachute. Paragliders descend from mountains and cliffs	Arroyo & Razin 2006

presence is intense and regular, birds may reduce their habitat use in the proximity of the disturbance, leading to local changes in their distribution and abundance (Patthey *et al.* 2008; Larson *et al.* 2019). Such effects can be long-term, especially when recreational activities are accompanied by construction of facilities such as buildings, cable cars, ski-lifts and ski-pistes that alter existing habitats, with effects that are detectable for many years due to the limited regeneration capacity of high elevation vegetation (Barni *et al.* 2007; Maliniemi & Virtanen 2021). There is a diverse range of winter-related activities that vary in terms of their intensity of potential disturbance and stress to wildlife. Table 7.1 presents a list of outdoor mountain activities with impacts that can vary significantly according to the site and the species considered. Similar activities are also present in summer in many areas, e.g., cycling, mountain biking, quadbiking, horse riding, canyoneering, rock climbing, paragliding and base jumping.

Mountains are also important for energy generation. The exploitation of the potential energy in mountain water sources through hydropower has been known for centuries and has been used to generate electricity for over a century. More recently, wind power, another resource that is particularly prevalent in mountain areas, has also been exploited for energy generation through the construction of arrays of wind turbines (so-called 'wind farms'). Both of these represent renewable energy resources and they typically form key components of strategies to reduce the use of fossil fuels and hence combat climate change. Currently, both wind power (GWEC 2015; EWEA 2016) and hydropower (Zarfl *et al.* 2015) are expanding rapidly worldwide with potential consequences for biodiversity through direct effects of the constructions of the energy plants themselves, and of associated infrastructure and disturbance. Although effects of these renewable energy sources have been studied in many areas, there is concern that the rate of development is outpacing ecological research. Thus many impacts still need to be fully evaluated and proper mitigation measures are slow to be implemented (Reid *et al.* 2019).

7.2 The Impact of Skiing on Birds

Within the leisure industry, skiing plays a prominent role in impacting the natural environment because of the large-scale changes it causes (Rixen & Rolando 2013). Since the beginning of the 1900s, but especially after World War II, ski tourism has become a popular activity, and the development of new ski resorts has significantly altered large parts of mountain ecosystems, where previously the only human activities were low-intensity agriculture and grazing. Worldwide, skiing represents probably the largest human impact on temperate mountains: globally around 60,000 km of slopes are served by more than 23,000 ski lifts (www.skiresort.info, accessed on 30 May 2021). In Europe alone, more than 76 million people ski (Vanat 2020). In the United States, there were 9.2 million active skiers and snowboarders in the period 2018/19, representing more than 59 million skier-days (i.e., one person purchasing a ticket for one day of skiing or snowboarding; www.nsaa.org). In the same period, there were more than 20 million skier-days in China, where the number of people practicing this sport is increasing exponentially (Wu 2020), and more than 2 million skier-days in Australia (http://asaa.org.au/stats/).

Skiing has a particularly significant impact on mountain habitats due to the construction of ski-pistes, which causes the removal of vegetation and part of the soil layer. Strictly speaking, a ski-piste is a ski track covered in snow and used by skiers, hence the ski track is usually the disturbance factor, rather than the piste *per se*. However, here we will use the more common, but slightly less accurate, term ski-piste to refer to both. The creation and use of ski-pistes involve significant consequences for mountain ecosystems if we consider the broad elevation range involved, with impacts on both forest and treeless areas and evident effects both at habitat and landscape levels (Rixen & Rolando 2013).

7.2.1 The Impact of Ski-Piste Creation on Birds

Ski-piste creation causes a wide range of negative effects on the natural environment (Rixen & Rolando 2013; Sato *et al.* 2013). The most evident are habitat degradation and destruction due to the removal and modification of the vegetation in the process of ski-piste construction, which reduces plant diversity (Figure 7.1), structural diversity and disrupts successional stages (Urbanska *et al.* 1998; Tsuyuzaki 2002). Habitat loss and degradation, in terms of decreasing cover or increasing predation risk, result in a lowered species richness and abundance of birds, not only on the piste itself, but also extending into adjacent habitat. A negative edge effect of ski-piste construction significantly reduces species richness and/or occurrence rates in habitats close to ski-pistes (Korňan 2020). This effect operates both in forests (Laiolo & Rolando 2005), where plots at edges of ski-pistes have a lower bird species richness and diversity than those located in the forest interior or at the edges of pastures, and in alpine grassland bird communities (Rolando *et al.* 2007), where plots at ski-piste edges show a lower abundance of grassland species. On the other hand, some species, like those that breed in forest edges created by natural disturbances, may benefit from ski-pistes creation. The abundance of Bicknell's thrush *Catharus bicknelli* in North American boreal forests was about 15 times higher close to ski-pistes and associated infrastructure compared to more distant areas, likely due to the creation of structurally suitable forest edge habitat (Hill & Campell 2019).

Figure 7.1 Examples of highly impacted ski-pistes in the Italian Alps where vegetation and topsoil has been removed as part of regular management or 'grooming'. A. and B. high elevation ski-pistes (photos: Enrico Caprio), C. and D. lower elevation ski-pistes through forest (photos: Antonio Rolando and Dan Chamberlain).

It is therefore clear that the effects of ski-piste creation extend beyond the ski-piste itself, exerting a mainly negative effect at a landscape scale which may impact on most populations, rather than just cause a local shift in bird distributions. In the Italian Alps, this was shown for grassland specialist species richness, and for the probability of occurrence of water pipit *Anthus spinoletta,* northern wheatear *Oenanthe oenanthe* and black redstart *Phoenicurus ochruros*, which decreased significantly with increasing extent of ski-piste edge (Caprio *et al.* 2011). The removal of much of the vegetation and rocks, and disturbance to the soil layer, creates a habitat that is almost totally unsuitable for nesting and that also provides extremely limited food resources for high alpine species that require both grass cover and rocks. Predictions of species occurrence, made by applying models of probability of occurrence to different scenarios of habitat change, showed detrimental impacts of a relatively small increase in ski-piste extent of 10 per cent, but also that grassland restoration on existing ski-pistes could result in significantly increased

Figure 7.2 Examples of partially vegetated (A. Photo: Enrico Caprio) and totally vegetated ski-pistes (B. Photo: Antonio Rolando).

occurrence rates of alpine grassland species (Caprio *et al.* 2011). Indeed, revegetation of ski-pistes (Figure 7.2) seems to provide a promising management intervention that may allow recovery of bird communities. However, grass on restored ski-pistes and natural grassland are not necessarily ecologically equivalent. Differences may still be great and significant in terms of density of grass species, which remains lower on restored ski-pistes, or in terms of occurrence of alien plant species, which is higher on revegetated ski-pistes, especially when hydroseeded (Barni *et al.* 2007). This means that, even though grass cover is high, the vegetation of restored ski-pistes is not equal to that of adjacent pastures and, therefore, is less attractive to grassland birds (Caprio *et al.* 2016). Moreover, most ski-pistes lack the heterogenous micro-habitat mosaic that benefits birds since they have been totally flattened by machinery (e.g., removal of rocks).

Another factor that is intrinsically linked to ski-piste construction is the associated transport infrastructure to take skiers to the start of the piste – typically ski lifts or cable cars. Some of this associated infrastructure may sometimes provide nest sites for alpine species (e.g., white-winged snowfinches *Montifringilla nivalis* nesting in cavities in pylons; Resano-Mayor *et al.* 2019; Nyffenegger 2021), but collision with cables associated with ski lifts and cable cars can be a significant source of mortality for mountain birds. There is much evidence to show that mortality due to collisions with cables has increased in local populations of black grouse *Lyrurus tetrix*, rock partridge *Alectoris graeca* and rock ptarmigan *Lagopus muta* (Miquet 1990; Watson & Moss 2004; Buffet & Dumont-Dayot 2013). Bevanger & Brøseth (2004) found 24 species of dead birds from a range of taxonomic groups (e.g., raptors, waders, passerines) below power lines in a subalpine area of Norway (grouse were the most commonly found group). While this study did not involve cables associated with ski lifts, the risks are likely to be similar, suggesting that ski cables may be a risk for many mountain bird species, although grouse may be at particular risk as they are poor fliers with their broad short wings and relatively high body mass (Rayner 1988). They are also easier to detect than smaller species, and it is likely that estimates of mortality rates for many species are significantly underestimated using standard search methods (Bech *et al.* 2012).

In summary, ski-piste construction poses a threat to biodiversity and efforts are needed to preserve native vegetation as much as possible in order to reduce the negative effects on many taxonomic groups. These results are of particular concern given the global extent of ski-pistes, most of which is concentrated in temperate mountains. Many high elevation species are already vulnerable and species such as common rock thrush *Monticola saxatilis*, Eurasian skylark *Alauda arvensis* and rock bunting *Emberiza cia* are declining (see Chapter 5, Table 5.1).

7.2.2 The Impact of Ski-Pistes on Bird Food Resources

The construction of ski-pistes may have subsequent impacts on birds via their important dietary components. The diet of large mountain birds, which have wide home ranges reaching far beyond ski-piste areas, is well documented (e.g., golden eagle *Aquila chrysaetos*, bearded vulture *Gypaetus barbatus*, black grouse). While we also know a fair amount about some characteristic mountain species such as alpine chough *Pyrrhocorax graculus*, red-billed chough, white-winged snowfinch and ring ouzel *Turdus torquatus* (Rolando & Patterson 1993; Rolando & Laiolo 1997; Laiolo & Rolando 1999; Resano-Mayor *et al.* 2019; Barras *et al.* 2021), very little is known about dietary niches in other passerines, in particular mountain generalists. For such species, we need to infer impacts on diet by analysing effects on likely prey groups. In this section, we consider impacts of ski-piste creation on animals that are known, or are likely, prey for several mountain birds. There are nevertheless biases in the research in that studies have focussed on ground-dwelling animals (terrestrial invertebrates, small mammals), rather than tree/shrub dwelling animals and aerial insects (with the exception Rolando *et al.* 2013 – see below), all of which may be important for certain bird species.

For many potential prey species, ski-pistes running through forest create a clear barrier to dispersal. A radiotelemetry study on *Carabus olympiae*, a brachypterous, ground-dwelling beetle, found that these invertebrates inhabit only forests and completely avoid open habitats: radio-tracked animals moved during the night in the forest, but when they arrived at the margin of ski tracks, they never crossed them (Negro et al. 2008). Strong et al. (2002) also found that ski-pistes acted as barriers to forest carabid species, whilst the piste itself was colonized by generalist species from lower elevations. Ski-pistes are also perceived as ecological barriers by some small forest mammals. For example, bank vole *Myodes glareolus*, Eurasian pygmy shrew *Sorex minutus* and common shrew *S. araneus* were virtually absent from ski-pistes in coniferous forests, while they occured in the adjacent woods (Negro et al. 2009). Based on a radiotelemetry study, Negro et al. (2013a) concluded that small mammals (European edible dormouse *Glis glis*, bank vole and yellow-necked mouse *Apodemus flavicollis*) perceived ski-pistes as semipermeable barriers. Animals crossed ski-pistes only if they were forced to (i.e., through translocation to other areas), suggesting they would only risk exposing themselves to predators by crossing open spaces in extreme circumstances (Negro et al. 2013a). Some small mammals that prefer open habitat structures may, however, be more abundant on ski-pistes. Hadley and Wilson (2004) found ski-pistes had lower densities of red-backed voles *Clethrionomys gapperi*, but higher densities of deer mice *Peromyscus maniculatus* and least chipmunks *Tamias minimus* than adjacent forest sites.

Skiing may also impact the quality and quantity of available habitat for prey species in the winter. Skiing and associated activity (surface ski lifts and pedestrian routes to pistes) result in compression of the snow surface and subsequent negative impacts on the sub-nivean space, which provides a crucial habitat for small mammals in winter. Sanecki et al. (2006) experimentally compressed the snowpack in order to mimic the action of skiing activities. This resulted in large declines (75–80 per cent) of two small mammal species that depend on the sub-nivean space in winter, illustrating how skiing can cause habitat loss for these species.

In more open habitats at high elevation, or in open pastures, the diversity of arthropods such as brachypterous carabids (with reduced wings or wingless), spiders, orthopterans and opilionids, is lower on ski-pistes than in the adjacent alpine grassland and meadows; the decrease is largely due to the low degree of herbaceous and shrub cover (Negro et al. 2010; Kessler et al. 2011). It should be noted, however, that the diversity of macropterous carabids, which are able to move in flight and have varied ecological needs, did not differ between ski-pistes and alpine grassland in the Italian Alps (Negro *et al.* 2010). Some invertebrate species groups that prefer more open habitats may be expected to benefit from ski-pistes that are constructed in forests, such as generalist carabid species (Strong *et al.* 2002) and herbivorous beetles associated with nitrophilous plants (Kašák *et al.* 2013). For invertebrates below the treeline, the abundance and species richness of brachypterous carabids decreased significantly from forest interior to open habitats (i.e., ski-pistes or pastures), while those of spiders and macropterous carabids (those able to fly) increased from forest interior to open habitats. The ski slopes are, however, a suboptimal open habitat for the latter groups – the diversity of spiders and macropterous carabids is lower in the ski-pistes than in the pastures of equal elevation, probably due to the low herbaceous cover on the former (Negro *et al.* 2009). Similarly, the occurrence of lizards may be affected by the extreme structural simplification of ski-piste habitat (Sato *et al.* 2014). Finally, one may expect that the availability of earthworms (Lombricidae) is reduced in the compacted soils of ski-pistes (Barras *et al.* 2021) which is likely to affect ring ouzel foraging ecology.

One of the few studies that sampled flying insects was also a rare example of potential positive impacts of ski-pistes on an invertebrate group. The abundance of butterflies was found to be greater on ski-pistes than on pastures in late summer (Rolando *et al.* 2013). This surprising result can be explained by the fact that the greater persistence of snow on pistes induces a delay in plant phenology. In late summer, the ski-pistes still offer flowers that are no longer present in the meadow-pastures of equal elevation and therefore the number of adult lepidopterans remains high. However, the diversity and species richness of lepidopterans was lower than in adjacent pastures because of the reduced number of plant species that colonize the pistes (Rolando *et al.* 2013). It remains to be seen what effect this has on the availability of caterpillars, which are the prey potentially most used by birds.

Ski-pistes are continually managed to level the soil and remove rocks and encroaching woody vegetation, and are also fertilized and/or seeded with plants (often non-native). There is evidence that a number of these practices can have negative impacts on invertebrates. For example, Kessler *et al.* (2011) found that grasshopper species richness and abundance on ski-pistes was lower than natural grassland, due to fertilization and bulldozing. The construction and management of ski-pistes, combined with the use of artificial snow and snow grooming, have severe effects on mountain soils, leading to the significant modification of their physical and chemical properties, such as higher pH, lower organic matter, loss of fine particles and aggregates and loss of moisture-holding capability (Pohl *et al.* 2009; Hudek *et al.* 2020). All of the above leads to a reduction in the abundance of wild herbaceous plants (Barni *et al.* 2007; Pintaldi *et al.* 2017) and likely also underground invertebrates such as earthworms (Barras 2021). Management to control vegetation (including burning) and to smooth the ski-piste surface has also been shown to have negative effects on the sub-nivean space and hence the quality of habitat for small mammals in winter (Sanecki *et al.* 2006).

The above evidence shows that ski-pistes are on the whole likely to be poor habitats in terms of invertebrate and small mammal prey for open habitat bird species. Furthermore, there are likely to be population-level impacts on such species if the ski-pistes cause significant fragmentation of their natural habitats (forest, grassland). However, there is evidence that management interventions can go some way to ameliorate negative effects. For forest ski-pistes, it may be possible to 'soften' the barrier effect by introducing boulder-filled and culvert-style wildlife crossings, which have been shown to increase their permeability to the threatened broad-toothed mouse *Mastacomys fuscus* in Australia (Schroder & Sato 2017). Hydroseeding ski-pistes, while creating a non-native vegetation cover, induces the recovery of some groups of arthropods – grasshoppers and brachypterous carabids immediately return to hydroseeded slopes. Spiders, on the other hand, avoided re-seeded ski-pistes. This group is especially sensitive to habitat alterations at high elevation and thus has the potential to be an excellent bioindicator of environmental alteration (Negro *et al.* 2013b).

7.2.3 Physiological Impacts of Skiing on Birds

Several studies provide evidence of a negative effect of winter recreational activities on tetraonids mediated through physiological effects. Outdoor winter recreation represents a major source of stress for black grouse (Arlettaz *et al.* 2007). Impacted areas translate to a substantial estimated reduction of 28 per cent in suitable wintering habitat when considering ski infrastructures and free ranging skiing activities in Switzerland (Braunisch *et al.* 2011) and a reduction of 10 per cent in Austria (Jäger *et al.* 2020). The presence of skiers in black grouse wintering grounds causes high concentrations of corticosterone metabolites in individual birds which may reduce individual fitness and ultimately result in the decline of the population (Formenti *et al.* 2015). Similar results have been found for the western capercaillie *Tetrao urogallus*, which showed markedly increased stress hormone levels closer to locations with winter recreation activity (Thiel *et al.* 2011). It has been estimated that in most disturbed areas, individuals may increase their daily energy expenditure by more than 10 per cent (Arlettaz *et al.* 2015), therefore in areas intensely used for winter sports, there is a need to establish undisturbed protection zones for affected species (Zeitler 2000; Braunisch *et al.* 2011; Thiel *et al.* 2011; Arlettaz *et al.* 2013). More recently, there has been a spread of skiing activities outside traditional ski resorts that is further impacting wildlife, notably ski mountaineering, snowboarding and snowshoeing. Their impacts have not been investigated in detail, except in black grouse (Braunisch *et al.* 2011) for which an additional significant fraction of their wintering habitat will be impacted by these new rapidly expanding outdoor winter sports.

7.3 The Impact of Other Recreational Activities

7.3.1 Indirect Effects of Recreational Activities

Tourism and recreational activities in mountain areas can have several effects on birds, some of which may actually be positive, at least in the short term. For example, species such as black redstart, white-winged snowfinch and alpine chough can breed in buildings and associated infrastructure in high elevation tourist resorts. Furthermore, corvid species such as alpine chough, carrion crow *Corvus corone* and northern raven *Corvus corax* regularly visit popular hiking trails, feeding readily on picnic remains. A study in the Bavarian Alps showed that corvids are able to adjust their range use opportunistically according to the availability of resources offered by tourists (Storch & Leidenberger 2003). Mountain huts and other places frequented by humans may thus provide additional food resources and contribute to an increased carrying capacity for corvids and carnivorous mammals (e.g., red fox *Vulpes vulpes*) at higher elevations with consequent threats for potential prey species. Other species may also benefit. At Cairn Gorm in Scotland (one of the few places that qualifies as truly alpine in the UK), more pied wagtails *Motacilla alba yarrelli*, gulls *Larus* spp. and snow buntings *Plectrophenax nivalis*, as well as corvids (crows and rooks *Corvus frugilegus*), were seen on disturbed than on undisturbed areas, often feeding on waste food (Watson 1979).

The availability of anthropogenic food may also influence bird behaviour. The opportunistic alpine chough is a characteristic bird of high elevation ski resorts, often fearlessly foraging on leftovers at restaurants

Figure 7.3 An alpine chough *Pyrrhocorax graculus* feeding on food remains at Plateau Rosa, Western Italian Alps, at 3,500 m (Photo E. Caprio).

and bar terraces at the top of ski-pistes (Figure 7.3). A study in the Italian Alps showed that the correlation between alpine chough flock size and the biomass of grasshoppers, their main natural prey in summer, was positive at a natural site and negative at a tourist site. This suggests that where there is a high level of human influence, other factors, such as the availability of human-provided food, may disturb the natural relationship between the birds and their key prey. Thus, flock size of foraging alpine choughs may reflect both grasshopper abundance and the degree of anthropogenic influence (Vallino *et al.* 2020). In winter, the link with human infrastructure at ski resorts was positive, although it varied according to the site in question. Considering three resorts in the Alps, flock size and time spent at ski resorts increased with the number of tourists and decreased with increasing temperature at two sites out of three (Vallino *et al.* 2021), suggesting that alpine choughs exploit these sites when there are likely more food resources and when natural food sources are scarcer due to lower temperatures in their natural habitat.

It is not yet known if short term gains for birds mask other disadvantages of feeding on anthropogenic food. There is evidence from urban environments that productivity may be affected by non-natural, human-provided, foods (e.g., Plummer *et al.* 2013, 2018). Furthermore, there may be wider effects on the community that can have far reaching consequences for more natural areas (Shutt & Lees 2021). Indeed, the attraction of potential predators to anthropogenic food at elevations where they would not otherwise occur may have major ramifications for other species through increased predation or competition. There is one such example from an alpine habitat in the Cairngorms in Scotland, where generalist carrion crows colonized a high elevation area after construction of a ski resort, causing increased nest predation in the local population of rock ptarmigan (Watson & Moss 2004).

7.3.2 Hiking and Climbing

There is evidence that apparently low-impact activities such as hiking can have negative effects on mountain birds. When exposed to human presence, animals may show important changes in their behaviour and physiology, for example by increasing vigilance and flushing distance and releasing stress hormones, which may affect individual fitness and the dynamics of animal populations (as happens with skiing – see above). For example, in the Chilean Andes, regular presence of humans within a distance of 200 m of their roosts disturbed Andean condors *Vultur gryphus* and typically prevented birds from using roost sites (Herrmann *et al.* 2010). In the European Alps, tourist presence negatively affected the intake rates and the amount of time spent in a foraging patch for alpine choughs, although there was some evidence that birds could habituate to human presence, since in more frequented sites, the flushing distances were shorter than in the less frequented areas (Vallino *et al.* 2019). Nonetheless, results of studies investigating effects of disturbance on mountain birds caused by humans using hiking trails have varied. Some studies show generally negative effects on, for example, species richness and diversity and the abundance or occurrence of individual species (Gutzwiller & Anderson 1999; Heil *et al.* 2007; Immitzer *et al.* 2014; Barros *et al.* 2015; Bötsch *et al.* 2018), although for many individual species, there appears to be little effect. In part, lack of impacts may be due to the difficulty of disentangling the effect of habitat modification due to trails from direct human presence. However, species seem to vary in their sensitivity to disturbance caused by recreational trails, probably due to particular traits (Morelli *et al.* 2015). In a comparison of bird communities on and off mountain trails in the Andes, there was a reduction in overall species richness and diversity, but impacts varied according to diet group (insectivores were most affected), and few individual species (6/28) showed negative effects (Heil *et al.* 2007).

A study conducted in the White Mountains, New Hampshire, USA showed no evidence that recreational hiking trails had adverse effects on the abundance, detection probabilities, recruitment or daily nest survival on the five most common species (blackpoll warbler *Setophaga striata*, Bicknell's thrush, boreal chickadee *Poecile hudsonicus*, Swainson's thrush *Catharus ustulatus* and yellow-bellied flycatcher *Empidonax flaviventris*; Deluca & King 2014). There also appears to be marked variation in disturbance effects among sites for some studies (Gutzwiller & Anderson 1999; Bötsch *et al.* 2018), which may to some extent be influenced by the intensity and predictability of recreational disturbance. Bötsch *et al.* (2018) compared high-use and low-use forest trails and showed that the response of the bird community was affected by human presence and mainly depended on the intensity of recreational activities. Low activity areas showed no effect, suggesting some degree of tolerance, but there were negative effects in high activity areas.

Rock climbing, in common with off-piste snowsport activities such as ski mountaineering, snowboarding and snowshoeing, has shown a rapid growth in popularity over the past two decades, although the evidence for effects on wildlife is currently sparse (Holzschuh 2016). For birds, there is some evidence that raptors may be negatively affected by the presence of rock climbers. A study in the Italian Alps showed that peregrine falcons *Falco peregrinus* nesting on cliffs where rock climbing took place had lower breeding success and productivity, although this effect was also dependent on the presence of northern ravens, another major source of disturbance for peregrine falcons (Brambilla *et al.* 2004). Such effects are likely for other raptor species such as golden eagle, although for the eagles, irresponsible nature photographers appear to be a more serious threat than recreationalists (Fasce *et al.* 2017). There is little evidence of impacts on other species, although Camp & Knight (1998) found a broad variation in responses (negative, positive and no effect) of the bird community to rock climbers in a non-mountain site.

A further aspect which has received little attention is the transport infrastructure associated with tourist activities, that is, the means by which tourists arrive at hiking trails, rock faces or ski-pistes. Although transport impacts may also be associated with other sources of human activity, we assume that tourism is the main source of traffic in most mountain areas. Increases in tourist infrastructure will inevitably include increases in transport infrastructure with potential negative effects. Roads are likely to have a significant negative impact on bird populations in general (e.g., Cooke *et al.* 2020), and avoidance of roads may effectively reduce the area of usable habitat available (e.g. Andean condors, Plaza & Lambertucci 2020). Other forms of transport may be sources of disturbance such as the widespread use of helicopters. This is little studied in birds, although it is thought likely that it will be a source of major disturbance (Herrmann *et al.* 2010; Plaza & Lambertucci 2020), as it is for chamois *Rupicapra rupicapra* in the European Alps (Brambilla & Brivio 2016). Other aerial snowsports such as paragliding and deltagliding, speed flying and base jumping are also sources of disturbance to wildlife, as demonstrated for effects of paragliding on chamois (Schnidrig-Petrig & Ingold 2001). There are reported cases of breeding failures of golden eagle caused by base jumping activities (S. Denis, pers. comm.).

In summary, the limited available evidence on recreational activities in summer suggests the need for their regulation in high mountain habitats, especially in areas of conservation concern. More studies with proper control treatments, ideally in an experimental set up, are needed to evaluate the impacts of hiking trails, rock climbing and other recreational activities on mountain bird species and communities, including the effects of associated transport infrastructure. In particular, many studies fail to adequately account for confounding variables, such as habitat quality, between disturbed and undisturbed sites (Holzschuh 2016).

7.4 Hunting and Persecution

Hunting, both legal and illegal, is undoubtedly a source of disturbance and stress as well as a direct cause of mortality in birds. It is considered a key threat to certain groups of mountain birds, especially raptors and grouse (Chamberlain *et al.* 2016). Alba *et al.* (2022) found hunting to have the most consistent negative impact across a range of mountain species in Europe. Hunting may also have an effect on mountain birds through management of habitat to promote quarry species (almost always gamebirds). Indeed, there is evidence that several thousand years ago mountain forests were opened up, often using fire, to create pastures which facilitated hunting in many areas (e.g., Kessler & Herzog 1998; Hope 2014), contributing to changes in structural diversity that altered bird communities. Due to the popularity and commercial interests of hunting in many areas, a considerable amount of research has been carried out to assess whether the consequent mortality affects the population size of quarry species (Newton 1998). Grouse have been a particular focus of research in North America and Europe, although there is relatively little published research on impacts of hunting specifically on mountain bird populations. Furthermore, existing studies on hunting impacts have focussed on grouse populations of mountain forests and timberline ecosystems (e.g., Hörnell-Willebrand et al. 2006; Åhlen et al. 2013; Zbinden et al. 2018). There have been very few that have concerned higher elevation species of the treeline and alpine zones (exceptions include McGowan 1975; Giesen & Braun 1993; Zbinden et al. 2018; Nilsen et al. 2020; Cannone et al. 2021). There is a considerable body of work from the UK uplands in highly managed habitat on effects of hunting on red grouse Lagopus lagopus scotica, including impacts on other species through habitat management and both legal and illegal control of competing species. However, this habitat is at the lower elevation limit of most mountain definitions, is highly modified, and it has also been well reviewed in earlier works (e.g., Newton 2020), so we do not focus on it in detail here.

Managed (and thus legal) hunting of birds does not necessarily lead to impacts on their population size due to the concept of compensatory mortality, whereby a 'doomed surplus' of birds is removed that would have died anyway through other causes. There are many examples of such cases, again in particular on grouse species (Newton 1998). The few studies carried out on mountain birds show fairly low overall rates of mortality caused by hunting. In montane forests of Sweden, 10 per cent of mortality for female western capercaillies was due to hunting, a rate considered sustainable (Åhlen et al. 2013). For rock ptarmigan in Alaska, there appeared to be no effect of autumn hunting on population size in the subsequent year, or on population trends over several years (McGowan 1975). There was an effect on spring numbers in the following year, but not on longer-term trends, suggesting that in general, there was compensatory mortality. Similarly, a study of juvenile survival of white-tailed ptarmigan Lagopus leucura found negligible differences between hunted and non-hunted populations (Giesen & Braun 1993).

However, there are also cases where mortality due to hunting appears to be additive (e.g., rock ptarmigan in Norwegian mountains; Nilsen et al. 2020). In some cases, this additive mortality may lead to biases in sex ratios due to selective hunting (fewer males in a hunted population of black grouse in the Alps; Rotelli et al. 2021). In the European Alps, there is demographic evidence that hunting mortality is additive for the black grouse (Zbinden et al. 2018), and Patthey et al. (2008) established an effect of hunting on black grouse abundance. The former study led to a new regulation establishing a ceiling to the number of authorized hunted black grouse cocks per hunter and season in the Canton of Ticino, Switzerland.

In some cases, legal hunting may have the goal of controlling a population which can have consequences beyond the target species. An interesting case study is provided by the kea *Nestor notabilis*, an alpine parrot. Due to occasional attacks on farm animals, a bounty was placed on this species in the late 1800s in New Zealand, which remarkably lasted until 1971 (Young *et al.* 2012). In addition to resulting in severe population declines, kea provide a key ecosystem service of seed dispersal as they regularly take long-distance flights between mountain ranges. The impact of control on this species is thus likely to have also impacted the alpine flora of the mountains in New Zealand (Young *et al.* 2012).

Raptors have been the group historically most affected by hunting in mountains, although it would be more accurately termed persecution as it is often illegal. Raptors have long been perceived as a threat to human livelihoods, especially those related to livestock. Typically, this perception is erroneous, as illustrated by the case of the bearded vulture, a scavenging species that specializes on consuming bone marrow, and which hence presents no threat to livestock. This species was once fairly widespread in the European Alps, but persecution led to its extirpation in the early twentieth century (Mingozzi & Estève 1997). In the late nineteenth century, the species was heavily persecuted in the Western Alps. For example, 25 individuals were known to have been shot in the period between 1890 and 1899, a significant number for such a long-lived, slowly reproducing species (Schaub *et al.* 2009). By 1910, the species had ceased to breed and the last individual known to have been shot in the region was in 1920 (Mingozzi & Estève 1997). Such impacts are sadly not a thing of the past – there are many recent examples of populations of raptors being severely affected by illegal persecution, e.g., shooting and nest destruction was a major contributor to the extinction of the Egyptian vulture *Neophron percnopterus* in Bulgaria (Milchev & Giorgiev 2014), mortality of hen harriers *Circus cyaneus* and other raptors is closely associated with illegal persecution on managed grouse moors in the UK uplands (Muragtroyd *et al.* 2019; Newton 2021). However, there is also some evidence that lower levels of persecution in recent decades has contributed to the recovery of raptor populations in some mountain areas. The golden eagle in the Western Italian Alps recovered from a population of one pair in 1972 to 144 pairs by 2008 (Fasce *et al.* 2011).

In addition to increased mortality, impacts of hunting may have other effects on mountain bird populations. Captive rearing and release of gamebirds for hunting, often of non-native species, is a common practice in many areas, and this can have consequences for native species. For example, grey partridges *Perdix perdix*, chukar partridges *Alectoris chukar* and hybrids of the latter species and red-legged partridge *A. rufa*, are commonly released for hunting in Europe, outside of their natural range. A study analysing DNA from rock partridges from the European Alps, the Apennines and Sicily found evidence of hybridization with chukars (up to 28 per cent of samples in the French Alps), raising concerns of disruption of local adaptations in rock partridge populations (Barilani *et al.* 2007).

There may be some positive effects of hunting, for example by creating habitat for species that prefer more open areas (see above). There is evidence from the Cantabrian Mountains that the spatio-temporal distribution of the griffon vulture *Gyps fulvus* is significantly affected by hunting activity. In particular, trophy hunting is common in the area, and typically, about 90 per cent of biomass of carcasses of hunted mammals (mostly red deer *Cervus elephus*) are left in the field, providing an important food source for the vultures (Mateo-Tomás & Olea 2010). However, hunting can be a source of lead in the environment, and poisoning from lead shot can have negative effects on individuals and populations (Gangoso *et al.* 2009). Indeed, a further effect of hunting may be through longer-term mortality when birds are not killed immediately, but the lead shot in their bodies eventually leads to toxic effects. This can have subsequent negative bioaccumulation effects for scavenging bird species.

7.5 Renewable Energy Development

7.5.1 Impacts of Hydropower on Mountain Birds

The construction of dams for hydropower has a range of effects on river characteristics, including changes to discharge, temperature, solutes, sediment transport, water depth and flow velocity and periodicity (Reid *et al.* 2019). These changes have important implications for biodiversity, including birds (Irving *et al.* 2018). For example, the black-necked crane *Grus nigricollis*, which winters in river valleys in the Himalayas, is likely to be susceptible to dam construction due to associated increases in water depth (Johnson *et al.* 2020). The blue duck *Hymenolaimus malacorhynchos* seems to be negatively affected by reduced water flow caused by hydropower plants fed by mountain rivers in New Zealand (King *et al.* 2000). Torrent ducks *Merganetta armata* in the Chilean Andes downstream of hydroelectric plants have lower density and reproductive success, presumably as a result of reduced water velocity as the species has a preference for fast flowing rapids (Pernollet *et al.* 2013). Roads are an additional disturbance affecting habitat use for torrent ducks which avoid stretches of river within 200 m of roads (Pernollet *et al.* 2013).

There is evidence that hydropower can affect a range of river-dwelling animals that may be prey for birds, in particular stream invertebrates (McIntosh *et al.* 2002; Colas *et al.* 2012). Bruno *et al.* (2009) found mostly negative impacts on the diversity and abundance of invertebrates due to hydropeaking, that is, the marked fluctuations in flow regimes characterized by periodic large discharges from power plants. Quadroni *et al.* (2021) found that richness of most benthic macroinvertebrates was lowered as a result of streamflow alterations associated with hydropower plants. However, no evidence was found of an effect of hydropower plants on the macroinvertebrate community available to torrent ducks (Pernollet *et al.* 2013) or on the diet of American dippers *Cinclus mexicanus* (Silverthorn *et al.* 2018a). In fact, the latter species seems to prefer the more stable habitat offered by the regulated flow and headponds associated with hydropower. Silverthorn *et al.* (2018b) found that American dippers had higher densities, a greater proportion of adults in the population and a higher tendency to remain resident through the winter on regulated streams associated with hydropower plants. However, there were fewer hatch–year birds in these areas compared to natural streams, suggesting a possible impact on productivity or survival.

In summary, the limited available evidence suggests that changes to water flow and disturbance as a consequence of hydropower plant construction in mountains are likely to negatively impact avian habitat suitability and sometimes their prey, but in a few instances these impacts may be positive. There may be longer-term demographic consequences of the changes caused by hydropower plants on mountain waterways. Currently, there is insufficient information, with too few species studied, to make general conclusions about the levels and directions of hydropower impacts on mountain birds.

7.5.2 Impacts of Wind Energy Installations on Mountain Birds

The development of energy generation facilities from wind turbines has grown steadily since the turn of this century (GWEC 2015; EWEA 2016), largely driven by strategies to increase the use of renewable energies and thus reduce greenhouse gas emissions. These trends are likely to increase in the future, and mountain regions are expected to contribute significantly to renewable energy expansion (Svadlenak-Gomez et al. 2013). There is concern that industrial wind turbines may have negative effects on avifauna, either through direct mortality due to collisions with turbine blades or towers and associated infrastructure such as power lines, or due to indirect effects of disturbance such as roads and traffic at turbine sites (Pearce-Higgins et al. 2012; Dai et al. 2015; Wang et al. 2015; Smith & Dwyer 2016; Schöll & Nopp-Mayr 2021; Taubmann et al. 2021). However, most research on the effects of onshore wind turbines on birds has been carried out in lowland, mostly agricultural, habitat with relatively few in mountains (Aschwanden et al. 2018). Existing studies tend to focus on grouse species such as black grouse (Zeiler & Grünschachner-Berger 2009) and western capercaillie (Coppes et al. 2020a). There are some examples from lower elevations in open grazed areas below the climatic treeline and 'upland' areas (Scottish and English moorland), that we consider here as we assume that effects in these habitats would be similar to those at higher elevations.

Raptors are common subjects for research on impacts of wind turbines on birds as they are particularly vulnerable (Watson et al. 2018). In mountainous areas, topographically suitable sites for wind energy generation, such as ridges, may also be used heavily by large raptors (e.g., Katzner et al. 2012; Johnston et al. 2013) which can lead to significant mortality in some sites (Watson et al. 2018). There is evidence that the presence of wind turbines alters the behaviour of golden eagles, suggesting that they can adapt to some degree to their presence, but this is influenced by weather conditions (Johnston et al. 2014), whether birds are migratory or resident (Katzner et al. 2012), and specific characteristics of individual sites (Miller et al. 2014). Avoidance behaviour may reduce mortality due to collisions, but the area in which a given wind farm is located will no longer be usable, resulting in functional habitat loss due to disturbance (Marques et al. 2020).

Research on wind turbine impacts for other avian groups in mountains is less common. Aschwanden et al. (2018) carried out a comprehensive study on the impacts of wind turbines on bird mortality in the Swiss Jura, considering the whole community. They found that mortality rates peaked during migration periods and that nocturnal migrant passerines were particularly affected. Ferreira *et al.* (2019) modelled the impacts of increasing the energy output of a wind farm on Eurasian skylark mortality in northern Portugal between c. 1,200–1,300 m in elevation. According to their simulations, there would be a significant impact on male Eurasian skylark mortality if the number of turbines were increased. However, 'repowering' the existing wind turbines using upgraded designs did not result in any predicted negative impacts. Grouse species could also be affected in mountains – several grouse species have been found to collide with wind turbines, in particular with the towers. Most common behavioural responses in relation to wind turbine facilities in seven grouse species included spatial avoidance and displacement of lek-king or nesting sites (Coppes *et al.* 2020b). Willow ptarmigan *Lagopus lagopus* was the most common species found dead under turbines at the Norwegian island of Smøla (Watson *et al.* 2018). This species is also found in mountainous areas, along with closely related species (*L. muta* and *L. leucura*), and it seems reasonable to assume that they would be similarly at risk in higher elevation habitats. Western capercaillie showed avoidance around wind turbines, with decreased probabilities of occurrence within a 650 m radius (Coppes *et al.* 2020a), resulting in a net loss of available habitat in the Austrian Styrian Alps.

Energy generated from wind is forecast to increase in the future (EWEA 2016), and it seems likely that high elevation areas will continue to be exploited. Compared to some early wind farms where there was little or no planning to mitigate environmental impacts, with a subsequent high avian mortality rate (e.g., Altamont Pass, California; Smallwood & Thelander 2008), our understanding of some of the factors that increase risk have increased greatly. For example, knowledge of habitat use and behaviour of birds can be used to construct new wind farms in habitats that are known to be unattractive for species at risk (Miller *et al.* 2014). Vignali *et al.* (2021, 2022) have recently published predictive models that should make developers, policy-makers and practitioners aware of areas in the Swiss Alps where the installation of wind turbines might represent major risks of collision for bearded vultures.

Many questions remain unanswered, notably concerning the extent to which large soaring raptors can adapt their flight behaviour to such infrastructures (Wang *et al.* 2015; Smith & Dwyer 2016). To date, the research focus has been on larger soaring birds, in particular raptors, although a recent distribution model for the red-billed chough in the Swiss Alps has been designed primarily with the objective to prevent the construction of turbines in their key habitats (Braunisch *et al.* 2021). Direct and indirect effects of wind power developments on smaller birds (and indeed impacts on wider biodiversity, such as bats) may be underestimated as they are more of a challenge to study. Nevertheless, research needs to be as comprehensive as possible, assessing impacts on the whole mountain avian and wildlife community, as well as continued research on slow life history strategists such as large-soaring birds whose populations are likely to suffer from any additive mortality caused by wind turbines.

7.6 Research and Conservation Perspectives

This chapter has reviewed a number of human activities which, through disturbance and alteration of habitats, may have some serious implications for mountain birds. In many cases, these pressures are growing. Disturbance caused by tourists is increasing in many regions, through increased participation in skiing and other outdoor winter sports in the last five years (Vanat 2020) and in nature tourism (Herrmann *et al.* 2010; Steven *et al.* 2011). Furthermore, the need to reduce carbon emissions through greater use of renewable energy is likely to lead to the expansion of wind and hydropower sectors in mountains. Legal hunting of mountain birds is generally declining in North America (U.S. Department of the Interior *et al.* 2018) and Europe (Hirschfeld *et al.* 2019), although some declining species are still under high hunting pressure. However, we have less idea of the impacts of illegal hunting or subsistence hunting in the developing world, which can have major impacts on mountain species (e.g., tropical montane forest; Sethi & Howe 2009; Palacio *et al.* 2019). There are additional pressures not considered in this chapter, such as changes in grazing practices (Chapters 1 and 4) and climate change (Chapter 6) that may also have significant implications for mountain birds.

The above factors are likely to be acting in synergy with other key drivers of environmental change. Potential conflicts between high elevation biodiversity and human use will continue to increase due to interactive effects, in particular through climate change. For example, skiing and related activities are likely to be impacted negatively by changes in precipitation regimes and increasing temperature (Behringer *et al.* 2000; Uhlmann *et al.* 2009). Due to decreasing snowfall and/or less reliable snow cover at lower elevations, the areas suitable for skiing are undergoing a range contraction and an upwards elevational shift, moving into areas that are currently undisturbed by human pressure (Brambilla *et al.* 2016), an already evident phenomenon in some areas in Europe (Marty 2013). Therefore, many species which are already facing climate change also have to cope with indirect impacts deriving from human adaptation to warmer conditions. The strong diversification of recreational activities (Table 7.1) will pose challenges in the future in addition to climate change.

Despite the potential threats of the activities reviewed in this chapter, there are already ways in which their effects can be lessened, or even reversed, through conservation initiatives. Tourism is undoubtedly a major source of income for people in mountains, so sustainable tourism needs to be developed. Ski-pistes can be managed in a more environmentally friendly way to lower their impact and increase their value to biodiversity, for example, by 'softening' ski-piste edges through mountain forest, and by re-seeding with locally adapted mixes and creating vegetation patches on ski-pistes ('safety islands'; Urbanska 1997), which benefit plants and are thus likely to have positive effects on mountain birds though plant and invertebrate food sources and nest sites. Better spatial planning could also minimize the effects of disturbance by identifying areas with important and potentially sensitive populations of mountain birds and making them off-limits to human activity (e.g., banning off-piste skiing in important areas for tetraonids; Zeitler 2000; Braunisch *et al.* 2011; Arlettaz *et al.* 2013), or preventing future ski-piste development in areas important for high elevation specialist birds (Brambilla *et al.* 2016). Further mitigation could be achieved by marking cables to reduce collision mortality, as has been successfully done with powerlines (Barrientos *et al.* 2011). Spatial planning to minimize potential impacts is also needed for wind farm development (e.g., Vignali *et al.* 2021, 2022). For bird populations severely impacted by hunting (including regional extirpation), reintroductions have proved to be successful for several raptor species and they may provide a useful tool by which populations can be restored where persecution is now much less than in previous decades (e.g., Margalida *et al.* 2013; Morandini & Ferrer 2017). However, reintroductions can fail. Three individual bearded vultures were introduced in Sardinia in 2008, but all were poisoned within one month (Grussu 2019), suggesting that enforcement and education need to be improved in some areas where reintroductions are carried out.

In order to achieve the goal of sustainable human use of mountains, we need to broaden the research on the impacts of human activities at high elevations. Two key gaps need to be addressed. First, while we have a good idea of population-level effects of hunting and persecution for some populations of mountain birds (mostly grouse and raptors), we do not fully understand the population consequences of many other human activities, nor the demographic mechanisms which might underpin population responses. Secondly, the current research base is very restricted geographically, with the majority of studies coming from European mountains (e.g., Sato *et al.* 2013). There are few examples of the impacts of human activities in tropical areas and in the southern hemisphere (but see Barros *et al.* 2015). In conclusion, if we are to allow continued growth of human activities in high mountains, and the potential benefits this can bring to mountain economies, we need a much wider consideration of their impacts both in terms of research topics and geographical area to enable us to develop sustainable strategies that can protect high mountain bird populations.

Acknowledgements

We are most grateful to Ursula Nopp-Meyr and Paola Laiolo whose comments greatly improved this chapter.

References

Åhlen, P.-E., Willebrand, T., Sjöberg, K. & Hörnell-Willebrand, M. (2013) Survival of female capercaillie *Tetrao urogallus* in northern Sweden. *Wildlife Biology*, **19**, 368–373.

Alba, R., Kasoar, T., Chamberlain, D., *et al.* (2022) Drivers of change in mountain bird populations in Europe. *Ibis*, **164**, 635–648.

Arroyo, B. & Razin, M. (2006) Effect of human activities on bearded vulture behaviour and breeding success in the French Pyrenees. *Biological Conservation*, **128**, 276–284.

Arroyo, B., Lafitte, J., Sourp, E., *et al.* (2021) Population expansion and breeding success of Bearded Vultures *Gypaetus barbatus* in the French Pyrenees: results from long-term population monitoring. *Ibis*, **163**, 213–230.

Arlettaz, R., Patthey, P., Baltic, M., *et al.* (2007) Spreading free-riding snow sports represent a novel serious threat for wildlife. *Proceedings of the Royal Society Series B*, **274**, 1219–1224.

Arlettaz, R., Patthey, P. & Braunisch, V. (2013) Impacts of outdoor winter recreation on alpine wildlife and mitigation approaches: a case study of the Black Grouse. In *The Impacts of Skiing and Related Winter Recreational Activities on Mountain Environments*. Rixen, C. & Rolando, A. (eds.). Bussum: Bentham eBooks, pp. 137–154.

Arlettaz, R., Nusslé, S., Baltic, M., *et al.* (2015) Disturbance of wildlife by outdoor winter recreation: allostatic stress response and altered activity-energy budgets. *Ecological Applications*, **25**, 1197–1212.

Aschwanden, J., Stark, H., Peter, D., *et al.* (2018) Bird collisions at wind turbines in a mountainous area related to bird movement intensities measured by radar. *Biological Conservation*, **220**, 228–236.

Barilani, M., Bernard-Laurent, A., Mucci, N., *et al.* (2007) Hybridisation with introduced chukars (*Alectoris chukar*) threatens the gene pool integrity of native rock (*A. graeca*) and red-legged (*A. rufa*) partridge populations. *Biological Conservation*, **137**, 57–69.

Barni, E., Freppaz, M. & Siniscalco, C. (2007) Interactions between vegetation, roots, and soil stability in restored high-altitude ski runs in the Alps. *Arctic, Antarctic, and Alpine Research*, **39**, 25–33.

Barras, A.G. (2021) *Assessing the Response of Mountain Birds to Rapid Environmental Change: Conservation Ecology of the Alpine Ring Ouzel (Turdus torquatus alpestris).* PhD thesis, University of Bern, Bern, Switzerland.

Barras, A.G., Niffenegger, C.A., Candolfi, I., Hunziker, Y.A. & Arlettaz, R. (2021) Nestling diet and parental food provisioning in a declining mountain passerine reveal high sensitivity to climate change. *Journal of Avian Biology*, **52**, e02649

Barrientos, R., Alonso, J. C., Ponce, C. & Palacin, C. (2011) Meta-analysis of the effectiveness of marked wire in reducing avian collisions with power lines. *Conservation Biology*, **25**, 893–903.

Barros, A., Monz, C. & Pickering, C. (2015) Is tourism damaging ecosystems in the Andes? Current knowledge and an agenda for future research. *Ambio*, **44**, 82–98.

Battisti, C., Poeta, G. & Fanelli, G. (2016) *An Introduction to Disturbance Ecology.* Cham: Springer.

Bech, N., Beltran, S., Boissier, J., *et al.* (2012) Bird mortality related to collisions with ski-lift cables: do we estimate just the tip of the iceberg? *Animal Biodiversity and Conservation*, **35**, 95–98.

Behringer, J., Buerki, R. & Fuhrer, J. (2000) Participatory integrated assessment of adaptation to climate change in Alpine tourism and mountain agriculture. *Integrated Assessment*, **1**, 331–338.

Bevanger, K. & Brøseth, H. (2004) Impact of power lines on bird mortality in a subalpine area. *Animal Biodiversity and Conservation*, **27**, 67–77.

Böhm, R., Auer, I., Brunetti, M., *et al.* (2001) Regional temperature variability in the European Alps: 1760–1998 from homogenized instrumental time series. *International Journal of Climatology*, **21**, 1779–1801.

Bötsch, Y., Tablado, Z., Scherl, D., *et al.* (2018) Effect of recreational trails on forest birds: human presence matters. *Frontiers in Ecology and Evolution*, **6**, 175.

Brambilla, A. & Brivio, F. (2018) Assessing the effects of helicopter disturbance in a mountain ungulate on different time scales. *Mammalian Biology*, **90**, 30–37.

Brambilla, M., Rubolini, D. & Guidali, F. (2004) Rock climbing and Raven *Corvus corax* occurrence depress breeding success of cliff-nesting Peregrines *Falco peregrinus*. *Ardeola*, **51**, 425–430.

Brambilla, M., Pedrini, P., Rolando, A. & Chamberlain, D.E. (2016) Climate change will increase the potential conflict between skiing and high-elevation bird species in the Alps. *Journal of Biogeography*, **43**, 2299–2309.

Brändle, J.M., Langendijk, G., Peter, S., Brunner, S.H. & Huber, R. (2015) Sensitivity analysis of a land-use change model with and without agents to assess land abandonment and long-term re-forestation in a Swiss mountain region. *Land*, **4**, 475–512.

Braunisch, V., Patthey, P. & Arlettaz, R. (2011) Spatially explicit modeling of conflict zones between wildlife and snow sports: prioritizing areas for winter refuges. *Ecological Applications*, **21**, 955–967.

Braunisch, V., Vignali, S., Oggier, P.A. & Arlettaz, R. (2021) Present in the western European Alps but absent in the eastern part: can habitat availability explain the differences in red-billed chough occurrence? *Journal of Avian Biology*, **52**, e02682.

Bruno, M.C., Maiolini, B., Carolli, M. & Silveri, L. (2009) Impact of hydropeaking on hyporheic invertebrates in an Alpine stream (Trentino, Italy). *Annales De Limnologie-International Journal of Limnology*, **45**, 157–170.

Buffet, N. & Dumont-Dayot, E. (2013) Bird collisions with overhead ski-cables: a reducible source of mortality. In *The Impacts of Skiing and Related Winter Recreational Activities on Mountain Environments*: Rixen, C. & Rolando, A. (eds.). Bussum: Bentham eBooks. pp. 123–136.

Camp, R.J. & Knight, R.L. (1998) Rock climbing and cliff bird communities at Joshua Tree National Park, California. *Wildlife Society Bulletin*, **26**, 892–898.

Canonne, C., Montadert, M. & Besnard, A. (2021) Drivers of black grouse trends in the French Alps: the prevailing contribution of climate. *Diversity and Distributions*, **27**, 1338–1352

Caprio, E., Chamberlain, D.E., Isaia, M. & Rolando, A. (2011) Landscape changes caused by high altitude ski-pistes affect bird species richness and distribution in the Alps. *Biological Conservation*, **144**, 2958–2967.

Caprio, E., Chamberlain, D. & Rolando, A. (2016) Ski-piste revegetation promotes partial bird community recovery in the European Alps. *Bird Study*, **63**, 470–478.

Chamberlain, D.E., Pedrini, P., Brambilla, M., Rolando, A. & Girardello, M. (2016) Identifying key conservation threats to Alpine birds through expert knowledge. *PeerJ*, **4**, e1723.

Clivaz, C. & Savioz, A. (2020) Glacier retreat and perception of climate change by local tourism stakeholders: the case of Chamonix-Mont-Blanc in the French Alps. *Via Tourism Review*, **18**, 6097.

Colas, F., Archaimbolt, V., Férard, J.-F., et al. (2012) Benthic indicators of sediment quality associated with run-of-river reservoirs. *Hydrobiologia*, **703**, 149–164.

Cooke, S.C., Balmford, A., Donalf, P.F., Newson, S.E. & Johnston, A. (2020) Roads as a contributor to landscape-scale variation in bird communities. *Nature Communications*, **11**, 1–10.

Coppes, J., Kämmerle, J.L., Grünschachner-Berger, V., et al. (2020a) Consistent effects of wind turbines on habitat selection of capercaillie across Europe. *Biological Conservation*, **244**, 108529.

Coppes, J., Braunisch, V., Bollmann, K., et al. (2020b) The impact of wind energy facilities on grouse: a systematic review. *Journal of Ornithology*, **161**, 1–15.

Dai, K., Bergot, A., Liang, C. Xiang, W.-N. & Huang, Z. (2015) Environmental issues associated with wind energy – a review. *Renewable Energy*, **75**, 911–921.

Dax, T., Schroll, K., Machold, I., et al. (2021) Land abandonment in mountain areas of the EU: an inevitable side effect of farming modernization and neglected threat to sustainable land use. *Land*, **10**, 591.

Deluca, W.V. & King, D.I. (2014) Influence of hiking trails on montane birds. *Journal of Wildlife Management*, **78**, 494–502.

Dobbs, C., Escobedo, F.J., Clerici, N., *et al.* (2019) Urban ecosystem services in Latin America: mismatch between global concepts and regional realities? *Urban Ecosystems*, **22**, 173–187.

Eurostat (European Commission), Kotzeva, M., Brandmüller, T. & Önnerfors, Å. (2017) *Eurostat Regional Yearbook: 2017 Edition*. Luxembourg: Publications Office of the European Union.

EWEA European Wind Energy Association (2016) *Wind in Power 2016 European Statistics*. Brussels: Wind Europe.

Fasce, P., Fasce, L., Villers, A., Bergese, F. & Bretagnolle, V. (2011) Long-term breeding demography and density dependence in an increasing population of Golden Eagles *Aquila chrysaetos*. *Ibis*, **153**, 581–591.

Fasce, L., Fasce, P. & Bergese, F. (2017) Status of the Golden Eagle *Aquila chrysaetos* in the Western Alps. *Avocetta*, **41**, 35–38.

Ferreira, D., Freixo, C., Cabral, J.A. & Santos, M. (2019) Is wind energy increasing the impact of socio-ecological change on Mediterranean mountain ecosystems? Insights from a modelling study relating wind power boost options with a declining species. *Journal of Environmental Management*, **238**, 283–295.

Flousek, J., Telenský, T., Hanzelka, J. & Reif, J. (2015) Population trends of central European montane birds provide evidence for adverse impacts of climate change on high-altitude species. *PLoS ONE*, **10**, e0139465.

Formenti, N., Viganó, R., Bionda, R., *et al.* (2015) Increased hormonal stress reactions induced in an Alpine Black Grouse (*Tetrao tetrix*) population by winter sports. *Journal of Ornithology*, **156**, 317–321.

Gangoso, L., Álvarez-Lloret, P., Rodríguez-Navarro, A., *et al.* (2009) Long-term effects of lead poisoning on bone mineralization in vultures exposed to ammunition sources. *Environmental Pollution*, **157**, 569–574

Giesen, K.M. & Braun, C.E. (1993) Natal dispersal and recruitment of juvenile White-Tailed Ptarmigan in Colorado. *Journal of Wildlife Management*, **57**, 72–77.

Grime, J.P. (1979) *Plant Strategies and Vegetation Processes*. Chichester: Wiley.

Grubb, T.G., Delaney, D.K., Bowerman, W.W. & Wierda, M.R. (2010) Golden eagle indifference to heli-skiing and military helicopters in northern Utah. *Journal of Wildlife Management*, **74**, 1275–1285.

Grussu, M. (2019) Evolution of the vulture population on a Mediterranean island. The Sardinian instance (Italy). *Vulture News*, **76**, 6–19.

Gutzwiller, K.J. & Anderson, S.H. (1999) Spatial extent of human-intrusion effects on subalpine bird distributions. *Condor*, **101**, 378–389.

GWEC (2015) *Global Wind Report. Annual Market Update*. Brussels: GWEC.

Hadley, G.L. & Wilson, K.R. (2004) Patterns of density and survival in small mammals in ski runs and adjacent forest patches. *Journal of Wildlife Management*, **68**, 288–298.

Herrmann, T.M., Costina, M.I. & Aron Costina A.M. (2010) Roost sites and communal behaviour of Andean Condors in Chile. *Geographical Review*, **100**, 246–262.

Heil, L., Fernández-Juricic, E., Renison, D., Cingolani, A.M. & Blumstein, D.T. (2007) Avian responses to tourism in the biogeographically isolated high Córdoba Mountains, Argentina. *Biodiversity and Conservation*, **16**, 1009–1026.

Hill, J.M. & Campbell, J. (2019) *Continued Exploration of the Relationship between Downhill Ski Area Edges and Bicknell's Thrush in the Northeastern U.S. Using Mountain Birdwatch Data (2016–2019).* White River Junction VT: Vermont Center for Ecostudies.

Hirschfeld, A., Attard, G. & Scott, L. (2019) Bird hunting in Europe: an analysis of bag figures and the potential impact on the conservation of threatened species. *British Birds*, **112**, 153–166.

Hobbs, R.J. & Huenneke, L.F. (1992) Disturbance, diversity, and invasion: implications for conservation. *Conservation Biology*, **6**, 324–337.

Hoffmann, E.M., Konerding, V., Nautiyal, S. & Buerkert, A. (2019) Is the push–pull paradigm useful to explain rural-urban migration? A case study in Uttarakhand, India. *PLoS ONE*, **14**, e0214511.

Holzschuh, A. (2016) Does rock climbing threaten cliff biodiversity? A critical review. *Biological Conservation*, **204**, 153–162.

Hope, J. (2014) The sensitivity of the high mountain ecosystems of New Guinea to climatic change and anthropogenic impact. *Arctic, Antarctic, and Alpine Research*, **4**, 777–786.

Hörnell-Willebrand, M., Marcström, V., Brittas, R. & Willebrand, T. (2006) Temporal and spatial correlation in chick production of willow grouse *Lagopus lagopus* in Sweden and Norway. *Wildlife Biology*, **12**, 347–355.

Hudek, C., Barni, E., Stanchi, S., *et al.* (2020) Mid and long-term ecological impacts of ski run construction on alpine ecosystems. *Scientific Reports*, **10**, 11654.

Immitzer, M., Nopp-Mayr, U. & Zohmann, M. (2014) Effects of habitat quality and hiking trails on the occurrence of Black Grouse (*Tetrao tetrix* L.) at the northern fringe of alpine distribution in Austria. *Journal of Ornithology*, **155**, 173–181.

Irving, G.J., Round, P.D., Savini, T., Lynam, A.J. & Gale, G.A. (2018) Collapse of a tropical forest bird assemblage surrounding a hydroelectric reservoir. *Global Ecology and Conservation*, **16**, e00472.

Jäger, H., Schirpke, U. & Tappeiner, U. (2020) Assessing conflicts between winter recreational activities and grouse species. *Journal of Environmental Management*, **276**, 111–194.

Johnson, K. & Lichter, D. (2019) *Rural Depopulation in a Rapidly Urbanizing America. The Carsey School of Public Policy at the Scholars' Repository.* 358. Durham: University of New Hampshire.

Johnson, J.A., Watham, T., Gopi, G.V. & Sivakumar, K. (2020) Development of habitat suitability criteria for conservation of the black-necked crane in Nyamjang Chu River in eastern Himalaya, India in connection with a proposed hydropower dam. *River Research and Applications*, **37**, 321–329.

Johnston, N.N., Bradley, J.E., Pomeroy, A.C. & Otter, K.A. (2013) Flight paths of migrating Golden Eagles and the risk associated with wind energy development in the Rocky Mountains. *Avian Conservation and Ecology*, **8**, 12.

Johnston, N.N., Bradley, J.E. & Otter, K.A. (2014) Increased flight altitudes among migrating Golden Eagles suggest turbine avoidance at a Rocky Mountain wind installation. *PLoS ONE*, **9**, e93030.

Kašák, J., Mazalová, M., Šipoš, J. & Kurus, T. (2013) The effect of alpine ski-slopes on epigeic beetles: does even a nature-friendly management make a change? *Journal of Insect Conservation*, **17**, 975–988.

Katzner, T.E., Brandes, D., Miller, T., *et al.* (2012) Topography drives migratory flight altitude of golden eagles: implications for on-shore wind energy development. *Journal of Applied Ecology*, **49**, 1178–1186.

Kessler, M. & Herzog, S.K. (1998) Conservation status in Bolivia of timberline habitats, elfin forest and their birds. *Cotinga*, **10**, 50–54.

Kessler, T., Cierjacks, A., Ernst, R. & Dziock, F. (2011) Direct and indirect effects of ski run management on alpine Orthoptera. *Biodiversity and Conservation*, **21**, 281–296.

King, T.M., Williams, M. & Lambert, D.M. (2000) Dams, ducks and DNA: identifying the effects of a hydro-electric scheme on New Zealand's endangered blue duck. *Conservation Genetics*, **1**, 103–113,

Korňan, M. (2020) Potential negative effects of construction of a high-mountain ski resort in the High Tatras, Slovakia, on breeding bird assemblages. *Community Ecology*, **21**, 213–226.

Laiolo, P. & Rolando, A. (1999) The diet of the Chough (*Pyrrhocorax pyrrhocorax*) and the Alpine Chough (*P. graculus*) in the Alps: seasonality, resource partitioning and population density. *Revue d'Ecologie (Terre et Vie)*, **54**, 133–147.

Laiolo, P., Dondero, F., Ciliento, E. & Rolando, A. (2004) Consequences of pastoral abandonment for the structure and diversity of the alpine avifauna. *Journal of Applied Ecology*, **41**, 294–304.

Laiolo, P. & Rolando, A. (2005) Forest bird diversity and ski-runs: a case of negative edge effect. *Animal Conservation*, **7**, 9–16.

Larson, C.L., Reed, S.E., Merenlender, A.M. & Crooks, K.R. (2019) A meta-analysis of recreation effects on vertebrate species richness and abundance. *Conservation Science and Practice*, **1**, e93.

Maggini, R., Lehmann, A., Zbinden, N., *et al.* (2014) Assessing species vulnerability to climate and land use change: the case of the Swiss breeding birds. *Diversity and Distributions*, **20**, 708–719.

Maharjan, A., Kochhar, I., Chitale, V.S., Hussain, A. & Gioli, G. (2020) Understanding rural outmigration and agricultural land use change in the Gandaki Basin, Nepal. *Applied Geography*, **124**, 102278.

Maliniemi, T. & Virtanen, R. (2021) Anthropogenic disturbance modifies long-term changes of boreal mountain vegetation under contemporary climate warming. *Applied Vegetation Science*, **24**, e12587.

Margalida, A., Carrete, M., Heglin, D., *et al.* (2013) Uneven large-scale movement patterns in wild and reintroduced pre-adult bearded vultures: conservation implications. *PLoS ONE*, **8**, e65857.

Marques, A.T., Santos, C.D., Hassan, F., *et al.* (2020) Wind turbines cause functional habitat loss for migratory soaring birds. *Journal of Animal Ecology*, **89**, 93–103.

Martina Hermmann, T.M., Costina, M.I. & Aron Costina, A.M. (2010) Roost sites and communal behaviour of Andean condors in Chile. *Geographical Review*, **100**, 246–262.

Marty, C. (2013) Climate change and snow cover in the European Alps. In *The Impacts of Skiing and Related Winter Recreational Activities on Mountain Environments*. Rixen, C. & Rolando, A. (eds.). Bussum: Bentham eBooks, pp. 30–44.

Mateo-Tomás, P. & Olea, P.P. (2010) When hunting benefits raptors: a case study of game species and vultures. *European Journal of Wildlife Research*, **56**, 519–528.

McGowan, J.D. (1975) Effect of autumn and spring hunting on ptarmigan population trends. *Journal of Wildlife Management*, **39**, 491–495.

McIntosh, M.D., Benbow, M.E. & Burky, A.J. (2002) Effects of stream diversion on riffle macroinvertebrate communities in a Maui, Hawaii, stream. *River Research and Applications*, **18**, 569–581.

Milchev, B. & Gregoriev, V. (2014) Extinction of the globally endangered Egyptian vulture *Neophron percnopterus* breeding in SE Bulgaria. *North-Western Journal of Zoology*, **10**, 266–272

Miller, T.A., Brooks, R.P., Lanzone, M., *et al.* (2014) Assessing risk to birds from industrial wind energy development via paired resource selection models. *Conservation Biology*, **28**, 745–755.

Mingozzi, T. & Estève, R. (1997) Analysis of the historical extirpation of the bearded vulture (*Gypaetus barbatus* L.) in the Western Alps (France-Italy): former distribution and causes of extirpation. *Biological Conservation*, **79**, 155–171.

Miquet, A. (1990) Mortality in black grouse *Tetrao tetrix* due to elevated cables. *Biological Conservation*, **54**, 349–355.

Montenegro Statistical Office (2012) *Poverty Analysis in Montenegro in 2011. Release No 329*. Montenegro: Podgorica.

Morandini, V. & Ferrer, M. (2017) How to plan reintroductions of long-lived Birds. *PLoS ONE*, **12**, e0174186.

Morelli, F., Jerzak, L., Pruscini, F., *et al.* (2015) Testing bird response to roads on a rural environment: a case study from Central Italy. *Acta Oecologica*, **69**, 146–152.

Mountain Agenda (1999) *Mountains of the World: Tourism and Sustainable Mountain Development*. Bern: Centre for Development and the Environment (CDE).

Murgatroyd, M., Redpath, S.M., Murphy, S.G., *et al.* (2019) Revealing patterns of wildlife crime using satellite tags: a case study of hen harriers *Circus cyaneus* in the UK. *Nature Communications*, **10**, 1094.

Negro, M., Casale, A., Migliore, L., Palestrini, C. & Rolando, A. (2008) Habitat use and movement patterns in the endangered ground beetle species *Carabus olympiae* (Coleoptera, Carabidae). *European Journal of Entomology*, **105**, 105–112.

Negro, M., Isaia, M., Palestrini, C. & Rolando A. (2009) The impact of forest ski-pistes on diversity of ground-dwelling arthropods and small mammals in the Alps. *Biodiversity and Conservation*, **18**, 2799–2821.

Negro, M., Isaia, M., Palestrini, C., Schoenhofer, A. & Rolando, A. (2010) The impact of high-altitude ski pistes on ground-dwelling arthropods in the Alps. *Biodiversity and Conservation*, **19**, 1853–1870.

Negro, M., Novara, C., Bertolino, S. & Rolando, A. (2013a) Ski-pistes are ecological barriers to forest small mammals. *European Journal of Wildlife Research* **59**, 57–67.

Negro, M., Rolando, A., Barni, E., *et al.* (2013b) Differential responses of ground dwelling arthropods to ski-piste restoration by hydroseeding. *Biodiversity and Conservation*, **22**, 2607–2634.

Newton, I. (1998) *Population Limitation in Birds*. San Diego: Academic Press.

Newton, I. (2020) *Uplands and Birds*. London: Collins.

Newton, I. (2021) Killing of raptors on grouse moors: evidence and effects. *Ibis*, **163**, 1–19.

Niffenegger, C.A. (2021) *Nest Site Selection of the White-winged Snowfinch* Montifringilla nivalis *in the Swiss Alps*. MSc Thesis, University of Bern, Bern, Switzerland.

Nilsen, E.B., Moa, P.F., Brøseth, H., Pedersen, H.C. & Hagen, B.R. (2020) Survival and migration of rock ptarmigan in Central Scandinavia. *Frontiers in Ecology and Evolution*, **8**, article 34.

Østby, G. (2016) Rural–urban migration, inequality and urban social disorder: evidence from African and Asian cities. *Conflict Management and Peace Science*, **33**, 491–515.

Palacio, R.D., Kattan, G.H. & Pimm, S.L. (2019) Bird extirpations and community dynamics in an Andean cloud forest over 100 years of land-use change. *Conservation Biology*, **34**, 677–687.

Patthey, P., Wirthner, S., Signorell, N. & Arlettaz, R. (2008) Impact of outdoor winter sports on the abundance of a key indicator species of alpine ecosystems. *Journal of Applied Ecology*, **45**, 1704–1711.

Pearce-Higgins, J.W., Stephen, L., Douse, A. & Langston, R.H. (2012) Greater impacts of wind farms on bird populations during construction than subsequent operation: results of a multi-site and multi-species analysis. *Journal of Applied Ecology*, **49**, 386–394.

Pernollet, C.A., Pavez, E.F. & Estades, C.F. (2013) Habitat selection by Torrent Ducks (*Merganetta armata armata*) in Central Chile: conservation implications of hydropower production. *Waterbirds*, **36**, 287–299.

Pickett, S.T.A. & Thompson, J.N. (1978) Patch dynamics and the design of nature reserves. *Biological Conservation*, **13**, 27–37.

Pickett, S.T.A., Kolasa, J., Armesto, J.J. & Collins, S.L. (1989) The ecological concept of disturbance and its expression at various hierarchical levels. *Oikos*, **54**, 129–136.

Pintaldi, E., Hudek, C., Stanchi, S., *et al.* (2017) Sustainable soil management in ski areas: threats and challenges. *Sustainability*, **9**, 2150.

Plaza, P.I. & Lambertucci, S.A. (2020) Ecology and conservation of a rare species: what do we know and what may we do to preserve Andean condors? *Biological Conservation*, **251**, 108782.

Plummer, K.E., Bearhop, S., Leech, D.I., Chamberlain, D.E. & Blount, J.D. (2013) Winter provisioning reduces breeding performance in a wild bird. *Scientific Reports*, **3**, article 2002.

Plummer, K.E., Bearhop, S., Leech, D.I., Chamberlain, D.E. & Blount, J.D. (2018) Effects of winter food provisioning on the phenotypes of breeding blue tits. *Ecology and Evolution*, **8**, 5059–5068.

Pohl, M., Alig, D., Körner, C. & Rixen, C. (2009) Higher plant diversity enhances soil stability in disturbed alpine ecosystems. *Plant Soil*, **324**, 91–102.

Quadroni, S., Salmaso, F., Gentili, G., Crosa, G. & Espa, P. (2021) Response of benthic macroinvertebrates to different hydropower off-stream diversion schemes. *Ecohydrology*, **14**, e2267.

Rayner, J.M.V. (1988) Form and function in avian flight. *Current Ornithology*, **5**, 1–66.

Reid, A.J., Carlson, A.K., Creed, I.F., *et al.* (2019) Emerging threats and persistent conservation challenges for freshwater biodiversity. *Biological Reviews*, **94**, 849–873.

Resano-Mayor, J., Korner-Nievergelt, F., Vignali, S., *et al.* (2019) Snow cover phenology is the main driver of foraging habitat selection for a high-alpine passerine during breeding: implications for species persistence in the face of climate change. *Biodiversity and Conservation*, **28**, 2669–2685.

Rixen, C. & Rolando, A. (2013) *The Impacts of Skiing and Related Winter Recreational Activities on Mountain Environments.* Bussum: Bentham eBooks.

Rolando, A. & Patterson, I.J. (1993) Foraging behaviour and diet of the Alpine Chough *Pyrrhocorax graculus* in the Italian Alps in summer. *Journal of Ornithology,* **134**, 181–187.

Rolando, A. & Laiolo, P. (1997) A comparative analysis of the diet of the Chough *Pyrrhocorax pyrrhocorax* and the Alpine Chough *P. graculus* co-existing in the Alps. *Ibis,* **139**, 388–395.

Rolando, A., Caprio, E., Rinaldi, E. & Ellena, I. (2007) The impact of high-altitude ski-runs on alpine grassland bird communities. *Journal of Applied Ecology,* **44**, 210–219.

Rolando, A., Negro, M., D'Entrèves, P. P., Balletto, E. & Palestrini, C. (2013) The effect of forest ski-pistes on butterfly assemblages in the Alps. *Insect Conservation and Diversity,* **6**, 212–222.

Rotelli, L., Bionda, R., Zbinden, N. & Schaub, M. (2021) Chick survival and hunting are important drivers for the dynamics of two Alpine black grouse *Lyrurus tetrix* populations. *Wildlife Biology,* **2021**, wlb.00874.

Sanecki, G.M. Green, K., Wood, H. & Lindenmayer, D.B. (2006) The implications of snow-based recreation for small mammals in the subnivean space in southeast Australia. *Biological Conservation,* **129**, 511–518.

Sato, C.F., Wood, J.T. & Lindenmayer, D.B. (2013) The effects of winter recreation on alpine and subalpine fauna: a systematic review and meta-analysis. *PLoS ONE,* **8**, e64282.

Sato, C.F., Wood, J.T., Schroder, M., Green, K. & Michael, D.R. (2014) The impacts of ski resorts on reptiles: a natural experiment. *Animal Conservation,* **17**, 313–322.

Schaub, M., Zink, R., Beissmann, H., Sarrazin, F. & Arlettaz, R. (2009) When to end releases in reintroduction programmes: demographic rates and population viability analysis of bearded vultures in the Alps. *Journal of Applied Ecology,* **46**, 92–100.

Schnidrig-Petrig, R. & Ingold, P. (2001) Effects of paragliding on alpine chamois *Rupicapra rupicapra rupicapra. Wildlife Biology,* **4**, 285–294.

Schöll, E.M. & Nopp-Mayr, U. (2021) Impact of wind power plants on mammalian and avian wildlife species in shrub and woodlands. *Biological Conservation,* **256**, 109037.

Schroder, M. & Sato, C.F. (2017) An evaluation of small-mammal use of constructed wildlife crossings in ski resorts. *Wildlife Research,* **44**, 259–268.

Sethi, P. & Howe, H.F. (2009) Recruitment of hornbill-dispersed trees in hunted and logged forests of the Indian Eastern Himalaya. *Conservation Biology,* **23**, 710–718.

Shutt, J.D. & Lees, A.C. (2021) Killing with kindness: does widespread generalised provisioning of wildlife help or hinder biodiversity conservation efforts? *Biological Conservation,* **261**, 109295.

Silverthorn, V.M., Bishop, C.A., Jardine, T., Elliot, J.E. & Morrissey, C.A. (2018a) Impact of flow diversion by run-of-river dams on American dipper diet and mercury exposure. *Environmental Toxicology,* **37**, 411–426.

Silverthorn, V.M., Bishop, C.A., Elliot, J.E. & Morrissey, C.A. (2018b) An assessment of run-of-river hydroelectric dams on mountain stream ecosystems using the American dipper as an avian indicator. *Ecological Indicators,* **93**, 942–951.

Smallwood, K.S. & Thelander, C. (2008) Bird mortality in the Altamont Pass Wind Resource Area, California. *Journal of Environmental Management*, **72**, 215–223.

Smith, J.A. & Dwyer, J.F. (2016) Avian interactions with renewable energy infrastructure: an update. *Condor*, **118**, 411–423.

Storch, I. & Leidenberger, C. (2003) Tourism, mountain huts and distribution of corvids in the Bavarian Alps, Germany. *Wildlife Biology*, **9**, 301–308.

Strong, A.M., Dickert, C.A. & Bell, R.T. (2002) Ski trail effects on a beetle (Coleoptera: Carabidae, Elateridae) community in Vermont. *Journal of Insect Conservation*, **6**, 149–159.

Summers, R.W., McFarlane, J. & Pearce-Higgins, J.W. (2007) Measuring avoidance by capercaillies *Tetrao urogallus* of woodland close to tracks. *Wildlife Biology*, **13**, 19–27.

Steven, R., Pickering, C. & Guy Castley, J. (2011) A review of the impacts of nature based recreation on birds. *Journal of Environmental Management*, **92**, 2287–2294.

Svadlenak-Gomez, K., Badura, M., Kraxner, F., *et al.* (2013) Valuing Alpine ecosystems: the recharge.green project will help decision-makers to reconcile renewable energy production and biodiversity conservation in the Alps. *Management and Policy Issues*, **5**, 51–54.

Taubmann, J., Kämmerle, J.-L., Andrén, H., *et al.* (2021) Wind energy facilities affect resource selection of capercaillie *Tetrao urogallus*. *Wildlife Biology*, **2021**, wlb.00737.

Thiel, D., Jenni-Eiermann, S., Braunisch, V., Palme, R. & Jenni, L. (2008) Ski tourism affects habitat use and evokes a physiological stress response in capercaillie *Tetrao urogallus*: a new methodological approach. *Journal of Applied Ecology*, **45**, 845–853.

Thiel, D., Jenni-Eiermann, S., Palme, R. & Jenni, L. (2011) Winter tourism increases stress hormone levels in the Capercaillie *Tetrao urogallus*. *Ibis*, **153**, 122–133.

Tsuyuzaki, S. (2002) Vegetation development patterns on ski slopes in lowland Hokkaido, northern Japan. *Biological Conservation*, **108**, 239–246.

Uhlmann, B., Goyette, S. & Beniston, M. (2009) Sensitivity analysis of snow patterns in Swiss ski resorts to shifts in temperature, precipitation and humidity under conditions of climate change. *International Journal of Climatology*, **29**, 1048–1055.

U.S. Department of the Interior, U.S. Fish and Wildlife Service, and U.S. Department of Commerce, U.S. Census Bureau (2018) 2016 National Survey of Fishing, Hunting, *and Wildlife-Associated Recreation*.

Urbanska, K.M. (1997) Restoration ecology research above the timberline: colonization of safety islands on a machine-graded alpine ski run. *Biodiversity and Conservation*, **6**, 1655–1670.

Urbanska, K.M., Erdt, S. & Fattorini, M. (1998) Seed rain in natural grassland and adjacent ski run in the Swiss Alps: a preliminary report. *Restoration Ecology*, **6**, 159–165.

Vanat, L. (2020) 2020 International Report on Snow & Mountain Tourism – Overview of the Key Industry Figures for Ski resorts. www.vanat.ch/RM-world-report-2020.pdf accessed on 30 May 2021

Vallino, C., Caprio, E., Genco, F., *et al.* (2019) Behavioural responses to human disturbance in an alpine bird. *Journal of Ornithology*, **160**, 763–772.

Vallino, C., Caprio, E., Genco, F., *et al.* (2020) Flocking of foraging Yellow-Billed Choughs *Pyrrhocorax Graculus* reflects the availability of grasshoppers and the extent of human influence in high elevation ecosystems. *Ardeola*, **68**, 53–70.

Vallino, C., Yoccoz, N.G., Rolando, A. & Delestrade, A. (2021) Webcams as a remote tool for eco-ethological research: a study on the Alpine Chough. *Frontiers in Environmental Science*, **9**, 659521.

Vignali, S., Lörcher, F., Hegglin, D., Arlettaz, R. & Braunisch, V. (2021) Modelling the habitat selection of the bearded vulture to predict areas of potential conflict with wind energy development in the Swiss Alps. *Global Ecology and Conservation*, **25**, e01405.

Vignali, S., Lörcher, F., Hegglin, D., Arlettaz, R. & Braunisch V. (2022) A predictive flight-altitude model for avoiding future conflicts between an emblematic raptor and wind energy development in the Swiss Alps. *Royal Society Open Science*, **9**, 211041.

Viterbi, R., Cerrato, C., Bassano, B., *et al.* (2013) Patterns of biodiversity in the northwestern Italian Alps: a multi-taxa approach. *Community Ecology*, **14**, 18–30.

Wang, S., Wang, S. & Smith, P. (2015) Ecological impacts of wind farms on birds: questions, hypotheses, and research needs. *Renewable and Sustainable Energy Reviews*, **44**, 599–607.

Watson, A. (1979) Bird and mammal numbers in relation to human impact at ski lifts on Scottish hills. *Journal of Applied Ecology*, **16**, 753–764.

Watson, A. & Moss, R. (2004) Impacts of ski-development on ptarmigan (*Lagopus mutus*) at Cairn Gorm, Scotland. *Biological Conservation*, **116**, 267–275.

Watson, R.T., Kolar, P.S., Ferrer, M., *et al.* (2018) Raptor interactions with wind energy: case studies from around the world. *Journal of Raptor Research*, **52**, 1–18.

White, P.S. & Pickett, S.T.A. (1985) Natural disturbance and patch dynamics: an introduction. In *The Ecology of Natural Disturbance and Patch Dynamics*. Pickett, S.T.A. & White, P.S. (eds.). New York: Academic Press, pp. 3–13.

Wohlgemuth, T., Jentsch, A. & Seidl, R. (2019) *Störungsökologie*. Bern: UTB/Haupt Verlag.

Wu, B. (2020) *2019 China Ski Industry* White Book. www.vanat.ch. accessed on 30 May 2021.

Young, L.M., Kelly, D. & Nelson, X.J. (2012) Alpine flora may depend on declining frugivorous parrot for seed dispersal. *Biological Conservation*, **147**, 133–142.

Zarfl, C., Lumsdon, A.E., Berlekamp, J., Tydecks, L. & Tockner, K. (2015) A global boom in hydropower dam construction. *Aquatic Sciences*, **77**, 161–170.

Zbinden, N., Salvioni, M., Korner-Nievergelt, F. & Keller, V. (2018) Evidence for an additive effect of hunting mortality in an alpine black grouse *Lyrurus tetrix* population. *Wildlife Biology*, **2018**, wlb.00418.

Zeiler, H.P & Gruenschachner-Berger, V. (2009) Impact of wind power plants on black grouse, *Lyrurus tetrix* in Alpine regions. *Folia Zoologica*, **58**, 173.

Zeitler, A. (2000) Human disturbance, behaviour and spatial distribution of black grouse in skiing areas in the Bavaria Alps. *Cahiers d'Ethologie*, **20**, 381–402.

8 · *Modelling Large-Scale Patterns in Mountain Bird Diversity and Distributions*

MATTIA BRAMBILLA, MATTHEW G.
BETTS, UTE BRADTER, HANKYU KIM,
PAOLA LAIOLO AND THOMAS SATTLER

8.1 Introduction

Modelling distributions of species is a key task for modern ecologists. Species distribution models (SDMs), aimed at quantitatively identifying factors driving occurrence and/or characterizing ecological niches (Guisan & Thuiller 2005), have replaced the largely descriptive investigations that dominated the discipline previously. SDMs have also become a key method for making predictions, usually of species distributions, under different future scenarios of environmental change and as such are important in conservation planning (Rodríguez *et al.* 2007). Similarly, spatially explicit modelling of communities has gained importance in ecology and conservation, with a progressive shift from a simple characterization of richness and diversity, to more nuanced investigations assessing the variation of functional, ecological and other life-history traits in relation to environmental drivers or time (Villéger *et al.* 2011; White *et al.* 2018).

Distribution modelling over broad scales poses several challenges to researchers because of potentially altered equilibrium between distribution and environmental characteristics, resulting in non-stationarity in space and time (Guisan & Thuiller 2005), due to, for example, interspecific interactions, dispersal limitation, demographic dynamics, key resources not adequately represented in the available information, and several types of environmental filtering (Zurell 2017). Birds represent a particular challenge for distribution modelling (Engler *et al.* 2017). They are generally highly mobile, often displaying important seasonal changes in distributions and ecological niches (Ponti *et al.* 2020). Long-distance migrant species may be affected by the climate in their wintering and/ or breeding areas, complicating the selection of factors influencing niches and therefore covariates used in distribution modelling (Eyres *et al.* 2017). They may also be subject to carry-over effects (conditions in one season that affect resources and/or survival in a subsequent season; Yu *et al.* 2010; Frey *et al.* 2016a; Latimer & Zuckerberg 2021). Furthermore, bird species respond to environmental drivers at different and potentially multiple spatial scales. Large raptors regularly roam over thousands of hectares, often travelling over several kilometres (and different valleys in mountain regions) in a single day, whereas small passerines may spend all their breeding season within one thousand square metres (a difference of several orders of magnitude). In addition, habitat selection in many bird species is a multi-scale process (Jedlikowski *et al.* 2016); this could be particularly true for mountain birds exploiting a habitat encompassing three-dimensions (e.g., Brambilla *et al.* 2010). Many bird species may require different habitats for the acquisition of various resources (Brambilla & Saporetti 2014; D'Elia *et al.* 2015), further complicating the identification of the drivers of distribution. All of these issues result in complex decisions about the best scale(s) to use and lead to multi-scale approaches to modelling species distributions and communities (Mertes & Jetz 2018; Brambilla *et al.* 2019a; Goljani Amirkhiz *et al.* 2021).

The above complications are exacerbated in the case of mountain birds because of the characteristics of mountain ecosystems and the effects they have on such endothermic, mobile organisms (García-Navas *et al.* 2020). Endothermy allows birds to extend the range of temperatures they can tolerate. In particular, if resources are adequate, they can buffer against lower temperatures, which are particularly frequent in mountains. This implies that the limit of mountain bird distributions may be affected by resource availability, especially at the lowest extreme (Engler *et al.* 2017). High mobility enables species to exploit highly seasonal, almost ephemeral, habitats and resources in high elevation sites, and to cope with environments that are subject to marked and abrupt temporal variation (Barras *et al.* 2021a). Multi-scale habitat selection may involve several drivers that are difficult to identify along the steep environmental gradients of mountain ecosystems, determined by the interaction between climate, topography and habitat. Key factors such as temperature, wind, humidity and solar radiation vary over much finer scales than in most other ecosystems. Finally, the harsh conditions found in high-elevation areas have resulted in a mix of adaptations (Barve *et al.* 2021; Chapter 2) and plasticity of organisms inhabiting such 'extreme' habitats. Such difficult conditions, and especially the difficulty in accessing many mountain areas, also impede intensive sampling and data collection. The high mobility of birds, coupled with the complex interactions involving rapid turnover in vegetation, topography and microclimate, make it difficult to collect data, but also to analyse them with a high degree of confidence when it comes to modelling distributions, community characteristics and monitoring mountain birds over time.

In this chapter, we deal with crucial issues for modelling bird distribution and diversity in mountains. Given that modelling species distributions is often undertaken at fairly large spatial scales, we consider a broad definition of mountain habitats that can encompass all vegetation zones (see Chapter 1, Table 1.1). We discuss the role of environmental constraints at different scales, the importance of interactions between species and among drivers in impacting bird distributions, and the factors shaping bird communities. We point out the major challenges for modelling distributions and community structure. We keep a prevalent focus on temperate mountains, given that a specific chapter of the book is dedicated to tropical mountains (Chapter 9). We conclude by discussing potential solutions to the main challenges, implications for research and conservation and future steps that could be envisioned to fill the remaining gaps in our knowledge of avian distribution and communities in mountain ecosystems.

8.2 Modelling Distributions of Mountain Birds

8.2.1 Environmental Constraints

Since the work of Alexander von Humboldt (von Humboldt & Bonpland 1807), mountains have been used as model systems to study the geographical distributions of species, specifically with respect to ecological niches. Their steep environmental gradients enable examination of species range limits without the need to cover large geographical distances. These steep environmental gradients have conferred similar potential benefits to bird species under climate change, as the potential exists for birds to disperse to locations that become suitable in terms of environmental niche. Indeed, upward shifts in the distribution of both avian and non-avian species towards mountain summits have been widely observed across mountain ranges of the world (Sheldon *et al.* 2011; Neate-Clegg *et al.* 2021), even if a lack of tangible shifts is also frequent (Chapter 6).

Furthermore, bird species distributions have often shifted more slowly than would be expected based on temperature change alone, likely because of other environmental constraints (Scridel *et al.* 2018).

Climate-envelope models relate species distributions to climatic (and often other environmental) variables and then project future distribution based on expected climate change over the coming decades (Thomas *et al.* 2004; Jantz *et al.* 2015; Scridel *et al.* 2021). Many of these models predict that mountain birds will lose habitat rapidly, and become imperilled under future climate warming as 'sky islands' shrink in size (Şekercioğlu *et al.* 2008, 2012). Shifting upslope often comes with the risk of extirpation or extinction, as habitat area shrinks with increasing shifts toward mountain peaks, although such effects vary according to the physical form of a mountain (Elsen & Tingley 2015; Chapter 6). The orientation and topographical complexity of mountains (concave 'bowls', convex 'mounds', gullies etc.) often results in complex thermal properties across elevations, with potential for 'microrefugia' that may buffer species from the effects of climate change, at least temporarily (Dobrowski 2011; Wolf *et al.* 2021). Therefore, species may not necessarily shift upwards under climate change – cooler patches may occur at lower elevations due to cold-air drainage (Pypker *et al.* 2007), or on pole-facing slopes where mountainsides receive less solar radiation due to shading (Feldmeir *et al.* 2020). This may lead to shifts toward 'cold spots' that are not necessarily upslope (Frey *et al.* 2016b). Distribution modelling of mountain birds should thus ideally include rather fine-scaled, temperature-relevant environmental information next to or instead of widely used, broader topographical variables serving as proxies for temperature (elevation, inclination, orientation).

Modelling the fundamental niche of a species, and thus its potential to adapt to changing climatic conditions, may be limited by the difficulty to approximate its 'true' fundamental niche as the current species distribution does not cover its overall climatic range. This may be due to species ranges moving more slowly than temperatures, e.g., due to site fidelity in many species. For long-lived species in particular, this may lead to an extinction debt at the trailing (retreating) edge of a species' niche (Devictor *et al.* 2008; Lehikoinen & Virkkala 2016). Furthermore, current species distribution is often limited by historical habitat loss or by former persecution, both of which lead to an underestimation of climate suitability for the species (Ratcliffe 2010; Brambilla *et al.* 2021).

Even when the fundamental niche is known, the capacity of bird species to follow it as the climate shifts will depend upon a number of important factors, few of which have been included in modelling efforts to date. First, the structural components of the habitat itself (e.g., forest type) must be present in the new area, otherwise nesting substrate or foraging surfaces will not be available. Second, interspecific interactions may limit the capacity of species to move (Section 8.2.2). If a more dominant competitor already occupies the new niche locations, colonization may not occur. Finally, the species must have the capacity for finding new habitat as the climate shifts. Birds use a variety of behaviours to find new habitat during natal or breeding dispersal, with some approaches more effective than others. For instance, using personal experience can be time consuming (Danchin *et al.* 2004), in comparison to social information (i.e., using information about the breeding success of others), which can be a very efficient mechanism for finding habitat under changing conditions (Betts *et al.* 2008).

In species distribution modelling, the broad environmental gradients afforded by mountain landscapes allow sampling across wide ranges of both climatic and vegetation predictor variables. Incorporating the full climatic and vegetation niches of species is likely to make models more transferable to other regions and future time periods (Yates *et al.* 2018).

8.2.2 The Importance of Biotic Interactions

Species distributions and abundances are not only shaped by abiotic (Burner *et al.* 2020), but also by biotic factors, which could significantly contribute to setting bird elevational range limits (e.g., Jankowski *et al.* 2013; Freeman *et al.* 2019). Interspecific interactions, such as competition, facilitation, prey availability or predation influence where species can persist and how abundant they are. Biotic interactions are, however, often neglected in SDMs (Guisan & Thuiller 2005; Zurell 2017). To obtain a better ecological understanding of spatial occurrence, it often makes sense to include the presence or absence (or probability of occurrence) of other species which are either advantageous or disadvantageous for the focal species. Some biotic interactions may involve food availability (e.g., earthworms for ring ouzel *Turdus torquatus*, Barras *et al.* 2021b), and providers of or competitors for a certain resource (e.g., common blackbirds *Turdus merula* as competitors for ring ouzels, von dem Bussche *et al.* 2008; woodpecker holes as nesting resources for different owl species, Heikkinen *et al.* 2007; Brambilla *et al.* 2020a). Interactions with potential predators may also be important. For example, in the boreal region, black grouse *Lyrurus tetrix* were more abundant further from nests of the northern goshawk *Accipiter gentilis*, a main predator (Tornberg *et al.* 2016). However, the proportion of black grouse hens with broods was higher close to goshawk nests, indicating that they may also have an indirect facilitation effect on black grouse by reducing the number of corvids which prey on their nests.

Therefore, including biotic interactions in distribution models is of great importance for understanding the ecological responses of species and their spatial distribution. In mountain systems, these models may shed light on the factors that promote zonation and species replacement observed along elevational gradients, and allow inferences about the occurrence of interactions that are otherwise difficult to disclose (such as competition and facilitation). This is normally performed by correlative models fitting species distribution and environmental data with patterns of co-occurrence among species (Zurell 2017). These correlative models look for excesses (possibly indicating positive interactions such as facilitation or mutualism) and deficits in co-occurrence (possibly indicating negative interactions, such as competition or predation; Dorman *et al.* 2018). Excesses and deficits are normally established based on null models of species distribution following abiotic and habitat factors alone. Among correlative models, joint species distribution models (jSDMs) infer the role of species associations in the residuals of the model, after controlling for abiotic and habitat factors (Pollock *et al.* 2014).

Bastianelli *et al.* (2017) used jSDMs to study the influence of interspecific competition in determining the spatial turnover between two pipit species (water pipit *Anthus spinoletta* and tree pipit *A. trivialis*) and two bunting species (yellowhammer *Emberiza citrinella* and ortolan bunting *E. hortulana*) in the Cantabrian Mountains in Spain, each species pair being made up of one relatively high and one relatively low elevation species along the gradient. The jSDMs for pipits highlighted divergent climate and habitat requirements, but also negative correlations between species not explained by environmental variables. Evidence from modelling was then compared with experimental evidence of interference competition obtained by means of playback experiments, but no evidence of interspecific aggressiveness was found. The significant residual correlation of jSDMs therefore possibly reflected forms of competition other than direct interference, or the influence of unmeasured environmental predictors. The jSDMs for buntings indicated shared habitat preferences, but a possible limitation to dispersal as a cause of the parapatric distribution of these congeneric species.

As an alternative to jSDMs, the sources of variation in species abundance can be modelled by taking into account environmental suitability and the occupancy and detection probabilities of other species (e.g., N-mixture models; Joseph *et al.* 2009). Using this approach, Brambilla *et al.* (2020a) modelled the potential distributions of black woodpecker *Dryocopus martius*, boreal owl *Aegolius funereus*, tawny owl *Strix aluco* and Ural owl *Strix uralensis* in montane and subalpine forests of the entire region of the European Alps, and tested whether the spatial patterns of the more widespread species were shaped by interspecific interactions. Models revealed an effect of interspecific interactions on current species abundance, especially in boreal owl (positive effects of black woodpecker because boreal owls breed in woodpecker holes; negative effects of tawny owl, which can prey on boreal owls and compete with them for nest holes and prey). Climate change is altering the pattern of co-occurrence and hence the potential interspecific relationships. For example, boreal owl is predicted to share a greater proportion of its range with tawny owl in the future, especially due to the latter's expansion along the elevational gradient, mainly promoted by warming temperatures (Brambilla *et al.* 2020a).

All this evidence suggests that ignoring interspecific interactions could hamper the ability of SDMs to predict species distributions. There are limitations on the inferences about interactions that can be drawn from these methods, and fundamental problems remain. Patterns in species distributions and abundances can often be explained by factors that suggest different underlying processes. Without detailed knowledge of the processes occurring, or subsequent experiments to confirm the hypotheses suggested by correlative methods, it is often difficult, or even impossible, to distinguish between the effects of biotic interactions and those of environmental covariates not included in the model (Dormann *et al.* 2012, 2018).

8.2.3 Challenges in Quantifying Microclimate and Microhabitat

Although some mountain bird species have exhibited range shifts in response to climate change (Tingley *et al.* 2009), many species have not been observed to track their climatic niche by adjusting their spatial distributions (Neate-Clegg *et al.* 2021; Chapter 6). One hypothesis for this mismatch between bird-climate envelope predictions and observed responses is that the climate data used to define suitable envelopes are collected at resolutions much coarser than those perceived and used by organisms in habitat selection (Plate 6, Storlie *et al.* 2014). Most temperature data are collected at scales 10^4-fold larger than the territory sizes of focal organisms (Potter *et al.* 2013), and there is high potential for hidden microclimate variation within broader regional patterns. This hidden microclimatic variation and its potential to affect distribution dynamics is often overlooked (Riddell *et al.* 2021), but is considered to be particularly relevant to mountain vertebrates. Additionally, lack of high-resolution climate data, particularly understorey temperatures (Scherrer *et al.* 2011), has prohibited effective testing of the role of microclimate in fine-scale distribution dynamics. In forests, measuring climate below the canopy is particularly important because this is the environment experienced by most bird species (Frey *et al.* 2016a) and likely has implications for their population trends (Betts *et al.* 2019).

Thankfully, microclimate is increasingly quantified in population and community ecology studies of mountain landscapes (de Frenne *et al.* 2021). However, quantification of microclimate involves substantial challenges. Because the microclimate is so variable, and it can be driven by a host of variables including microtopography and forest structure (Plate 6), data loggers must be deployed in large numbers to enable spatial extrapolation of temperature and humidity variables. Data loggers are often relatively inexpensive, but the logistics of data download, storage and handling can be considerable. Recent advances indicate that microclimate can be estimated even without extensive on-the-ground devices, by means of highly refined downscaling based on the information of fine-scale variation in solar radiation, albedo, vegetation, topography and coastal effects (Maclean *et al.* 2019; Kearney *et al.* 2020). If effective, such microclimate modelling approaches could result in an explosion of new microclimate studies that use existing long-term bird distribution or abundance data along with back-cast microclimate predictions.

It is important to note that even studies that purportedly quantify microclimate may not necessarily do so at scales relevant to the species or individuals under study. Frequently, loggers are deployed at a set level above the ground (e.g., 1.5 m; Frey *et al.* 2016b) which is not necessarily relevant to birds nesting or foraging either at ground level or in the canopy. Indeed, there is still substantial climatic variability even within the forest canopy if one considers tree cavities, sun spots and shaded areas that are available for highly mobile birds, thereby enabling a behavioural buffering against weather and climate conditions (Shaw & Flick 1999). Micro-loggers are already available to track the body temperatures and ambient conditions surrounding the animal (air temperatures) for larger bird species (Kerr *et al.* 2004; Chmura *et al.* 2018). When it becomes available, such technology will shed new light on microclimate habitat use by smaller birds. Other potential advances include use of thermal imaging to determine microclimate availability in forests (Kim *et al.* 2018) along with radio-telemetry (Hadley & Betts 2009) to quantify habitat selection in relation to very fine-scale microclimate features.

All these advances will also make it easier to investigate the short-term (i.e., within the same season) adjustments in species' distribution (Betts *et al.* 2008), with those occurring within the breeding season being of particular importance for conservation in hilly and mountain areas (Brambilla & Rubolini 2009). Likely because of the strong gradients and seasonality of mountain environments, within-season changes in local or regional distribution of breeding birds have been observed in forests (Frey *et al.* 2016a), meadows (Brambilla & Pedrini 2011) and along broad habitat gradients, spanning from subalpine forest to high-elevation alpine grassland and rocky habitats (Ceresa *et al.* 2020).

Finally, it will be important to link microclimate use and bird distributions to key avian demographic stages such as reproduction and survival. To our knowledge, few, if any, studies have linked microclimate use by mountain birds to overall population dynamics across space, but there are studies that relate it to some key demographic variables, highlighting, for example, that inclement weather may have varying stage-specific impacts on offspring development (and hence on breeding success) among alpine songbirds with diverging traits (de Zwaan *et al.* 2020). Long-term studies on avian population trends will also be hugely beneficial as they integrate these demographic parameters to address the direct and indirect effects of mountain climate change on bird populations (e.g., Strinella *et al.* 2020; Kim *et al.* 2022).

8.2.4 Challenges and Opportunities for Modelling Distribution and Abundance in Mountain Birds

Advances in the spatial, temporal and thematic resolution of remote sensing data may prove to be particularly useful for modelling mountain bird distributions in the future. Mountain habitats can be snow covered for long periods, and frequent cloud cover can limit the collection of data with optical sensors from airborne or satellite platforms. High revisit frequencies of satellite platforms are therefore particularly important to provide full data coverage to enable mapping of mountain habitats or the monitoring of changes in vegetation and phenology. Several recent and planned satellite missions have high revisit frequencies, high spatial resolutions and spectral channels suitable for mapping and monitoring vegetation (Feilhauer *et al.* 2013; Rapinel *et al.* 2019). High revisit frequencies should also result in greater availability of multi-temporal imagery in frequently cloud-covered areas. Furthermore, the reflectance of vegetation varies temporally due to changes in the chemical compositions of plants, the structure of the plant tissue and the structure of the canopy (Lillesand *et al.* 2008; Thenkabail *et al.* 2011). Such temporal variation can be captured by multi-temporal imagery and can improve the accuracy with which habitat classes can be mapped (Wakulinska & Marcinkowska-Ochtyra 2020). Studies using data from airborne or satellite platforms in upland and mountain habitats have already shown the potential for mapping vegetation at the high thematic and spatial resolutions relevant for bird distribution modelling (Bradter *et al.* 2011; Wakulinska & Marcinkowska-Ochtyra 2020).

Another potentially major limitation to species modelling is the lack of knowledge of how species are affected by ecological processes. Species distributions emerge from the underlying demographic processes determining reproduction, survival, immigration and emigration, which in turn are affected by abiotic and biotic conditions and interactions. Due to the often difficult logistics, the ecology of many mountain birds is less well studied compared to some species in more accessible regions (Chamberlain *et al.* 2012; Chapter 1).

Whether a lack of ecological knowledge limits the modelling of mountain bird distributions depends on the aim of the study. If the aim of modelling is to produce a map of the distribution or abundance of a species for the area and time in which sample data were collected (interpolation), incomplete knowledge of ecological processes does not necessarily result in less accurate mapping. Well-performing distribution maps can be produced by using spatial predictors to substitute unknown abiotic or biotic processes (Bahn & McGill 2007), for example using distance-based eigenvectors (Borcard & Legendre 2002; Dray *et al.* 2006). Therefore, mapping applications to facilitate conservation planning or prioritization can often produce the desired results despite some of the limitations highlighted above.

If the aim of the study is to identify ecological processes from observed patterns, a lack of ecological knowledge may hamper progress. As discussed above, selected covariates in correlative analysis methods express associations, not necessarily causation (Dormann *et al.* 2012; Hawkins 2012). The realism of associations between a species and abiotic or biotic covariates suggested by models needs to be assessed through the filter of ecological knowledge or verified by independent experiments and are otherwise often better seen as suggested hypotheses of potential associations. Moreover, a lack of knowledge of relevant ecological processes can lead to specifying a covariate wrongly, for example at an incorrect spatial scale, which can lead to biased regression coefficients, and consequently biased conclusions, even if spatial models are used to eliminate residual spatial autocorrelation (de Knegt *et al.* 2010).

Lack of ecological knowledge can be a limitation for the increasingly important field of projecting distributions into the future, or to other areas (Wenger & Olden 2012; Urban *et al.* 2016; see below). Some other disciplines make greater use of process-based or mechanistic models avoiding the limitations of correlative approaches. However, they require comprehensive ecological knowledge and population data (Urban *et al.* 2016; Singer *et al.* 2018), often acquired from intensive studies. Usually, such intensive data collection is less feasible in logistically challenging mountain areas.

8.3 Modelling Bird Diversity in Mountains

Many fundamental concepts of ecology, biogeography and evolution, such as species richness–environment relationships, species turnover across life zones and speciation, originate from models of species diversity in montane regions, often with birds as the target system (McCain 2009). Modelling diversity serves two major functions (Scheiner *et al.* 2011). The first is to produce quantitative estimations related to α-, β- and/or γ-diversity for descriptive comparisons, for instance among different mountain chains, habitats or time periods. The second is to explore the causes of different diversity patterns, that is, to understand the ecological, stochastic and historical processes underlying diversity relationships. Linking diversity metrics to environmental and climatic parameters is key to understanding changes in avian communities in response to climate and habitat changes, providing further insights into the understanding of biodiversity drivers in mountains, and providing knowledge complementary to that relative to species distributions for conservation. Modelling diversity in a mountain environment requires disentangling the complex interactions among drivers along the elevational and topographical gradients.

Species richness, a common measure of bird diversity, is estimated as the number of species for a particular spatial or temporal grain. It generally shows a monotonic decline with elevation, reflecting the effect of temperature and productivity on species abundance (Laiolo *et al.* 2018). The grain and the sampling design can have important effects on the observed patterns, and should be formulated *a priori* to respond to different questions. Here, we will focus on the conceptual and methodological aspects of diversity modelling. The methods used for field sampling may also affect results, an issue that is dealt with in Box 8.1. The spatial decomposition of species richness into α-, β- and γ-diversity has been the subject of a rich literature (Whittaker 1960; Tuomisto 2010). Briefly, α-diversity refers to the diversity of local communities and γ- diversity to the total species diversity of all local communities. β- diversity encompasses many aspects of compositional heterogeneity, from species turnover to community nestedness (Anderson *et al.* 2011; Tuomisto 2010).

Box 8.1 *Collecting and Analysing Observations of Birds in Mountain Regions*

Modelling the distribution and diversity of species requires data on the occurrence or abundance of species, often over large areas. Many countries collect data each year through systematic bird monitoring programmes that follow specific survey designs and protocols to produce representative and comparable data, specifying when, what, where, how and how often, to survey and to report (Chapter 5).

National bird monitoring protocols may be tailored to the specific requirements and logistical challenges of a country, but mountain ranges are often shared by multiple countries. Differences across national survey protocols can include the recording units (pairs or individuals) or the survey type (point count stations or line transects). A simple way to analyse data collected with different protocols is to degrade the data to a common standard, such as conversion from counts to the detection or non-detection of a species. However, this involves the loss of potentially valuable information. Alternatively, modelling methods can increasingly account for differences in data characteristics (Bowler *et al.* 2019; Isaac *et al.* 2020).

An alternative type of data comprises species observations collected without a survey protocol. Such opportunistic data are often referred to as Citizen Science data, although this term may also refer to systematic data collected by volunteers. Opportunistic data are increasingly available for regions and species for which little or no systematic data exist (Hochachka *et al.* 2012; Amano *et al.* 2016). Common breeding bird monitoring programmes often collect relatively little data for rarer species or those occurring in localized areas. On the other hand, bird watchers are often particularly interested in the rarer species. For example, for the Eurasian dotterel *Charadrius morinellus* in Norway (Figure B8.1), the number of records from the Norwegian breeding bird monitoring programme Norsk hekkefuglovervåking (co-ordinated by the Norwegian Institute for Nature Research and BirdLife Norway) is small (309 records) compared to records available from the Norwegian Citizen Science portal Artsobservatjoner during the same time period (c. 1250 records for the period 1st June – 10th July 2006–2020).

Opportunistic data may reflect large variation in recording intensity in time and space, and in observer skills, and often are spatially biased towards areas that are easily accessible or popular (Mair & Ruete 2016; Tye *et al.* 2017). Species records may have complementary information on species non–detections and recording intensity, or may be unstructured without this information (Sullivan *et al.* 2009). Appropriate data preparation and modelling increasingly account for the challenges of opportunistic data (Jackson *et al.* 2015; Bradter *et al.* 2018; Johnston *et al.* 2018, 2021). Additionally, methods to model jointly systematic and opportunistic data to combine the strengths of both are being developed (Fithian *et al.* 2015; Fletcher *et al.* 2019). Habitat suitability is commonly modelled based on unstructured detection-only records with presence-background methods such as MaxEnt (Phillips *et al.* 2006; Elith *et al.* 2011; Yackulic *et al.* 2013). However, the inclusion of species non–detection data is preferable (Royle *et al.* 2012; Bradter *et al.* 2018, 2021; Johnston *et al.* 2021). Occurrence probability can only be estimated from detection–only data if randomly sampled in space, and from detections paired with the background or non–detections if the data reflect the prevalence of the species (Elith *et al.* 2006; Royle *et al.* 2012). Occupancy models can account for imperfect detection in both systematic and opportunistic data, but require repeat observations and suitable information on the reporting intensity to account for the reporting bias of opportunistic data (MacKenzie *et al.* 2003; Kéry *et al.* 2010a, b; Isaac *et al.* 2014; Bradter *et al.* 2021).

Figure B8.1 Eurasian dotterel *Charadrius morinellus* (Photo: Ute Bradter).

The definitions above are suited to species richness data, but may also include variation beyond this component of diversity. Diversity descriptors can be calculated by weighting the contribution of each species to richness by its abundance, biomass or other adaptive phenotypic traits, or by phylogenetic relatedness. These functional and phylogenetic facets of diversity, reflecting, respectively, the diversity of morphological, physiological and ecological traits, and the diversity of biogeographic histories, have been used to predict biodiversity contributions to ecosystem functions. Models assume, for instance, that functional diversity equates to resource use complementarity, so that differences in how species gain resources is the variation represented by functional diversity (Petchey & Gaston 2002). Foraging birds exert important ecosystem functions (e.g., seed dispersal by frugivorous birds; pest control by insectivorous birds and birds of prey, nutrient recycling by avian scavengers), thus bird functional diversity can represent the diversity of services birds can provide, and be associated with their economic value (Şekercioğlu et al. 2016). Quantifying these metrics may serve to track temporal changes in bird functional contributions to the (alpine) ecosystem (García-Navas et al. 2020), or the occurrence of spatial or habitat barriers to specific bird functions (Altamirano et al. 2020), and geographic patterns of phylogenetic and functional structure of bird communities (Boyce *et al.* 2019). Notably, scale can also affect results when evaluating functional traits (Laiolo *et al.* 2017).

8.4 Assessing and Predicting Impacts of Environmental Changes and Implications for Conservation

8.4.1 Working with Relevant Scales and Drivers

The widespread occurrence of steep gradients in mountains represents a challenge in modelling bird distributions at high elevation. In part, this is due to restrictions on data availability at appropriate spatial and temporal scales (Section 8.2.3), but also due to the high mobility and multi-scale habitat selection of birds. Distribution models integrating multiple scales could help identify the individual spatial scales at which the ecological responses by mountain birds are most likely (Mertes & Jetz 2018; Brambilla *et al.* 2019a). Nevertheless, approaches based on univariate evaluation of the scale-dependency in the effect of single predictors may lead to a partial or an incorrect view of their ecological and spatial relevance (Brambilla *et al.* 2020b). Here, the use of PCA-based methods (Bettega *et al.* 2020) or multi-scale approaches (e.g., Bradter *et al.* 2013) may help. For some species that require different resources for different purposes, the use of approaches based on the partition of the ecological niche into functional habitats may greatly help both modelling and conservation (Brambilla & Saporetti 2014; D'Elia *et al.* 2015). However, detailed data allowing such an approach are rarely available. When high-resolution data are available, in terms of the accuracy and spatial and temporal precision of bird records, microhabitat and microclimate modelling may provide more direct 'mechanistic' assessments of habitat use by mountain birds (e.g., Frey *et al.* 2016a; Barras *et al.* 2020), allowing deeper insights into species' ecology.

Assessing the effect of distribution drivers at the relevant scale is key to identifying robust relationships (e.g., de Knegt *et al.* 2010), and for obtaining meaningful model extrapolations to other geographical or temporal contexts. The covariation of climate and other, sometimes more direct, environmental traits may lead to an overestimation of the importance of climate, and this risk likely grows as the discrepancy increases between the spatial scale at which a predictor is evaluated (and entered into models) and the scale at which it actually affects a species. Large-scale evaluation of climatic drivers of occurrence or distribution in mountain birds, based on environmental predictors measured over sample units of several square kilometres, is unlikely to capture accurately the true nature of species-climate relationships, with consequences for estimates of potential future impacts of climate change (Trivedi *et al.* 2008; Randin *et al.* 2009; Meineri & Hylander 2017). Assessments over different spatial scales may be needed to pinpoint robust, causal effects, or alternatively to identify (and hence discard) non-causal, indirect impacts of other potential drivers of occurrence.

Scale is an essential feature when assessing species-environment relationships, as these are often relevant only at particular spatial scales, especially in birds (e.g., Jedlikowski *et al.* 2016). Direct effects of climatic features on species should be consistent across all, or most, spatial scales. For indirect associations between a species and climate, the modelled species-variable relationships are much more likely to show scale-dependent variations (Brambilla *et al.* 2019a). Furthermore, species-specific differences in the relevance of spatial scales may also complicate the use of jSDMs, where variables are considered over the same scale(s) for all species. For a species for which a direct effect of a climatic predictor could be expected, the modelled effects should be consistent across scales, and the predictions well outside the study area should be accurate (as for the white-winged snowfinch *Montifringilla nivalis*, Box 8.2).

For territorial species during the breeding season, the territory scale is likely to be a highly relevant scale, because territory holders need to find many relevant resources within the limited area that they actively defend and exploit (Jedlikowski *et al.* 2016). Studies working at such a scale based on high-resolution records have provided biologically reliable and ecologically relevant results for birds in complex mountain habitats (e.g., Chamberlain *et al.* 2013, 2016; Brambilla *et al.* 2016; Jähnig *et al.* 2018; Barras *et al.* 2021b), but could still miss some potentially relevant ecological patterns taking place at other scales (Lenoir *et al.* 2017). Integrating microclimate/microhabitat measurements with downscaled macroclimate/macrohabitat patterns would likely provide a definitive perspective for the analysis of species–environment relationships, with relevant implications for modelling distributions and the relative dynamics of communities (Zellweger *et al.* 2019).

The temporally dynamic nature of mountain bird communities and habitats also present a challenge to modelling. Communities vary in their composition and structure not only within the year, but also within the breeding season, because of the progressive settlement of species with different phenologies: as an example, at high elevation in the European Alps, rock ptarmigan *Lagopus muta* may initiate territoriality

Box 8.2 *Modelling the Ecology and Distribution of the White-Winged Snowfinch*

For some species particularly adapted to cold, high-elevation habitats, the link with climatic parameters (especially with temperature) and climate-sensitive habitats and resources may be evident through different spatial scales (Brambilla *et al.* 2019a). In recent years, the white-winged snowfinch is likely one of the species that has gathered the highest interest of ornithologists studying the impacts of climate change on mountain birds in the Old World. Several research initiatives have addressed habitat selection and habitat use over different spatial scales, breeding phenology, demography, social behaviour and distribution at regional and continental (European) scales.

Fine-scaled models describing habitat use during the critical nestling-rearing phase have revealed an association with snow patches (Brambilla *et al.* 2017a, 2019b; Resano-Mayor *et al.* 2019; Schano *et al.* 2021) and other climate-sensitive habitats, such as low-sward alpine grassland (Brambilla *et al.* 2018a, b). Microhabitat selection has also been shown to be affected by microclimate, with foraging individuals adjusting habitat use according to air temperature (Alessandrini *et al.* 2022). All of these results have provided support for fine-scale associations with rather cold habitats which are perfectly mirrored at a larger scale by consistent effects of temperature on the broad species distribution: models developed at different spatial scales, from a 100 m radius to 2 x 2 km cells, have revealed a consistent link with low temperature (Brambilla *et al.* 2020c; de Gabriel-Hernando *et al.* 2021), which remained constant outside the areas used for model calibration (Brambilla *et al.* 2016, 2017b), to the point that distribution models performed well even when projected to distant areas (Brambilla *et al.* 2022).

Adult survival was also found to be affected by climate, with female mortality increasing during warm and dry summers (Strinella *et al.* 2020). Snowfinch ecology and behaviour also appear to be particularly related to temperature outside the breeding season (Bettega *et al.* 2020; de Gabriel-Hernando *et al.* 2021; Delgado *et al.* 2021). The use of fine-tuned, presence-background models based on heterogeneous data sources (a combination of research data and Citizen Science) proved successful in predicting the white-winged snowfinch distribution across its European range (Brambilla *et al.* 2020c).

Figure B8.2 White-winged snowfinches *Montifringilla nivalis* (Photo: Mattia Brambilla).

at the beginning of April, while several songbirds do not occupy their breeding sites before mid-May, or even later in the case of prolonged snow cover. This means that for community studies, it is essential to focus on the most relevant breeding season period, within which all the breeding species are likely to have settled and before species enter their post-breeding phase. The use of data from multiple years may contribute to overcoming limitations due to dynamic patterns resulting from short-term responses to varying environmental conditions when pairing avian data with climatic predictors. Nevertheless, matching as precisely as possible bird and climate data would provide more accurate and robust insights into the potential effects and importance of climatic predictors (Lembrechts *et al.* 2019; Perez-Navarro *et al.* 2021; Section 8.2.3). The increasing availability of spatially and temporally accurate datasets and methods for local estimation of microclimate (Hannah *et al.* 2014; Kearney *et al.* 2020) would definitely promote accuracy in distribution modelling (He *et al.* 2015; Lembrechts *et al.* 2018). Scaling-up from fine-scale to regional or even macroecological levels is particularly important for birds in mountain regions, for all the previously mentioned reasons. We likely need to capitalize on the continuous spatio-temporal information that remote sensing provides for many factors key to avian distribution (Randin *et al.* 2020). The occurrence and hence distribution of many mountain bird species is affected simultaneously by climatic, topographic, land-cover and biotic interactions (Braunisch *et al.* 2014; Barras *et al.* 2021b; Chamberlain *et al.* 2016; Brambilla *et al.* 2020a, b). A proper evaluation of relevant environmental predictors is crucial to understand the impact of global change: if a relevant driver is not taken into account, then the importance of the others could be overestimated, and their effect inaccurately modelled.

A first requirement for correctly modelling the effects of determinants of species distribution or abundance in complex mountain environments is therefore to consider simultaneously the potential impact of multiple drivers. More advanced approaches causally link the effect of microclimate and vegetation by means of structural equation modelling (Duclos *et al.* 2019), disentangling the direct effects of climate from those mediated by the vegetation characteristics, which are largely affected by climate. There are only a few studies that explicitly aim to disentangle the direct impacts of climate on birds (e.g., by effects on habitat selection, phenology or thermoregulatory behaviour) from the indirect impacts, especially through the effect of climate on habitat via an impact on vegetation compositional and structural features. As an example, Ceresa *et al.* (2021) showed the predominant effect of vegetation over temperature for several species along an elevation gradient in the Alps. This approach is important because species distribution changes and shifts in elevation can be due to climate tracking in the case of direct effects, or to habitat tracking in the case of indirect effects. In addition, there may also be synergies between direct and indirect effects. This has obvious implications for our understanding of ongoing and future changes; studies considering the unique and synergistic effects of climate and land-use changes will better predict variation in abundance of several species than of climate alone (e.g., Betts *et al.* 2019). These synergistic effects could be particularly relevant for mountain birds.

8.4.2 Possible Reasons for Deviations of SDMs from Observed Patterns in the Real World

SDMs have proved to be an important tool for many real-world applications, providing useful information for fieldwork, conservation, evaluation of potential interactions and predictions of range variations, among others (Engler *et al.* 2017), and of course this is also the case for mountain birds. However, being models, SDMs may sometimes diverge from the 'true' distribution (i.e., observed patterns in the real world). Thorough model evaluation should be part of any SDM project. Model evaluation regarding realism, accuracy and generality is a broad research field (Araújo *et al.* 2019), which goes beyond the scope of this chapter. We refer the reader to specific literature (Araujo & Guisan 2006; Fourcade *et al.* 2018).

There are several possible reasons why predicted distributions may diverge from observed patterns in the field: inappropriately chosen variables for particular species, both in terms of predictors and responses; the wrong spatial or temporal scale; species that are in a non-equilibrium state with their environment; and spatial autocorrelation. Such divergence may have implications for the potential use of SDMs for conservation, planning and research and hence understanding some of the causes of divergence may be useful to improve our ability in modelling mountain bird distributions. In the following, we explore several potential solutions to the above issues, which we consider particularly relevant for mountain birds.

Species-Specific Environmental Variables
Poor model performance may arise due to inappropriate environmental input variables for a given species, in particular when the same set of variables is applied across all species. Interactions are also important. For predictive studies, information on expected (i.e., modelled) climate change and land-use change needs to be integrated (Sirami *et al.* 2017; Vincent *et al.* 2019). Direct, physiological effects of climate change may be altered indirectly by (possibly less-responsive) habitat variables (Braunisch *et al.* 2014; Crase *et al.* 2014), such as lagged treeline shifts (Gehrig-Fasel *et al.* 2007; Duclos *et al.* 2019).

The development of species-specific habitat variables has not always received sufficient attention. Sometimes, the selection of habitat variables is driven simply by their availability in (accessible) databases (Araujo & Guisan 2006; Braunisch *et al.* 2013). In most cases, and especially when aiming for an ecological understanding of the distribution rather than for a descriptive pattern, SDMs profit from the inclusion of species-specific variables (Mod *et al.* 2016), and this could be particularly true in the case of mountain birds. As an example, the distribution of ring ouzel in Switzerland is affected not only by climate and land-cover, but also by low-productivity pasture and the number of solitary trees (Barras *et al.*

2021b). Brambilla *et al.* (2020c) found that, depending on species, next to climate and habitat, human management may be important to model species adequately, with red-backed shrike *Lanius collurio* and Eurasian skylark *Alauda arvensis* being sensitive to the occurrence of grazing and ski-pistes, respectively, in mountain grassland in central Italy.

The development of species-specific variables may be challenging, but they are essential to ecologically understand (also in a quantitative way) the factors determining the distribution of species (Fourcade *et al.* 2018). For mountain birds, this can include grassland type (Hotta *et al.* 2019) or the progress of melting of snow fields as a surrogate for food availability (Tipulidae larvae for white-winged snowfinch, Resano-Mayor *et al.* 2019; earthworms for ring ouzel, Barras *et al.* 2021b). Also, environmental variables specific to periods other than the breeding season may be relevant (de Gabriel Hernando *et al.* 2021), including human disturbance in winter (e.g., black grouse and winter outdoor sports; Braunisch *et al.* 2011).

Novel Remote Sensing Environmental Data
Remote sensing has provided new environmental data (e.g., satellite images) that are helpful to distinguish new habitats (He *et al.* 2015; Randin *et al.* 2020), and to model the distributions of mountain birds (e.g., rock ptarmigan in Austria, Zohmann *et al.* 2013), down to very fine scales. As an example, Alessandrini *et al.* (2022) evaluated foraging habitat selection in white-winged snowfinches (Figure B8.2), highlighting a preference for intermediate vegetation cover, snow patches and higher heterogeneity and an avoidance of extremely warm or cold microclimates. Results matched previous knowledge based on accurate field measurements, and highlighted behavioural buffering against 'hot' conditions. Air-borne lidar-data has great potential to get novel spatial information on habitat structure, and has important explanatory power in SDMs (e.g., in mountain forest birds; Zellweger *et al.* 2013; Huber *et al.* 2016). Such data may also help model three-dimensional habitats, e.g., species breeding in rocky habitats (Brambilla *et al.* 2010). Often, satellite data are provided to global databases, meaning they are particularly helpful for studies encompassing many countries (He *et al.* 2015).

Finer Scales of Resolution
Fine-grained, ecologically functional species-habitat relationships are particularly valuable in a mountain context where environmental

conditions change markedly over small spatial scales (e.g., Barras *et al.* 2021b). Sun-exposed and pole-facing slopes may be very different, but there are also less evident (but still important) habitat changes for mountain birds induced by topography or geology. Grain size of spatial models can be decisive in determining which environmental variables are important for the distribution of a species (Guisan *et al.* 2007; Brambilla *et al.* 2019a), and modelling may be useful to better understand spatial patterns (Jombart *et al.* 2009; Revermann *et al.* 2012). Fine-scaled modelling approaches, e.g., at the territory scale (Hotta *et al.* 2019; Barras *et al.* 2021a), shed additional light on species-environment relationships and species interactions.

Non-Equilibrium State with the Environment

SDMs assume that a species occupies its environmental niche wherever this niche is present. However, empirical studies show that this equilibrium state with the environment is the exception rather than the norm (Araujo & Pearson 2005). Species may be in a non-equilibrium state with their environment for multiple reasons (Ewing *et al.* 2020), with some populations in their breeding range limited by drivers other than environmental factors. Populations may be in decline due to deteriorating habitat on migration or overwintering areas (Vickery *et al.* 2014, Zurell *et al.* 2018; Marcacci *et al.* 2020), hunting or persecution (Pernollet *et al.* 2015), diseases or additional factors. On the contrary, species in a non-equilibrium state may have undergone a population decline in the past for any of the above-mentioned reasons and are now recovering, that is, a species has an expanding population that has not yet occupied all suitable habitat (e.g., bearded vulture *Gypaetus barbatus*; Hirzel *et al.* 2004; Schaub *et al.* 2009; Margalida *et al.* 2020). Additionally, in many cases, missing important environmental (habitat) variables that describe the spatial patterns of species may also add to a non-equilibrium model.

Spatial Autocorrelation

Spatial autocorrelation is inherent in most ecological data and the effects of ignoring it in SDMs has received considerable attention (Segurado *et al.* 2006; Dormann 2007; Guélat & Kéry 2018). Five categories of factors can drive the presence of spatial autocorrelation in model residuals: ecological data and processes, scale and distance, missing variables, sampling design and assumptions and methodological approaches (Gaspard *et al.* 2019).

Considering spatial variables (e.g., Moran's eigenvectors maps) that account for spatial autocorrelation may be of particular importance when modelling future climate impacts (Crase *et al.* 2014) and failure to include them may have dramatic effects (Guélat & Kéry 2018). Conditional autoregressive (CAR) models (Besag *et al.* 1991) and geoadditive models (Kammann & Wand 2003), which use splines to model spatial structure, have performed well in complex simulations (Guélat & Kéry 2018). Recently, penalized 2D splines were successfully implemented to model spatial autocorrelation both in regional (Knaus *et al.* 2018) and continental (Keller *et al.* 2020) bird distribution atlases that included many mountain birds. Including such spatial variables in modelling may account for missing environmental variables, although whether this is desirable depends on specific study goals. Modelling the spatial structure (i.e., considering spatial autocorrelation) might be a feature required by atlas projects which aim mainly to describe the distributional patterns found in the field. Studies aimed at understanding the spatial ecology of species should possibly try to generate species-specific environmental variables rather than spatial variables for their models. This is especially true when studies are focussed on species conservation and/or the development of management strategies (Hoffmann *et al.* 2015; Brambilla *et al.* 2017b, 2020b). In these cases, model transferability would be highly relevant to ensure likely effectiveness over broader scales.

8.4.3 Implications for Predicting Future Changes

Climate envelope models (Section 8.2.1) explicitly or implicitly assume niche conservatism (i.e., the ecological niche of the species does not change with time). In addition to the issues relating to distribution modelling already noted (e.g., Sections 8.2.3 and 8.4.2), such an approach is also underpinned by various assumptions about whether or not species will be able to keep pace with niche shifts. Although climate envelope models have been successful to some degree in predicting bird species range shifts in mountains and across latitudes (Illán *et al.* 2014), predictions do not always correlate well with observed trends (Betts *et al.* 2019). These 'fall-downs' in model prediction success may have severe consequences for species conservation planning as the climate changes, thus identification of priority areas or candidate species may be flawed.

How can models that predict the fate of birds in mountain landscapes under climate and land-use change be improved? The sections above have foreshadowed the suggestions here. First, modelling bird responses to climate change will need to include more of the key non-environmental, biological parameters known to influence species distributions and demography. Particularly important will be models that incorporate information about the distributions of competitors, mutualists and other elements of the biotic environment. New jSDMs are now available to incorporate these aspects, but a number of important challenges remain (Poggiato et al. 2021). Dispersal and habitat selection are also critical parameters to include in order to enable more accurate forecasting of avian distributions under climate change. 'Process-based' models that incorporate dispersal have been available for some time (Morin et al. 2007). Models that account for imperfect detection, including dynamic occupancy models (MacKenzie et al. 2003), open-population Dail-Madsen models (Dynamic N-mixture Models; Dail & Madsen 2011; Hostetler & Chandler 2015) and multi-state dynamic occupancy models (MacKenzie et al. 2009) are often used to explicitly include population processes. Some of these would allow for the spatially explicit modelling of dispersal processes (Sutherland et al. 2014; Broms et al. 2016). These models were developed to model dynamic processes in abundance and occurrence of unmarked populations, hence they have their own limitations for estimating demographic parameters that would be available from a marked population study (i.e., true mortality/survival, fecundity, immigration and emigration). More recent developments even enable emigration to be distinguished from survival and reproduction, although restrictive assumptions about dispersal capability remain (Zhao et al. 2017).

Given the wide range of uncertainty about the scale(s) and drivers associated with bird dispersal and other demographic processes, such highly parameterized models can still be a challenge to produce for many species, particularly migratory species. Only now are we seeing the first models that incorporate changes in habitat and climate across the full annual cycle (breeding, migration and wintering locations; Culp et al. 2017; Rushing et al. 2020). The ecology of natal dispersal and breeding dispersal processes of long-distance migrant species remains as a big gap in our knowledge of population processes for many smaller migratory species.

Increasing accessibility to Bayesian approaches, combined with developments in hierarchical, multilevel models, would open more windows for explicitly modelling processes that could improve prediction for occupancy or abundance of mountain birds in the future (Kéry & Royle 2016). Nevertheless, these 'mechanistic' or 'process-based' models would require well-thought designs that can address the potential biases and errors associated with mountain environments. Additional field data collection is critical for improved analysis of relationships between distributions of mountain bird species and the ecological processes that drive them, and hence better predictions. In this context, elevational gradients are crucial to predict the effect of climate change, as they provide a potential space-for-time substitution, which is frequently needed because of the widespread lack of historical data to determine rates of change in elevational distributions. Of course, such space-for-time data come with the assumption that mechanisms operating across space adequately reflect the same mechanisms over time.

A robust approach must therefore include, as some of its irreplaceable features:

1. elevational gradients and microtopography (i.e., aspect, slope, elevational position), along with other variables of interest, such as vegetation and microclimate;
2. the temporal gradient, as the phenology of plants and animals in the mountain environment changes along the elevational gradient and across different topographies;
3. stratified sampling to take into account potential biases, elevation and topography;
4. the interactions among species and among biotic and abiotic environmental drivers;
5. a range of climate change and land-cover change scenarios, which would be necessary to predict potential range change and available habitat change in the future.

8.4.4 Implications for Conservation

Distribution, habitat and community modelling are powerful tools for conservationists. However, as described in this chapter, the complexities and challenges of modelling avian species in mountains make the use of such tools potentially more difficult in these environments and call for additional caution. Evaluating the ecological realism of models and their transferability over independent data (ideally, distant areas) may give indications about their potential reliability and robustness in the face of the complexities that characterize mountain systems. Reliable models should show both realistic evaluations of the species-environment relationships and the ability to predict distributions based on independent data. Such models are likely to be the most useful to predict distributions under different scenarios (e.g., future climates) and hence for conservation, when it comes to identifying potential climate refugia (Brambilla *et al.* 2022) or future conflicts with human activities (Brambilla *et al.* 2016). Disentangling the effects of climate and other environmental changes is very important (Ceresa *et al.* 2021), not only for modelling and predicting current and future impacts, but also for conservation-oriented management of mountain environments, because climate change is a particular concern for mountain ecosystems (Nogués-Bravo *et al.* 2007). Long-term monitoring data can help distinguish the effects of climate change from other environmental changes. If birds are tracking habitat rather than climate, then *ad hoc* habitat management (e.g., Brambilla *et al.* 2018a) or targeted habitat conservation or restoration (e.g., Braunisch *et al.* 2016) may greatly enhance their persistence probabilities under a changing climate. However, if birds are mostly affected by climate, modelling trends of relevant climatic variables becomes crucial to conservation because of their direct effect (e.g., impact of heat waves on model species and the non-uniform spatio-temporal patterns at the regional scale, Cunningham *et al.* 2013).

Scales also matter: if microclimate and microhabitats play a crucial role in driving distributions of mountain species (e.g., Frey *et al.* 2016b; Ceresa *et al.* 2020), fostering generalizable models at fine scales could promote conservation too, by allowing the identification of the characteristics (and their spatial arrangement) that make a site suitable for a species (e.g., Barras *et al.* 2020; Alessandrini *et al.* 2022). On the other hand, at the landscape level, potential climate refugia (Morelli *et al.* 2020), and the main 'corridors' connecting them from current to future occurrence sites (Brambilla *et al.* 2017b), represent key elements for conservation planning at this larger scale (Morelli *et al.* 2017). These elements provide significant advances compared to static visions of sites of conservation relevance, and can be used to test for the robustness of networks of protected areas in the face of climate change (e.g., Scridel *et al.* 2021). Combining modelling outcomes from multiple scales may allow prediction of local priority areas for conservation, that is, suitable microhabitats, microclimates and fine-scale refugia, within landscape units that are, and/or will be, suitable for a target species or community under current and future conditions, that is, 'landscape-scale' refugia (Brambilla *et al.* 2022).

Ideally, such approaches, usually based on (multiple) species-specific models, should be complemented with models describing the likely changes of species diversity and community traits. This would allow development of conservation strategies aimed at maintaining highly diverse and functionally unique species assemblages.

Acknowledgements

We are grateful to two anonymous reviewers for constructive comments on a first draft of the chapter. We are also indebted to several colleagues and co-authors for their irreplaceable contribution in developing studies on mountain bird distributions and communities. Data for Plate 6 were provided by the HJ Andrews Experimental Forest and Long Term Ecological Research programme, administered cooperatively by the USDA Forest Service Pacific Northwest Research Station, Oregon State University and the Willamette National Forest. This material is based upon work supported by the National Science Foundation under Grant No. DEB-1440409.

References

Alessandrini, C., Scridel, D., Boitani, L., Pedrini, P. & Brambilla, M. (2022) Remotely sensed variables explain microhabitat selection and reveal buffering behaviours against warming in a climate-sensitive bird species. *Remote Sensing in Ecology and Conservation,* **8**, 615–628.

Altamirano, T.A., de Zwaan, D.R., Ibarra, J.T., Wilson, S. & Martin, K. (2020) Treeline ecotones shape the distribution of avian species richness and functional diversity in south temperate mountains. *Scientific Reports,* **10**, 1–13.

Amano, T., Lamming, J.D.L. & Sutherland, W.J. (2016) Spatial gaps in global biodiversity information and the role of Citizen Science. *Bioscience,* **66**, 393–400.

Anderson, M.J., Crist, T.O., Chase, J.M. *et al.* (2011) Navigating the multiple meanings of β diversity: a roadmap for the practicing ecologist. *Ecology Letters,* **14**, 19–28.

Araújo, M.B. & Guisan, A. (2006) Five (or so) challenges for species distribution modelling. *Journal of Biogeography,* **33**, 1677–1688.

Araújo, M.B., Anderson, R.P., Barbosa, A.M., *et al.* (2019) Standards for distribution models in biodiversity assessments. *Science Advances,* **5**, eaat4858.

Araújo, M.B. & Pearson, R.G. (2005) Equilibrium of species' distributions with climate. *Ecography,* **28**, 693–695.

Bahn, V. & Mcgill, B.J. (2007) Can niche-based distribution models outperform spatial interpolation? *Global Ecology and Biogeography,* **16**, 733–742.

Barras, A.G., Marti, S., Ettlin, S., *et al.* (2020) The importance of seasonal environmental factors in the foraging habitat selection of Alpine Ring Ouzels *Turdus torquatus alpestris. Ibis,* **162**, 505–519.

Barras, A.G., Liechti, F. & Arlettaz, R. (2021a) Seasonal and daily movement patterns of an alpine passerine suggest high flexibility in relation to environmental conditions. *Journal of Avian Biology,* **52**, e02860.

Barras, A.G., Braunisch, V. & Arlettaz, R. (2021b) Predictive models of distribution and abundance of a threatened mountain species show that impacts of climate change overrule those of land use change. *Diversity and Distributions,* **27**, 989–1004.

Barve, S., Ramesh, V., Dotterer, T.M. & Dove, C.J. (2021) Elevation and body size drive convergent variation in thermo-insulative feather structure of Himalayan birds. *Ecography*, **44**, 680–689

Bastianelli, G., Wintle, B.A., Martin, E.H., Seoane, J. & Laiolo, P. (2017) Species partitioning in a temperate mountain chain: segregation by habitat vs. interspecific competition. *Ecology and Evolution*, **7**, 2685–2696.

Besag, J., York, J. & Mollié, A. (1991) Bayesian image restoration, with two applications in spatial statistics. *Annals of the Institute of Statistical Mathematics*, **43**, 1–20.

Bettega, C., Fernández-González, Á., Ramón Obeso, J. & Delgado, M.D.M. (2020) Circannual variation in habitat use of the White-winged Snowfinch *Montifringilla nivalis nivalis*. *Ibis*, **162**, 1251–1261.

Betts, M.G., Hadley, A.S., Rodenhouse, N. & Nocera, J.J. (2008) Social information trumps vegetation structure in breeding-site selection by a migrant songbird. *Proceedings of the Royal Society Series B*, **275**, 2257–2263.

Betts, M.G., Gutierrez Illan, J., Thomas, C.D., Shirley, S. & Yang, Z. (2019) Synergistic effects of climate and land-cover change on long-term bird population trends of the western USA. *Frontiers in Ecology and Evolution*, **7**, 186.

Borcard, D. & Legendre, P. (2002) All-scale spatial analysis of ecological data by means of principal coordinates of neighbour matrices. *Ecological Modelling*, **153**, 51–68.

Bowler, D.E., Nilsen, E.B., Bischof, R., *et al.* (2019) Integrating data from different survey types for population monitoring of an endangered species: the case of the Eld's deer. *Scientific Reports*, **9**, 7766.

Boyce, A.J., Shakya, S., Sheldon, F.H., Moyle, R.G. & Martin, T.E. (2019) Biotic interactions are the dominant drivers of phylogenetic and functional structure in bird communities along a tropical elevational gradient. *Auk*, **136**, ukz054.

Bradter, U., Thom, T.J., Altringham, J.D., Kunin, W.E. & Benton, T.G. (2011) Prediction of National Vegetation Classification communities in the British uplands using environmental data at multiple spatial scales, aerial images and the classifier random forest. *Journal of Applied Ecology*, **48**, 1057–1065.

Bradter, U., Kunin, W.E., Altringham, J.D., Thom, T.J. & Benton, T.G. (2013) Identifying appropriate spatial scales of predictors in species distribution models with the random forest algorithm. *Methods in Ecology and Evolution*, **4**, 167–174.

Bradter, U., Mair, L., Jönsson, M., *et al.* (2018) Can opportunistically collected Citizen Science data fill a data gap for habitat suitability models of less common species? *Methods in Ecology and Evolution*, **9**, 1667–1678.

Bradter, U., Ozgul, A., Griesser, M., *et al.* (2021) Habitat suitability models based on opportunistic citizen science data: evaluating forecasts from alternative methods versus an individual-based model. *Diversity and Distributions*, **27**, 2397–2411.

Brambilla, M. & Pedrini, P. (2011) Intra-seasonal changes in local pattern of Corncrake *Crex crex* occurrence require adaptive conservation strategies in Alpine meadows. *Bird Conservation International*, **21**, 388–393.

Brambilla, M. & Rubolini, D. (2009) Intra-seasonal changes in distribution and habitat associations of a multi-brooded bird species: implications for conservation planning. *Animal Conservation*, **12**, 71–77.

Brambilla, M. & Saporetti, F. (2014) Modelling distribution of habitats required for different uses by the same species: implications for conservation at the regional scale. *Biological Conservation*, **174**, 39–46.

Brambilla, M., Bassi, E., Ceci, C. & Rubolini, D. (2010) Environmental factors affecting patterns of distribution and co-occurrence of two competing raptor species. *Ibis*, **152**, 310–322.

Brambilla, M., Pedrini, P., Rolando, A. & Chamberlain, D.E. (2016) Climate change will increase the potential conflict between skiing and high-elevation bird species in the Alps. *Journal of Biogeography*, **43**, 2299–2309.

Brambilla, M., Cortesi, M., Capelli, F., *et al.* (2017a) Foraging habitat selection by Alpine White-winged Snowfinches *Montifringilla nivalis* during the nestling rearing period. *Journal of Ornithology*, **158**, 277–286.

Brambilla, M., Caprio, E., Assandri, G., *et al.* (2017b) A spatially explicit definition of conservation priorities according to population resistance and resilience, species importance and level of threat in a changing climate. *Diversity and Distributions*, **23**, 727–738.

Brambilla, M., Resano-Mayor, J., Scridel, D. *et al.* (2018a) Past and future impact of climate change on foraging habitat suitability in a high-alpine bird species: management options to buffer against global warming effects. *Biological Conservation*, **221**, 209–218.

Brambilla, M., Capelli, F., Anderle, M., *et al.* (2018b) Landscape-associated differences in fine-scale habitat selection modulate the potential impact of climate change on White-winged Snowfinch *Montifringilla nivalis*. *Bird Study*, **65**, 525–532.

Brambilla, M., Gustin, M., Cento, M., Ilahiane, L. & Celada, C. (2019a) Predicted effects of climate factors on mountain species are not uniform over different spatial scales. *Journal of Avian Biology*, **50**, e02162.

Brambilla, M., Scridel, D., Sangalli, B., *et al.* (2019b) Ecological factors affecting foraging behaviour during nestling rearing in a high-elevation species, the White-winged Snowfinch (*Montifringilla nivalis*). *Ornis Fennica*, **96**, 142–151.

Brambilla, M., Scridel, D., Bazzi, G., *et al.* (2020a) Species interactions and climate change: how the disruption of species co-occurrence will impact on an avian forest guild. *Global Change Biology*, **26**, 1212–1224.

Brambilla, M., Gustin, M., Cento, M., Ilahiane, L. & Celada, C. (2020b) Habitat, climate, topography and management differently affect occurrence in declining avian species: implications for conservation in changing environments. *Science of the Total Environment*, **742**, 140663.

Brambilla, M., Resano-Mayor, J., Arlettaz, R., *et al.* (2020c) Potential distribution of a climate sensitive species, the White-winged Snowfinch *Montifringilla nivalis* in Europe. *Bird Conservation International*, **30**, 522–532.

Brambilla, M., Gubert, F. & Pedrini, P. (2021) The effects of farming intensification on an iconic grassland bird species, or why mountain refuges no longer work for farmland biodiversity. *Agriculture, Ecosystems & Environment*, **319**, 107518.

Brambilla, M., Rubolini, D., Appukuttan, O., *et al.* (2022) Identifying climate refugia for high-elevation Alpine birds under current climate warming predictions. *Global Change Biology*, **28**, 4276–4291.

Braunisch, V., Patthey, P. & Arlettaz, R. (2011) Spatially explicit modeling of conflict zones between wildlife and snow sports: prioritizing areas for winter refuges. *Ecological Applications*, **21**, 955–967.

Braunisch, V., Coppes, J., Arlettaz, R., *et al.* (2013) Selecting from correlated climate variables: a major source of uncertainty for predicting species distributions under climate change. *Ecography*, **36**, 971–983.

Braunisch, V., Coppes, J., Arlettaz, R., *et al.* (2014) Temperate mountain forest biodiversity under climate change: compensating negative effects by increasing structural complexity. *PLoS ONE*, **9**, e97718.

Braunisch, V., Patthey, P. & Arlettaz, R. (2016) Where to combat shrub encroachment in Alpine timberline ecosystems: combining remotely sensed vegetation information with species habitat modelling. *PLoS ONE*, **11**, e0164318.

Broms, K.M., Hooten, M.B., Johnson, D.S., *et al.* (2016) Dynamic occupancy models for explicit colonization processes. *Ecology*, **97**, 194–204.

Burner, R.C., Boyce, A.J., Bernasconi, D., *et al.* (2020) Biotic interactions help explain variation in elevational range limits of birds among Bornean mountains. *Journal of Biogeography*, **47**, 760–771.

Ceresa, F., Brambilla, M., Monrós, J.S. & Kranebitter, P. (2020) Within-season movements of Alpine songbird distributions are driven by fine-scale environmental characteristics. *Scientific Reports*, **10**, 5747.

Ceresa, F., Kranebitter, P., Monrós, J.S., Rizzolli, F. & Brambilla, M. (2021) Disentangling direct and indirect effects of local temperature on abundance of mountain birds and implications for understanding global change impacts. *PeerJ*, **9**, e12560.

Chamberlain, D., Arlettaz, R., Caprio, E., *et al.* (2012) The altitudinal frontier in avian climate change research. *Ibis*, **154**, 205–209.

Chamberlain, D.E., Negro, M., Caprio, E. & Rolando, A. (2013) Assessing the sensitivity of alpine birds to potential future changes in habitat and climate to inform management strategies. *Biological Conservation*, **167**, 127–135.

Chamberlain, D., Brambilla, M., Caprio, E., Pedrini, P. & Rolando, A. (2016) Alpine bird distributions along elevation gradients: the consistency of climate and habitat effects across geographic regions. *Oecologia*, **181**, 1139–1150.

Chmura, H.E., Glass, T.W. & Williams, C.T. (2018) Biologging physiological and ecological responses to climatic variation: new tools for the climate change era. *Frontiers in Ecology and Evolution*, **6**, 92.

Crase, B., Liedloff, A., Vesk, P.A., Fukuda, Y. & Wintle, B.A. (2014) Incorporating spatial autocorrelation into species distribution models alters forecasts of climate-mediated range shifts. *Global Change Biology*, **20**, 2566–2579.

Culp, L.A., Cohen, E.B., Scarpignato, A.L., Thogmartin, W.E. & Marra, P.P. (2017) Full annual cycle climate change vulnerability assessment for migratory birds. *Ecosphere*, **8**, e01565.

Cunningham, S.J., Kruger, A.C., Nxumalo, M.P. & Hockey, P.A. (2013). Identifying biologically meaningful hot-weather events using threshold temperatures that affect life-history. *PLoS ONE*, **8**, e82492.

D'Elia, J., Haig, S.M., Johnson, M., Marcot, B.G. & Young, R. (2015) Activity-specific ecological niche models for planning reintroductions of California condors (*Gymnogyps californianus*). *Biological Conservation*, **184**, 90–99.

Dail, D. & Madsen, L. (2011) Models for estimating abundance from repeated counts of an open metapopulation. *Biometrics*, **67**, 577–587.

Danchin, É., Giraldeau, L.A., Valone, T.J. & Wagner, R.H. (2004) Public information: from nosy neighbors to cultural evolution. *Science*, **305**, 487–491.

de Frenne, P., Lenoir, J., Luoto, M., et al. (2021) Forest microclimates and climate change: importance, drivers and future research agenda. *Global Change Biology*, **27**, 2279–2297.

de Gabriel Hernando, M., Fernández-Gil, J., Roa, I., et al. (2021) Warming threatens habitat suitability and breeding occupancy of rear-edge alpine bird specialists. *Ecography*, **44**, 1191–1204.

de Knegt, H.J., Van Langevelde, F., Coughenour, M.B., et al. (2010) Spatial autocorrelation and the scaling of species-environment relationships. *Ecology*, **91**, 2455–2465.

de Zwaan, D.R., Drake, A., Greenwood, J.L. & Martin, K. (2020) Timing and intensity of weather events shape nestling development strategies in three alpine breeding songbirds. *Frontiers in Ecology and Evolution*, **8**, 570034.

Delgado M., Arlettaz, R., Bettega, C., et al. (2021) Spatio-temporal variation in the wintering associations of an alpine bird. *Proceedings of the Royal Society Series B*, **288**, 20210690.

Devictor, V., Julliard, R., Couvet, D. & Jiguet, F. (2008) Birds are tracking climate warming, but not fast enough. *Proceedings of the Royal Society Series B*, **275**, 2743–2748.

Dobrowski, S.Z. (2011) A climatic basis for microrefugia: the influence of terrain on climate. *Global Change Biology*, **17**, 1022–1035.

Dormann, C.F. (2007) Promising the future? Global change projections of species distributions. *Basic and Applied Ecology*, **8**, 387–397.

Dormann, C.F., Schymanski, S.J., Cabral, J., et al. (2012) Correlation and process in species distribution models: bridging a dichotomy. *Journal of Biogeography*, **39**, 2119–2131.

Dormann, C.F., Bobrowski, M., Dehling, D.M., et al. (2018) Biotic interactions in species distribution modelling: 10 questions to guide interpretation and avoid false conclusions. *Global Ecology and Biogeography*, **27**, 1004–1016.

Dray, S., Legendre, P. & Peres-Neto, P.R. (2006) Spatial modelling: a comprehensive framework for principal coordinate analysis of neighbour matrices (PCNM). *Ecological Modelling*, **196**, 483–493.

Duclos, T.R., DeLuca, W.V. & King, D.I. (2019) Direct and indirect effects of climate on bird abundance along elevation gradients in the Northern Appalachian mountains. *Diversity and Distributions*, **25**, 1670–1683.

Elith, J., Graham, C.H., Anderson, R.P., et al. (2006) Novel methods improve prediction of species' distributions from occurrence data. *Ecography*, **29**, 129–151.

Elith, J., Phillips, S.J., Hastie, T., et al. (2011) A statistical explanation of MaxEnt for ecologists. *Diversity and Distributions*, **17**, 43–57.

Elsen, P.R. & Tingley, M.W. (2015) Global mountain topography and the fate of montane species under climate change. *Nature Climate Change*, **5**, 772–776.

Engler, J.O., Stiels, D., Schidelko, K., et al. (2017) Avian SDMs: current state, challenges, and opportunities. *Journal of Avian Biology*, **48**, 1483–1504.

Ewing, S.R., Baxter, A., Wilson, J.D., *et al.* (2020) Clinging on to alpine life: investigating factors driving the uphill range contraction and population decline of a mountain breeding bird. *Global Change Biology*, **26**, 3771–3787.

Eyres, A., Böhning-Gaese, K. & Fritz, S.A. (2017) Quantification of climatic niches in birds: adding the temporal dimension. *Journal of Avian Biology*, **48**, 1517–1531.

Feilhauer, H., Thonfeld, F., Faude, U., *et al.* (2013) Assessing floristic composition with multispectral sensors – A comparison based on monotemporal and multiseasonal field spectra. *International Journal of Applied Earth Observation and Geoinformation*, **21**, 218–229.

Feldmeier, S., Schmidt, B.R., Zimmermann, N.E., *et al.* (2020) Shifting aspect or elevation? The climate change response of ectotherms in a complex mountain topography. *Diversity and Distributions*, **26**, 1483–1495.

Fithian, W., Elith, J., Hastie, T. & Keith, D.A. (2015) Bias correction in species distribution models: pooling survey and collection data for multiple species. *Methods in Ecology and Evolution*, **6**, 424–438.

Fletcher Jr, R.J., Hefley, T.J., Robertson, E.P., *et al.* (2019) A practical guide for combining data to model species distributions. *Ecology*, **100**, e02710.

Fourcade, Y., Besnard, A.G. & Secondi, J. (2018) Paintings predict the distribution of species, or the challenge of selecting environmental predictors and evaluation statistics. *Global Ecology and Biogeography*, **27**, 245–256.

Freeman, B.G., Tobias, J.A. & Schluter, D. (2019) Behavior influences range limits and patterns of coexistence across an elevational gradient in tropical birds. *Ecography*, **42**, 1832–1840.

Frey, S.J.K., Hadley, A.S., Betts, M.G. & Robertson, M. (2016a) Microclimate predicts within-season distribution dynamics of montane forest birds. *Diversity and Distributions*, **22**, 944–959.

Frey, S.J.K., Hadley, A.S., Johnson, S.L., *et al.* (2016b) Spatial models reveal the microclimatic buffering capacity of old-growth forests. *Science Advances*, **2**, e1501392.

García-Navas, V., Sattler, T., Schmid, H. & Ozgul, A. (2020) Temporal homogenization of functional and beta diversity in bird communities of the Swiss Alps. *Diversity and Distributions*, **26**, 900–911.

Gaspard, G., Kim, D. & Chun, Y. (2019) Residual spatial autocorrelation in macroecological and biogeographical modeling: a review. *Journal of Ecology and Environment*, **43**, 1–11.

Gehrig-Fasel, J., Guisan, A. & Zimmermann, N.E. (2007) Tree line shifts in the Swiss Alps: climate change or land abandonment? *Journal of Vegetation Science*, **18**, 571–582.

Goljani Amirkhiz, R., Dixon, M.D., Palmer, J.S. & Swanson, D.L. (2021) Investigating niches and distribution of a rare species in a hierarchical framework: Virginia's Warbler (*Leiothlypis virginiae*) at its northeastern range limit. *Landscape Ecology*, **36**, 1039–1054.

Guélat, J. & Kéry, M. (2018) Effects of spatial autocorrelation and imperfect detection on species distribution models. *Methods in Ecology and Evolution*, **9**, 1614–1625.

Guisan, A. & Thuiller, W. (2005) Predicting species distribution: offering more than simple habitat models. *Ecology Letters*, **8**, 993–1009.

Guisan, A., Graham C. & Elith, J. (2007) Sensitivity of predictive species distribution models to change in grain size. *Diversity and Distributions,* **13,** 332–340.

Hadley, A.S. & Betts, M.G. (2009) Tropical deforestation alters hummingbird movement patterns. *Biology Letters,* **5,** 207–210.

Hannah, L., Flint, L., Syphard, A.D., *et al.* (2014) Fine-grain modeling of species' response to climate change: holdouts, stepping-stones, and microrefugia. *Trends in Ecology & Evolution,* **29,** 390–397.

Hawkins, B.A. (2012) Eight (and a half) deadly sins of spatial analysis. *Journal of Biogeography,* **39,** 1–9.

He, K.S., Bradley, B.A., Cord, A.F., *et al.* (2015) Will remote sensing shape the next generation of species distribution models? *Remote Sensing in Ecology and Conservation,* **1,** 4–18.

Heikkinen, R.K., Luoto, M., Virkkala, R., Pearson, R.G. & Körber, J. (2007) Biotic interactions improve prediction of boreal bird distributions at macroscales. *Global Ecology and Biogeography,* **16,** 754–763.

Hirzel, A.H., Posse, B., Oggier, P.A., *et al.* (2004) Ecological requirements of reintroduced species and the implications for release policy: the case of the bearded vulture. *Journal of Applied Ecology,* **41,** 1103–1116.

Hochachka, W.M., Fink, D., Hutchinson, R.A., *et al.* (2012) Data-intensive science applied to broad-scale citizen science. *Trends in Ecology & Evolution,* **27,** 130–137.

Hoffmann, D., Vasconcelos, M.F. de & Martins, R.P. (2015) How climate change can affect the distribution range and conservation status of an endemic bird from the highlands of eastern Brazil: the case of the Gray-backed Tachuri, *Polystictus superciliaris* (Aves, Tyrannidae). *Biota Neotropica,* **15,** e20130075.

Hostetler, J.A. & Chandler, R.B. (2015) Improved state-space models for inference about spatial and temporal variation in abundance from count data. *Ecology,* **96,** 1713–1723.

Hotta, M., Tsuyama, I., Nakao, K., *et al.* (2019) Modeling future wildlife habitat suitability: serious climate change impacts on the potential distribution of the rock ptarmigan *Lagopus muta japonica* in Japan's northern Alps. *BMC Ecology,* **19,** 23.

Huber, N., Kienast, F., Ginzler, C. & Pasinelli, G. (2016) Using remote-sensing data to assess habitat selection of a declining passerine at two spatial scales. *Landscape Ecology,* **31,** 1919–1937.

Illán, J.G., Thomas, C.D., Jones, J.A., *et al.* (2014) Precipitation and winter temperature predict long-term range-scale abundance changes in Western North American birds. *Global Change Biology,* **20,** 3351–3364.

Isaac, N.J.B., van Strien, A.J., August, T.A., de Zeeuw, M.P. & Roy, D.B. (2014) Statistics for citizen science: extracting signals of change from noisy ecological data. *Methods in Ecology and Evolution,* **5,** 1052–1060.

Isaac, N.J.B., Jarzyna, M.A., Keil, P., *et al.* (2020) Data integration for large-scale models of species distributions. *Trends in Ecology & Evolution,* **35,** 56–67.

Jackson, M.M., Gergel, S.E. & Martin, K. (2015) Citizen science and field survey observations provide comparable results for mapping Vancouver Island white-tailed ptarmigan (*Lagopus leucura saxatilis*) distributions. *Biological Conservation,* **181,** 162–172.

Jähnig, S., Alba, R., Vallino, C., et al. (2018) The contribution of broadscale and finescale habitat structure to the distribution and diversity of birds in an Alpine forest-shrub ecotone. *Journal of Ornithology*, **159**, 747–759.

Jankowski, J.E., Londoño, G.A., Robinson, S.K. & Chappell, M.A. (2013) Exploring the role of physiology and biotic interactions in determining elevational ranges of tropical animals. *Ecography*, **36**, 1–12.

Jantz, S.M., Barker, B., Brooks, T.M., et al. (2015) Future habitat loss and extinctions driven by land-use change in biodiversity hotspots under four scenarios of climate-change mitigation. *Conservation Biology*, **29**, 1122–1131.

Jedlikowski, J., Chibowski, P., Karasek & T. & Brambilla, M. (2016) Multi-scale habitat selection in highly territorial bird species: exploring the contribution of nest, territory and landscape levels to site choice in breeding rallids (Aves: Rallidae). *Acta Oecologica*, **73**, 10–20.

Johnston, A., Fink, D., Hochachka, W.M. & Kelling, S. (2018) Estimates of observer expertise improve species distributions from citizen science data. *Methods in Ecology and Evolution*, **9**, 88–97.

Johnston, A., Hochachka, W.M., Strimas-Mackey, M.E., et al. (2021) Analytical guidelines to increase the value of community science data: an example using eBird data to estimate species distributions. *Diversity and Distributions*, **27**, 1265–1277.

Jombart, T., Dray, S. & Dufour, A.B. (2009) Finding essential scales of spatial variation in ecological data: a multivariate approach. *Ecography*, **32**, 161–168.

Joseph, L.N., Elkin, C., Martin, T.G. & Possingham, H.P. (2009) Modeling abundance using N-mixture models: the importance of considering ecological mechanisms. *Ecological Applications*, **19**, 631–642.

Kammann, E.E. & Wand, M.P. (2003) Geoadditive models. *Journal of the Royal Statistical Society: Series C (Applied Statistics)*, **52**, 1–18.

Kearney, M.R., Gillingham, P.K., Bramer, I., Duffy, J.P. & Maclean, I.M.D. (2020) A method for computing hourly, historical, terrain-corrected microclimate anywhere on earth. *Methods in Ecology and Evolution*, **11**, 38–43.

Keller, V., Herrando, S., Voříšek, P., et al. (2020) *European Breeding Bird Atlas 2: Distribution, Abundance and Change*. Barcelona: European Bird Census Council & Lynx Edicions.

Kerr, G.D., Bull, C.M. & Cottrell, G.R. (2004) Use of an "on board" datalogger to determine lizard activity patterns, body temperature and microhabitat use for extended periods in the field. *Wildife Research*, **31**, 171–176.

Kéry, M. & Royle, J.A. (2016). *Applied Hierarchical Modeling in Ecology: Analysis of Distribution, Abundance and Species Richness in R and BUGS: Volume 1: Prelude and Static Models*. Amsterdam: Elsevier/AP.

Kéry, M., Gardner, B. & Monnerat, C. (2010a) Predicting species distributions from checklist data using site-occupancy models. *Journal of Biogeography*, **37**, 1851–1862.

Kéry, M., Royle, J.A., Schmid, H., et al. (2010b) Site-occupancy distribution modeling to correct population-trend estimates derived from opportunistic observations. *Conservation Biology*, **24**, 1388–1397.

Kim, Y., Still, C.J., Roberts, D.A. & Goulden, M.L. (2018) Thermal infrared imaging of conifer leaf temperatures: comparison to thermocouple measurements and assessment of environmental influences. *Agricultural and Forest Meteorology*, **248**, 361–371.

Kim, H., McComb, B.C., Frey, S.J., Bell, D.M. & Betts, M.G. (2022) Forest microclimate and composition mediate long-term trends of breeding bird populations. *Global Change Biology*, **28**, 6180–6193.

Knaus, P., Antoniazza, S., Wechsler, S., *et al.* (2018) Swiss Breeding Bird Atlas 2013–2016. *Distribution and Population Trends of Birds in Switzerland and Liechtenstein.* Sempach: Swiss Ornithological Institute.

Laiolo, P., Seoane, J., Obeso, J.R. & Illera, J.C. (2017) Ecological divergence among young lineages favours sympatry, but convergence among old ones allows coexistence in syntopy. *Global Ecology and Biogeography*, **26**, 601–608.

Laiolo, P., Pato, J. & Obeso, J.R. (2018) Ecological and evolutionary drivers of the elevational gradient of diversity. *Ecology Letters*, **21**, 1022–1032.

Latimer, C.E. & Zuckerberg, B. (2021) Habitat loss and thermal tolerances influence the sensitivity of resident bird populations to winter weather at regional scales. *Journal of Animal Ecology*, **90**, 317–329.

Lehikoinen, A. & Virkkala, R. (2016) North by north-west: climate change and directions of density shifts in birds. *Global Change Biology*, **22**, 1121–1129.

Lembrechts, J.J., Nijs, I. & Lenoir, J. (2018) Incorporating microclimate into species distribution models. *Ecography*, **42**, 1267–1279.

Lembrechts, J.J., Lenoir, J., Roth, N., *et al.* (2019) Comparing temperature data sources for use in species distribution models: from in-situ logging to remote sensing. *Global Ecology and Biogeography*, **28**, 1578–1596.

Lenoir, J., Hattab, T. & Pierre, G. (2017) Climatic microrefugia under anthropogenic climate change: implications for species redistribution. *Ecography*, **40**, 253–266.

Lillesand, T.M., Kiefer, R.W. & Chipman, J.W. (2008) *Remote Sensing and Image Interpretation, 6th ed.* New York: Wiley.

MacKenzie, D.I., Nichols, J.D., Hines, J.E., Knutson, M.G. & Franklin, A.B. (2003) Estimating site occupancy, colonization, and local extinction when a species is detected imperfectly. *Ecology*, **84**, 823–835.

Mackenzie, D.I., Nichols, J.D., Seamans, M.E. & Gutiérrez, R.J. (2009) Modeling species occurrence dynamics with multiple states and imperfect detection. *Ecology*, **90**, 823–835.

Maclean, I.M., Mosedale, J.R. & Bennie, J.J. (2019) Microclima: an r package for modelling meso-and microclimate. *Methods in Ecology and Evolution*, **10**, 280–290.

Mair, L. & Ruete, A. (2016) Explaining spatial variation in the recording effort of citizen science data across multiple taxa. *PLoS ONE*, **11**, e0147796.

Marcacci, G., Gremion, J., Mazenauer, J., *et al.* (2020) Large-scale versus small-scale agriculture: disentangling the relative effects of the farming system and semi-natural habitats on birds' habitat preferences in the Ethiopian highlands. *Agriculture, Ecosystems & Environment*, **289**, 106737.

Margalida, A., Jiménez, J., Martínez, J.M., *et al.* (2020) An assessment of population size and demographic drivers of the bearded vulture using integrated population models. *Ecological Monographs*, **90**, e01414.

McCain, C.M. (2009) Global analysis of bird elevational diversity. *Global Ecology and Biogeography*, **18**, 346–360.

Meineri, E. & Hylander, K. (2017) Fine-grain, large-domain climate models based on climate station and comprehensive topographic information improve microrefugia detection. *Ecography*, **40**, 1003–1013.

Mertes, K. & Jetz, W. (2018) Disentangling scale dependencies in species environmental niches and distributions. *Ecography*, **41**, 1604–1615.

Mod, H.K., Scherrer, D., Luoto, M. & Guisan, A. (2016) What we use is not what we know: environmental predictors in plant distribution models. *Journal of Vegetation Science*, **27**, 1308–1322.

Morelli, T.L., Maher, S.P., Lim, M.C.W., *et al.* (2017) Climate change refugia and habitat connectivity promote species persistence. *Climate Change Responses*, **4**, 1–12.

Morelli, T.L., Barrows, C.W., Ramirez, A.R., *et al.* (2020) Climate-change refugia: biodiversity in the slow lane. *Frontiers in Ecology and Environment*, **18**, 228–234.

Morin, X., Augspurger, C. & Chuine, I. (2007) Process-based modeling of species' distributions: what limits temperate tree species' range boundaries? *Ecology*, **88**, 2280–2291.

Neate-Clegg, M.H.C., Jones, S.E.I., Tobias, J.A., Newmark, W.D. & Şekercioğlu, Ç.H. (2021) Ecological correlates of elevational range shifts in tropical birds. *Frontiers in Ecology and Evolution*, **9**, 215.

Nogués-Bravo, D., Araújo, M.B., Errea, M.P. & Martínez-Rica, J.P. (2007) Exposure of global mountain systems to climate warming during the twenty-first Century. *Global Environmental Change*, **17**, 420–428.

Perez-Navarro, M.A., Broennimann, O., Esteve, M.A., *et al.* (2021) Temporal variability is key to modelling the climatic niche. *Diversity and Distributions*, **27**, 473–484.

Pernollet, C.A., Korner-Nievergelt, F. & Jenni, L. (2015) Regional changes in the elevational distribution of the Alpine Rock Ptarmigan *Lagopus muta helvetica* in Switzerland. *Ibis*, **157**, 823–836.

Petchey, O.L. & Gaston, K.J. (2002) Functional diversity (FD), species richness and community composition. *Ecology Letters*, **5**, 402–411.

Phillips, S.J., Anderson, R.P. & Schapire, R.E. (2006) Maximum entropy modeling of species geographic distributions. *Ecological Modelling*, **190**, 231–259.

Poggiato, G., Münkemüller, T., Bystrova, D., *et al.* (2021) On the interpretations of joint modeling in community ecology. *Trends in Ecology & Evolution*, **36**, 391–401.

Pollock, L.J., Tingley, R., Morris, W.K., *et al.* (2014) Understanding co-occurrence by modelling species simultaneously with a Joint Species Distribution Model (JSDM). *Methods in Ecology and Evolution*, **5**, 397–406.

Ponti, R., Arcones, A., Ferrer, X. & Vieites, D.R. (2020) Seasonal climatic niches diverge in migratory birds. *Ibis*, **162**, 318–330.

Potter, K.A., Arthur Woods, H. & Pincebourde, S. (2013) Microclimatic challenges in global change biology. *Global Change Biology*, **19**, 2932–2939.

Pypker, T.G., Unsworth, M.H., Mix, A.C., *et al.* (2007) Using nocturnal cold air drainage flow to monitor ecosystem processes in complex terrain. *Ecological Applications*, **17**, 702–714.

Randin, C.F., Engler, R., Normand, S., *et al.* (2009) Climate change and plant distribution: local models predict high-elevation persistence. *Global Change Biology*, **15**, 1557–1569.

Randin, C.F., Ashcroft, M.B., Bolliger, J., *et al.* (2020) Monitoring biodiversity in the Anthropocene using remote sensing in species distribution models. *Remote Sensing of Environment,* **239**, 111626.

Rapinel, S., Mony, C., Lecoq, L., *et al.* (2019) Evaluation of Sentinel-2 time-series for mapping floodplain grassland plant communities. *Remote Sensing of Environment,* **223**, 115–129.

Ratcliffe, D.A. (2010) *Bird Life of Mountain and Upland.* Cambridge: Cambridge University Press.

Resano-Mayor, J., Korner-Nievergelt, F., Vignali, S., *et al.* (2019) Snow cover phenology is the main driver of foraging habitat selection for a high-alpine passerine during breeding: implications for species persistence in the face of climate change. *Biodiversity Conservation,* **28**, 2669–2685.

Revermann, R., Schmid, H., Zbinden, N., Spaar, R. & Schröder, B. (2012) Habitat at the mountain tops: how long can Rock Ptarmigan (*Lagopus muta helvetica*) survive rapid climate change in the Swiss Alps? A multi-scale approach. *Journal of Ornithology,* **153**, 891–905.

Riddell, E.A., Iknayan, K.J., Hargrove, L., *et al.* (2021) Exposure to climate change drives stability or collapse of desert mammal and bird communities. *Science,* **371**, 633–636.

Rodríguez, J.P., Brotons, L., Bustamante, J. & Seoane, J. (2007) The application of predictive modelling of species distribution to biodiversity conservation. *Diversity and Distributions,* **13**, 243–251.

Royle, J.A., Chandler, R.B., Yackulic, C. & Nichols, J.D. (2012) Likelihood analysis of species occurrence probability from presence-only data for modelling species distributions. *Methods in Ecology and Evolution,* **3**, 545–554.

Rushing, C.S., Royle, A.J., Ziolkowski, D.J. & Pardieck, K.L. (2020) Migratory behavior and winter geography drive differential range shifts of eastern birds in response to recent climate change. *Proceeding of the National Academy of Sciences,* **117**, 12897–12903.

Schano, C., Niffenegger, C., Jonas, T. & Korner-Nievergelt, F. (2021) Hatching phenology is lagging behind an advancing snowmelt pattern in a high-alpine bird. *Scientific Reports,* **11**, 1–11.

Schaub, M., Zink, R., Beissmann, H., Sarrazin, F. & Arlettaz, R. (2009) When to end releases in reintroduction programmes: demographic rates and population viability analysis of bearded vultures in the Alps. *Journal of Applied Ecology,* **46**, 92–100.

Scheiner, S.M., Chiarucci, A., Fox, G.A., *et al.* (2011) The underpinnings of the relationship of species richness with space and time. *Ecological Monographs,* **81**, 195–213.

Scherrer, D., Schmid, S. & Körner, C. (2011) Elevational species shifts in a warmer climate are overestimated when based on weather station data. *International Journal of Biometeorology,* **55**, 645–654.

Scridel, D., Brambilla, M., Martin, K., *et al.* (2018) A review and meta-analysis of the effects of climate change on Holarctic mountain and upland bird populations. *Ibis,* **160**, 489–515.

Scridel D., Brambilla, M., de Zwaan, D., *et al.* (2021) A genus at risk: current and future potential distribution of all three *Lagopus* species reveal sensitivity to climate change and efficacy of protected areas. *Diversity and Distributions*, **27**, 1759–1774.

Segurado, P., Araújo, M.B. & Kunin, W.E. (2006) Consequences of spatial autocorrelation for niche-based models. *Journal of Applied Ecology*, **43**, 433–444.

Şekercioğlu, Ç.H., Schneider, S.H., Fay, J.P. & Loarie, S.R. (2008) Climate change, elevational range shifts, and bird extinctions. *Conservation Biology*, **22**, 140–150.

Şekercioğlu, Ç.H., Primack, R.B. & Wormworth, J. (2012) The effects of climate change on tropical birds. *Biological Conservation*, **148**, 1–18.

Şekercioğlu, Ç.H., Wenny, D.G. & Whelan, C.J. (2016) *Why Birds Matter: Avian Ecological Function and Ecosystem Services*. Chicago: University of Chicago Press.

Shaw, D. & Flick, C. (1999) Are resident songbirds stratified within the canopy of a coniferous old-growth forest? *Selbyana*, **20**, 324–331.

Sheldon, K.S., Yang, S. & Tewksbury, J.J. (2011) Climate change and community disassembly: impacts of warming on tropical and temperate montane community structure. *Ecology Letters*, **14**, 1191–1200.

Singer, A., Schweiger, O., Kühn, I. & Johst, K. (2018) Constructing a hybrid species distribution model from standard large-scale distribution data. *Ecological Modelling*, **373**, 39–52.

Sirami, C., Caplat, P., Popy, S., *et al.* (2017) Impacts of global change on species distributions: obstacles and solutions to integrate climate and land use. *Global Ecology and Biogeography*, **26**, 385–394.

Storlie, C., Merino-Viteri, A., Phillips, B., *et al.* (2014) Stepping inside the niche: microclimate data are critical for accurate assessment of species' vulnerability to climate change. *Biology Letters*, **10**, 20140576.

Strinella, E., Scridel, D., Brambilla, M., Schano, C. & Korner-Nievergelt, F. (2020) Potential sex-dependent effects of weather on apparent survival of a high-elevation specialist. *Scientific Reports*, **10**, 8386.

Sullivan, B.L., Wood, C.L., Iliff, M.J., *et al.* (2009) eBird: a citizen-based bird observation network in the biological sciences. *Biological Conservation*, **142**, 2282–2292.

Sutherland, C.S., Elston, D.A. & Lambin, X. (2014) A demographic, spatially explicit patch occupancy model of metapopulation dynamics and persistence. *Ecology*, **95**, 3149–3160.

Thenkabail, P.S., Lyon, J.G. & Huete, A. (2011) Advances in hyperspectral remote sensing of vegetation and agricultural croplands. In *Hyperspectral Remote Sensing of Vegetation*. Thenkabail, P.S. & Lyon, J.G. (eds.). Boca Raton: CRC Press, pp. 3–26.

Thomas, C.D., Cameron, A., Green, R.E., *et al.* (2004) Extinction risk from climate change. *Nature*, **427**, 145–148.

Tingley, M.W., Monahan, W.B., Beissinger, S.R. & Moritz, C. (2009) Birds track their Grinnellian niche through a century of climate change. *Proceedings of the National Academy of Sciences*, **106** (Suppl. 2), 19637–19643.

Tornberg, R., Rytkönen, S., Välimäki, P., Valkama, J. & Helle, P. (2016) Northern Goshawk (*Accipiter gentilis*) may improve Black Grouse breeding success. *Journal of Ornithology*, **157**, 363–370.

Trivedi, M.R., Berry, P.M., Morecroft, M.D. & Dawson, T.P. (2008) Spatial scale affects bioclimate model projections of climate change impacts on mountain plants. *Global Change Biology*, **14**, 1089–1103.

Tuomisto, H. (2010) A diversity of beta diversities: straightening up a concept gone awry. Part 1. Defining beta diversity as a function of alpha and gamma diversity. *Ecography*, **33**, 2–22.

Tye, C.A., McCleery, R.A., Fletcher, R.J., Greene, D.U. & Butryn, R.S. (2017) Evaluating citizen vs. professional data for modelling distributions of a rare squirrel. *Journal of Applied Ecology*, **54**, 628–637.

Urban, M.C., Bocedi, G., Hendry, A.P., *et al.* (2016) Improving the forecast for biodiversity under climate change. *Science*, **353**, aad8466.

Vickery, J.A., Ewing, S.R., Smith, K.W., *et al.* (2014) The decline of Afro-Palaearctic migrants and an assessment of potential causes. *Ibis*, **156**, 1–22.

Villéger, S., Novack-Gottshall, P.M. & Mouillot, D. (2011) The multidimensionality of the niche reveals functional diversity changes in benthic marine biotas across geological time. *Ecology Letters*, **14**, 561–568.

Vincent, C., Fernandes, R.F., Cardoso, A.R., *et al.* (2019) Climate and land-use changes reshuffle politically-weighted priority areas of mountain biodiversity. *Global Ecology and Conservation*, **17**, e00589.

von dem Bussche, J., Spaar, R., Schmid, H. & Schröder, B. (2008) Modelling the recent and potential future spatial distribution of the Ring Ouzel (*Turdus torquatus*) and Blackbird (*T. merula*) in Switzerland. *Journal of Ornithology*, **149**, 529–544.

von Humboldt, A. & Bonpland, J.R. (1807) *Ideen zu einer Geographie der Pflanzen nebst einem Naturgemälde der Tropenländer*. Tübigen: F.G. Costa/F. Schoell.

Wakulińska, M. & Marcinkowska-Ochtyra, A. (2020) Multi-temporal sentinel-2 data in classification of mountain vegetation. *Remote Sensing*, **12**, 2696.

Wenger, S.J. & Olden, J.D. (2012) Assessing transferability of ecological models: an underappreciated aspect of statistical validation. *Methods in Ecology and Evolution*, **3**, 260–267.

White, H.J., Montgomery, W.I., Storchová, L., Hořák & D. & Lennon, J.J. (2018) Does functional homogenization accompany taxonomic homogenization of British birds and how do biotic factors and climate affect these processes? *Ecology and Evolution*, **8**, 7365–7377.

Whittaker, R.H. (1960) Vegetation of the Siskiyou Mountains, Oregon and California. *Ecological Monographs*, **30**, 279–338.

Wolf, C., Bell, D.M., Kim, H., *et al.* (2021) Temporal consistency of undercanopy thermal refugia in old-growth forest. *Agricultural and Forest Meteorology*, **307**, 108520.

Yackulic, C.B., Chandler, R., Zipkin, E.F., *et al.* (2013) Presence-only modelling using MAXENT: when can we trust the inferences? *Methods in Ecology and Evolution*, **4**, 236–243.

Yates, K.L., Bouchet, P.J., Caley, M.J., *et al.* (2018) Outstanding challenges in the transferability of ecological models. *Trends in Ecology & Evolution*, **33**, 790–802.

Yu, H., Luedeling, E. & Xu, J. (2010) Winter and spring warming result in delayed spring phenology on the Tibetan Plateau. *Proceedings of the National Academy of Sciences*, **107**, 22151–22156.

Zellweger, F., Braunisch, V., Baltensweiler, A. & Bollmann, K. (2013) Remotely sensed forest structural complexity predicts multi species occurrence at the landscape scale. *Forest Ecology and Management*, **307**, 303–312.

Zellweger, F., De Frenne, P., Lenoir, J., Rocchini, D. & Coomes, D. (2019) Advances in microclimate ecology arising from remote sensing. *Trends in Ecology & Evolution*, **34**, 327–341.

Zhao, Q., Royle, J.A. & Boomer, G.S. (2017) Spatially explicit dynamic N-mixture models. *Population Ecology*, **59**, 293–300.

Zohmann, M., Pennerstorfer, J. & Nopp-Mayr, U. (2013) Modelling habitat suitability for alpine rock ptarmigan (*Lagopus muta helvetica*) combining object-based classification of IKONOS imagery and Habitat Suitability Index modelling. *Ecological Modelling*, **254**, 22–32.

Zurell, D. (2017) Integrating demography, dispersal and interspecific interactions into bird distribution models. *Journal of Avian Biology*, **48**, 1505–1516.

Zurell, D., Graham, C.H., Gallien, L., Thuiller, W. & Zimmermann, N.E. (2018) Long-distance migratory birds threatened by multiple independent risks from global change. *Nature Climate Change*, **8**, 992–996.

9 · The Alpine Avifauna of Tropical Mountains

JON FJELDSÅ, JESPER SONNE
AND CARSTEN RAHBEK

9.1 Introduction

Alexander von Humboldt was the first to describe how the environmental conditions changed as he ascended from the tropical lowlands to near the peak of Mount Chimborazo in Ecuador in 1802, and to suggest that the elevational ecological gradient was comparable to the latitudinal gradient from the equator towards the poles (von Humboldt & Bonpland 1807). Both gradients have been characterized as a correlation between biodiversity and the contemporary climate (e.g., Stevens 1989; Lomolino 2001), but the variation in species richness with elevation can actually take many forms, most often with a mid-elevation peak (Rahbek 1995; Chapter 1). Recent advances in macroecology have revealed profound differences between high and low latitudes, both in ecological stability, speciation dynamics and life history traits. In a global analysis, where species richness was regressed against productivity, unexpectedly high residual values were found in tropical mountains (Rahbek et al. 2019a, b). Thus, the view of mountains as hotspots of biodiversity and speciation (Rahbek & Graves 2001; Orme et al. 2005; Igea & Tanentzap 2021) applies mainly at low latitudes (Fjeldså et al. 2012).

The biological diversity of the tropical mountains of the world had already been described in the book 'High Altitude Tropical Biogeography' (Vuilleumier & Monasterio 1986). However, with the recent development of large biodiversity databases and new analytical tools, we can now draw conclusions of greater generality, especially concerning how the variation in biodiversity in montane regions was generated over time (Pulido-Santacruz & Weir 2016; Quinteiro & Jetz 2018; Rangel et al. 2018; Jarzyna et al. 2021).

In this chapter, we will focus mainly on how tropical mountains differ from those at higher latitudes. First of all, we need to emphasize some differences in physical conditions between the alpine environments at low and high latitudes. We will then, with reference to new macroecological and macroevolutionary research, look at how this affects rates and patterns of diversification (Box 9.1). We will also review characteristics of the endemic avifauna of high tropical mountains and its narrow association with specific elevational zones. Finally, we will outline the biogeographic history of tropical alpine avifaunas and how evolutionary processes contributed to the build-up of the immense diversity and local turnover of species in tropical mountains.

Box 9.1 *Tropical Mountain Regions are the Avian Hotspots of the World*

Mountain regions are global hotspots of extraordinary richness, with 85 per cent of the world's species of amphibians, birds, and mammals in merely c. 25 per cent of the global land area. Tropical mountain regions hold many species with narrow geographical distributions, and a recent global analysis (Rahbek *et al.* 2019a, b) aimed to identify the driving factors.

Mountain regions that are larger, more productive, and topographically more complex have more species, many more small-ranged species and a greater proportion of mountain endemics than smaller, less productive and topographically more homogeneous mountain regions. However, area, productivity and topographic complexity in themselves are far from enough to explain the enormous species diversity of certain tropical mountain regions. Climate undoubtedly shapes patterns of diversity in time and space through its impact on ecological and evolutionary processes. Mosaics of distinct climates, which can be maintained over time in rugged landscapes in regions with low seasonality, are fundamentally different from the featureless lowlands as well as from environments at higher latitudes. In tropical mountains, distinct climate zones replace each other over very short distances, compared to thousands of kilometres across the latitudinal gradient. Therefore, tropical mountain regions can encompass a remarkable volume of different climate types within relatively small areas. The Northern Andes, the most avian species-rich region in the world, encompass approximately half of the world's temperature–precipitation climate space – much more than the adjacent, much larger, Amazon region (Figure B9.1). The complexity of mountain climates promotes the origination, differentiation and persistence of species while enabling the coexistence of many species with slightly different climatic niches in relatively small areas and facilitates dense packing of species at local scales. Over time, the complexity of the landscapes and local climates combined with long-term climate oscillations and tectonic dynamism led to rapid and repeated splitting (and fusion) of species ranges, thus stimulating diversification. The speciation dynamics are therefore tightly linked with earth history dynamics.

Geological heterogeneity has been suggested to play an important role, but simple metrics of geological heterogeneity only show a weak correlation with species richness in mountains. Interestingly, an empirical pattern has emerged showing that tropical mountain regions with an admixture of rock types that originated deep in the

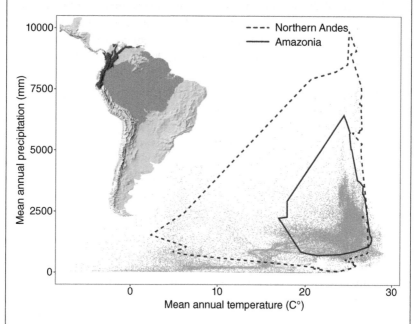

Figure B9.1 A comparison of the climate volume of one particular mountain region (Northern Andes, dark grey area) with the largest tract of tropical lowland forest (Amazon region, light grey area). The Northern Andes encompasses a very large proportion of the continent's climates (dashed line), represented here by dots in 30 arc. sec. resolution of the entire Neotropical land area. The much larger Amazon area encompasses a smaller proportion of the Neotropical climates (solid line).

earth's crust (with unusual mineral compositions and little available phosphorus) are particularly specious (Rahbek *et al.* 2019b). Unusual soil types may constrain plant growth and lead to high levels of phenols and lignin in leaves and could drive specialized dietary adaptations of herbivores and cause evolutionary cascades across trophic levels, including birds. Understanding such relationships will require new kinds of research. Overall, understanding the variation in mountain biodiversity requires in-depth studies of evolutionary and ecological processes.

9.2 Outlining Tropical Alpine Regions

As already emphasized in Chapter 1, there is no simple way of defining mountains or alpine zones. The elevational zonation depends on the mountain mass. The largest tropical highlands have the highest heat retention (the Massenerhebung effect), with timberlines generally located above 3,500 m. In contrast, small tropical mountains under strong oceanic influence can have exceptionally high adiabatic lapse rates, with dripping wet cloud forests from below 1,000 m and timberlines around 2,000 m (Lovett 1993; Foster 2001; Karger *et al.* 2019). Here, the absence of forest near the summits has been associated with nightly freezing conditions (Lovett 1993), but it is difficult to rule out that anthropogenically-set fires also play a role. Many moderate-sized mountains in the interior of Africa have sparsely vegetated habitats as a consequence of dryness, and the low and scrubby vegetation of the Tepuis mountains of Venezuela (at 1,000–3,000 m) can mainly be attributed to nutrient-poor soils. Since the position of timberlines in tropical mountains can have different causes, we found it most practical here to focus on the timberlines of the major mountain ranges, at around 3,500 m, as being the typical borderline towards the tropical alpine zone. However, in order to avoid the inclusion of too many bird species, which are only marginally associated with above-timberline habitats, we will deal only with species that have been recorded breeding at 4,000 m, or above. Thus, we define 'alpine birds' more narrowly than in Chapter 3 (Table 3.1) which includes a range of alpine habitats, from the upper treeline ecotone to the higher alpine and nival zones.

Most attempts to analyze how biological diversification varies with latitude have focused on the Western Hemisphere. An orocline with extensive alpine habitat follows the entire montane 'backbone' of western North and South America, punctuated only in Central America (e.g., Weir *et al.* 2009). This environment provides a high degree of physical connectedness among alpine environments at different latitudes. The situation in the Eastern Hemisphere is strikingly different, as the main mountain ranges are oriented west to east on the borderline between the subtropical and temperate zones, with only scattered and isolated 'sky islands' with alpine habitat within the tropics (Elsen & Tingley 2015; see Plates 1–4). In order to make up for the small area of tropical highlands in the Eastern Hemisphere, we include the Sino-Himalayan Mountains in this overview. However, we recognize that this is a subtropical/temperate inter-zonal borderline (White *et al.* 2019) under the climatic influence of the tropical monsoon system.

9.2.1 The Neotropics

Within the Neotropics, continuous and extensive areas from northern Argentina to northern Peru reach 3,500–5,000 m, as well as smaller and less continuous highlands (páramos) extending from northern Peru to Venezuela, and as isolated mountains in Central America up to the transcontinental volcanic belt of southern Mexico (Chapter 3, Sections 3.2.2–3.2.3). In Bolivia and Peru, the Western Cordillera had already uplifted from the late Eocene, providing plenty of time for the evolution of highland biota. Since the early Neogene, volcanoes and carbonate sediments were accreted along the western plate boundary from Peru to Colombia to form a mountainous 'proto-Andean Peninsula' (Garzione *et al.* 2008) with cool cloud forest environments. However, the uplift of other mountain ranges has been a highly diachronous process (varying in age spatially), and the formation of alpine (páramo) habitats in the northern Andes appeared mainly since the Late Miocene (Pérez-Escobar *et al.* 2022).

9.2.2 The Afrotropics

The mountains of tropical Africa are mostly solitary sky islands (with the fold mountains of North Africa and the Cape regions being outside the tropics; see Chapter 3, Section 3.2.6). Most mountains are capped with forest, and the larger mountains with alpine vegetation on the top have been characterized as an archipelago-like region of extreme biotic impoverishment, widely separated from other alpine zones (White 1978). They comprise scattered volcanoes and up-thrusted blocks of ancient bedrock with variable vegetation types (Rehm & Feeley 2015a), including moderately high plateaus and walls fringing the rift valleys. Huge volcanoes existed from c. 30 million years ago, but the individual volcanoes were rapidly eroded down. Present volcanoes with truly alpine habitats (Kilimanjaro, Mount Meru, Mount Kenya, Mount Elgon, Rwenzori, Virungas, Ethiopia Highlands) are too young to have accumulated significant endemism, except for the larger highland areas in Ethiopia.

9.2.3 Tropical and Subtropical Asia

The landmass above 3,500 m in tropical and subtropical Asia is almost entirely located in the Himalayas and adjacent south-western China, right on the borderline towards the cold highlands in the interior of Asia. The Tibetan Plateau was probably uplifted above 4,000 m in the late Eocene (Favre *et al.* 2015), but the uplift of the Himalayas and Hengduan Mountains came later. Many avian species have their elevation records in Yunnan and western Sichuan, which is outside the subtropics, but which is affected by the monsoon system, as warm and humid air is funneled into the area through the many north–south-oriented valleys. However, mountains at similar latitudes in Pakistan and Iran are outside the influence of these humid winds and will not be discussed here. Southern Asia and the Malaysian Archipelago have only widely scattered, very small and recently uplifted highlands (only Mount Kinabalu on Borneo and a few places in New Guinea exceed 4,000 m).

9.3 The Physical Environment of Tropical Mountains

As first emphasized by Janzen (1967), tropical mountains differ from those at higher latitudes as the seasonal variation in temperature is insignificant compared with the altitudinal temperature gradient (see also Ghalambor *et al.* 2006). The stable temperatures allow for whole-year segregation of species in distinct elevation zones. Such segregation can even be maintained over significant periods of evolutionary time, which implies that groups of closely related species could evolve by isolation in different places within the same elevational zone (Cadena *et al.* 2012; Cadena & Cespedes 2020; Linck *et al.* 2021). It also means that local topographic barriers, or distinct local climates, can significantly isolate local populations and drive the process of biological diversification. For these reasons, tropical mountains have provided fundamentally different evolutionary opportunities from mountains at high latitudes. Firstly, most species could evolve and adapt within local environments, and secondly, they did not have to move thousands of kilometres to track seasonal and long-term climate change.

Because of the slight seasonal variation in solar radiation near the equator (Troll 1959; Sarmiento 1986), the tropical alpine zones have a long growth season (although it is somewhat constrained by seasonal drought stress and El Niño type climatic oscillations). Except on the highest peaks, the ground is rarely covered by snow for more than a few days. At the same time, however, the areas above the timberline experience strong night-day oscillations in temperature, humidity, cloudiness and winds (Hedberg 1964; Sarmiento 1986). Those who have camped for long periods in the tropical mountains will know that diurnal variation is modest as long as they stay under canopy cover, but it changes abruptly if the camp site is moved out in the open, where the nights are freezing cold. Species inhabiting the alpine zone must endure heat stress by day (with soil surface temperatures above 30°C) and freezing conditions by night. With 'day-summer/night-winter' rather than seasonal variation, species can specialize in staying within their preferred elevational zone (Chan *et al.* 2016).

Rainfall tends to decline with elevation, but it can increase in some regions (Bruinzeel *et al.* 2010; Schawe *et al.* 2010). This variation is related to the location of mist zones caused by the interaction of atmospheric flows and local topography. The location of cloud immersion is difficult to predict from generalized climate models (Sayre *et al.* 2020), which assume a uniform lapse-based drop in temperature with elevation and ignore local phenomena such as rain shadow zones or mist zones caused by local atmospheric inversions. A special situation is related to the large wetlands on the high plains of the Central Andes (Junín and the Peruvian–Bolivian Altiplano). Because of the intense solar radiation and thermal capacity of water, all water bodies (except small and shallow ponds) up to 5,000 m elevation remain ice-free throughout the year and have a buffering effect on the local climate, making it milder and moister. The enormous wetlands that existed on the Altiplano during Pleistocene glacial periods appear to have been permanently ice-free (while the surrounding peaks were capped with ice, with glacier tongues extending down below 3,000 m in certain valleys). These persistent wetlands allowed the evolution of distinct biota in the surrounding landscapes (Hansen *et al.* 1984; Fjeldså 1985; Argolfo & Mourguiart 2000).

9.3.1 Tropical Alpine Vegetation

The tropical alpine vegetation is characterized by stiff bunchgrasses and low, matted vegetation where much of the biomass is kept below ground level as a protection against extreme UV radiation and nightly frost (Troll 1959). The flora shares many plant genera with the mountains at higher latitudes, with migratory birds possibly being dispersal agents for some plant groups (e.g., Hedberg 1986). Because of the extreme radiation at the highest elevations, the plants have often evolved bizarre growth forms such that it can be difficult to see their relatedness with congeneric taxa in the lower mountains at high latitudes. Only the flowers remain 'normal', although the flowerheads develop in the top-soil and unfold right on the surface.

Five life forms of plants are recognized in the tropical alpine zone: tussock grasses, which can dominate over vast areas (called 'puna' in the Andes), sclerophyllous scrub ('tola' heaths in the Andes), compact cushion plants (illustrated in Plate 7), acaulescent rosette plants with no visible stem, and some giant rosette plants. The latter type comprises forms with a thick basal stem, often isolated by thick layers of dead leaf sheaths, lifting the leafy parts and the inflorescence above the coldest air near the ground. This plant type includes the famous giant puyas (*Puya* spp.) and espeletias (*Espeletia* spp.) in the Andes (Figure 9.1), and giant *Lobelias* and *Senecio* species, and red-hot pokers (*Kniphofia* spp.), in the Afromontane areas. They are all extremely slow-growing and when they finally bloom, some of these plants have thousands of nectar-producing flowers.

The páramo zone of the northern Andes is floristically unique and extremely diverse, with up to 60 per cent of its 3,000–4,000 plant species being endemic. In terms of rates of evolution of new species, it is the world's fastest evolving biome (Madriñán *et al.* 2013; Hoorn *et al.* 2018), with remarkable numbers of closely related species of *Astragalus*, *Espeletia*, *Hypericum* and *Lupinus*; the latter genus varies from tree-like forms to tiny, prostrate plants with two to three flowers (Hughes & Eastwood 2006). Bogs ('bofedales'), which are characteristic of flat and waterlogged valley bottoms below high ice-capped mountains, have peaty soils and compact cushions of rosette plants (Plate 7). The New Guinea highlands are distinct in terms of very humid conditions (see Chapter 3, Section 3.2.11).

9.3.2 Patches of Woody Vegetation

Above the timberline ('*ceja de monte*' in Andean terminology), a unique vegetation mosaic with small and large thickets ('elfin forests') extends

Figure 9.1 High Andean habitats: A. Humid *Festuca* grassland with flowering *Chuquiragua* scrub at 3,600 m on Cerro de Arcos, southwestern Ecuador (Photo: Jesper Sonne). B. Stands of giant puyas *Puya raimondii*, including an eight-meter tall flowering specimen, and some *Polylepis* trees, in an area with otherwise very short, matted vegetation at 4,160 m near Putina in Puno, Peru (Photo: Jon Fjeldså). C. Páramo vegetation with abundant espeletias, *Espeletia* spp., around 3,500 m on Sumapaz, Colombia (Photo: Jesper Sonne). D. The interior of a *Polylepis* forest at 4,400 m east of Abancay in southern Peru (Photo: Jesper Sonne).

up to the ultimate treeline. This subalpine vegetation (Figure 9.1) is interesting for two reasons: first of all, because it is home to a special guild of birds, with many local endemics. Second, many birds of the cloud forest will move up into this transitional zone at certain times to profit from flowering shrubs, berries and rich insect fauna, and often breed there (Section 9.4). Only plains, where cold air accumulates at night, are devoid of woody vegetation.

Körner (2003) assumed the position of the treeline to be associated with the mean temperature, the 5°C tissue formation threshold. Moreover, Körner & Paulsen (2004) found that mean soil temperatures during the growing season were generally the same (6.4–7.8°C) for treelines all over the world (although it was lower for their three tropical study sites). However, there are many problems with these interpretations (Harsh & Bader 2011; Rehm & Feeley 2015a, b; Bader *et al.* 2017). The nightly freezing conditions make it difficult for trees to germinate in the open land, and the tropical timberlines also appear to be highly modified by human activities, including anthropogenically-set fires, used for hunting or for creating good pasture for livestock (Lægaard 1992; Wakeling *et al.* 2012; van Breugel *et al.* 2015; see also Chapter 4). The effect of burning is often manifested in how distinct patches of trees and scrub are restricted to deep stream ravines, rocky slopes or areas with boulder scree (see Chapter 1, Figure 1.1B), which are avoided by grazing livestock and where fires do not easily spread. In the Andes, some patches of *Polylepis* trees grow arbitrarily on grassy slopes with ordinary compact soils, high up on hillsides and sometimes near villages, suggesting that they have been actively conserved to secure soil humidity, firewood or medicinal plants. Pollen analyses suggest that *Polylepis* woodlands were widespread in many parts of the highlands during the early Holocene (as still seen in the sparsely populated arid puna zone of western Bolivia, where scattered *Polylepis* woodlands can extend up to 5,000 m on some volcanoes; Hoch & Körner 2005). It is now believed that the present distribution of such woodlands is determined primarily by human activities (Kessler & Herzog 1998; Fjeldså 2002). Today, in Peru and Bolivia, a gradual (natural) transition between forest and truly alpine habitat is only observed in very few places (where humans rarely have access), suggesting that human activity has otherwise caused the treelines to be lowered by several hundred meters in elevation.

It is unclear to what extent grasslands on moderate-sized African mountains are natural (determined by climate extremes or edaphic conditions) or caused by human-induced fires (e.g., Wesche *et al.* 2000). Above the timberline, there are occasional patches of *Hagenia* and *Podocarpus* woodlands and a zone of gigantic heathers (*Erica*, *Philippia*) up to 4,100 m. Some places in south-western China have tall coniferous forests well above 4,000 m, and high ridges often have low and gnarled shrubs (*Juniperus*, *Rosa*, *Berberis* and *Cotoneaster* spp., dwarf bamboos and dwarf rhododendrons).

9.4 The Birds of High Tropical Mountains

Defining the avifauna of the tropical alpine zone is not straightforward, since many species are flexible and distributed across many life zones, and they reach the alpine zone only sporadically or locally (Chapters 2 and 3).

Some widespread species, mostly at moderate elevations in the northern temperate zone, reach 4,000 m at the southern border of their geographical range (in the Himalayas or in southern Mexico). However, most of the endemic species of tropical montane environments are quite narrowly associated with specific elevation zones (Linck *et al.* 2021). An immense diversity of species occupies the upper cloud forests of tropical mountains, but the species diversity drops sharply as we pass the timberline. Observations suggest approximately 1,000 avian species breed at 3,500 m, but in order to avoid including too many marginal records of cloud forest birds, we will focus here on those breeding at a minimum elevation of 4,000 m and above. According to our worldwide inventory of elevation distributions (based on on-line data, see Quintero & Jetz 2018 and supplemented by field records by JF), this amounts to 665 avian species, of which 618 are in the tropical and subtropical zones up to the Himalayas. Here, we have excluded some records, such as observations of nuthatches (*Sitta* spp.) and siskins (*Spinus* spp.) in treeless alpine environments, which presumably represent post-breeding dispersal (see Chapter 2).

The tropical alpine avifauna is phylogenetically highly clustered, with most species nested in a few taxonomic groups, while other groups are not represented at all (Table 9.1). Jarzyna *et al.* (2021) demonstrated that there is also a high degree of functional clustering, as many species which co-occur in tropical alpine environments are closely related forms with similar ecological roles. This is the case with the many species of sparrows and finches that co-occur in the high mountains of Asia, and the many sparrow-like tanagers that co-occur in the Andean highlands. In contrast, the avifaunas of high latitude mountains are functionally overdispersed.

The larger highlands have some ancient species, suggesting a long history of accumulation of species diversity (although ancient species are, over all, more characteristic of the lower montane zones). Phylogenetically isolated species in the high parts of the Andes comprise some shorebirds: seedsnipes (*Thinocorus* and *Attagis* spp., the latter browsing on cushion-plants up to the snowline), diademed sandpiper-plover *Phegornis mitchelli*, *Metriopelia* ground-doves, giant hummingbird *Patagona gigas* and white-cheeked cotinga *Zaratornis stresemanni*. Ancient species in Asia are ibisbill *Ibidorhyncha struthersi*, choughs *Pyrrhocorax* spp., Przevalski's finch *Urocynchramus pylzowi*, wallcreeper *Tichodroma muraria* and grandala *Grandala coelicolor*; and in New Guinea, eastern crested berrypecker *Paramythia montium* (see Fjeldså *et al.* 2020 for dated phylogenies).

High tropical mountains have many precocial birds, which comprise some of the most ancient lineages in the phylogeny of modern birds,

Table 9.1 Species diversity and number of species breeding in alpine environments above 4,000 m per taxonomic group (as defined by Cracraft 2013 for non-passerines and Fjeldså et al. 2020 for passerines). The alpine species are divided by geographical region (Neotropics, Afrotropics, tropical Asia and Australasia, Sino-Himalayan Mountains and 'extra-tropical areas'; note that this regionalization differs from that in Chapter 3). Groups where >10 per cent of the species reach 4,000 m are shown in bold type, but note that some avian orders do not reach alpine environments at all. Many Sino-Himalayan species extend their geographical ranges into the highlands of Central Asia or beyond (and some species of the Tropical Andes also occur in the southern cone of the continent). Such species appear in two or more columns, but are placed in brackets where they do not reach 4,000 m.

Taxonomic group	Total species	Spp. above 4,000 m	Neotropics	Afrotropics	Trop.Orient/ Malaysia	Sino-Himalaya	Extratropical
Paleognaths, Ratitae	60	7	7	0	0	0	0
Waterfowl, Anseriformes	168	15	9	3	1	1	4(4)
Landfowl, Galliiformes	298	30	1	3	1(1)	15	15(3)
Flamingos + grebes, Phoenicopterimorphae	29	8	6	1(2)	0(1)	2	4(2)
Nightbirds, Caprimulgiformes (s.s.)	130	1	0	0	0	0	0(1)
Swifts, Apodiformes	117	12	2	2	3(3)	5(1)	1(6)
Hummingbird, Trochiliformes	363	37	37	0	0	0	0(1)
Musophagi-/Otidi-/Cuculiformes	198	1	0	0	0	1	0(1)
Pigeons et al., Columbimorphae	367	14	5	4	0(3)	5	4(4)
Core gruiforms, Gruiformes	189	14	9	2	0(1)	2	4(3)
Shorebirds, Charadriiformes	387	23	14	3	0	4	7(4)
Core waterbirds, Aequornithia	249	8	6	1(2)	0(2)	(1)	1(1)
Hawks, Accipitriformes	266	24	4	10(1)	0(4)	11	7(10)
Owls, Strigiformes	248	16	9	3(1)	1(1)	3	6(7)
Trogoni-/Buceroti-/Coraciiformes	295	0	0	0	0	0	0
Woopeckers et al., Piciformes	445	11	7	4	0(3)	4	5(2)
Falcons, Falconiformes	66	10	5	4	0(3)	4	5(2)

(cont.)

Table 9.1 (*cont.*)

Taxonomic group	Total species	Spp. above 4,000 m	Neotropics	Afrotropics	Trop.Orient/ Malaysia	Sino-Himalaya	Extratropical
Parrots, Psittaciformes	398	5	4	0	0(1)	1	0
Old World suboscines, Eurylaimides	60	0	0	0	0	0	0
Antbirds et al., Thamnophiloidea	253	0	0	0	0	0	0
Antpittas, tapalulos + furnariids, Furnarioidea	453	70	70	0	0	0	2(12)
Manakins, Pipridae + cotingas, Cotingidae	118	2	2	0	0	0	0
New World flycatchers, Tyrannoidea	475	30	28	0	0	0	4(11)
Basal songbirds: Menurides, Climacterides, Meliphagides	294	7	0	0	7	0	0
Crow-like birds, Corvides; excl. Corvidae	685	6	0	0	0(4)	5	1(3)
Crows, Corvidae	133	15	1(1)	5	0(3)	9	2(6)
Deep lineages among higher songbirds, Passerides	108	2	0	0	2	0	0
Tits et al., Paroidea	73	4	0	0	3	2	0
Warblers et al., excl. Phylloscopidae	1129	56	0	1	5(11)	36(2)	15(8)
Leaf warblers, Phylloscopidae	80	15	0	1	(2)	13	8(4)
Creepers and wrens, Certhioidea	166	14	9	0	0	7	1(6)
Mockingbirds, Mimidae, + starlings, Sturnidae	152	3	1	2	0	0	0
Chats, flycatchers, Muscicapidae, + thrushes, Turdidae	482	53	4	9	3(5)	29(2)	18(3)
Sunbirds and other basal passeroids	185	5	0	2	2(1)	2	1
Sparrows, weavers + accentors	403	35	4	2	2(3)	17	22(5)
Finches, Fringillidae	230	46	8	4	4	29	20(12)
New World nine-primaried Oscines	820	64	60	0	0	3	3(9)

such as paleognaths, waterfowl, landfowl (Galliformes), shorebirds and rails. They are characterized by the advanced development of newly hatched young, which (mostly) are mobile and can find their own food. These groups do not follow the general correlation between species diversity and environmental productivity, as their highest species diversity is found in open habitats (savanna, wetlands, tundra and high montane zones; Fjeldså *et al.* 2020). Several species of ducks and geese (Anseriformes) and some rails (Rallidae) and shorebirds (Charadriiformes) are associated with alpine wetlands. Some paleognaths (lesser rhea *Rhea pennata* and tinamous, Tinamidae) inhabit grassland and scrubland in the High Andes. The Himalayas and mountains of south-western China are centers of diversification of gallopheasants (the genera *Lophophorus, Tragopan, Ithaginis, Crossoptilon* and *Catreus*; Cai *et al.* 2018), with many species foraging by digging for subterranean tubers.

Tropical mountains harbour a fair number of species that search for their food in flight, namely swifts, swallows and various raptors. The raptors find safe nest-sites in the rugged alpine landscapes, but include extensive areas of valleys and high plateaus in their hunting territories. Thus, Andean condors *Vultur gryphus*, which breed high up in the cordilleras, may descend daily down to the lowlands or to the Pacific coast to search for carcasses of large animals, including sea lions and dolphins. Among nightjars and their allies, only a single species (the band-winged nightjar *Systellura longirostris* of South America) reaches the alpine zone, and also many other groups of higher land-birds are absent (or virtually so) from this zone (Table 9.1).

9.4.1 Birds of the High Tropical Andes

We recorded 315 species as representatives of the Andean alpine zone. The diversity peak at around 15°S (Figure 9.2) reflects the larger area of alpine habitat in Peru, compared with the more restricted area of páramo habitat in the northern Andes. The Peruvian Andes are also characterized by complex landscapes, with ice-free high-elevation refuges during the Pleistocene and a significant number of range-restricted avian species, even in the alpine zone.

A large number of wetlands in the central and southern Andes are important bird areas because of the large biomass of submerged vegetation and invertebrates which may reflect the generally small populations of competing fish species (Fjeldså 1985), but the northern Andes, and tropical mountains in other parts of the world, have few wetlands and

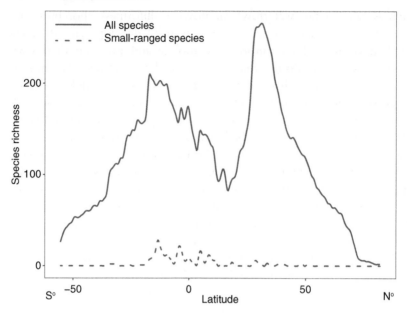

Figure 9.2 Latitudinal variation in the number of species recorded above 4,000 m at least locally within their range. The lower dashed line shows species distributed in only 1–10 map grid-cells of 1 x 1 geographical degrees (corresponding to the quartile of avian species with the smallest geographical distributions). The peak around 30°N derives from the diversity hotspots in the Himalayas and mountains of south-western China. The species diversity near the equator appears less prominent since the individual species have more restricted geographical distributions, with less geographical overlap among them. The diversity peak at 15°S corresponds to south-eastern Peru's extensive and topographically complex highland.

waterbirds. One of the most spectacular Andean waterbirds is the giant coot *Fulica gigantea* (Plate 7), which feeds on the abundant waterweed in the lake shallows, and is so heavy that it may become incapable of flight at the time of sexual maturity. It then becomes sedentary and apparently stays for the rest of its life at its enormous nest (Fjeldså 1981). Other characteristic birds include grebes (*Rollandia* and *Podiceps* spp.), several dabbling ducks (*Lophonetta, Anas* and *Spatula* spp.), Andean duck *Oxyura ferruginea*, Andean avocet *Recurvirostra andina* (Plate 7) and Andean gull *Chroicocephalus serranus*. The reed marshes have highland populations of black-crowned night herons *Nycticorax nycticorax*, rails (especially plumbeous rail *Pardirallus sanguinolentus*) and a couple of specialized passerines (many-coloured rush tyrant *Tachuris rubigastra* and wren-like rushbird *Phleocryptes melanops*). Characteristic birds of the surrounding shore meadows include ibises (Andean ibis *Theristicus branickii*, puna ibis *Plegadis ridgwayi*), Andean goose *Chloephaga melanoptera* and Andean lapwing *Vanellus resplendens*, and some of the high-elevation bogs are the home of the distinctive diademed sandpiper-plover (Plate 7). For part of the year, the shore meadows can also be staging areas for large populations of Nearctic migratory shorebirds. Finally, some of the salt lakes of the Altiplano are breeding sites for enormous numbers of flamingos (*Phoenicopterus*, *Phoenicoparrus*), although they conduct a rather nomadic life during the dry season. Flocks of more than one hundred thousand Wilson's phalaropes *Phalaropus tricolor* can be seen foraging commensally with Chilean flamingos *Phoenicopterus chilensis* in some of the saline lakes.

The fauna of smaller land-birds is dominated by rather few groups (Fjeldså & Krabbe 1990), while others are prominently under-represented. There are few parrots (e.g., mountain parakeets of the genus *Bolborhynchus*), and among the coraciiform and piciform birds, only a few woodpecker species reach the alpine zone. The most prominent case is the Andean flicker *Colaptes rupicola*, which is one of the characteristic resident birds of the Andean puna zone, foraging in grassland and excavating its nest-holes in earth banks and in the walls of adobe houses. Thirty-seven species of hummingbird appear to breed above 4,000 m. Among them, seven species of hillstars (*Oreotrochilus*) replace each other in different parts of the Andean highlands, typically in alpine habitats, with females defending territories in thickets rich in flowers while males search for more scattered floral resources in the open grassland, sometimes up to 5,000 m (Carpenter 1976).

Among the ancient suboscine passerine groups, the antpittas (Grallaridae), tapaculos (Rhinocryptidae) and ovenbirds and their allies (Furnarioidea) have a long history of diversification in Andean cloud forests (Derryberry *et al.* 2011; Fjeldså *et al.* 2020), and a few genera in these groups also diversified in the alpine zone: the ground ovenbird genera *Cinclodes* and *Upucerthia*, and various spinetails, notably many species of *Asthenes* in puna grassland and scrubby vegetation. These are mostly insectivores, some of which probe the ground or the matted vegetation with long, pointed and often somewhat curved bills. Among the New World flycatchers, small agile tit-tyrants (*Anairetes*) and some chat-tyrants (*Ochthoeca*) are common birds in subalpine shrub and elfin forests, and the Xolmini clade of open-land flycatchers is well represented in the open habitats of the high Andes (notably many ground-tyrants of the genus *Muscisaxicola*).

Among oscines (songbirds), only some families of the infraorder Passerides (the 'higher songbirds'; Fjeldså *et al.* 2020) are well established in alpine environments. Most species are nine-primaried oscines in the large group of finch-billed passerines (Fringilloidea). Patches of woody vegetation in the highland have various siskins in the genus *Spinus* and conebills (*Conirostrum*), flowerpiercers (*Diglossa*) and warbling-finches (*Poospiza, Poospizopsis*). Some brushfinches (*Atlapetes*), and colourful mountain tanagers can also be found in patches of elfin forest in the subalpine zone. The open habitats of the puna zone are home to many similar-looking species of yellow finches (*Sicalis*) and sierra finches, a group of generally greyish or cryptically coloured 'sparrows', which, according to recent DNA data (Fjeldså *et al.* 2020), represent a polyphyletic assemblage of tanagers, now divided in the genera *Phrygilus, Geospizopsis, Ephippiospingus, Rhodospiza, Corydospiza* and *Idiopsar*. Some of these genera are distributed along nearly the entire length of the Andes. The rufous-collared sparrow *Zonotrichia capensis* is found in a broad range of open habitats over large parts of the South American continent, including in the Andes.

9.4.2 Birds of African Mountains

We recorded 63 species for the tropical alpine zone. Only few species have their core habitat in the alpine zone: for example, brown woodland warbler *Phylloscopus umbrovirens*, a couple of cisticolas (*Cisticola* spp.), scarlet-tufted sunbird *Nectarinia johnstoni*; and in the Ethiopian Highlands, moorland francolin *Scleroptila psilolaema*, blue-winged goose *Cyanochen cyanoptera*, white-collared pigeon *Columba albitorques*, Rouget's rail *Rougetius rougetii*, spot-breasted lapwing *Vanellus melanocephalus*, wattled ibis *Bostrychia carunculata*, thick-billed raven *Corvus crassirostris* and a few species of finches (*Crithagra, Serinus*).

9.4.3 Birds of Tropical Asian Mountains

Extremely few avian species are narrowly associated with the tiny patches of alpine habitat in tropical Asia. New Guinea has only a limited alpine avifauna, such as the Snow Mountain quail *Synoicus monorthonyx*, a few members of the oldest songbird groups (honeyeaters, Meliphagidae, eastern crested berrypecker and Snow Mountain robin *Petroica archboldi*) and four representatives of the 'higher songbirds' (Papuan grassbird *Cincloramphus macrurus*, island thrush *Turdus poliocephalus*, alpine pipit *Anthus gutturalis* and western alpine mannikin *Lonchura montana*).

A much greater diversity of species is found in the Sino-Himalayan Mountains (Figure 9.2), especially in the eastern part (Lei *et al.* 2015). Among the 225 species recorded, typical birds of the alpine meadows include choughs (*Pyrrhocorax* spp.) and the peculiar ground tit *Pseudopodoces humilis*. A large diversity of 'higher songbirds' comprise many chats and robins (Muscicapidae), some thrushes (*Turdus, Zoothera* and *Grandala* spp.) and laughing-thrushes (Leiotrichidae; Cai *et al.* 2019), and mountain finches (Pyrrhulini; Päckert *et al.* 2020). These groups have their highest diversities in the montane forest, but they are also well represented in the rhododendron zone and even higher up, in low shrubby vegetation (i.e., transition zone). A subgroup of the speciose genus of leaf-warblers (*Phylloscopus* spp.; Alström *et al.* 2018) is specifically associated with scrubby vegetation on the highest ridges. The treeless habitats have many rosefinches (Carpodacini), accentors (Prunellidae), pipits (*Anthus* spp.) and sparrows (Passeridae), some of the latter continuing up to the tundra of the Tibetan plateau (notably snowfinches *Montifringilla* and *Pyrgilauda* spp.; Päckert *et al.* 2020).

The avifaunas of the Andes, the Afrotropics and the Sino-Himalayan Mountains mostly represent different phylogenetic lineages (Table 9.1), but Dorst & Vuilleumier (1986) claimed convergence and similarities of guilds, for example, *Thinocorus* seedsnipes in the Andes vs *Syrrhaptes* sandgrouse in Tibet, miners and earthcreepers (*Geositta, Upucerthia* spp.) vs ground tit; *Anairetes* tit-tyrants vs *Leptopoecile* tit-warblers, *Muscisaxicola* ground tyrants vs chats (*Oenanthe, Pinarochroa* spp.); sierra-finches vs snowfinches. Dorst and Vuilleumier (1986) also emphasized similar habits for roosting and breeding in rodent burrows, but further work is needed to determine whether similarity in functional traits reflects a truly convergent evolution, or whether it is a simple consequence of filtering, where only certain ecological types find opportunities at the highest elevations.

9.4.4 Birds that Specialize on Carbohydrate Foods

Birds at all latitudes consume some fruits and other sugary plant parts opportunistically, but specialization on such food is mainly possible at low latitudes with little seasonality. Altogether, 10 per cent of birds feed on floral nectar, especially hummingbirds (Box 9.2 and Plate 8), lories (Loriini; Psittacidae), sunbirds (Nectariniidae) and honeyeaters (Meliphagidae); also some berrypeckers (Dicaeidae), Hawaiian honeyeaters (Drepanidini), tanagers (Thraupidae), white-eyes (Zosterpidae) and myzornis (*Myzornis*, Paradoxornithidae), with some other groups being

Box 9.2 *The High Andes as a Hotspot for Specialized Bird Pollination*

Few avian groups have radiated as successfully in tropical mountains as the hummingbirds. While all 360 species are restricted to the Americas, most of the species belong to a monophyletic group that primarily radiated in the Andean cloud forest zone (McGuire *et al.* 2014). This group evolved unique adaptations to cope with the high-elevation climates, and many species even specialized to live in the alpine zone.

Hummingbirds are obligate nectarivores, with specialized adaptations including long and slender beaks, a long brush-tipped tongue and an ability to sustain hovering flight. Most of the lowland hummingbirds represent early-diverged lineages with long and slightly decurved bills, well suited for feeding on flowers with long corollas such as *Centropogon*, *Drymonia* and *Heliconia* (Sonne *et al.* 2019). However, most abnormal bill morphologies aggregate in the Andean group. The species such as those depicted in Plate 8 (upper panel) thrive from the upper cloud forest zone to the páramo above the timberline. Purple-backed thornbill *Ramphomicron microrhynchum* and the helmetcrests (*Oxypogon* spp.) have the shortest bills of all hummingbirds, well suited to probe nectar from open flowers and glean the vegetation for arthropods. The helmetcrests thrive above the treeline among the tall *Espeletia* shrubs. Unusually for hummingbirds, short-billed species rarely forage while hovering in the air, but instead use an energy-saving foraging strategy as they walk on the ground or cling to the vegetation. The sharply upturned bill of mountain avocetbill *Opisthoprora euryptera* is suited for nectar robbing, piercing the corollas of *Centropogon* flowers, the nectar being otherwise unreachable by legitimate visitation. Most highland hummingbirds have straight bills, with the single exception of the mountain velvetbreast *Lafresnaya lafresnayi,* which often visits curved flowers such as *Centropogon*, *Siphocampylus* (Campanulaceae) and *Salvia* (Lamiaceae), thereby complementing other hummingbirds' foraging preferences (Tinoco *et al.* 2017; Sonne *et al.* 2019). The *Coeligena* lineage (starfrontlets) comprises eleven species adapted to exploit nectar resources unavailable to most other hummingbirds. The sword-billed hummingbird *Ensifera ensifera* has the longest bill in the world relative to body size. The bill reaches 10 cm in length, matching long tubular flowers such as, for example, *Brugmansia, Datura* (Solanaceae) and

Passiflora (Passifloraceae), none of which can be reached by other competing hummingbirds. The Andean highlands are also home to the giant hummingbird, the largest of all hummingbirds. Its exceptionally long wings enable it to fly long distances in search of nectar-rich flowers of agaves (Agavaceae), puyas (Bromeliaceae) and *Lobelias* (Campanulaceae).

While the Andean foothills also comprise unique bill shapes, the morphological diversity is driven by a single ancient lineage Phaethornithinae (Plate 8, lower panel). By contrast, the highland's specialists represent seven different evolutionary origins within the montane clade, meaning that we can probably rule out niche conservatism as an explanation for the variation in bill morphologies (Sonne *et al.* 2019). An alternative suggestion could be that low temperatures and high humidity in the cloud forest zone (and freezing temperatures above the treeline) are unfavourable for large pollinating insects (Poulsen 1996; Aizen 2003). The absence of these insects means that flowering plants could optimize their reproductive fitness by specializing to attract endothermic avian pollinators instead. As such, it appears that hummingbirds have exploited ecological opportunities in the high elevation environment resulting in a large diversity of bill types (Sonne *et al.* 2019).

partly nectarivorous. These groups are generally well represented in the montane forest zones, and some of them even favour the alpine zone (37 species of hummingbird, three lories, two sunbirds and three honeyeaters). Despite their susceptibility to energetic stress, small nectar-feeding birds are important members of high-elevation tropical ecosystems (Wolf & Gill 1986). Flowers are abundant, especially in second-growth vegetation. They have low nectar production rates, but are longer-lived than flowers at lower elevations (Carpenter 1976), and flower nectar is available for most or all of the year, unlike in the mountains at high latitudes. The *Chuquiragua* scrub (Figure 9.1A), which is the main food plant for most populations of hillstar hummingbirds, flowers at all seasons. Titlike dacnis *Xenodacnis parina*, plain-tailed warbling finch *Microspingus alticola* and conebills appear to feed much on sugary excretions on the leaves of *Gynoxys* bushes. There is also some feeding on fruit in the treeline zone, and the white-cheeked cotinga is a specialist in eating mistletoe berries in the highest woodland patches in Peru's western cordillera.

9.5 Adaptations and Life History Strategies

Adaptations of birds of alpine environments are discussed at length in Chapter 2, and we therefore focus here only on aspects that are specific to the tropical alpine avifauna. With our focus on birds which breed above 4,000 m, we would assume a stronger degree of specialization to endure hypoxic conditions and UV radiation (see Chapter 2, Section 2.3) than in the birds of the generally lower mountains at high latitudes. In spite of this, Feinsinger *et al.* (1979) found only slight signs of adjustment of metabolism and wing-disc loading with elevation in hummingbirds. In a study of Himalayan birds, haemoglobin concentrations and haematocrit were found to correlate with elevation, but the relationship for haematocrit was only significant for altitudinal migrants (Barve *et al.* 2016). The generally low responses to elevation reflect the efficiency of the avian respiratory system.

Freeman (2017) found little evidence of increasing body mass with elevation in a broad analysis of size variation in tropical passerines. Nevertheless, a few highland birds have evolved to enormous size relative to congeners (giant coot and horned coot *Fulica cornuta*, giant hummingbird, giant conebill *Conirostrum binghami*, and some populations in the *Cranioleuca baroni* complex of spinetails; García-Moreno *et al.* 1999) and of tit-like dacnis. These examples suggest that gigantism can evolve in rare bursts (Landis & Schraiber 2017), although it remains an open question why this happens only in a few lineages of species.

Most songbirds of the alpine zone belong to the 'higher oscines' (infraorder Passerides), a monophyletic group with a shared, unique blood supply system for the eyes and brain (Mayr 2019). The ophthalmic artery of birds, which provides heat exchange for the eyes and brain, generally passes through the same bony channel as the ophthalmic vein, potentially causing a loss of heat. However, the artery and vein are placed in separate channels in most species of the Passerides group, which could be an adaptation to minimize loss of heat of the arterial blood before it reaches the networks of fine blood vessels that warm the eyes and brain (Mayr 2019). Most songbirds of alpine environments (the 11 lower lines in Table 9.1) are nested within this infraorder, which originated during the cold Oligocene period and primarily radiated in the montane regions of Asia, with subsequent expansion across the entire Northern Hemisphere and onwards to tropical mountains (Fjeldså *et al.* 2020, and see Section 9.6).

Hummingbirds save energy during cold nights by entering torpor (Chapter 2) and sleeping in caves. Several small alpine birds sleep in rock crevices or caves, and many ground-living birds are closely associated with rodents, sleeping or nesting in their burrows (see also Chapter 3). Many Andean birds use the numerous holes in earth banks that have been excavated by the Andean flicker or by various furnariids (thus avoiding the nightly frost mainly by behavioural adaptations). The glacier finch *Idiopsar speculifer* will, at least in some areas, nest in cavities in glaciers (Hardy & Hardy 2008; see Chapter 1, Box 1.1).

Disregarding hummingbirds, which generally do not form pairs, birds of tropical alpine environments appear to be socially monogamous, mostly appearing in pairs or family groups of three to four individuals. Many furnariids show a long-term (and possibly year-round) association with their nesting sites, using the nests as common dormitories. Although detailed life history data are still available only for a few tropical birds, it is clear that their investment in annual egg production is generally low (Chapter 2), as their life may be influenced more by stress hormones than by sex hormones (Hau *et al.* 2010). Many tropical birds lay clutches of only two eggs, and to further reduce the clutch size would mean laying only a single egg; in fact, this is what many birds do at high-elevation sites in the tropics (Boyce *et al.* 2015).

9.5.1 Seasonality

Most birds of tropical mountains appear to be year-round residents. Those inhabiting patches of elfin forest or *Polylepis* woodland tend to stay on their territories even during periods of snow, and tapaculos can even survive snowstorms under the snow, among boulders (Fjeldså 1991). Some of the highland hummingbirds can sweep away the snow that covers the flowers of vines and shrubs with their wings. However, the cloud forest hummingbirds, which only visit the elfin forest zone opportunistically, appear to flee down to lower elevations during snowfall. Periods with snow rarely last more than a couple of days in tropical mountains, but they force many ground-feeding birds (especially grain-eating sierra finches and yellow finches) to gather in groups and move around to search for places with little snow or to move some hundred metres downslope to warmer sites.

Longer periods with bad weather (such as seasonal drought or long-lasting rain) can force birds to leave their territories to join multi-species foraging parties, which move around within a few square kilometres (Poulsen 1996). Seasonal movements to lower elevations may mainly affect frugivores, granivores and nectarivores (Herzog *et al.* 2003). Such movements are often perceived as being analogous to the regular migratory programme of temperate-zone birds (Winger *et al.* 2018), only at a more local scale. However, we may consider whether some movements may actually be more comparable with nomadism (non-regular movements as an immediate response to local lack of food). Judging from information on the tags of large numbers of museum specimens, tropical alpine birds appear rarely to accumulate subdermal fat reserves, except for the tit-like dacnis (JF, unpubl. data).

Some bird populations breeding near the southern boundary of the tropical zone in the highlands of Bolivia/Argentina are truly migratory, wintering closer to the equator (but still within the same elevational zone). Similarly, many of the insectivorous birds at the northern boundary towards the temperate zone (Sino-Himalayan Mountains) undertake regular down-slope population movements (Chapter 2), or they may even migrate to lowlands in the tropical orient (as seen in certain *Phylloscopus* leaf warblers).

Most tropical alpine birds breed in the rainy season, with some exceptions relating to the flowering rhythm of their favoured food plants. Many species appear to have a fairly long breeding season, but the amount of information available in the literature is still too fragmentary for quantitative analyses. More data are available for Andean waterbirds (Fjeldså & Krabbe 1990). Most of these species lay their eggs in the rainy season (thus, from November through January for the Peruvian highland), but dabbling ducks also have an egg-laying peak in June to July. Coots breed mainly in this part of the year (when water levels are low), with some clutches also in the rainy season, and a few species, such as grebes of the genus *Rollandia*, appear to be able to breed at any time of the year. Waterbirds need to be flexible in their habitat selection and breeding, as their shallow wetland habitats are often of an ephemeral nature. As these wetlands dry up or become filled with sediments, their inhabitants have to find alternative sites. This leads to some dispersal between highland and lowland sites, with Andean waterbirds sometimes turning up in lagoons along the Pacific coast. Some species may actually have breeding populations around 4,000 m as well as near sea level (Fjeldså 1985; Fjeldså & Krabbe 1990). For these birds, shallow water and the abundance of food appear to be more important than a particular climate.

9.6 Origin and Diversification of Tropical Alpine Avifaunas

Many ancient avian lineages diversified mainly in tropical lowlands. They are assumed to be constrained by thermal niche conservatism (Borregaard *et al.* 2020), and the cold alpine environments should accordingly represent sink habitats for them. However, the niche conservatism appears to be asymmetrical, as lineages with a long evolutionary history at high latitudes tend to be thermally flexible (Stager *et al.* 2015). This pattern applies, for instance, to landfowl (Galliformes), with the large diversity of pheasants originating in the Sino-Himalayan Mountains (Cai *et al.* 2018), and to the 'higher songbirds' (see below). For such groups, mountain regions appear to act as cradles of species diversity (Jarzyna *et al.* 2021).

Passerine birds are suited for further interpretation since they represent a large sample (147 families and 6,200 species), with most species well placed in time-calibrated molecular phylogenies (Fjeldså *et al.* 2020). Most lineages, which represent deep branches in the passerine phylogeny, diversified mainly in the lowlands and rarely evolved the degree of cold tolerance needed in high mountains. Among suboscine birds (Tyranni), a few lineages may have been uplifted since the early phase of Andean exhumation (cotingas, antpittas, tapaculos and some furnariid groups), and have reached a high diversity in the Andean cloud forest, with rapid diversification during the last 10–12 million years in a few genera (Harvey *et al.* 2020). Adaptations to open alpine habitats are especially seen in *Cinclodes, Upucerthia, Asthenes* and among the Xolmini tribe of flycatchers, notably in ground tyrants (Fjeldså *et al.* 2018). Apparently, this rapid diversification happened as birds of austral subtropical or temperate grassland biomes colonized the alpine environments of the Andes, following the formation of new páramo habitats during the final uplift of the northern Andes.

The oldest songbird lineages (Menurides, Climacterides, Meliphagides) reside mainly in Australasian lowlands, with a few independent cases of lineages being uplifted during the formation of the central highlands of New Guinea since the late Miocene. Also, the cohort of crow-like birds (infraorder Corvides), which dispersed to other parts of the world, are mainly lowland birds, although some ancient (relict) lineages survive today in the highlands of New Guinea, and a few large-bodied species adapted to cold environments in other continents (Table 9.1).

The 'higher songbirds' differ (Passerides, total of 3,900 species globally). Most of the deep phylogenetic lineages in this group are found in the Sino-Himalayan mountains, suggesting that the evolution of the group was rooted in the highlands of Central Asia since the Oligocene period (Fjeldså 2013; Fjeldså *et al.* 2020). It is mainly within the Passerides group that many lineages expanded to breed all over the Northern Hemisphere, with highlands representing important cradles for diversification (Päckert *et al.* 2015, 2020). Phylogenetic studies suggest a gradual saturation of species diversity in the centre of origin (Himalayas; Price *et al.* 2014; Cai *et al.* 2020), with multiple cases of colonization to isolated tropical mountains (e.g., Alström *et al.* 2015), and a gradual expansion across the northern continents and onwards to the Neotropics (with non-adaptive radiation and a long period with a continuously high diversification rate). Migratory sparrows and tanagers settled to breed, first of all in the tropical Andes region, but rapidly expanding to all parts of South America, with a gradually slower rate of diversification towards the present (Barker *et al.* 2015).

The enormous expansion of higher songbirds may have been possible thanks to three adaptational changes (Fjeldså *et al.* 2020). These changes include their breeding system, with the relatively short formation of social pairs (but mixed mating strategies; Lifjeld *et al.* 2019), while for most of the year, the birds move around in social groups. This breeding system is, in turn, associated with pervasive and flexible migratory behaviour, where some migrating populations can settle down and become residents in stopover sites in their annual migratory programme, which provide suitable conditions (Winger *et al.* 2014, 2018; Rolland *et al.* 2015; Päckert *et al.* 2020). Finally, the group combined cold tolerance and high thermal flexibility (Mayr 2019), as already mentioned. Lineages of finch-billed birds that settled in the northern Andes from around 10 million years ago could rapidly expand to all over the Neotropics (Barker *et al.* 2015), and parallel cases of establishment of resident populations in tropical mountains have also been revealed for the Old World (Fjeldså *et al.* 2020).

Due to the paucity of well-preserved avian fossils from the interior of Asia, we can only guess how many of the avian lineages, which today constitute the Sino-Himalayan diversity peak in Figure 9.2, may have originated further north in Asia. Better evidence is available for the mammalian megafauna, where a good fossil record reveals that lineages, which today inhabit warm climates, were widespread in northern and central Eurasia before the Pleistocene (Weigold 1949).

9.6.1 The Speciation Process

Mountains can be barriers or bridges for dispersal, depending on the ecological requirements of the individual avian lineages. The generally sedentary behaviour and specialization on particular ecological zones mean that many populations will evolve within restricted areas (Box 9.1). However, changes in the connectivity of habitat patches in response to Pleistocene climatic fluctuations and glaciations have been assumed to drive the speciation of tropical alpine birds (Vuilleumier 1969), a process referred to as a 'flickering connectivity' between habitat patches (Flantua *et al.* 2019). Even in the rather homogeneous puna grassland of the high plains of Peru and Bolivia, there is a significant turnover in species composition across sites, a sign of historical isolation (Vuilleumier & Simberlov 1980).

While Pleistocene glaciations affected tropical mountains only during the last million years (Pérez-Escobar *et al.* 2022), the large number of molecular phylogenies that have now been generated (Oliveros *et al.* 2019; Fjeldså *et al.* 2020) documents that the diversification of tropical alpine avifaunas proceeded over a much longer period. Examples of rapid diversification during the Pleistocene exist for *Muscisaxicola* ground tyrants (Fjeldså *et al.* 2018), various groups of spinetails (García-Moreno *et al.* 1999; Derryberry *et al.* 2011) and the *Atlapetes* brush-finches (Sanchez-Gonzales *et al.* 2014). Despite the apparent dispersal barriers, phylogeographic data suggest fairly high levels of gene flow among isolated mountains for some Afromontane birds (Fjeldså & Bowie 2008).

The most intensive differentiation of local populations is seen in the upper part of the elevation gradient (Fjeldså & Irestedt 2009; Quintero & Jetz 2018), and Graves (1988) related this to stochastic fragmentation (and divergence) of populations inhabiting the long and extremely narrow band of ecotonal treeline habitat. Using comprehensive molecular phylogenetic data, Cadena *et al.* (2012) demonstrated that sister species among Andean birds generally inhabit the same elevational zone (i.e., they have a conserved climatic niche, in contrast to the situation at high latitudes). Segregation in different elevation zones comes secondarily, often delayed by several million years, when species have expanded to become sympatric and then segregate in different habitats or ecological zones (e.g., Cadena & Cespedes 2020). A global analysis of passerine diversification (van Els *et al.* 2021) demonstrated how the great accumulation of species in montane regions proceeded with greater amounts of down-slope (rather than up-slope) shifts in elevational distributions, leading to a dominance of old and widespread species at mid-elevation (Quintero & Jetz 2018; Sonne *et al.* 2022). The down-slope colonization can, for instance, be seen in the phylogenetic relationships in the genera *Geositta, Cinclodes, Asthenes, Leptasthenura* (Furnarioidea), mountain finches and in siskins of the genus *Spinus*, where lowland species are nested within groups with a highland origin.

9.7 Climate Change and the Future of Tropical Alpine Birds

With global warming, it is generally assumed that vegetation zones will move upwards, pushing many mountain endemics towards mountain peaks. In this situation, mountaintop species would have nowhere to go (La Sorte & Jetz 2010; Dullinger *et al.* 2012; Chapter 6). Climate change is, however, moderate near the equator (White *et al.* 2019), and can be quite difficult to predict for large and complex mountain regions (Elsen & Tingley 2015) where empirical data, rather than theoretical models, will be needed to find out how the changing weather interacts with the complex topography.

Climate warming has been associated with increasing bird abundance at the highest elevations, but for tropical mountains, this has only been documented from within the montane forest zone (e.g., Harris *et al.* 2014; Dulle *et al.* 2016; Freeman *et al.* 2018; Neate-Clegg *et al.* 2021). Unlike in temperate mountains (Chapters 4 and 6), only a few studies have been able to document an upslope expansion of tropical treelines (Forero-Medina *et al.* 2011; Harsh & Bader 2011; Lutz 2013; Rehm & Feeley 2015a). Tropical timberlines appear to be remarkably stationary (Bader *et al.* 2017), implying a disequilibrium with the warmer present-day climate. This absence of upslope expansion of forest applies also to the remaining patches of *Polylepis* forest in the Andes (Byers 2000, and our own scrutiny of recent satellite images). Deciding factors could be regular burning, grazing by livestock, as well as the intense radiation (Bader *et al.* 2017) and freezing night temperatures that prevent forest expansion into open land (Wakeling *et al.* 2012; Rehm & Feeley 2015b). We know of no published empirical evidence of the upslope expansion of birds associated with the subalpine ecotone, but we have some circumstantial evidence. In an unpublished field study in Peru and Bolivia, from 1997–2001, we compiled quantitative data on avian community composition at seven sites with a diffuse (and relatively undisturbed) transition between montane forest and low alpine vegetation, and eight sites with an abrupt timberline, which appears to have been maintained by frequent burning. The comparison suggested a repeated pattern: the 'undisturbed' sites had generally high densities of range-restricted species of hummingbirds, tapaculos, spinetails, thistletails, etc (contrary to the general theory on occupancy–abundance relationships; Brown 1984), while the 'disturbed' sites were dominated by widespread species (but with no significant difference in species richness). Thus, it seems that the most dispersive and geographically widespread cloud forest birds can take over wherever human-induced fires determine the position of the timberline. By contrast, it is difficult for the range-restricted birds to maintain populations in the absence of a natural transitory subalpine habitat mosaic.

Population changes can also be expected for Andean wetlands. Here, the rapid melting of glaciers has caused an increase in water availability in the adjacent outwash plains (Vuille 2013). Periglacial land is mainly colonized by anemochorous plants (Zimmer et al. 2018). However, the observed positive trend in the area of periglacial wetland is likely to be reversed in the near future as many small glaciers disappear or diminish to become insignificant (Rabatel et al. 2013; Huss et al. 2017; Bosson et al. 2019). Presently, the greatest abundance and diversity of waterbirds is found in the largest and most complex wetlands. Therefore, we must infer that diversity will decline without a supply of glacial meltwater. The disappearance of meltwater may have consequences, for example, for the glacier finch (Box 1.1) and diademed sandpiper-plover (Plate 7). Another problem is the introduction of rainbow trout *Ognorhynchus mykiss*, which has caused a collapse of limnic food chains in many Andean lakes, and which now threatens some of the ecosystems where flamingos breed in the Andes (Hurlbert et al. 1996).

9.8 Concluding Remarks

While birds breeding in the mountains at high latitudes may have to move large distances to track seasonal or long-term climate changes, those of tropical mountains can in many cases live their entire lives within a well-defined ecological zone, where the seasonal temperature variation is generally less than the day-night amplitude. Closely related species can evolve in different (but adjacent) highlands and gradually adapt to coexist in the same places or expand into other ecological zones. These mountains can therefore play important roles as biodiversity cradles, which recruit species to the broader regional biota. In order to better understand how species adapt and persist in the high tropical mountains, we now need to collect more (and better) life history data. Permanent plots should be established to document how rare and range-restricted birds respond to changing climates or changes in land use. However, some documentation could also be obtained by revisiting sites where past explorers documented the avifauna, such as conducted by Freeman *et al.* (2018). Such revisits would provide knowledge about changes in the vegetation and avian communities at the temporal scale of decades, necessary information to document how mountain birds respond to climate change.

Acknowledgements

The authors thank the Villum Foundation for supporting the Center for Global Mountain Biodiversity (grant number 25925).

References

Aizen, M.A. (2003) Down-facing flowers, hummingbirds and rain. *Taxon*, **52**, 675–680.

Alström, P., Jønsson. L.A., Fjeldså, J., *et al.* (2015) Dramatic niche shifts and morphological change in two insular motacillid birds. *Royal Society Open Science*, **2**, 140364.

Alström, P., Rheindt, F.E., Zhang, B., *et al.* (2018) Complete species-level phylogeny of the leaf warbler (Aves, Phylloscopidae) radiation. *Molecular Phylogenetics and Evolution*, **126**, 141–152.

Argolfo, J. & Mourguiart, P. (2000) Late Quaternary climate history of the Bolivian Altiplano. *Quaternary International*, **72**, 37–51.

Bader, M.Y., van Geloof, J. & Rietkerk, M. (2017) High solar radiation hinders tree regeneration above the alpine treeline in northern Ecuador. *Plant Ecology*, **191**, 33–45.

Barker, F.K., Burns, K.J., Klicka, J., Lanyon, S.M. & Lovette, I.J. (2015) New insights into New World biogeography: an integrated view from the phylogeny of blackbirds, cardinals, sparrows, tanagers, warblers, and allies. *Auk*, **132**, 333–348.

Barve, S., Dhondt, A.A., Mathur, V.B. & Cheviron, Z.A. (2016) Life-history characteristics influence physiological strategies to cope with hypoxia in Himalayan birds. *Proceedings of the Royal Socety Series B*, **283**, 1843.

Borregaard, M.K., Graves, G.R. & Rahbek, C. (2020) Dispersion fields reveal the compositional structure of South American vertebrate assemblages. *Nature Communications*, **11**, 491.

Bosson, J.B., Huss, M. & Osipova, E. (2019) Disappearing world heritage glaciers as a keystone of nature conservation in a changing climate. *Earth's Future*, **7**, 469–479.

Boyce, A.J., Freeman, B.G., Mitchell, A.E. & Martin, T.E. (2015) Clutch size declines with elevation in tropical birds. *Auk*, **132**, 424–432.

Brown, J.H. (1984) On the relationship between abundance and distribution of species. *American Naturalist*, **124**, 255–279.

Bruijnzeel, L.A., Scatena, F.N. & Hamilton, L.S. (2010) *Tropical Montane Cloud Forests*. Cambridge: Cambridge University Press.

Byers, A.C. (2000) Contemporary landscape change in the Huascarán National Park and buffer zone, Cordillera Blanca, Peru. *Mountain Research and Development*, **20**, 52–63.

Cadena, C.D., Kozak, K.H., Gómez, J.P., et al. (2012) Latitude, elevational climatic zonation and speciation in New World vertebrates. *Proceedings of the Royal Society Series B*, **279**, 194–201.

Cadena, C.K. & Cespedes, L.N. (2020) Origin of elevational replacements in a clade of nearly flightless birds: most diversity in tropical mountains accumulates via secondary contact following allopatric speciation. In *Neotropical Speciation*. Rull, V. & Carnaval, A.C. (eds.). Berlin: Springer, pp. 635–659.

Cai, T., Fjeldså, J., Wu, Y., et al. (2018) What makes the Sino-Himalayan mountains the major diversity hotspots for pheasants? *Journal of Biogeography*, **45**, 640–651.

Cai, T., Cibois, A., Alström, P., et al. (2019) Near-complete phylogeny and taxonomic revision of the World's babblers (Aves: Passeriformes). *Molecular Phylogenetics and Evolution*, **130**, 346–356.

Cai, T., Shao, S., Kennedy, J.D., et al. (2020) The role of evolutionary time, diversification rates and dispersal in determining the global diversity of a large radiation of passerine birds. *Molecular Phylogenetics and Evolution*, **47**, 1612–1625.

Carpenter, F.L. (1976) Ecology and evolution of an Andean hummingbird (*Oreotrochilus estella*). *University of California Publications in Zoology*, **196**, 1–74.

Chan, W-P., Chen, I.C., Colwell, R.K., et al. (2016) Seasonal and daily climate variation have opposite effects on species elevational range-size. *Science*, **351**, 1437–1439.

Cracraft, J. (2013) Avian higher-level relationships and classification: nonpasseriforms. In *The Howard and Moore Complete Checklist of the Birds of the World*. 4th edition, Vol. 1. Dickinson, E.C. & Remsen, J.V. (eds.). Eastbourne: Aves Press, pp. xxi–xli.

Derryberry, E.P., Claramunt, S., Derryberry, G., et al. (2011) Lineage diversification and morphological evolution in a large-scale continental radiation: the Neotropical ovenbirds and woodcreepers (Aves: Furnariidae). *Evolution*, **65**, 2973–2986.

Dorst, J. & Vuilleumier, F. (1986) Convergence in bird communities at high altitudes in the tropics (especially the Andes and Africa) and at temperate latitudes (Tibet). In *High Altitude Tropical Biogeography*. Vuilleumier, F. & Monasterio, M. (eds.). New York: Oxford University Press, pp. 120–149.

Dulle, H.I., Ferger, S.W., Cordeiro, N.J., et al. (2016) Changes in abundances of forest understorey birds on Africa's highest mountain suggest subtle effects of climate change. *Diversity and Distributions*, **22**, 288–299.

Dullinger, G., Gattringer, A., Thuiller, W., et al. (2012) Extinction debt of higher mountain plants under twenty-first-century climate change. *Nature Climate Change*, **2**, 619–622.

Elsen, P.R. & Tingley, M.W. (2015) Global mountain topography and the fate of montane species under climate change. *Nature Climate Change*, **5**, 772–776.

Favre, A., Päckert, M., Pauls, S.U., et al. (2015) The role of the uplift of the Qinghai-Tibetan Plateau for the evolution of Tibetan biotas. *Biological Reviews*, **90**, 236–253.

Feinsinger, P., Colwell, R.K., Terborgh, J. & Chaplin, S.B. (1979) Elevation and the morphology, flight energetics and foraging ecology of tropical humming-birds. *American Naturalist*, **113**, 181–197.

Fjeldså, J. (1981) Biological notes on the Giant Coot *Fulica gigantea*. *Ibis*, **123**, 423–437.

Fjeldså, J. (1985) Origin, evolution and status of the avifauna of Andean wetlands. *Ornithological Monographs*, **36**, 85–112.

Fjeldså, J. (1991) The activity of birds during snowstorms in high-level woodlands in Peru. *Bulletin of the British Ornithologists Club*, **111**, 4–11.

Fjeldså, J. (2002) *Polylepis* forests – vestiges of a vanishing ecosystem in the Andes. *Ecotropica*, **8**, 111–123.

Fjeldså, J. (2013) The global diversification of songbirds (Oscines) and the build-up of the Sino-Himalayan diversity hotspot. *Chinese Birds*, **4**, 132–143.

Fjeldså, J. & Bowie, R.C.K. (2008) New perspectives on Africa's ancient forest avifauna. *African Journal of Ecology*, **46**, 235–247.

Fjeldså, J. & Irestedt, M. (2009) Diversification of the South American avifauna: patterns and implications for conservation in the Andes. *Annals of the Missouri Botanical Garden*, **96**, 398–409.

Fjeldså, J. & Krabbe, N.K. (1990) *Birds of the High Andes*. Copenhagen: Zoological Museum and Apollo Books.

Fjeldså, J., Bowie, R.C.K. & Rahbek, C. (2012) The role of mountain ranges in the diversification of birds. *Annual Review of Ecology and Systematics*, **43**, 244–265.

Fjeldså, J., Ohlson, J.I., Batalha-Filho, H., Ericson, P.G.P. & Irestedt, M. (2018) Rapid expansion and diversification into new niche space by fluvicoline fly-catchers. *Journal of Avian Biology*, **49**, e01661.

Fjeldså, J., Christidis, L. & Ericson, P.G.P. (2020) *The Largest Avian Radiation. The Evolution of Perching Birds, or the Order Passeriformes*. Barcelona: Lynx Edicions.

Flantua, S.G.A., O'Dea, A, Onstein, R., Giraldo, C. & Hooghiemstra, H. (2019) The flickering connectivity system of the north Andean páramos. *Journal of Biogeography*, **46**, 1808–1825.

Forero-Medina, G., Terborgh, J., Socolar, S.J. & Pimm, S.L. (2011) Elevational ranges of birds on a tropical montane gradient lag behind warming tempera-tures. *PLoS ONE*, **6**, e28535.

Foster, P. (2001) The potential negative impacts of global climate change on tropical montane cloud forests. *Earth-Science Reviews*, **55**, 73–106.

Freeman, B.G. (2017) Little evidence for Bergmann's rule body size clines in passerine birds along tropical elevational gradients. *Journal of Biogeography*, **44**, 502–510.

Freeman, B.G., Scholer, M.N., Ruiz-Gutierrez, V. & Fitzpatrick, J.W. (2018) Climate change causes upslope shifts and mountaintop extirpations in a tropical bird community. *Proceedings of the National Academy of Sciences*, **115**, 11982–11987.

García-Moreno, J., Arctander, P. & Fjeldså, J. (1999) A case of rapid diversifica-tion in the Neotropics: phylogenetic relationships among *Cranioleuca* spinetails (Aves: Furnariidae). *Molecular Phylogenetics and Evolution*, **12**, 273–281.

Garzione, C.N., Hoke, G.D., Libarkin, J.C., et al. (2008) Rise of the Andes. *Science*, **320**, 1304–1307.

Ghalambor, C.K., Huey, R.B., Martin, P.H., Tewksbury, I.J. & Wang, G. (2006) Are mountain passes higher in the tropics? Janzen's hypothesis revisited. *Integrative and Comparative Biology*, **46**, 5–17.

Graves, G.R. (1988) Linearity of geographic range and its possible effect on the population structure of Andean birds. *Auk*, **105**, 47–52.

Hansen, P.C.S., Wright, H.E. & Bradbury, J.P. (1984) Pollen studies in the Junín area, central Peruvian Andes. *Geological Society of America Bulletin*, **95**, 1454–1465.

Hardy, D.R. & Hardy, C.P. (2008) White-winged Diuca-finch (*Diuca speculifera*) nesting on Querccaya Ice Cap, Peru. *Wilson Journal of Ornithology*, **120**, 613–617.

Harsh, M.A. & Bader, M.Y. (2011) Treeline form – a potential key to understanding treeline dynamics. *Global Ecology and Biogeography*, **20**, 582–596.

Harris, J.B.C., Dwi Putra, D., Gregory, S.D., et al. (2014) Rapid deforestation threatens mid-elevational endemic birds but climate change is most important at higher elevations. *Diversity and Distributions*, **20**, 773–785.

Harvey, M.G., Bravo, G.A., Claramunt, S., et al. (2020) The evolution of a tropical biodiversity hotspot. *Science*, **370**, 1343–1348.

Hau, M., Ricklefs, R.E., Wikelski, M., Lee, K.A. & Brown, J.D. (2010) Corticosterone, testosterone and life history strategies of birds. *Proceedings of the Royal Society Series B*, **277**, 3203–3212.

Hedberg, O. (1964) *Features of Afroalpina Plant Ecology*. Uppsala: Arnquist & Wikson.

Hedberg, O. (1986) Origins of the Afroalpine flora. In *High Altitude Tropical Biogeography*. Vuilleumier, F. & Monasterio, M. (eds.). New York: Oxford University Press, pp. 443–468.

Herzog, S.K., Soria, A.R. & Matthysen, E. (2003) Seasonal variation in avian community composition in a high-Andean *Polylepis* (Rosaceae) forest fragment. *Wilson Bulletin*, **115**, 438–447.

Hoch, G. & Körner, C. (2005) Growth, demography and carbon relations of *Polylepis* trees at the World's highest treeline. *Functional Ecology*, **19**, 74–51.

Hoorn, C., Perrico, A. & Antonelli, A. (2018) *Mountains, Climate, and Biodiversity*. Oxford: Wiley & Sons Ltd.

Hughes, C. & Eastwood, R. (2006) Island radiation on a continental scale: exceptional rates of plant diversification after uplift of the Andes. *Proceedings of the National Academy of Sciences*, **103**, 10334–10339.

Hurlbert, S.H., Loayza, W. & Moreno, T. (1996) Fish-flamingo-plankton interactions in the Peruvian Andes. *Limnology and Oceanography*, **31**, 457–463.

Huss, M., Bookhagen, B., Huggel, C., et al. (2017) Toward mountains without permanent snow and ice. *Earth's Future*, **5**, 418–435.

Igea, J. & Tanentzap, A.J. (2021) Global topographic uplift has elevated speciation in mammals and birds over the last 300 million years. *Nature Ecology and Evolution*, **5**, 1530–1535.

Janzen, D.H. (1967) Why mountain passes are higher in the tropics. *American Naturalist*, **101**, 233–249.

Jarzyna, M.A., Qintero, L. & Jetz, W. (2021) Global functional and phylogenetic structure of avian assemblages across elevation and latitude. *Ecology Letters*, **24**, 196–207.

Karger, D.N., Kessler, M., Conrad, O., *et al.* (2019) Why tree lines are lower on islands – Climate and biogeographic effects hold the answer. *Global Ecology and Biogeography*, **28**, 839–850.

Kessler, M. & Herzog, S.K. (1998) Conservation status in Bolivia of timberline habitats, elfin forest and their birds. *Cotinga*, **10**, 50–54.

Körner, C. (2003) *Alpine Plant Life*. 2nd ed. Heidelberg: Springer.

Körner, C. & Paulsen, J. (2004) A world-wide study of high altitude treeline temperatures. *Journal of Biogeography*, **31**, 713–732.

Lægaard, S. (1992) Influence of fire in the grass páramo vegetation of Ecuador. In *Páramo. An Andean Ecosystem under Human Influence*. Balslev, H. & Luteyn, J. (eds.). Århus: Academic Press, pp. 151–170.

La Sorte, F.A. & Jetz, W. (2010) Projected range contractions of montane biodiversity under global warming. *Proceedings of the Royal Society Series B*, **277**, 3401–3410.

Landis, M.J.J. & Schreiber, J.G. (2017) Pulsed evolution shaped modern vertebrate body sizes. *Proceedings of the National Academy of Sciences*, **114**, 13224–13229.

Lei, F., Qu, Y., Song, G., Alström, P. & Fjeldså, J. (2015) The potential drivers in forming avian biodiversity hotspots in the East Himalaya Mountains of Southwest China. *Integrative Zoology*, **10**, 171–181.

Lifjeld, J.T., Gohli, J., Albrecht, T., *et al.* (2019) Evolution of female promiscuity in Passerides songbirds. *BMC Evolutionary Biology*, **19**, 169.

Linck, E.B., Freeman, B.G., Cadena, C.D & Ghalambor, C.K. (2021) Evolutionary conservatism will limit responses to climate change in the tropics. *Biology Letters*, **17**, 20210363.

Lomolino, M. (2001) Elevation gradients of species diversity: historical and prospective views. *Global Ecology and Biogeography*, **10**, 3–13.

Lovett J.C. (1993) Eastern Arc moist forest flora. In *Biogeography & Ecology of the Rain Forests of Eastern Africa*. Lovett, J.C. & Wasser, S.K. (eds.). Cambridge: Cambridge University Press, pp. 33–55.

Lutz, D.A. (2013) Four decades of Andean timberline migration and implications for biodiversity loss with climate change. *PLoS ONE*, **8**, e74496.

Madriñán, S., Cortés, A.J. & Richardson, J.E. (2013) Paramó is the world's fastest evolving and coolest biodiversity hotspot. *Frontiers in Genetics*, **4**, 192.

Mayr, G. (2019) A previously unnoticed vascular trait of the middle ear suggests that a cranial heat-exchange structure contributed to the radiation of cold-adapted songbirds. *Journal of Ornithology*, **160**, 173–184.

McGuire, J.A., Witt, C.C., Remsen Jr, J.V., *et al.* (2014) Molecular phylogenetics and the diversification of hummingbirds. *Current Biology*, **24**, 910–916.

Neate-Clegg, M.H.C., Jones, S.E.I., Tobias, J.A., Newmark, W.D. & Şekercioğlu, Ç.H. (2021) Ecological correlates of elevational range shifts in tropical birds. *Frontiers in Ecology and Evolution*, **9**, 621749.

Oliveros, C.H., Field, D.J., Ksepka, D.T., *et al.* (2019) Earth history and the passerine superradiation. *Proceedings of the National Academy of Sciences*, **116**, 7916–7925.

Orme, C.D.L., Davies, R.G., Burgess, M., *et al.* (2005) Global hotspots of species richness are not congruent with endemism or threat. *Nature*, **436**, 1016–1020.

Päckert, M., Martens, J., Sun, Y.-H. & Tietze, D.T. (2015) Evolutionary history of passerine birds (Aves: Passeriformes) from the Qhinghai-Tibetan plateau: from a pre-Quaternary perspective to an integrative biodiversity assessment. *Journal of Ornithology*, **156** S1, 355–365.

Päckert, M., Favre, A., Schnitzler, J., *et al.* (2020) "Into and out of" the Quinghai-Tibet Plateau and the Himalayas: centers of origin and diversification across five clades of Eurasian montane and alpine passerine birds. *Ecology and Evolution*, **10**, 9283–9300.

Pérez-Escobar, O.A., Zizka, A., Bermúdez, M.A., *et al.* (2022) The Andes through time: evolution and distribution of Andean floras. *Trends in Plant Science*, **27**, 364–378.

Poulsen, B.O. (1996) Relationships between frequency of mixed-species flocks, weather and insect activity in a montane cloud forest in Ecuador. *Ibis*, **138**, 466–470.

Price. T.D., Hooper, D.M., Buchanan, C.D., *et al.* (2014) Niche filling slows the diversification of Himalayan songbirds. *Nature*, **509**, 222–225.

Pulido-Santacruz, P. & Weir, J.T. (2016) Extinction as a driver of avian latitudinal diversity gradients. *Evolution*, **70**, 860–872.

Quintero, J. & Jetz, W. (2018) Global elevational diversity and diversification of birds. *Nature*, **553**, 246–250.

Rabatel, A., Francou, B., Soruco, A., *et al.* (2013) Current state of glaciers in the tropical Andes: a multi-century perspective on glacier evolution and climate change. *Cryosphere*, **7**, 81–102.

Rahbek, C. (1995) The elevational gradient of species richness: a uniform pattern? *Ecography*, **18**, 200–205.

Rahbek, C. & Graves, G.R. (2001) Multiscale assessment of patterns of avian species richness. *Proceedings of the National Academy of Sciences*, **98**, 4534–4539.

Rahbek, C., Borregaard, M.K., Colwell, R.K., *et al.* (2019a) Humboldt's enigma: what causes global patterns of mountain biodiversity? *Science*, **365**, 1108–1113.

Rahbek, C., Borregaard, M.K., Antonelli, A., *et al.* (2019b) Building mountain biodiversity: geological and evolutionary processes. *Science*, **365**, 1114–1119.

Rangel, R.F., Edwards, N.R., Holden, P.B., *et al.* (2018) Modelling the ecology and evolution of biodiversity: biogeographic cradles, museums and graves. *Science*, **361**, eaar5462.

Rehm, E.M. & Feeley, K.J. (2015a) The inability of tropical cloud forest species to invade grassland above treeline during climate change: potential explanations and consequences. *Ecography*, **38**, 1167–1175.

Rehm, E.M. & Feeley, K.J. (2015b) Freezing temperatures as a limit to forest recruitment above tropical Andean treelines. *Ecology*, **96**, 1856–1865.

Rolland, J, Jiguet, F., Jønsson, K.A., Condamine, F.L. & Morlon, H. (2015) Settling down of seasonal migrants promotes bird diversification. *Proceedings of the Royal Society Series B*, **281**, 20140473.

Sánchez-González, L.A., García-Moreno, J., Navarro-Sigüenza, A.G., Krabbe, N.K. & Fjeldså, J. (2014) Diversification in a Neotropical montane bird: the *Atlapetes* brush-finches. *Zoologica Scripta*, **44**, 135–152.

Sarmiento, G. (1986) Ecological features of climate in high tropical mountains. In *High Altitude Tropical Biogeography*. Vuilleumier, F. & Monasterio, M. (eds.). New York: Oxford University Press, pp. 11–45.

Sayre, R., Karagulle, D., Frye, C., *et al.* (2020) An assessment of the representation of ecosystems in global protected areas using new maps and World Climate Regions and World Ecosystems. *Global Ecology and Conservation*, **21**, e00860.

Schawe, M., Gerold, G., Bach, K. & Gradstein, S.R. (2010) Hydrometeorological patterns in relation to montane forest types along an elevational gradient in the Yungas of Bolivia. In *Tropical Montane Cloud Forests*. Bruijnzeel, L.A., Scatena, F.N. & Hamilton, L.S. (eds.). Cambridge: Cambridge University Press, pp. 199–216.

Sonne, J., Zanata, T.B., Martín González, A.M., *et al.* (2019) The distributions of morphologically specialized hummingbirds coincide with floral trait matching across an Andean elevational gradient. *Biotropica*, **51**, 205–218.

Sonne, J., Dalsgaard, B., Borregaard, M.K., *et al.* (2022) Biodiversity cradles and museums segregating within hotspots of endemism. *Proceedings of the Royal Society Series B*, **289**, 20221102.

Stager, M., Pollock, H.S., Benham, P.M., *et al.* (2015) Disentangling environmental drivers of metabolic flexibility in birds: the importance of temperature extremes versus temperature variability. *Ecography*, **39**, 787–795.

Stevens, G.C. (1989) The latitudinal gradient in geographical range: how so many species coexist in the tropics. *American Naturalist*, **133**, 240–256.

Tinoco, B.A., Graham, C.H., Aguilar, J.M. & Schleuning, M. (2017) Effects of hummingbird morphology on specialization in pollination networks vary with resource availability. *Oikos*, **126**, 52–60.

Troll, C. (1959) Die Tropischen Gebirge, ihre dreidimensionale klimatische und pflanzengeographische Zonierung. *Bonner geographische Abhandlungen*, **25**, 1–93.

van Breugel, P., Friis, I., Demissew, S., Lillesø, J.-P. & Kindt, R. (2015) Current and future fire regimes and their influence on natural vegetation in Ethiopia. *Ecosystems*, **19**, 369–386.

van Els, P., Herrera-Alsine, L., Pigot, A.L. & Etienne, R. (2021) Dynamical analysis of the global diversity gradient in passerine birds reveals a prominent role for highlands as species pumps. *Nature Ecology and Evolution*, **5**, 1259–1265.

von Humboldt, A. & Bonpland, J.R. (1807) *Ideen zu einer Geographie der Pflanzen nebst einem Naturgemälde der Tropenländer*. Tübigen: F.G. Costa/F. Schoell.

Vuille, M. (2013) Climate change and water resources in the tropical Andes. Inter-American Development Bank Environmental Safeguards Unit Technical Note No. IDB-TN-515. *Inter-American Development Bank*.

Vuilleumier, F. (1969) Pleistocene speciation in birds living in the High Andes. *Nature*, **223**, 1179–1180.

Vuilleumier, F. & Simberloff, D. (1980) Ecology vs. history as determinants of patchy and insular distribution in high Andean birds. *Evolutionary Biology*, **12**, 235–379.

Vuilleumier, F. & Monasterio, M. (1986) *High Altitude Tropical Biogeography*. New York and Oxford: Oxford University Press.

Wakeling, J.L., Cramer, M.D. & Bond, W.J. (2012) The savanna-grassland 'treeline': why don't savanna trees occur in upland grasslands? *Journal of Ecology*, **100**, 381–391.

Weigold, H. (1949) Tibet einst en Entwicklungszentrum. In *Ornithologie als Biologische Wissenschaft*. Mayr, E. & Schüz, E. (eds.). Heidelberg: Stresemann-Festschrift, pp. 92–107.

Weir, J.T., Bermingham, B. & Schluter, D. (2009) The Great American Biotic Interchange in birds. *Proceedings of the National Academy of Sciences*, **106**, 21737–21742.

Wesche, K., Miehe, G. & Kaeppell, M. (2000) The significance of fire for Afroalpine ericaceous vegetation. *Mountain Research and Development*, **20**, 340–347.

White, F. (1978) *The Vegetation of Africa*. Paris: UNESCO.

White, A.E., Dey, K.K., Mohan, D., Stephens, M. & Price, T.D. (2019) Regional influences on community structure across the tropical-temperate divide. *Nature Communications*, **10**, 2646.

Winger, B.M., Barker, F.K. & Ree, R.H. (2014) Temperate origins of long-distance seasonal migration in New World songbirds. *Proceedings of the National Academy of Sciences*, **111**, 12115–12120.

Winger, B.M., Auteri, G.G., Pegan, T.M. & Weeks, B.C. (2018) A long winter for the Red Queen: rethinking the evolution of seasonal migration. *Biological Reviews*, **94**, 737–753.

Wolf, L.L & Gill, F.B. (1986) Physiological and ecological adaptations in high montane sunbirds and hummingbirds. In *High Altitude Tropical Biogeography*. Vuilleumier, F. & Monasterio, M. (eds.). New York: Oxford University Press, pp. 103–119.

Zimmer, A., Meneses, R.I., Rabatel, A., *et al.* (2018) Time lag between glacial retreat and upward migration alters tropical alpine communities. *Perspectives in Plant Ecology, Evolution and Systematics*, **30**, 89–102.

10 · *Priorities for Information, Research and Conservation of Birds in High Mountains*

KATHY MARTIN, DAN CHAMBERLAIN AND ALEKSI LEHIKOINEN

10.1 High Mountain Birds, Avian Adaptations and Key Habitats

High mountain habitats attract and inspire us, whether we are artists, poets, natural or social scientists, recreationalists or agricultural users. Perhaps mountains intrigue us because we get a bird's eye view of the surrounding landscape when we scale their summits. Their imposing landmass presents barriers and opportunities for human landuse. Regardless, high mountains are special habitats, that despite their rugged terrain and short growing seasons, surprise us with their impressive biodiversity. Cumulatively, we have spent over 75 years studying alpine birds and we never fail to be impressed with how successfully high mountain birds cope with their extreme living conditions. This book has been such a pleasure to produce in part because of the extensive new knowledge we have learned about the ecology and conservation of high mountain birds globally.

Birds in high mountains have global significance because:

1. Mountains tend to support disproportionately high biodiversity
2. Mountains cover an estimated one quarter of the global land surface (Kapos *et al.* 2000; Körner *et al.* 2017)
3. Mountains support about one-third of terrestrial biodiversity (Körner 2004; Körner *et al.* 2011)
4. Mountains harbour almost 50 per cent of terrestrial biodiversity hot-spots globally (Myers *et al.* 2000; Rahbek *et al.* 2019).

Much of our focus is on the open areas of high mountain habitat above the natural elevational limit of continuous forest, with the treeline ecotone as our lower limit of interest (Nagy & Grabherr 2009). High mountain habitats support exceptional levels of biodiversity and often high endemism, because as different life zones succeed one another with increasing elevation, a wide range of ecosystem types are compressed into relatively close proximity, diversifying niche availability (Grabherr 2000), especially in high mountain habitats at lower latitudes (Chapter 9). Within several hundred meters, alpine habitats can include persistent or permanent snowfields, rocky ridges, occasional wind-shaped trees and scattered to continuous tundra vegetation. The adjoining treeline eco-tone with woody shrubs and the upper limits of small trees can provide early season forage, and the upper montane forest comprised of open parklands may provide cover and other resources for birds breeding in or migrating to high mountain habitats (Boyle & Martin 2015). Alpine habi-tats are often thought to support low numbers of species, but recent stud-ies in temperate systems in the Americas have shown that high mountain habitats can support 40 to 60 per cent of the local species pool, and 12 per cent of the global species pool, in addition to supporting high proportions of endemic species (Martin 2001; Araneda *et al.* 2018; Martin *et al.* 2021; de Zwaan *et al.* 2022a; Chapters 3 and 9). Despite a global significance for avian biodiversity, relatively little research has been conducted on birds in mountains compared to other habitats, especially for tropical mountain birds in Asia and Africa. If considering only research on higher eleva-tions (treeline and above), the output over the past decade is amongst the lowest of major habitat types, and comparable to the extreme (and low diversity) desert and Antarctic/Arctic/boreal ecosystems (Chapter 1).

Chapter 1 defines what we consider to be 'mountains' and 'mountain birds', a critical requirement to assess the importance of mountains to global avifaunal diversity. We identify key research and conservation needs given that in addition to resident birds, a significant proportion of the global avifauna use high mountains for at least some part of their annual cycle during breeding, winter or post-breeding migratory stop-overs from higher latitudes or low elevations (Boyle & Martin 2015). We focus on key influences of avian community assembly and variation along elevation gradients encompassing a wide range of habitats from relatively low elevations at high latitudes to the highest alpine peaks. Reliable mapping to determine ecologically relevant high mountain habitats globally is needed urgently to address habitat availability with respect to species distributions and species-habitat associations (Sayre *et al.* 2018). High mountain habitats are challenging to describe and classify given the variety of global and local influences exerted on the treeline and alpine habitats, such as latitude (alpine habitats are at lower elevations at high latitudes), longitude (continental vs oceanic influences), strong environmental gradients, barriers to dispersal and a wide range of anthropogenic activities (Testolin *et al.* 2020).

10.1.1 Avian Adaptations for High Mountain Living

High mountain ecosystems support a diverse array of birds during breeding and post-breeding seasons (Martin 2001; Blyth *et al.* 2002; Boyle & Martin 2015). Birds living in high mountains must cope with a wide range of rigorous abiotic, energetic and ecological challenges. These challenges increase with elevation as most of the key abiotic factors such as temperature, wind, solar radiation and partial pressure of oxygen change quickly over relatively small distances, imposing strong influences on avian biology and life history. With increasing elevation, the time for breeding decreases and environmental stochasticity increases; at the highest elevations, hypoxic conditions add additional energetic living costs especially for developing embryos in the egg. A combination of environmental factors results in short, intense breeding seasons for birds in high mountain habitats. Since few temperate species live in the alpine zone year-round, birds need to make seasonal movements from breeding habitats above the treeline to wintering areas at lower elevations and lower latitudes. Additionally, many species move to high elevations to forage post-breeding or during migration (Boyle & Martin 2015; Boyle 2018; Martin *et al.* 2021).

To cope with difficult environmental conditions, birds breeding in high mountain habitats have developed physiological, morphological and behavioural adaptations to improve cold tolerance, conserve energy and improve crypticity to avoid predation in open landscapes. An active area of current research involves the genetic and physiological adaptations that adjust morphology, energy metabolism, hypoxia response, immune function, feather structure and olfaction to enable birds to persist better in high mountain ecosystems (Ke & Lu 2009; Qu *et al.* 2015). For example, ground tits *Pseudopodoces humilis* on the Tibetan Plateau have transitioned from carbohydrate-based metabolism at low elevations to lipid-based metabolism in the alpine zone (Qu *et al.* 2013). In some high mountain areas, bird populations have adopted a slower life history strategy that includes lower reproductive rates, delayed offspring development and maturity, and greater investment in parental care such that they produce fewer offspring annually compared to close relatives or intra-specific populations living at lower elevations. Additionally, greater annual survival and longevity allows mountain birds more attempts to replace themselves over more years despite a lower annual reproductive output (Badyaev & Ghalambor 2001; Sandercock *et al.* 2005; Camfield *et al.* 2010).

10.1.2 Key Habitats

Alpine habitats support an impressive diversity of bird species and communities. Chapter 3 provides an overview of these habitats above the treeline across 12 major global regions, as well as the diversity and characteristics of the avian communities that inhabit them. Globally, at least 1,310 species of birds breed in alpine habitats (12 per cent of extant species; de Zwaan *et al.* 2022a). Little is known about the distribution, ecology, movements and conservation status of most species, nor of the ecological and geographic variation across high mountain habitats. Elevation generalists are predominant as about 85 per cent of species breed across broad elevational ranges. About 15 per cent of species are considered alpine or tundra habitat specialists, with the highest proportion of alpine specialists in the tropical and temperate Andes, Himalayas and Tibet, and alpine–tundra specialists concentrated in high-latitude regions of North America and Eurasia. The proportion of species within each region that are resident or short-distance migrants ranges from 42 per cent (Nearctic) to 99 per cent (Australasian). While many species of mountain birds build open cup nests, species using cavity or domed nests are prevalent in certain regions.

Some of the main environmental and ecological influences shaping alpine communities include climate, vegetation structure, food availability and species interactions. Although living and breeding in open alpine habitats may be costly in terms of an increased risk of detection by predators when searching for food or cover, alpine birds may experience less predation pressure relative to lower elevation habitats, as well as reduced interspecific competition and habitat degradation from anthropogenic land use (Boyle *et al.* 2016, but see Freeman 2020). Rapid climate change remains a central concern for alpine birds, exerting additional challenges such as disrupted snow dynamics, which play a critical role in maintaining many alpine bird communities.

Treeline bird communities (Chapter 4) are made up of overlapping communities from the upper montane forest and alpine zones, but despite the diversity of habitat elements, treeline habitats tend to support few specialist species. The ratio of forest to alpine species varies according to geographic location, with the treeline ecotone in subtropical regions mostly consisting of forest birds at their upper elevational limit (Lloyd *et al.* 2012; Romanov *et al.* 2019; Altamirano *et al.* 2020). In temperate regions the treeline zone is occupied by species originating from both the montane and alpine zones (Martin *et al.* 2021). Except for studies of species richness and a few studies on breeding success, limited research has been done on birds living in this mountain habitat. Regardless, treeline habitats often support a high diversity of species relative to adjacent habitats, and may function as ecological and phylogenetic refugia for both alpine and montane birds given their strategic location on mountain systems where they can provide options for both connectivity and barriers to dispersal.

The treeline is a dynamic habitat that has been driven upwards and downwards repeatedly during glaciation events, and in recent times has been driven upwards by environmental change (rising tree and shrublines, Myers-Smith & Hik 2018), or downward by anthropogenic activities (e.g., grazing, logging, fire; Rössler *et al.* 2008). Thus, treeline habitats support a diversity of potentially critical ecological functions, and may serve an integral role in connectivity, perhaps enabling or reducing gene flow of lineages across elevations.

Tropical and subtropical mountains comprise about one third of the earth's mountain ecosystems (Nagy & Grabherr 2009) and they support 43 per cent of the global alpine breeding species, with considerably more diversity yet to be discovered. Tropical high mountain regions include the Neotropics (the extended mountain chain from Peru to Venezuela), the Afrotropics (mostly sky islands and scattered volcanoes) and tropical and subtropical Asia bordering the cold Himalayan highlands (the greatest elevational gradient on Earth) that support many restricted range species and show high species turnover across mountain ranges and sites. Chapter 9 reviews the variation in avian diversity in tropical high mountains, the characteristics and adaptations of the endemic tropical alpine avifauna, and contrasts patterns of diversification with high latitude mountains.

At a global scale, tropical mountains stand out with an over-representation of both recently diverged and ancient species, making them both cradles and museums of biodiversity. Most tropical alpine birds represent young radiations (e.g., ground tyrants), but the extensive Eurasian highlands have a few ancient species (e.g., shorebirds, rails) that suggest a long history of accumulating species diversity. The highest levels of diversification and local endemism are found in the treeline zone, but a few avian families also diversified in the alpine zone. Species inhabiting the tropical alpine zone experience strong night-day oscillations in temperature, humidity, cloud cover and winds (heat stress by day and freezing conditions by night), a pattern of climatic variation that allows species to specialize for residency within narrow elevational bands. The tropical alpine habitats with the highest avian richness are wetlands, bogs and grasslands, with a predominance of precocial species.

Most birds of tropical mountains are year-round residents, although they may leave their territories to follow multi-species foraging flocks during periods with food shortages or inclement weather. In other geographic areas, birds have a range of seasonal movements, especially in the Sino-Himalayan Mountains. Relatively little is known about the impacts of climate change for the majority of tropical alpine birds, but the key elements of climate and habitat change appear to be glacier melt and desiccation of wetland habitat for the predominance of waterbirds, rather than shifting treeline habitats.

10.2 Monitoring and Modelling

Population trends and distributional changes are critical for understanding the conservation status of species. Early detections of declining abundance can be key to effective conservation planning and restoration success if population changes can be predicted by detecting patterns of decline in abundance and range size, and associated traits such as migratory behaviour (short vs long distance), species climatic niche (cold vs warm dwellers) and the degree of specialisation to mountain habitats (specialists vs generalists; Chapter 5). Systematic monitoring of mountain bird populations is challenging because the habitats are remote and difficult to access. A mountain bird indicator for Europe, which summarized the population trends of 44 alpine species, suggests a slight overall increase in population numbers during the past two decades (Chapter 5). In Europe, cold-dwelling mountain birds have less favourable population trends than warm-dwelling species. For North America, regional indicators based on seven alpine species showed declining trends during the past 50 years. Long term, large scale systematic monitoring is critical to detecting population trends, but there is poor knowledge of population trends in most mountain areas, with the greatest needs for monitoring outside Europe and North America.

Chapter 8 evaluates the recent methodologies developed to monitor and model avian populations in the complex topographies and stochastic and temporally variable environmental conditions of high mountain habitats. Researchers are developing more realistic species distribution models (SDMs) that include biotic interactions (such as competition, facilitation, prey availability, predation), as well as joint SDMs that include the role of species associations after abiotic and habitat factors have been accounted for. Mechanistic and process-based models that incorporate individual-based traits such as dispersal, and models that account for imperfect detection, including dynamic occupancy models, are being used to improve predictions of the population viability of birds in mountain landscapes under climate and land-use change. Overall, the field of projecting distributions to future times or other geographic areas enable us to make more informed and accurate projections into the future which have major value for conservation. SDMs have become a crucial component of spatial aspects in conservation planning. The next steps involve the need to incorporate ecological mechanisms, other demographic processes and Citizen Science data to improve our predictive models (Bradter *et al.* 2021).

10.3 Climate Change Impacts and Other Anthropogenic Influences

A growing body of evidence indicates that climate change is impacting the distribution, abundance and status of many high mountain birds, from individuals to populations and communities (Chapter 6). More detailed population studies are needed to identify the likely mechanisms underlying these environmental changes that will allow us to assess the future vulnerability of mountain birds to climate change. Temperature and precipitation are key elements of environmental change in mountains, with tropical mountains being moisture-dominated and temperate or boreal mountains being more temperature-limited. Key climate change sensitivities include threats for environmental change predicted to have impacts on habitat availability, breeding phenology, reproductive success, annual survival and full life cycle needs of alpine birds.

We observe variability in avian responses to environmental change elements within and across species given geospatial and elevation complexities, and also due to life history traits (migration strategies, cold vs warm dwelling, generalist vs specialist and tropical vs temperate ecosystems). Effects of climate change can also act through altered vegetation, food availability, diversity and abundance of predators, parasites, and competitors. Many studies have documented asymmetrical changes in leading and trailing range margins, with some influences being driven by climate and others by habitat change. Impacts can occur across the full annual cycle for high mountain birds, whereby different climate change effects on low elevation wintering grounds or high elevation breeding sites may exacerbate or mitigate impacts on subsequent reproduction or survival via carry-over effects (de Zwaan *et al.* 2019, 2022b). For example, both annual fluctuations and long-term trends in breeding populations of long-distance migrants may vary across large areas in response to changes in rainfall conditions in the tropical winter sites, ultimately influencing breeding phenology and success. Global warming outcomes may vary temporally as the growth, survival and breeding success of many birds is enhanced by warmer conditions, but warming may have longer-term negative impacts on bird populations such as the temperature- or precipitation-mediated reductions in the abundance of key food resources (Bradter *et al.* 2022).

Given variation among species in elevation range shifts, evidence is building that climate change has already changed bird community composition, in one study altering the proportion of generalists and specialists in mountain avifaunal communities (Neate-Clegg *et al.* 2021; Chapter 6). Changing climatic limits to distribution and abundance may 'rescue' some low elevation species in decline that are able to move upslope in response to habitat loss at lower elevations. A full understanding of the impacts of climate change on mountain bird species relies on good ecological understanding, given the many potential vulnerabilities to direct and indirect effects of climate change.

For centuries, mountain ecosystems and their wildlife communities have played an important role in maintaining a sustainable flow of mountain resources to the lands below, including forestry, mining, water and agricultural products, in addition to hunting and recreational activities (Chapter 7). Over the course of the last century, there have been great social changes in mountain areas, reflecting a shift in the human population of many parts of the world from rural areas to cities. Resident human populations in mountain areas have decreased, while seasonal visitors have increased, such that mountain habitats now experience seasonal increases in human populations by 5 to 10 times.

The main modern anthropogenic activities in mountains include recreational tourism, hunting and energy generation, all of which have potential negative impacts on high mountain birds. Increases in industrial and recreational activities and infrastructures such as those associated with wind farms, skiing (both through habitat alteration and disturbance), hunting and rock climbing also have adverse impacts on alpine birds. The majority of these potential impacts have not yet been measured, so we know little about effects on key demographic parameters (reproduction, survival) and whether infrastructures in the mountains such as ski resorts have a localized effect, or whether they impact populations at a broader scale which might occur if they support increased generalist predator populations.

10.4 Impacts, Adaptations and Vulnerabilities to Climate Change and Interactions with Other Stressors: Modelling, Predicting and Mitigating

Mountain habitats are experiencing globally significant increases in climate warming, extreme weather and rising tree- and shrub-lines (Myers-Smith & Hik 2018), resulting in increasingly unpredictable conditions for birds at high elevations (Chapter 6). Sympatric congeneric species can have different responses to environmental conditions based on their life history traits (Wilson & Martin 2010; Martin *et al.* 2017). Birds living in alpine patches that are shrinking will have smaller populations and be required to disperse longer distances to other alpine patches, or face the consequences of not dispersing (Martin *et al.* 2000). Some subalpine species will experience an increase in habitat availability, but many alpine species will need to cope with further reductions and fragmentation of their naturally patchy habitats (Jackson *et al.* 2015; Scridel *et al.* 2021). Both will also experience increased competition from species invading and shifting upslope from lower elevations (Jankowski *et al.* 2010; Freeman *et al.* 2018a). With limited data for baseline conditions, we are poorly positioned to detect future changes in ecological processes, subsequent ecological costs, or even population declines at an early stage, especially if ecological processes such as predation or competition are shifting at large cross-habitat scales.

Global modelling studies suggest that climate change vulnerability in mountain birds is a combination of the magnitude of climate change, mountain topography, isolation and habitat extent (Pepin *et al.* 2022). Despite the variation in model projections of future conditions and avian responses, there is good consensus that the increasing magnitude of warming will threaten increasing numbers of species with extinction or significantly reduce range extent and abundance. Şekercioğlu *et al.* (2008) modelled the impacts of warming on the extinction risk of landbirds, mediated through changes in elevational distribution and habitat loss. Under a 2.8°C warming scenario, 400–550 species were estimated to become extinct, with an additional 100–500 species added for every further degree of warming. Across the Western Hemisphere, projected extinction rates varied from 1.3 per cent under 1.1°C of warming to 30 per cent with an increase of 6°C temperature (Şekercioğlu *et al.* 2008), with tropical mountain endemics identified as particularly vulnerable. With more specific modelling for over 1,000 mountain bird species, La Sorte & Jetz (2010) concluded that species with narrow elevational distributions, especially tropical mountain endemics, are highly threatened if they are dispersal-constrained, with at least one third of mountain bird species projected to suffer more than 50 per cent declines in range extent.

What does a warmer future hold for mountain birds? The most cold-adapted and highest elevation species will likely be the most threatened by warming, especially if species occurrence is linked with snow cover for camouflage or food availability (e.g., white-winged snowfinch *Montifringilla nivalis*, ptarmigan spp.; Scridel *et al.* 2017; Chapter 5). Population declines of willow grouse *Lagopus lagopus* in low elevation boreal landscapes are driven, at least partially, by a decrease in snow cover making grouse with their normally camouflaged white winter plumage more evident to predators (Melin *et al.* 2020). A similar colour mismatch of white plumage against a largely snow-free background occurs in alpine ptarmigan. However, mountain environments may become increasingly important refuges for elevational generalists as the cold upper limits on such species distributions are relaxed, with formerly unsuitable habitats potentially supporting species that have lost their more productive lower elevations. Thus, despite the threats by climate change, mountain ecosystems may, with appropriate management, become more important centres for bird conservation in a changing climate than they are at present (Chapter 6, Box 10.1).

Ski resorts, tourist centres and their associated activities during winter can impact adversely the foraging activities of resident species and fall migration stopovers by restricting the areas or times when wildlife can feed without harassment or stress (Chapter 7). Improved access to food waste for both bird and mammal predators can change the local bird species composition year-round. For example, increasing populations of food-subsidized corvid and red fox *Vulpes vulpes* in Fennoscandia (Kaisanlahti-Jokimäki *et al.* 2012; Marolla *et al.* 2019) and corvids in Scotland (Watson & Moss 2004) may increase the risk of predation for alpine and subalpine specialist species, as well as for those 'upward shifted' elevational generalist species. The use of artificial snow may

Box 10.1 *Mountains as Climate and Habitat Refugia*

Devin R. de Zwaan

Under climate change, nearly all ecosystems will shift to an altered climatic state, driving the redistribution of bird species trying to remain within their climatic niche (Mora *et al.* 2013). While some species are already moving to cooler climates at higher elevations and latitudes, many may be unable to track changing conditions (Freeman *et al.* 2018b; Mamantov *et al.* 2021). Refugia are habitats with slower rates of climate change, offering potential havens for species persistence (Keppel *et al.* 2012). Mountains have a high probability of supporting refugia, with complex topography and rapid turnover of environmental conditions across elevations allowing species to maintain consistent climatic conditions without having to move large distances (Loarie *et al.* 2009; Carroll *et al.* 2017).

Climate refugia vary by spatial scale and temporal resilience. Macrorefugia occur at coarse spatial scales, tending to concentrate at higher elevations, where complex topography generates greater environmental heterogeneity (Carroll *et al.* 2017). Microrefugia, on the other hand, are defined by fine-scale landscape features that support optimal conditions relative to the deteriorating regional climate (Dobrowski 2011). Species may use microrefugia for certain behaviours, such as nesting or shade-seeking which can improve their ability to persist within a habitat even when average conditions are no longer tolerable (Huey *et al.* 2012).

Temporal resilience is a metric of climatic inertia (i.e., how long a given refugium may retain a relatively unaltered climate; Hannah *et al.* 2014). The stability of refugia over time may be influenced by regional factors regulating climate variation, such as proximity to the ocean (Stralberg *et al.* 2020). While the conservation value of long-lasting 'hold-out' refugia is clear, less stable refugia, with conditions that will likely deteriorate in the coming decades (e.g., hill-tops or ravines within low, arid habitats), can play important roles in maintaining habitat connectivity and assisting species range shifts as 'stepping-stones' (Morelli *et al.* 2016). The presence and location of hold-out and stepping-stone refugia in the landscape are therefore vital components of a refugia network, minimizing dispersal costs and promoting range shifts to more favourable climatic conditions at higher latitudes or elevations (Littlefield *et al.* 2019).

In addition to climate refugia, high mountain landscapes may also be important strongholds of declining habitat under land-use change. Mountains support a disproportionate number of avian species that use high elevation habitats to breed, forage, or stopover during migration, including species of conservation concern that breed across a range of elevations (Martin *et al.* 2021). Habitat loss and degradation tends to be greater at lower elevations (Ibarra *et al.* 2017; Elsen *et al.* 2020), leading to precipitous declines in many common species (Rosenberg *et al.* 2019). Accounting for the relatively greater habitat loss at low elevations, species moving upslope in response to climate change will often benefit from increased remaining available habitat, despite decreases in total land area (Elsen *et al.* 2020), suggesting high elevation habitats function as potential refugia from both climate and land-use change processes (Guo *et al.* 2018).

Ultimately, mountain ranges offer conservation opportunities and challenges. In many regions, a relatively low human impact at higher elevations and north–south connectivity (e.g., the Americas) highlight the potential of mountains to act as corridors for bird populations to shift to higher latitudes. However, while mountain habitats are often disproportionately protected, connectivity from valley bottom to high mountains is often fragmented, foreshadowing potential barriers as species simultaneously move upslope and northward (Elsen *et al.* 2020). Refugia are still largely unaccounted for in conservation initiatives as protected area networks are not designed to enhance climate resilience (Tingley *et al.* 2014). Incorporating scale, temporal resilience, and connectivity among refugia in conservation planning is critical to allow species to move to and use refugia, promoting climate resilience and species persistence (Robillard *et al.* 2015).

disrupt the ecology of a site, particularly if birds are staying at higher elevations for longer or moving upslope; the impacts of using artificial snow to maintain skiing activities on alpine birds are completely unstudied. The adverse impacts of ski operations on populations such as increased mortality due to collisions with ski cables or powerlines, or disruption of their foraging activities and snow burrowing behaviours by skiers, will have a greater impact on bird populations with lower reproductive potential and slower rates of population recovery (slower life history; Martin 2013).

Given the uncertainties in modelling future scenarios for species responses to climate change and other stressors, good monitoring data from high mountain environments are needed to track and predict the changes that occur and to attribute them to climate change and/or other stressors. Forecasts of climate change impacts are typically based on fairly coarse-scale distribution data that are likely inappropriate to predict the rapid changes in conditions (and thus of the bird community) along elevation gradients over small scales. Predictive models require data from detailed autecological studies to understand the requirements of species and how those are changing (Chapters 2, 5 & 9). We need to develop better understanding of demographic drivers of populations to forecast potential impacts and develop conservation strategies; achieving this requires a major change in research effort for high mountain systems. This is a necessary first step to inform how we should alter our management of mountain environments to help mountain birds adapt to climate change and other disturbance factors and thus help maintain high elevation habitats as long-term, stable refugia.

10.5 Key Knowledge Gaps and Research Priorities for High Mountain Bird Ecology and Conservation Problems

We have identified 10 major knowledge gaps (KGs) arising from the reviews of mountain birds in our chapters. We propose a set of priorities for ecological and conservation research that will help to ensure persistence of alpine birds in high mountain ecosystems (Table 10.1). Our priorities are to increase our knowledge of mountain birds to protect and enhance existing populations, and to facilitate the adaptation and dispersal of populations in the face of environmental change. Ultimately, we aim to promote resistance and resilience for high mountain birds (Walker *et al.* 2004).

Knowledge Gap 1 (KG-1). A Global List of High Mountain Avian Diversity

There is a profound lack of knowledge of the birds that depend on mountains for at least one key stage of their annual cycle. Despite being highly valued for their intrinsic beauty and rich biodiversity, alpine birds and high mountain habitats are a neglected area for research and management (Chapter 1). Global tallies for several continents indicate that

Table 10.1 *Key knowledge gaps and research priorities for high mountain birds.*

Knowledge gap	Description	Related research priorities
1. Low state of knowledge of which species occur in high mountains and in which seasons – a global list	12 per cent of birds use high mountains globally; biodiversity inventories are lacking. In most regions, little is known about which bird species use, and depend on, high mountain areas, particularly outside the breeding season	A compilation of existing knowledge of birds that use mountains for at least a part of their annual cycle
2. Mountain bird species in the under-studied regions of the world	Strong geographical bias in high mountain research to north temperate regions; studies especially lacking for globally significant hotspots for alpine avifauna in tropical and subtropical systems	More research, including basic information on species distributions, especially in mountains of the Global South
3. Population trends of mountain birds	Little information on long-term population trends of mountain birds outside Europe and North America; more long-term repeatable surveys are needed in all regions	Establish monitoring programmes in the main mountain ranges; develop Citizen Science programmes to enhance coverage
4. Limits on physiological adaptations	The limits of elevation that birds can reach given known and immutable atmospheric constraints (air pressure, hypoxia, UV radiation) are largely unknown	Identify the factors that constrain colonization of new climatically suitable high mountains
5. Ecological mechanisms and demographic rates that influence species distributions and population change	Life history traits, demographic parameters, population status or trends are known for very few species outside Europe and North America, especially for the Global South; this knowledge allows for better planning and forecasting for conservation intervention (see #9)	Studies of individuals and populations to determine key drivers of species distribution, population change and connectivity
6. Mountains as habitat and climate refugia	Need to determine whether and how mountains can support refugia with suitable climatic conditions that can enable species to persist	Identify refugia locations, and determine their habitat and environmental characteristics

(cont.)

Table 10.1 (cont.)

Knowledge gap	Description	Related research priorities
7. Role of protected areas	Many protected areas are located in high mountains – these may function as biodiversity reservoirs for mountain birds	Assess whether current protected areas meet their purpose; identify areas to be protected in future to anticipate changes in species distributions
8. Response to climate change and other stressors	Alpine birds are considered vulnerable to climate change and yet show good resilience to environmental variability; we lack understanding of variable mountain bird responses to climate change, and how these responses interact with other threats and stressors	Need improved predictions for how alpine birds will cope with changing climates and environmental condition
9. Conservation actions	Mountain bird conservation and management research programmes lack critical information on practical management interventions, interactions and synergisms of climate change with other stressors and other global change drivers	Experimental conservation interventions; develop evidence-based conservation strategies for multiple geographical areas
10. Socio-cultural considerations	Most current mountain bird research fails to incorporate expertise, knowledge and approaches from local and Indigenous peoples into research questions and programmes	Diversify funding options to support researchers from under-studied global regions; expand research teams to include under-represented sectors and expertise

mountains support diverse communities in terms of species richness and endemism. The first global estimate of avian biodiversity for high mountain ecosystems indicated that 12 per cent of all birds breed in alpine and treeline ecotone habitats (de Zwaan *et al.* 2022a; Chapter 3). Extensive species tallies across elevational habitats are missing for most continents, but in North America, over one third of the avifauna use alpine or sub-alpine habitats at some period in their annual cycle (Boyle & Martin 2015; Boyle 2018). At least 40 per cent of certain regional species pools are found to breed above 1,000 m in temperate North American mountains, and over 60 per cent in the temperate mountains of the Southern Andes (Martin *et al.* 2021). Thus, we expect that more species will be recorded in comprehensive surveys of high mountain species, especially for elevation generalist species where the majority of studies occur at lower elevations.

Knowledge Gap 2 (KG-2). Geographical Biases in High Mountain Bird Research

It may be possible to address KG-1 for some temperate mountain bird communities by collating existing information. However, little is known about the avifauna of many of the world's mountains, especially in alpine habitats (*sensu* Chapter 3). In relation to the percentage of mountain area contained in each continent, research on high mountain birds is the most strongly under-represented in Asia and can be considered over-represented in Europe (Chapter 1). The Antarctic continent and Greenland (Plate 4) include globally significant high mountain areas which we do not cover in this book because there is virtually no information on birds in these mountain systems. In fact, some of the mountain classification systems do not even include these areas (Chapter 1). Tropical alpine birds and their habitats are a key understudied mountain ecosystem, especially given that tropical and subtropical alpine habitats represent over one-third of the global mountain landbase (Nagy & Grabherr 2009), and tropical mountains represent many globally significant hotspots for alpine avifauna (Chapter 9). Furthermore, much of the research carried out in tropical mountains has been on montane forest, with still little research on birds at or above the treeline. Much ecological, systematic and conservation research is needed on most tropical alpine systems which promise to yield exciting and insightful results for alpine birds and high mountain science given their biodiversity, including high levels of avian endemism.

Knowledge Gap 3 (KG-3). Population Trends of High Mountain Birds

Outside Europe and North America, little is known about population trends of mountain bird species over time (Chapter 5). Even in North America, the existing programmes such as the Breeding Bird Survey and Christmas Bird Count do a poor job of monitoring alpine bird status and trends. Thus, we have little idea of the potential impacts of environmental change on high elevation bird species over much of the globe. This knowledge gap is particularly concerning for tropical mountains that harbour a high level of avian diversity and endemism with many specialist species (Chapter 9). Regular monitoring would act as an early warning system for species that are being negatively impacted by environmental change, thus allowing time for the development of potential conservation actions. However, occasional repeat surveys such as conducted by Freeman *et al.* (2018a) decades after an initial survey can yield important information about species and communities, especially for tropical mountains. Improved monitoring over a broader scale would also address KG-1 and KG-2, and improve our ability to better predict future impacts of environmental change on populations.

Knowledge Gap 4 (KG-4). Limitations Regarding Physiological Adaptations

We have much to learn about the physiological and other adaptations and general behaviours that birds use to solve the problems of living in high mountain habitats, as well as which abiotic and ecological factors present the greatest challenges to birds. Research priorities include investigating the paths birds have developed to live in mountain habitats, the limits to their coping mechanisms and the costs associated with these adaptations (Martin & Wiebe 2004). Research is needed to determine the important ecological processes required by birds such as research on trophic ecology to determine the potential links between climate change and changes in breeding phenology. Although it is difficult to generalize about the relative reproductive success and survival for species that live at high and low elevations, the few ecological studies of birds conducted across elevational gradients suggest there is greater local adaptation and life history diversity than previously realized. Some bird species may have differentiated into high elevation ecotypes or subspecies that have yet to be described.

Knowledge Gap 5 (KG-5). Limitations Regarding Ecology, Life History, Movement and Full Life Cycle

Despite the impressive species richness and extensive endemism supported in high mountain habitats, basic demographic parameters, life history traits and detailed understanding of the ecological mechanisms that dictate distributions and population trends are known for few species outside Europe and North America, and especially for the Global South. Life history studies are needed for alpine generalist species that are experiencing extensive habitat loss at low elevations. Most research for temperate alpine fauna has been done in spring and summer, thus our knowledge of their use of mountain areas in other seasons is limited. To accurately characterize the importance of the biodiversity of mountain ecosystems and the threats to its persistence, we need to consider species requirements at different stages of the annual cycle. A better understanding is needed of the importance of maintaining connectivity across time and space for species with seasonal altitudinal shifts (Powell & Bjork 1994). Connectivity is a key ecological process for alpine bird populations that needs to be maintained (i) among patchy habitat islands for breeding populations, (ii) along mountain corridors for north–south migrants, and (iii) between alpine and adjacent lower elevation habitats including valley bottoms for both breeding populations and migrants in tropical and temperate mountains. Alpine habitats support impressive levels of biodiversity globally throughout the annual cycle. Their role in supporting avian biodiversity will almost certainly increase as lower elevation habitats are lost or degraded (Elsen *et al.* 2020; Martin *et al.* 2021; Chapter 2).

Knowledge Gap 6 (KG-6). Mountains as Refugia from Climate and Habitat Change

Mountains are experiencing significant environmental change from both global climate warming and habitat loss, but many areas are likely to retain good natural conditions because they are unsuitable for other land uses such as cultivated crops. Refugia are habitats with slower rates of climate and habitat change that can offer potential security for species persistence (Box 10.1). Mountains have a high probability of supporting refugia because their complex topography and rapid climate turnover across elevations may allow species to maintain consistent climatic conditions without having to move long distances. Additionally, high alpine habitats represent areas of high biodiversity value as they can provide climate and habitat refugia for generalist species experiencing extensive habitat loss and climate change in their low elevation range, especially for birds that are on lists of national or international conservation concern.

Knowledge Gap 7 (KG-7). The Role of Mountain Protected Areas for Biodiversity Maintenance

Considerable research is devoted to the conservation values of protected areas currently and going forward. A few studies have shown that some protected areas have limited conservation value at present, but their role is predicted to increase with continued habitat loss at lower elevations and near mountain areas that lack protection for ptarmigan and other mountain birds (Scridel *et al.* 2021). Current networks of protected areas are static which makes them vulnerable to changing species distributions. A dynamic conservation plan for mountain birds should try to identify and protect new sites to expand the network of protected areas needed for climate and habitat refugia for the future.

Knowledge Gap 8 (KG-8). Responses to Climate Change and Other Stressors

It is critical to determine the vulnerabilities of high mountain birds to climate change and other anthropogenic stressors to mitigate impacts and manage for their persistence in high mountain habitats. High elevation species (especially in temperate mountains) may be quite resilient to climate change as they are adapted not only to cold temperatures, but also to the unpredictability of the alpine environment given the high variability in temperature and precipitation year-round (Martin *et al.* 2017; Scridel *et al.* 2018). One of the main threats for these species is likely to be loss of habitat, rather than direct climate effects. For example, a scenario of increased temperature, but no change in habitat, results in very little predicted change in distribution for several mountain species in the Italian Alps (Chamberlain *et al.* 2013). Most high elevation species in the Alps such as the water pipit *Anthus spinoletta* (Mermillon *et al.* 2022) show broad habitat-temperature niches suggesting a degree of tolerance to changing environmental conditions. Some species such as white-winged snowfinch have a narrow temperature–habitat niche and thus may be more vulnerable to climate change. In the longer-term, alpine birds are likely to have limited capacity to cope with significant increases in warmer temperatures, particularly given the range of biotic mechanisms discussed in Chapter 6.

Knowledge Gap 9 (KG-9). Effective Conservation Actions

Alpine and subalpine areas have increased in value as wildlife habitat, given habitat loss and changes in ecological processes at low elevations. Our lack of knowledge of population drivers and demographic mechanisms hampers our ability to deliver effective conservation strategies and implement management actions. Successful conservation planning initiatives should include identifying and incorporating new protected areas into an expanded network with climate and habitat refugia. To achieve the goal of sustainable human use of mountains we need to develop mitigation strategies that can protect alpine bird populations by expanding the range and focus of research topics and monitoring programmes to measure the direct and indirect impacts of human activities at high elevations for more geographical areas (Section 10.6).

Knowledge Gap 10 (KG-10). Incorporate Local Knowledge, Expertise and Socio-Cultural Considerations into Mountain Bird Research

This final knowledge gap addresses the geographic omissions and social considerations for who is involved in and leads mountain bird research. Scientists from the Global South are typically under-represented in research efforts, especially in leadership positions (Asese *et al.* 2022), a situation that exacerbates the geographic biases in knowledge gaps (KG-2). Additionally, many mountain bird research and conservation networks and partnerships do not involve or include local and Indigenous peoples and the non-profit sector. Mountain bird researchers from developed nations need to develop opportunities to include and support researchers from under-studied global regions and under-represented sectors, and to make funds available for local researchers to reduce the geographic and socio-cultural biases in knowledge gaps.

10.6 Conservation and Management Research Priorities for Birds Living in High Mountains

To address the Knowledge Gaps (KGs) listed in Table 10.1, we propose seven key research priorities (RPs) below, which are inter-linked and can cover more than one KG. Although some priorities may be applicable to bird species generally, these priorities are more pressing for mountain bird populations due to the generally poor coverage of high elevation treeline and alpine habitats, especially in the mountains of the Global South.

Research Priority 1 (RP-1). Complete a Detailed Biodiversity Inventory of High Mountain Birds, Especially for Habitats at and Above the Treeline to Determine Critical Knowledge Gaps and Conservation Concerns for the Global Avian Diversity Supported by High Mountain Habitats (KGs 1, 2 & 5)

For a full assessment of avian biodiversity for treeline and alpine habitats, we need a balanced global coverage of species occurrence and how they use high mountain environments. Assessing biodiversity will involve determining the best approaches to assemble a comprehensive list of bird species, including subspecies variation, degree of endemism, the extent and nature of habitat use for breeding and year-round, the role of connectivity and migration, and other ecological functions across elevations for the full annual life cycle. de Zwaan *et al.* (2022a) provide a useful starting point with their global list of mountain birds for various regions based on current knowledge, but this list needs to be greatly expanded.

Research Priority 2 (RP-2). Establish Long-Term Monitoring Programmes at Larger Geographical Scales (KGs 2 & 3)

To detect and predict the ecological effects of global climate change, it will be crucial to establish new standardized monitoring programmes, e.g., a worldwide GLORIA (Global Observation Research Initiative in Alpine Environments) project for birds (Chamberlain *et al.* 2012), and to maintain existing long-term mountain habitat and species monitoring programmes similar to those in Europe (Chapter 5). A much greater geographic scope for monitoring programmes is needed, targeting especially tropical mountains and high elevation habitats at and above the treeline. Coordination of monitoring is needed in mountain systems that cross national boundaries. More cross-continental collaborations are needed, ideally with comparable sampling protocols to facilitate data sharing and analyses. We need to be able to make better use of unstructured data from Citizen Science programmes to increase avian biodiversity knowledge in high mountain habitats, including eBird, or BirdTrack (UK) which could provide an effective way to increase coverage (Box 10.2; Sullivan *et al.* 2009; Chamberlain *et al.* 2012; Alba *et al.* 2022).

Box 10.2 *Mountain Bird Monitoring in the Climate Change Era: An Important Role for Citizen Science*

Benjamin G. Freeman

High mountain birds are predicted to be imperiled by climate change (Şekercioğlu *et al.* 2008). Species at all elevations are predicted to move upslope as temperatures climb. However, high elevation species are constrained by the physical mountaintop, so cannot balance local population declines and extirpations with the colonization of higher elevation environments. High elevation species are therefore predicted to be on an 'escalator to extinction' that could lead to global extinctions. Worryingly, there are examples where an escalator to extinction is already in action for high mountain birds in the tropics (Freeman *et al.* 2018a, 2021) and other global systems (Chapter 6). However, empirical data to assess these dire predictions are not available for most mountain bird species. In the absence of monitoring and status assessment data, we cannot identify which species in which places are vulnerable to the escalator to extinction, let alone craft management programmes to assist species that are declining.

Citizen Science provides one solution to the challenge of monitoring mountain birds, and there are two main types of Citizen Science projects. First, projects can be explicitly designed to monitor birds, and work with trained volunteers to collect standardized data. Examples of these 'structured' projects include the Breeding Bird Survey in North America, Breeding Bird Atlases at national or provincial levels, and Mountain Birdwatch in northeastern North America. Structured data collection facilitates data analysis, but can also limit the scope of the project. For example, high elevation environments are poorly represented within the road-based Breeding Bird Survey (Lawler & O'Connor 2004).

Second, Citizen Science projects may not be explicitly designed to monitor mountain birds. For birds, eBird is the dominant example of such a 'semi-structured' project. eBird participants submit checklists of the species they detect while birding, with varying observer quality and effort (Sullivan *et al.* 2009). Nevertheless, the huge amount of eBird data allows for sophisticated modeling of species' distributions at broad spatiotemporal scales. Recent advances permit abundance

modeling and the inference of population trends over time (https://
science.ebird.org/en/status-and-trends).

Moving forward, data from both structured and semi-structured
Citizen Science projects will be key for monitoring how mountain
birds respond to climate change and other environmental changes.
Breeding bird atlases have documented population changes in
mountain birds (Popy *et al.* 2010; Kirchman & Van Keuren 2018),
while Mountain Birdwatch has documented population declines
for several species of conservation concern (https://mountainbirds
.vtecostudies.org/). One promising approach is to combine structured Citizen Science projects with the available infrastructure of
eBird. Breeding bird atlases and Breeding Bird Survey data are now
often input via eBird, while structured projects to monitor mountain birds can be designed for use by eBirders. For example, the
Mountain Bird Network is an effort to monitor species' elevational
ranges along mountain slopes by asking participants to submit point
counts with precise locality information via eBird. As proof of concept, Mountain Bird Network participants conducted 273 point
counts to document the distribution and abundance of species at
Mount Seymour, near Vancouver, Canada. More generally, efforts
to persuade eBird users to submit checklists with fine-scale locality
information (e.g., point counts, traveling checklists with distances
less than 1 km) are useful, as these more structured data assist statistical analysis. For example, analyses of eBird checklists with fine-
scale elevation data are a promising approach to testing the escalator
to extinction model (Girish & Srinivasan 2022). Taken together,
Citizen Science projects clearly have tremendous potential to play
an important role in monitoring high mountain birds, and provide
key information on which mountain birds in which places are on an
escalator to extinction as temperatures continue to climb.

**Research Priority 3 (RP-3). Enhance Our Understanding of High
Mountain Bird Ecology through Focal Population Studies (KGs 4 & 5)**

New approaches are required to assess crucial factors operating for
mountain birds, such as drivers of reproductive success and survival, key
food sources, important predators, connectivity, species interactions,
phenology, dispersal and movement in response to climate change for
high mountain bird communities. Such information would facilitate the
development of conservation and management strategies and enhance

our ability to make predictions under different scenarios of environmental change. High mountain bird field research should target how to minimize the potential negative impacts on mountain bird populations under anthropogenic pressure and to maintain the normal balance of predator-prey dynamics in mountain areas (i.e., avoid subsidizing the food supply to generalist predators during times of normal food shortages). We recommend targeting field studies for high mountain systems to mitigate climate-driven changes to alpine habitats.

Research Priority 4 (RP-4). Modelling Advances to Predict Avian Distribution and Abundance (KGs 6–8)

Continued advances in analytical techniques are needed to incorporate the role of environmental constraints at different temporal and spatial scales. Improved monitoring (RP-2) is needed in conjunction with better modelling. We recommend development of analytical programs and modelling approaches to address the large spatial and temporal scales required for conservation planning, species interactions and predicting impacts of environmental change for high mountain birds. Predictive models require data from detailed autecological studies (RP-3) to understand the requirements of species and how those are changing. Most predictive models are based on species occurrence or more rarely with counts of individuals (Bradter *et al.* 2022), and usually lack other ecological data. We need to develop better understanding of demographic drivers of populations to forecast potential impacts and to develop conservation strategies. Modelling climatic and microclimatic niches is critical to predicting current and future species distributions (Scridel *et al.* 2021). Technological advances are needed, both in terms of available spatial data for environmental conditions from higher resolution remote-sensing and Lidar systems, and the modelling techniques available to analyse these 'big data' sets. In addition, there are analytical needs to determine species thermal niches (e.g., climate envelope models) and in time, the role of evolutionary mechanisms (e.g., niche-based and neural networks) in shaping bird communities in mountain habitats and across elevation gradients.

Research Priority 5 (RP-5). Conservation: Develop Practical Interventions and Evidence-Based Strategies (KG-9)

Research should prioritize 'evidence-based conservation', whereby management interventions and conservation strategies are based on verifiable scientific evidence (Sutherland *et al.* 2004). We identify four areas that we think are particular priorities for such interventions in Box 10.3. However, our current knowledge of mountain bird populations and ecology hampers our ability to develop sound conservation strategies. Direct assessments are needed of the impacts of management interventions on bird populations in alpine habitats, such as the study by Clarke & Johnson (1990) who compared demographic performance of white-tailed ptarmigan *Lagopus leucura* in their native range and in their introduced range after translocation. The precautionary principle is strongly advised for managing alpine and subalpine communities since we lack comprehensive understanding of what is required to maintain ecological processes in alpine habitats, and have limited experience and success in restoring these sensitive ecosystems. Expert opinion also has a role to play; ideally expert opinion approaches should be used to identify potential priority species and threats (Chamberlain *et al.* 2016), and to propose key research topics to assess practical conservation interventions.

Box 10.3 *Priority Areas for Conservation Management Interventions in Alpine Habitat*

1) Identification and management of refugia
Two types of refugia might assist with population shifts to newly suitable habitats in the face of climate change: holdouts (stable refugia) and stepping-stones (temporary refugia; Box 10.1). Mountain refugia could be central to deciding where to protect birds and for how long. Thus, identifying existing refugia and creating new refugia through improved spatial planning and habitat management will be key challenges.

2) Interventions to maintain habitat openness
In many mountain regions, there has been a net loss of open habitat over the past few decades, driven both by changes in grazing practices and treeline shifts caused by climate change (Chapter 4). There have been calls for sustainable management interventions (Laiolo *et al.* 2004), especially through targeted grazing, to slow down or even reverse shrub encroachment and upward shifts in the treeline (Chamberlain *et al.* 2013; Jähnig *et al.* 2018; Brambilla *et al.* 2019). However, we are unaware of any practical trials that have been carried out to assess their effects on the bird community in alpine habitats. Such trials have been conducted for other taxa (e.g., Coleoptera, Tocco *et al.* 2013; plants, Pittarello *et al.* 2016). Similar designs at larger scales could be adopted for birds.

3) Management and mitigation actions to counter negative impacts of human disturbance

Several potential types of disturbance are increasing in many mountain areas including recreational activities and renewable energy infrastructure (Chapter 7). These may bring vital benefits to local economies, but they need to be managed in a sustainable way to maintain the integrity of mountain ecosystems. Strategies exist to minimize impacts of renewable energy on birds (Arnett & May 2016; Bevanger & Brøseth 2001; Stokke et al. 2020) and they should be applied where new infrastructure is created at high elevation. For skiing activities, practices can be adopted to minimize impacts on plants, such as creating habitat patches that promote colonization (Urbanska 1997), but the research on management and mitigation for birds is currently lacking.

4) Restoration of threatened high elevation habitats

Some high elevation habitats are under particular threat, especially in the tropics (Chapter 9) and hence warrant specific conservation action for protection and restoration. For example, in the mid- and high-elevation tropical regions of the Andes, endemic *Polylepis* trees are in critical decline. Acción Andina, a network of grassroots conservation partnerships co-founded by Global Forest Generation and Peruvian-based NGO ECOAN aim to restore 500,000 hectares of high Andean forest by replanting 300,000 *Polylepis* trees in buffer zones and important areas downslope from glaciers (https://ecologi .com/projects/restoring-andean-forests-in-ecuador). The impact of the *Polylepis* replanting project on the bird communities has yet to be measured. However, since *Polylepis* patches are considered essential to maintaining connectivity across the alpine matrix for many bird species (Lloyd & Marsden 2011), there is strong potential that this project will restore critical connectivity for this tropical alpine bird community.

Research Priority 6 (RP-6). Conservation: Enhance Protected Area Networks (KGs 7 & 9)

For protected areas, we first need to know whether the current network in mountain regions is fit-for-purpose. Does a given protected area hold viable populations of mountain bird species? If not, how can it be improved? Furthermore, should some unprotected areas that hold important populations of mountain birds be given protected area status? Such information can be obtained through targeted research in protected areas, but may also be gained from monitoring programmes that include unprotected areas (RP-2). In the longer-term, we need to know whether protected areas will continue to be fit-for-purpose in the future, where new protected areas should be located, and whether they can mitigate the negative impacts of climate change and other threats. Modelling techniques already exist to predict potentially important bird areas in mountains, for example those that would enhance species resistance and resilience (Brambilla *et al.* 2017) and those that would minimize conflict with human disturbance (Brambilla *et al.* 2016). Such techniques, enhanced with advances in modelling methods (RP-4) and a greater availability of data (RPs 1 & 2), will provide us with powerful means to develop strategies to establish robust protected area networks. These networks could aim to balance conflicting interests for mountain areas such as protecting biodiversity hotspots versus developing areas for renewable energy that are close to markets. Such strategies would require proper management and enforcement of legal protection to fully achieve their objectives, and should be clearly communicated and policy-relevant (Sutherland & Freckleton 2012).

Research Priority 7 (RP-7). Socio-cultural Considerations: Diversify Research Team Dynamics and Funding Arrangements (KG-10)

Funds should be made available for research to address the geographic biases in knowledge gaps, and to address the biases in who leads the research (Asese *et al.* 2022). We need to ensure that local researchers are full partners involved in decision making processes and in leading high mountain bird research and monitoring programmes, especially in under-researched areas such as many tropical mountain systems. We will derive the most benefit if mountain bird researchers from the Northern Hemisphere and the Global South work collaboratively and build capacity to pose the critical questions, generate new data, collate existing data, conduct analyses and co-develop and interpret the results. Successful research and monitoring projects should include local communities as major partners, and make full use of Indigenous and local knowledge (Jessen *et al.* 2022). Large and diverse research networks, such as the Canadian Mountain Network (www.canadianmountainnet work.ca) with education and training components co-led by local communities, academic researchers, governments, Indigenous organizations and communities, and the non-profit sector, will have the longest and largest legacy to promote the health, conservation and resilience of high mountain systems and their associated avian wildlife communities.

10.7 Concluding Summary

As we worked on this book, we have been astounded at the high levels of avian biodiversity and the breadth of important services that high mountain systems provide when viewed from a global perspective. We conclude with a reminder that maintaining and restoring mountain biodiversity is important from ecological, evolutionary and cultural points of view, and worth protecting for a diversity of sectors. Mountains have exceptional value for biodiversity and people, because alpine habitats provide a wealth of ecosystem services – such as fresh water supply, energy generation, and agricultural, industrial, forestry, recreational, cultural and hunting activities. The social values of alpine biodiversity are well established in countries like Japan and Nepal where high mountain ecosystems are venerated for their spiritual values. Mountain ecosystems and the high elevation specialist species that they support are sensitive to environmental perturbations, and thus mountain biodiversity can be an important barometer of environmental sustainability.

We need to invest in research to safeguard the critical social and economic values of mountain systems into the future. To fulfill our conservation research and management priorities, strong support is needed from the scientific community, policy makers, politicians and local communities. To highlight the importance of protecting high elevation species, and the conservation of mountain biodiversity, we need to improve communication of the social values of biodiversity, in particular why mountain biodiversity is important and worth protecting. Maintaining and restoring alpine bird populations is a critically important component for the management and conservation of mountain biodiversity and high mountain ecosystems.

Acknowledgements

We are very grateful to Brett Sandercock, Michael Usher and Elizabeth Krebs for their insightful comments.

References

Alba, R., Kasoar, T., Chamberlain, D., *et al.* (2022) Drivers of change in mountain and upland bird populations in Europe. *Ibis*, **164**, 635–648.

Altamirano, T.A., de Zwaan, D.R., Ibarra, J.T. Wilson, S. & Martin, K. (2020) Treeline ecotones shape the distribution of avian species richness and functional diversity in south temperate mountains. *Scientific Reports*, **10**, 18428.

Araneda, P., Sielfeld, W., Bonacic, C. & Ibarra, J.T. (2018) Bird diversity along elevational gradients in the Dry Tropical Andes of northern Chile: the potential role of Aymara indigenous traditional agriculture. *PLoS ONE*, **13**, e0207544.

Arnett, E.B. & May, R.F. (2016) Mitigating wind energy impacts on wildlife: approaches for multiple taxa. *Human–Wildlife Interactions*, **10**, 28–41.

Asese, A., Mzumara-Gawa, T.I., Owino, J.O., Peterson, A.T. & Saupe, E. (2022) Replacing "parachute science" with "global science" in ecology and conservation biology. *Conservation Science and Practice*, **4**, e517.

Badyaev, A. & Ghalambor, C.K. (2001) Avian life-history strategies in relation to elevation: evidence for a trade-off between fecundity and parental care. *Ecology*, **82**, 2948–2960.

Bevanger, K. & Brøseth, H. (2001) Bird collisions with power lines – an experiment with ptarmigan (*Lagopus* spp.). *Biological Conservation*, **99**, 341–346.

Boyle, A.W. (2018) Altitudinal bird migration in North America. *Auk*, **134**, 443–465.

Boyle, A.W. & Martin, K. (2015) The conservation value of high elevation habitats to North American migrant birds. *Biological Conservation*, **192**, 461–476.

Boyle, W.A., Sandercock, B.K. & Martin, K. (2016) Patterns and drivers of intraspecific variation in avian life history along elevational gradients: a meta-analysis. *Biological Reviews*, **91**, 469–482.

Bradter, U., Ozgul, A., Griesser, M., *et al.* (2021) Habitat suitability models based on opportunistic citizen science data – evaluating forecasts from alternative methods versus an individual-based model. *Diversity and Distributions*, **27**, 2397–2411.

Bradter, U., Johnston, A., Hochachka, W.M., *et al.* (2022) Decomposing the spatial and temporal effects of climate on bird populations in northern European mountains. *Global Change Biology*, **28**, 6209–6227.

Brambilla, M., Pedrini, P., Rolando, A. & Chamberlain, D.E. (2016) Climate change will increase the potential conflict between skiing and high-elevation bird species in the Alps. *Journal of Biogeography*, **43**, 2299–2309.

Brambilla, M., Caprio, E., Assandri, G., *et al.* (2017) A spatially explicit definition of conservation priorities according to population resistance and resilience, species importance and level of threat in a changing climate. *Diversity and Distributions*, **23**, 727–738.

Brambilla, M., Scridel, D., Sangalli, B., *et al.* (2019) Ecological factors affecting foraging behaviour during nestling rearing in a high-elevation species, the White-winged Snowfinch (*Montifringilla nivalis*). *Ornis Fennica*, **96**, 142–151.

Blyth, S., Groombridge, B., Lysenko, I., Miles, L. & Newton, A. (2002) *Mountain Watch*. Cambridge: UNEP World Conservation Monitoring Centre.

Camfield, A.F., Pearson, S. & Martin, K. (2010) Life history variation between high and low elevation subspecies of horned larks *Eremophila spp. Journal of Avian Biology*, **41**, 273–281.

Carroll, C., Roberts, D.R., Michalak, J.L., *et al.* (2017) Scale-dependent complementarity of climatic velocity and environmental diversity for identifying priority areas for conservation under climate change. *Global Change Biology*, **23**, 4508–4520.

Chamberlain, D., Arlettaz, R., Caprio, E., *et al.* (2012) The altitudinal frontier in avian climate change research. *Ibis*, **154**, 205–209.

Chamberlain, D., Negro, M., Caprio, E. & Rolando, A. (2013) Assessing the sensitivity of alpine birds to potential future changes in habitat and climate to inform management strategies. *Biological Conservation*, **167**, 127–135.

Chamberlain, D.E., Pedrini, P., Brambilla, M., Rolando, A. & Girardello, M. (2016) Identifying key conservation threats to Alpine birds through expert knowledge. *PeerJ*, **4**, e1723.

Clarke, J.A. & Johnson, R.E. (1990) Biogeography of white-tailed ptarmigan (*Lagopus leucurus*): implications from an introduced population in the Sierra Nevada. *Journal of Biogeography*, **17**, 649–656.

de Zwaan, D.R., Wilson, S. Gow, E.A. & Martin, K. (2019) Sex-specific spatiotemporal variation and carry-over effects in a migratory alpine songbird. *Frontiers in Ecology and Evolution*, **7**, article 285.

de Zwaan, D.R., Scridel, D., Altamirano, T.A., *et al.* (2022a) GABB: a global dataset of alpine breeding birds and their ecological traits. *Scientific Data*, **9**, 627, https://doi.org/10.1038/s41597-022-01723-6.

de Zwaan, D.R., Drake, A., Camfield, A.F., MacDonald, E.C. & Martin, K. (2022b) The relative influence of cross-seasonal and local weather effects on the breeding success of a migratory songbird. *Journal of Animal Ecology*, **91**, 1458–1470.

Dobrowski, S.Z. (2011) A climatic basis for microrefugia: the influence of terrain on climate. *Global Change Biology*, **17**, 1022–1035.

Elsen, P.R., Monahan, W.B. & Merenlender, A.M. (2020) Topography and human pressure in mountain ranges alter expected species responses to climate change. *Nature Communications*, **11**, 1–10.

Freeman, B.G. (2020) Lower elevation animal species do not tend to be better competitors than their higher elevation relatives. *Global Ecology and Biogeography*, **29**, 171–181.

Freeman, B.G., Scholer, M.N., Ruiz-Gutierrez, V. & Fitzpatrick, J.W. (2018a) Climate change causes upslope shifts and mountaintop extirpations in a tropical bird community. *Proceedings of the National Academy of Sciences*, **115**, 11982–11987.

Freeman, B.G., Lee-Yaw, J.A., Sunday, J.M. & Hargreaves, A.L. (2018b) Expanding, shifting and shrinking: the impact of global warming on species' elevational distributions. *Global Ecology and Biogeography*, **27**, 1268–1276.

Freeman, B.G., Song, Y., Zhu, K. & Feeley, K.J. (2021) Montane species track rising temperatures better in the tropics than in the temperate zone. *Ecology Letters*, **24**, 1697–1708.

Girish, K. & Srinivasan, U. (2022) Community science data provide evidence for upward elevational range shifts by Eastern Himalayan birds. *Biotropica*, **54**, 1457–1465.

Grabherr, G. (2000) Biodiversity of mountain forests. In *Forests in Sustainable Mountain Development: A State of Knowledge Report for 2000*. Price, M.F. & Butt, N. (eds.). Wallingford: CABI International, pp. 28–38.

Guo, F., Lenoir, J. & Bonebrake, T.C. (2018) Land-use change interacts with climate to determine elevational species redistribution. *Nature*, **9**, 1–7.

Hannah, L., Flint, L., Syphard, A.D., *et al.* (2014) Fine-grain modeling of species' response to climate change: holdouts, stepping-stones, and microrefugia. *Trends in Ecology & Evolution*, **29**, 390–397.

Huey, R.B., Kearney, M.R., Krockenberger, A., et al. (2012) Predicting organismal vulnerability to climate warming: roles of behaviour, physiology and adaptation. *Philosophical Transactions of the Royal Society B*, **367**, 1665–1679.

Ibarra, J.T., Gálvez, N., Altamirano, T.A., et al. (2017) Seasonal dynamics of avian guilds inside and outside core protected areas in an Andean Biosphere Reserve of southern Chile. *Bird Study*, **64**, 410–420.

Jackson, M.M., Gergel, S.E. & Martin, K. (2015) Effects of climate change on habitat availability and configuration for an endemic coastal bird. *PLoS ONE*, **10**, e0142110.

Jähnig, S., Alba, R., Vallino, C., et al. (2018) The contribution of broadscale and finescale habitat structure to the distribution and diversity of birds in an Alpine forest-shrub ecotone. *Journal of Ornithology*, **159**, 747–759.

Jankowski, J.E., Robinson, S.K. & Levey, D.J. (2010) Squeezed at the top: interspecific aggression may constrain elevational ranges in tropical birds. *Ecology*, **91**, 1877–1884.

Jessen, T.D., Ban, N.C., Claxton, N. & Darimont, C.T. (2022) Contributions of Indigenous Knowledge to ecological and evolutionary understanding. *Frontiers in Ecology and the Environment*, **20**, 93–101.

Kaisanlahti-Jokimäki, M.-L., Jokimäki, J., Huhta, E. & Siikamäki, P. (2012) Impacts of seasonal small-scale urbanization on nest predation and bird assemblages at tourist destinations. In *Urban Bird Ecology and Conservation. Studies in Avian Biology 45*. Lepczyk, C.A. & Warren, P.S. (eds.). Berkely: University of California Press, pp. 93–110.

Kapos, V., Rhind, J., Edwards, M., Price, M.F. & Ravilious, C. (2000) Developing a map of the world's mountain forests. In *Forests in Sustainable Mountain Development: A State of Knowledge Report for 2000*. Price, M.F. & Butt, N. (eds.). Wallingford: CABI International, pp. 4–9.

Ke, D. & Lu, X. (2009) Burrow use by Tibetan Ground Tits *Pseudopodoces humilis*: coping with life at high altitudes. *Ibis*, **151**, 321–331.

Keppel, G., Van Niel, K.P., Wardell-Johnson, G.W., et al. (2012) Refugia: identifying and understanding safe havens for biodiversity under climate change. *Global Ecology and Biogeography*, **21**, 393–404.

Kirchman, J.J. & Van Keuren, A.E. (2018) Altitudinal range shifts of birds at the southern periphery of the boreal forest: 40 years of change in the Adirondack Mountains. *Wilson Journal of Ornithology*, **129**, 742–753.

Körner, C. (2004) Mountain biodiversity, its causes and function. *Ambio, Special Report*, **13**, 11–17.

Körner, C. & Ohsawa, M. (2006) Mountain systems. In *Ecosystem and Human Well-being: Current State and Trends. Millennium Ecosystem Assessment*. Vol. 1. Hassan, R., Scholes, R. & Ash, N. (eds.). Washington DC: Island Press, pp. 681–716.

Körner, C., Paulsen, J. & Spehn, E.M. (2011) A definition of mountains and their bioclimatic belts for global comparisons of biodiversity data. *Alpine Botany*, **121**, 73–78.

Körner, C., Jetz, W., Paulsen, J., et al. (2017) A global inventory of mountains for bio-geographical applications. *Alpine Botany*, **127**, 1–15.

La Sorte, F.A. & Jetz, W. (2010) Projected range contractions of montane biodiversity under global warming. *Proceedings of the Royal Society of London Series B*, **277**, 3401–3410.

Laiolo, P., Dondero, F., Ciliento, E. & Rolando, A. (2004) Consequences of pastoral abandonment for the structure and diversity of the alpine avifauna. *Journal of Applied Ecology*, **41**, 294–304.

Lawler, J. & O'Connor, R. (2004) How well do consistently monitored breeding bird survey routes represent the environments of the conterminous United States? *Condor,* **106**, 801–814.

Littlefield, C.E., Krosby, M., Michalak, J.L. & Lawler, J.J. (2019) Connectivity for species on the move: supporting climate-driven range shifts. *Frontiers in Ecology and the Environment*, **17**, 270–278.

Loarie, S.R., Duffy, P.B., Hamilton, H., *et al.* (2009) The velocity of climate change. *Nature*, **462**, 1052–1055.

Lloyd, H. & Marsden, S.J. (2011) Between-patch bird movements within a high-Andean *Polylepis* woodland/matrix landscape: implications for habitat restoration. *Restoration Ecology*, **19**, 74–82.

Lloyd, H., Sevillano-Ríos, S., Marsden, S.J. & Valdéz-Velásquez, A. (2012) Bird community composition across an Andean tree-line ecotone. *Austral Ecology*, **37**, 470–478.

Mamantov, M.A., Gibson-Reinemer, D.K., Linck, E.B. & Sheldon, K.S. (2021) Climate-driven range shifts of montane species vary with elevation. *Global Ecology and Biogeography*, **30**, 784–794.

Marolla, F., Aarvak, T., Øien, I.J., *et al.* (2019) Assessing the effect of predator control on an endangered goose population subjected to predator-mediated food web dynamics. *Journal of Applied Ecology*, **56**, 1245–1255.

Martin, K. (2001) Wildlife in alpine and sub-alpine habitats. In *Wildlife-Habitat Relationships in Oregon and Washington*. Johnson, D.H. & O'Neil, T.A. (Manag. Dirs.). Corvallis, Oregon: Oregon State University Press, pp. 285–310.

Martin, K. (2013) The ecological values of mountain environments and wildlife. In *The Impact of Skiing on Mountain Environments*. Rixen, C. & Rolando, A. (eds.). Bessum: Bentham eBooks, pp. 3–29.

Martin, K. & Wiebe, K.L. (2004) Coping mechanisms of alpine and arctic breeding birds: extreme weather and limitations to reproductive resilience. *Integrative and Comparative Biology*, **44**, 177–185.

Martin, K., Stacey, P.B. & Braun, C.E. (2000) Recruitment, dispersal and demographic rescue in spatially-structured White-tailed Ptarmigan populations. *Condor*, **102**, 503–516.

Martin, K.M., Wilson, S., MacDonald, E., *et al.* (2017) Effects of severe weather on reproduction for sympatric songbirds in an alpine environment: interactions of climate extremes influence nesting success. *Auk*, **134**, 696–709.

Martin, K., Altamirano, T.A, de Zwaan, D.R., *et al.* (2021) Avian ecology and community structure across elevation gradients: the importance of high latitude temperate mountains for conserving biodiversity in the Americas. *Global Ecology and Conservation*, **30**, e01799.

Melin, M., Mehtätalo, L., Helle, P., Ikonen, K. & Packalen, T. (2020) Decline of the boreal willow grouse (*Lagopus lagopus*) has been accelerated by more frequent snow-free springs. *Scientific Reports*, **10**, 6987.

Mermillon, C., Jähnig, S., Sander, M.M., *et al.* (2022) Variations in niche breadth and position of alpine birds along elevation gradients in the European Alps. *Ardeola*, **69**, 41–58.

Mora, C., Frazier, A.G., Longman, R.J., *et al.* (2013) The projected timing of climate departure from recent variability. *Nature*, **502**, 183–187.

Morelli, T.L., Daly, C., Dobrowski, S.Z., *et al.* (2016) Managing climate change refugia for climate adaptation. *PLoS ONE,* **11**, e0159909.

Myers, N., Mittermeier, R.A., Mittermeier, C.G., da Fonseca, G.A.B. & Kent, J. (2000) Biodiversity hotspots for conservation priorities. *Nature*, **403**, 853–858.

Myers-Smith, I.H. & Hik, D.S. (2018) Climate warming as a driver of tundra shrubline advance. *Journal of Ecology*, **106**, 547–560.

Nagy, L. & Grabherr, G. (2009) *The Biology of Alpine Habitats*. Oxford: Oxford University Press.

Neate-Clegg, M.H.C., Stuart, S.N., Mtui, D., Şekercioğlu Ç.H. & Newmark. W.D. (2021) Afrotropical montane birds experience upslope shifts and range contractions along a fragmented elevational gradient in response to global warming. *PLoS ONE*, **16**, e0248712.

Pittarello, M., Probo, M., Lonati, M. & Lombardi, G. (2016) Restoration of sub-alpine shrub-encroached grasslands through pastoral practices: effects on vegetation structure and botanical composition. *Applied Vegetation Science*, **19**, 381–390.

Pepin, N.C., Arnone, E., Gobiet, A., *et al.* (2022) Climate changes and their elevational patterns in the mountains of the world. *Reviews of Geophysics*, **60**, e2020RG000730.

Popy, S., Bordignon, L. & Prodon, R. (2010) A weak upward elevational shift in the distributions of breeding birds in the Italian Alps. *Journal of Biogeography*, **37**, 57–67.

Powell, G. & Bjork, R. (1994) Implications of altitudinal migration for conservation strategies to protect tropical biodiversity: a case study of the Resplendent Quetzal *Pharomacrus mocinno* at Monteverde, Costa Rica. *Bird Conservation International*, **4**, 161–174.

Qu, Y., Zhao, H., Han, N., *et al.* (2013) Ground tit genome reveals avian adaptation to living at high altitudes in the Tibetan plateau. *Nature Communications*, **4**, 2071.

Qu, Y., Tian, S., Han, N., *et al.* (2015) Genetic responses to seasonal variation in altitudinal stress: whole-genome resequencing of great tit in eastern Himalayas. *Scientific Reports*, **5**, 14256.

Rahbek, C., Borregaard, M.K., Antonelli, A., *et al.* (2019) Building mountain biodiversity: geological and evolutionary processes. *Science*, **365**, 1114–1119.

Robillard, C.M., Coristine, L.E., Soares, R.N. & Kerr, J.T. (2015) Facilitating climate-change-induced range shifts across continental land-use barriers. *Conservation Biology*, **29**, 1586–1595.

Romanov, A.A., Astakhova, M.A., Miklin, N.A. & Shemyakin E.V. (2019) Geography of avifauna in the northern parts of the Koryak Highland. *Moscow University Bulletin. Series 5. Geography*, **1**, 53–60. [In Russian]

Rosenberg, K.V., Dokter, A.M., Blancher, P.J., *et al.* (2019) Decline of the North American avifauna. *Science*, **366**, 120–124.

Rössler, O., Bräuning, A. & Löffler, J. (2008) Dynamics and driving forces of treeline fluctuation and regeneration in central Norway during the past decades. *Erdkunde*, **62**, 117–128.

Sandercock, B.K., Martin, K. & Hannon, S.J. (2005) Life history strategies in extreme environments: comparative demography of arctic and alpine ptarmigan. *Ecology*, **86**, 2176–2186.

Sayre, R., Frye, C., Karagulle, D., *et al.* (2018) A new high-resolution map of world mountains and an online tool for visualizing and comparing characterizations of global mountain distributions. *Mountain Research and Development*, **38**, 240–249.

Scridel, D., Bogliani, G., Pedrini, P., *et al.* (2017) Thermal niche predicts recent changes in range size for bird species. *Climate Research*, **73**, 207–216.

Scridel, D., Brambilla, M., Martin, K., *et al.* (2018) A review and meta-analysis of the effects of climate change on Holarctic mountain and upland bird populations. *Ibis*, **160**, 489–515.

Scridel, D., Brambilla, M., de Zwaan, D., *et al.* (2021) A genus at risk: predicted current and future distribution of all three *Lagopus* species reveal sensitivity to climate change and efficacy of protected areas. *Diversity and Distributions*, **27**, 1759–1774.

Şekercioğlu, Ç.H., Schneider, S.H., Fay, J.P. & Loarie, S.R. (2008) Climate change, elevational range shifts and bird extinctions. *Conservation Biology*, **22**, 140–150.

Stokke, B.G., Nygård, T., Falkdalen, U., Pedersen, H.C. & May, R. (2020) Effect of tower base painting on willow ptarmigan collision rates with wind turbines. *Ecology and Evolution*, **10**, 5670–5679.

Stralberg, D., Arseneault, D., Baltzer, J.L., *et al.* (2020) Climate-change refugia in boreal North America: what, where, and for how long? *Frontiers in Ecology and the Environment*, **18**, 261–270.

Sullivan, B.L., Wood, C.L., Iliff, M.J., *et al.* (2009) eBird: a citizen-based bird observation network in the biological sciences. *Biological Conservation*, **142**, 2282–2292.

Sutherland, W.J. & Freckleton, R.P. (2012) Making predictive ecology more relevant to policy makers and practitioners. *Philosophical Transactions of the Royal Society B*, **367**, 322–330.

Sutherland, W.J., Pullin, A.S., Dolman, P.M. & Knight, P.M. (2004) The need for evidence-based conservation. *Trends in Ecology & Evolution*, **19**, 305–308.

Testolin, R., Attore, F. & Jiménez-Alvaro, B. (2020) Global distribution and bioclimatic characterization of alpine biomes. *Ecography*, **43**, 779–788.

Tingley, M.W., Darling, E.S. & Wilcove, D.S. (2014) Fine-and coarse-filter conservation strategies in a time of climate change. *Annals of the New York Academy of Sciences*, **1322**, 92–109.

Tocco, C., Probo, M., Lonati, M., *et al.* (2013) Pastoral practices to reverse shrub encroachment of sub-alpine grasslands: dung beetles (Coleoptera, Scarabaeoidea) respond more quickly than vegetation. *PLoS ONE*, **8**, e83344.

Urbanska, K.M. (1997) Restoration ecology research above the timberline: colonization of safety islands on a machine-graded alpine ski run. *Biodiversity and Conservation*, **6**, 1655–1670.

Watson, A. & Moss, R. (2004) Impacts of ski-development on ptarmigan (*Lagopus mutus*) at Cairn Gorm, Scotland. *Biological Conservation*, **116**, 267–275.

Walker, B., Holling, C.S., Carpenter, S.R. & Kinzig, A. (2004) Resilience, adaptability and transformability in social-ecological systems. *Ecology and Society*, **9**, 5.

Wilson, S. & Martin, K. (2010) Variable reproductive effort for two ptarmigan species in response to spring weather in a northern alpine ecosystem. *Journal of Avian Biology*, **41**, 319–326.

Bird Species Index

All bird species names follow the IOC 2022 World Bird List

Subject Index